ISLAMIC ECONOMICS

Critical Concepts in Economics

Other titles in this series

The Economics of Innovation
Edited and with a new introduction by
Cristiano Antonelli
4 volume set

Public Sector Economics
Edited and with a new introduction by
Richard W. Tresch
4 volume set

Feminist Economics
Edited and with a new introduction by
Drucilla K. Barker and Edith Kuiper
4 volume set

Islamic Banking and Finance
Edited and with a new introduction by
Amer al-Roubaie and Shafiq Alvi
4 volume set

Twentieth-Century Economic History
Edited and with a new introduction by
Lars Magnusson
4 volume set

Urban and Regional Economics
Edited and with a new introduction by
Philip McCann
4 volume set

Agricultural Economics
Edited and with a new introduction by
Gail L. Cramer
4 volume set

Economic Reform in Modern China
Edited and with a new introduction by
Zhang Wei
4 volume set

The Great Depression
Edited and with a new introduction by
Geoffrey Wood and Forrest Capie
5 volume set

Transport Economics
Edited and with a new introduction by
David Hensher
4 volume set

China and Globalization
Edited and with a new introduction by
Linda Yueh
4 volume set

Political Economy
Edited and with a new introduction by
Norman Schofield, Dino Falaschetti
and Andrew R. Rutten
4 volume set

The Rise of Econometrics
Edited and with a new introduction by
Duo Qin
4 volume set

Forthcoming titles:

Behavioural Economics
Edited and with a new introduction by
Kumaraswamy Velupillai
4 volume set

e-Commerce Economics
Edited and with a new introduction by
David Vanhoose
4 volume set

Economic Development of India
Edited and with a new introduction by
Pulin B. Nayak
4 volume set

Economics of Natural Resources
Edited and with a new introduction by
Barry Field and Gardner Brown
4 volume set

Evolutionary Economics
Edited and with a new introduction by
Andreas Pyka
4 volume set

Experimental Economics
Edited and with a new introduction by
Kumaraswamy Velupillai and
Shu-Heng Chen
4 volume set

Human Capital
Edited and with a new introduction by
Pedro Teixeira
4 volume set

Information Economics
Edited and with a new introduction by
David Sappington and Michael Baye
4 volume set

International Trade
Edited and with a new introduction by
Bharat Hazari and Yin Wong Cheung
4 volume set

Labour Economics
Edited and with a new introduction by
George J. Borgas
4 volume set

Women's Economic Writing 1760–1900
Edited and with a new introduction by
Janet Seiz
6 volume set

ISLAMIC ECONOMICS

Critical Concepts in Economics

Edited by
Shafiq Alvi and Amer Al-Roubaie

Volume I
Evolution of Islamic Economics

Routledge
Taylor & Francis Group

LONDON AND NEW YORK

First published 2014
by Routledge
2 Park Square, Milton Park, Abingdon, Oxon OX14 4RN

Simultaneously published in the USA and Canada
by Routledge
711 Third Avenue, New York, NY 10017

Routledge is an imprint of the Taylor & Francis Group, an informa business

British Library Cataloguing in Publication Data
A catalogue record for this book is available from the British Library

Library of Congress Cataloging in Publication Data
Islamic economics : critical concepts in economics / Edited by Shafiq Alvi
and Amer Al-Roubaie.
   volumes cm
  Includes bibliographical references and index.
  ISBN 978-0-415-51960-1 (set : alk. paper) – ISBN 978-0-415-52839-9
(v. 1 : alk. paper) – ISBN 978-0-415-52840-5 (v. 2 : alk. paper) –
ISBN 978-0-415-52841-2 (v. 3 : alk. paper) – ISBN 978-0-415-52842-9
(v. 4 : alk. paper)   1. Economics–Religious aspects–Islam.
2. Islam–Economic aspects.   I. Alvi, Shafiq.   II. Al-Roubaie, Amer.
  BP173.75.I828 2013
  330.088′297–dc23

                                                            2012046168

ISBN: 978-0-415-51960-1 (Set)
ISBN: 978-0-415-52839-9 (Volume I)

Typeset in 10/12pt Times NR MT
by Graphicraft Limited, Hong Kong

Publisher's Note
References within each chapter are as they appear in the original complete work

Printed and bound in Great Britain by
TJ International Ltd, Padstow, Cornwall

CONTENTS

CONTENTS

CONTENTS

CONTENTS

CONTENTS

CONTENTS

VOLUME III ISLAMIC ECONOMICS: THEORIES AND MARKET STRUCTURE

CONTENTS

CONTENTS

CONTENTS

CONTENTS

ACKNOWLEDGEMENTS

The publishers would like to thank the following for permission to reprint their material:

Journal of Research in Islamic Economics for permission to reprint Muhammad Arif, 'Toward a Definition of Islamic Economics: Some Scientific Considerations', *Journal of Research in Islamic Economics*, 2, 2, 1985, 79–93.

S. M. Hasanuzzaman for permission to reprint S. M. Hasanuzzaman, 'Economic Policy in the Early Islamic Period', *The Journal: Rabitat Al-Alam Al-Islami*, 6, 8, 1979, 22–26.

Emerald Group Publishing for permission to reprint Sami M. Abbasi, Kenneth W. Hollman and Joe H. Murrey, Jr., 'Islamic Economics: Foundations and Practices', *International Journal of Social Economics*, 16, 5, 1989, 5–17.

Islamic Research Institute, Islamabad, Pakistan for permission to reprint Faẓlur Raḥmān, 'Economic Principles of Islam', *Islamic Studies*, 8, 1, 1969, 1–8.

The Islamic Research and Training Institute for permission to reprint Khurshid Ahmad, 'Nature and Significance of Islamic Economics', *Lectures on Islamic Economics* (Jeddah: Islamic Development Bank, 1992), pp. 19–31.

Brill for permission to reprint Volker Nienhaus, 'Islamic Economics: Dogma or Science?', in Kay Hafez (ed.), *The Islamic World and the West*, trans. Mary Ann Kenny (Leiden: Brill, 2000), pp. 86–99.

John Wiley & Sons for permission to reprint Salah El-Sheikh, 'The Moral Economy of Classical Islam: A FiqhiConomic Model', *The Muslim World*, 98, 1, 2008, 116–144.

John Wiley & Sons for permission to reprint M. Umer Chapra, 'Mawlana Mawdūdī's Contribution to Islamic Economics', *The Muslim World*, 94, 2, 2004, 163–180.

Islamic Research Institute, Islamabad, Pakistan for permission to reprint Anwar Iqbal Qureshi, 'Islam's Concept of Life Regarding Economic Matters', *Islamic Studies*, 11, 4, 1972, 297–308.

Islamic Research Institute, Islamabad, Pakistan for permission to reprint Masudul Alam Choudhury, 'Principles of Islamic Economics', *Islamic Studies*, 21, 2, 1982, 89–107.

Salman Ahmed Shaikh for permission to reprint Salman Ahmed Shaikh, 'Thesis of Religion: Normative Basis of Islamic Economics', *Journal of Islamic Banking and Finance*, 28, 4, 2011, 27–38.

Islamic Research Institute, Islamabad, Pakistan for permission to reprint Max Horten, 'Die Philosophie des Islam', trans. V. June Hager, 'Phases in the Development of an Islamic World View', *Islamic Studies*, 11, 4, 1972, 231–249.

The Institute of Objective Studies for permission to reprint Mohammad Anwar, 'Islamic Economic Methodology', *Journal of Objective Studies*, 2, 1, 1990, 28–46.

Journal of Islamic Economics for permission to reprint Muhammad Akram Khan, 'Methodology of Islamic Economics', *Journal of Islamic Economics*, 1, 1, 1987, 17–33.

King Abdulaziz University for permission to reprint Shamim Ahmad Siddiqi, 'A Suggested Methodology for the Political Economy of Islam', *Journal KAAU: Islamic Economics*, 13, 1, 2001, 3–27.

King Abdulaziz University for permission to reprint Muhammad Anas Zarqa, 'Islamization of Economics: The Concept and Methodology', *Journal KAAU: Islamic Economics*, 16, 1, 2003, 3–42.

Syed Nawab Haider Naqvi for permission to reprint Syed Nawab Haider Naqvi, 'Choice of Policy Instruments: Specific Issues', in *Ethics and Economics: An Islamic Synthesis* (Markfield: Islamic Foundation, 1981), pp. 129–141.

Islamic Research Institute, Islamabad, Pakistan for permission to reprint S. M. Hasanuzzaman, 'Shihāb al-Dīn ibn Abī'l-Rabī': On Management of Personal and Public Wealth', *Islamic Studies*, 31, 3, 1992, 365–374.

Duke University Press for permission to reprint Abdol Soofi, 'Economics of Ibn Khaldun Revisited', *History of Political Economy*, 72, 2, 1995, 387–404. Copyright, 1995, Duke University Press.

Journal of Markets & Morality for permission to reprint Giovanni Patriarca, 'A Medieval Approach to Social Sciences: The Philosophy of Ibn Khaldun: Some Historical Notes and Actual Reflections', *Journal of Markets & Morality*, 13, 1, 2010, 175–188.

ACKNOWLEDGEMENTS

King Abdulaziz University for permission to reprint Abdul Azim Islahi, 'Ibn Taimiyah's Concept of Market Mechanism', *Journal of Research in Islamic Economics*, 2, 2, 1985, 51–60.

Oxford University Press for permission to reprint Ahmad Al-Hasan, 'The Financial Reforms of the Caliph al-Mu'taḍid (279–89/892–901)', *Journal of Islamic Studies*, 18, 1, 2007, 1–13.

Oxford University Press for permission to reprint Rodney Wilson, 'The Contribution of Muḥammad Bāqir al-Ṣadr to Contemporary Islamic Economic Thought', *Journal of Islamic Studies*, 9, 1, 1998, 46–59.

Disclaimer

Chronological table of reprinted articles and chapters

Date	Author	Article/chapter	Reference	Vol.	Chap.
1924	Max Horten	Phases in the development of an Islamic world view	*Islamic Studies*, 11:4 (1972): 231–49. Translated by V. June Hager from *Die Philosophie des Islam*, Munich: Ernst Reinhardt.	I	13
1954	W. Montgomery Watt	Economic and social aspects of the origin of Islam	*Islamic Quarterly*, 1:2, 90–103.	II	49
1964	S. D. Goitein	Commercial and family partnerships in the countries of medieval Islam	*Islamic Studies*, 3:3, 315–37.	III	61
1969	S. Hasanuzzaman	Study of price and price fluctuations in early Islamic period	*Finance Taxation & Company Law*, 1:7–8, 333–6.	III	74
1969	Fazlur Rahmān	Economic principles of Islam	*Islamic Studies*, 8:1, 1–8.	I	4
1971	Ziauddin Ahmed	Socio economic values of Islam, and their significance and relevance to the present day world	*Islamic Studies*, 10:4, 343–55.	IV	105
1972	Anwar Iqbal Qureshi	Islam's concept of life regarding economic matters	*Islamic Studies*, 11:4, 297–308.	I	10
1977	Irfan Mahmud Ra'ana	Commerce and trade	I. M. Ra'ana, *Economic System under Umar the Great*, Lahore: Shaikh Muhammad Ashraf Publishers, pp. 34–48.	IV	85
1977	Irfan Mahmud Ra'ana	Distribution of wealth	I. M. Ra'ana, *Economic System under Umar the Great*, Lahore: Shaikh Muhammad Ashraf Publishers, pp. 125–38.	IV	98
1979	S. M. Hasan-uz-Zaman	Economic policy in the early Islamic period	*The Journal: Rabitat Al-Alam Al-Islami*, 6:8, 22–6.	I	2
1979	Seyyed Hossein Nasr	Reflections on Islam and modern thought	*Islamic Quarterly*, 23, 119–31.	II	34
1981	Syed Nawab Haider Naqvi	Choice of policy instruments: specific issues	S. N. H. Naqvi, *Ethics and Economics: An Islamic Synthesis*, Markfield: Islamic Foundation, pp. 129–41.	I	18

Chronological table continued

Date	Author	Article/chapter	Reference	Vol.	Chap.
1981	Syed Nawab Haider Naqvi	The Islamic ethical system	S. N. H. Naqvi, *Ethics and Economics: An Islamic Synthesis*, Markfield: Islamic Foundation, pp. 45–57.	II	40
1982	Masudul Alam Choudhury	Principles of Islamic economics	*Islamic Studies*, 21:2, 89–107.	I	11
1982	Rodney Wilson	Economic change and re-interpretation of Islamic social values	*British Journal for Middle Eastern Studies*, 9:2, 107–13.	II	53
1983	F. R. Faridi	Theory of fiscal policy in an Islamic state	*Journal of Research in Islamic Economics*, 1:1, 15–30.	III	65
1984	Muhammad Arif	Towards establishing the microfoundations of Islamic economics: the basis of the basics	*Islamic Quarterly*, 38:2, 61–72.	IV	79
1985	Muhammad Arif	Toward a definition of Islamic economics: some scientific considerations	*Journal of Research in Islamic Economics*, 2:2, 79–93.	I	1
1985	Abdul Azim Islahi	Ibn Taimiyah's concept of market mechanism	*Journal of Research in Islamic Economics*, 2:2, 51–60.	I	23
1986	Timur Kuran	The economic system in contemporary Islamic thought: interpretation and assessment	*International Journal of Middle East Studies*, 18:2, 135–64.	II	33
1987	Muhammad Akram Khan	Methodology of Islamic economics	*Journal of Islamic Economics*, 1:1, 17–33.	I	15
1987	Seyyed Vali Reza Nasr	Towards a philosophy of Islamic economics	*The Muslim World*, LXXVII, 175–96.	II	47
1987	Muhammad Yasin Mazhar Siddiqui	Economic imbalances and the role of Islam – an essay in Qur'ānic interpretation	*Hamdard Islamicus*, X:2, 35–46.	II	52
1988	Zaidi Sattar	The ethics of profits in the Islamic economic system: a socioeconomic analysis	*Islamic Quarterly*, 32:2, 69–76.	II	46
1989	Sami M. Abbasi, Kenneth W. Hollman and Joe H. Murrey, Jr	Islamic economics: foundations and practices	*International Journal of Social Economics*, 16:5, 5–17.	I	3

Chronological table continued

Date	Author	Article/chapter	Reference	Vol.	Chap.
1994	Shamim A. Siddiqui	Some controversies in contemporary macroeconomics: an Islamic perspective	Review of Islamic Economics, 3:1, 19–50.	IV	84
1995	Mohammad A. Elgari Bin Eid	Ethics and economics, an Islamic perspective	Journal of Objective Studies, 7:2, 28–36.	II	42
1995	Abdol Soofi	Economics of Ibn Khaldun revisited	History of Political Economy, 72:2, 387–404.	I	20
1996	Irfan Ul Haq	Economic doctrines of Islam: introduction and philosophy	I. U. Haq, International Doctrines of Islam, Herndon, Va.: International Institute of Islamic Thought, pp. 81–9.	II	35
1996	Muhammad Ramzan Akhtar	Towards an Islamic approach for environmental balance	Islamic Economic Studies, 3:2, 57–76.	IV	100
1996	Mohammad A. Muqtedar Khan	The philosophical foundations of Islamic political economy	American Journal of Islamic Social Sciences, 13:3, 389–400.	II	48
1996	Muhammad Nejatullah Siddiqi	Role of fiscal policy in controlling inflation in Islamic framework	Jeddah: Centre for Research in Islamic Economics, King Abdulaziz University, 10pp.	III	69
1997	Muhammad Lawal Ahmad Bashar	Price control in an Islamic economy	Journal KAAU: Islamic Economics, 9:1, 29–52.	III	77
1997	Syed Abul A'ala Maududi	Re-codification of economic laws in modern times	S. A. A. Maududi, Economic System of Islam, Lahore: Islamic Publications, pp. 295–310.	II	50
1998	Muhammad M. El-Ghirani	The Islamic economic order and the right to social security	Journal of Objective Studies, 10:2, 1–15.	IV	95
1998	Nadeem Ul Haque and Abbas Mirakhor	The design of instruments for government finance in an Islamic economy	IMF: Working Paper, WP/98/54, pp. 1–18.	III	70
1998	Rodney Wilson	The contribution of Muhammad Bāqir al-Ṣadr to contemporary Islamic economic thought	Journal of Islamic Studies, 9:1, 46–59.	I	25

Chronological table continued

Date	Author	Article/chapter	Reference	Vol.	Chap.
2004	Masudul Alam Choudhury and Mohammad Ziaul Hoque	Ethics and economic theory	*International Journal of Social Economics,* 31:8, 790–807.	II	41
2004	Abul Hassan	Islamic ethical responsibilities for business and sustainable development	*Islamic Quarterly,* 48:4, 31–46.	II	45
2004	Zamir Iqbal and Abbas Mirakhor	Stakeholders model of governance in Islamic economic system	*Islamic Economic Studies,* 11:2, 43–63.	III	63
2005	Shafiq Alvi and Amer Al-Roubaie	The alternate growth strategy: Islamic perspective	*Islamia,* II:5, 86–98.	IV	89
2005	Partha Dasgupta	The economics of social capital	*Economic Record,* 81: S1–S16.	II	32
2005	Osman Güner	Poverty in traditional Islamic thought: is it virtue or captivity?	*Studies in Islam and the Middle East,* 2:1, 1–12.	II	37
2005	Thomas O. Nitsch	Economics, social justice and the common good: Roman-Catholic perspectives	*International Journal of Social Economics,* 32:6, 554–69.	II	27
2005	Sayed Afzal Peerzade	Towards self-enforcing Islamic tax system: an alternative to current approaches	*Journal KAAU: Islamic Economics,* 18:1, 3–12.	III	72
2005	Asad Zaman	Towards a new paradigm for economics	*Journal KAAU: Islamic Economics,* 18:2, 49–59.	III	55
2007	Nur Barizah Abu Bakar and Abdul Rahim Abdul Rahman	A comparative study of *zakah* and modern taxation	*Journal KAAU: Islamic Economics,* 20:1, 25–40.	III	68
2007	Ahmad Al-Hasan	The financial reforms of the Caliph al-Mu'taḍid (279–89/892–901)	*Journal of Islamic Studies,* 18:1, 1–13.	I	24
2007	Donald K. Gates and Peter Steane	Historical origins and development of economic rationalism	*Journal of Management History,* 13:4, 330–58.	III	56
2008	Toseef Azid, Mehmet Asutay and Muhammad Junaid Khawaja	Price behaviour, vintage capital and Islamic economy	*International Journal of Islamic and Middle Eastern Finance and Management,* 1:1, 52–68.	III	75
2008	M. Umer Chapra	Ibn Khaldun's theory of development: does it help explain the low performance of the present-day Muslim world?	*Journal of Socio-Economics,* 37:2, 836–63.	IV	86

Chronological table continued

Date	Author	Article/chapter	Reference	Vol.	Chap.
2011	Masudul Alam Choudhury	A critique of economic theory and modeling: a meta-epistemological general-system model of Islamic economics	*Social Epistemology*, 25:4, 423–46.	IV	82
2011	Petur O. Jonsson	On utilitarianism *vs* virtue ethics as foundations of economic choice theory	*Humanomics*, 27:1, 24–40.	III	54
2011	Muhammad Akbar Khan	Consumer protection and the Islamic law of contract	*Islamabad Law Review*, 2:2.	III	60
2011	William Marty Martin and Karen Hunt-Ahmed	Executive compensation: the role of *Shari'a* compliance	*International Journal of Islamic and Middle Eastern Finance and Management*, 4:3, 196–210.	III	78
2011	Amartya Sen	Uses and abuses of Adam Smith	*History of Political Economy*, 43:2, 257–71.	III	57
2011	Salman Ahmed Shaikh	Thesis of religion: normative basis of Islamic economics	*Journal of Islamic Banking and Finance*, 28:4, 27–38.	I	12
2011	Edward Peter Stringham	Embracing morals in economics: the role of internal moral constraints in a market economy	*Journal of Economic Behavior & Organization*, 78:1–2, 98–109.	II	28
2011	Mohamed Ali Trabelsi	The impact of the financial crisis on the global economy: can the Islamic financial system help?	*Journal of Risk Finance*, 12:1, 15–25.	IV	102
2011	Frans Wijsen	Religion, development and security: a mission studies perspective	*Exchange*, 40: 274–87.	II	29
2012	Masudul Alam Choudhury	The "impossibility theorems" of Islamic economics	*International Journal of Islamic and Middle Eastern Finance and Management*, 5:3, 179–202.	II	38
2012	Salman Ahmed Shaikh	Examining theories of growth & development & policy response based on them from Islamic perspective	*Journal of Islamic Banking and Finance*, 29:2, 1–15.	IV	87

GENERAL INTRODUCTION

Shafiq Alvi and Amer Al-Roubaie

Knowledge is cumulative; it evolves, spreads and keeps on advancing as time passes. Economics as a branch of knowledge has existed as long as the human race. Even in very primitive times humans engaged, though in the crudest form, in such economic activities as production, consumption and exchange. History bears testimony that economic knowledge has reconstituted itself and evolved periodically into an improved and modified self to reflect the needs of the time.

Each progressive society periodically evaluates and modifies the operations of its economic and other social institutions with the idea of enhancing human welfare. The conventional or capitalist economic system, and its offshoot socialism, emerged with the advent of the Industrial Revolution in Europe during the fifteenth and sixteenth centuries. This system, designed and advanced by the inquisitive human intellect, is still a dominant operational force worldwide. It prides itself on global economic and social progress and, despite recent crises, remains a crucial factor in human progress.

With the recent demise of the socialist economic system, the capitalist system heaved a sigh of relief as it was rid of a formidable competing economic ideology, little realizing that it too could pass through turbulent waters. The global currency crisis of the 1990s left a deep scar on the face of the world economy. It had barely recouped its original self from this crisis than it found itself again engulfed, this time in an economic and financial crisis of greater magnitude. This crisis started around 2007 and, unfortunately, still reverberates. The repeated failures of the contemporary economic system have made it imperative that 'all thinking and feeling individuals question its very bases and norms' (Ahmed, 2000). This crisis is one of the main reasons for the revival of Islamic economics.

The Islamic economic system, as a subset of a comprehensive social system, is based on the Divine injunctions and Shari'ah. It was devised soon after the establishment of the Islamic state in the early seventh century. The two main objectives for setting up this system were a) to meet fiscal and other requirements of the newly set up state, and to 'implement and promote human welfare (*falah*) by organizing the resources of earth on the basis of cooperation and

1

participation' (Khan, 1984: 55), and b) to provide a framework of norms and practices by which economic and business activities were to be carried out based on ethical and moral standards. From this modest start, it evolved gradually by the fourteenth century into a comprehensive economic system.

The economic doctrine of Islam is closely related to and is part of the Islamic concept of life. It is based on a network of interrelated concepts of God, of humanity, of man's relationship with his fellow man. It is evident that the prevalent system is lacking in its objective of creating a progressive and human-friendly world. Loud cries are being heard for ethical safeguards against corruption, pollution, shortage of energy and a serious threat to the well-being of humanity. At a time like this, it is argued, Islamic economics may be considered as a system that can provide not only the ethical guidelines for economic behaviour but also compelling motivation for improvements.

Islamic economics is not entirely a new subject; it has been developed as an integral part of the wider subject of Islamic jurisprudence (*fiqh*). It is as old as the Islamic way of life. Islamic jurisprudence covers different aspects of economic activities such as market organization, sales contracts, financial dealings, types of company structures in production and consumer protection. It despises inequalities, injustices, misuse of resources and exploitation. The system is not based on scarcity of commodities or lack of efficient organization of the means and sources of production and distribution. Rather, it softens human greed and selfishness, and calls for social justice and mutual responsibilities.

The development of Islamic economics, like all other intellectual endeavours, came to a halt with the disintegration of the Islamic state and the decline of Islamic civilization together with the rising power of European social and economic systems. For various reasons, western economists did not recognize, or decided to ignore, the Islamic system of economics, which remained dormant during the evolutionary period of western economic thought. However, the post-Second World War era and the recent economic crises have accelerated the revival of Islamic economics.

Even with the collapse of communism and the crises facing capitalism, most western economists do not seem particularly enthusiastic to explore the possibility of any other economic system that might be sitting on the shelf collecting dust. Those following particular western ideologies seem content with their own views, theories and operational procedures tainted with their own way of thinking. While Islamic influences on the development of knowledge of philosophy and natural sciences have been widely accepted, there has been a grudging resistance among western intellectuals to investigate the impact of other branches of knowledge. The Islamic economic system, as a result, has become almost a forgotten entity. Muslim economists and those of other persuasions have been unable to get their ideas across to most of the scholars of the two dominant ideas in western thinking – capitalism and socialism.

It is quite appropriate at this juncture to acknowledge that western economists were hard at work developing new economic theories, debating their ideas in public discourses and challenging the relevance of the economic notions of the bygone era. Complacent towards the Islamic economic ideas, they advanced their own, which culminated in the birth of the science of economics and new schools of thought. For their own part, most Islamic scholars were either busy criticizing the western type of economic thinking or trying to assimilate and convert it into operational tools to be applied in their own system. Little effort was made, until recently, by most Islamic scholars to put forth Islamic economic ideas as a legitimate contender for a competing economic system. By and large, they failed to promote the principles of Islamic economics.

Each economy necessarily functions within the confines of a particular social framework, which is defined by its distinctive moral philosophy and legal systems. The western global world view is conditioned by the ideologies of secularism, liberalism and materialism. As portrayed by the classical economists, and further developed by its successors, the founding principles of the conventional economics are the doctrine of laissez-faire, right of private property, operations of a free market where individuals make rational decisions and division of labour. In contrast, socialism believed in state intervention in every facet of social life, collective ownership of property, market control and liberation of the working class from oppressive exploitation. Thus both seek economic justice. Yet each of them is a one-sided, unbalanced expression of justice.

Humankind was created with a possessive instinct, an insatiable thirst for accumulating wealth and a tendency to cling to possessions. The current global financial system and the ensuing economic crises brought us face to face with the imperative of searching for better responses to pressing issues. Islam provides alternative responses that can help address some of the evidently problematic aspects of the conventional economic system. It believes in human freedom and individual liberty. Like capitalism, it fully acknowledges the right of ownership and entitles each to the fruits of his labour. The Islamic injunctions work against the concentration of wealth by means of *Zakah* and alms on savings, trade and crops and certain other properties. Yet it does not resent limited state intervention when necessary as a lever against boundless greed and corruption. In spite of several challenges, the revival of these dynamics is manifesting itself in the phenomenon of the 'revivalism of Islamic economics'. There is no room now for complacency about the inherent benefits of the Islamic economic system. Its alternative vision deserves attention (Ahmed, 1971).

Encouraged by Routledge, we decided to prepare a comprehensive study on critical concepts in Islamic economics. Its stated objective is to stimulate interest in the new paradigm of Islamic economics. It is expected to encourage recognition in western economic circles and provide an alternate economic system for further evaluation from economists of all persuasions (Presley and Sessions, 1994). We sincerely hope it takes its due place as a significant addition to existing human knowledge.

The study presents a little over 100 scholarly pieces which outline a variety of views on Islamic economics. They represent the ongoing efforts to reintroduce an economic system which originated some fifteen centuries ago and evolved as a response to the requirements of that time. The collection includes a combination of classical, medieval and modern Islamic economic views using modern tools of economic analysis. It is divided into four volumes, each containing research papers based on the requirements of the evolutionary process. Though mutual exclusivity of several critical areas of Islamic economics is not possible, each volume is further subdivided into four sections representing a critical area of Islamic economics.

Volume I comprises 25 articles expressing views of some of the renowned scholars of Islamic economics. The aim of these essays is to outline the meaning and the basics of the principles of Islamic economics. For the sake of sequential necessity, these are arranged in three subsections of definition, basis and methodology of Islamic economics. The fourth part outlines the ideas of some of the early Islamic scholars who advanced the basic tenets of Islamic economics. With slightly different approaches to the subject matter, these views offer a repertoire of information about the meaning (Arif, 1985), foundation (Abbasi et al., 1989) and principles (Choudhury, 1982) of Islamic economics. As well, readers will find explanations of the concept and methodology of an important branch of learning.

Anthropologists and historians would argue that economic ideas existed long before the advent of classical and even Islamic economics. They emerged with growing human needs and the ensuing economic activities such as trade and exchange. Indeed, these activities were carried out in the crudest form in the distant past compared to what exists today. However, each era modified and improved them to suit the needs of the time. Many western economists seem to hold the view that the basic principles of economics, as we know them today, have their roots in the thinking that prevailed during the era of the Industrial Revolution in Europe. This treatise might lead them to change their views.

Part 4 on 'Pioneers of Islamic Economics' brings to the attention of the readers some of the fundamental ideas and theories of economics that were enunciated long before the advent of European thinking on the subject. For instance, Ibn Taimiyah presented his distinct views on the economic role and functions of the state. Promotion of socio-economic justice, he contended, had to be its supreme goal and it had to strike a balance between private interests and public pursuits. Some of his ideas are amplified in the article by Islahi (1985). Wilson in his essay (1998) dwells upon the ideas of another pioneer, al-Ṣadr.

It is generally agreed, even by some modern economists, that Ibn Khaldun was the first and foremost economist, who systematically developed and presented in the fourteenth century a number of economic theories that are the precursors of modern economic ideas. For instance, modern European thinking accepts that the division of labour and its benefits to the national economy are explained by Adam Smith in the first chapter of his book *Wealth of Nations*. Weiss (1995), however, informs the readers that 'Ibn Khaldun presented almost exactly the same arguments 400 years earlier (than Smith's idea)'. He elaborated on the theories of production, value, distribution and business cycle.

Ibn Khaldun is now rightly regarded as a pioneer economist and as a pioneer social scientist with considerable insight and expertise in public finance and community development. Besides, he discovered a number of other economic notions centuries before their birth in modern times. Soofi (1995) and Patriarca (2010) have attempted in their essays to give further accounts of Ibn Khaldun's contributions to economic knowledge.

Every branch of knowledge has its own philosophical base upon which its edifice is constructed. Islamic economics is no exception. Volume II presents 28 research pieces that outline the foundation of Islamic economics. The basic theme of the subject is further divided into four sections, the first of which deals with a general but brief comparison of the philosophies of modern and Islamic economics together with the ethical and moral aspects of the latter.

One of the basic principles of modern economics is laissez-faire. It means individuals behave rationally in the pursuit of their economic interests. It might be true for the founder of conventional economics Adam Smith, but does not seem to hold in modern times, where one finds human greed and selfishness rampant, thus contradicting what perhaps Smith's belief was. Of the several articles included in this section, readers' attention is particularly drawn to those by Zaratiegui (1999), Stringham (2011) and De Soto (1999). The views portrayed in these articles are the testimonies of the basic ills of the modern economy.

For the sake of justice and human welfare, Islam devised a comprehensive social system with economics as an integral part. The remaining three sections throw light on the most important aspect of Islamic social life, namely the acceptance of its moral and ethical standards in all human dealings. This is amplified, among others, by Chapra (2001), Naqvi (1981), Choudhury and Hoque (2004), Nasr (1987) and Reilly and Zangeneh (1990). Space and time do not permit us to elucidate further on the ideas expressed in these articles. That task is left for the readers.

The cornerstone of conventional economics is the formulation, discussion and propagation of the theories and thoughts of economics. Through the unending efforts of western economists, much success has been achieved in this regard. The revival of the system of Islamic economic thought is still in its infancy. No doubt, efforts are steadily being made to revive and polish it up. Recent economic and financial crises have given impetus to these efforts.

A selected few articles on modern economic theories are explained in the first subsection of Volume III. They serve as a backdrop to our main discussion and are an excellent source of information, particularly those articles by Jonsson (2011), Zaman (2005) and Storr (2009). Ideas contained in these writings provide a wealth of knowledge to the reader.

No economic system can operate successfully without devising and implementing a proper fiscal policy. Faridi (1983) attempts a theoretical exposition of the fiscal dynamics of an Islamic economy. Islam pays special attention to market structure and income distribution and treats them as two very important pillars of its economic system. Research by Zaman (1993) and Peerzade (2005) elucidate their importance in theory and practice. Islamic economics is emphatic for maintaining fairness in income distribution and justice. Lack of them is abhorred. The principle of factor pricing and its impact on functional income distribution is addressed by Sadeq (1989) whereas Bashar's piece (1997) deals with the administration of prices in the Islamic system.

Volume IV is composed of 27 articles that explain some of the crucial elements of the current global economic and financial crises. A few of them also venture into advancing some of the solutions that the Islamic economic system offers for their remedies. Spread over four parts, this volume introduces research findings of various well-known authors in terms of the theoretical foundation of Islamic economics, trade and economic growth, Islamic distributive justice and, of course, the opportunities and challenges that lie ahead for the Islamic system. Though showing the unanimity of thoughts at the end, the selected articles also offer different approaches the authors have taken in presenting their views on some of the critical issues of Islamic economics. All of them are stimulating and thought provoking.

In terms of the expressed views, Haneef and Furqani (2009) seem rather apprehensive about the operation of the Islamic economic system as it is currently being practised and point out its 'missing dimensions'. To them the system should be implemented as designed by the Divine injunctions. On his part Ahmed (2000) goes as far as suggesting that there is a global need for Islamic economics as an alternate to the current system. It is a well-known fact that trade and commercial dealings were in vogue even before medieval times. Local, regional and even multinational exchanges of goods were carried out in order to satisfy human needs and requirements. Exchanges like these were also responsible for instituting growth, or lack of it, in local and regional economies. According to a leading Islamic economist (Chapra, 2008), they still are.

In their article, Alvi and Al-Roubaie (2005) suggest an alternate Islamic growth theory that embodies both material and spiritual elements. Unlike the modern emphasis on material goods and services alone as the engine of economic growth, they would like to include spiritualism as a determinant of growth and development.

The Islamic social system lays great importance on justice and human welfare. It regards distribution of material requisites of human life and distributive justice as the two founding pillars of the Islamic economic system. The introduction of compulsory *Zakah* or alms in the very early stages of Islamic administration was to achieve redistribution of income and promote social justice especially for the downtrodden in society. A good description of various aspects of *Zakah*, its operational procedure and its effectiveness is given in Zein al-Abdin (2003) while Yusuf (1990) and Islahi (1993) explain the theory and practice of consumption and distribution of wealth.

At present, the Islamic economic system faces a number of challenges to its acceptance and success. Apart from many less informed citizens even some western intellectuals seem to be oblivious to it. Furthermore, even many Muslims do not seem enthusiastic about it and do not practise it fully. Weiss (1989) has singled out the struggle that a viable Islamic system has been facing. Only Heaven knows what lies ahead for this system or whether it can be accepted as a supplement or substitute for the troubled modern economic system. In his presentation, Trabelsi (2011) suggests that the Islamic system be considered as a possible alternative.

The study at hand is a special issue dealing with *critical concepts* of Islamic economics. Sourcing material for a study of this nature and scope is a monumental task. After searching, collecting, reading and identifying more than 250 research articles and relevant book chapters, 105 of them were finally included in this study. This process also required contacting dozens of authors, publishers, editors and copyright holders. It provided us with an opportunity to create new contacts and enlarge the circle of writers and scholars with a common intellectual pursuit. We see the forging of these contacts as a very special beneficial experience and express our gratitude to all the scholars and writers for their valuable help and cooperation. The paucity of space prohibits us from mentioning their names here, but some of them have, indeed, been identified in the Acknowledgements.

Apart from the authors, writers and organizations to whom the material of this study belongs, we owe special gratitude to Professor (Dr) S. M. Hasanuz Zaman, former Associate, Islamic Research and Training Institute, Jeddah; Professor Khurshid Ahmad, a well-known scholar and an Associate, Institute of Policy Studies, Islamabad, Pakistan; Professor (Dr) Ugi Suharto, Visiting Professor, Ahlia University, Kingdom of Bahrain; and Professor Masudul Alam Choudhury, Professor of Economics and Finance, Sultan Qaboos University, Muscat, Sultanate of Oman. These scholars succumbed to our continued pressure and agreed to write introductions for each volume and for that we owe them many thanks.

Apart from encouragement, a treatise of this magnitude needs technical and research facilities. Dr Abdullah Al-Hawaj, President of Ahlia University, Kingdom of Bahrain, was kind enough to provide us with both of them. We offer our appreciation of his help and heartfelt thanks for his cooperation.

In the preparation of this collection, we also received timely and very helpful advice and guidance from a number of Islamic studies scholars. Two of them, Khaliq A. Alvi and Rafat Noor Khan, merit special mention. Our sincere thanks go to Dr Richard Cummings for going through the manuscript and making certain important linguistic improvements.

Montreal's Concordia University library staff members were extremely cooperative and helped us secure some of the much needed research material. We feel greatly indebted to all of them for their assistance. Without their help, we might still be probing in the dark. Publication of a work of this magnitude is a collective effort of not only visible scholars, writers and publishers but also of a host of invisible hands in the production department. Through Simon Alexander of Routledge, we offer our sincere gratitude to all these 'unsung heroes'.

In the preparation of this collection, we gained valuable experience of editing and producing a study of this size. We hope and expect that *Islamic Economics (Critical Concepts in Economics)* will be welcome as a timely contribution towards advancing a contemporary and comparative understanding of the Islamic and conventional approaches to some of the pressing economic issues facing humanity.

In the end, though admirably assisted by Simon Alexander, Chief Editor of Major Works at Routledge, we take full responsibility for the final editorial decisions in terms of selecting, arranging and presenting views of learned scholars. The material included in this collection, indeed, belongs to literally dozens of authors and writers. They are the sole proprietors of their creation. The editors and publishers disclaim any responsibility for its authenticity.

Additional references

Khan, Muhammad Akram (1984), 'Islamic economics: nature and need', *Journal of Research in Islamic Economics* 1(2): 51–5.

Presley, John R. and Sessions, John G. (1994), 'Islamic economics: the emergence of a new paradigm', *Economic Journal* 104: 584–96.

INTRODUCTION

S. M. Hasanuz Zaman

Enormous literature in Islamic economics has appeared since the Second World War. The current study is yet another contribution to it. The appearance of *Islamic Economics (Critical Concepts in Economics)*, comprising around one hundred scholarly essays, arranged in four volumes, is a welcome move. Its editors, Professors Shafiq Alvi and Amer Al-Roubaie, have painstakingly assembled the research findings of some of the world's outstanding Islamic scholars. These findings provide a detailed insight into some of the crucial issues of Islamic economics.

This volume contains 25 essays, sequentially arranged into four sections. The first three sections give readers undisputed basic knowledge of the founding principles of Islamic economics. The fourth one brings into the spotlight contributions of some of the eminent pioneers of Islamic economics, such as al-Ṣadr, Ibn Taimiyah and Ibn Khaldun.

As mentioned above, this collection deals with basic conceptual issues of Islamic economics. Up to the fourth decade of the twentieth century, the terms 'Islamic economics' and the 'economic system of Islam' were unfamiliar in academic circles. Before this, the subjects that engaged Muslim minds were their personal affairs, such as the legality of the sources of one's earnings, items of the levy of *Zakah* and application of the law of inheritance and so forth. These were generally the issues that Muslims had to grapple with. These issues were referred to the *ulema*, religious scholars who responded to these queries on the authority of the opinions expressed long, long ago.

It was perhaps the challenge of aggressive socialism and communism in the 1940s that led Muslim academicians to think in terms of a counter economic doctrine that could be derived from the Qur'an (the book revealed to the Prophet Muhammad) and the Sunnah (sayings and the actions of the Prophet) and had so far been totally ignored. A number of scholars came forward to prove the superiority of the Islamic economic system over capitalism and socialism. For this purpose, they propagated their ideas in the form of debates and publications. A number of good books on the subject of Islamic social and economic systems were produced by a number of *ulema* (religious and knowledgeable authorities). But all of them except two were

9

written in Urdu. This, however, paved the way for more scholars to make new inroads in the direction and bring more sophistication to their work on the subject. Many scholars devoted themselves to subsidiary aspects of the Islamic economic system. This was being done in several languages, Urdu, English and Arabic simultaneously.

Until the 1970s, the attempts to illuminate the different aspects of the Islamic economic system were really useful but much was of ephemeral value or mere repetition of some sound work already produced. To pursue this objective further, a number of international conferences and symposia were organized in various parts of the Islamic world. The scholarly gatherings assembled a large number of Muslim economists under one roof to deliberate over different aspects of the subject. This was instrumental in creating enthusiasm to work more seriously on the subject. The modus operandi of these conferences was and is to call for papers on different aspects of a particular topic. This practice set a much needed direction for the study and research of various aspects of Islamic economics. One of the consequences of such endeavours was the production and availability of enormous literature on Islamic economics and related issues.

The papers included in this volume discuss critical concepts relevant to the Islamic economic system. Although much more has been written on these concepts, the editors have picked up as many articles as could be accommodated in the compilation. There is still more room to add to these subjects and equally much more room to expose them to criticism. It should, however, be kept in mind that the basic principles on which Islamic concepts rest are fixed and invariable as they are derived from the Qur'an and the Sunnah. This automatically implies that in Islamic economics the normative aspect is more pronounced than the positive one. This idea is amplified by Shaikh (2011) in his article on 'Thesis of Religion: Normative Basis of Islamic Economics'.

The fact of being normative does not mean the absence of any differences among scholars and administrators. There may be differences in interpreting the injunctions in the Qur'an. In many cases these may not be differences in interpretation but in determining policy and strategy. For example, *Zakah* (poor tax) proceeds are to be disbursed among eight heads of expenditure as laid down in the Qur'an. Difference in interpretation may arise in determining the meaning of some specified head. The policy-makers may even have differences in the method of its distribution. The strategy may be to pay a lump sum for purchase of machinery/tool or to award such things on hire-purchase basis, in which case a down payment and some initial instalments are paid from the *Zakah* fund while the remaining is to be arranged by the beneficiary himself on a pay-as-you-earn basis. Differences are also bound to arise due to social and regional differences.

Islamic economics is a subset of a broad-based social system. Its important tenets are economic well-being, social and economic justice, and equitable distribution of income and wealth. It strictly upholds ethical and moral standards in all social and economic dealings. Every discipline is based on certain fundamentals and their significance. Both Ahmad (1992) and Choudhury (1982) have explained some of these principles and why they should be followed in every walk of human life. Part 3 of the volume presents several excellent articles that deal with the methodology of Islamic economics. Those by Anwar (1990) and Khan (1987) are full of information for the benefit of the reader.

A very interesting and informative part of this volume is the collection of papers that deal with some of the pioneers of Islamic economics and their contributions. It may be surprising for some modern economists to know that the pioneers of Islamic economics had already developed, centuries ago, many of the fundamentals of economics. For instance, Abī'l-Rabī' developed and presented to the world the early Theory of Personnel Management (Zaman, 1992) while Ibn Taimiyah presented his ideas of markets and market mechanism a long, long time ago.

Historians and modern economists are slowly discovering Ibn Khaldun, a fourteenth-century Muslim economist, sociologist and social scientist who produced a well-known treatise *History of the World* (*Kitab al-ibar*) and its famous introduction *Muquddima*. It is argued that Ibn Khaldun was the first scholar to present the idea that prices and values are determined by supply and demand – the two fundamentals of economics. It was Ibn Khaldun, not Karl Marx, who first introduced the idea of a 'labour theory of value'. In his *Muquddima* (2:311), he writes: 'Profit is the value realized from human labour' (Weiss, 1995). Readers may also get enormous information from Wilson (1998), Al Roubaie and Alvi (2001) and others.

In conclusion, the material assembled in this volume provides an overview of the basic principles of Islamic economics. The editors deserve our appreciation for having tried to include most of those basic concepts that are not susceptible to different opinions.

Part 1

ISLAMIC ECONOMICS: DEFINITION AND MEANING

1

TOWARD A DEFINITION OF ISLAMIC ECONOMICS

Some scientific considerations

Muhammad Arif

Source: *Journal of Research in Islamic Economics*, 2:2 (1985), 79–93.

The contributions of Dr. Hasanuz Zaman and Mr. M. Akram Khan in the Winter 1404/1984 issue of the JRIE (pp.51–61) are timely attempts to recognise the importance of defining Islamic economics. Since the definitions of Islamic economics proposed by these two scholars will be discussed below, it seems appropriate to reproduce them here.

> "Islamic economics is the knowledge and application of injunctions and rules of the *Shari'ah* that prevent injustice in the acquisition and disposal of material resources in order to provide satisfaction to human beings and enable them to perform their obligations to Allah and the society."
>
> (Zaman, p.51)

> "Islamic economics aims at the study of human *falah* achieved by organising the resources of earth on the basis of cooperation and participation."
>
> (Akram Khan, p.55)

Since economics is a mature science any attempt to define Islamic economics necessitates a clear statement of the scientific justification for the study and development of Islamic economics.

It also requires discussion of the scientific traditions that can be helpful in presenting the definition of Islamic economics in a clear, concise and convincing way so that our position is well understood by the profession in general. Lastly, we need a statement of the basic economic problem for the

15

study and solution of which Islamic economics deserves to be developed. The basis of our efforts to develop Islamic economics lies in the fact that the paradigm of Islamic economics is different from the other economics paradigms. This statement needs further elaboration.

We start with acknowledging the fact that economics is a normal science. "Normal science means research firmly based upon one or more past scientific achievements that some particular community acknowledges for a time as supplying the foundation for its further practice. Today such achievements are recounted, though seldom in their original form, by science textbooks, elementary and advanced." (Kuhn, p.10). Within a community of scientists involved in research in a given normal science there may exist different paradigms. The term paradigm is defined as. "some accepted examples of actual scientific practice – examples which include law, theory, application, and instrumentation together – provide models from which spring particular coherent traditions of scientific research." (Kuhn, p.10). In the context of the science of economics, two widely known paradigms at present are: the Marxian paradigm of socialism and the market economy paradigm of capitalism. The paradigm of Islamic economic system is the *Shari'ah* which is fundamentally different from the above two. Every paradigm in economics is based on certain philosophic foundations and is a system of belief. (Edwards, Reich, and Weiskopf, 1978).

The structure of economic science is shown in chart no. 1. This chart is drawn on the basis of the structural organization of a normal science as discussed by Thomas Kuhn in, *The Structure of Scientific Revolutions* (1970). This chart shows that an economic system is the outcome of the paradigm that it follows. The choice of the paradigm is reflected by the behavioural pattern of the individual units in the society. The behaviour of the individual units is, in fact, the basis of the micro foundations of the system. The philosophy in which the individual unit believes is crystallized by its behaviour.

Using the structure of economic science, chart no.2 shows the place of Islamic economic system vis-a-vis capitalism and socialism. This chart shows that the philosophic foundations of capitalism are in laissez faire. The behaviour of the members of a society that believes in laissez faire is symbolized by the 'economic man'. The economic man believes in utilitarian rationality. The behaviour of the economic man is the basis of the micro foundations that logically lead to the market economy paradigm. Using this paradigm the conventional economic theory builds the economic system known as capitalism.

A society based on the philosophic foundations of dialectical materialism chooses a different course. In this case the basis of the micro foundations lies in the fact that private ownership of the factors of production is not allowed. The resulting relationships lead to the Marxian paradigm of economics. This paradigm builds the economic system called socialism whose structure in the context of economic science is shown in chart no.2.

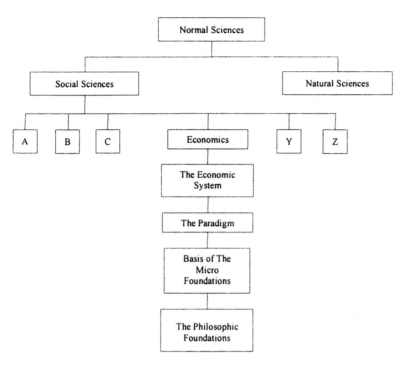

Chart No.1   The structure of a normal science: the case of economics.

A society whose members adopt Islam as their way of life will develop the Islamic economic system. The scientific structure of Islamic economics is shown in chart no.2. Like the other economic systems, the economic system of Islam is also rooted in certain philosophic foundations such as the following:

i)   *Tawhid*: God's Unity and Sovereignty.
ii)   *Rububiyyah*: Divine arrangements for nourishment and directing things towards their perfection.
iii) *Khilafah*: Man's role as God's vicegerent on the earth.
iv)   *Tazkiyah*: Purification plus growth.
v)   Accountability: Belief in accountability on the day of judgement and its implications for the life in this world and in the hereafter. (Khurshid Ahmad, p.230; and Arif, 1983).

As a result of these philosophic foundations the behaviour of the representative economic agent in an Islamic society can best be characterised as the "Muslim, i.e., one who submits to Allah". The behaviour of the Muslim man is very different from that of the long celebrated 'economic man'. Qur'an's position on the economic man's attitude towards life is very clearly stated:

17

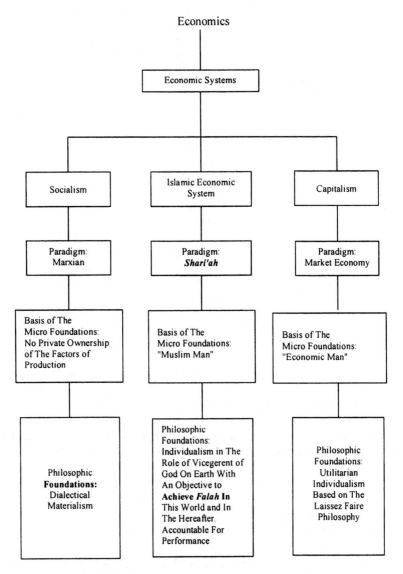

Chart No.2 The basis of the micro foundations and its implications for the economic system.

"Some say, 'Our Lord, give us all the good things here in this world. Such people shall have no share in the Hereafter.'" (2: 200)*

Qur'an also gives a clear description of the behaviour of a Muslim:

"Then there are those who say, 'Our Lord, give us what is good in this world and also what is good in the Hereafter and save us from the torment of Fire.' Such people will have their due share (in both worlds) according to what they earn. And Allah is swift at settling accounts." (2: 201–202)

Qur'an frequently mentions that the individual who believes in Islam and practices it as well, shall have only one course of life i.e. obedience to Allah and His prophet Muhammad (peace be upon him). The references of some of the verses emphasizing this are: (3:32), (3:132), (5:92–93), (8:1), (8:20–21), (9:71), (24:54–56), and (58:13).

A Muslim is the one whose purpose in life is to achieve *falah* by being successful in his role as the vicegerent of God on this earth. His success in this role depends among many other things, on the acquisition, allocation and disposition of the resources, which are a trust, according to the consent of Allah.

Thus it is the Muslim man's behaviour which serves as the basis of the micro foundations that logically lead to the *Shari'ah* paradigm. This micro foundations' link between the human behaviour and the *Shari'ah* paradigm (in an Islamic society) is the scientific basis of our efforts to develop Islamic economic system. Our efforts to develop Islamic economic system based on *Shari'ah* paradigm are fully consistent with the scientific traditions of paradigm building.

After having shown the scientific basis for the development of Islamic economics, we look at the traditions of the science of economics that will be useful. We find that the practitioners involved in the development of a paradigm observe three traditions. In the context of the development of Islamic economics these three traditions mean that:

i)   we should differentiate between the definition of Islamic economics and that of its paradigm
ii) we should develop an appropriate terminology which describes the concept unique to Islamic economics without any ambiguity
iii) our proposed definition of Islamic economics should state basic economic problem as a built-in phenomenon of human life; and not as an exogenous scenario being imposed upon the economic agents. The implications of each of these traditions will be discussed in greater detail in the following:

i) Defining Islamic economics and not its paradigm

We should be aware of the fact that there is a difference between Islamic economics and its paradigm. The definition of Islamic economics is the *Statement* of the Basic Economic Problem and it need not explicitly mention the paradigm involved. The paradigm involved should be defined separately. According to the structure of a normal science, anything that involves the law, theory, instruments and practices concerning the solution of the problem is included in the paradigm. (Kuhn, p.10); also see chart no. 1. In the case of Islamic economics *Shari'ah* is the paradigm.

But in the profession, the *Shariah* paradigm will be used by those economists only who define the basic economic problem in a certain way. Thus a paradigm is a means, and it will be followed by those practitioners only who share a common definition of the basic problem. Hence it becomes clear that it is our outlook towards the basic economic problem that tells us that the best way to solve this problem is to follow *Shari'ah* paradigm. Therefore, our definition of Islamic economics should be a statement of our understanding of the basic economic problem and not a statement of the means to solve that problem in a certain way.

ii) Use of the appropriate terminology

The established scientific traditions tell us that the choice of appropriate terminology plays a key role in the smooth development of a paradigm. A kit of appropriate terminology to express a phenomenon which is unique in one paradigm, enables the reader to clearly distinguish the nature and characteristics of this paradigm from that of the other competing paradigms. For example the terms like: Surplus Value, Proletariat Class, Bourgeoisie Class, etc; are representative of the Marxian paradigm. The reader reading these terms, is able to recognize immediately that the paradigm being mentioned here is Marxian. Thus when defining Islamic economics we should also try to develop and use the terms that represent the distinct nature of the *Shari'ah* paradigm without any ambiguity. This would allow both the scholars and the students to use a term without the additional burden of qualifying statements to save the reader from potential ambiguity. Once the readers and the critics of Islamic economics understand this sharply distinct terminology they will not confuse Islamic economics with something else. They will be able to appreciate the fact better that we are not trying to make certain adjustments in the existing paradigm of capitalism to accommodate Islam or vice-versa. Instead, the use of the appropriate terminology, representing the particular Islamic concepts, would make it obvious that ours is an effort to develop the *Shari'ah* paradigm of Islamic economics. This clear vision of our efforts would allow them to appreciate the fact that the *Shari'ah* paradigm is capable of achieving certain goals which the other paradigms are unable to achieve. It is, however, worth mentioning here that the new terminology will be needed only where there is a disagreement on the use of the existing terminology/concepts; or concepts alien to the existing paradigms are introduced. Thus we find that one of the important responsibilities of the builders of a paradigm is to coin an easy but distinct terminology capable of distinguishing their perspective from that of the other prevalent paradigms. Terminology, in the final analysis, plays a vital role in advocating a particular viewpoint towards the economic problem at hand. Selection of terminology is also suggestive of the possible measures to solve the problem. The moment we come across a particular set of terms being used in the analysis, we immediately recognize the paradigm that is being referred to; and our mind can picture the paradigmic implications of the terminology being used.

iii) Constructing the definition of Islamic economics which states the basic economic problem as a built-in phenomenon of human life; and not as an exogenous scenario being imposed upon the individual

The definition of Islamic economics is nothing but the statement of the basic economic problem; as viewed by an economic agent in the Islamic society. Attempts to define Islamic economics call for stating the basic economic problem in such a way that it is expressed as an integral part of human life. This way the statement of the problem itself leads the individual to a logical approach for its solution. The one who follows this logical approach is normal and rational.

Lionell Robins defined economics as, "the science which studies human behaviour as a relationship between ends and scarce means which have alternative uses". But Robbins meant a very specific pattern of human behaviour. In this book (1935) he perfected the concept of economic man as the truly representative economic agent of a society based on the philosophy of laissez faire. Since the human behaviour, as represented by the rationality of the economic man, is a response to the basic economic problem (as viewed by the economic man) therefore, utilitarian efficiency considerations logically build the capitalistic economic system. Here we find that Robbins very skillfully knitted the problem and its solution together, and made it an integral part of the economic man's rational behaviour.

Thus any statement of the basic economic problem to be used as the definition of Islamic economics should also take into account the role played by the individual in the solution of the stated problem.

If we define Islamic economics as the knowledge and application of injunctions and rules of *Shari'ah*, then what type of individuals do we expect out there in the society – who will be eager to embrace the *Shari'ah* guidelines and principles in their activities. Or if we define Islamic economics as the study of human *falah* – again we are faced with the same question; namely: what type of individuals do we expect to be out there in the society who will be happy only when they achieve *falah*?

A proper description of the representative economic agent in our definition of Islamic economics thus becomes a scientific necessity in the development of the *Shari'ah* paradigm. Such an identification enables us to meet all the scientific requirements of paradigm building.

21

First, it provides the scientific justification to develop a separate paradigm of Islamic economics: as the behaviour of the economic agents is the basis of the micro foundations of an economic system. Second, it eases the task of the Islamic economists who are engaged in research and analysis to formulate the hypotheses and theories that best describe the *falah* oriented behaviour of this representative unit. Third, a clear understanding of the behaviour of this representative unit would enable the society to create and establish an institutional framework conducive to his *falah* oriented activities. Fourth, it saves our critics from unnecessary trouble too; and they wouldn't launch the criticism that is caused by nothing but sheer ambiguity.

The representative economic unit in an Islamic society is a Muslim – one obedient to Allah. His spirit of obedience demands that he follows the path of Islam by acquiring the knowledge of *Shari'ah* and applying it to solve all his problems including the economic ones. Thus Islamic rational behaviour is built into his personality and thinking. Consequently he always follows the injunctions and the rules of the *Shari'ah* in all walks of his life.

The need to recognize the human behaviour as the basis of the micro foundations of the system

The argument is that the human behaviour should be duly recognized as the basis of the micro foundations of Islamic economic system. If we accept that the Islamic economic system is based on *Shari'ah* paradigm, then what interests us, as economists, is the behaviour of the economic agents in an Islamic society. This means that the element of human behaviour will contribute to the functioning of the Islamic economic system in a variety of ways. For example let us look at the theory of consumer behaviour in an Islamic society. Suppose a consumer has a certain level of income, and prices are given. He is a Muslim. Assume that his income is much above the subsistence level. Thus he saves some part of his income and pays *Zakat* on it. He follows *Shari'ah* in his spending decisions and spends with moderation.

He fully knows that he should not be a spendthrift because Allah declares that spendthrifts are the brethren of Satan (Qur'an, 17:27). Thus he is following *Shari'ah*: he has already allocated a certain amount for savings: out of the remainder he is spending with moderation. Suppose this spending with moderation means that he is still left with some (disposable) amount. He now has the following options to use this remaining amount:

a) he can use it for his consumption spending
b) he can add it to his savings and pay *Zakat* on it
c) he can spend it for the sake of Allah in a variety of ways; for example: helping the poor and the needy in the society, spending on the social welfare projects like schools, hospitals, education, training of the unskilled, etc.
d) he can invest it.

As far as option (a) above is concerned our consumer will not choose it because he is a Muslim. He knows that according to the *Shari'ah* his consumption has already reached the maximum level allowed with moderation. Now if his consumption exceeds this moderate limit, it is undesirable to Allah and will make a negative contribution to his *falah* (for detailed treatment of the consumer theory in an Islamic society see: Arif, 1983). Here we find that our consumer has followed the *Shari'ah* by maintaining a moderate level of consumption. Now he can choose any of the remaining three options; namely the options, (b), (c) and (d). As a matter of fact our consumer can choose any one of these remaining three options or any combination of them. By doing so he will remain within the limits of *Shari'ah*. But whatever decision he makes, his micro level choice will have its implications for the entire economic system at the macro level.

Assume that he chooses option (b) and adds the remainder amount to his savings. In such a case he pays *zakat* on these additional savings as well. This means that Islam's built-in mechanism of social justice becomes effective. This redistributive effect of *zakat* has its macroeonomic implications for the system as a whole.

If he chooses option (c) i.e. he decides to spend the remainder amount for the sake of Allah, then we see the dynamics of Islam's theory of welfare. We find that Islam's theory of welfare is much more superior to the welfare theory of conventional economics which is based on the Pareto optimal approach. Here this consumer is giving a portion of his income to the other members of the society without asking anything in exchange from them. But still his *falah* is increasing. This decision has increased the *falah* of all: the one who spends in the way of Allah, his *falah* increases; one who receives this amount his *falah* also increases; and the *falah* of the entire society also increases by such an act. This could never happen in a world governed by Pareto optimal rules.

If he chooses option (d); and decides to invest this remainder amount, then economic development takes place with purity. This happens because he is a Muslim and will not invest in any project which is undesirable to Allah. The choice of this option highlights the built-in dynamics of Islamic Growth Theory. But as Islamic economists our job is only half done if we stop at this observation. We know that given the options (b), (c) and (d) whatever he decides is permitted under *Shari'ah* but still we are equally concerned with his actual choice because this micro decision has important macro implications for the functioning of the system. Now our interest in the study of his behaviour is generated because of the fact that option (b) has distributive implications, option (c) has welfare implications and option (d) has growth implications for the economy. The way he behaves now, affects the entire system. Thus his behaviour forms the basis of the micro foundations of the Islamic economic system and must, therefore, be studied despite the satisfaction that he is following *Shari'ah*. If we were interested only in the implementation of *Shari'ah* then we wouldn't study his actual choice out of the three options, namely: (b), (c) and (d).

A policy maker will always be seriously interested in the study of the factors that affect a Muslim's choice of the options in the above situation. Because if the policy maker can fully understand the nature and effectiveness of such factors, then he will be in a position to use them in his macro policies to achieve certain desired goals for the society as a whole. In the conventional economic theory the macro policy makers, (assuming a simple closed economy model) are limited to two policies only, namely: the fiscal policy and the monetary policy. But in the Islamic economic system, an understanding of the Muslim man's behaviour tells that he will be allocating some resources for the sake of Allah as well. A study of the factors that motivate him to make such a decision would allow the policy makers to create the institutions and adopt the measures which facilitate such decisions by the economic agents in the society. This way the policy makers in the Islamic economic system gain access to one more macro policy, namely the *falah* policy which is non-existent in the non-Islamic economic systms.

The *falah* policy can be used to affect the aggregate demand in an Islamic economy. This is obvious from the components of aggregate demand as shown below:

$$\text{Aggregate Demand} = \bar{C} + D + J + G + A$$

where

$\bar{C}$ = Subsistence level of consumption. If the individual is unemployed or his income is below subsistence, then the *Bait-ul-Mal* will support him with the means to meet the subsistence requirements.

D = Desirable consumption: consumption over and above the subsistence level but within the moderate limits as prescribed by the *Shari'ah*.

I = Investment.

G = Government spending.

A = Direct voluntary spending for the sake of Allah. This expenditure by the individual can be influenced if the government can demonstrate the ability to formulate and implement a policy that motivates the individual to undertake such spendings. This is another potential macro policy which can legitimately be called the *falah* policy (and can be considered one more tool for the policy makers in an Islamic society)

We know that in a recession when the rate of unemployment is high and private investment is not forthcoming due to the pessimism about the market, the aggregate demand in the economy can be increased by using the appropriate expansionary fiscal and/or monetary policies. But such policy activism has been criticised on the ground that it would cause inflation in the long run and would lead the system to instability. If non-activist approach is adopted then flexible prices and quantity adjustments will eventually restore the full employment equilibrium in the long run but after a huge cost in terms of human misery. In an Islamic economy the policy maker is equipped with three policies to stabilise the economy, namely: fiscal policy, monetary policy and the *falah* policy. Of these three, the *falah* policy is least inflationary because this policy uses the measures to motivate those who have enough, to spend for the sake of Allah. Thus without the fears of deficit financing and increase in the money supply, significant use can be made of this policy by creating appropriate institutions and using the appropriate measures that motive this kind of spending.

Similarly to curb inflation, in addition to the fiscal and monetary policies, *falah* policy can also be used. This will be done by stressing the negative implications for *falah* if the consumption exceeds moderate limits. Thus we find that in Tinbergin's targets and tools framework, the Islamic economics gives us one more policy tool, and improves the efficiency of the system. This tool is lacking in the conventional economic theory.

All this becomes possible only when we recognize the behaviour of a Muslim as the basis of the micro foundations of Islamic economics. An economic system which is not centrally planned, is very strongly affected by the behaviour of its individual economic units. This is true for Islamic economic system as well. It is founded on the philosophy of economic individualism based on a Muslim's role as the vicegerent of Allah. This role calls for some unique behavioural characteristics that manifest themselves in his economic decision making, and have very far reaching implications from the macroeconomic point of view. If Islamic economics fails to recognize these characteristics of a Muslim, which, in fact, are the basis of the micro foundations of the system, then it will be difficult to develop a macro policy package consistent with the nature and the demands of the *Shari'ah* paradigm, and necessary for its efficient functioning.

A look at the two proposed definitions of Islamic economics

The two definitions of Islamic economics mentioned above are the attempts to meaningfully state the basic economic problem. But it may be pointed out that both of them share a common fundamental weakness. In response to both of these definitions it can be argued that what if the economic agents are interested neither in the *Shari'ah* injunctions and rules, nor in the human *falah*. The weakness of these definitions is that they give an impression that the *Shari'ah* based system or the *falah* criteria is being imposed upon the individual from the outside. If the representative economic agent is the 'economic man' type, guided by his utility oriented self-interest, then he does not find any appeal either in *Shari'ah* or in *falah*. Thus there is no scientific justification to develop Islamic economics. But if we clearly recognise a

Muslim man who is the representative economic agent of the Islamic society then the need for the establishment of *Shari'ah* and the achievement of falah gets built into his behaviour, and these proposed definitions acquire the desired relevance. This recognition provides us the scientific basis to develop the *Shari'ah* paradigm of Islamic economics. This is fully consistent with the scientific traditions of paradigm building. The recognition of a Muslim as the representative economic unit in our paradigm, internalizes the process of Islamization. This internalization manifests itself in the rational behaviour of a Muslim. He is the one whose purpose in life is to achieve *falah*. Thus his quest for the knowledge of *Shari'ah* injunctions and rules, and his commitment to apply them in his real life provides the real scientific bases to formulate theories and test hypotheses of Islamic economics which are different from the conventional economic theory. The natural outcome of the study of a Muslim's rational behaviour is nothing else but the development of the *Shari'ah* paradigm of Islamic economics. Given the above scientific bases of Islamic economics, we can now define it as follows:

> *Islamic economics is the study of Muslim's behaviour who organises the resources, which are a trust, to achieve falah.*

This definition follows the scientific tradition of limiting itself to the statement of the basic economic problem only. It does not explicitly mention the *Shari'ah* paradigm or some of its characteristics, like: prevention of injustice, cooperation or participation, etc. The very fact that the economic unit is a Muslim, makes the knowledge and application of *Shari'ah* built into his rational behaviour. This implies that his activities and decisions will be based on *Shari'ah* and will demonstrate a number of characteristics, of which prevention of injustice, cooperation and participation are only a few. This definition replaces the term satisfaction' in Dr. Zaman's definition with the term *falah*. As a matter of fact at the end of his paper Dr. Zaman explains the meaning of the term satisfaction' with Islamic qualifications (Zaman, pp. 52–53). But to the profession of economics, in general, the term 'satisfaction' remains synonymous to the concept of the term 'utility' as used in conventional economics. Standard textbooks on economic theory use the terms satisfaction and utility interchangeably. For example, in his well-known textbook on microeconomics Ferguson writes, "A consuming unit – either an individual or household derives *satisfaction or utility* from each good or service consumed during a given time period". (Ferguson, p. 18). We know that the use of the terms which have the potential of causing ambiguity in understanding of the concepts is the violation of the second scientific tradition of paradigm building as discussed above. Thus we propose to use the term *falah* in our definition instead of the term satisfaction.

The expression in Dr. Zaman's definition, ". . . to provide satisfaction to human beings and enable them to perform their obligations to Allah and the society" needs further analysis. Here, in principle, we fully agree with the spirit of this statement but on technical grounds we have reservations about the way this spirit is being phrased. Here three things are being mentioned:

i)   providing satisfaction to human beings.
ii) enabling them to perform their obligations to Allah.
iii) enabling them to perform their obligations to the society.

To the Western economists the separate mention of the three may sound to be very much in line with the principle of the separation of Church and the real life activities. Thus they may argue that the efforts to meet all the three obligations are fully allowed in the capitalist system as well. Some of them may even argue that in fact it is only capitalism which gives complete freedom to the individual to pursue the activities that enable him to meet his obligations to God and to the society. They would hold that this is actually the true purpose and spirit of laissez faire to establish a system which guarantees such freedom for all the members of the society. Thus again here we find that lack of appropriate terminology may cause confusion for other economists. Since Islam is a '*Din*, it considers human life in its totality, without making a separation between the Church, the state and the real life. One is accountable for all his deeds and therefore, a Muslim looks for the best of both the worlds. (Quran, 2:201–202). Thus all the activities of an individual in the Islamic society, even if they pertain to different aspects of one's life, are directed towards the achievement of one single goal only i.e. to achieve the consent of Allah. From education production and sales to politics, recreation and entertainment: all activities have to be performed in such a way that one achieves Allah's consent which brings *falah* to him. The person who does so, is nothing but a Muslim' and his goal is nothing else but to achieve *falah*. This concept of the purposiveness of life has to be made built into the definition of Islamic economics. The definition proposed in this note attempts to do the job by using the appropriate terminology. Once these terms are introduced and properly explained critics will have no scientific basis to offer an adjusted form of capitalism as a substitute for Islamic economic system. Of course they reserve the right to disagree with us and are free to follow any paradigm of their choice.

Mr. Akram Khan's definition rightly tries to focus on the statement of the basic problem but it falls short of making the problem and its solution built into the human life. If the individual is the 'economic man' type then neither he will be interested in achieving *falah* nor his behaviour will be characterized by *falah* seeking activities. Thus an explicit mention of the kind of individual interested in seeking *falah* is a necessary scientific condition to make the proposed definition consistent with the *Shari'ah* paradigm of economics. The use of the terms 'cooperation' and 'participation' in Mr. Akram Khan's definition can be criticized on the following grounds:

i) The definition of Islamic economics, scientifically speaking, should be limited to the statement of the basic economic problem. It should not include the features of the likely paradigm to be followed in the Islamic economy. The terms 'cooperative' and 'participative' are not indicative of the basic problem, but represent features of the *Shari'ah* paradigm in an Islamic economy. These terms should be mentioned in the definition or explanation of the paradigm and not in the definition of Islamic economics as such.

ii) Operationally speaking the inclusion of cooperation and participation may turn out to be unnecessary constraints for an Islamic economy. If all the economic activities have to be performed on the basis of cooperation and participation, then what happens to human initiative? It may so happen that an enterprising economic unit sees the opportunity or the need for a certain venture or activity which is allowed by *Shari'ah* but involves a very high degree of uncertainty.

Now the question is:

a) Should the others in the system cooperate with this unit and hence participate in this activity or not? If we accept the organization of resources on the basis of cooperation and participation it becomes mandatory for the others to do so whether they consider the project feasible or not. Should this always be the case in the Islamic economic system?

b) Let us look at the other aspects of this phenomenon. Suppose in the above case the others do not cooperate with this unit. Then the question is: should this enterprising unit take the initiative and undertake the activity on his own (if possible) or not? If cooperation and participation is the required condition then it should not.

c) If the terms cooperation and participation are used to describe the nature of the market that will exist under the *Shari'ah* paradigm, then again technically speaking, it is irrelevant to introduce these terms in the definition of Islamic economics. Cooperation and participation will have the place in the *Shari'ah* paradigm of Islamic economics similar to that of perfect competition in the market economy paradigm of economics based on laissez faire philosophy. As a matter of fact, cooperation, participation, honesty, justice and fairness – all these features of the *Shari'ah* paradigm are built into the behaviour of the Muslim. Once we recognize the Muslim as the representative economic unit of the Islamic society, the behavioural implications of this assumption naturally make all such attributes built into the Islamic economic system.

iii) "Organizing the resources of earth" is a very narrow statement in Khan's definition. It limits the scope of Islamic economics and contradicts the very spirit of its paradigm. The Muslim man believes that his life is purposive: and the purpose of his life is to be successful in his role as the vicegerent of Allah on this earth. The expression 'vicegerent of Allah on earth' does not mean that his activities should be limited to this earth only. It is the duty of the Muslim to design and administer the world in such a way that the rule of Allah is established. Thus our job is to apply Islam not only in our individual lives and on the Islamic society in a given country; but in fact, as the vicegerent of Allah, we are responsible for leading the entire humanity towards/on the path of *falah*. If the resources of the other planets become accessible and their organization helps us, we should treat them the same way as we treat the resources of this earth.

Conclusion

It seems appropriate to examine the definition of Islamic economics, as proposed in this note, to see if it is in line with the three scientific traditions of paradigm building as laid down above.

Firstly, we find that the definition of Islamic economics, as proposed in this note, limits itself to the statement of the basic economic problem only.

Secondly, our proposed definition uses the appropriate terminology which enables the reader to understand the concepts without any ambiguity.

Thirdly, our proposed definition recognizes the Muslim man as the representative economic agent. This recognition makes the basic economic problem and its solution logically built into his rational behaviour. (Is there any other way to achieve *falah* if one is NOT a Muslim indeed?). A Muslim's Islamic rationality demands obedience to Allah. This leads him to acquire the knowledge of *Shariah* and motivates him to apply it towards the solution of the basic economic problem. Thus our proposed definition maintains the third scientific tradition as well. It internalizes the process of Islamization. Here Islamization, in the final analysis, is the natural outcome of the rational behaviour of the economic agents in an Islamic society. For any paradigm of economics, in which individual units are allowed to make decisions, micro theory is crucial and must be founded on the rational behaviour of the micro units. The recognition of the Muslim man as the representative unit enables us to develop Islamic economics with consistency because his rational behaviour:

a) serves as the subject matter of Islamic microeconomics.
b) serves as the basis of the micro foundations of Islamic economics.

According to this definition the basic economic problem faced by the members of the Islamic society is that the resources are a trust of Allah, and man as His vicegerent wants to obey Him in the organization of these resources so that he is able to achieve *falah* by establishing His rule.

Note

* This and the following translation from the Qur'an are taken from S. Abul A'la Moudoodi's "The Meaning of Qur'an".

References

Ahmad, Khurshid, "Economic Development in an Islamic Framework". In *Islamic Perspectives: Studies in Honour of Mawlana Sayyid Abul A'la Mawdudi*, edited by Khurshid Ahmad and Zafar Ishaq Ansari. UK: The Islamic Foundation in Association with Saudi Publishing House, Jeddah, 1980.

Arif, Muhammad, "Towards Establishing the Micro foundations of Islamic Economics: A Contribution to the Theory of Consumer Behaviour in an Islamic Society". A paper presented at the 12th Annual Conference of the Association of Muslim Social Scientists, held at the University of Illinois, Urbana Champaign, November, 1983.

Edwards, R. C., M. Reich, and T. E. Weisskopf, *The Capitalist System*, 2nd ed. Englewood Cliffs, New Jersey: Prentice Hall, 1978.

Ferguson, C. E., *Microeconomic Theory*, 3rd ed., Homewood, Illinois: Richard D. Irwin, Inc. 1972.

Khan, M. Akram, "Islamic Economics: Nature and Need". *Journal of Research in Islamic Economics*. Vol. 1, No. 2; Winter 1404H/1984CE.

Kuhn, Thomas S., *The Structure of Scientific Revolutions*, 2nd ed., enl. Chicago: University of Chicago Press, 1970.

Zaman, S. M. Hasanuz, "Definition of Islamic Economics". *Journal of Research in Islamic Economics*, Vol. 1, No. 2; Winter 1404H/1984CE.

2

ECONOMIC POLICY IN THE EARLY ISLAMIC PERIOD

S. M. Hasan-uz-Zaman

Source: *The Journal: Rabitat Al-Alam Al-Islami*, 6:8 (1979), 22–6.

The Qur'an and the Sunnah give the basic principles which underlie the economic system of Islam. These were the principles which guided the early caliphs to consciously lay down an economic policy and which they pursued during their caliphate. The change in strategy was often necessitated due to changed socio-economic institutions in the newly conquered lands but this fact did not bring about a change in the policy. The levy and collection of poll-tax, the administration of land-tax and the introduction of Zakat are suggestive of the government's policy of removing injustice, relieving the burden of the oppressed classes and bringing about a forced distribution of wealth among the poor of the society. The expenditure of government revenues over different sectors of the economy gives an idea of the government's desire for economic growth and public welfare in addition to increase its defence potential. What in precise terms were the policy objectives which the early rulers intended to achieve can be laid down in the following lines:

The Qur'an enjoins the cardinal values of equity, justice, mutual co-operation and self-sacrifice for reorganizing the socio-economic milieu of the society.[1] The Holy Prophet has said: "If God makes anyone in charge of some job of the Muslims and he neglects their requirement, He will also neglect him in time of his need".[2] He has further said: "An office is a trust; it is a humiliation except for those who rise equal to the task and pay every one his due".[3] Again, "If somebody in a community sleeps hungry until the next morning, Allah will withdraw His security from that community"[4] It was on this basis that Caliph Umar declared: "(Umar) the son of Khattab would be answerable (to God) if a camel starves to death along the Euphrates"[5]

A study of the teachings of the Qur'an and the Holy Prophet's sayings suggests the objective of setting up an economic order which enforces justice, stops exploitation and sets up a contented, satisfied society. It is a real welfare state. What the early Islamic governments did to achieve this objective can be reproduced in the following lines:

Pattern of consumption

Islam discarded the contemporary outlook of an ever increasing higher standard of living[6] as the object of economic pursuits. While officially it seeks to increase produciton and distribute incomes and wealth on a broader level, it does not allow its followers to make it an ultimate object of their life. Firstly, the Qur'an and the Hadith prohibit the use of many luxurious items of wealth like precious metals, and silken clothes for men and strong drinks for everybody. Secondly, simplicity is made a norm[7] and austerity treated to be commendable. The Pious Caliphs set their own examples before other government officials to emphasise simplicity and austerity.[8] Works on Islamic history are replete with innumerable instances to suggest that in spite of increase in opulence after the conquests of Persia, Iraq, Syria and Egypt the level of consumption of the common man did not substantially change from simple mode of living. The frequent reports about distinguished persons' large bequests[9] suggest that large incomes were not lavishly spent and consumed. This simple living was inspired by Islamic teachings and by the examples of the rulers in contrast with the living of the well-to-do Persians who were accustomed to a high standard of big beautiful houses, costly robes, sumptuous dishes and expensive jewellery.

Distribution of income and wealth

The Qur'anic policy of distribution helps a lot in introducing a broader basis of the distribution of income and wealth and discouraging accumulations and concentrations. It assures that in the process of distribution none of the factors of produciton is deprived of its share nor does it exploit the other. Land, labour and capital jointly create value. As a result the land owners, the labourers and the owners of capital should jointly share in their produciton. In addition to this policy it compulsorily retains a portion of this produced wealth for those who are detained from contributing their share in production due to any social, physical or economic handicap.

The former aim was achieved by the Holy Prophet (peace be upon him) and the caliphs through prohibiting a very large number of exploitative and unjust techniques in trade.[10] A study of Hadith literature is suggestive of those measures which include disciplinary restrictions on landlord and the farmer, the employer and the employee, and the producer and the trader.

The latter aim was achieved by the rulers through the levy of taxes[11] including the impost of Zakat and to enact the laws of sustenance *(nafaqat)*, in addition to the emphasis on philanthropy and generosity.

Distribution of incomes and wealth acquired by man is perhaps the most distinguishing feature of Islamic economic system. The frequent emphasis on spending for noble cause, occurring in the Qur'an,[12] is not only voluntary but also to an extent compulsory. Moreover, Islam encourages such institutions as lead to wider distribution of wealth. The concept of the *Bayt-al-Mal* as a trust in the hands of the ruler retained for expending for the betterment of the public warrants for distributive bias of the financial policy of the State.[13] The levy of Zakat is a unique impost in the sense that its direct *quid-pro-quo* is prohibited for the tax-payer. The Islamic law of sustenance binds all the Muslims to share their wealth with their kinsmen. The State may, if need arises, extend this law to cover even the neighbourers and remote relations.[14] The prohibition of interest accommodates for those possible alternatives of investment which distribute the return on capital on a broader basis.[15] Even if these distributive measures leave some accumulations of wealth and large holdings, the law of inheritance compulsorily sub-divides them in relatively smaller fragments.[16] While the former measures are a regular though mild technique of distribution, the last is a long term process and takes a generation to substantially disintegrate accumulations. It is a process of this redistribution through which the sharers of the inherited wealth have to restart their economic struggle and prove their entrepreneurial genius. A really capable enterpreneur may exceed his legator but an incapable person may lose his existing resources. Thus the privilege of being wealthy is not monopolised by a few fortunate for ever.

Stability of prices

Another objective of the economic policy of the state was price stability. Free market economy prevailed in the early medieval societies. Price generally reflected the point of equilibrium between aggregate supply and effective demand. It was, therefore, natural that the increase in opulence should increase the demand for goods and hence the price. In the early Islamic period the increase in demand was generally met from import of goods from the newly conquered provinces. But due to slow means of transport supply often lagged behind the demand. Moreover, increased incomes and urbanisation also influenced the standard of living of the people. As a result the prices began to rise sharply. A rise in prices, without a rise in incomes is more detrimental to the poor than to the rich. But the government's policy did not allow these factors affect the people adversely due to a number of reasons: Firstly, the state provided them free rations.[17] Secondly, all able bodied persons were granted annual pensions.[18] Thirdly, the very poor were supported from general budget as well as from Zakat funds.[19] Fourthly, the rulers made it a point to ensure that prices of essential goods did not rise beyond the reach of the common man.[20] In some cases they controlled prices while sometime they restricted the rate of profit. Control on prices and security of the supply of essential goods ensured stability of the prices over a long period although prices of other non-essential items rose very sharply during the same period.

Security of supply

The security of supply was ensured by improved means of communication and transport. As already mentioned, it was Governor Amr b. al-Aas who first proposed the construction of a canal linking Mediterranean and Red Sea. Caliph Umar though disagreed with it, however, advised him to reopen the choked up canal linking the Nile to Red Sea,[21] for facilitating the transport of food grains. In Iraq many canals were as broad as to be used for transport.[22]

Founding of new cities implied the construciton of godowns[23] for storage of food grain and providing roads for quick transport of goods from one city to another.[24] This was extensively done by the rulers and the supply of goods was ensured. The supply was further facilitated by ensuring safety of the caravan routes which were, before the conquest, exposed to a number of hazards. Credit also goes to the organization of the efficient means of communication throughout the Muslim empire. Muawiya and his governor Ziyad spent huge funds on organizing a mail service.[25] The network of this service had become so effective by Hajjaj's time that his message from Kufa could reach Sind within three days.[26]

Expansion in production

Egypt and Iraq were already surplus areas; the former fed the Byzantines and the latter Persians, before Islam. Their conquest added to the vast food resources of the Islamic state. But the early rulers did not relie on the existing bounty; they continued to add to their resources. New lands were reclaimed and brought under cultivation by the Pious Caliphs and later rulers.[27] This not only added to the coffers of the state but also provided large quantities of food grains for the population and for export. There are reports to suggest the existence of 120000 canals around Basra (presumably including water courses and field channels). In Egypt more than one hundred thousand persons were employed to maintain dams and canals in working condition.[28]

A very large number of canals, dams and water courses were built by the rulers. A historian mentions of the construcion of a dam in the first century of Islam, along river Indus in the present day province of Sind in Pakistan. The dam Sakr-al-Mid was built to canalize the water of the river.[29]

Apart from efforts to increase agricultural production mining was also encouraged by exempting minerals from tax. Oil and mica are reported by some historians as an example in Iraq.[30] Handicrafts were not subject to tax and they flourished because contrary to food items, they were not subject to the policy of price controls.

Welfare activities

After food and clothing another basic necessity for man is housing. The early instances of founding new cities abound in number.[31] The basic policy was to avoid density of population as far as possible. This urbanization started since Caliph Umar's time and continued for centuries. The foundation of a city called for the basic establishments and amenities of life like offices, mosques, houses, godowns, roads, markets, bathhouses, communications, water supply and pastures for the cattle.[32] Some of these facilities were supplied by the inhabitants while some others were provided to the wayfarers by constructing rest-houses and inns and providing meal-houses and supplying fresh water.[33] Free medical service was institutionalised by Walid (A.H.85) when he inaugurated a *bimaristan* and also set up a number of leprosy clinics. Many of such hospitals as were set up in the first and the second centuries of Islam were also used as teaching hospitals.[34]

In addition to the policy of providing the above facilities the rulers made it a point to ensure that nobody was handicapped in his economic pursuits or social accomplishments simply for want of essential necessities of social requirements. The government gave direct and indirect support to the needy by advancing loans, relieving the undischarged debtor, and offering financial assistance. This welfare oriented behaviour of the government can be summed up in the words of historians which shed sufficient light on the policy and approach. A historian observed the behaviour of Caliph Umar's Governor in the following words: "Collects for the people grains like an ant; behaves affectionately like a mother; is a Bedouin in his care for date-trees and Nabaetean in supervising taxes; distributes equally and arbitrates justly". Another observer summed up the conduct of the Governor of Egypt thus: "He gives a camel if somebody loses his own; gives a salve if somebody misses one; gives money if somebody is needful of it."[35]

Population planning

It may be a point of argument if the Islamic approach to population is inspired by religious motives or economic requirements or both. The Holy Prophet's sayings allude to the desirability of increase in population.[36] The religious justification for this policy is beyond doubt because the strength of a religion lies in the number of its followers which could increase either by force, or by preaching or by multiplying. Islam did not advocate direct pressure of force; it made use of the last two devices. Preaching was made a religious duty.[37] Polygamy favoured increase in birth rate. Permission to marry non-Muslim female Scriptuaries[38] further increased the net reproduction rate of the Muslims with a negative effect on non-Muslims.

Besides this religious factor the Qur'anic condemnation of 'killing' the offsprings for fear of poverty[39] alludes to the disapproval of freely practising birth control measures on economic grounds. The planning of population that was practised in the early Islamic period not only aimed at an increase in the size of the population but also at changes in the structure of population. Large scale migrations and emigrations were organized and encouraged by the early Islamic governments, sometimes also for strategic and social reasons. The economic effects of these religious, social and strategic reasons were an increase in human capital and employment of extensive production techniques.

Protection for consumer

It was not only the setting up of market which the government took upon itself in the early period; it also ensured, as already mentioned in the above lines, that the trader did not exploit the buyer. The government interest in the market condition developed into the institution of *hisab*, the department of inspection which was responsible for stopping adulteration, under-weighing, over-work by the employees, employment in risky jobs, encroachment on thoroughfares, unhealthy trades, unlawful professions and cruelty to animals.[40] This department, headed by a *muhtasib*, performed more functions then the present day local government. There are numerous instances to suggest that the government intervened if the rules of justice and fairplay were violated. The Holy Prophet's treaties with the Thaqif, Hawazin and the people of Najran required a ban on the transactions involving interest.[41] Transactions involving uncertainty and any possibility of dispute were also banned in the Hadith.[42] The Holy Prophet not only appointed an inspector to ensure that the unlawful transactions were avoided but also himself visited the market advising the traders to observe moral principles in trade.[43] His successors were also active in controlling trade and commerce. Serious action was taken against adulteration.[44] Minting of coins was so regulated as to prevent debasement and dishonesty and save the general public from being defrauded.[45] Most of the rulers were vigilant about prices of different commodities in different markets.[46]

Defence

The Qur'anic emphasis on defence by laying down: "And make ready for them all thou canst of (armed) force and horses tethered, that thereby ye may dismay the enemy of Allah and your enemy, and others besides them whom ye know not",[47] inspired the Muslims to be always ready with their striking power. Actually it was treated to be the duty of every adult Muslim to take part in warfare. But manpower was not the only requirement for war. It needed a large number of riding animals, workshops for manufacturing conventional weapons, efficient communication system, cantonments and forts, and if necessary, manufacture of warships. A full account of the activities of the government in this regard as are given by the early historians,[48] are suggestive of its very keen interest in this sector and also a high degree of accomplishment as compared with their adversaries. The above lines discuss the objectives of the economic policy that was pursued by the early rulers consciously. These objectives include:

(1) Improvement in the pattern of consumption
(2) Improvement in the distribution of income and wealth
(3) Stability of prices of essential goods
(4) Security of supply
(5) Expansion in production
(6) Satisfaction of collective needs and other welfare activities
(7) Population planning
(8) Protection and safeguard of consumer
(9) Defence.

Notes and references

1 For example the Qur'an provides:

"Those who, if We give them power in the land establish worship and pay the poor due and enjoin right conduct and forbid indecency . . .".
(22:41)

"Lo: Allah commandeth you that ye restore deposits to their owners, and if ye judge between mankind, then ye judge justly . . .".
(4:58)

"Oye who believe: Be staunch in justice, witness for Allah, even though it be against yourself or (your) parents or (your) kindred, whether (the case be of) a rich man or a poor man, for Allah is nearer unto both (than ye are)."
(4:135)

"O ye who believe: Be steadfast witness for Allah in equity, and let not hatred of any people seduce you that ye deal not justly. Deal justly, that is nearer to your duty."
(5:8)

"Say: My Lord enjoineth justice."
(7:29)

"Give full measure and be not of those who give less than the due. And weigh with true balance. Wrong not mankind in their goods, and do no evil, making mischief in the earth . . .".
(26: 181–183)

"Allah forbiddeth you not, those who warred not against you on account of religion and drove you not out from your homes that ye should show them kindness and deal justly with them. Lo Allah loveth the just dealers."
(60:8)

2 Abu Daud: *Sunan:* Quran Mahal, Karachi, n.d. 2,465.
3 Sahih *Muslim:* Vol. 2, p. 209.
4 *Musnad* Ahmad Ibn Hanbal, Cairo 1333A. H., Vol. 2, p. 466.
5 At-Tabari, *Tarikh*, Cairo 1939 (1357 AH) Vol.3, p.272.
6 The Qur'an and the Sunna make a disparate approach to the issue of the standard of living. While they give due congnizance to natural tendencies in man which operate as a stimulus to work, to earn, and to spend; they equally use the force of their eschatological beliefs and edification to suppress the tendencies which expose man to depravity. To achieve this purpose it does not shirk from authorising the state to legislate for the same.
7 *Sunan* Ibn Maja: Qur'an Mahal, n.d. Vol. 2, p.543.
8 It is not possible here to cite the numerous examples of simplicity and austerity demonstrated in the early Caliphate as are reported by the historians. The reader may find such accounts in any work on them.
9 For some of such examples see my booklet *"Trading in Islam: Principles and Practices."* Motamar publications, n.d. PP 37–48.
10 Ibid, PP 20–24.
11 The most important of these taxes was land-tax which formed major part of general budget. Among other levies the fifth of the booty and the *fay* also acted as redistributive measures.
12 For example, suras 2:271–73, 280; 17:26; 92:6 etc.
13 The very concept of the Bayt-al-Mal is the concept of trust; the wealth of Bayt-al-Mal to be treated as God's wealth or Muslims' wealth, as against the imperial treasury as used to be known during the medieval period. This concept implied that monies paid into the treasury were God's trust and the common property of the Muslims and that the ruler was only in the position of a trustee, whose duty it was to expend them on the common concerns of Muslims while allowing for himself nothing more than a fixed stipend.
14 The law not only provides for the subsistence share of wife, children and other near relations but also pet animals, in the wealth of the guardian if he can afford it.
15 According to Islamic Law the owner may offer his land or capital to worker on the basis of share-cropping or partnership on the condition of sharing with the worker profit as well as loss.
16 For a broad outline of the law of inheritance see the Qur'an 4: 11–12.
17 Ibn Saad, *At-Tabaqat*, Leiden III (1) p. 203.
18 *Ibid* pp 213 sqq.
19 *Sunan* Nasai 5, 89, Sahih Bukhari, Zakat, 102, Abu Ubayd: *Kitab al-Ammal.* para 1803, 1804, 1805, 1912, 1914.
20 Tabari, *Tarikh*, Leiden 1893, Vol. 1, 2718 Ibn Saad, op cit., III (1) pp.18,40 etc.
21 Ibn Abdal-Hakam, *Futuh Misr*, Baghdad 1920, p 163. Aldo see Suleman Nadvi, *Arbon Ki Jahaz Rani*, Azamgarh, 1934.
22 Istakhri, *Masalik wa'l-Mamalik*, Cairo, 1938, p 80.
23 Yaqubi: *Kitab al-Buldan*, Leiden, 1967, 2,145 Baladhuri *Futuh al-Buldan*, al-Azhar Press, 1932 pp 191, 209–247.
24 Al-Kharbutti: *Tarikh al Iraq* p.419.
25 Baladhuri, 424.
26 Baladhuri, 288, 291, 325, 356 etc; Aghnides: *Muhammadan Theories of Finance, N.Y.*, 1916 p. 509.
27 Baladhuri, 352–53; Ibn Abd al Hakam, op. cit. 163. Lanepole: *A History of Egypt*, Part VI, London, 1901, 20.
28 Baladhuri, 432.
29 Alk harbutli, 360.

30 For a comprehensive work on the subject see Maruf Naji: *Uruba al-Mudun al-Islamiyya*, Baghdad, 1964.
31 Op cit.
32 Baladhuri, 64–65, 150, 415, Ibn Said 5, 258.
33 Yaqubi, 3, 36, Tabari 2, 1199: Istakhri, 241.
34 Ibn Ubayd paras 621, 659: Ibn Saad III (i) 1, 198: etc.
35 Muslim, 12, 212: Baladhuri, 279.
36 Abu Daud 2, 123.
37 For example the Qur'an 3; 104; 3:110; 16:112, etc.
38 The Qur'an 5:5.
39 The Qur'an 6:151, 17:31.
40 For a comprehensive work on the subject see Ibn al-Ukhuwwa: *Kitab Maalim al-Qurba fi ahkam a-Hisba*, Ed, Reuben Levy, Cambridge University Press, 1938.
41 Abu Ubayd, 469, 506 Baladhuri 67.
42 op cit.
43 Tirmidhi: Jami, Cairo, 1931–34 6, 35, 39.
44 Ibn Abd al-Hakam: *Sira Umar Ibn Abd al-Aziz*. Damascus 1966, 22.
45 Baladhuri, 455.
46 Tabari, 1, 2718; Ibn Saad III(1) 18, 40; Baladhuri, 25; etc.
47 8:60.
48 Ibn Saad III(i) 151, 220; Abu Ubayd, para 742; Tabari, 1, 2452 and 2, 1347; etc.

3

ISLAMIC ECONOMICS

Foundations and practices

Sami M. Abbasi, Kenneth W. Hollman and Joe H. Murrey, Jr

Source: *International Journal of Social Economics*, 16:5 (1989), 5–17.

Recent events in the Islamic world have captured the attention of the general public in the west to an unprecedented degree. Many of these events are widely misunderstood or misconstrued by them. This could be attributed to the ignorance of westerners concerning things Islamic, including the culture, art, geography, history and politics of Islamic countries as well as the precepts and conditions of the Islamic religion. Westerners often fail to comprehend the unshakeable conviction that Muslims have in the superiority of their religion; the Islamic belief that there is but one God who is the sole creator and ruler of the destiny of men; the belief in the necessity for manifest acts of common worship and devotional requirements for the Islamic faithful; and the belief that conscientious application of the sacred law of Islam is not only necessary for one's ultimate salvation and deliverance but also for the fulfilment of human existence on earth. To the Muslim faithful, a mere intellectual grasp of the religion is not sufficient; thanks must be rendered and obedience must be shown in the most profound manner[1,2,3, p. 7,4,5,6].

Today's business executive or manager should have a fundamental understanding of Islam, not merely to expand his/her intellectual horizons but as a practical business necessity[2,7,8,9]. He/she needs to comprehend the whole posture of Islam in its historical and environmental context. This is true for several reasons. First, there is a growing economic, political and cultural interdependence in the world; Muslim and non-Muslim nations of the world are becoming increasingly and inextricably linked. A significant share of the world's fossil fuel resources, which are of crucial importance to western economies, are located in and controlled by Muslim countries. Second, many Islamic countries, particularly those in the OPEC group, have proven to be of extraordinary strategic military importance to the west. Third, the oil-fuelled boom of the mid-1970s caused many Arab and Muslim countries to experience a rise in national income and in cash balances available for investment worldwide. The impact of these developments on world financial and trading patterns is immeasurable.

A final reason why managers need to understand Islamic economics is that there are about 720 million adherents of Islam in the world; they comprise approximately 20 per cent of the world's population and represent all known races. Muslims constitute a majority in over 35 countries and inhabit a nearly contiguous stretch of land from the shores of the Atlantic in the west to the confines of China and Malaysia in the east. Further, the religion is spreading or being revived in many parts of the world. Unfortunately, the forms of revivalism all too often have conformed to and reinforced the stereotypical image of the Muslim in the west: extreme theological ethnocentrism, strident fundamentalism, and religious chauvinism[3, p. 2,4,5,9,10,11].

The purpose of this article is to help broaden the understanding of contemporary business people of the principles of Islamic economics. The first section is an introduction to Islam and the second contains a general discussion of the Islamic religion. Emphasis is placed on the basic principles and key ethical practices of the religion and the ways that it differs from other great western religions. The third section focuses first on the general economic tenets and then on the economic basics of Islam. Specifically, this section explains how a system forbidding the payment or receipt of interest is being made viable in the modern world. The final section brings together the major findings of the study and presents the conclusions.

Islamic religious foundations

To Islamic believers, there is great pride in belonging to a unifying faith that has contributed to the social solidarity and cultural development of such a large part of the world. They see their religion first as a guide for a righteous way of life and for an eternal reward in the hereafter. They also see it as the generator of an original and rich civilisation [12, p. 7].

The Islamic ideology was first pronounced through the Prophet Muhammad in Mecca in the Holy Book, The Koran (or Qu'ran), in 610 AD, much later than either Christianity or Judaism. Muslims consider Muhammad to be the messenger of Islam — the appointed mouthpiece of God. The Koran is the principal inspiration and basic guidance of Islam. It not only yields dependable historical information on the life and genius of Muhammad, but it is thought to be the law of God, the literal word of God, since it came directly from heaven. It represents the supreme embodiment of the sacred beliefs of Islam[3,11,12, pp. 78–107].

Islam brought together Muslims regardless of colour, national origin, or economic or social status in a fellowship constructed on monotheism and egalitarianism — a faith in one God (Allah), equality among men, and the subjection of the individual to the good of the greater societal whole. The term "Islam" means submission, that is, the believer's submission to Allah. In the eyes of believers, Muhammad, like Abraham, Moses and Jesus, was a prophet who delivered the message of the true God. However, unlike the Christian conception of Jesus (the Son of God), Muslims do not consider Muhammad to be a divine figure, though he has earned the respect and reverence of countless millions of people. Rather, Muhammad was a mortal commissioned by God to deliver God's sacred message to mankind. Muhammad's objective was not to supplant but rather to complement the mission of his predecessors, Jesus and, especially, Abraham. In fact, Muhammad taught that Jesus and Moses were the most important bearers of God's hallowed message to his people in the Testaments and the Torah[3,12, pp. 88–105,13, p. 2].

Islam, like Christianity and Judaism, is regarded as a basic variant of the Abrahamic faith. Some observers see in all three the same religious themes. Islam bears particularly close historical and theological ties to Christianity, derived as they were from the common fount of Judaic and Hellenic beliefs. However, there are important differences, including the fact that Christianity clearly places less emphasis on communal solidarity than does Islam[12, pp. 3,27].

The powerful appeal of Islam lies in the fact that it is an all-embracing way of life governing the totality of the Muslim's being. As God's surrogate in this world, a person is not a totally free agent but is circumscribed by religious principles — a code of conduct for interpersonal relations — in his/her social and economic activities. Religion is paramount in all areas of life, even the most trivial; the moral and spiritual element is not divorced from everyday behaviour. The Muslim lives within a social structure shaped by Islamic values and is guided in his/her daily affairs by standards and rules of moral conduct forged in the cauldron of Islam. There are numerous Islamic dictates and prohibitions regarding secular transactions and human relationships. Islam is as much a socio-economic-political system as it is a religion [1,2,6,7, p. 11,9,11,13, p. 119].

Islamic theology is primarily based on writings in the Koran — the final recension (or review) of God's testament. It is also based on complementary information from: (a) prophetic sayings (the *hadith* or traditions — utterances and unspoken approvals attributed to Muhammad by reliable witnesses), and (b) ideal human conduct (the *Sunna* or way — reported acts and allowances of the Prophet). In addition to these non-canonical texts, another source of Islamic guidance is the *shari'a* — the laws derived from both the Koran and the Sunna. The shari'a is considered sacred law grounded in divine revelation.

There is general agreement among Muslims on these primary sources of guidance though the different Islamic sects or branches may disagree over the liturgical authenticity of many hadith. The Koran, hadith and Sunna in combination shaped the institutions attending the rise of Islam to socio-economic and political heights of attainment[2,3,6,14].

There are also two secondary sources of guidance in Islam. The first is the *ijma* — a historical consensus of qualified legal scholars regarding the adoption of existing doctrine to new socio-economic conditions. This art has significance in many Muslim countries today. The second is the *ra'y*, which is one's own determination of right and wrong based on analogical reasoning. This art is now largely discredited[2,3,6,14].

Islam is a religion studded with socio-religious injunctions and ordinances based on logic and rationality. The themes of reason, proof and deduction emanating from within a predetermined frame of reference are found throughout the Koran. A holy verse states that God called reason a religious law, and another states that he called the mind religion. Muhammad contended that there was congruence between revelations mentioned in the Holy Book that were received at different times and through different prophets. Similarly, Islamic exegetes (*Ulama*) today contend that there is internal coherence between Koranic writings and the hadith[1,3].

A cardinal principle of Islam is that there is to be no coercion in religion. In most Muslim countries, Islam is a religion with the strongest claim to human rights. The Prophet himself as well as the early caliphate (his successors) ordained it to be the duty of the state to protect the rights, property and churches of subjects, regardless of nationality or place of abode, Muslim and non-Muslim alike. Even when the early Islamic state was expanding, albeit by the sword, the conquered Jews and Christians became protected minorities who could practise their own religion and exercise some degree of autonomy under their religious head. It would be difficult to find a system, including democracy, that is so tolerant of minorities or which puts the state so completely at their service. One of the foundation-stones of the Islamic religion is the responsibility of the individual to the welfare of others in the world society[2,9,11,13, p. 2,15].

In countries where Islam is the state religion, the belief in Islam and its civil and ceremonial codes creates consensus; there is no distinction between secular and religious law; and religion permeates the whole fabric of society, both public and private. The dichotomy of church and state is alien in a truly Islamic context. Islam is considered to be the final revelation and the primal religion, not just "a" religion. The Koran has all the religious and moral truth required of mankind from birth to judgement. This belief has set the tone for Muslim scholarship and serves as the foundation for the Muslim states' prohibition on the practices of non-Muslim religion [1,3,8,11].

The following are considered to be the basic fundamentals of Islam (do's and don'ts):

(1) Acknowledging there is no god whatsoever but God. This is the essence of Islam:

> There is no God, but God.
>
> Thy Lord hath decreed, that ye worship none save Him . . .
>
> Set not up with Allah any other God . . . lest thou sit down reproved, forsaken.

The Islamic religion has as its foundation submission and obeisance to the will of the omnipotent and omniscient creator, the one and only God, who admits of no consorts or associates in the worship and adoration of him[12, pp. 103,112].

(2) Honouring and respecting parents:

> And lower unto them the wing of submission through mercy, and say: My Lord! Have mercy on them, seeking mercy from the Lord, for which thou hopest, then speak unto them a reasonable word.
>
> If one or both of them attain old age with thee, say not "Fie" unto them nor repulse them, but speak unto them a gracious word.

No message which the Prophet received from Allah is so thoroughly underscored in the revelations as honouring and respecting parents. In this area, the familiar and communal responsibility of believers is expressed in its purest form[12, pp. 112,126].

(3) Respecting the rights of others:

> Give the kinsman his due, and the needy, and the wayfarer . . .
> But if thou turn away from them, seeking mercy from the Lord,
> for which thou hopest, then speak unto them a reasonable word.

The Koran speaks often against such injustices as the wealthy lording their wealth over the poor, or the strong taking advantage of the weak and helpless[12, p. 112].

(4) Being generous but not a squanderer:

> . . . squander not (thy wealth) in wantonness. Lo! the squanderers were ever brothers of the devil, and the devil was ever an ingrate to his Lord.

And let not thy hand be chained to thy neck nor open it with a complete opening, lest thou sit down rebuked, denuded. Lo! thy Lord enlargeth the provision for whom He will, and straiteneth (it for whom He will)[12, p. 113].

(5) Avoiding killing except for justifiable cause:

Allah defendeth those who are true . . . sanction is given unto those who fight because they have been wronged . . . Those who have been driven from their homes unjustly only because they said: Our Lord is Allah.

Slay not the life which Allah hath forbidden save with right. Who so is slain wrongfully. We have given power unto his heir, but let him not commit excess in slaying[12, pp. 50,113].

(6) Not committing adultery:

And come not near unto adultery. Lo! it is an abomination and an evil way[12, p. 113].

(7) Safeguarding the possessions of orphans:

Come not near the wealth of the orphan save with that which is better till he come to strength; and keep the covenant. Lo! of the covenant it will be asked.

Muhammad himself was born to a father who died soon afterwards, and with the death of his mother was orphaned at age six. He undoubtedly understood very well what poverty accompanied by orphanage meant. Revelations regarding orphans, minors, the needy and destitute, as well as slaves and their treatment and liberation form the cornerstone of the social structure of Islam[12, pp. 38,112].

(8) Dealing justly and equitably:

Fill the measure when ye measure, and weigh with a right balance; that is meek, and better in the end.

And if you give your word, do justice thereunto . . .

The faithful are enjoined to be honest in their dealings with others, to be true to their commitments, to honour their promises and to be truthful, trustworthy and reliable[12, pp. 113,128].

(9) Being of pure heart and mind:

> Your Lord is best aware of what is in your minds. If ye are
> righteous then lo! He was ever forgiving unto those who turn
> (unto Him).

> It is your righteousness that reaches him.

A firm commandment of Islam is to be beneficent, to be good in communal relations and to act rightly in all circumstances. The faithful are
admonished to be constantly mindful of God's will in all dealings[12,
p. 113].
(10) Being humble and unpretentious:

> And walk not in the earth exultant. Lo! thou canst not rend
> the earth, nor canst thou stretch to the height of the hills . . . and
> follow not that whereof thou hast no knowledge. Lo! the hear-
> ing and the sight and the heart — of each of these it will be
> asked. Unto me it has been revealed that you should be humble
> that ye may not be proud over others. The faithful slaves of
> the Beneficent are they who walk upon the earth modestly and
> when the foolish address them answer: Peace[12, pp. 113,130].

Islamic economics

In recent years, many Islamic countries have proposed an Islamic economic
system which reasserts traditional Islamic values. These countries want a
complete system that covers specific patterns and areas of social and economic
behaviour for believers which does not involve a reformulation of Islamic
ideology or a compromise of its tenets. Economic practices are made
to conform to Koranic dictates, with no reinterpretation of the basic
doctrine[5,6].

The process of Islamisation of economic systems involves a stamping
of economic institutions with a particular Islamic identity. The process
seems to be gaining momentum over time. New institutions have been established, such as Islamic banks and development assistance agencies, with the
aim of translating Islamic economic ideals into practical business solutions
[8,16,17].

As noted previously, Islamic economics is closely related to and is part of
the Islamic concept of life. Both the Koran and Sunna have much to say on
economic questions. The welfare of people while on this earth and their
welfare in the hereafter are inextricably intertwined. Islamic teaching in the
economic sphere deals with a wide-ranging set of welfare issues: justice,
mercy, well-being, wisdom, and stress on fraternity and equality. It also

addresses purely economic issues such as the system of economic decision making, saving, investment, capital accumulation, the incentive system, the proper role of government, property rights, inheritance laws, the allocation of resources, the types of economic freedom man enjoys and other fundamental economic issues which have a deep-rooted significance for the Muslim faithful[1,3,11,13, p. 119,16,17].

In sum, the moral teachings of Islam lay down ethical guidelines for the effective control of all economic behaviour. Economic institutions should facilitate the achievement of the goals and objectives of Islam. Economic activities and undertakings are assessed and measured in moral terms and must be conducted in consonance with the ethos and norms of the Islamic value system. There must be a positive line of action leading towards the ultimate aim of welfare dispensed judiciously and tempered with wisdom. Specific ordinances, some obligatory and others prohibitive, serve as guides to economic actions.

Principles governing economic practices

It is Islamically legitimate to engage in material pursuits aiming at welfare. Commercial institutions relating to the sale of goods, hiring of workers, warehousing goods, wages, interest, exchange, banking and the like have been well understood in the Islamic world for many centuries. Many have Islamic origins.

There are several basic principles that serve as the foundation of Islamic economics. First, Islamic economics contraindicates acts resulting in harm, corruption and exploitation of the weak. Islamic economics, more than capitalism or socialism, emphasises man as part of a collectivity and attempts to balance and harmonise the individual's spiritual and material needs equitably against the needs of society at large. Islam stresses the virtue of total integration of morality in man's dealings with other human beings in any endeavour undertaken. It literally encompasses the relationship of Islamic adherents to each other and to their society from birth to death. In the area of economic activity as well as personal morality, Islam places great emphasis on selflessness as a form of gratitude towards God[1,3,7, p. 11,12, p. 1].

An overriding concern with social justice, stress on contractual obligations, the sanctity of one's word and the correct patterns of income and wealth distribution pervades Islamic economic thought. This is the basis of repeated admonitions regarding the needy, destitute, prisoners, wayfarers, orphans and one's parents and relatives; the appropriate tax policy and general orientation of government expenditures; the importance of meeting one's contractual obligations; and the precise execution of very strict trust and inheritance laws. In Islam, no individual or institution is left a victim of human vagaries and uncontrolled greed. The selfishness of the rich and powerful is denounced repeatedly[1,2,7, p. 11,11].

Second, Muslims are not averse to legitimate profit through trade and other kinds of business. Muhammad was not hostile to commerce as he himself was a businessman for most of his life, and some of his most eminent followers were merchants who imported, exported, and facilitated the transit of goods. The merchant has always been a respected member of the Islamic community, and like the artisan and members of other professions receives particular commendation in the Koran[3,5,6,7, p. 13,11].

While giving express approbation to certain occupations, the Koran sanctions any other licit occupational pursuit based on free will that does not involve usury, fraud and profiteering. In economics as in other areas, the belief is that Allah in his divine justice allows man the freedom to pursue actions on which he will be judged. Man is the author of his own economic vices and virtues and thus of his own crimes and punishment. Man's economic actions rest on the basis of his good deeds, his faith in Allah and his own conscience. There is clear reasoning behind this thinking. Muhammad wrote that a wide range of economic choices motivates man to be creative and to use his intellectual and physical endowments for the betterment of his life and his society. With the exception of certain doctrinally unacceptable practices (gambling, speculating, or trading in prohibited items such as alcohol or arms), man should be free to choose his trade or business of his own volition[7, p. 13,11,12, p. 172].

Third, Muslims have what seems to westerners to be a unique concept of property. Islam assumes that wealth is a favour from Allah, who created and so owns everything. Man is merely an agent with only temporal possession of material things. This belief is demonstrated in an often-quoted Koranic verse: "To him belongs whatever is in the heavens and whatever is in the earth and whatever is in between and whatever is beneath the soil". The shari'a provides commandmerits on how this trust is to be fulfilled. Those holding property are regarded as trustees or bondsmen who are entitled to receive profits therefrom. However, they are admonished to honour and please Allah by managing and using property entrusted to them in a responsible, righteous, socially beneficial and prudent manner; and to neither abuse, destroy, nor waste it. Wealth is to be used in moderation and is to be shared with the less fortunate through payment of the *Zakat* and the discreet giving of alms to the poor and needy generally[3,4,6,7, p. 6,9].

Those holding wealth are particularly admonished not to misuse it for dubious pleasure. Allah does not look with favour on those who spend and use resources wastefully and extravagantly. Further, property is not to be hoarded or accumulated as an end in itself; rather, it is to be viewed as a means of serving society as a whole. Avariciousness, cupidity and indifference to the poor and needy are cardinal sins [7, p. 6,9,13, p. 127].

Fourth, it should be noted that the Koran speaks approvingly of demarcated free enterprise, while quite straightforwardly discouraging the kind of central planning that characterises socialistic and communistic economies.

A relevant Koranic verse reads: "O ye who believe, consume not your property between yourselves unlawfully; it being lawful to acquire property through trade with mutual consent". Another quotation sanctions the acquisition of legitimate wealth: "Wealth rightly acquired is a good thing for the righteous man". The Koran does not condemn the accumulation of wealth, only the failure to use it to help others[1,3,4,9,11].

The protection of the rights to property, including ownership of the means of production, is deeply embedded in Islamic ideology. Private property is not to be confiscated, even at death. This contradiction to socialist philosophy is seen clearly in a passage dealing with laws of descent and distribution: "For everyone leaving an inheritance we have appointed heirs, parents, and near relations, and also husbands and wives with whom you have made firm covenants. So give each of them appointed shares." Even if the inheritance laws do not have a socialistic intent, they ensure that substantial estates soon get dispersed and prevent the concentration of wealth through massive inter-generational transfers to heirs and beneficiaries of the testator's choosing. Obviously, the inheritance laws serve as a major check on the accumulation of property[1,3,4,9,11,13, p. 120].

The Islamic emphasis on private property and individual initiative manifests itself in other ways. The Koran says that all men are created equal, but that some are endowed with more talent, energy, ambition and wealth, so there are bound to be differences in degrees of economic success. Simply put, some people possess more personal ability, aspirations and resources than others. There is no Koranic objection to pecuniary incentive and no assumption is made that all citizens in an Islamic society should consume at the same level. Thus, the Islamic religion accepts maldistribution of wealth and income and justifies it in the interests of efficiency, with the caveat that the wealthier people in society should be aware of their obligations to poorer people [1,4,6,9,15].

While the Holy Word speaks of the obligatory payment by the affluent of levies to feed and help the needy and wayfarers, it discourages transfers intended solely to equalise wealth. A relevant injunctive Koranic passage reads: "Allah has favoured some of you above others in the matter of worldly provision; but those more favoured will by no means restore a portion of their provision to those under their control". Such an injunction is again contrary to socialist thinking. Here is one reason why the Zakat, a capital levy or wealth tax designed to cover most of the activities of a modern welfare state, but very regressive in character, is favoured over income tax, a progressive tax whose effect is to redistribute income and wealth[6,9,15,18].

Basic characteristics

The full impact of the Islamic religion can be derived only from the political, social and economic institutions it sired. In the area of economics, ten fundamental characteristics — dictates, prohibitions, and injunctions — which distinguish the Islamic economic system from others are as follows:

(1) Muslims must pay an annual Zakat, an alms or poor tax that is assessed as a capital levy, not as a graduated income tax. Zakat means giving back to Allah a portion of his bounty as a means of purification or expiation for what the believer keeps for himself. It is also a means of avoiding the sufferings of the next life. Paying the Zakat — which is in many ways similar to the Christian tithe — is not only a commendable virtue but an imperative religious obligation. It is a duty rather than a mere ritual act. While the mode of paying the Zakat and the percentage levied are worked out according to carefully laid down and specifically defined rules, generally, peasants must pay from 5–10 per cent of their produce and others must pay 2.5 per cent of their income and savings. The Zakat contribution is over and above the secular tax.

(2) An obligation consecrated in Islam is that believers must pay food, clothing and other maintenance costs for certain categories of relatives, including one's wife, needy parents, and female children until they are married and male children until they reach the age of puberty.

(3) Believers are obliged (have an inalienable right and a communal responsibility) to provide charitable assistance to relatives, orphans, neighbours and the destitute. Individual fortunes are intertwined with and inseparable from the fortunes of the family and the entire community.

(4) Muslims are enjoined to work diligently to earn their own livelihood and to provide for dependants.

(5) Workers earning a wage or salary, employers earning a profit, and administrators are urged to do their work faithfully and loyally, and to exert the utmost effort to produce the highest quality product or service possible.

(6) The faithful are exhorted to observe the conditions laid down in the shari'a for the validity of business and financial transactions. These laws facilitate the exchange of goods, help remove miscomprehension and misunderstanding in business dealings and help promote a climate of peace between the contracting parties.

(7) Solemn and binding agreements such as pledges or trusts concluded with other parties must be fulfilled.

(8) Muslims must respect Koranic ordinances concerning the devolution of one's estate to heirs, including the surviving spouse, surviving parent(s) and all surviving children.

(9) Usury is condemned and usurious practices are considered to be the gravest of sins.

(10) Muslims are admonished to observe the property rights of others and to abstain from deception, exploitation, sharp trade practices and disruptive transgressions such as gambling, monopoly, pornography and

the like. Gaining profit through expediency and making unethical use of others for one's own advantage is condemned[3,4,6,11,14,15,18].

Ban on interest

In the economic arena, in particular, the Islamic religion is seen not as a set of rudimental beliefs but as an all-encompassing complex framework of theological reference. A particularly important principle is the unbending Koranic prohibition of the payment or receipt of interest, which is considered usury (*riba*).

Though there are few hadiths on the subject, Muslim scholars interpret riba as the increasing of a capital sum before repayment — the predetermined return on the use of money. Dicta regarding riba are more than mere moral exhortations; they are straightforward condemnations. To accept riba is to commit the very grave sin of *haram*. The moral distaste by Muslims for riba cannot be overstated and the penalty for not observing the rule is clear. Practitioners of the black art of usury are warned on pain of hell-fire to abstain; the giver and the taker are equally damned[2,3,5,6,15,16].

Riba is sometimes defined as "excessive" interest, but Moslem scholars today almost universally hold it to mean all interest. The Koran says that the incentive for interest is to accumulate money, to make more and more of it and to secure its rates at the expense of those who need the money. It stultifies the best humanitarian propensities. There is a holy verse which removes all doubt of the condemnation of interest: "Ye who believe! Fear God and give up what remains of your demand for usury, if ye are indeed believers". Another passage compares riba unfavourably with the Zakat when it says "Allah will wipe out riba and will foster charity", and another reads "O believer, devour not usury, doubled and redoubled". Clearly, the Koran implies that the creditor who does not seek to profit from his loan is performing an act of pious munificence which pleases Allah greatly[2,3,6,16,18,19,20, p. 53].

Riba is scorned and forbidden because of its pernicious effects. The faithful believe that it is useless and a reward gained without productive effort. No benefit comes from it. Its abolition is a consideration of equity — it was intended to protect the poor and weak against exploitation and unwarranted hardship and at the same time to encourage investors and labourers to combine their resources in joint ventures. Muslim scholars usually accept this prohibition to mean not only interest for the use of money, but any fixed or guaranteed interest payment on cash advances or on deposits. However, as noted above, no Koranic passage admonishes the faithful to shun trade which, unlike interest, involves an uncertain rate of return. The Koranic concern with the differentiation between riba and lawful commercial transactions can be sensed in the following passage: "They keep saying: the business of buying and selling is also like riba; whereas Allah has made buying and selling lawful and riba unlawful" [1,5,6,15,17,20, p. 33,21].

Thus, it is Koranically acceptable to sell goods and commodities and participate in other business transactions. Further, it is acceptable to lend money, but only if the return for the use of money fluctuates according to the actual profits made from such use. Capital should earn a profit only if it is invested in productive enterprise or in the provision of tangible services involving human effort and an element of risk.

It is interesting to note that riba is not viewed as a commercial concept; rather, it is always referred to in a moral context. This is in keeping with the Islamic concept of unity that emphasises man's role in a larger societal context and his moral obligation not to take advantage of other human beings. Society benefits little when debtors live in indebtedness from which there is no hope of escape. Similarly, society does not benefit when creditors hoard wealth for personal use and security and do not recirculate it in the community.

To protect the interest of both parties and to reduce the risk of fraudulent dealings, the Koran suggests that creditors have the terms of their loan put in writing and have it witnessed by two neutral parties. The relevant Koranic passage reads: "Believers, when you contract a debt for a fixed period, put it in writing. Let a scribe write it down for you with fairness . . .". Furthermore, creditors should be understanding to debtors who get into difficulty with repayments. An applicable Koranic verse states: "Should a debtor be in strained circumstances, then grant him respite, in respect of the repayment of capital sum, till a time of ease. But if, in such a case, you remit the capital sum also as a charity, it will be better for you." This verse suggests, first, that burdensome debt should be settled through peaceful bilateral negotiations and, second, that interest is a source of misery and should be prohibited. It is a vehicle through which the wealthy can exploit rather than help the needy[5,6,7,13,16,17,20, p. 34].

Financial techniques

In addition to a strong determination to establish an economic order in line with the teaching of Islam, there has been a revival of interest in Islamic banking in recent years. In general, an Islamic bank is one which does not charge or pay interest rates on loans or deposits. To skirt the ban on interest, Islamic banks use a profit-sharing system to replace interest on borrowed or loaned money. In contrast to western-inspired banks, an Islamic bank enables the Muslim faithful to conduct financial operations in accordance with their deeply held religious beliefs without resorting to the subterfuge of calling interest by another name and condoning it, or engaging in other practices which the faithful find repugnant[5,15,17,22,23].

On the liability side of the balance sheet, there are two types of accounts: demand deposit accounts, which earn no interest but entitle the holder to certain services, and savings deposit accounts, which may (after a period of three to six months) earn a return for the depositor. The savings depositor in essence purchases an equity position in whatever activity the bank uses the capital for. Deposits are treated as shares and their nominal value is not guaranteed. Thus, depending on the type of account, the depositor may be entitled to share in the profit from the bank's investment after the account is maintained for a given period. This type of savings account is in keeping with the Koran's interdiction of interest charges or payments[3,5,6,7, p. 27,15,16].

On the asset side of the balance sheet, the system is symmetrical in that there is equitable risk-sharing between the provider of capital and the entrepreneur who uses it. That is, profits and losses are shared between banks and economic agents according to certain predefined rules. The banks are in effect investing money rather than lending and they are sharing the risks with their clients. Muslim apologists insist that the active involvement of the bank with the entrepreneur through profit-sharing is more efficient than loan financing as a way to channel capital into productive outlets.

Thus, the Islamic bank does not charge a fixed rate of interest but does become a partner to the borrower on investment projects. Co-operation with and advice to the borrower is a primary responsibility of the bank, since it faces great risk on any investment project it finances. The advice includes both technical and economic aspects of the investment. These kinds of loans offer many advantages, albeit there are many risks and requirements for participating banks[4,5,6,15,16,17,24].

It remains to be seen whether the act of abolishing riba is a powerful enough force to engineer a smooth transition from an interest-based banking system to an exploitation-free Islamic banking system. Fundamentalist Islamic countries in which riba is prohibited are using a variety of traditional Islamic techniques on both the asset and liability sides of the balance sheet to achieve profit goals within Koranic-imposed constraints. Many Muslims sense and believe that this is an opportunity to have the shari'a guide and direct their lives, not only in family and social matters but also in economic and business matters. The fresh evaluation and new interpretation of original shari'a principles is providing a reassertion of shari'a as a valid and relevant corpus of law within which modern-day banking and business transactions can be conducted.

Conclusion

Like the Bible, the Koran is concerned primarily with spiritual matters of an abstract nature. Unlike the Bible, which concentrates on temporal teaching of social relations, the Koran deals with how believers should conduct their everyday lives. Indeed, for the Muslim faithful, no task, commitment, performance, journey, or business transaction is undertaken without the involvement of Allah.

Koranic proscriptions and ordinances are replete with strong but not always distinguishable ethical undertones which motivate Islamic social and economic behaviour. Morality as ordained by the Koran is not only a strong binding and unifying element among the Islamic faithful all over the world, but it serves as the foundation for all social and economic behaviour. In the social arena, the moral element is particularly evident in the stress on family ties, the respect for elders and the injunctions in the Koran prescribing behaviour for women. In the economic arena, the moral element surfaces in the emphasis placed on justice and fidelity in dealings, the distribution of property on inheritance, the sanctity of oath and trust, the honouring of one's covenants, the avoidance of riba and the general prevalence of an egalitarian sentiment. The moral element, reinforced with continual emphasis on the need for religion in one's daily life and in all commercial and occupational pursuits, is one of the most important factors which distinguish Islamic economics from other economic systems.

References

1. Kassem, O., "Arab Aid Funds Represent the Spirit of Islam", *Euromoney*, December 1981, pp. 140–46.
2. Jensen, L., "Shari'a: The Foundation of Islamic Law", *Business America*, 30 June 1980, pp. 12–13.
3. Abdul-Rauf, M., *The Islamic Doctrine of Economics and Contemporary Economic Thought: Highlight of a Conference on Theological Inquiry into Capitalism and Socialism*, American Enterprise Institute, Washington DC, 1979, pp. 1–23.
4. Pryor, F. L., "The Islamic Economic System", *Journal of Comparative Economics*, June 1985, pp. 197–222.
5. Khouri, R. G., "Islamic Banking: Knotting A New Network", *Aramco World Magazine*, May–June 1987, pp. 14–28.
6. Cooper, R., "A Calculator in One Hand and the Koran in the Other", *Euromoney*, November 1981, pp. 44–54.
7. Ali, M. (Ed.), *Islamic Banks and Strategies of Economic Cooperation*, New Century Publishers, London, 1984.
8. Looney, R. E., "Saudi Arabia's Islamic Growth Model", *Journal of Economic Issues*, June 1982, pp. 453–9.
9. Hoadley, W. E., "Business Should Tax Opportunities in Moslem Nations — Particularly in East Asia", *Dun's Business Month*, December 1983, p. 66.
10. Moore, A., "Will Gulf Investors Use Their Own Banks?", *The Banker*, December 1980, pp. 83–93.
11. Welling, K. M., "Clash of Values: A Seminar Weighs the Impact of Religion on Business", *Barron's*, 25 June 1979, pp. 9, 21–2.
12. Farah, C. E., *Islam: Beliefs and Observances*, Barron's Educational Series, New York, 1970.
13. MacEoin, D. and Al-Shahi, A. (Eds.), *Islam in the Modern World*, St Martin's Press, New York, 1983.
14. Graham, D., "Sharia Loses Its Grip", *Euromoney*, May 1987, pp. 137–8.

15. Davids, L. E., "Understanding Arab Banking', *The Bankers Magazine*, May–June 1983, pp. 62–72.
16. Karsten, I., "Islam and Financial Intermediation", *International Monetary Fund Staff Papers*, Vol. 29 No. 1, March 1982, pp. 108–42.
17. Khouri, R., "The Spread of Banking for Believers", *Euromoney*, May 1987, pp. 145–6.
18. Briston, R. and El-Ashker, A., "Religious Audit: Could It Happen Here?", *Accountancy*, October 1986, pp. 120–21.
19. Weiss, G., "Reconciling God, Mammon, and the Koran", *Barron's*, 20 May 1985, pp. 57–8.
20. Saleh, N. A., *Unlawful Gain and Legitimate Profit in Islamic Law*, Cambridge University Press, Cambridge, 1986.
21. "Double Jeopardy", *The Economist*, 3 May 1986, p. 98.
22. Wilson, R., *Banking and Finance in the Arab Middle East*, St Martin's Press, New York, 1983.
23. Thorn, P., "Jostling for Position in the Middle East", *The Banker*, April 1977, pp. 127–30.
24. Osborn, N., "Can Arab Banking Fulfill Its Vision?", *Institutional Investor*, June 1983, pp. 131–42.

4

ECONOMIC PRINCIPLES OF ISLAM

Fazlur Raḥmān

Source: *Islamic Studies*, 8:1 (1969), 1–8.

I—Economic values and social order

The purpose of Islam is the creation of conditions wherein every individual shall find maximum facilities for an active development and expression of his personality. For the purpose, as has been pointed out in different ways previously, a social context is necessary. Such a social context cannot, by its very nature, be that of a *laissez faire* society, but has to be directed towards *this* end. In a *laissez faire* society, disparity, exploitation in various forms and deformities arise and, as a consequence, the ultimate defeat of the very purpose of Islam is bound to occur. If the citizens of an Islamic State were true Muslims, the need for controls would obviously be proportionately less, and, theoretically, one could imagine their reaching a zero point where every-body behaved fairly and justly to everybody else. But this is somehow not yet visible on the horizon of our present-day society. While, therefore, a drive to instil a sense of Islamic responsibility must be undertaken in full vigour, the Islamic social order cannot be established immediately without there being a *directed* society.

The full expression of an individual, according to Islam, is obviously not just an economic expression.[1] The attempt to regard a human being as a purely economic entity is, in fact, a bitter satire on human nature, or, rather on the total historic performance of man.[2] However, without the establish-ment of socio-economic justice, it is inconceivable that the individuals of a society or the society as a whole can develop. Further, economic justice is the cornerstone even of social justice although, of course, social justice is much more than that. That is why we have ceaselessly reiterated, as the most basic principle of Islamic social order, the establishment of economic justice. Once a person's economic needs are secured, his personality will inevitably ooze out into creative scientific, intellectual, artistic and moral channels, because man is a thinking machine whose physical fuel is the economic factor. To imagine, therefore, that men in general will develop without the economic basis, is tantamount to committing treachery with human nature.

This is the reason why the Qur'ān lays so much emphasis on the economic and material side of life. In fact, whenever the Qur'ān mentions wealth, it mostly uses such adjectival names for it as "the good" (*Khayr*) and the "bounty of God" (*Faḍl Allāh*). The provision of sustenance or *Rizq* and other essential securities against disease, danger, ignorance etc., are continuously upheld as the most obvious blessings of God on man.[3] The Qur'ān exhorts the Faithful to earn and enjoy wealth and regards the infliction of poverty and straitened circumstances as a definite scourge from God.[4] Economic values, then, form the base of the Islamic social order. This fact invests the pursuit of wealth and production of material goods with a unique *moral* quality. A Muslim, who is engaged in the pursuit of producing and generating wealth, is, in consequence, engaged in a basic service to God or '*Ibādah*'. The Prophet is reported to have said that indigence verges on rejection of Truth (*Kufr*).

كاد الفقر ان يكون كفراً

Since, however, economic values, although absolutely necessary and basic for realising the Islamic purpose in society, are, nevertheless, essentially means to an end, it follows that the economic order has to be controlled and directed under the guidelines of other and more ultimate values. If, for example, in the pursuit of wealth, man begins to eat his fellow-man, the entire purpose is defeated. The avenues of economic production and distribution have, therefore, to be strictly controlled and engineered. This is what the principle of *Kasb Ḥalāl* precisely yields. It must be firstly borne in mind that wealth *is to be earned*. With the exception of such relatively small benefits as may accrue to the immediate family by the earning capacity of the head of that family during the latter's life or after his death or, again, such small transfers of benefits as may be gifted from person to person (all of which are allowed in Islam), all wealth has to be earned.[5]

The key-note of the Islamic economic endeavour of *Kasb Ḥalāl* is labour whether manual, mental or moral (whereby we mean various imperceptible and non-physical services to the community). The basic principle in this connection is laid down by the Qur'ān in IV: 29–32: "O you Faithful! devour not your wealth among yourselves through unjust means, unless it be on the basis of an agreed upon trade pact between you; and do not commit (economic and social) suicide (by devouring of wealth through unjust means). And set your eyes not greedily on that whereby God has given distinction to some of you (economically) over others; men and women shall share in what they have earned, and ask God of His bounty......"

It is thus clear that, whereas the Qur'ān patently recognises differences in capacities and skills among people because of native endowment and, consequently, in the economic gains because of these differences, it clearly lays down that all wealth must be earned through exercise of these capacities whatever they may be. The nature of the relationship between labour and its reward shall be discussed a little more fully in the following section.

Although Islam recognises great differences among people in their capabilities nevertheless it is obvious that in order to satisfy its requirements of economic and social justice, certain basic necessities must be guaranteed to every citizen of the State. These include food, clothing, shelter, health services and education. No citizen, even if his earning capacities are close to zero point, may be Islamically denied these rights.[6] There are various compelling reasons why this is so. Firstly, all these basic necessities are part of a human being *qua* human. A denial of any of these provisions would render a person in a definite sense subhuman. The Qur'ān regards a human being as honourable. The second reason, closely allied to the first, is that the Islamic requirements for the development of human individuals cannot be satisfied unless everyone gets a chance. Now if a person is denied any of these basic necessities, his chances to develop his individuality are thereby dimmed and may be negated. In fact, the establishment of economic and social justice is necessary for this very purpose.

This being so, it is obvious that an Islamic State shall establish a strict order of priorities as more or less successive targets of economic development. In other words, since human wants are unlimited and the economic avenues of satisfying them at any moment are limited, an order of priorities has to be prescribed for the satisfaction of these wants. More specifically, *since the economic order itself is a necessary means to the achievement of a total social order, the economic productive machine cannot be allowed to run riot and produce what it pleases and as it pleases.* The basic necessities have to be produced and satisfied first. Only we must add that the list of basic necessities mentioned above are strictly individual so far as the consumer is concerned, viz, food, clothing, etc. For the society as such, there is still another need which has to be satisfied even more primordially than all of these and this is the necessity of defence. An Islamic State will thus create adequate means for satisfying the needs of defence, food, clothing, shelter, health and education. Only when these are ensured, will it be possible for the society to move towards the Islamic ideal.

II—Methods of production and distribution of wealth

The key-note of economy in Islam, as we have said, is its concept of labour. Labour may be defined as that human exertion which is directly or indirectly involved in the production of wealth and is conducive to progress. According to this definition, not only will the manual labour be included in the concept "labour" but also all the managerial efforts required for running an economic venture. But this is not all; for, labour, according to this definition, includes all such intellectual and moral endeavour as makes for the progress of the society and also necessarily rebounds on the economic life with positive results. Thus, not only is a scientist, working in his laboratory, a labourer on this view, but so is a preacher who endeavours to resuscitate the moral fibre of the society in order to maintain its moral strength for the struggle required for the forward march. In sum, all constructive and creative endeavour is "labour."[7] Endeavour must have its reward.

That endeavour cannot and must not go unrewaded is a most fundamental principle of Islam.[8] Indeed, Islam insists that labour-reward principle is operative not only in the material sphere, but equally in the spiritual sphere. Further, it is not only true of the individual but of peoples and nations as well.[9] It is in this wide context that the Qur'ān uses terms like *Kasb* (earning), *Jazā'* (recompense), *Ajr* (wages or reward) etc. According to the Qur'ān, the entire universe works on this principle and every action has its necessary and inalienable consequences. *Justice is the name for the successful operation of the principle of labour and reward.* A society, therefore, which neglects this principle violates a most fundamental law of nature and inevitably suffers from its consequences. An Islamic State, therefore, works out exactly and justly the terms of the recompense of all forms of labour.

In spite of this vital Islamic principle, no one can deny that particularly later centuries of Muslim history constitute its flagrant violation. Disproportionate exploitation of power—economic, political, spiritual and social (including the sexual) has been rampant in our society and our masses are still bleeding from its consequences. Landlordism, political authoritarianism and spiritual exploitation have left the masses in shambles. To remedy this state of affairs as quickly and effectively as possible would probably be the most obvious touchstone of an Islamic State.[10] Important questions will have to be answered in settling a just scale. The shares of physical labour, of capital, of managerial and other services will have to be decided (in a flexible manner) in the light of a set of relevant social conditions. We give an illustration by citing a typical question. In the disorganized and inefficient and, indeed, really non-existent marketing conditions in the Pakistan of today, the middle man seems to be perhaps the major beneficiary of the entire economic process from production to consumption, even though his labour is often insignificant compared to his reward. Can this be allowed to go on or should intelligent marketing be established as soon as possible?

We have said before[11] that Islam is not identical either with doctrinaire socialism or capitalism. If the dilapidated condition of the society can be remedied without resorting to wholesale socialization and by keeping the freedom of the individual initiative intact, Islam would undoubtedly prefer this. *If, however, it is found that the state of the society is economically irremediable in the visible future without the State's taking over direct management of industry, Islam would not only not forbid this but would obviously enjoin this upon the State as a most imperative duty.* It should be pointed out that the Meccans before Islam paid little regularly towards social welfare out of the wealth they earned because they regarded their earned wealth as entirely their own individual possession. The Qur'ān, however, told them that there was a part of their wealth over which they had no right of ownership and which *belonged* to the society, even if they had earned it.[12] This yields to us the principle that *in the basic interest of the socio-economic justice, the State shall interfere with private wealth to the extent that socio-economic justice demands.*

If it is found necessary to nationalise industry, it has to be borne in mind that to nationalise labour would be a necessary consequence of this. To nationalise industries without the corresponding mobilization and regimentation of labour, as has been experimented by some of the developing countries as a halfway house measure, is not only ineffectual but is patently illogical and absurd.[13] It yields little fruit and creates more confusion. If avenues of production are controlled in this manner, then all labour will have to be regimented. In a general state of conscription for national work, nobody has the right to say, in the name of alleged freedom, that he will not work or that he will not do the job assigned to him.

There is nothing in Islam against this total mobilization of capital and labour. We have stated repeatedly in the body of this work that Islam provides a charter for interference in society and that Islamic society is a directed and controlled society.[13] When a child is young and understands very little of the demands of life, being ignorant of both the latent possibilities and dangers of the future, his life is fully regimented by his parents. But it would be absurd to say that the child is not free and that he is a slave. This is because freedom and its lack are expressions which are applicable only within certain suitable contexts meaningfully. If a sane adult in perfect possession of his intellectual and moral faculties is put in bondage, he would be said to be enslaved or enchained. This is because, left to himself, he is capable of that conduct which is expected of him. In a society, therefore, which may be economically and intellectually so backward that it is not easy for it even to realise what lies ahead of it, purposefully applied direction is absolutely requisite and is in no real sense against the concept of freedom. In fact, it is in order to make people free that such a measure is undertaken.

Nevertheless, it must be fully realised that such a total assumption of direction on the part of the State, if necessary, shall be by its very nature temporary. As soon as enough wealth is generated in the country, social and economic justice is established, and people are on the road to intellectual and moral self-awareness and confidence, external reins must be relinquished to bring out from within people their best.

If, however, the society has a good chance of building itself on a free-enterprise basis and is capable of redeeming its economic position fast, Islam would welcome this. The Qur'ān, in fact, assumes all-through that people do and can own wealth and have the right to produce wealth for themslves and for the society at large. The nearest form of free enterprise to the teaching of the Qur'ān is undoubtedly a kind of cooperative industry in the form of joint stock companies. This would liberalise the economic base. It would keep the freedom of the initiative intact, which would, in turn, be a factor in the fast generation of wealth; it would avoid the gross form of capitalistic exploitation symbolized by cartels. The wealth thus generated will partly be distributed among the investors and partly through fiscal measures over the society as a whole.

In our opinion, Islam does not deny share to the capital in the production of wealth, provided this capital and its share are kept subordinate to the overriding principle of economic justice operative in the society as a whole. The theory that capital is no more than congealed labour of the past generations, seems to us untenable on Islamic and rational principles. Islam has patently allowed share to capital in production. If everything were to be explained with reference to past factors, as the Communist theory explains capital, then this would be true not only of capital but of everything in the world. For, after all, everything existent in the world is a product of past factors. But this would be obviously stretching things too far. As for the contention that capital by itself does not produce anything, but man does by his labour, it would be equally true to say that man would not be able to produce anything by himself unless he has materials to produce from and through.

It is on the same basis that we must dismiss the extreme contention which seeks to reject bank interest on Islamic grounds. If capital has a share in the production of wealth, bank interest must be allowed. What cannot be allowed is economic exploitation (*Ẓulm*).[14] So far as the share of the capital is concerned, two things have to be ensured. Firstly, that the share that goes to capital whether as interest or otherwise is strictly regulated by other relevant factors in society and it cannot claim a disproportionate share of the net produce. Secondly, that the capital is lent out for productive purposes and not for purely consumptive purposes. It is when money is loaned out for purposes of consumption only and on exorbitant rental prices that interest becomes usury and economically harmful and morally reprehensible. The Qur'ān had prohibited usury and not legitimate interest. To stretch this ban to cover transactions like those of commercial banking is again doctrinaire and un-Islamic. It is not morality but moral diabetes.

Notes

1 See my article, "The Qur'ānic Solution of Pakistan's Educational Problems," Section I, quotations from the Qur'ān, in *Islamic Studies*, Journal of the Islamic Research Institute, Vol. VI, No. 4, December, 1967. This is the Qur'ānic critique of a purely materialistic outlook on life.

2 The Qur'ān itself has often criticized the persistent human tendency towards a narrow-minded and short-sighted material self-interest, *e.g.*, "Man has been created timid; when evil befalls him, he panicks but when good comes to him, he prevents it from reaching others" (LIX: 19–21). This criticism, however, presupposes that this initial trend is curable and, indeed, reversible under suitable training and with proper human initiative.

3 This is a frequent theme in the Qur'ān; in CVI: 4 God's blessing is particularly upheld in the removal of hunger and immunity from danger. The Qur'ān, however, also recurrently inveighs against those who are proud of their prosperity and smug in their worldly acquisitions (*māl wa'l banūn*—wealth and children) to the detriment of higher values of life. Similarly, there are innumerable verses of the Qur'ān citing knowledge as a special favour of God. Knowledge as source of goodness and power is, in fact, a patent Qur'ānic theme. In XXVI: 80 disease is regarded as an affliction which is removed by God.

4 E. G. II: 155; "The devil promises poverty" while "God promises amplitude" (II: 268).

5 II: 203 etc., also "Man shall get but what he has striven for" (LIII: 39).

6 This is also necessarily implied by the Qur'ānic dicta cited in Notes 3 and 4 above, which bring out the elemental importance of these necessities of life. This is precisely why their privation is regarded as the scourge of God *i.e.* they detract from the integrity of a man as man. It is the elemental nature of these factors in human life that has been clearly brought out by Shāh Waly Allāh under the term "*Irtifāq*" in his system of thought.

7 The most common Qur'ānic term is *'amal* (work) or *kasb* (earning, desert), and *sa'y* (endeavour); so are *jazā'* and *ajr* (reward). The Qur'ān uses them in a wider sense including the economic: see Qur'ān, *S. V.*

8 "Whosoever does the grain's worth of good, shall find its reward and whosoever does a grain's worth of evil, shall have its requital (IC: 7).

9 It is true that the Qur'ān regards the individual as a locus of ultimate moral responsibility which is irreducible and indissoluble. Thus, in a sense, every *individual person* is accountable for his deeds. But the Qur'ān equally regards collective responsibility as irreducible and inescapable. Indeed, the Qur'ān, in view of its general teaching, seems more concerned with collective responsibility and fates of societies as a whole. "That is a people of a bygone age; they were responsible for what they earned and you shall be answerable for what you perform and you shall not be held responsible for what they did" (II: 134, 141); "Thus have We rendered attractive to every people its behaviour" (VI: 108); "Every people has a life-term" (VII: 34). Thus, both the human individual and human society are irreducible entities.

10 See my article, "Some Reflections on the Reconstruction of Muslim Society in Pakistan", sections II and III, in *Islamic Studies*, Vol. VI, No. 2, June, 1967.

11 See article cited in the preceding note, section I.

12 *Ibid.*, pp. 109–11.

13 *Ibid.*, p. 107.

14 The Qur'ānic judgment on usury is principally contained in II: 275–279. The system of *Ribā*, as it was prevalent in the Prophet's day, was, in fact, a terrible form of exploitation.

5

NATURE AND SIGNIFICANCE OF ISLAMIC ECONOMICS

Khurshid Ahmad

Source: *Lectures on Islamic Economics*, Jeddah: Islamic Development Bank, 1992, pp. 19–31.

I

During the last 70 years or so, particularly after the First World War, quite a sizeable literature on themes relating to Islamic economics has been produced[1]. One can discern an evolution of thought and widening of the scope of subjects and themes people have addressed themselves to. We started with an effort to understand the economic teachings of Islam as expounded in the Qur'an and the *Sunnah* and the later Islamic literature. Gradually we have moved from an exposition of Islamic economic teachings towards the development of what can be described as the emerging science of Islamic economics. The two are not synonymous. "Islamic Economics" represents a systematic effort to try to understand the economic problem and man's behavior in relation to that problem from an Islamic perspective. This systematization of thought is gradually taking place. However, I would humbly submit that amongst different areas and themes relating to economic teachings of Islam expounded so far, perhaps what can be described as the science of Islamic economics remains the least developed.

It may not be far too wrong to suggest that even if we look into the history of the evolution of economic analysis in the West, we find that the subject and its major themes were developed first and the systematization of the theoretical framework followed suit. A somewhat similar trend can be discerned even in other disciplines, particularly in social sciences. We start with ideas; with propositions; develop them into theories and explanations; refine them further and that is how crystallization of thought in the form of a discipline takes place over a period of time. Islamic economics is also passing through similar phases. That is why it would be easier to speak on how Islam looks upon the problems of property, *Ribā*, *Zakāh*, social security, even employer/employee relationships, monetary policy, population strategy and development activities. But it is more difficult to spell out precisely the nature and significance of Islamic economics as a discipline, as a science in the making of which all the above could act as building blocs.

In the literature on Islamic economics, we find that some effort has been made in this direction. Amongst the pioneers, the founding fathers, Syed Mawdūdī and Bāqir al-Ṣadr have touched upon the subject[2]. Syed Mawdūdī, particularly in his lecture on "*the Economic Problem of Man and its Islamic Solution*" and Bāqir al-Ṣadr in his "*Iqtiṣādunā*" (our economics) have tried to define the nature of the economic problem from an Islamic viewpoint and in this context have thrown some light on the nature of Islamic economics, taking care of both the ideological perspectives and the technical relationships. While the founding fathers spelled out the moral and the human aspect in greater detail, they only touched upon the technical aspects. In later writings, Nejatullah Siddiqi in a number of articles dealing with the theory and spirit of Islamic economics tried to spell out the main concerns of Islamic economics, major areas of its study, and its unique approach to the economic problems[3]. He has also tried to highlight how the historical, analytical, descriptive and the prescriptive aspects of economics may be taken care of in an Islamic framework. In more recent writings, a number of articles have appeared in the *Journal of Research in Islamic Economics* starting with two papers produced by M. Akram Khan and Hasanuzzaman followed by the papers of M. A. Mannan and Muhammad Ariff. Monzer Kahf has also produced a short note on the subject and Anas Zarqa's paper in *Studies in Islamic Economics*, also touches upon the same theme. Naqvi's *Economics and Ethics: An Islamic Synthesis* represents an effort to develop an axiomatic approach to the subject. These, among others, are some of the major efforts that focus on the nature and significance of Islamic economics[4]. However, this is an area to which more thought has to be given and new literature has to be produced to fully articulate the nature, the scope, and the significance of Islamic economics as a rigorous discipline.

II

Historically speaking, Islamic economics has developed from the perspective of either *Kalām* (I am not using the word theology, because there is no theology as such in Islam), or *Fiqh. Kalām* unveils and expounds the *Ḥikmah*, or the rationale, behind Islamic teachings while *Fiqh* deals, *inter alia*, with the practical relationships, modes of behavior and conduct of a Muslim individual operating in a society. While this has been the context of the origin of Islamic economics, in our own times, Islamic economics is not a branch of either *Kalām* or *Fiqh*. Though it has grown out of that background yet it is a discipline in its own right. The challenge that we face as Muslim economists is that while developing an economic system based on Islam, we have to study different areas of economic activity for which Islam has provided concrete guidance, in a professional manner, and develop tools of analysis which would enable us to examine human behavior under different conditions and also to evolve tools of policy which would help in influencing things in the desired direction. All this has to be done with professional rigor and in a language that could even be understood by a non-Muslim economist.

This approach is necessary to make a systematized formulation of Islamic economics, to spell out the assumptions on which it is based, to develop the methodology it adopts and to find out its predictive capacities, so that we can have a framework for description and explanation as well as for prediction of human behavior in a given context; and, finally, to formulate policy recommendations highlighting its prescriptive role. That is the problem facing us and unless it is addressed in this manner the systematic development of Islamic economics as a science may not take place.

III

Let us now quickly cast a glance upon the mainstream economics in the context of which we are trying to make our effort. This is essential, first, because most of us have been trained in modern economics and, whether we like it or not, we are somehow conditioned by that thought, training and experience. If we can make some of the implicit assumptions of modern economics more explicit, that would help us in developing a better understanding of the subject. In fact, one of the concerns about the mainstream economics is that it has always tried to conceal many of its value based assumptions and has tried to put up a face that may not be in total conformity with reality. Persons like Jacob Viner, Gunnar Myrdal, Paul Streeten, John Galbraith, Lester Thurow, Heilbroner and others have realized it and have established that all that is being presented in the name of positive economics is not necessarily value-free. So a quick look at the scenario, from which we are trying to move, could be helpful to understand the departure that we, as Muslim economists, might have to make from the traditional economics, if we want to do justice to Islamic economics.

It is well known that economics has passed through many phases. The earliest efforts to grapple with economic problems were made by moral philosophers and reformers beginning with Aristotle, if not earlier and going through the Greco-Roman-Christian period in the West and the Islamic era in the East. The origin of economics is to be primarily found in ethics. Even Aristotle's basic ideas on economics have been presented in the context of ethics. And it is very interesting that the founder of modern economics, Adam Smith, who was primarily a professor of moral philosophy, also begins from the same background. *An Inquiry into the Nature and Causes of the Wealth of Nations (1776)* was preceded by his *Theory of Moral Sentiments (1759)*. The idea of self-interest, as it develops and unfolds itself in the *Wealth of*

Nations, can be traced back to the concept of "prudence" which he spells out in the *Theory of Moral Sentiments*. Thus, historically speaking, the origins of economics has to be traced to the background of ethics. The difference is that in the pre-18th century phase, the economic problem, economic analysis and its relation with ethical values, and norms were intertwined. They almost merged into each other. It is in the post-18th century developments, despite its moral origins, that economics seems to have grown into a self-contained discipline.

It would be difficult to deny the social-moral paradigm in which economic analysis was situated. Its birth, evolution and growth remain rooted in a set of metaphysical assumptions and moral values and attitudes. However, they were taken as given. No effort was made to expressly demonstrate whether they were desirable or not, equitable or not, in consonance with the needs and aspirations of mankind or not and to what extent a second look on them was needed. Nonetheless, it was in the background of the utilitarian philosophy of the 18th and 19th century, that economic science grew as a scientific discipline. Its later development, despite the moral origins, was more of a engineering growth; a growth that was more concerned with the mechanical relationships, with internal consistency, with efficient allocation, etc. Gradually, efficiency became the key concept around which the whole stream of economic thought somehow clustered. During this period, secularism held sways all the world over and there was no significant development either in the context of Islamic thought or even in the context of religious thought of Christianity, Judaism or other religions; with the result that the moral case went out by default. The only exception to this perhaps was Shāh Walīullah who tried to reconstruct Muslim thought and looked at the whole spectrum of man's social existence from the Islamic perspective[5]. But even that did not spark off any intellectual movement which could lead to a fundamental review of economic thought. It is only a recent phenomenon that Muslims have started undertaking this exercise.

IV

Self-interest, as one finds in the original writings of Adam Smith, is a much wider concept that the narrow and more limited view taken later in 19th century economic analysis and then its development and somewhat 'perfection' or stratification in the neo classical tradition. 'Prudence' in Adam Smith represented wisdom understanding and self-discipline. All three were regarded as essential parts of the whole exercise of self-interest. This width is conspicuous, by its absence, in later developments. Whatever efforts were made to add some kind of a moral dimension to economics, somehow, always remained outside the mainstream. With the expanding hegemony of capitalism, it seems that systematic efforts were made to eschew the moral dimension altogether.

To take one example, we find that, in the context of the inequities of the industrial revolution and the capitalist enterprise, there emerged some serious concern for basic human needs, for essential conditions for human living and for distributive justice, particularly in the writings of Tawney, Pigou, Dalton and others. A new world began to be opened up in the form of welfare economics. But very soon even that was sucked into a not-too-different utilitarian framework. Comparison of inter-personal utility was considered to be somehow outside the scope of economics. And finally we arrived at Pareto optimality, which very much brought welfare economics nearer to the utilitarian background in which mainstream economics had developed. The prospects of a restructuring of economics somehow collapsed into a search merely for making others better off without making somebody else worse off. A very promising development was nipped in the bud. Instead of influencing the mainstream, welfare economics remained a by-lane of little consequence. Strangely enough, there is an influence of mainstream economics on welfare economics but there is very little that welfare economics has done to influence the nature of mainstream economics.

The Keynesian revolution represents another important departure. It created a concern for the economy and its global dimensions. It is very interesting that Lionel Robbins' *Nature and Significance of Economic Science* and *Keynes' General Theory* appeared almost in the same climate and in the same politico-economic context. Robbins tried to salvage economics from the morass of the ethics aiming at perfecting the tools in a manner that the blames of economic failure could some how not fall upon the shoulders of economics. He makes a very clear statement that ethics and economics are strange bedfellows: there cannot be any link between the two. They can only be juxtaposed, not integrated. Keynes on the other hand, was concerned with the economy and the failures of capitalism. His thought leads to the development of a positive role for the state and new concerns for public policy and social economics. A freshness was breathed into economics, but again we find that, instead of a reformulation of the paradigm, changes began to be made within the paradigm and the end result is that within the neo-classical tradition, we have a burgeoning macroeconomics, while the moral assumptions and the micro-foundations of economics, remain as they were. The back-waters of economics remain unchanged.

Yet another major challenge came from development economics, again an area where the issue of changing the whole social system was involved. The multiplicity of factors, which ordinarily was not taken into account in economic analysis, had to be now taken account of. But again we find that the mainstream economics proves strong enough to suck in development economics and to put it in the same strait-jacket of capital-formation as the key to growth.

John Hicks, in his interesting essay, "A Manifesto", which has been published in his *Essays in World Economics* and reprinted in *Wealth and Welfare* makes the courageous claim that the rationale for economic freedom is not merely in economic efficiency as mainstream economists would make us believe. This is no more than a secondary support to freedom[6]. Economic freedom is important in its own right and if it is important in its own right then it means that it has an intrinsic value and note merely instrumental value. The very idea of intrinsic value and how to take note of it in economic analysis is a challenging idea. As I will show later on, this is where Islamic economics has to make a significant contribution.

The very idea of basic needs, whether in the context of welfare economics or development economics, is important not merely because of concern for needs, but, in my view, because of the foundation on which this concern is expressed and this is different from the limited framework of self-interest and of personal gain and pain on which bulk of the economic calculus is based. And if the idea of intrinsic value of things is accepted and accommodated, then, this would mean a major departure from the framework in which the mainstream economics has been developed. This digression primarily was with a view to invite attention to the way economics has developed and how a Muslim economist may look upon that.

V

The ideal of 'economic rationality' is primarily rooted in self-interest, at best, in the context of social achievement but nonetheless to be evaluated, understood and explained in the context of individual choice. This is germane to the mainstream economics. That is why major concern in economic analysis is on internal consistency so that resources are used optimally. There is some concern with external consistency also; that is a consistency between means and wants as they have been expressed, i.e. revealed preferences. Hardly anything beyond that is considered. When we try to reflect on this central problem of economics from an Islamic perspective, we find that the concept of rationality would have to be reconsidered. But before I come to that, let me in passing refer to the economic world view or the paradigm within which mainstream economics has developed. If I try to put it in a summary form, I would say that it consists of three elements.

Firstly, individual motivation is to be self-interest; personal gain or loss. That is the real motivating force. It is not merely an assumption. It has also become the objective. And that is how, moving between assumption and objective along with the primary consideration of self-interest, the economic analysis, economic description and economic prediction have developed.

Secondly, the individual is assumed to be operating in the context of a market framework; a framework where he has the opportunity to make his effort, to compete with others, to utilize scarce resources. This context of freedom and opportunity or this framework of competition and market is also an essential element of that paradigm.

The third element which had not originally been there, but has been added, is the role of state, involving a slight widening of the concept of rationality, to take into view individual rationality along with social or national rationality. These are the three main elements which reign supreme in the mainstream economic analysis.

VI

The Islamic paradigm is different. It is different not necessarily by denying all these but by spelling out its own unique world view and approach in the context of which analysis has to take place in Islamic economics.

Rationality in Islam does not deny the need for internal consistency. It does not deny that self-interest is one of the factors which influence human behavior. What it challenges is the assumption of the mainstream economics that for all practical purposes it is self-interest alone that would explain human wants and that would determine individual and social choice. I have very strong reservations if this is even factually true. There is ample evidence in the literature within mainstream economics which casts doubts upon this view of man and upon the assumption that self-interest alone is the most important and the most decisive factor in decision-making by the individual.

George Stigler, in his lecture on "Economics or Ethics", has claimed that the assumption of the mainstream economics is empirically true[7] but others have challenged this thesis and a number of alternative explanations are being offered in literature[8]. An equally strong case can be made for the possibility as well as rationality of rule-based behavior. Even within the framework of a market economy the possibility of different motivations can be demonstrated, not merely theoretically, but on the basis of empirical evidence. There is strong empirical evidence from Japan suggesting that systematic departures from self-interest based behavior to the direction of duty, loyalty, family traditions, cultural mores, goodwill and sense of belonging have played important role in its industrial successes. What Michio Morishima has described as 'the Japanese ethos' cannot be explained simply by the calculus of self-interested behavior[9]. There is a strong case for plurality of motives. While self-interest remains an important factor influencing human behavior, it is very difficult to conclusively prove that this is the only factor exclusively determining human behavior in all cultural settings. If it is incorrect to argue that people always act selflessly, it is equally unsubstantiated to assume that their behavior is always determined by self-interest alone. If it can be demonstrated that the plurality of motivations is a more rational proposition and can be substantiated by actual behavior of people living in different social systems, then the whole edifice of mainstream economics will have to be looked upon differently. If ethical values, Islamic or otherwise, have any influence on human conduct, and if we are interested in actual human behavior, and not simply assumed human behavior, then, the whole matrix of economic analysis would have to be redrawn. So, in my view, the first question we have to face is: What motivates man? What is the fundamental principle of rationality? Is it self-interest alone as assumed by the mainstream economics? Is this assumption philosophically tenable? Is it morally acceptable? Is it actually so? Is it empirically establishable? The studies by H. A. Simon[10] on human motivation and behavior, and also the evidence offered by the Dutch School, emphasizing the psychological approach to economics, empirically demonstrating multiplicity of motives, seem nearer to the human situation than the one-dimensional approach that is found in the mainstream economics.

The other aspect of self-interest is that it looks upon man primarily from the background that whatever he wants, is only for himself. 'Utility' and 'well-being' have almost been equated in economic literature. But is it really so? Is well-being coexistent with utility maximization? Is it possible to achieve well-being in ways other than utility maximization? Another aspect which deserves to be considered is "Does utility maximization always lead to well-being"?

Let us examine the question from another angle. Man operates at two levels. At one level, he is the object, and, at the other level, he is an instrument or he is an agent. For example, if I am prepared to give my life for my country or my faith, then, here, I am operating as an agent, pursuing an objective that is beyond my own physical well-being but something that I value. In welfare economics, the highest that we can think of is making others better off without making somebody worse off. But would that really always serve the interests of equity and justice, of social well-being, of human prosperity? If I am prepared, through my own volition, to be physically worse off to see that others are well-off, how would I take view of this approach? So, man whose behavior we examine in economics, has to be looked upon in both of these positions and not merely in one. One is that of him being an object, where self-interest may be the major motivating force and the other, where he is an agent; or should we use an Islamic term, a *Khalī fah*; where he is living for certain objectives. Nonetheless, the choice is his own according to his own evaluation. Yet, what he is trying to contribute is relevant to his economic behavior and to the economic consequences of his actions. Now this instrumental or agency role has not been taken into view by the mainstream economic analysis.

Similarly, on the question of rights, we find that a very utilitarian view of rights has been developed. Rights are valuable as instruments. Freedom is important as an instrument. In economic theory, whether in exchange or consumption, endowments or social security, the question of rights as having intrinsic value is ignored, yet, if there are rights with intrinsic value, then, it is something over and above the self-interest calculus. In that case, norms, rights and values would have to be integrated with otherwise mechanistic methodology of economics. So, when we look upon the issue of rationality from all these angles, we come to the conclusion that the narrow self-interest approach is a very limited approach. Although it is rich with a number of insights and capable of explaining many areas of activity and behavior, yet there are equally important areas which have been neglected or ignored or which are incapable of explanation within the narrow limits of its framework. As a result, thereof, we must admit that some falsification has also taken place in economic analysis and this has resulted in an impoverishment of economics.

Amartya Sen[11] has rightly emphasized that "moral acceptance of rights (especially rights that are valued and supported and not just respected in the form of constraints) may call for systematic departures from self-interested behavior. Even a partial and limited move in that direction in actual conduct can shake the behavioral foundations of standard economic theory. The impoverishment of economics related to its distancing from ethics affects both welfare economics (narrowing its reach and relevance) and predictive economics (weakening its behavioral foundations)".

The Islamic concept of rationality would not deny self-interest but would put self-interest in perspective with social responsibility and with behavior in the context of rules and norms. Again, it may be mentioned in passing that in the mainstream economics there is, *prima facie*, hardly any scope for rule-based behavior. But we do find that there are societies where self-interest alone has not been the most decisive factor. It has been supplemented by rule-based behavior: loyalty, sacrifice, restraint, altruism, service, respect for values of the society. This is not merely a moral proposition; it is an empirical reality. One can cite as examples, the early Muslim societies or even the Japanese and Chinese societies in the twentieth century. There are many factors that have played important role in shaping human behavior, which has led to economic activity and progress. There is some recognition of these factors in contemporary literature, even though it may be at the periphery. But these areas deserve to be considered seriously and that is what Islam does.

In Islam, self-interest has been put into the context of moral values, norms and rules. And all of these norms, rules and values are not necessarily man-made. They are not merely mechanically 'revealed preferences' of human behavior but Divinely revealed preferences and norms. They are based on the Qur'an and the *Sunnah*. They are part of the belief-system and moral commitment of the individual and the society. So, we find that we have several tiers or rationality. First, an internal consistency which is essential for efficiency. Second, an external consistency which takes care of the relationship between means and ends, i.e. optimal use of resources for fulfilment of preferences, wants and needs. Over and above that, there is a third level which takes care of moral and material, individual and social, national and international requirements.

In the mainstream economics, wants as given. In Islam, wants may not be taken as given. They are also choice-based. But here choice is based on the moral values, on *Shari'ah*, on the criterion of *Ḥalāl* (the permitted) and *Ḥarām* (the prohibited); and that is how the third level is developed. For want of a better term, this may be called the 'harmonizing consistency' which would ensure harmony between wants and values; between the 'revealed preferences' and the 'revelational preferences', between the actual and the desirable behavior in the framework of *Ḥalāl* and *Ḥarām*. Our concern is not confined to an equation between means and wants. The whole exercise has to take place in the context of a process preparing us to want what we should want. Harmonization between wants and needs, between wants and values and norms is as important as efficient allocation at the technical level.

The level of wants is also influenced. There is a framework in which these needs and wants have to take place. Muslim thinkers have tried to develop needs-profiles. Shāṭabi and Imām Al-Ghazālī are early examples. Shāh Walīullāh has discussed it in the context of *Irtifāqāt* and *Sa'ādah*. Bāqir-al-Ṣadr has touched upon this in the context of *'Adl* (justice) and *Ẓulm* (exploitation).

The criminal law of a country is always the protector of the social values of a people. Generally, in the criminal law of other civilizations and societies, there are long lists of crimes and punishments prescribed for them. In Islam, we find that *Ḥudūd* are very limited, just seven. When we reflect upon them, we find that perhaps there is a very close relationship between the Islamic concept of needs and values and the *Ḥudūd*. In the Islamic scheme, the first major value is the protection of *Īmān* and *Dīn* (faith and religion) because they constitute the basis on which the Muslim society, individual and the community, rest. And *Riddah* is the *Ḥadd* for that. Then comes *'Aql*, man's level of consciousness and we find there is *Ḥadd* for use of *Khamr*, (intoxication), which negates consciousness. Then comes life, the protection of human body, *Nafs*, and here we find the *Ḥudūd* of *Qiṣāṣ* and *Diyat*. Then we have the moral dimension of honor, of chastity, of protection of family and integrity, and we have the *Ḥadd* for *Zinā* and *Qadhf*. Then comes protection of property, *Māl* and we have the *Ḥadd* for *Sarqah* and *Hirābah*. These are the only seven *Ḥudud* in Islam. The rest are *Ta'zīrāt*. This gives us a scheme for the real values or needs of a society which have to be protected and these are *Īmān*, *'Aql*, *Nafs*, honor and property. Different scholars have tried to develop this scheme further and many more refinements may take place. The whole spectrum of *Ḥalāl* and *Ḥarām* provides that framework.

This third tier is unique to the Islamic system and merges into a fourth tier of rationality highlighting consistency between the action in this world and the Hereafter. So the Islamic paradigm would consist of these values and then the behavior of the individual would have to be studied, examined and analyzed in this context.

VII

These submissions suggest a new approach to the economic problem, based not on total negation of what man has done so far, but, to provide a new framework and develop a new paradigm within which to assimilate what can fit into the framework and leave out what is abhorrent to it. In a way, the development of socialist economics represented a not too dissimilar effort, although, the extent of change Islam visualizes is far grater and more fundamental. Marxist concern was confined to structural change. Islam stands for structural change as well as textural change within men and society.

Marx tried to develop a new paradigm, however, Marx did not expound what could be described as the whole matrix of socialist economics. What he gave was a new paradigm and a new approach which later on led to the development of economics of socialism. His contribution lies in giving a new economic philosophy, an exposition of what he saw as laws of social evolution, based on a particular principle of historical materialism and in the light of that a vision of the future; how things are destined to move and grow. One fails to find the nitty gritty of economics of socialism in the writings of Karl Marx. In that context, Ludwig Von Mises and Fredrick Hayek were correct in raising certain fundamental questions about the impossibility of socialist economics but they were incorrect in assuming that Marx did not give a new economics. He did give a new approach and a new paradigm. We are in a similar position. Our paradigm is different from the paradigm of Marxism but the problem is very similar. Since we have a different paradigm, we have to adopt a new approach, a new methodology, and then only would we be able to produce a new content of economics.

I will not go into the other aspects of this paradigm which deals with certain other critical issues like property rights, the role of state, network of incentives, *Waqf*, social subsistence (*Kifālah-al-'Āmmah*), etc. It may suffice to submit that the incentive of personal interest has been fully harnessed by Islam but not as the only or necessarily the most important factor or even the dominant factor. That is why personal interest is supplemented by other factors and that is why the concerns of Islamic economics, as also its points of intervention, start not merely with behavior or institutions but with motives. Now Islamic economics has a positive aspect, suggesting that it would be studying economic behavior as it is. But that is not all. It also has an equally important normative aspect. It is also interested in what ought to be. If moral values influence human conduct, and they do, then changed human behavior should also articulate itself in space and time. Our tools should be capable of comprehending that. We must not operate on the assumption that there is only one factor determining behavior. Ethically-based choice, ethically-based social behavior and ethically-based public policy fall as much within the scope of Islamic economics as different aspects of positive behavior. So the normative and the positive dimensions are poised together; both have to be there. In any way the normative dimensions come first as it is the starting point for the study of positive behavior which remains crucial.

In the study of the normative aspect, we rely upon *Shari'ah*, the Qur'an and *Sunnah*, the revealed guidance, as the primary source. Secondary sources include *Ijmā'*, *Ijtihād*, '*Urf*, etc. Interaction between the two sets of sources would enable the Muslim intellectual to be always engaged in an unceasing effort to remain rooted in his spiritual sources and yet keep up-to-date with the problems and exigencies of the time.

On the positive side we have to study economic behavior as it is and also as it would be as a result of ethics-based choice, ethics-based incentives, ethics-based effort and ethics-based policy. So ethics-based behavior and departures, therefrom, are to be empirically studied and capacity developed to predict the same. Our tools of analysis and our methodology has to be such that it takes into view both positive and normative dimensions. Recent developments in economics throwing light on behavior under uncertainty may, among others, provide some pointers to the methodology that might be needed to study these types of behavior.

One of the problems that beset economics, as also other social sciences, relate to an uncritical extensions of natural science methodology to this science of man. Scientific methodology is no doubt important. Observation and experiment are important tools in our kit but blind use of the methodology of natural sciences in the realm of social sciences, particularly in economics, is at the root of the poverty of thought in our times. It has been a major mistake that has to be rectified, not by denying the methodology of experiment and observation but by supplementing it and putting it into context.

In Islamic economics, self-interest based behavior and rule-based behavior and interaction between the two have to be studied simultaneously. Similarly, in the realm of policy-analysis and policy-formation, the challenge lies in developing policy-based operational tools and development of techniques to study individual and institutional behavior in the light of these policy objectives and interaction between them. These are the areas where Muslim economists will have to make original contributions. They will have to develop their own models. They will have to skillfully use statistics, mathematics, econometrics, etc. They will have to make use of static as well as dynamic analysis. In these efforts they will have to seek truth with scientific integrity. In this quest, tentative results, learning from experience and verification through practice, would be as relevant as in any other exercise. Yet I must emphasize that all these would be relevant within the context of this new value-framework.

Value judgements come into economics in a number of ways: through personal biases of the researcher, through assumptions on which his approach or that of the economics is based, in the form of the paradigm in the context of which he is thinking and behaving, in the formulation of the problem, in the choice of methodology, etc. I think Islam's contribution lies in making many of these hidden assumptions and values open and explicit. That makes the Islamic approach more scientific because we articulate our values and we share the framework with others. The paradigm is more comprehensive and complete. And all that has gone to make it, is expressly stated. Then we are prepared to examine all the inter-relationships from internal consistency to external consistency and what has been described as 'harmonizing consistency' which looks into the relationship between values and morals and objectives and the divinely revealed norms and rules to which we have to conform. It is a more scientific approach. Definitely, it would have to be a more comprehensive, all-embracing, and dynamic approach and a multidimensional methodology would be required because the required methodology cannot be limited to observation, experimentation and verification. They would continue to be important instruments of the tool kit but not its only instruments.

VIII

Finally, the significance of Islamic economics, if whatever has been said about its nature is correct, lies in enabling the Muslims to fashion their lives, particularly their economic system, in accordance with the Divine commandments. Its significance, however, does not lie merely for Muslims. There is no doubt that the development of Islamic economics is going to enrich the whole field of economics as such. It is destined to develop a new critique of economics, exposing some of its weaknesses and paving the way for its rectification. It would be able to throw fresh light on some of the areas which remain dark and virtually ignored in contemporary economics, at least in the mainstream economics. This may enhance the contribution that economics can make towards the solution of human problems. These insights which have been expressed but not fully availed of and the agonies and concerns that have been expressed by a number of economists but left unresponded may now be tackled in the new framework. The Muslim economists would be able to present a different tool kit, a more comprehensive framework for analysis and I hope a more realistic approach to what human behavior is and to what human behavior ought to be, and how the two interact with each other and how the society on the whole may be able to actualize the real objectives of *Falāḥ*, *Khayr*, goodness and well-being. In economics, despite all the lip-service paid to equality, the fact remains that efficiency has remained the prime consideration. Taking into view the inter-temporal aspects, though the growth dimension was added, yet equity and maximization of goodness and virtue and well-being in the society have never been properly and fully integrated within the framework of analysis as well as of prescription. At best it is at periphery and mostly even outside the periphery: either a trickle down effect or a by-product, never the real objective.

Our approach would integrate equity, efficiency and growth. Here, the objective would be *Khayr* and *Falāḥ*. Efficiency would have an instrumental role. Though, Islam would still be concerned with efficiency and with the judicious use of resources, yet the target would be maximization of *Khayr* and *Falāḥ*, the establishment of justice in all aspects of living and, with that objective, the individual and the collective behavior of the economic agents would be studied as well as influenced. It is through such interaction that a better society, a more equitable economy and a world which would be a better place to live in and which would be a stepping stone to success in *Ākhirah* (the hereafter) can be achieved. That is the objective we are setting before ourselves that represents our tryst with destiny.

Notes

1 "Contemporary Literature on Islamic Economics" by Nejatullah Siddiqi, in *Studies in Islamic Economics*, ed. by Khurshid Ahmad, Leicester, the Islamic Foundation, 1980. See also M. Akram Khan, *Islamic Economics: Annotated Sources in English and Urdu*, Leicester, The Islamic Foundation, 1983; Tariqullah Khan, *Islamic Economics: A Bibliography*, Jeddah, Islamic Research and Training Institute, 1984. Volker Nienhaus, *Literature on Islamic Economics in English and German*, Cologne, 1982.

2 S. Ābul A'la Mawdūdī, *Ma'āshīyāt-e-Islām*, Lahore: Islamic Publications, 1969 (edited by Khurshid Ahmad); S. M. Bāqir al-Ṣadr, *Iqtiṣadunā*, (Arabic), Urdu translation, (Hamārī Iqtiṣadiyāt), Lahore.

3 M. Nejatullah Siddiqi, *Some Aspects of Islamic Economy*, Lahore: Islamic Publications, 1970.

4 Also see: Khurshid Ahmad, "A Muslim Response" in J. Gremillion & William Ryan, *World Faiths and the New World Order*, Washington, Inter-religious Peace Colloquim, 1978.

5 See: Shāh Walīullāh, *Ḥujjatullāh al-Bālighah*; and M. M. Sharif, (ed.). *A History of Muslim Philosophy*, Vol.II.

6 J. R. Hicks, *Wealth and Welfare*, Oxford: Blackwell, 1981.

7 G. J. Stigler, "Economics or Ethics?" in S. Mcmurrin (ed.), *Tanner Lectures on Human Values*, Vol.II, Cambridge University Press, 1981.

8 See: A. K. Sen, "Labor Allocation in a Cooperative Enterprise", in *Review of Economic Studies*, 33, 1966; idem, "Behavior and the Concept of Preference", *Economica*; 40, 1973; idem "Choice, Orderings and Morality", in S. Korner (ed.), *Practical Reason*, Oxford, Blackwell, 1974; A. O. Hirschman, "Against Parsimony: Three Easy Ways of Complicating Some Categories of Economic Discoveries", *American Economic Review*, 74, 1984; T. Nagal, *The Possibility of Altruism*, Oxford: Clarenden Press, 1970; T. Scitovsky, *The Joyless Economy*, New York: Oxford University Press, 1976.

9 Michio Morishima, *Why Has Japan 'Succeeded'? Western Technology Ethos*, Cambridge University Press, 1982. Also see: Ronald Dore, *Authority and Benevolence: The Confucian Recipe for Industrial Success*, The McMillum Lecture, Pembroke College, Oxford, 1984.

10 H. A. Simon, *Models of Man*, New York, Wiley, 1957.

11 Amartya Sen, *On Ethics and Economics*, Oxford Basil Blackwell, 1987, p.57.

6

ISLAMIC ECONOMICS

Dogma or science?

Volker Nienhaus

Source: Kay Hafez (ed.), *The Islamic World and the West*, trans. Mary Ann Kenny, Leiden: Brill, 2000, pp. 86–99.

Islam is a religion which concerns itself with much more than the after-life: it is a comprehensive world view, and as such it endeavours to provide an answer to all questions of human existence. For every world view, consistency and coherence are of paramount importance. In the past, Islamic jurists used to ensure that Islam met these criteria. The dramatic social and economic transformation of the Islamic world in the twentieth century means, however, that their traditional body of knowledge is no longer sufficient to fully understand contemporary developments and changes.

The capacity to understand and explain phenomena is a precondition for sound judgements and rational evaluations. Max Weber, who is known in the West for being the first to insist in the 1920s that social science should be value-free, did not deny the possibility of applying the tools of rational analysis and reasonable argument to the sphere of values. Indeed, he explicitly recognised the importance of this type of debate. He did argue, however, that philosophers rather than social scientists should concern themselves with such matters. While Western economists have tended therefore to withhold value judgements and have only begun to return to the treatment of normative questions in the last few years, "Islamic economics," in contrast, has always defined itself as a science which makes explicit value judgements and links them to the findings of positive economics.

The fundamental principles of "Islamic economics"

The proponents of Islamic economics tend to create the impression that only one Islamic economic system exists and that this is uniform, final and closed.

In point of fact, the reverse is true. Islamic economics, in both theory and practice, comprises a wide variety of positions on important questions such as the permissibility of certain banking operations, the ideal social security system and the type and levels of taxation in the Islamic state. In spite of these differences, advocates of Islamic economics agree that the Koran and the *Sunna* must guide the behaviour of both the individual and the state. All practical recommendations and theoretical explanations must therefore refer to the regulations outlined in these primary Islamic sources. But this is by no means sufficient to resolve concrete problems such as the following when designing an Islamic system:

- The Koran and the *Sunna* contain very few prescriptions which are directly applicable to specific economic issues. The most notable exception are the laws of inheritance.
- Many of the concepts employed in the primary sources are based on terms which require interpretation. The most important example in this context is the word *riba*, which may be translated as "interest" or "usury."
- Even the first four "Rightly Guided" caliphs in the early days of Islam arrived at diverging interpretations of the primary sources, recommending, for example, different practices with respect to *zakat* (Islamic taxation), which is mentioned in the Koran. The method of analogy yields disparate answers depending on which passage in the Koran and *Sunna* is cited, and on how the similarity between the problem at hand and a previously solved case is established.
- In making an analogy, individual judgement comes into play, as does the individual's understanding of the theoretical background to the economic issue in question. As a result, different recommendations may be made while referring to the same passage in the *Sunna* or the Koran.
- Finally, the specific circumstances of a particular contemporary case also require consideration. Concrete recommendations may vary greatly even when starting from identical Koran citations, an identical theoretical background and an identical methodology in justifying the analogy. The appropriate practical implementation of Islamic taxation (*zakat*), for example, will depend on whether it is to be imposed in an oil-rich and sparsely populated country or in one that is densely populated and lacking in resources.

Thus the term "Islamic economics" represents a broad spectrum of differing positions. Politically, they range from justifying the status quo along strictly conservative lines to demands for social revolution, a radical transformation of property rights and ownership of the means of production, and a strong state with direct control over the economy. Notwithstanding this diversity of viewpoints, there is increasing evidence for the emergence of a mainstream viewpoint, which is shaped by recognised Muslim economists and further disseminated by respected Islamic institutions like Islamic universities and the *Islamic Development Bank*. The following deliberations will concentrate on this perspective and will also consider those theoretical concepts of Islamic economics in the areas of Islamic banking and taxation (*zakat*) which have been implemented in a number of Islamic countries.

Interest and morality in the early days of Islam

One of the best known economically relevant rules of Islam is the prohibition of interest or usury. There is some disagreement about the modern meaning of the old Arabic term *riba*, which is used in the Koran. In the days of the Prophet, credit was usually granted in times of need, when the debtor was forced to secure his own and his family's livelihood as a result of illness or crop failure or having lost his work tools or his wares through theft. Only moderate rates or no interest at all was charged. However, the loans had to be repaid in full within a relatively short period. If the debtor was unable to meet the deadline—which was frequently the case due to the short maturity of the loan—an extension was granted, but the sum was doubled. This process was repeated either until the debt had been repaid, which became more and more difficult, or until the debtor—and his family and children—had become the creditor's bondservants. This type of usury is not only immoral, it is also detrimental to the economy and to society as a whole.

It is widely accepted that at the time of the Prophet the term *riba* referred to usury of this type. Its contemporary significance is less clear, however. One argument holds that the prohibition of *riba* is confined to the form of usury outlined above and that moderate interest is permissible, particularly on loans for the financing of productive investments. Against this, it is argued that the Koran is the direct and eternal word of God and that the starting point for all interpretations must therefore be the abstract meaning of the relevant terms, rather than their significance in particular historical situations. *Riba* literally means "growth." Thus the prohibition of *riba* on loans means the prohibition of any kind of growth or advantage to the lender. The latter is merely entitled to full repayment of the loan by the agreed maturity date. This second, stricter interpretation of the prohibition of *riba* has gained general acceptance in Islamic economics and is the underlying principle of demands for an interest-free economic system.

Islamic finance today: between revolution and conservatism

Some Islamic authors interpret efforts to abolish *riba* at the time of the Prophet as a fundamental rejection of capitalist economic practices.

Supporters of this radical, socialist position favour state control over capital investment and over the economy as a whole. They emphasise the exploitative nature of the debtor-creditor relationship and use selected passages from the Koran to substantiate their criticism of private ownership of the means of production. Whereas these arguments were once more widespread, they are of minor importance in Islamic economics today and will not be considered in further detail here.

A second group of authors also advocates an interest-free economy and criticises interest-based credit relations. They consider it unjust and immoral that the creditor makes a financial gain by lending money at no entrepreneurial risk. Unlike the radical-socialist camp, this group does not question private ownership of the means of production per se. Nor do they reject the productivity of private capital. Their objective is to replace risk-free, interest-based financial practices with a system which ensures that the capital owner and the entrepreneur have a fair and just share in the risks and opportunities of the project. They suggest a system based on "partnership contracts," whereby the provider of capital and the entrepreneur agree to share the profits and losses of the project according to a pre-determined ratio. This is a modern version of a type of business contract which was common in the days of the Prophet, and which is adapted to modern-day needs. At the time of the Prophet, traders tended to use equity capital rather than loans to finance their transactions. They and their business partners contributed the necessary capital for the implementation of the project, and subsequently shared both gains and losses on the basis of their financial contributions. Advocates of the *profit/loss-sharing system* consider it superior to the conventional interest-based economy, not only morally and from the point of view of justice, but also economically, i.e. in terms of distribution, efficiency and stability.

A third group of Islamic economists base their ideas on the profit-sharing model, but focus specifically on its potential in terms of development. The most important criteria in a profit/loss-sharing system are the quality of the proposed project and the partner's integrity, rather than the security he can offer. Conventional banks, it is argued, lay so much emphasis on collateral that potential entrepreneurs with good ideas but insufficient cover have little chance of realising their projects. Banks operating on the principle of profit-sharing could, and should, ignore collateral considerations and rely on the quality of the project proposal. Advocates of this approach point out that the widespread adoption of Islamic banking practices would lead to an expansion of the entrepreneurial base in the national economy. A greater number of socially beneficial transactions and projects would be financed than is the case under the conventional banking system. Thus, Islamic finance could contribute significantly to a reform of the economy and of society in general.

A fourth group, finally, consists mainly of Islamic business people and bankers, who are not openly opposed to such reforms. However, they adopt a "legalistic" approach which implies a *de facto* adherence to the economic and social status quo. Bank practitioners are quick to point out that the principle of profit-sharing means sharing the risks as well as the opportunities. It stands to reason that entrepreneurs embarking on risky ventures will be interested in finding partners willing to share the risks, while those with safe projects will prefer to concentrate on their own profits and pay their creditors a fixed rate of interest. Interest-free banks can avoid the resulting problems by employing financing techniques which are essentially risk-free: Islamic jurists confirm the view of bank practitioners that the prohibition on interest only relates to loans of *money* and that profit resulting from leasing and trading with goods is permitted by the Koran. The bank should therefore act as a trader on behalf of the enterprise seeking funding: instead of granting a loan which will be used to buy raw materials, commodities or machines, the bank buys the goods and sells them on to the enterprise at a later date with an agreed surcharge on the cost price (*mark-up financing*). The mark-up is seen as legitimate trading profit rather than prohibited interest-based gain, as it is based not on money-lending, but on the delayed payment of the purchase price in what is in essence a trade or rental transaction.

It is obvious that while such profit may not legally be interest, in economic terms it is. Under this system, profit-sharing is limited to the deposit business of the interest-free banks: savers do not earn interest on their deposits, but share in the profits (or losses) of the bank. With mark-up financing, the *economic* difference between conventional and interest-free banking largely disappears, and conventional and interest-free banks finance the same transactions and the same projects for the same customers. In practice, at least 80 per cent of the financing techniques used by interest-free banks are surcharge-based and the same kind of commercial transactions are financed by them as by conventional banks.

Financing techniques based on such an interpretation of the prohibition of interest, are unlikely to promote development in the Islamic world. Because the difference between mark-up financing and interest-based transactions is legal rather than economic, this approach has little to offer either in terms of macro-economics, i.e. efficiency and stability, or with respect to equity and development. Western observers and Islamic economists alike are critical of the often careless use of the adjective "Islamic." For them, it should mean more than interest-free in a legalistic sense. They point to the danger of conservative legal experts using Islamic labels to sanction capitalist banking practices, in which case Islamic economics and Islamic banking are no more than an ideological veneer for a dogmatic adherence to the economic status quo.

Most Islamic economists, all too aware of the widespread underdevelopment of the Islamic world and the often extreme inequality in the distribution of income and wealth, reject legalistic and conservative positions, whose effect is to keep existing structures in place. They call for extensive reform and adherence to the primary sources of the Islamic world view which, they believe, reveal the necessity and the direction of economic and social change.

Interest-free banking. A bridge between Western and Islamic economic systems

Many Islamic economists are critical of the discrepancy between the ideology and practice of Islamic banking. This is particularly striking in the case of Pakistan, which began to Islamise its entire banking system in 1981 and officially completed the process in 1985. In 1991, however, the country's Supreme *Sharia* Court declared the practice of interest-free banking un-Islamic and demanded the abolition or radical revision of the underlying legal decrees (which has yet to happen, for political reasons). Criticism focused on the fact that what had become the standard technique in the financing business was, in fact, a combination of two types of financing originally designed for different types of transaction: a) the purchase and resale of goods at a higher than cost-price and b) the purchase of assets with a buy-back agreement.

The first method of financing corresponds to the mark-up financing out-lined above: customer A asks bank B to buy goods from supplier C and to sell them onto him with an agreement on deferred payment at a fixed mark-up on the cost price. In the second type of transaction—the purchase and resale of assets—only customer A and bank B are involved. The latter type of transaction was intended to secure claims from more long-term projects (such as the construction of a building), with purchase and repurchase occurring at different times. Rather than buying from supplier C, however, the standard technique used by Pakistani banks in about 80 per cent of all financing business was to buy customer A's goods—his stock for example—and to resell it to him immediately at a higher price. In this way, the bank was effectively giving the client an interest-bearing loan, which he could use for whatever purpose he chose. The practise involving two parties, rather than three as in the case of genuine trade financing, continued a tradition dating back to classical Islamic law of circumventing the prohibition of interest by means of legal tricks, a tradition which the *Sharia* court was not prepared to follow. It consequently rejected as un-Islamic the financing practices of Pakistan's banks.

There is no evidence to suggest that questionable practices of this kind are used by Islamic banks in other countries. It may be assumed therefore that what they practise is genuine trade financing—with three participants. Yet this too is criticised by Islamic economists for falling short of the ideal of profit/loss-sharing and because it differs only marginally in economic terms from interest-based commercial lending. Yet while criticism of this kind may be justified on a theoretical level, it should not be overstated: the particular circumstances under which Islamic banks operate in most parts of the Muslim world should also be taken into consideration.

With the exception of Pakistan, Iran and Sudan, all Islamic countries have conventional interest-based fiscal systems. Approximately 120 Islamic banks and financial institutions (mainly investment and insurance companies) are in existence today. They are generally of marginal importance in these systems, with shares of the market of between less than one and 10 per cent, and only in exceptional cases of up to 25 per cent. Governments and central banks in most Islamic countries are Western-oriented and approach the Islamic banks with more than a touch of scepticism. One notable exception is Malaysia, where the government and central bank have given their full backing to the development of a *dual banking system* since the beginning of the 1990s, in which conventional and Islamic banking practices are on an equal footing. Islamic banking in Malaysia is carried by one exclusively Islamic bank and separate Islamic departments in many of the conventional banks.

Islamic banks in most mixed systems defend the practice of markup financing by pointing to the danger of accumulating negative risks under a profit-sharing system. They maintain that in order to secure deposits, which are affected by the bank's profits *and* losses, there should be a strict limitation on high-risk profit/loss-sharing practices. The maturity structure is also seen as problematic: deposits are mainly short-term in nature, yet profit-sharing tends to be middle to long-term, and it runs counter to sound banking principles to finance long-term projects with short-term deposits. A further issue is that the Islamic banks must offer their depositors competitive returns, particularly in the first years of their existence. Yet while conventional trade financing yields relatively rapid returns, profits from projects financed on the basis of profit-sharing often emerge only after a long gestation period. In most countries, finally, responsibility for financing development projects is carried not by the commercial banks, which include the Islamic banks, but by special banks, which are established and supported by the state.

Against this background, criticism of the legalistic interpretation of the prohibition of interest seems less fundamental. Indeed it can be argued that co-operation between the two banking systems becomes relatively straightforward when the Islamic substance of financing contracts is restricted to *legal* issues, while the entrepreneurial decisions by the management of both Islamic and conventional banks are based on the same criteria of profitability and liquidity. In practice, Islamic and Western banks working on an international level have intensified their contacts over the last number of years. Western banks have become progressively more interested in the Islamic banks' market, and growing numbers of conventional banks are offering their Muslim clients "Islamic products," opening Islamic departments and, in some cases, establishing Islamic subsidiaries in the Gulf region. They are also offering services and financing models to the Islamic banks which allow them to make interest-free, but profitable short-term placements of surplus funds. Whether *Sharia* experts would approve of all the types of "Islamic products" and cooperation currently in existence is open to question. It is undeniable however that Islamic financing practices are no longer viewed as a curiosity in the West, and that they are receiving growing recognition in both banking and business circles. Thus the legalistic interpretation of the interest ban has, in fact, helped to forge links between the Islamic and Western economic systems.

Islamic economics and political opposition

Not all Islamic economists welcome this "convergence of systems." Some see it as a reinforcement of existing conditions which are clearly a hindrance to development. With a view to introducing change, they demand a stronger adherence to Islamic ideals involving more competition, a reduction in privileges and a limitation of the power of the state to the reinforcement of the principles of law, justice and equal participation. An Islamic economic system, they argue, means more than interest-free financial practices. It presupposes a transformation of the economic and social power structures, a transformation which would have to be more radical in some Islamic states than in others.

A clash between the proponents of an Islamic economic system and the ruling elite is often inevitable. The latter essentially dictate the form in which the Islamic opposition expresses its demands. Either the opposition is involved in the parliamentary system and given the opportunity to make constructive criticism and contribute to the decision-making process, or it is forced into a fundamentalist, extra-parliamentary position in militant opposition to the status quo. The more radical the opposition, the more important the mobilising power of Islamic ideologies, which operate on an emotional level and whose promises of salvation have a far greater appeal than the intellectually sophisticated concepts underlying the Islamic economic system.

The more politicised and radical Islam is in a particular country, therefore, the more simplistic and lacking in substance are demands for an "Islamic system." It is regrettable that the Western media's perception of Islam tends to be coloured by the most radical slogans, which can easily be misrepresented as applying to the Islamic world as a whole. There is little inclination in the West to look beyond the political agitation, and even political decision-makers regularly display considerable reluctance to come to an understanding of Islamic concepts. The tragedy is that such concepts could ultimately be demonstrated to justify a system which comes much closer to Western notions of development than the rigid and frequently repressive systems currently in existence in many countries.

Islamic economics: rigid dogma or dynamic science?

It is beyond question that Islamic economics is open to serious investigation. Far from being a monolithic and closed doctrine resting on irrefutable principles, or a rigid dogma open to change only on the most trivial details, it defines itself as a new academic discipline, which is practical in focus and uses rational methods to explain and advise on economic phenomena in the Islamic world. In the past, concrete recommendations regarding appropriate human behaviour and the best organisations and structures were made by Islamic jurists, who referred to the Koran and *Sunna* as the primary sources of the Islamic world view. While Islamic economists endeavouring to make similar recommendations today cannot afford to ignore the solutions contained in Islamic law, this does not mean that it is impossible to arrive at new answers.

The methods employed in Islamic economics differ from those used in Islamic jurisprudence and are derived from modern, i.e. Western, economics. When dealing with a problem for which Islamic jurisprudence has already found a solution, the Islamic economist who arrives at an alternative recommendation must be prepared to enter into a discussion on method. He must be able to demonstrate on the basis of rational argument why his method is superior to that of the Islamic jurists. For this, he needs to be familiar with legal methods, and to have a sound knowledge of Arabic language and history. In its approach, therefore, Islamic economics is an inter- or multi-disciplinary science, under the umbrella of the discipline of economics.

In the early years of Islamic economics, from its origins in the 1950s until the 1970s, much study was devoted to the construction of *ideal worlds*. That these models were superior to the imperfect reality of Western socialist and capitalist systems, not to mention the real existing systems of the Islamic world, is neither surprising nor methodologically relevant. Since the mid-1980s, this phase, which was characterised by a strong ideological polarisation, has given way to a growing *realism*. This development was influenced to a large degree by the implementation since the mid-1970s of some of the doctrines of Islamic economics, such as interest-free banking. As a result, it has become possible to examine the experiences of Islamic banks working in a conventional environment and to analyse attempts to Islamise the economies of Pakistan, Iran and Sudan.

What has become apparent is that most Muslims are less influenced in their economic behaviour by Islamic rules such as the prohibition of interest and the mandatory payment of *zakat* than had been assumed in earlier models of ideal systems. If the prohibition of interest were rigidly adhered to by all Muslims, it would be difficult to explain why Islamic banks in countries with a mixed fiscal system have not secured a much bigger market share in the ten or more years they have been in operation, or why the majority of the population continue to conduct their business with conventional banks. Analyses of banking practices in the Islamised systems of Pakistan and Iran have also produced sobering results, particularly with regard to the behaviour of the bank management there. Developments in Malaysia, finally, raise further doubts as to the influence of Islamic rules on the economic behaviour of Muslims. Government support for the introduction of Islamic departments in conventional banks has not been matched by Malaysian depositors, who continue by and large to opt for conventional banking schemes.

Financing policy and social security is a further area with considerable influence on economic development which has begun to reflect a greater approximation of reality. It has become obvious in recent years that Islamic law in this area is in need of considerable modification and extension. For while there are numerous and detailed expositions on the taxation of the spoils of war, of camel and sheep, and of dates and honey, the imposition of taxes on wages and salaries or on portfolio investments is rarely dealt with, and then in a contradictory manner. A discussion of the imposition of *zakat* in the modern age is long overdue, as is the creation of a wider consensus on the basic principles.

Islamic economics defines itself more through its methodology than its object of study. It is therefore somewhat surprising that the methods employed by modern-day economists, when defining the basis and rates for the levy of *zakat*, differ widely from those used by Islamic jurists in the past. The literature produced today on the subject of *zakat* contains a large number of false statements, questionable analogies and subjective evaluations, including the claim that the basis of assessment for *zakat* and the rates to be imposed were established once and for all in the Koran. In point of fact, most regulations were not even drawn up by the Prophet, but by the first caliphs, who in some cases modified the rules laid down by their predecessors. Furthermore it is argued that as landowners must pay a certain percentage of their crop in tax, *zakat* is a form of income tax. However, since the harvest is an indicator of the value of the agricultural land, it is more plausible to treat the landowners' contribution as a form of *property* tax, all the more so since the individual costs of cultivating the land are not taken into consideration. Subjective evaluations also colour discussions on the correct treatment of completely new types of income and property, such as wages and salaries and portfolio investments. As yet, there has been no clarifying discussion and no criticism of methodologically unsound studies.

Western literature on Islamic economics occasionally creates the impression that the great scholars from the early days of Islam and the Islamic Middle Ages provided an answer to all the important questions, leaving us with what is in essence a closed doctrinal system, inflexible on all but the most peripheral matters. While it may be true that modern-day Islamic economists frequently refer to earlier solutions, this does not imply that all questions have been answered or that Islamic economics is merely repetitive and uncreative. As suggested above, there are no definitive answers even to important questions such as the correct interpretation and implementation of the prohibition of interest or the rules governing *zakat*. To overlook the dynamism of Islamic economics would therefore be misguided.

Nevertheless, it must be remembered that scientific freedom and a critical attitude towards existing conditions are not encouraged by the governments and ruling classes in many Muslim countries. Thus it is difficult, and in some cases impossible, to conduct an open exchange of views. Frequently it is left to Western institutions to create a suitable forum for discussion. Islamic institutions in the West also have an important contribution to make to the future development of Islamic economics. But despite the fact that progress is slow and not always continuous, Islamic economics is clearly beginning to establish itself as a *science*, which will not allow itself to degenerate into an ideology of social revolution or a veneer for conservative dogmatism.

Constructive dialogue cannot be conducted with dogmatists or ideologues. Science, on the other hand, has developed techniques to deal with disagreements and differences of opinion not by physical force but by means of rational argument. In the field of science, the "Clash of Civilizations" need not end in destruction and defeat: both sides stand to gain from a critical but rational intellectual examination of their own world view.

Bibliography

Ahmad, Ausaf, and Kazim Raza Awan, (eds.). 1992. *Lectures on Islamic Economics.* Jeddah: Islamic Research and Training Institute.

Ahmad, Khurshid (ed.). 1980. *Studies in Islamic Economics.* Jeddah/Leicester: International Centre for Research in Islamic Economics and The Islamic Foundation.

Ahmed, Z., M. Iqbal, and M. F. Khan (eds.). 1983. *Fiscal Policy and Resource Allocation in Islam.* Islamabad: Institute of Policy Studies.

Al-Harran, Saad (ed.). 1995. *Leading Issues in Islamic Banking and Finance.* Petaling Jaya: Pelanduk Publications.

Ariff, Mohammad (ed.). 1982. *Monetary and Fiscal Economics of Islam.* Jeddah: International Center for Research in Islamic Economics, King Abdulaziz University.

Chapra, Muhammad Umar. 1985. *Towards a Just Monetary System.* Leicester: The Islamic Foundation.

Chapra, M. Umer. 1993. *Islam and Economic Development.* Islamabad: International Institute of Islamic Thought and Islamic Research Institute.

Choudhury, Masudul Alam. 1997. *Money in Islam: A Study in Islamic Political Economy.* London: Routledge.

El-Ashker, Ahmed Abdel-Fattah, and Muhammad Sirajul Haq (eds.). 1995. *Institutional Framework of Zakah: Dimensions and Implications.* Jeddah: Islamic Research and Training Institute.

Federal Shariat Court. 1992. *Federal Shariat Court Judgement on Interest (Riba).* Vol. XLIV. Lahore: The All Pakistan Legal Decisions.

Gulaid, Mahamoud A., and Mohamed Aden Abdullah (eds.). 1995. *Readings in Public Finance in Islam.* Jeddah: Islamic Research and Training Institute.

Haque, Ziaul. 1995. *Riba: The Moral Economy of Usury, Interest and Profit.* Petaling Jaya: Ikraq.

Haneef, Mohamed Aslam. 1993. *Contemporary Islamic Economic Thought: A Selected Comparative Analysis.* Petaling Jaya: Ikraq.

Jomo, K. S. (ed.). 1993. *Islamic Economic Alternatives—Critical Perspectives and New Directions.* Kuala Lumpur: Ikraq (previously published: London: Macmillan 1992).

Khan, M. Fahim. 1995. *Essays in Islamic Economics.* Markfield: The Islamic Foundation.

Kuran, Timur, James D. Montgomery, and Erich Schanze. 1997. Islam and Underdevelopment: An Old Puzzle Revisited. *Journal of Institutional and Theoretical Economics* 1: 41–71.

Mannan, M. A. 1986. *Islamic Economics: Theory and Practice,* rev. ed. Sevenoaks: Hodder and Stoughton.

Mannan, M. A., Monzer Kahf, and Ausaf Ahmad (eds.). 1992. *International Economic Relations from Islamic Perpectives.* Jeddah: Islamic Research and Training Institute.

Nienhaus, Volker. 1997. "Taxation and Public Finance." *International Review of Comparative Public Police,* Vol. 9: Islam and Public Policy, edited by Sohrab Behdad, Farhad Nomani, 249–275. Greenwich/London: JAI Press.

Nienhaus, Volker. 1998. "The Financial System of Malaysia." In *Asian Financial Markets—Structures, Policy Issues and Prospects,* edited by Lukas Menkhoff and Beate Reszat, 187–221. Baden-Baden: Nomos.

Nomani, Farhad, and Ali Rahnema. 1994. *Islamic Economic Systems.* London/New Jersey: Zed Books.

Sadar, Ziauddin. 1979. *The Future of Muslim Civilisation.* London: Croom Helm.

Sadeq, A. H. M. 1990. *Economic Development in Islam.* Petaling Jaya: Pelanduk Publications.

Siddiqi, Muhammad Nejatullah. 1983. *Banking without Interest.* Leicester: The Islamic Foundation.

Wilson, Rodney (ed.). 1990. *Islamic Financial Markets.* London: Routledge.

Wilson, Rodney J. A. 1997. *Economics, Ethics and Religion: Jewish, Christian and Muslim Economic Thought.* Basingstoke: Macmillan.

Zaidi, Nawazish Ali. 1987. *Eliminating Interest from Banks in Pakistan.* Karachi: Royal Book Company.

7

ISLAMIC ECONOMICS

What it is and how it developed

M. Umer Chapra

Source: EH.Net Encyclopedia, ed. Robert Whaples, 16 March 2008, at http://eh.net/encyclopedia/article/chapra.islamic.

Islamic economics has been having a revival over the last few decades. However, it is still in a preliminary stage of development. In contrast with this, conventional economics has become a well-developed and sophisticated discipline after going through a long and rigorous process of development over more than a century. Is a new discipline in economics needed? If so, what is Islamic economics, how does it differ from conventional economics, and what contributions has it made over the centuries? This article tries to briefly answer these questions.

It is universally recognized that resources are scarce compared with the claims on them. However, it is also simultaneously recognized by practically all civilizations that the well-being of *all* human beings needs to be ensured. Given the scarcity of resources, the well-being of all may remain an unrealized dream if the scarce resources are not utilized efficiently and equitably. For this purpose, every society needs to develop an effective strategy, which is consciously or unconsciously conditioned by its worldview. If the worldview is flawed, the strategy may not be able to help the society actualize the well-being of all. Prevailing worldviews may be classified for the sake of ease into two board theoretical constructs (1) secular and materialist, and (2) spiritual and humanitarian.

The role of the worldview

Secular and materialist worldviews attach maximum importance to the material aspect of human well-being and tend generally to ignore the importance of the spiritual aspect. They often argue that maximum material well-being can be best realized if individuals are given unhindered freedom to pursue their self-interest and to maximize their want satisfaction in keeping with their own tastes and preferences.[1] In their extreme form they do not recognize any role for Divine guidance in human life and place full trust in the ability of human beings to chalk out a proper strategy with the help of their reason. In such a worldview there is little role for values or government intervention in the efficient and equitable allocation and distribution of resources. When asked about how social interest would be served when everyone has unlimited freedom to pursue his/her self-interest, the reply is that market forces will themselves ensure this because competition will keep self-interest under check.

In contrast with this, religious worldviews give attention to both the material as well as the spiritual aspects of human well-being. They do not necessarily reject the role of reason in human development. They, however, recognize the limitations of reason and wish to complement it by revelation. They do not also reject the need for individual freedom or the role that the serving of self-interest can play in human development. They, however, emphasize that both freedom and the pursuit of self-interest need to be toned down by moral values and good governance to ensure that everyone's well-being is realized and that social harmony and family integrity are not hurt in the process of everyone serving his/her self-interest.

Material and spiritual needs

Even though none of the major worldviews prevailing around the world is totally materialist and hedonist, there are, nevertheless, significant differences among them in terms of the emphasis they place on material or spiritual goals and the role of moral values and government intervention in ordering human affairs. While material goals concentrate primarily on goods and services that contribute to physical comfort and well-being, spiritual goals include nearness to God, peace of mind, inner happiness, honesty, justice, mutual care and cooperation, family and social harmony, and the absence of crime and anomie. These may not be quantifiable, but are, nevertheless, crucial for realizing human well-being. Resources being limited, excessive emphasis on the material ingredients of well-being may lead to a neglect of spiritual ingredients. The greater the difference in emphasis, the greater may be the difference in the economic disciplines of these societies. Feyerabend (1993) frankly recognized this in the introduction to the Chinese edition of his thought-provoking book, *Against Method*, by stating that "First world science is only one science among many; by claiming to be more it ceases to be an instrument of research and turns into a (political) pressure group" (p.3, parentheses are in the original).

The Enlightenment worldview and conventional economics

There is a great deal that is common between the worldviews of most major religions, particularly those of Judaism, Christianity and Islam. This is because, according to Islam, there is a continuity and similarity in the value systems of all Revealed religions to the extent to which the Message has not been lost or distorted over the ages. The Qur'an clearly states that: "Nothing has been said to you [Muhammad] that was not said to the Messengers before you" (Al-Qur'an, 41:43). If conventional economics had continued to develop in the image of the Judeo-Christian worldview, as it did before the Enlightenment Movement of the seventeenth and eighteenth centuries, there may not have been any significant difference between conventional and Islamic economics. However, after the Enlightenment Movement, all intellectual disciplines in Europe became influenced by its secular, value-neutral, materialist and social-Darwinist worldview, even though this did not succeed fully. All economists did not necessarily become materialist or social-Darwinist in their individual lives and many of them continued to be attached to their religious worldviews. Koopmans (1969) has rightly observed that "scratch an economist and you will find a moralist underneath." Therefore, while theoretically conventional economics adopted the secular and value neutral orientation of the Enlightenment worldview and failed to recognize the role of value judgments and good governance in the efficient and equitable allocation and distribution of resources, in practice this did not take place fully. The pre-Enlightenment tradition never disappeared completely (see Baeck, 1994, p. 11).

There is no doubt that, in spite of its secular and materialist worldview, the market system led to a long period of prosperity in the Western market-oriented economies. However, this unprecedented prosperity did not lead to the elimination of poverty or the fulfillment of everyone's needs in conformity with the Judeo-Christian value system even in the wealthiest countries. Inequalities of income and wealth have also continued to persist and there has also been a substantial degree of economic instability and unemployment which have added to the miseries of the poor. This indicates that both efficiency and equity have remained elusive in spite of rapid development and phenomenal rise in wealth.

Consequently there has been persistent criticism of economics by a number of well-meaning scholars, including Thomas Carlyle (*Past and Present*, 1843), John Ruskin (*Unto this Last*, 1862) and Charles Dickens (*Hard Times*, 1854–55) in England, and Henry George (*Progress and Poverty*, 1879) in America. They ridiculed the dominant doctrine of laissez-faire with its emphasis on self-interest. Thomas Carlyle called economics a "dismal science" and rejected the idea that free and uncontrolled private interests will work in harmony and further the public welfare (see Jay and Jay, 1986). Henry George condemned the resulting contrast between wealth and poverty and wrote:

"So long as all the increased wealth which modern progress brings goes but to build great fortunes, to increase luxury and make sharper the contrast between the House of Have and the House of Want, progress is not real and cannot be permanent" (1955, p. 10).

In addition to failing to fulfill the basic needs of a large number of people and increasing inequalities of income and wealth, modern economic development has been associated with the disintegration of the family and a failure to bring peace of mind and inner happiness (Easterlin 2001, 1995 and 1974; Oswald, 1997; Blanchflower and Oswald, 2000; Diener and Oshi, 2000; and Kenny, 1999). Due to these problems and others the laissez-faire approach lost ground, particularly after the Great Depression of the 1930s as a result of the Keynesian revolution and the socialist onslaught. However, most observers have concluded that government intervention alone cannot by itself remove all socio-economic ills. It is also necessary to motivate individuals to do what is right and abstain from doing what is wrong. This is where the moral uplift of society can be helpful. Without it, more and more difficult and costly regulations are needed. Nobel-laureate Amartya Sen has, therefore, rightly argued that "the distancing of economics from ethics has impoverished welfare economics and also weakened the basis of a good deal of descriptive and predictive economics" and that economics "can be made more productive by paying greater and more explicit attention to ethical considerations that shaped human behaviour and judgment" (1987, pp. 78–79). Hausman and McPherson also conclude in their survey article "Economics and Contemporary Moral Philosophy" that "An economy that is engaged actively and self-critically with the moral aspects of its subject matter cannot help but be more interesting, more illuminating and, ultimately, more useful than the one that tries not to be" (1993, p. 723).

Islamic economics – and how it differs from conventional economics

While conventional economics is now in the process of returning to its pre-Enlightenment roots, Islamic economics never got entangled in a secular and materialist worldview. It is based on a religious worldview which strikes at the roots of secularism and value neutrality. To ensure the true well-being of all individuals, irrespective of their sex, age, race, religion or wealth, Islamic economics does not seek to abolish private property, as was done by communism, nor does it prevent individuals from serving their self-interest. It recognizes the role of the market in the efficient allocation of resources, but does not find competition to be sufficient to safeguard social interest. It tries to promote human brotherhood, socio-economic justice and the well-being of all through an integrated role of moral values, market mechanism, families, society, and 'good governance.' This is because of the great emphasis in Islam on human brotherhood and socio-economic justice.

The integrated role of the market, families, society, and government

The market is not the only institution where people interact in human society. They also interact in the family, the society and the government and their interaction in all these institutions is closely interrelated. There is no doubt that the serving of self-interest does help raise efficiency in the market place. However, if self-interest is overemphasized and there are no moral restraints on individual behavior, other institutions may not work effectively – families may disintegrate, the society may be uncaring, and the government may be corrupt, partisan, and self-centered. Mutual sacrifice is necessary for keeping the families glued together. Since the human being is the most important input of not only the market, but also of the family, the society and the government, and the family is the source of this input, nothing may work if families disintegrate and are unable to provide loving care to children. This is likely to happen if both the husband and wife try to serve just their own self-interest and are not attuned to the making of sacrifices that the proper care and upbringing of children demands. Lack of willingness to make such sacrifice can lead to a decline in the quality of the human input to all other institutions, including the market, the society and the government. It may also lead to a fall in fertility rates below the replacement level, making it difficult for society not only to sustain its development but also its social security system.

The role of moral values

While conventional economics generally considers the behavior and tastes and preferences of individuals as given, Islamic economics does not do so. It places great emphasis on individual and social reform through moral uplift. This is the purpose for which all God's messengers, including Abraham, Moses, Jesus, and Muhammad, came to this world. Moral uplift aims at the change in human behavior, tastes and preferences and, thereby, it complements the price mechanism in promoting general well-being. Before even entering the market place and being exposed to the price filter, consumers are expected to pass their claims through the moral filter. This will help filter out conspicuous consumption and all wasteful and unnecessary claims on resources. The price mechanism can then take over and reduce the claims on resources even further to lead to the market equilibrium. The two filters can together make it possible to have optimum economy in the use of resources, which is necessary to satisfy the material as well as spiritual needs of all human beings, to reduce the concentration of wealth in a few hands, and to raise savings, which are needed to promote greater investment and employment. Without complementing the market system with morally-based value judgments, we may end up perpetuating inequities in spite of our good intentions through what Solo calls inaction, non-choice and drifting (Solo, 1981, p. 38).

From the above discussion, one may easily notice the similarities and differences between the two disciplines. While the subject matter of both is the allocation and distribution of resources and both emphasize the fulfillment of material needs, there is an equal emphasis in Islamic economics on the fulfillment of spiritual needs. While both recognize the important role of market mechanism in the allocation and distribution of resources, Islamic economics argues that the market may not by itself be able to fulfill even the material needs of all human beings. This is because it can promote excessive use of scarce resources by the rich at the expense of the poor if there is undue emphasis on the serving of self-interest. Sacrifice is involved in fulfilling our obligations towards others and excessive emphasis on the serving of self-interest does not have the potential of motivating people to make the needed sacrifice. This, however, raises the crucial question of why a rational person would sacrifice his self-interest for the sake of others?

The importance of the hereafter

This is where the concepts of the innate goodness of human beings and of the Hereafter come in – concepts which conventional economics ignores but on which Islam and other major religions place a great deal of emphasis. Because of their innate goodness, human beings do not necessarily always try to serve their self-interest. They are also altruistic and are willing to make sacrifices for the well-being of others. In addition, the concept of the Hereafter does not confine self-interest to just this world. It rather extends it beyond this world to life after death. We may be able to serve our self-interest in this world by being selfish, dishonest, uncaring, and negligent of our obligations towards our families, other human beings, animals, and the environment. However, we cannot serve our self-interest in the Hereafter except by fulfilling all these obligations.

Thus, the serving of self-interest receives a long-run perspective in Islam and other religions by taking into account both this world and the next. This serves to provide a motivating mechanism for sacrifice for the well-being of others that conventional economics fails to provide. The innate goodness of human beings along with the long-run perspective given to self-interest has the potential of inducing a person to be not only efficient but also equitable and caring. Consequently, the three crucial concepts of conventional economics – rational economic man, positivism, and laissez-faire – were not able to gain intellectual blessing in their conventional economics sense from any of the outstanding scholars who represent the mainstream of Islamic thought.

Rational economic man

While there is hardly anyone opposed to the need for rationality in human behavior, there are differences of opinion in defining rationality (Sen, 1987, pp. 11–14). However, once rationality has been defined in terms of overall individual as well as social well-being, then rational behavior could only be that which helps us realize this goal. Conventional economics does not define rationality in this way. It equates rationality with the serving of self-interest through the maximization of wealth and want satisfaction. The drive of self-interest is considered to be the "moral equivalent of the force of gravity in nature" (Myers, 1983, p. 4). Within this framework society is conceptualized as a mere collection of individuals united through ties of self-interest.

The concept of 'rational economic man' in this social-Darwinist, utilitarian, and material sense of serving self-interest could not find a foothold in Islamic economics. 'Rationality' in Islamic economics does not get confined to the serving of one's self-interest in this world alone; it also gets extended to the Hereafter through the faithful compliance with moral values that help rein self-interest to promote social interest. Al-Mawardi (d. 1058) considered it necessary, like all other Muslim scholars, to rein individual tastes and preferences through moral values (1955, pp. 118–20). Ibn Khaldun (d.1406) emphasized that moral orientation helps remove mutual rivalry and envy, strengthens social solidarity, and creates an inclination towards righteousness (n.d., p.158).

Positivism

Similarly, positivism in the conventional economics sense of being "entirely neutral between ends" (Robbins, 1935, p. 240) or "independent of any particular ethical position or normative judgment" (Friedman, 1953) did not find a place in Muslim intellectual thinking. Since all resources at the disposal of human beings are a trust from God, and human beings are accountable before Him, there is no other option but to use them in keeping with the terms of trust. These terms are defined by beliefs and moral values. Human brotherhood, one of the central objectives of Islam, would be a meaningless jargon if it were not reinforced by justice in the allocation and distribution of resources.

Pareto optimum

Without justice, it would be difficult to realize even development. Muslim scholars have emphasized this throughout history. Development Economics has also started emphasizing its importance, more so in the last few decades.[2] Abu Yusuf (d. 798) argued that: "Rendering justice to those wronged and eradicating injustice, raises tax revenue, accelerates development of the country, and brings blessings in addition to reward in the Hereafter" (1933/34, p. 111: see also pp. 3–17). Al-Mawardi argued that comprehensive justice "inculcates mutual love and affection, obedience to the law, development of the country, expansion of wealth, growth of progeny, and security of the sovereign" (1955, p. 27). Ibn Taymiyyah (d. 1328) emphasized that "justice towards everything and everyone is an imperative for everyone, and injustice is prohibited to everything and everyone. Injustice is absolutely not permissible irrespective of whether it is to a Muslim or a non-Muslim or even to an unjust person" (1961–63, Vol. 18, p. 166).

Justice and the well-being of all may be difficult to realize without a sacrifice on the part of the well-to-do. The concept of Pareto optimum does not, therefore, fit into the paradigm of Islamic economics. This is because Pareto optimum does not recognize any solution as optimum if it requires a sacrifice on the part of a few (rich) for raising the well-being of the many (poor). Such a position is in clear conflict with moral values, the raison d'être of which is the well-being of all. Hence, this concept did not arise in Islamic economics. In fact, Islam makes it a religious obligation of Muslims to make a sacrifice for the poor and the needy, by paying Zakat at the rate of 2.5 percent of their net worth. This is in addition to the taxes that they pay to the governments as in other countries.

The role of state

Moral values may not be effective if they are not observed by all. They need to be enforced. It is the duty of the state to restrain all socially harmful behavior[3] including injustice, fraud, cheating, transgression against other people's person, honor and property, and the non-fulfillment of contracts and other obligations through proper upbringing, incentives and deterrents, appropriate regulations, and an effective and impartial judiciary. The Qur'an can only provide norms. It cannot by itself enforce them. The state has to ensure this. That is why the Prophet Muhammad said: "God restrains through the sovereign more than what He restrains through the Qur'an" (cited by al-Mawardi, 1955, p. 121). This emphasis on the role of the state has been reflected in the writings of all leading Muslim scholars throughout history.[4] Al-Mawardi emphasized that an effective government (Sultan Qahir) is indispensable for preventing injustice and wrongdoing (1960, p. 5). Say's Law could not, therefore, become a meaningful proposition in Islamic economics.

How far is the state expected to go in the fulfillment of its role? What is it that the state is expected to do? This has been spelled out by a number of scholars in the literature on what has come to be termed as "Mirrors for Princes."[5] None of them visualized regimentation or the owning and operating of a substantial part of the economy by the state. Several classical Muslim scholars, including al-Dimashqi (d. after 1175) and Ibn Khaldun, clearly expressed their disapproval of the state becoming directly involved in the economy (Al-Dimashqi, 1977, pp. 12 and 61; Ibn Khaldun, pp. 281–83). According to Ibn Khaldun, the state should not acquire the character of a monolithic or despotic state resorting to a high degree of regimentation (ibid., p. 188). It should not feel that, because it has authority, it can do anything it likes (ibid, p. 306). It should be welfare-oriented, moderate in its spending, respect the property rights of the people, and avoid onerous taxation (ibid, p. 296). This implies that what these scholars visualized as the role of government is what has now been generally referred to as 'good governance'.

Some of the contributions made by Islamic economics

The above discussion should not lead one to an impression that the two disciplines are entirely different. One of the reasons for this is that the subject matter of both disciplines is the same, allocation and distribution of scarce resources. Another reason is that all conventional economists have never been value neutral. They have made value judgments in conformity with their beliefs. As indicated earlier, even the paradigm of conventional economics has been changing – the role of good governance has now become well recognized and the injection of a moral dimension has also become emphasized by a number of prominent economists. Moreover, Islamic economists have benefited a great deal from the tools of analysis developed by neoclassical, Keynesian, social, humanistic and institutional economics as well as other social sciences, and will continue to do so in the future.

The fallacy of the 'Great Gap' theory

A number of economic concepts developed in Islamic economics long before they did in conventional economics. These cover a number of areas including interdisciplinary approach; property rights; division of labor and specialization; the importance of saving and investment for development; the role that both demand and supply play in the determination of prices and the factors that influence demand and supply; the roles of money, exchange, and the market mechanism; characteristics of money, counterfeiting, currency debasement, and Gresham's law; the development of checks, letters of credit and banking; labor supply and population; the role of the state, justice, peace, and stability in development; and principles of taxation. It is not possible to provide comprehensive coverage of all the contributions Muslim scholars have made to economics. Only some of their contributions will be highlighted below to remove the concept of the "Great Gap" of "over 500 years" that exists in the history of conventional economic thought as a result of the incorrect conclusion by Joseph Schumpeter in *History of Economic Analysis* (1954), that the intervening period between the Greeks and the Scholastics was sterile and unproductive.[6] This concept has become well embedded in the conventional economics literature as may be seen from the reference to this even by the Nobel-laureate, Douglass North, in his December 1993 Nobel lecture (1994, p. 365). Consequently, as Todd Lowry has rightly observed, "the character and sophistication of Arabian writings has been ignored" (See his 'Foreword' in Ghazanfar, 2003, p. xi).

97

The reality, however, is that the Muslim civilization, which benefited greatly from the Chinese, Indian, Sassanian and Byzantine civilizations, itself made rich contributions to intellectual activity, including socio-economic thought, during the 'Great Gap' period, and thereby played a part in kindling the flame of the European Enlightenment Movement. Even the Scholastics themselves were greatly influenced by the contributions made by Muslim scholars. The names of Ibn Sina (Avicenna, d. 1037), Ibn Rushd (Averroes, d. 1198) and Maimonides (d. 1204, a Jewish philosopher, scientist, and physician who flourished in Muslim Spain) appear on almost every page of the thirteenth-century summa (treatises written by scholastic philosophers) (Pifer, 1978, p. 356).

Multidisciplinary approach for development

One of the most important contributions of Islamic economics, in addition to the above paradigm discussion, was the adoption of a multidisciplinary dynamic approach. Muslim scholars did not focus their attention primarily on economic variables. They considered overall human well-being to be the end product of interaction over a long period of time between a number of economic, moral, social, political, demographic and historical factors in such a way that none of them is able to make an optimum contribution without the support of the others. Justice occupied a pivotal place in this whole framework because of its crucial importance in the Islamic worldview. There was an acute realization that justice is indispensable for development and that, in the absence of justice, there will be decline and disintegration.

The contributions made by different scholars over the centuries seem to have reached their consummation in Ibn Khaldun's *Maquddimah*, which literally means 'introduction,' and constitutes the first volume of a seven-volume history, briefly called *Kitab al-'Ibar* or the *Book of Lessons* [of History].[7] Ibn Khaldun lived at a time (1332–1406) when the Muslim civilization was in the process of decline. He wished to see a reversal of this tide, and, as a social scientist, he was well aware that such a reversal could not be envisaged without first drawing lessons ('ibar) from history to determine the factors that had led the Muslim civilization to bloom out of humble beginnings and to decline thereafter. He was, therefore, not interested in knowing just what happened. He wanted to know the how and why of what happened. He wanted to introduce a cause and effect relationship into the discussion of historical phenomena. The *Muqaddimah* is the result of this desire. It tries to derive the principles that govern the rise and fall of a ruling dynasty, state (dawlah) or civilization ('umran).

Since the centre of Ibn Khaldun's analysis is the human being, he sees the rise and fall of dynasties or civilizations to be closely dependent on the well-being or misery of the people. The well-being of the people is in turn not dependent just on economic variables, as conventional economics has emphasized until recently, but also on the closely interrelated role of moral, psychological, social, economic, political, demographic and historical factors. One of these factors acts as the trigger mechanism. The others may, or may not, react in the same way. If the others do not react in the same direction, then the decay in one sector may not spread to the others and either the decaying sector may be reformed or the decline of the civilization may be much slower. If, however, the other sectors react in the same direction as the trigger mechanism, the decay will gain momentum through an interrelated chain reaction such that it becomes difficult over time to identify the cause from the effect. He, thus, seems to have had a clear vision of how all the different factors operate in an interrelated and dynamic manner over a long period to promote the development or decline of a society.

He did not, thus, adopt the neoclassical economist's simplification of confining himself to primarily short-term static analysis of only markets by assuming unrealistically that all other factors remain constant. Even in the short-run, everything may be in a state of flux through a chain reaction to the various changes constantly taking place in human society, even though these may be so small as to be imperceptible. Therefore, even though economists may adopt the ceteris paribus assumption for ease of analysis, Ibn Khaldun's multidisciplinary dynamics can be more helpful in formulating socio-economic policies that help improve the overall performance of a society. Neoclassical economics is unable to do this because, as North has rightly asked, "How can one prescribe policies when one does not understand how economies develop?" He, therefore, considers neoclassical economics to be "an inappropriate tool to analyze and prescribe policies that will induce development" (North, 1994, p. 549).

However, this is not all that Islamic economics has done. Muslim scholars, including Abu Yusuf (d. 798), al-Mawardi (d. 1058), Ibn Hazm (d. 1064), al-Sarakhsi (d. 1090), al-Tusi (d. 1093), al-Ghazali (d. 1111), al-Dimashqi (d. after 1175), Ibn Rushd (d. 1187), Ibn Taymiyyah (d.1328), Ibn al-Ukhuwwah (d. 1329), Ibn al-Qayyim (d. 1350), al-Shatibi (d. 1388), Ibn Khaldun (d. 1406), al-Maqrizi (d. 1442), al-Dawwani (d. 1501), and Shah Waliyullah (d. 1762) made a number of valuable contributions to economic theory. Their insight into some economic concepts was so deep that a number of the theories propounded by them could undoubtedly be considered the forerunners of some more sophisticated modern formulations of these theories.[8]

Division of labor, specialization, trade, exchange and money and banking

A number of scholars emphasized the necessity of division of labor for economic development long before this happened in conventional economics. For example, al-Sarakhsi (d. 1090) said: "the farmer needs the work of the weaver to get clothing for himself, and the weaver needs the work of the farmer to get his food and the cotton from which the cloth is made . . . , and thus everyone of them helps the other by his work . . ." (1978, Vol. 30, p. 264). Al-Dimashqi, writing about a century later, elaborates further by saying: "No individual can, because of the shortness of his life span, burden himself with all industries. If he does, he may not be able to master the skills of all of them from the first to the last. Industries are all interdependent. Construction needs the carpenter and the carpenter needs the ironsmith and the ironsmith needs the miner, and all these industries need premises. People are, therefore, necessitated by force of circumstances to be clustered in cities to help each other in fulfilling their mutual needs" (1977, pp. 20–21).

Ibn Khaldun ruled out the feasibility or desirability of self-sufficiency, and emphasized the need for division of labor and specialization by indicating that: "It is well-known and well-established that individual human beings are not by themselves capable of satisfying all their individual economic needs. They must all cooperate for this purpose. The needs that can be satisfied by a group of them through mutual cooperation are many times greater than what individuals are capable of satisfying by themselves" (p. 360). In this respect he was perhaps the forerunner of the theory of comparative advantage, the credit for which is generally given in conventional economics to David Ricardo who formulated it in 1817.

The discussion of division of labor and specialization, in turn, led to an emphasis on trade and exchange, the existence of well-regulated and properly functioning markets through their effective regulation and supervision (hisbah), and money as a stable and reliable measure, medium of exchange and store of value. However, because of bimetallism (gold and silver coins circulating together) which then prevailed, and the different supply and demand conditions that the two metals faced, the rate of exchange between the two full-bodied coins fluctuated. This was further complicated by debasement of currencies by governments in the later centuries to tide over their fiscal problems. This had, according to Ibn Taymiyyah (d. 1328) (1961–63, Vol. 29, p. 649), and later on al-Maqrizi (d. 1442) and al-Asadi (d. 1450), the effect of bad coins driving good coins out of circulation (al-Misri, 1981, pp. 54 and 66), a phenomenon which was recognized and referred to in the West in the sixteenth century as Gresham's Law. Since debasement of currencies is in sheer violation of the Islamic emphasis on honesty and integrity in all measures of value, fraudulent practices in the issue of coins in the fourteenth century and afterwards elicited a great deal of literature on monetary theory and policy. The Muslims, according to Baeck, should, therefore, be considered forerunners and critical incubators of the debasement literature of the fourteenth and fifteenth centuries (Baeck, 1994, p. 114).

To finance their expanding domestic and international trade, the Muslim world also developed a financial system, which was able to mobilize the "entire reservoir of monetary resources of the mediaeval Islamic world" for financing agriculture, crafts, manufacturing and long-distance trade (Udovitch,

1970, pp. 180 and 261). Financiers were known as sarrafs. By the time of Abbasid Caliph al-Muqtadir (908–32), they had started performing most of the basic functions of modern banks (Fischel, 1992). They had their markets, something akin to the Wall Street in New York and Lombard Street in London, and fulfilled all the banking needs of commerce, agriculture and industry (Duri, 1986, p. 898). This promoted the use of checks (sakk) and letters of credit (hawala). The English word check comes from the Arabic term sakk.

Demand and supply

A number of Muslim scholars seem to have clearly understood the role of both demand and supply in the determination of prices. For example, Ibn Taymiyyah (d. 1328) wrote: "The rise or fall of prices may not necessarily be due to injustice by some people. They may also be due to the shortage of output or the import of commodities in demand. If the demand for a commodity increases and the supply of what is demanded declines, the price rises. If, however, the demand falls and the supply increases, the price falls" (1961–3, Vol. 8, p. 523).

Even before Ibn Taymiyyah, al-Jahiz (d. 869) wrote nearly five centuries earlier that: "Anything available in the market is cheap because of its availability [supply] and dear by its lack of availability if there is need [demand] for it" (1983, p. 13), and that "anything the supply of which increases, becomes cheap except intelligence, which becomes dearer when it increases" (ibid., p. 13).

Ibn Khaldun went even further by emphasizing that both an increase in demand or a fall in supply leads to a rise in prices, while a decline in demand or a rise in supply contributes to a fall in prices (pp. 393 and 396). He believed that while continuation of 'excessively low' prices hurts the craftsmen and traders and drives them out of the market, the continuation of 'excessively high' prices hurts the consumers. 'Moderate' prices in between the two extremes were, therefore, desirable, because they would not only allow the traders a socially-acceptable level of return but also lead to the clearance of the markets by promoting sales and thereby generating a given turnover and prosperity (ibid, p. 398). Nevertheless, low prices were desirable for necessities because they provide relief to the poor who constitute the majority of the population (ibid, p. 398). If one were to use modern terminology, one could say that Ibn Khaldun found a stable price level with a relatively low cost of living to be preferable, from the point of view of both growth and equity in comparison with bouts of inflation and deflation. The former hurts equity while the latter reduces incentive and efficiency. Low prices for necessities should not, however, be attained through the fixing of prices by the state; this destroys the incentive for production (ibid, pp. 279–83).

The factors which determined demand were, according to Ibn Khaldun, income, price level, the size of the population, government spending, the habits and customs of the people, and the general development and prosperity of the society (ibid, pp. 398–404). The factors which determined supply were demand (ibid, pp. 400 and 403), order and stability (pp. 306–08), the relative rate of profit (ibid, pp. 395 and 398), the extent of human effort (p. 381), the size of the labor force as well as their knowledge and skill (pp. 363 and 399–400), peace and security (pp. 394–95 and 396), and the technical background and development of the whole society (pp. 399–403). All these constituted important elements of his theory of production. If the price falls and leads to a loss, capital is eroded, the incentive to supply declines, leading to a recession. Trade and crafts also consequently suffer (p. 398).

This is highly significant because the role of both demand and supply in the determination of value was not well understood in the West until the late nineteenth and the early twentieth centuries. Pre-classical English economists like William Petty (1623–87), Richard Cantillon (1680–1734), James Steuart (1712 –80), and even Adam Smith (1723–90), the founder of the Classical School, generally stressed only the role of the cost of production, and particularly of labor, in the determination of value. The first use in English writings of the notions of both demand and supply was perhaps in 1767 (Thweatt, 1983). Nevertheless, it was not until the second decade of the nineteenth century that the role of both demand and supply in the determination of market prices began to be fully appreciated (Groenewegen, 1973). While Ibn Khaldun had been way ahead of conventional economists, he probably did not have any idea of demand and supply schedules, elasticities of demand and supply and most important of all, equilibrium price, which plays a crucial role in modern economic discussions.

Public finance

Taxation

Long before Adam Smith (d. 1790), who is famous, among other things, for his canons of taxation (equality, certainty, convenience of payment, and economy in collection) (see Smith, 1937, pp. 777–79), the development of these canons can be traced in the writings of pre-Islamic as well as Muslim scholars, particularly the need for the tax system to be just and not oppressive. Caliphs Umar (d. 644), Ali (d. 661) and Umar ibn Abd al-Aziz (d. 720), stressed that taxes should be collected with justice and leniency and should not be beyond the ability of the people to bear. Tax collectors should not under any circumstances deprive the people of the necessities of life (Abu Yusuf, 1933/34, pp. 14, 16 and 86). Abu Yusuf, adviser to Caliph Harun al-Rashid (786–809), argued that a just tax system would lead not only to an increase in revenues but also to the development of the country (Abu Yusuf, 1933/34, p. 111; see also pp. 14, 16, 60, 85, 105–19 and 125).

Al-Mawardi also argued that the tax system should do justice to both the taxpayer and the treasury – "taking more was iniquitous with respect to the rights of the people, while taking less was unfair with respect to the right of the public treasury" (1960, p. 209; see also pp. 142–56 and 215).[9]

Ibn Khaldun stressed the principles of taxation very forcefully in the *Muqaddimah*. He quoted from a letter written by Tahir ibn al-Husayn, Caliph al-Ma'mun's general, advising his son, 'Abdullah ibn Tahir, Governor of al-Raqqah (Syria): "So distribute [taxes] among all people making them general, not exempting anyone because of his nobility or wealth and not exempting even your own officials or courtiers or followers. And do not levy on anyone a tax which is beyond his capacity to pay" (p. 308).[10] In this particular passage, he stressed the principles of equity and neutrality, while in other places he also stressed the principles of convenience and productivity.

The effect of taxation on incentives and productivity was so clearly visualized by Ibn Khaldun that he seems to have grasped the concept of optimum taxation. He anticipated the gist of the Laffer Curve, nearly six hundred years before Arthur Laffer, in two full chapters of the *Muqaddimah*.[11] At the end of the first chapter, he concluded that "the most important factor making for business prosperity is to lighten as much as possible the burden of taxation on businessmen, in order to encourage enterprise by ensuring greater profits [after taxes]" (p. 280). This he explained by stating that "when taxes and imposts are light, the people have the incentive to be more active. Business therefore expands, bringing greater satisfaction to the people because of low taxes . . . , and tax revenues also rise, being the sum total of all assessments" (p. 279). He went on to say that as time passes the needs of the state increase and rates of taxation rise to increase the yield. If this rise is gradual people become accustomed to it, but ultimately there is an adverse impact on incentives. Business activity is discouraged and declines, and so does the yield of taxation (pp. 280–81). A prosperous economy at the beginning of the dynasty, thus, yields higher tax revenue from lower tax rates while a depressed economy at the end of the dynasty, yields smaller tax revenue from higher rates (p. 279). He explained the reasons for this by stating: "Know that acting unjustly with respect to people's wealth, reduces their will to earn and acquire wealth . . . and if the will to earn goes, they stop working. The greater the oppression, the greater the effect on their effort to earn . . . and, if people abstain from earning and stop working, the markets will stagnate and the condition of people will worsen" (pp. 286–87); tax revenues will also decline (p. 362). He, therefore, advocated justice in taxation (p. 308).

Public expenditure

For Ibn Khaldun the state was also an important factor of production. By its spending it promotes production and by its taxation it discourages production (pp. 279–81). Since the government constitutes the greatest market for goods and services, and is a major source of all development (pp. 286 and 403), a decrease in its spending leads to not only a slackening of business activity and a decline in profits but also a decline in tax revenue (p. 286). The more the government spends, the better it may be for the economy (p. 286).[12] Higher spending enables the government to do the things that are needed to support the population and to ensure law and order and political stability (pp. 306 and 308). Without order and political stability, the producers have no incentive to produce. He stated that "the only reason [for the accelerated development of cities] is that the government is near them and pours its money into them, like the water [of a river] that makes green everything around it, and irrigates the soil adjacent to it, while in the distance everything remains dry" (p. 369).

Ibn Khaldun also analyzed the effect of government expenditure on the economy and is, in this respect, a forerunner of Keynes. He stated: "A decrease in government spending leads to a decline in tax revenues. The reason for this is that the state represents the greatest market for the world and the source of civilization. If the ruler hoards tax revenues, or if these are lost, and he does not spend them as they should be, the amount available with his courtiers and supporters would decrease, as would also the amount that reaches through them to their employees and dependents [the multiplier effect]. Their total spending would, therefore, decline. Since they constitute a significant part of the population and their spending constitutes a substantial part of the market, business will slacken and the profits of businessmen will decline, leading also to a decline in tax revenues . . . Wealth tends to circulate between the people and the ruler, from him to them and from them to him. Therefore, if the ruler withholds it from spending, the people would become deprived of it" (p. 286).

Economic mismanagement and famine

Ibn Khaldun established the causal link between bad government and high grain prices by indicating that in the later stage of the dynasty, when public administration becomes corrupt and inefficient, and resorts to coercion and oppressive taxation, incentive is adversely affected and the farmers refrain from cultivating the land. Grain production and reserves fail to keep pace with the rising population. The absence of reserves causes supply shortages in the event of a famine and leads to price escalation (pp. 301–02).

Al-Maqrizi (d. 1442) who, as muhtasib (market supervisor), had intimate knowledge of the economic conditions during his times, applied Ibn Khaldun's analysis in his book (1956) to determine the reasons for the economic crisis of Egypt during the period 1403–06. He identified that the political administration had become very weak and corrupt during the Circassian period. Public officials were appointed on the basis of bribery rather than ability.[13]

To recover the bribes, officials resorted to oppressive taxation. The incentive to work and produce was adversely affected and output declined. The crisis was further intensified by debasement of the currency through the excessive issue of copper fulus, or fiat money, to cover state budgetary deficits. All these factors joined hands with the famine to lead to a high degree of inflation, misery of the poor, and impoverishment of the country.

Hence, al-Maqrizi laid bare the socio-political determinants of the prevailing 'system crisis' by taking into account a number of variables like corruption, bad government policies, and weak administration. All of these together played a role in worsening the impact of the famine, which could otherwise have been handled effectively without a significant adverse impact on the population. This is clearly a forerunner of Sen's entitlement theory, which holds the economic mismanagement of illegitimate governments to be responsible for the poor people's misery during famines and other natural disasters (Sen, 1981). What al-Maqrizi wrote of the Circassian Mamluks was also true of the later Ottoman period (See Meyer, 1989).

Stages of development

Ibn Khaldun stated the stages of development through which every society passes, moving from the primitive Bedouin stage to the rise of village, towns and urban centers with an effective government, development of agriculture; industry and sciences, and the impact of values and environment on this development (*Muqaddimah*, pp. 35, 41–44, 87–95, 120–48, 172–76). Walliyullah[14] (d. 1762) later analyzed the development of society through four different stages from primitive existence to a well-developed community with khilafah (morally-based welfare state), which tries to ensure the spiritual as well as material well-being of the people. Like Ibn Khaldun, he considered political authority to be indispensable for human well-being. To be able to serve as a source of well-being for all and not of burden and decay, it must have the characteristics of the khilafah. He applied this analysis in various writings to the conditions prevailing during his life-time. He found that the luxurious life style of the rulers, along with their exhausting military campaigns, the increasing corruption and inefficiency of the civil service, and huge stipends to a vast retinue of unproductive courtiers, led them to the imposition of oppressive taxes on farmers, traders and craftsmen, who constituted the main productive section of the population. These people had, therefore, lost interest in their occupations, output had slowed down, state financial resources had declined, and the country had become impoverished (Waliyullah, 1992, Vol. I, pp. 119–52). Thus, in step with Ibn Khaldun and other Muslim scholars, al-Maqrizi and Waliyullah combined moral, political, social and economic factors to explain the economic phenomena of their times and the rise and fall of their societies.

Muslim intellectual decline

Unfortunately, the rich theoretical contribution made by Muslim scholars up until Ibn Khaldun did not get fertilized and irrigated by later scholars to lead to the development of Islamic economics, except by a few isolated scholars like al-Maqrizi, al-Dawwani (d. 1501), and Waliyullah. Their contributions were, however, only in specific areas and did not lead to a further development of Ibn Khaldun's model of socio-economic and political dynamics. Islamic economics did not, therefore, develop as a separate intellectual discipline in conformity with the Islamic paradigm along the theoretical foundations and method laid down by Ibn Khaldun and his predecessors. It continued to remain an integral part of the social and moral philosophy of Islam.

One may ask here why the rich intellectual contributions made by Muslim scholars did not continue after Ibn Khaldun. The reason may be that, as indicated earlier, Ibn Khaldun lived at a time when the political and socio-economic decline of the Muslim world was underway.[15] He was perhaps "the sole point of light in his quarter of the firmament" (Toynbee, 1935, Vol. 3, p. 321). According to Ibn Khaldun himself, sciences progress only when a society is itself progressing (p. 434). This theory is clearly upheld by Muslim history. Sciences progressed rapidly in the Muslim world for four centuries from the middle of the eighth century to the middle of the twelfth century and continued to do so at a substantially decelerated pace for at least two more centuries, tapering off gradually thereafter (Sarton 1927, Vol. 1 and Book 1 of Vol. 2). Once in a while there did appear a brilliant star on an otherwise unexciting firmament. Economics was no exception. It also continued to be in a state of limbo in the Muslim world. No worthwhile contributions were made after Ibn Khaldun.

The trigger mechanism for this decline was, according to Ibn Khaldun, the failure of political authority to provide good governance. Political illegitimacy, which started after the end of khilafah in 661 gradually led to increased corruption and the use of state resources for private benefit at the neglect of education and other nation-building functions of the state. This gradually triggered the decline of all other sectors of the society and economy.[16]

The rapidly rising Western civilization took over the torch of knowledge from the declining Muslim world and has kept it burning with even greater brightness. All sciences, including the social sciences, have made phenomenal progress. Conventional economics became a separate academic discipline after the publication of Alfred Marshall's great treatise, *Principles of Economics*, in 1890 (Schumpeter, 1954, p. 21),[17] and has continued to develop since then at a remarkable speed. With such a great achievement to its credit, there is no psychological need to allow the 'Great Gap' thesis to persist. It would help promote better understanding of Muslim civilization in the West if textbooks started giving credit to Muslim scholars. They were "the torchbearers of ancient learning during the medieval period" and "it was from them that the Renaissance was sparked and the Enlightenment kindled" (Todd Lowry in his 'Foreword' in Ghazanfar, 2003, p. xi). Watt has been frank enough to admit that, "the influence of Islam on Western Christendom is greater than is usually realized" and that, "an important task for Western Europeans, as we move into the era of the one world, is . . . to acknowledge fully our debt to the Arab and Islamic world" (Watt, 1972, p. 84).

Conventional economics, however, took a wrong turn after the Enlightenment Movement by stripping itself of the moral basis of society emphasized by Aristotelian and Judeo-Christian philosophies. This deprived it of the role that moral values and good governance can play in helping society raise both efficiency and equity in the allocation and distribution of scarce resources needed for promoting the well-being of all. However, this has been changing. The role of good governance has already been recognized and that of moral values is gradually penetrating the economics orthodoxy. Islamic economics is also reviving now after the independence of Muslim countries from foreign domination. It is likely that the two disciplines will converge and become one after a period of time. This will be in keeping with the teachings of the Qur'an, which clearly states that mankind was created as one but became divided as a result of their differences and transgression against each other (10:19, 2:213 and 3:19). This reunification [globalization, as it is now called], if reinforced by justice and mutual care, should help promote peaceful coexistence and enable mankind to realize the well-being of all, a goal the realization of which we are all anxiously looking forward to.

Notes

1 This is the liberal version of the secular and materialist worldviews. There is also the totalitarian version which does not have faith in the individuals' ability to manage private property in a way that would ensure social well-being. Hence its prescription is to curb individual freedom and to transfer all means of production and decision making to a totalitarian state. Since this form of the secular and materialist worldview failed to realize human well-being and has been overthrown practically everywhere, it is not discussed in this paper.

2 The literature on economic development is full of assertions that improvement in income distribution is in direct conflict with economic growth. For a summary of these views, see Cline, 1973, Chapter 2. This has, however, changed and there is hardly any development economist now who argues that injustice can help promote development.

3 North has used the term 'nasty' for all such behavior. See the chapter "Ideology and Free Rider," in North, 1981.

4 Some of these scholars include Abu Yusuf (d. 798), al-Mawardi (d. 1058), Abu Ya'la (d. 1065), Nazam al-Mulk (d.1092), al-Ghazali (d. 1111), Ibn Taymiyyah (d. 1328), Ibn Khaldun (d. 1406), Shah Walliyullah (d. 1762), Jamaluddin al-Afghani (d. 1897), Muhammad 'Abduh (d. 1905), Muhammad Iqbal (d. 1938), Hasan al-Banna (d. 1949), Sayyid Mawdudi (d. 1979), and Baqir al-Sadr (d. 1980).

5 Some of these authors include al-Katib (d. 749), ibn al-Muqaffa (d. 756) al-Nu'man (d. 974), al-Mawardi (d. 1058), Kai Ka'us (d. 1082), Nizam al-Mulk (d. 1092), al-Ghazali (d. 1111), al-Turtushi (d. 1127). (For details, see Essid, 1995, pp.19–41.)
6 For the fallacy of the Great Gap thesis, see Mirakhor (1987) and Ghazanfar (2003), particularly the "Foreword" by Todd Lowry and the "Introduction" by Ghazanfar.
7 The full name of the book (given in the bibliography) may be freely translated as "The Book of Lessons and the Record of Cause and Effect in the History of Arabs, Persians and Berbers and their Powerful Contemporaries." Several different editions of the *Muqaddimah* are now available in Arabic. The one I have used is that published in Cairo by al-Maktabah al-Tijarriyah al-Kubra without any indication of the year of publication. It has the advantage of showing all vowel marks, which makes the reading relatively easier. The *Muqaddimah* was translated into English in three volumes by Franz Rosenthal. Its first edition was published in 1958 and the second edition in 1967. Selections from the *Muqaddimah* by Charles Issawi were published in 1950 under the title, *An Arab Philosophy of History: Selections from the Prolegomena of Ibn Khaldun of Tunis (1332–1406)*.
   A considerable volume of literature is now available on Ibn Khaldun. This includes Spengler, 1964; Boulakia, 1971; Mirakhor, 1987; and Chapra, 2000.
8 For some of these contributions, see Spengler, 1964; DeSmogyi, 1965; Mirakhor, 1987; Siddiqi, 1992; Essid, 1995; Islahi, 1996; Chapra, 2000; and Ghazanfar, 2003.
9 For a more detailed discussion of taxation by various Muslim scholars, see the section on "Literature on Mirrors for Princes" in Essid, 1995, pp. 19–41.
10 This letter is a significant development over the letter of Abu Yusuf to Caliph Harun al-Rashid (1933/34, pp. 3–17). It is more comprehensive and covers a larger number of topics.
11 These are "On tax revenues and the reason for their being low and high" (pp. 279–80) and "Injustice ruins development" (pp. 286–410).
12 Bear in mind the fact that this was stated at the time when commodity money, which it is not possible for the government to 'create,' was used, and fiduciary money, had not become the rule of the day.
13 This was during the Slave (Mamluk) Dynasty in Egypt, which is divided into two periods. The first period was that of the Bahri (or Turkish) Mamluks (1250–1382), who have generally received praise in the chronicles of their contemporaries. The second period was that of the Burji Mamluks (Circassians, 1382–1517). This period was beset by a series of severe economic crises. (For details see Allouche, 1994.)
14 Shah Walliyullah al-Dihlawi, popularly known as Walliyullah, was born in 1703, four years before the death of the Mughal Emperor, Aurangzeb (1658–1707). Aurangzeb's rule, spanning a period of forty-nine years, was followed by a great deal of political instability – ten different changes in rulers during Walliyullah's life-span of 59 years – leading ultimately to the weakening and decline of the Mughal Empire.
15 For a brief account of the general decline and disintegration of the Muslim world during the fourteenth century, see Muhsin Mahdi, 1964, pp. 17–26.
16 For a discussion of the causes of Muslim decline, see Chapra, 2000, pp. 173–252.
17 According to Blaug (1985), economics became an academic discipline in the 1880s (p. 3).

References

Abu Yusuf, Ya 'qub ibn Ibrahim. *Kitab al-Kharaj*. Cairo: al-Matab'ah al-Salafiyyah, second edition, 1933/34. (This book has been translated into English by A. Ben Shemesh. *Taxation in Islam*. Leiden: E. J. Brill, 1969.)

Allouche, Adel. *Mamluk Economics: A Study and Translation of Al-Maqrizi's Ighathah*. Salt Lake City: University of Utah Press, 1994.

Baeck Louis. *The Mediterranean Tradition in Economic Thought*. London: Routledge, 1994.

Blanchflower, David, and Andrew Oswald. "Well-being over Time in Britain and USA." NBER, Working Paper No. 7487, 2000.

Blaug Mark. *Economic Theory in Retrospect*. Cambridge: Cambridge University Press, 1985.

Boulakia, Jean David C. "Ibn Khaldun: A Fourteenth-Century Economist." *Journal of Political Economy* 79, no. 5 (1971): 1105–18.

Chapra, M. Umer. *The Future of Economics: An Islamic Perspective*. Leicester, UK: The Islamic Foundation, 2000.

Cline, William R. *Potential Effects of Income Redistribution on Economic Growth*. New York: Praeger, 1973.

DeSmogyi, Joseph N. "Economic Theory in Classical Arabic Literature." *Studies in Islam* (Delhi), (1965): 1–6.

Diener E., and Shigehiro Oshi. "Money and Happiness: Income and Subjective Well-being." In *Culture and Subjective Well-being*, edited by E. Diener and E. Suh. Cambridge, MA: MIT Press, 2000.

Dimashqi, Abu al-Fadl Ja'far ibn 'Ali al-. *Al-Isharah ila Mahasin al-Tijarah*, Al-Bushra al-Shurbaji, editor. Cairo: Maktabah al-Kulliyat al-Azhar, 1977.

Duri, A. A. "Baghdad." *The Encyclopedia of Islam*, 894–99. Leiden: Brill, 1986.

Easterlin, Richard. "Does Economic Growth Improve the Human Lot? Some Empirical Evidence." In *Nations and Households in Economic Growth: Essays in Honor of Moses Abramowitz*, edited by Paul David and Melvin Reder. New York: Academic Press, 1974.

Easterlin, Richard. "Will Raising the Income of All Increase the Happiness of All?" *Journal of Economic Behavior and Organization* 27, no. 1 (1995): 35–48.

Easterlin, Richard (2001), "Income and Happiness: Towards a Unified Theory" in Economic Journal, 111: 473 (2001).

Essid, M. Yassine. *A Critique of the Origins of Islamic Economic Thought*. Leiden: Brill, 1995.

Feyerabend, Paul. *Against Method: Outline of an Anarchistic Theory of Knowledge*. London: Verso, third edition, 1993.

Fischel, W. J. "Djahbadh." In *Encyclopedia of Islam*, volume 2, 382–83. Leiden: Brill, 1992.

Friedman, Milton. *Essays in Positive Economics*. Chicago: University of Chicago Press, 1953.

George, Henry. *Progress and Poverty*. New York: Robert Schalkenback Foundation, 1955.

Ghazanfar, S. M. *Medieval Islamic Economic Thought: Filling the Great Gap in European Economics*. London: Routledge Curzon, 2003.

Groenewegen, P. D. "A Note on the Origin of the Phrase, 'Supply and Demand.'" *Economic Journal* 83, no. 330 (1973): 505–09.

Hausman, Daniel, and Michael McPherson. "Taking Ethics Seriously: Economics and Contemporary Moral Philosophy." *Journal of Economic Literature* 31, no. 2 (1993): 671–731.

Ibn Khaldun. *Muqaddimah*. Cairo: Al-Maktabah al-Tijariyyah al-Kubra. See also its translation under Rosenthal (1967) and selections from it under Issawi (1950).

Ibn Taymiyyah. *Majmu' Fatawa Shaykh al-Islam Ahmad Ibn Taymiyyah.* 'Abd al-Rahman al-'Asimi, editor. Riyadh: Matabi' al-Riyad, 1961–63.

Islahi, A. Azim. *History of Economic Thought in Islam*. Aligharh, India: Department of Economics, Aligharh Muslim University, 1996.

Issawi, Charles. *An Arab Philosophy of History: Selections from the Prolegomena of Ibn Khaldun of Tunis (1332–1406)*. London: John Muray, 1950.

Jahiz, Amr ibn Bahr al-. *Kitab al-Tabassur bi al-Tijarah*. Beirut: Dar al-Kitab al-Jadid, 1983.

Jay, Elizabeth, and Richard Jay. *Critics of Capitalism: Victorian Reactions to Political Economy*. Cambridge: Cambridge University Press, 1986.

Kenny, Charles. "Does Growth Cause Happiness, or Does Happiness Cause Growth?" *Kyklos* 52, no. 1 (1999): 3–26.

Koopmans, T. C. (1969), "Inter-temporal Distribution and 'Optimal' Aggregate Economic Growth", in Fellner et. al., Ten Economic Studies in the Tradition of Irving Fisher (John Willey and Sons).

Mahdi, Mohsin. *Ibn Khaldun's Philosophy of History*. Chicago: University of Chicago Press, 1964.

Maqrizi, Taqi al-Din Ahmad ibn Ali al-. *Ighathah al-Ummah bi Kashf al-Ghummah*. Hims, Syria: Dar ibn al-Wahid, 1956. (See its English translation by Allouche, 1994).

Mawardi, Abu al-Hasan 'Ali al-. *Adab al-Dunya wa al-Din*. Mustafa al Saqqa, editor. Cairo: Mustafa al-Babi al Halabi, 1955.

Mawardi, Abdu al-Hasan. *Al-Ahkam al-Sultaniyyah wa al-Wilayat al-Diniyyah*. Cairo: Mustafa al-Babi al-Halabi, 1960. (The English translation of this book by Wafa Wahba has been published under the title, *The Ordinances of Government*. Reading: Garnet, 1996.)

Mirakhor, Abbas. "The Muslim Scholars and the History of Economics: A Need for Consideration." *American Journal of Islamic Social Sciences* (1987): 245–76.

Misri Rafiq Yunus al-. *Al-Islam wa al-Nuqud*. Jeddah: King Abdulaziz University, 1981.

Meyer, M. S. "Economic Thought in the Ottoman Empire in the 14th–Early 19th Centuries." *Archiv Orientali* 4, no. 57 (1989): 305–18.

Myers, Milton L. *The Soul of Modern Economic Man: Ideas of Self-Interest, Thomas Hobbes to Adam Smith*. Chicago: University of Chicago Press, 1983.

North, Douglass C. *Structure and Change in Economic History*. New York: W.W. Norton, 1981.

North, Douglass C. "Economic Performance through Time." *American Economic Review* 84, no. 2 (1994): 359–68.

Oswald, A. J. "Happiness and Economic Performance," *Economic Journal* 107, no. 445 (1997): 1815–31.

Pifer, Josef. "Scholasticism." *Encyclopedia Britannica* 16 (1978): 352–57.

Robbins, Lionel. *An Essay on the Nature and Significance of Economic Science.* London: Macmillan, second edition, 1935.

Rosenthal, Franz. *Ibn Khaldun: The Muqaddimah, An Introduction to History.* Princeton, NJ: Princeton University Press, 1967.

Sarakhsi, Shams al-Din al-. *Kitab al-Mabsut.* Beirut: Dar al-Ma'rifah, third edition, 1978 (particularly "Kitab al-Kasb" of al-Shaybani in Vol. 30: 245–97).

Sarton, George. *Introduction to the History of Science.* Washington, DC: Carnegie Institute (three volumes issued between 1927 and 1948, each of the second and third volumes has two parts).

Schumpeter, Joseph A. *History of Economic Analysis.* New York: Oxford University Press, 1954.

Sen, Amartya. *Poverty and Famines: An Essay on Entitlement and Deprivation.* Oxford: Clarendon Press, 1981.

Sen, Amartya. *On Ethics and Economics.* Oxford: Basil Blackwell, 1987.

Siddiqi, M. Nejatullah. "History of Islamic Economic Thought." In *Lectures on Islamic Economics,* Ausaf Ahmad and K. R. Awan, 69–90. Jeddah: IDB/IRTI, 1992.

Smith, Adam. *An Inquiry into the Nature and Causes of the Wealth of Nations.* New York: Modern Library, 1937.

Solo, Robert A. "Values and Judgments in the Discourse of the Sciences." In *Value Judgment and Income Distribution,* edited by Robert A. Solo and Charles A. Anderson, 9–40. New York, Praeger, 1981.

Spengler, Joseph. "Economic Thought in Islam: Ibn Khaldun." *Comparative Studies in Society and History* (1964): 268–306.

Thweatt, W. O. "Origins of the Terminology, Supply and Demand." *Scottish Journal of Political Economy* (1983): 287–94.

Toynbee, Arnold J. *A Study of History.* London: Oxford University Press, second edition, 1935.

Udovitch, Abraham L. *Partnership and Profit in Medieval Islam.* Princeton; NJ: Princeton University Press, 1970.

Waliyullah, Shah. *Hujjatullah al-Balighah.* M. Sharif Sukkar, editor. Beirut: Dar Ihya al-Ulum, second edition, two volumes, 1992. (An English translation of this book by Marcia K. Hermansen was published bu Brill, Leiden, 1966.)

Watt, W. Montgomery. *The Influence of Islam on Medieval Europe.* Edinburgh: Edinburgh University Press, 1972.

Part 2

RELIGIOUS BASIS OF ISLAMIC ECONOMICS

8

THE MORAL ECONOMY OF CLASSICAL ISLAM

A FiqhiConomic model

Salah El-Sheikh[1]

Source: *Muslim World*, 98:1 (2008), 116–44.

Down out of the heaven, He sendeth water, and the wadis overflow each in its measure: So the torrent beareth (on its back) a mounting froth, akin to that froth (emitting) from what they smelted in the fire for making ornaments or wares. **Thus Allah depicteth the true and the false**: The froth is cast away a vanishing dross, but **that which benefits mankind abides in the earth**. So doth Allah coin His similitudes.

Qur'ān, 13:17

The inner meaning of history . . . involves speculation and an attempt to get at the truth, subtle explanation of the causes and origins of existing things, and deep knowledge of the how and why of events. History, therefore, is firmly rooted in philosophy . . . It takes critical insight to sort out the hidden truth; it takes knowledge to lay truth bare . . .

Ibn Khadūn's *Muqaddimah*

Let the *sūq* of this world below do no injury to the *sūq* of the Hereafter, and the *sūqs* of the Hereafter are the mosques.

Al-Ghazāli's *Ihyā'*

Each economy necessarily functions within the confines of a particular social framework, which is defined by its distinctive moral philosophy and legal system. What makes an economy "Islamic" is Sharī'ah:[2] a huge corpus of moral and legal discourses, which was intended by scholars (jurists and theologians) of the second and third Islamic centuries to guide Muslims in their pursuit of a good and virtuous life (and which also qualifies them for paradise in the life after). As such, Sharī'ah defined the moral economy of classical Islam, shaped its micro and macro institutions, and modulated its actual performance. Recently, it has become both a symbol and a basis for revivalist Islamic movements in their attempts to Islamicize their polities and economies.

The moral/legal framework

Sharī'ah was molded by the theological and jurisprudential debates that began towards the end of the eighth century.[3] The Mu'tazila, a rationalist school of *kalām* (philosophical theology) and self-designated as Ahl al-'Adl (Advocates/People of Justice), adopted a doctrine of teleological ethics and law, arguing that humans — with their divine gift of *'aql* (reason) alone — are capable not only of recognizing good and evil acts, but also of legislating good laws to regulate their lives, at least in the domain of *mu'amallat* (social and economic transactions).[4] In this they were bitterly opposed by the pietistic disposition and literalist bent of Ahl al-Hadith (the Traditionists).[5] The Mu'tazila gradually lost its primacy after the termination of a *mihna* (inquisition) enacted by Caliph al-Ma'mūn (d.218/833) in a failed attempt by the state to impose Mu'tazili theological doctrine on its officials, notably the judges.[6] It was in the midst of a resurgent traditionalism that the Ash'ariya school was founded by a former Mu'tazilite, Abul-Hassan al-Ash'ari (d.324/935), who worked out a "reconcilement" that largely accepts the rationalist doctrine and method of the Mu'tazila, but rejects their views in the all-important area of ethics and law.[7] In this realm, the Ash'arites accepted the Traditionists' doctrine that "God does not command an act because the act is just and good; it is His command (*amr*) which makes it just and good," as Gardet puts it.[8] Eventually, the Ash'ariya gained ascendancy and has since become the official *kalām* of Sunni orthodoxy, thereby providing the theological justification for its classical legal theory of *usul al-fiqh* (Sources/Roots of Jurisprudence).

Intertwined with the raging theological debate, the jurisprudential debate ultimately brought about an "idealist" concept of Sharī'ah as being an all-embracing system of "divine commands," which the classical jurists (*fuqaha*) set out to construct with their theory of the four sources.[9] Only two of these, the Qur'ān and the Prophet's Traditions (hadith), are material sources: the former is divine, the latter quasi-divine. The third is a rational hermeneutic method that enabled the *fuqaha* to interpret the material sources, and extend the embrace of the sources' positive content to span the entire range of human experience. This formal method, centering on *qiyās* (essentially, analogical syllogistics), was intended to safeguard the integrity of divine commands from the vagaries of personal prejudice. The entire structure of their brilliantly reasoned edifice hangs on the fourth root:[10] *Ijmā'* (consensus of the jurists), an authoritative (albeit informal and dialectical) sanctioning process which was deemed necessary for adjudicating the epistemological

THE MORAL ECONOMY OF CLASSICAL ISLAM

status of the material sources as well as the fruits of their juristic effort (*ijtihād*). When this highly competitive and geographically diffuse community of jurists reached a consensus, the substance of their *ijmāʿ* was classed as *ʿilm* (indubitable knowledge), and when they did not, the substance was considered *zann* (conjecture/opinion).

The classical jurists, who belonged to a number of competing schools (*madhāhib*), often disagreed, not least in the area of economic and commercial law. Nevertheless, they considered their variant opinions equally valid according to their doctrine of *ikhtilāf*, a correlative term to *ijmāʿ*.[11] The jurists also recognized that a mechanistic and strict application of their analogical syllogistics might lead to injustice. This was particularly so because the conclusion of their *qiyās* depended critically on the *ʿilla* (cogent reason); this was more of a reason in the logical sense (ratio), rather than a cause in the ontological sense (causa), or *hikma*.[12] In his celebrated *Muqaddimah*, the jurist and philosopher of history Ibn Khaldūn (d. 808/1406) gave an incisive re-statement of the logical hazards of this classical method:[13]

> Analogical reasoning (*qiyās*) and comparison are well known to human nature. They are not safe from error. Together with forgetfulness and negligence, they sway man from his purpose and divert him from his goal. Often, someone who has learned a good deal of past history remains unaware of the changes that conditions have undergone . . .

Hence, in their pursuit of *tawhīdi* justice, the classical jurists invoked the material sources (especially the Qurʾān) and often exercised their analytical/ speculative (as opposed to formal *qiyās*) reasoning. In so doing, I believe they must have drawn on the concepts of the Muʿtazila theory of divine justice: namely, that Allah, being necessarily just, only wills what is morally good (*hasan*), and that His motive in imposing the Law on His creatures is their welfare/benefit (*salah*).[14]

The first concept (*hasan*) was the root of *istihsān* ("seeking the most equitable solution"), the juristic method of the Hanafis (who tended to be Muʿtazilis); the second (*salah*) was the root of *istislāh* ("seeking the best solution for public welfare") of the Mālikīs.[15] The Hanafi and Mālikī schools viewed their respective methods as a kind of *qiyās khafī* (hidden analogy), considered them as subsidiary sources/roots, and often employed them when the solution issuing from formal *qiyās* entailed injustice or harm (*darar*), not the least in the area of economic dealings and business contracts.[16] In spite of the idealist nature of their enterprise, the classical jurists also exhibited an acute understanding of their economic and business environment, one that enabled them to articulate the moral foundations and efficient legal institutions of a highly successful Islamic economy. This fact led the economic historian Abraham Udovitch, in a meticulous and well-reasoned study of those institutions, to conclude that:[17]

The prominence of the Muslim world in the trade of the early Middle Ages, if not attributable to, was certainly reinforced by the superiority and flexibility of the commercial techniques available to its merchants. Some of the institutions, practices and concepts already found fully developed in the Islamic legal sources of the late eighth century did not emerge in Europe until several centuries later.

The preceding synopsis, which only highlights the nature of Sharī'ah, its principles, and how it came to be, is particularly important for recognizing that ill-conceived tendency among many Islamists to hypostatize Sharī'ah and separate it from its historical context, be it socio-economic, political, or technological. This tendency is evident in much of the body of literature designated as "Islamic Economics": a vast body that is more accurately rendered as "MawdūdīConomics," in view of the defining influence of the activist/scholar Abu'l-A'la Mawdūdī (d.1979), the founder of Pakistan's Islamist movement *Jama'at-e-Islami* and the first to articulate the doctrine that continues to dominate this literature (especially in English); as such, he is considered the intellectual progenitor of its contributors.[18] The above-mentioned tendency is no more evident than in the wholesale adoption by (what I will call) "MawdūdiConomists" of the doctrine of *Riba* as a pivotal principle in their prescriptive paradigm of the Islamic economy. In the interest of clarity, I will use the term *Riba* (with capital "R") to signify the generic moral meaning of the term, a principle/essence of economic inequity, and the term *riba* (with small "r") to signify a species of the genus *Riba*, notably loan interest (as estimated by the classical jurists).

In this article, I attempt to sketch out a verbal "model" of the "classical" economy of historical Islam, one that assembles what is known of its basic "building blocks" in a coherent system that highlights its moral and legal philosophy, and encapsulates its fundamental principles and "laws of motion" in theory as well as its *modus operandi* in practice.[19] In the process, the broad lines of this model are juxtaposed against the revivalist views and doctrines espoused by "MawdūdiConomists." In implementing this objective — besides the introduction — the article consists of four other sections. In section II, Islam's work ethic of "legitimate/justified gain" is expounded to reveal a doctrine of economic justice that underpins the juristic effort of the classical jurists. This doctrine is employed in section III, "The Sharī'ah Market Model," to delineate and typify the economic structure of classical *sūqs*, their moral and social embeddedness, their legal framework, and their operational and policy institutions. Section IV then addresses the microeconomic institutions of business association and financing as well as the macroeconomic conduits of financial intermediation between savers and investors. Finally, in Section V, the article ends with a perspective summary and concluding remarks regarding the nature of the socio-economic system typified here.

Economic morality and the classical doctrine of *Riba*

In their pursuit of *tawhīdi* justice and good, classical jurists found in their material sources (Qur'ān and Sunna) a divine sanction for economic activity and the work ethic in general.[20] They also found persistent exhortation for fair and just economic exchange.[21] On this basis, they formulated a meritorious doctrine of economic justice as fairness in economic dealings.[22] This doctrine rests on two fundamental maxims: (1) The avoidance of *gharar* (unjustified *jahl* or absence of necessary knowledge); (2) The avoidance of "unjustified enrichment" (*fadl māl bilā 'iwad*).

(a) Gharar

Intended essentially for obviating the possibility that a party to exchange gains an unfair advantage over the other (*ghubn*) due to a lack of necessary information, the prohibition of *Gharar* was sanctioned by *ijmā'*. But jurists disagreed over the content and nature of this necessary knowledge, the conditions for securing it, and the implications of their respective views to various types of sale contracts and practices. Their disagreements centered mainly on questions regarding the actual existence of the exchanged countervalues at contracting time, the actual control of the parties over those countervalues, the quantum and specification of the countervalues (precisely expressed in a genus/differentia pattern), and the question of future performance of exchange dealings with regard to the risks and uncertainties involved.[23] Viewed in its totality, the idealized world of the classical jurists ensures a complete knowledge (of exchanged objects), one that negates avoidable risks and uncertainties (hence potential deceits) regarding performance. As such, their world — it seems — is akin to the perfect-knowledge and perfect-foresight requirements of perfect competition, the central concept of the idealized market system of modern economics (explained below). In both worlds the community's economic welfare is sought, notwithstanding the difference in their respective moral justification.

(b) Unjustified enrichment and Riba

The prohibition of *gharar* eliminates a significant source of unjustified advantage or enrichment. *Riba*, generically understood, is every kind of excess or unjustified disparity between the exchanged objects or countervalues, essentially any kind of unjustified gain, a source of unjustified enrichment.[24] As such, in its specific sense, *Riba* assumes two different types: (1) *Riba al-Fadl*, and (2) *Riba al-Nasī'a*, according to the classical jurists.[25]

The first type is also called "*Sale riba*" (*buyū'*) because it is occasioned by a sale or exchange transaction, and is again called *Sunna riba* because its prohibition is regulated principally by Traditions of the Prophet. According to these Traditions, in bartering certain goods, the exchange of articles of the "same genus" (*jins*) is legitimate when the exchanged countervalues are quantitatively equal, and their delivery is not deferred.[26] The violation of this rule produces *riba*, an illegitimate or illicit excess or gain. The Traditions named only six goods (consisting of two types of precious metals, gold and silver; and four types of foodstuffs, wheat, barley, dates, and salt); and the jurists exercised their analogical syllogistics to extend the umbrella of the rule's applicability, but disagreed in specifying the *'ilia* (cogent reason), the distinguishing attributes of these particular goods. The rigor and complexities of their syllogistic differences and conclusions are compounded by their disagreements in defining the genus/species configurations (and their concrete content in each case) as well as the affinity of these differences with their variant views on *Riba*.[27]

(c) Riba *and interest*

Called *nasi'a* by the classical jurists, the second type of *Riba* is occasioned by deferring the delivery of a countervalue, regardless of whether the exchanged object is within or without the same species of the countervalue, and whether it does or does not generate *fadl* (gain/disparity). If the *nasi'a* transaction stipulates a gain manifestly, this gain is an "Explicit (*Jali*) *Riba*," in effect, a loan interest.[28] The latter is also called Qur'ānic *riba* because the classical jurists reached a "consensus" (*ijma'*) that the Qur'ān prohibited it. It is noteworthy, however, that this type of *Riba* is addressed in a number of Qur'ānic verses; given the accepted/traditional interpretation of these verses, the Qur'ānic position ranges from acceptance to prohibition.[29] The consensus prohibition by the jurists was only a consequence of their doctrine of abrogation (*naskh*).[30] Based on the chronology of revelation, their juristic technique (and its application in this case), although sanctioned by *ijma'*, is open to question, for it implicitly assumes a paradoxical and unsatisfactory theology regarding the nature of God and His Law, a fact that seems to be lost on or overlooked by modern scholars.

All pre-modern jurists advocate the prohibition against loan interest: To them, the only licit loan is an interest-free loan, this being either *qard hassan*, a loan of fungible objects (notably money), or *'ariyya*, a usufruct (*manfa'a*) loan of non-fungible objects.[31] They disagreed, however, on the scope and licitness of other types of *Riba*. They also employed their subsidiary methods of *istihsān* and *istislāh* to accommodate economic and business imperatives. Towards this accommodation, the jurists, especially the Hanafis, went further and produced treatises and manuals of legal devices (*hiyal*) to circumvent the prohibition's deleterious effect on the economy. Modern Muslim jurists tend to reject the *hiyal*, but disagree on the licitness of loan interest. As well, modern Muslim economists disagree on the prohibition: Muslim secularists and Islamic modernists reject the entire doctrine of *Riba*. In this they are vehemently opposed by MawdūdiConomists, who have been influential in the Islamic banking movement.

The *Sharī'ah* market model

The idealist worldview of the classical jurists is particularly evident in their distinctively Islamic vision of the market. Perhaps it is illustrated best by the previously stated maxim:[32] "Let the *sūk* [market] of this world below do no injury to the *sūks* of the Hereafter, and the *sūks* of the Hereafter are the mosques," the abode of *tawhīsd*-qua-harmony. Rendered by Abu Hamid al-Ghazali (d.505/1111), the great jurist/theologian (and anti-*falsafa* philosopher), this maxim is an apt representation of the Qur'ānic view of social and economic transactions (*mu'āmalāt*) of *al-umma* (the Islamic *gemeinschaff*):[33] That is, a consensual, free, and moral exchange, one that would establish the necessary conditions not only for a prosperous life, but also for "social harmony" and spiritual attainment (Qur'ān, IV:29).[34] Ghazāli's worldly *sūqs* are morally and "socially embedded" *à la* Polanyi; they provide the fora for a moral economic exchange that was carefully analyzed and systematized by the classical jurists.[35]

(a) The Bay' model of exchange

Translated "Sale," in fact *bay'* is a normative Qur'ānic concept which is divinely juxtaposed against "unjustified enrichment" (Qur'ān, II: 275). The classical jurists saw it as such, and developed the *bay'* contract with so much thought and sophistication that it became "the core of the Islamic law of obligations."[36] Indeed, it was viewed as a paradigm of various types of contracts, including the marriage contract, not to mention the "implicit contract" between the believer and Allah as well as the "social contract" between the Umma and the Caliph (*bay'ā*).[37] Asked: "How is it that you have not written anything concerning . . . *zuhd* (asceticism)?" Muhammad al-Shaybānī (d.189/805) answered: "I have already composed the Book of Sale" (*Bay'*).[38] What the great architect of Hanafi law meant was that the best way of seeking God is not by the hermetic abandonment of the community's material life, but rather by seeking a good livelihood and opportunity for one's family (within the community), and above all, according to the law. With this kind of engagement, the fruits of social cooperation proliferate, and in the process enrich the community at large. Abū Bakr al-Rāzī (d. 313/925), the well-known philosopher/medical scientist, put it best:[39]

> When many men agree to co-operate and help each other, they parcel out the various sorts of profitable endeavor among themselves; each labors upon a single business until he achieves its complete fulfillment, so that every man is simultaneously a servant and served,

toiling for others and having others toiling for him. In this way all enjoy an agreeable life and all know the blessings of plenty, even though there is a wide difference between them and an extensive variety of rank and accomplishment; nevertheless there is not one who is not served and labored for, or whose needs are not wholly sufficed.

This socio-economic philosophy of *tawhīd*-qwa-harmony — which imbues basic Qur'ānic concepts and injunction — underpins the jurists' careful analysis and meticulous articulation of the *bay'* contract and the law of sale in general.[40] First, the sale has to meet their procedural theory of justice by minimizing, if not eliminating, "unjustified enrichment." As such, it has to be *gharar*-free and *Riba*-free. In fact, the classical doctrines of *gharar* and *Riba* were developed in conjunction with the jurists' theory of sale.[41] In addition, the exchange process itself has to be genuinely consensual, fair, and endowed with safeguards and mechanisms to ensure these requirements.[42] All in all, in the ideal world of the classical jurists, the sale conditions, process, and contract ought to minimize, if not obviate, legal dispute and inequity among the parties, thereby enhancing overall social harmony, and in the process create the necessary conditions for the good of community members *à la* Shaybānī.

The classical jurists recognized however that their *bay'* was an ideal prototype; and they were fully aware of the substantial transaction cost of its procedures, as well as the immense information cost the doctrines of *gharar* and *Riba* entailed. With this awareness they exhibited a profound appreciation and acute understanding of the productive aspects of the "practices and customs/conventions" ('*ādāt* and '*urf*) of the business community, its "implicit contracts," an area that modern economics has begun to analyze and fathom only recently.[43] They deployed their juristic method of *qiyās* to accommodate and regulate the economic and business facts of life; and when *qiyās* failed to comprehend the necessary facts, they resorted to *istihsān, istislāh, darūra,* and *hiyal*. A case in point, they went against their ideal rules of evidence and accepted the necessity of written sale contracts to the functioning of a complex, vibrant and large economy. Again, guided by their *bay'* prototype, they developed or Islamicized a variety of practical contractual instruments which suited the complexities of economic life, albeit with the necessary informational and procedural safeguards for protecting the exchange parties and the community at large.

Among the above-mentioned instruments, the following variants of the *bay'* contract stood out:[44] (1) *salam bay'*, a sale that involves immediate payment, but deferred delivery; (2) *nasi'a bay'*, a sale that involves immediate delivery but deferred payment; (3) *bay'juzāf*, a sale whereby the good or/and price are assessed by mere viewing; (4) *murābaha*, a form of cost-plus resale with a specified "fair/normal" profit margin; (5) *istisnā'*, a form of salam contract used for commissioning the production of manufactured goods; (6) *ijāra*, a hire/lease contract, construed as sale of usufruct (*manfaʿa*); and (7) *sarf*, a currency exchange contract.

It is noteworthy that many of these contractual arrangements have been recently reworked and extensively used by MawdūdiConomists in the theory and practice of modern Islamic banking, along with the classical contracts of business association (treated below).

(b) The classical Sūq

Long before Ghazāli's time, the Islamic city planner did perceive and take his maxim seriously.[45] They located in the center of their city plan the great *Jamiʿ* (academy mosque), that great "*Sūq* (market) of the Hereafter" where the jurists dwelled, taught, practiced and reflected on the law. Next to the *Jamiʿ* was *Dar al-Imāra* (House of the Government), the abode of caliphal authority and guardian of the law: A kind of "political *sūq*" where the democratic transactions of *shūra* and *bayʿā* should take place,[46] and one that Ghazāli was painfully aware of, but did not include in the maxim.[47] Thus, socially and morally embedded, the "political *sūq*" along with the "Hereafter *sūq*" were both physically encircled by the (likewise embedded) "worldly *sūq*" according to a geometrical pattern, wherein the city's economic function — as producer of wealth and facilitator of exchange (both local and beyond) — was centered. In this pattern, the city's thoroughfares emanated from the central circle (towards the gates) and accommodated the bookmakers, merchants, financiers, currency-changers, manufacturers, etc., whose degree of proximity to the center reflected their intellectual, economic, and environmental priority to the city's welfare.[48] In addition to these "linear *sūqs*" the pattern included the great conglomerations (variously called *Khan, Qaysariya, Wakala, Funduq*, etc.) which facilitated inter-city and international trade.[49]

According to our current state of knowledge, those classical *sūqs* functioned efficiently, and served their cities and the larger community well.[50] In performing their economic function, they varied in their objects of exchange and scale of operations in such a manner that reflected the occupational structures of the commercial, industrial, and agricultural sectors of the economy. As such, they are classified into three types: (1) The weekly and daily *sūqs*, held inside the city's districts and outside its walls, for supplying fresh foodstuffs and other locally produced products; (2) The central *sūq* (near the great mosque), which permanently supplied in larger quantities a great variety of products, largely of greater value and luxurious vintage, that were mostly imported from other regional *sūqs*; and (3) A yearly or seasonal *sūq*, a sort of international trade fair, for the diffusion of manufactured, imported, and transit products, accommodated in the above-mentioned conglomerations.[51]

(c) The market and the state

Again, given the jurists' moral philosophy of socioeconomic harmony, the system of *sūqs* caricatured above had to be "socially/morally embedded" *à la* Polanyi: In effect, a "microcosm" of the larger society it inhabited and functioned in.[52] As such, the operation, economic transactions, and terms of trade set in the classical *sūqs* had to abide by the precepts of the jurists' doctrine of economic justice as fairness with its twin maxims: the avoidance of *gharar* (unjustified absence of knowledge) and the avoidance of *Riba* (unjustified gain, any advantage without equivalent countervalue). And logically this brought to the fore weighty economic questions of price formation and "fair" pricing in these *sūqs*, a subject that received considerable juristic attention and thought.

Prophet Muḥammad is reported to have rejected (during an episode of severe food shortage) price fixing, on grounds of justice: "The Musaʿir (He who sets prices) is Allah," said the wise Prophet, with his first-hand knowledge and understanding of the workings of markets (both local and international) as a merchant.[53] Naturally, this doctrine of a divine "Invisible Hand," to borrow a Smithonian metaphor, was accepted — in principle — by the classical jurists, for it was compatible with the above-mentioned Qur'ānic ideal of a free, consensual, fair, and ultimately harmonious exchange, the central principle of their *gharar*-free and *Riba*-free *bayʿ* model: A model — it is recalled — that insists on clear, detailed, and near perfect information (on the objects and terms of exchange) in order to preclude the possibility of "unjustified enrichment" (*Riba*) due to *jahl* (lack of information).[54] As I hinted earlier, this *bayʿ* type of economic operation and trading is akin to a divinely inspired world of "perfect competition," the "ideal type" of modern economics, which was justified by the moral theory of Adam Smith and his "invisible hand" (resting on self-interest and competitive markets).[55]

In this regard, it is again recalled that in enjoining consensual exchange (*tijāra*), the Qur'ān (II: 275, IV: 29) juxtaposes *bayʿ*, the ideal type of fair exchange, with *riba* (*buyūʿ*), which is castigated as iniquity, and classed as *harām* (forbidden). Analyzed by classical jurists,[56] this essential Qur'ānic categorization of consensual exchange/trade into *bayʿ* and *riba* reveals an affinity to another Qur'ānic distinction: namely, between *Ribh/kasb* (justified/earned gain) and *Riba* (unjustified/excessive gain).[57] The latter distinction is akin to a fundamental one made in modern economics between "normal profit" and "abnormal/economic profit": The former obtains under competitive market conditions, while the latter — an "excess" beyond the "normal" — is obtained and maintained (through market power) under monopolistic conditions. Being the basis of fair-pricing in modern regulation theory, the "normal/fair" profit concept was also critical of the licitness of various species of classical *bayʿ* transactions in general and the *murābaha* contract in particular.[58] It appears (from what is known) that the socially embedded fora of these transactions, the three categories of classical *sūqs* typified above, had functioned efficiently and competitively (with their prices reflecting market forces) enough to give rise to the superior economy of classical Islam.[59]

It has to be recognized, however, that the superior performance of this economy was not necessarily because the behavior of economic agents was *gharar*-free and *Riba*-free by inclination, an assumption that is often made by MawdūdiConomists in their work, and aptly construed as Homo Islamicus.[60] In fact, the thorough system of legal mechanisms and procedural safeguards, which the classical jurists structured in their sales contracts, assumed that the contracting parties were not inherently Homo Islamicus. The great Ghazāli remarked that ninety percent of his contemporaries — to whom he was addressing his maxim, I assume — did "let the *sūq* of this world do injury to the *sūqs* of the Hereafter," to use his phrase.[61]

Ghazāli's observation and the previous information on the structure of classical *sūqs* suggest then that the superior performance of the classical Islamic economy is explainable by its efficient and competitive "worldly *sūqs*." But to this, one must add the jurists and "political *sūqs*" which endowed that economy with its viable legal/institutional framework and competent economic governance. Being part of the classical doctrine of Islamic governance, this point was elegantly and insightfully expressed — in a law-like manner — by a later historian/jurist, the famed Ibn Khaldun (d. 808/1406), in his *Muqaddimah*:[62]

> Dynasty and government serve as the world's marketplace (*sūq*), attracting to it the products of scholarship and craftsmanship alike . . . Whatever is in demand in this market is in general demand everywhere else. Now, whenever the established dynasty avoids injustice . . . , the wares on its market are as pure silver and fine gold. However, when it is influenced by selfish interests and rivalries, or swayed by vendors of tyranny and dishonesty, the wares of its marketplace become as dross and debased metals.

A case in point is the institution of the *muhtasib*, an important element in the matrix of Islamic economic governance. An Islamicized outgrowth of the institution of *'amil al- sūq* (The Market Inspector) — which existed in the Prophet's era and received his sanction (according to traditional sources)[63] — the classical *muhtasib* was a judicial office with a much wider mandate.[64] The mandate covered the broad area of public morality and health, but economic morality figured steadily and prominently in it.[65]

The classical *muhtasib* was responsible for checking weights, measures, and currencies, investigating and dealing with fraud and generally unlawful market practices, including illicit speculation and misleading information. In effect, the *muhtasib* was in charge of what is now called fair trade and competition policy.[66] Appointed by, and accountable to the *qāḍi* (the judiciary), the *muhtasib's* moral and technical qualifications were enormous. The jurists prepared specialized manuals to facilitate the task, and the *muhtasib* depended on trustworthy associates (*'ariflamīn*) who were recruited for their expertise in the various branches of industry.[67] The producers of manufactured goods (*sunnā'*: artisans) were highly organized in "guilds" (professional corporations) with a potential for exercising monopoly power, and the specialized associates paid attention to their quality standards and pricing practices for good effect.[68]

To perform this mandate of economic morality effectively, the *muhtasib's* offices were located in the city's central market, near the *dar al-imāra* (the "political *sūq*") and the great mosque (the Hereafter *sūq*). Judging by the known results, it appears that the state's "visible hand," Smith's "invisible hand," and the Prophet's "divine hand" worked well, hand in hand.

Business association and finance

Effective operation of any economy is predicated on the availability of efficient and flexible economic institutions: institutions that facilitate the collaboration between workers and employers, between labor and capital, and between savers and investors, as it does generally between buyers and sellers. In the previously sketched market economy of classical Islam, those institutions were developed (or Islamicized) from current and pre-Islamic material, thoughtfully analyzed, and rigorously formulated and systematized by the jurists (with a view to obviate *Riba* and *gharar*). But again the classical jurists disagreed on the particular formulations of those institutions, and in making them licit, they often suspended *qiyās*, and invoked their subsidiary methods of *istihsān* or *istislāh*, and innovated *hiyal* (legal devices) to accommodate economic and business imperatives. The Hanafis in particular exhibited an insightful understanding of those imperatives, and their formulations were often economically superior to the other schools as the above-cited work of Udovitch has demonstrated.[69] It is not surprising therefore that the Hanafi doctrine was later adopted by the Ottoman Empire to become the most widely accepted of the classical schools in the Islamic world. The following brief rendering of the main forms of business association relies primarily on the Hanafi formulations of those institutions.

(a) Business partnership and capital

In facilitating the collaboration between human and financial/capital resources, the classical Islamic economy had at its disposal three basic forms of business association (*sharikāt*: companies): *mufāwada*, *'inān*, and *mudārabal qirād*, which were rigorously analyzed and systematized by the jurists in theoretical treatises and practical manuals.[70] All based on a principle of "fidelity" (*'aqd amāna*), these partnerships varied in their characteristics as regards each partner's "agency powers" (*wakāla*) and "surety" (*kafāla*), as well as the scope and nature of investment (capital) shares, profit/risk distribution, and authorized business activities.[71] Their differentiation endowed them with varied configurations which accorded with the particular needs of different sectors of the economy.

The Hanafi *mufāwada* is characterized as an "unlimited" investment partnership with full powers of mutual "agency" and "surety" among the partners, who also have to be "equal" in wealth and freedom of action (among other things).[72] Consequently, the partners share profit and loss equally, and are equally and mutually liable in their business dealing with outside (third) parties. As such, the Hanafi *mufawada* anticipates the modern concept of corporation, albeit with unlimited liability. The freedom of action includes each partner's prerogative to independently enter *'inān* or *mudāraba* partnerships with outside parties, and — with the other partner's consent — *mufāwada* partnerships as well: an interesting feature that enables the partners to expand the capital base, and diversify the operations of their enterprise.[73]

By contrast, the Hanafi *'inān* is a "restricted" form of investment partnership, albeit with unlimited liability like *mufāwada*.[74] Unlike the latter, however, the *'inān* partner is merely a mutual agent (*wakīl*), not a guarantor (*kafīl*), of other partners. This mutual agency applies only to the scope of business operation specified in the partnership contract, which can either be a class of goods (*khass*: specific) or all goods (*'amm*: general). Moreover, the partner's "equality" stipulation is restricted here to the area of legal competence. Yet, like *mufāwada*, the *'inān* partner can invest in a *mudārada* to further the interests of the enterprise.[75]

An interesting aspect of both *mufāwada* and *'inān* was the complex and varied concept of what I call the company's "common/corporate capital," the *sharika's māl* which is formed by *khalt*, "mingling" of the (possibly diverse) assets contributed by the partners.[76] Being the basis of profit/risk sharing among partners, this concept received a great deal of analysis and thought. The basic form of investment was made in gold and silver coins or/ and bullion: their lack of uniformity forced the jurists — in specifying the investment shares while abiding by the doctrines of *Riba* and *gharar* — to explore notions of equivalence, an exploration that often revealed acute economic analysis.[77] Another form of "common/corporate capital" was skilled labor, the basis of labor cooperatives/partnerships (*sharikāt al-sanā'i'*), which were formed for producing manufactured goods. Again their juristic theorizing here reveals a concept of "human capital" that modern economics started to investigate only recently.[78] Moreover, their juristic examination of credit cooperatives/partnerships (*sharikāt al-wujūh*) reveals a third concept of "common/corporate capital" consisting in pooling the business and moral credentials contributed by the partners, a kind of "human/moral capital" which qualified those *mafalīs* (literally, penniless folks) to be granted credit for financing their business.[79]

(b) Mudāraba *and banking*

Unlike *mufāwada* and *'inān*, the formulations of *mudāraba* partnership exhibited near uniformity among the classical schools, presumably because this indigenously Arabian mode of collaboration was also practiced by the Prophet himself (as *mudārib*).[80] In any event, the Hanafi *mudāraba* consists in a contract of "fidelity" (*amāna*) between *rabb al-māl* (The Capital Owner/Investor), a silent partner, and the *mudārib* (an entrepreneurial agent/manager), who is not liable for investment loss, in the normal course of business.[81] In its basic form, *mudāraba* does not involve a "common/corporate capital" in the usual sense, although it is often aptly rendered as a "partnership of profit" (*sharikāt al-ribb*):[82] Profit shares have to be specified proportionally to avoid *riba*; and, in case of loss, the liability of the agent/manager does not go beyond the human effort expended, while that of the investor (towards a third party) is normally limited to the capital invested.

The full agency powers enabled the classical *mudārib* to freely and independently pursue profit opportunities using any "legitimate" practice or transaction, in any licit field of economic activity, be it industrial or commercial; analogous associational contracts, *muzāra'a* and *musāqat*, were also available for agricultural activity.[83] The Hanafī *mudārib* can also enter *mudāraba* and other arrangements (with other partners) for enhancing profit opportunities.[84] This flexibility and innovative profit/risk distribution of the *mudāraba* rendered it an ideal arrangement for long-distance and international trade.[85] It is not surprising that it later became an essential business arrangement in the rise of European trade as it assumed a Europianized form known as *commenda*.[86]

The innovative features of *mudāraba* betrays its fundamental economic function of combining human and financial resources in a stark manner. This vital economic role is underscored by the *māliki* and *shāfi'ī* rendering of it as *qirād/muqārada*, literally loan provision/acquiring, a licit lending mechanism/instrument that escapes the prohibition against *riba*. And yet, unlike the Māliki and Shāfi'ī, the Hanafi *mudārib* — when endowed with an "unlimited mandate" (*i'mal fīhī bira'ika*) — was able to invest the *mudāraba* capital (combined with his own) in another *mudāraba*, or even a partnership (*sharika*), with third parties.[87]

It was this flexible mingling of associational arrangements, as well as the licitness of a multiplicity of "agents" and "investors" in a single *mudāraba* contract,[88] that made possible the mobilization and pooling of large amounts of financial resources, and ultimately the emergence of the classical banking houses, the *jahābidha*, around the end of the ninth century.[89] The evolution of the *jahābidha* into bankers (in the modern sense), a part of the general

'Abāssīd scientific, economic, and technological progress,[90] culminated in the enactment (ca. 302/913) of the first state/central bank, Jahābidhat al-Hadra.[91] Centered in the capital, Baghdad, probably in Darb al-'Awn (the financial district) of its central *Sūq* (near Dar al-Imāra),[92] this banking "partnership" appears to have effectively employed a *mudāraba-sharika* networking arabesque in mobilizing funds from the capital and other cities of the vast 'Abbāsīd caliphate for meeting the then growing financial demands of the state.[93]

In view of the preceding, it is not surprising that — along with the *'inān* partnership (*mushāraka*) — the *qirād/mudāraba* method of financing figures prominently in the modern theory and practice of Islamic banking, given the latter's aim of avoiding interest and operating on the basis of profit-loss sharing (PLS). In this, the modern Islamic banks also employ formulations of the classical exchange practices mentioned above, notably the *murābaha*, *ijāra, nasi'a bay'*, and *istisnā'*; and this modern banking movement has been remarkably influential.[94] Three countries (Iran, Pakistan, and Sudan) have "Islamicized" their entire banking systems, and Islamic banking has achieved significant inroads in over seventy countries. And yet, the Islamic banks have not been successful in fulfilling their stated primary goals. A case in point — as recent studies indicate — they scarcely supply long-term financing, and the bulk of their lending is directed to the short-term financing of trade. Moreover, only a minor part of their lending activity is PLS-based.[95] The reason hinges essentially on the classical jurists' problem of *gharar*, the information and agency problems which modern economists call principal-agent problems, moral hazard, and adverse selection, among others.[96]

A recent mathematical model by Aggarwal and Yusuf demonstrates (among other things) that the failure of Islamic banks in the PLS area is a rational response to this type of agency/information problem.[97] This type of problem (among others) goes far in explaining the recent data reported by the International Association of Islamic Banks: that less than twenty percent of bank lending is PLS based.[98] Curiously, this figure is remarkably close to Ghazali's above-mentioned estimation that only ten percent of his contemporaries "let the *sūq* of this world do no injury to the *sūqs* of the Hereafter." It appears, nine centuries after the great Ghazāli, that in the "real world," the actual behavior of Muslims bears little resemblance to the Homo Islamicus of MawdūdiConomists, a behavior that has been remarkably stable and heterodox, at least in the "*sūqs* of this world."[99]

Summary and conclusions

In attempting to typify the moral economy of classical Islam in its historical context, I have been generally guided by the three quotations I started with: among them they highlight the rationalist trend in Islam's moral philosophy and its scholarly (social-science) tradition. Ibn Khaldūn (d. 1406) restated the standard of that tradition brilliantly in his *Muqaddimah*:[100]

> Therefore, today, the scholar in this field needs to know the principles of politics, the nature of things, and the differences among nations, places, and periods with regard to ways of life, character qualities, customs, sects, schools (*Madhābib*), and everything else. He further needs a comprehensive knowledge of present conditions in all these respects. He must compare similarities or differences between present and past conditions. He must know the causes of the similarities in certain cases and of the differences in others.

Indeed this is a very modern standard, like "today," a "tall order" that I have attempted to cope with inasmuch as it is possible for me within the space of a journal article.

The main objective of this article has been the construction of a verbal "model" of the historical economy of "classical" Islam, one that assembles what is known of its basic "building blocks" in a coherent system that highlights its moral and legal philosophy, and encapsulates its fundamental principles and "laws of motion" in theory as well as its *modus operandi* in practice. In order to achieve this objective, I started (Section I) by presenting a synoptic review of the nature of Sharī'ah discourses, the moral and legal framework of that economy, one that highlights the moral and epistemological doctrine of the classical jurists as well as the jurisprudential theory and method they adopted in molding this framework. In Section II, Islam's work ethic of "legitimate gain" was expounded to reveal a concept of economic justice that underpinned the juristic effort (*ijtihād*) of the classical *fuqaha*: A meritorious doctrine of "justice as fairness" in economic exchange and dealings (*mu'āmalāt*), one which is "procedural" in nature, as it rests on two fundamental maxims, namely, the avoidance of "unjustified enrichment" (*fadl māl bila 'iwad*) and "unjustified absence of knowledge" (*jahl; gharar*).

This was followed by Section III, the "Sharī'ah Market Model," in which the "classical *sūq*" was characterized, and its "social embeddedness" highlighted (within the context of the jurists' concept of justice and its underlying *tawhīdi* philosophy of harmony) in terms of their normative contract of *Bay'* (sale/exchange) and its variants. As well, the actual *modus operandi* of the classical *sūq*, its legal framework, and policy institutions (notably *ihtisāb*) were sketched so as to reveal a *tawhīdi* doctrine of perfectly competitive markets and pricing, which are deemed "efficient" in the estimation of modern economic theory. Section IV, "Business Partnership and Finance," then addressed the all-important question of business association (*vis à vis* the deployment of human and non-human resources) within the parameters of the above-mentioned concept of justice. It briefly described the three basic forms of business association (*sharikāt*) formulated by the classical jurists (namely, *mufāwada*, *'inān*, and *mudārabalqirād*), and expounded the innovative, differentiated, and flexible set of legal instruments they had supplied for facilitating the efficient collaboration between human and financial/capital resources in commerce, industry, and agriculture. As well, the related macro-economic mechanism of financial intermediation was briefly reviewed to show how the jurists' formulations, which allowed flexible mingling of as-sociational (*mudāraba/sharika*) contracts, had facilitated the emergence of the classical banking institutions of Islam (*al-jahābidha*) and the first state/central bank (*jahābidhat al-hadra*) in history.

In the main, I have argued that — in theory — the economic system crafted by the classical *fuqaha* was essentially a "perfectly competitive market system," albeit with a difference; a difference that stemmed from their *tawhīdi* philosophy of social harmony, which motivated their doctrine of economic justice. Thus, by contrast with Adam Smith and his philosophy of self-love, the motive force of his "invisible hand," which animates and orchestrates the "unembedded" competitive markets of modern capitalism, the classical *fuqaha* had attempted (by their *bay'* model) to "re-embed" the competitive *sūqs* of classical Islam into the community (Umma), locally and beyond.[101]

In this article, I concerned myself primarily with typifying the institutions and workings of *fiqhi sūq* system, and shied away from the "ism" question of comparative economic systems:[102] a complex question that some specialists like Pryor did not find "profitable to focus on."[103] Nevertheless, the market system I have typified is compatible both with capitalism and "market socialism."[104] Indeed other scholars attempted to interpret the classical Islamic system in terms of these modern categories, especially that of capitalism.[105] Thus, examining the question from a Weberian viewpoint, Rodinson for instance concluded that the "merchants of the Muslim Empire conformed perfectly to Weber's criteria for capitalistic activity."[106] Adopting the same perspective, albeit with a Neo-Orientalist bent, Labib found that "Islamic capitalism was mainly a commercial and consumer-credit capitalism," render-ing it as "Oriental Capitalism."[107] Again, Rodinson examined the question using a Marxian conceptual framework, and concluded that "the Muslim . . . capitalistic sector . . . was apparently the most extensive and highly developed in history . . . until the sixteenth century."[108]

In contrast, others, including some MaudūdiConomists, emphasize the socialistic/egalitarian strand in Islamic doctrine and history to argue for an "Islamic Socialism," but historical studies in this area are meager (to the best of my knowledge).[109] An interesting line of research in this direction is the historical experience of the sunnā' (producers of manufactured goods) and whether their "professional corporations" (*asnāf*) constituted a form of "guild socialism."[110]

Finally, the preceding (modern) interpretations of the economic system of classical Islam, among others, are all interesting and plausible, each com-manding an element of truth, some more so than others. This judgment may suggest a different "type," one that combines these elements in a manner that is truer to the "animus" of that economy, and to its historical, cultural, and technological setting.[111] But, alas, the search for this "type" goes beyond the objective of this article.

Endnotes

1 A slightly different version of this article was read at the 34th Annual Conference of the Association of Muslim Social Scientists held at Temple University, Philadelphia, Pa. (30 September–2 October, 2005), at the Institute of Islamic Studies, McGill University, Montreal, Canada (22 November, 2005) in the Institute's Visiting Lecturer program, and at the 38th International Congress of Asian and North African Studies, held in Ankara, Turkey (10–15 September, 2007). I value the clarifying and encouraging comments received at these fora. I am particularly grateful for those of Wael B. Hallaq of McGill University, and owe much to his path-breaking work on *usūl al-fiqh* as well as his scientific dedication to de-Orientalizing Islamic legal theory and history. Naturally, the conventional disclaimer applies.

2 For a good overview of the concepts, structure, and development of Sharī'ah, see N. Calder and M. B. Hooker, "Sharī'a," *Encyclopaedia of Islam*, New Edition, Vol. IX (1997): 321–328, and H. A. R. Gibb, *Mohammedanism: An Historical Survey*, (Revised) 2nd Edition (London: Oxford University Press, 1970), ch. 6.

3 On these debates, see the classic survey by W. Montgomery Watt, *The Formative Period of Islamic Thought* (Edinburgh: Edinburgh University Press, 1973).

4 As D. Gimaret, "Mu'tazila," *Encyclopaedia of Islam*, New Edition, Vol. VII (1993): 792, puts it, to the Mu'tazila, "the revelation can only confirm that which reason tells us . . . [although] the latter is not sufficient to make us aware of everything that is evil (i.e., forbidden), nor everything that is obligatory, for example to perform a prayer to God, according to a certain ritual. . . ." On the Mu'tazila, see also R. C. Martin and M. P. Woodward, with D. S. Atmaja, *Defenders of Reason in Islam: Mu'tazilism from Medieval School to Modern Symbol* (Oxford: Oneworld, 1997), chs. 1–2, and Watt, *The Formative Period of Islamic Thought*, chs. 7–8; and on *kalām* in general, see L. Gardet, "'Ilm al-Kalām," *Encyclopaedia of Islam*, New Edition, Vol. III (1986): 1141–1150.

5 On Ahl al-Hadīth, and the context of the development of their doctrine, see F. Rahman, *Islam*, Second Edition (Chicago: University of Chicago Press, 1979), ch. 3, J. Schacht, "Ahl al-Hadīth," *Encyclopaedia of Islam*, New Edition, Vol. I (1986): 258–259, and Watt, *The Formative Period of Islamic Thought*, chs. 3–5.

6 On the Mihna, see M. Hinds, "Mihna," *Encyclopaedia of Islam*, New Edition, Vol. VII (1993): 2–6, and Martin and Woodward, *Defenders of Reason in Islam*, 28–29, and on its aftermath, see Watt, *The Formative Period of Islamic Thought*, ch. 10.

7 On the emergence of al-Ash'ari and his doctrine, see Watt, *The Formative Period of Islamic Thought*, 303–312, and Gardet, "'Ilm al-Kalām," 1144–45.

8 Gardet, "Ilm al-Kalam," 1144.

9 On the nature, structure, and development of Islamic jurisprudence, see Wael B. Hallaq, *A History of Islamic Legal Theories: An Introduction to Sunnī Usūl al-Fiqh* (Cambridge: Cambridge University Press, 1997), and the earlier works by Joseph Schacht, *An Introduction to Islamic Law* (London: Oxford University Press, 1964), N. J. Coulson, *Conflicts and Tensions in Islamic Jurisprudence* (Chicago: University of Chicago Press, 1969), and N. J. Coulson, *A History of Islamic Law, 3rd Edition* (Edinburgh: Edinburgh University Press, 1978).

10 The resulting Sharī'ah discourses are considered, "from the point of view of logical perfection, one of the most brilliant essays of human reasoning,"

according to the eminent Orientalist scholar Gibb, *Mohammedanism: An Historical Survey*, 62.

11 Hence *ikhtilāf* and *ijmā'* were considered in practice equally important, both epistemologically and morally. The former, *ikhtilāf* rested on the authority of Prophet Muḥammad himself, according to hadith: "Difference of opinion within my community (*ummati*) is a sign of the grace/bounty of Allāh"; hence the juristic maxim: *"man lā ya'raf al-ikhtilāf lam yashumma rā'ihata 'l-fiqh"* (He/She who does not apprehend *ikhtilāf* has not captured the true scent of jurisprudence.); quoted in Coulson, *Conflicts and Tensions in Islamic Jurisprudence*, 20–21. On this point see also Coulson, *Conflicts and Tensions in Islamic Jurisprudence*, ch. 2; and on the signification of *ikhtilāf* and *ijmā'*, see J. Schacht, "Ikhtilāf," *Encyclopaedia of Islam*, New Edition, Vol. III (1971): 1061–1062, and M. Bernand, "Idjmā'," *Encyclopaedia of Islam*, New Edition, Vol. III (1986): 1023–1026, respectively.

12 On this point see J. Van Ess, "The Logical Structure of Islamic Theology," in G. E. von Grunebaum, Ed., *Logic in Classical Islamic Culture* (Wiesbaden: Otto Harrassowitz, 1970), 27–39; see also M. Bernand, "Kiyās," *Encyclopaedia of Islam*, New Edition, Vol. V (1986): 238–242, and H. Fleisch and L. Gardet, "'Illa," *Encyclopaedia of Islam*, New Edition, Vol. III (1986): 1127–1132.

13 Ibn Khaldūn, *'Abd-ar-Rahman, The Muqaddimah: An Introduction to History*; Translated by Franz Rosenthal; abridged and edited by N. J. Dawood (Princeton, N.J.: Princeton University Press, 1974), 26. Centuries later, this same epistemological hazard was noted by Sir Henry Maine, *Ancient Law* (New York, 1887), 18, who "observed that the application of analogy tends to infuse customs which may in their inception have been rational with non-rational elements," says Abraham L. Udovitch, *Partnership and Profit in Medieval Islam* (Princeton, N.J.: Princeton University Press, 1970), 251. The original Arabic text of *Muqaddimah* was consulted, but the page reference (here and elsewhere in this article) is to the abridged English translation stated above.

14 On the centrality of these two concepts in the Mu'tazila theory, see Gimaret, "Mu'tazila," 790–791. Applied by the main schools, this juristic approach was the hallmark of the Hanafis, especially in dealing with conflicts between *qiyās* and economic imperatives. The term *tawhīdi* is used here in its *kalāmi* sense, *'ilm al-tawhīd* (Science of Unity) being synonymous with *kalām*, Islam's philosophical/dialectical theology.

15 For a good overview of these juristic methods, see R. Paret, "Istihsān and Istislāh," *Encyclopaedia of Islam*, New Edition, Vol. IV (1990): 255–259, and M. Khadduri, "Maslaha," *Encyclopaedia of Islam*, New Edition, Vol. VI (1991): 738–40.

16 They also invoked their formalist technique of *hiyal* (Legal devices) as well as a Qur'ānic doctrine of *Darūra* (necessity); for an overview, see J. Schacht, "Hiyal," *Encyclopaedia of Islam*, New Edition, Vol. III (1986): 510–513, and Y. Linant De Bellefonds, "Darūra," *Encyclopaedia of Islam*, New Edition, Vol. II (1983): 163–164, respectively.

17 Udovitch, *Partnership and Profit in Medieval Islam*, 261. Besides this study of Udovitch, which draws on his earlier work, see also A. E. Lieber, "Eastern Business Practices and Medieval European Commerce," *Economic History Review* (Second Edition), Vol. XXI (1968): 230–243.

18 On Mawdūdi, see F. C. R. Robinson, "Mawdūdī," *Encyclopaedia of Islam*, New Edition, Vol. VI (1991): 872–874, and S. V. R. Nasr, *Mawdudi and the Making of Islamic Revivalism* (New York: Oxford University Press, 1996); and for a critical examination of the literature on "Islamic Economics," see T. Kuran, "Islamic Economics and the Islamic Subeconomy," *Journal of Economic Perspectives*,

Vol. 9 (1995): 155–173, T. Kuran, "On the Notion of Economic Justice in Contemporary Islamic Thought," *International Journal of Middle East Studies*, Vol. 21 (1989): 171–191, and Fredric L. Pryor, "The Islamic Economic System," *Journal of Comparative Economics*, Vol. 9 (1985): 197–223.

19 The economic history of classical Islam is yet to be written, yet enough is already known to warrant the present attempt at theorizing. For an overview of the state of historical research, see C. E. Bosworth, W. Heffening and M. Shatzmiller "Tidjāra," *Encyclopaedia of Islam*, New Edition, Vol. X (2000): 469–475, especially their Bibliography section.

20 This basic point, an old object of contention in Orientalist literature, was examined and conclusively affirmed in recent scholarship, notably by Maxime Rodinson, *Islam and Capitalism, Translator Brian Pearce* (Austin: University of Texas Press, 1978), especially chs. 2–4.

21 For a review and critical assessment of the literature on economic justice, see Kuran, "On the Notion of Economic Justice in Contemporary Islamic Thought," and Rodinson, *Islam and Capitalism*, ch. 2; and on Islam's classical moral theory in general, see R. Walzer and H. A. R. Gibb, "Akhlāk," *Encyclopaedia of Islam*, New Edition, Vol. I (1986): 325–329. Refer also to notes (22), (24) and (40) below.

22 This doctrine is complemented by another doctrine of "distributive justice" that rests on the Qur'ānic concepts and institutions of *sadaqa* and *zakāt*, a complementarity that is highlighted by their juxtaposition in the Qur'ānic verses II: 276–277; on *sadaqa* and *zakāt*, see the overviews by T. H. Weir and A. Zysow, "Sadaka," *Encyclopaedia of Islam*, New Edition, Vol. VIII (1995): 708–716, and A. Zysow, "Zakāt," *Encyclopaedia of Islam*, New Edition, Vol. XI (2002): 406–422, respectively. For a brief exposition of the modern concepts of distributive economic justice and economic justice in general, see E. S. Phelps, "Distributive Justice," *The New Palgrave: A Dictionary of Economics*, Vol. 1 (1987): 886–888, and A. Sen, "Justice," *The New Palgrave: A Dictionary of Economics*, Vol. 2 (1987): 1039–1043, respectively; and on justice as fairness (and the related economic concept of "equity" as absence of "envy"), see John Rawls, *A Theory of Justice* (Cambridge, Massachusetts: Harvard University Press, 1971) and P. J. Hammond, "Envy," *The New Palgrave: A Dictionary of Economics*, Vol. 2 (1987): 164–166; and on the structure of the modern theory of justice (and moral theory) in general, see W. K. Frankena, *Ethics*, second Edition (Englewood Cliffs, N.J.: Prentice-Hall, 1973), and the textbook treatment by E. L. Miller, *Questions That Matter: An Invitation to Philosophy*, second Edition (New York: McGraw-Hill, 1987), chs. 16–19 and 22.

23 On the doctrine of *gharar* and the syllogistic differences among the main jurists of Sunni schools, see Nabil A. Saleh, *Unlawful Gain and Legitimate Profit in Islamic Law: Riba, Gharar and Islamic Banking* (Cambridge, U.K.: Cambridge University Press, 1986), ch. 3; and on the modern economic concepts of "risk" and "uncertainty," see M. J. Machina and M. Rothschild, "Risk," *The New Palgrave: A Dictionary of Economics*, Vol. 4 (1987): 201–206, and P. M. Hammond, "Uncertainty," *The New Palgrave: A Dictionary of Economics*, Vol. 4 (1987): 728–733, respectively.

24 On the jurists' generic meaning of *Riba* as "unjustified enrichment" (*fadl māl bilā 'iwad*), a fundamental criterion of economic injustice/inequity (*zulm*), and on its Qur'ānic (e.g. IV: 161 and II: 279) and Hadīth basis, see Schacht, *An Introduction to Islamic Law*, 145–146, and M. S. al-Fanjari, "On the Licitness of Interest on Bank Deposits," *L'Egypte Contemporaine*, Vol. LXX, no. 378 (1979): 154–155, in Arabic; and on *Zulm* and 'Adl, see R. Badry and B. Lewis "Zulm," *Encyclopaedia of Islam*, New Edition, Vol. XI (2002): 567–569, and

E. Tyan, "'Adl," *Encyclopaedia of Islam*, New Edition, Vol. I (1960): 209–210, respectively.

25 For a brief history of this classification, see al-Fanjari, "On the Licitness of Interest on Bank Deposits," 155–156, and Saleh, Unlawful Gain and Legitimate Profit in Islamic Law, 13–14; and for an overview of the doctrine, see J. Schacht, "Ribā," *Encyclopaedia of Islam*, New Edition, Vol. VIII (1995): 491–493, and F. Rahman, "Ribā and Interest," *Islamic Studies*, Vol. 3 (1964): 1–43.

26 Saleh, *Unlawful Gain and Legitimate Profit in Islamic Law*, 13. There seems to be some disagreement on whether the category involved is "species" (*naw'*) or "genus" (*jins*). The literature in English often employs "species"; see for instance Coulson, *A History of Islamic Law*, 79, and Schacht, *An Introduction to Islamic Law*, 145. In Arabic, however, al-Fanjari, "On the Licitness of Interest on Bank Deposits," 158–159, argues for employing the term *jins*. The main (Arabic) hadīth text, which he quotes (156), uses the plural of "genus" (*'ajnās*).

27 The intricacies of these differences are catalogued (in English) by Saleh, *Unlawful Gain and Legitimate Profit in Islamic Law*, ch. 1, but only for the Sunni schools; see also al-Fanjari, "On the Licitness of Interest on Bank Deposits," 153–170.

28 This is in contrast with the *fadl/buyū' riba*, which is characterized as *Riba kbafī* (hidden) and is occasioned by a sale/exchange transaction; see al-Fanjari, "On the Licitness of Interest on Bank Deposits," 156.

29 Chronologically arranged according to "traditional dating," these verses are: XXX: 39 (Meccan); IV: 161, III: 130, and II: 275–279 (Median). For a brief overview of the scholarship on dating techniques and criticism, both "traditional" and European, see A. T. Welch and J. D. Pearson, "Al-Kur'ān," *Encyclopaedia of Islam*, New Edition, Vol. V (1986): 415–419.

30 For an overview of the doctrine and techniques of Naskh, see J. Burton, "Naskh," *Encyclopaedia of Islam*, New Edition, Vol. VII (1993): 1009–1012, and Hallaq, *A History of Islamic Legal Theories: An Introduction to Sunnī Usūl al-Fiqh*, 68–74.

31 On the juristic elaborations of this position (and its variations among the Sunni schools) towards loans (*qard*), see Saleh, *Unlawful Gain and Legitimate Profit in Islamic Law*, ch. 2.

32 Quoted in Th. Bianquis, P. Guichard, A. Raymond and others, "Sūk," *Encyclopaedia of Islam*, New Edition, Vol. IX (1997): 787; the quotation originates in the celebrated *Ihyā' 'ulūm al-Dīn*, Cairo 1326, ii, 48ff., by al-Ghazāli. On al-Ghazāli and his immense and varied contributions, see W. M. Watt, "al-Ghazālī," *Encyclopaedia of Islam*, Vol. II (1983): 1038–1141.

33 For an overview of the juristic signification of *mu'āmalāt* vis à vis *'ibadāt* (worshiper's rituals and duties), and the classical "juristic philosophies" (*kalām fiqhi*), see M. Bernand, "Mu'āmalāt," *Encyclopaedia of Islam*, New Edition, Vol. VII (1993): 255–257. The Qur'ānic concept of al-Umma is akin to the concept of "community" (*gemeinschaft*) articulated by F. Tönnies, Fundamental Concepts of Sociology (*gemeinschaft und gesellschaft*), translated and supplemented by C. P. Loomis (New York: American Book Company, 1940), 37–39. Often misunderstood by modern writers, Al-Umma is a technical term which refers to the Islamic community as defined by sunnah, the traditions of the Prophet. In particular, it is defined in *al-Sahifah*, the Constitution of Medina, to include the Muslims, Christians, Jews, and pagans who agreed to its provisions with the Prophet in the two *bay'ās* (constitutional conferences) of *'aqabah*. Amended after the Immigration, the *Sahifah* was preserved by Ibn Ishaq, a biographer of the Prophet, and consists of 47 provisions which regulate the rights and duties of

the various constituencies. See W. M. Watt, *Muhammad At Medina* (London: Oxford University Press, 1956), ch. 7, for an English translation of the Arabic document, its signification, and historical context.

34 For a summary of the Islamic vision of moral exchange (in Qur'ān, Sunna, and ethical works), see Bosworth, Heffening and Shatzmiller, "Tidjāra," 466–469, and Bernand, "Mu'āmalāt," 255–257. Refer also to notes (40) below, and (21), (22), and (24) above.

35 On Polanyi's concept, see K. Polanyi, C. M. Arensberg, and H. W. Pearson, Eds., *Trade and Market in the Early Empires: Economics in History and Theory* (London: Collier-Macmillan, 1957), notably ch. 13, his own article "The Economy as Instituted Process."

36 See Schacht, *An Introduction to Islamic Law*, 151–154, and J. Schacht, "Bay'," *Encyclopaedia of Islam*, New Edition, Vol. I (1986): 1111–1113.

37 On marriage in the Classical Islamic law, see J. Schacht, "Nikāh," *Encyclopaedia of Islam*, New Edition, Vol. VIII (1995): 26–29; and on *bay'ā*, see E. Tyan, "Bay'a," *Encyclopaedia of Islam*, New Edition, Vol. I (1960): 1113–1114.

38 Quoted in Abraham L. Udovitch, "Islamic Law and the Social Context of Exchange in the Medieval Middle East," *History and Anthropology* 1 (1985): 459. On al-Shaybānī, see E. Chaumont, "al-Shaybānī," *Encyclopaedia of Islam*, New Edition, Vol. IX (1997): 392–394, and on Zuhd, see G. Gobillot, "Zuhd," *Encyclopaedia of Islam*, New Edition, Vol. XI (2002): 559–562.

39 Quoted in D. Waines, Ed., *Patterns of Everyday Life, The Formation of the Classical Islamic World*, Vol. 10 (Burlington, VT: Ashgate/Variorum, 2002), xi. On al-Rāzī, and his varied and influential contributions, see L. E. Goodman, "Al-Rāzī, Abū Bakr Muhammad B. Zakariyyā," *Encyclopaedia of Islam*, New Edition, Vol. VIII (1995): 474–477.

40 The Islamic quest for harmony is evident in the concept of Umma as a Community guided by the ideals of justice, fraternité and cooperation; as it is also evident in the institutions of *zakat* and *sadaqa* which cement those ideals (refer to notes 21, 22, 24 and 33 above). The same quest for harmony again manifests itself in the juristic doctrines of *ijmā'* and *ikhtilaf* (explained above) as well as the rendering of *kalām* (Islam's philosophical theology) as *'ilm al-tawhīd*, "The Science of Unity"; see Gardet, "'Ilm al-Kalām", 1141–1150.

41 On this point, see Schacht, "Ribā," 493, and Saleh, *Unlawful Gain and Legitimate Profit in Islamic Law*, 50–52.

42 See Schacht, An Introduction to Islamic Law, ch. 21, especially 151–155; Schacht, "Bay'," 1111–1113, and Udovitch, *Islamic Law and the Social Context of Exchange in the Medieval Middle East*, 448–460.

43 See Coulson, *Conflicts and Tensions in Islamic Jurisprudence*, ch. 4, and on *'urf* and *'adāt*, see G. Libson and F. H. Stewart, "'Urf," *Encyclopaedia of Islam*, New Edition, Vol. X (2000): 887–892, and G.-H. Bousquet, "'Āda," *Encyclopaedia of Islam*, New Edition, Vol. I (1986): 170–172, respectively; see also Udovitch, "Islamic Law and the Social Context of Exchange in the Medieval Middle East," 445–465. On the modern economic theory of contracts, see C. Azariadis, "Implicit Contracts," *The New Palgrave: A Dictionary of Economics*, Vol. 2 (1987): 733–737, O. Hart, "Incomplete Contracts," *The New Palgrave: A Dictionary of Economics*, Vol. 2 (1987): 752–759, and E. P. Lazear, "Incentive Contracts," *The New Palgrave: A Dictionary of Economics*, Vol. 2 (1987): 744–748.

44 On the details of these variants, see Saleh, *Unlawful Gain and Legitimate Profit in Islamic Law*, chs. 3–4, Udovitch, *Partnership and Profit in Medieval Islam*, chs. 4–6, and Schacht, "Bay'," 1111–1113.

45 On the Islamic city planning and constitution, see for instance the studies in A. H. Hourani, and S. M. Stern, Eds., *The Islamic City: A Colloquium* (Oxford:

Pruno Cassirer, 1970), G. E. Von Grunebaum, "The Structure of the Muslim Town," in Von Grunebaum, *Islam: Essays in the Nature and Growth of a Cultural Tradition* (New York: Barnes & Noble, 1961), and M. Bonine, "Urban Studies in the Middle East," *Middle East Studies Association Bulletin*, Vol. 10/3 (1976): 1–37.

46 On the traditional signification of *bay'ā*, see Tyan, "Bay'a," 1113–1114, and on *shūrā* and *mashwara*, see C. E. Bosworth, M. Marin and A. Ayalon, "Shūrā," *Encyclopaedia of Islam*, New Edition, Vol. IX (1997): 504–506, and B. Lewis, "Mashwara," *Encyclopaedia of Islam*, New Edition, Vol. VI (1990): 724–725, respectively.

47 On al-Ghazālī and the tumultuous religio-political climate of his time (including the Sūfi ascendancy and a Batinite threat), see Watt, "al-Ghazālī," 1038–1141, W. M. Watt, *Islamic Philosophy and Theology: An Extended Survey* (Edinburgh: University Press, 1987), ch. 13, and Van Ess, "The Logical Structure of Islamic Theology," 47–50.

48 This typification is based on the references in note (45), and that given by Bianquis *et al.*, "Sūk," 788–789. The model continued to exist in a modernized form in parts of the Muslim World, notably Morocco; see for instance the meticulous ethnographic study of Sefrou by C. Geertz. "Suq: The Bazaar Economy in Sefrou," in C. Geertz, H. Geertz, and L. Rosen, *Meaning and Order in a Moroccan Society* (Cambridge: Cambridge University Press, 1979), 123–313, who gives a detailed account of its evolution during the 20th Century, with emphasis on the *sūq's* cultural/social embeddedness.

49 On the institutional and architectural aspects of these conglomerations, see M. Streck, "Kaysāriyya," *Encyclopaedia of Islam*, New Edition, Vol. IV (1990): 840–841, H. Elisséeff, "Khān," *Encyclopaedia of Islam*, New Edition, Vol. IV (1990): 1010–1017, and R. LeTourneau, "Funduk," *Encyclopaedia of Islam*, New Edition, Vol. II (1983): 945.

50 For a literature review, see Bianquis *et al.*, "Sūk," 786–801, Bosworth *et al.*, "Tidjāra," 466–475, and Rodinson, *Islam and Capitalism*, 33–35.

51 On this point, see for instance Bosworth *et al.*, "Tidjāra," 471ff.

52 Udovitch, "Islamic Law and the Social Context of Exchange in the Medieval Middle East," 459, restates Polayni's economic/anthropological concept of "social embeddedness" by concluding that the classical jurists saw in the *sūq* "a kind of microcosm of society as a whole and the religious and ethical values by which it was supposed to live." Udovitch, however, does not refer to Polanyi but is ostensibly influenced by the work of the cultural/economic anthropologist C. Geertz, "Local Knowledge: Fact and Law in Comparative Perspective," in C. Geertz *Local Knowledge: Further Essays in Interpretive Anthropology* (New York: Basic Books, 2000), 167–234, which motivated his own study. For in his Moroccan study, "Suq: The Bazaar Economy in Sefrou," Geertz, who does not use Polanyi's term either, does illustrate it thoroughly, and states that: "if one is going to indulge in ['characterizing whole civilizations in terms of one of their leading institutions'] it is for the Middle East and North Africa the bazaar . . ." (123).

53 On this aspect of the Prophet's early career, see the meticulous work of W. M. Watt, *Muhammad at Mecca* (London: Oxford University Press, 1953), 33–39. This hadith is quoted in M. Y. Izzi Dien, "Tas'īr," *Encyclopaedia of Islam*, New Edition, Vol. X (2000): 358, and Bosworth *et al.* "Tidjāra," 467.

54 Udovitch, "Islamic Law and the Social Context of Exchange in the Medieval Middle East," 451, highlights this *Encyclopaedia of Islam*, New Edition, Vol. X (2000): 358, and Bosworth *et al.* "Tidjāra," 467. Critical role of information stating that: "This compulsion for 'knowing' and this abhorrence for 'ignorance'

in economic exchange is both a requirement of Islamic law, an inherent principle ..., and a reflection of the day-to-day transactions in the market place."

55 On Smith's invisible hand in relation to his moral theory of "self-love" and free, competitive markets, see K. I. Vaughn, "Invisible Hand," *The New Palgrave: A Dictionary of Economics*, Vol. 2 (1987): 997–999; and on their elaboration in the development of the concept of perfect competition and perfectly competitive markets in relation to socio-economic efficiency/welfare in modern economics, see G. J. Stigler, "Competition," *The New Palgrave: A Dictionary of Economics, Vol. 1* (1987): 531–536, M. A. Khan, "Perfect Competition," *The New Palgrave: A Dictionary of Economics, Vol. 3* (1987): 831–834 and J. Roberts, "Perfectly and Imperfectly Competitive Markets," *The New Palgrave: A Dictionary of Economics, Vol. 3* (1987): 837–841.

56 This was done for instance by the great Hanafi jurist al-Sarakhsī (d.483/1095) in his celebrated *Mahsūt, Vol. VII*, which is quoted on this point in Udovitch, "Islamic Law and the Social Context of Exchange in the Medieval Middle East," 459. On Sarakhsī, see N. Calder, "al-Sarakhsī," *Encyclopaedia of Islam*, New Edition, Vol. IX (1997): 35–36.

57 The term *Ribh* (in verbal form) occurs only once (II: 16) in the Qur'ān; but the cognates of *kasb* pervades its text, according to the verse listing of M. F. Abdel-Baqi, *Al-Mu'jam Al-Mufahras Li Alfāz Al-Qur'ān Al-Kareem (Concordance of Terms of The Glorious Qur'ān)* (Cairo: Dar Al-Sha'b Press, 1945), 604–605. On Kasb and its signification, see Cl. Cahen and L. Gardet, "Kasb," *Encyclopaedia of Islam*, New Edition, Vol. IV (1990): 690–694. On the meaning and role of normal/abnormal profit in modern economics, see M. Desai, "Profit and Profit Theory," *The New Palgrave: A Dictionary of Economics, Vol. 3* (1987): 1014–1021.

58 Based on cost-plus pricing, the *murābaha* fixed-profit premium (and implicit cost elements) had to be imputed in the light of *'urf al-tujjar*, literally the prevailing/known practices of merchants, what amounts to an opportunity-cost imputation of "normal/fair profit." On this point, see Udovitch, "Islamic Law and the Social Context of Exchange in the Medieval Middle East," 452–458, and Saleh, *Unlawful Gain and Legitimate Profit in Islamic Law*, 94–97. On the signification in modern economics of the notion of just/fair price, and the juxtaposition between competitive and monopolistic conditions, see D. D. Friedman, "Just Price," *The New Palgrave: A Dictionary of Economics, Vol. 2* (1987): 1043–1044, and J. Roberts, "Perfectly and Imperfectly Competitive Markets," 837–841, respectively.

59 On the "stylized" pattern and movements of those prices, see Bosworth *et al.*, "Tidjāra," 472, who also note (469) the fact that these patterns and movements were observed and analyzed by Muslim theorists such as al-Dimashqī' and Ibn Khaldūn. Ibn Khaldūn, *The Muqaddimah: An Introduction to History*, 276–278, in particular analyzed the pattern of prices and their movements (implicitly) using a model not unlike that of modern economics, over six centuries ago. On the superior economy of classical Islam and its business institutions, see Udovitch, *Partnership and Profit in Medieval Islam*, especially ch. VII.

60 On the prevalence of this assumption in MaudūdiConomics, see Kuran, "Islamic Economics and the Islamic Subeconomy," 159–160. This type is ostensibly constructed in juxtaposition to that of Homo Oeconomicus of modern economics; and on the latter, see S. Hargreaves-Heapand and M. Hollis, "Economic Man," *The New Palgrave: A Dictionary of Economics, Vol. 2* (1987): 54–55.

61 This estimate, which is made via a parable (in Ghazāli's *Ihyā'*) that is given in Rodinson, *Islam and Capitalism*, 112.

62 Ibn Khaldūn, *The Muqaddimah: An Introduction to History*, 23.

63 It is reported that — upon entering Mecca — the Prophet appointed Sa'īd b.al-'ās to serve as Mecca's *'amil 'alā al-sūq*; meanwhile in his city state of Medina, women also served as *'amila 'alā al-sūq*, see Bianquis *et al.*, "Sūq", 787.

64 Called also *sāhib al-sūq* and *wāli al-sūq*, the institution was renamed about the time of Caliph al-Ma'mūn (d. 218/833) as part of the Islamicization process engineered by the Mu'tazila school under the 'Abbasīd. However, the old name continued in the Maghrib and Spain as they remained under Ummayad rule.

65 The expanded mandate was justified by the Qur'ānic verse 9:71 (variations of which are given in 7:157, 31–17, 9:112, and 22:41), and although the terms *hisba/muhtasib* do not occur in the Qur'ān, the cognates of these terms, which connote accounting/calculation, recur repeatedly; see the verse listing of Abdel-Baqi, *Al-Mu'jam Al-Mufahras Li Alfāz Al-Qur'ān Al-Kareem*, 200–201. For a brief history of this evolution, see Cl. Cahen, M. Talbi, R. Mantran, A. K. S. Lambton and A. S. Bazmee Ansari, "Hisba," *Encyclopaedia of Islam*, New Edition, Vol. III (1986): 487.

66 On the economic mandate of the classical Muhtasib, see Cahen *et al.*, "Hisba," 487–488, and A. Ghabin, "Sinā'a," *Encyclopaedia of Islam*, New Edition, Vol. IX (1997): 628. This mandate varied somewhat under different dynasties, but a core economic mandate was remarkably stable, as was shown in the above-mentioned anthropological study by Geertz, "Suq: The Bazaar Economy in Sefrou," of a 20th century Moroccan case (182–197, and note 12). On competition policy in modern economics, see A. Hughes, "Competition Policy," *The New Palgrave: A Dictionary of Economics, Vol. 1* (1987): 550–552, and O. E. Williamson, "Antitaist Policy," *The New Palgrave: A Dictionary of Economics, Vol. 1* (1987): 95–98.

67 On the legal status and qualifications of the classical *muhtasib* and his associates, see Cahen *et al.*, "Hisba," 487–488.

68 For an overview of the artisans and their "professional corporations," see Ghabin, "Sinā'a," 625–629, and A. Raymond, W. Floor, and Ö Nutku, "Sinf," *Encyclopaedia of Islam*, New Edition, Vol. IX (1987): 644–646.

69 Refer to note (17) above.

70 On the nature and signification of *sharikāt*, and their categories, see M. Izzi Dien, "Sharika," *Encyclopaedia of Islam, New Edition, Vol. IX* (1997): 348–349, J. D. Latham, "Mufāwada," *Encyclopaedia of Islam, New Edition, Vol. VII* (1993): 310–312, Udovitch, *Partnership and Profit in Medieval Islam*, ch. II, and Schacht, *An Introduction to Islamic Law*, ch. 21.

71 This generalization is based on detailed scrutiny of a variety of sources, notably Udovitch, *Partnership and Profit in Medieval Islam*, and Saleh, *Unlawful Gain and Legitimate Profit in Islamic Law*, ch. 4.

72 Inadmissible on the basis of *qiyās*, this Hanafi version was justified by *istihsān* reasoning, based on the Prophet who was reported to say: "Enter into partnerships by reciprocity (*fāwidū*), for it is most conducive to prosperity"; quoted in Udovitch, *Partnership and Profit in Medieval Islam*, 43. Besides Udovitch, *Partnership and Profit in Medieval Islam*, chs. III and V, see also Latham, "Mufāwada," 310–312, on the position of other schools. It is notable that its principles and the Prophet's term *fāwidū*, both conjure the Polanyi *et al.*, *Trade and Market in the Early Empires: Economics in History and Theory*, ch. 13, concept of "reciprocity," especially as they base business association on *amāna* and *kafāla*.

73 In this direction, the partners are also free to enter other types of business relations/contracts with outside parties, including *'ariyya* loans, deposits, pledges, and *ibdā'*; see Udovitch, *Partnership and Profit in Medieval Islam*, 97–118. Described by Udovitch, *Partnership and Profit in Medieval Islam*, 101–104, *ibdā'* was a common "informal commercial cooperation or Quasi-agency" whereby a

business person authorizes another to take over part of his capital to perform a business task for him as a favor without return. Amounting to an informal *mudāraba* (without a profit share), this common Islamic practice illustrates again Polanyi's concept of "reciprocity" mentioned above.

74 On the Hanafi *'Inān*, see Udovitch, *Partnership and Profit in Medieval Islam*, ch. IV; and see ch. V on the Māliki version. See also Saleh, *Unlawful Gain and Legitimate Profit in Islamic Law*, 92–94, on the positions of other schools.

75 As in the case of *mufāwada*, the *'inān* partner can engage in loan, deposit, pledge, and *ibdāʿ* transactions, among others; Udovitch, *Partnership and Profit in Medieval Islam*, 139–140.

76 On this defining notion of *khalt*, see Izzi Dien, "Sharika," 349, and Udovitch, *Partnership and Profit in Medieval Islam*, 51–64. I use the term "common/corporate capital" here to signify the outcome of *khalt*, a concept that Udovitch, *Partnership and Profit in Medieval Islam*, variously calls "joint capital" (51–64) and "social capital" (171). While "joint capital" is adequate, it does not convey the full meaning of the concept; whereas the term "social capital" commands a distinctly different meaning in recent economic thinking and terminology; refer to note (79) below.

77 The complexity was compounded when other goods were contributed as investment. On these explorations, see the account given in Udovitch, *Partnership and Profit in Medieval Islam*, 48–64 and 147–157.

78 On the Hanafi and Māliki versions of this type of partnership, see Udovitch, *Partnership and Profit in Medieval Islam*, 65–76, 159–163; also accepted by Hanbalis, it was rejected by the Shāfiʿīs (p. 66); see also Izzi Dien, "Sharika," 348, on this. And on the concept and analysis of "human capital" in modern economics, see S. Rosen "Human Capital," *The New Palgrave: A Dictionary of Economics, Vol. 2* (1987): 681–690.

79 On this type of partnership, which was rejected by the Mālikis and Shāfiʿīs, see Udovitch, *Partnership and Profit in Medieval Islam*, 77–86, 158–159. On the concept of "moral/social capital" and its emerging significance in development economics, see for instance O. Mehmet, M. Tahiroglu, and A. L. Li, "Social Capital Formation in Large-Scale Development Projects," *Canadian Journal of Development Studies, Vol. XXIII* (2002): 335–357; and for a critical literature review of the concept, its uses, potentialities, and limitations, see J. Sobel, "Can We Trust Social Capital?" *Journal of Economic Literature, Vol. XL* (2002): 139–154.

80 Tradition reports that his wife-to-be Khadīja was *rabb al-māl*; and that leading Companions participated in *mudāraba* partnerships as well; Udovitch, *Partnership and Profit in Medieval Islam*, 172. Not surprisingly then, it was justified by Sunna, *ijmāʿ*, and *qiyās* (by the Shāfiʿīs) as well as "the practical grounds of its economic function in society"; Udovitch, *Partnership and Profit in Medieval Islam*, 175–176.

81 This basic structure applies to all fiqh Schools, yet in its formulation and elaboration, the Hanafi version "emerges as at once the most comprehensive, practical, and flexible form," as Udovitch, *Partnership and Profit in Medieval Islam*, 176, puts it.

82 And indeed this term can be easily construed (in modern economics) as "common/corporate capital," which can be imputed from the profit shares through capitalization (by means of present-value calculations). On various aspects of the Hanafi *mudāraba* (compared with other Sunni schools), see Saleh, *Unlawful Gain and Legitimate Profit in Islamic Law*, 101–114, Udovitch, *Partnership and Profit in Medieval Islam*, ch. VI, A. L. Udovitch, "Kirād," *Encyclopaedia of Islam, New Edition, Vol. V* (1986): 129–130, and J. A. Wakin, "Mudāraba," *Encyclopaedia of Islam, New Edition, Vol. VII* (1993): 284–285.

83 On these types of agricultural partnerships, see M. J. L. Young, "Musākat," *Encyclopaedia of Islam, New Edition, Vol. VII* (1993): 658, and M. J. L. Young, "Muzāraʿa," *Encyclopaedia of Islam, New Edition, Vol. VII* (1993): 822–823.

84 These include all variants of the *bayʿ* contracts/transactions (detailed above) as well as *ibdāʿ*, deposits, and pledges, among others; Udovitch, *Partnership and Profit in Medieval Islam*, 204ff.

85 S. Y. Labib, "Capitalism in Medieval Islam," *Journal of Economic History, Vol. 29* (1969): 91, for instance reported on a *mudāraba* partnership document between an Alexandrian and a Venetian in the early 15th century.

86 On this point, see A. L. Udovitch, "At the Origins of the Western Commenda: Islam, Israel, Byzantium," *Speculum*, Vol. 37 (1962): 198–207, and Lieber, "Eastern Business Practices and Medieval European Commerce," 230–243.

87 On the distinction between the "limited" and "unlimited" mandate in Hanafi law (and on the more restricted Māliki and Shāfiʿī Qirad), see Udovitch, *Partnership and Profit in Medieval Islam*, 204–215.

88 On the licitness and modalities of these complexities, and on the Hanafi jurists acute analysis in configuring the profit/risk shares therein, see Udovitch, *Partnership and Profit in Medieval Islam*, 225–233.

89 The story of the rise and fall of classical Islamic banking (even more than that of the Islamic economy at large) is yet to be written, but for our purposes here the early explorations of W. Fischel, "The Origin of Banking in Mediaeval Islam: A contribution to the economic history of the Jews of Baghdad in the tenth century (parts I–IV)," *Journal of the Royal Asiatic Society*, (1933): 339–352, W. Fischel, "The Origin of Banking in Mediaeval Islam: A contribution to the economic history of the Jews of Baghdad in the tenth century (parts V–)," *Journal of the Royal Asiatic Society*, (1933): 569–603, which were later summarized in W. Fischel, "Djahbadh," *Encyclopaedia of Islam*, New Edition, Vol. II (1983): 382–383, are valuable in understanding its beginnings, development, and virtual extinction.

90 A similar development occurred in Egypt with the growth of the Fātimid empire, as the weight of economic and political power gradually shifted from Baghdad to Cairo. A case in point is the *karīmī* business class, which emerged in the eleventh century, and continued to prosper under the Ayyūbid and Mamlūk sultans until the fifteenth century. Centered in Cairo, the *karīmī* merchants and financiers managed to mobilize huge amounts of financial resources through their special type of trading and banking houses, which operated on a global scale that ranged — at their peak — from the Maghrib to China. See Labib, "Capitalism in Medieval Islam," 79–96, and S. Y. Labib, "Kārimī," *Encyclopaedia of Islam*, New Edition, Vol. IV (1990): 640–643, on this development.

91 This date and a brief summary is given in Fischel, "Djahbadh," 382–383; the details are given in Fischel, "The Origin of Banking in Mediaeval Islam: A contribution to the economic history of the Jews of Baghdad in the tenth century (parts I–IV)," 339–352. Nearly eight centuries later (1694), the Bank of England was similarly incorporated (as a privately owned state bank) in a strikingly similar (fiscal/political/war) context to that of Jahabidhat al-Hadra; but the first state/central bank in Europe was the Swedish Riksbank (1668). On the beginning and evolution of central banking in Europe in general, see C. Goodhart, "Central Banking," *The New Palgrave: A Dictionary of Economics*, Vol. 1 (1987): 385–387, and on the Bank of England in particular, see the brief overview in the *The New Encyclopaedia Britannica*, Vol. 4 (1988): 497.

92 This location of the bank was suggested in Fischel, "The Origin of Banking in Mediaeval Islam: A contribution to the economic history of the Jews of Baghdad in the tenth century (parts I–IV)," 350.

93 On the nature and duration of this "partnership," see Fischel, "The Origin of Banking in Mediaeval Islam: A contribution to the economic history of the Jews of Baghdad in the tenth century (parts I–IV)," 349–352, and on the operations and activities of this official banking house, see Fischel, "The Origin of Banking in Mediaeval Islam: A contribution to the economic history of the Jews of Baghdad in the tenth century (parts V–)," 571–591. The operations described by Fischel — it is noted — do not seem to cover the full range of modern central banking, nor should they, given the different type of economy this first central bank served, especially its tri-metallic monetary system. And as indicated in Goodhart, "Central Banking," 385–387, this lesser central banking mandate was typical of the later-to-emerge state/central banks of Europe, although some of the more modern central bank functions were assumed by other classical institutions of Islamic economic governance, notably *Dār al-Darb* (Minting House) and *Bayt al-Māl* (Treasury House), among others; on these classical institutions, see A. S. Ehrenkreutz, H. Inalcik and J. Burton-Page, "Dar al-Darb," *Encyclopaedia of Islam*, New Edition, Vol. II (1983): 117–121, N. J. Coulson and Cl. Cahen, "Bayt al-Māl," *Encyclopaedia of Islam*, New Edition, Vol. I (1986): 1141–1147.

94 For a juristic review of their banking instruments and practices, see Saleh, *Unlawful Gain and Legitimate Profit in Islamic Law*, ch. 4, and for different reviews of their expansion and activities by economists, see Kuran, "Islamic Economics and the Islamic Subeconomy," 155–173, and Mohsin S. Khan and Abbas Mirakhor "Islamic Banking: Experiences in the Islamic Republic of Iran and in Pakistan," *Economic Development and Cultural Change* 38/2 (1990): 353–375.

95 H. A. Dar and J. R. Presley, "Lack of Profit Loss Sharing in Islamic Banking: Management and Control Imbalances," ERF Sixth Annual Conference (Cairo, Egypt: Economic Research Forum, 1999), examine this problem from a financial management perspective. This and other problems are also examined in Kuran, "Islamic Economics and the Islamic Subeconomy," and in Khan and Mirakhor, "Islamic Banking: Experiences in the Islamic Republic of Iran and in Pakistan."

96 On these, see J. E. Stiglitz, "Principal and Agent (ii)," *The New Palgrave: A Dictionary of Economics*, Vol. 3 (1987): 966–972, R. Guesnerie, "Hidden Actions, Moral Hazard and Contract Theory," *The New Palgrave: A Dictionary of Economics*, Vol. 2 (1987): 646–651, Y. Kotowitz, "Moral Hazard," *The New Palgrave: A Dictionary of Economics*, Vol. 3 (1987): 549–551, and C. Wilson, "Adverse Selection," *The New Palgrave: A Dictionary of Economics*, Vol. 1 (1987): 32–34.

97 R. K. Aggarwal and T. Yousef, "Islamic Banks and Investment Financing," *Journal of Money, Credit, and Banking* 32/1 (2000): 93–120.

98 This figure is reported in Dar and Presley, "Lack of Profit Loss Sharing in Islamic Banking: Management and Control Imbalances," 1.

99 See the evidence amassed by Rodinson, *Islam and Capitalism*, 35–45.

100 Ibn Khaldun, *The Muqaddimah: An Introduction to History*, 24.

101 I use the term 're-embed' because, as Rodinson in his *Islam and Capitalism*, 28, puts it: "The society in which Islam was born . . . was already a centre of capitalistic trade . . . It was indeed an "unembedded" economy."

102 On the criteria used by economists for classifying economic systems, see E. Neuberger, "Classifying Economic Systems," in M. Bornstein, Editor, *Comparative Economic Systems: Models and Cases*, Fourth Edition (Homewood, Illinois: Richard D. Irwin, Inc., 1979), 19–27, and J. B. Rosser, Jr., and M. V. Rosser, *Comparative Economics in a Transforming World Economy* (Chicago: Irwin, 1995), ch. 1.

103 Pryor, "The Islamic Economic System," 219–221, reached this conclusion in his attempt to characterize the "Islamic economic system" in the writings of MaudūdiConomists.

104 For an overview of the economic theory and practice of "market socialism," see W. Brus, "Market Socialism," *The New Palgrave: A Dictionary of Economics*, Vol. 1 (1987): 337–342.

105 This should not be surprising in view of the rationalist orientation of Islamic thought at the time, which is comparable to the situation later in Europe when modern capitalism rose. On the problematic nature of the "meaning of capitalism" in modern economic literature, see F. C. Lane, "Introductory Note," "Meanings of Capitalism," *Journal of Economic History*, Vol. 29 (1969): 1–12.

106 Rodinson, *Islam and Capitalism*, 30.

107 Labib, "Capitalism in Medieval Islam," 93, 96.

108 Rodinson, *Islam and Capitalism*, 56.

109 Often this kind of argument is based on re-interpreting certain Qur'ānic verses (e.g. 41:10) on the nature of ownership (of the means of production) as well as the historical experiences of "socialist figures" (e.g. Abu Dharr al-Ghifari) and the Ismaili sect (especially the Qarmatians), among others.

110 On Asnāf, see Raymond, Floor, and Nutku, "Sinf," 644–646, and Ghabin, "Sinā'a," 625–629. Of particular interest here is a new study by Ines Aščerić-Todd, "The Noble Traders: the Islamic Tradition of "Spiritual Chivalry" (futuwwa) in Bosnian Trade-Guilds (16th–19th Centuries)," *The Muslim World*, 97/12 (2007): 159–173; it highlights and documents the Islamic guilds' "code of honorable conduct" (and training) designed to instill in their membership the values of bravery, generosity, humility, honesty, and above all cooperation and harmony, with an egalitarian spirit.

111 Additional elements of this "type" are the jurists doctrine of distributive justice (alluded to in note (22) above) and the classical fiscal regime (in theory and practice), and the role of the institution of *Awqāf/hubus* as a form of community ownership, among others.

9

MAWLANA MAWDŪDĪ'S CONTRIBUTION TO ISLAMIC ECONOMICS*

M. Umer Chapra

Source: *Muslim World*, 94:2 (2004), 163–80.

Mawdūdī was a reformer, not a professional economist. Therefore, we cannot expect him to have been focused on theoretical discussions in economics. His main concern was the well being of mankind in keeping with the central objective of the *Sharī'ah*. Accordingly, he tried to analyze the problems and offer solutions in light of Islamic teachings. His immediate concern was the Muslim *ummah*, which had become engulfed in a number of difficult problems as a result of several centuries of Muslim degeneration followed by exploitative foreign occupation.[1]

These problems were all-encompassing and included moral laxity, political illegitimacy, stagnation of *fiqh*, poverty, illiteracy and lack of education, overall economic decline, inequalities of income and wealth, social tensions, and anomie. Since these problems were in utter conflict with the ethos of Islam, they were extremely disturbing for someone like Mawdūdī, who was concerned with the well being of his society. Nevertheless, little could be done during the period of foreign occupation. The independence of most of these countries in the middle of the twentieth century offered a long-awaited opportunity to mend these affairs.

At this stage, the most crucial task that needed to be performed was to find a proper strategy that would help solve the problems of these countries. The strategy could not, however, be laid down without first specifying the society's vision — its dream of what it would like to be in the future and the goals to which it aspired. It is the vision that enables a society to channel its resources and energies in the desired direction and thereby prevent their ineffective and wasteful use. The vision may be difficult to realize; nevertheless, it serves to inspire society to persist in the struggle for its realization and keep faith in the future perennially kindled. At the same time, the vision is itself a reflection of the society's worldview, which answers questions about how the universe came into existence, the meaning and purpose of human life, the ultimate ownership and objective of the limited resources at the disposal of human beings, and the relationship of human beings to each other (including their rights and responsibilities) and to their environment.

The worldview, vision, and strategy are all, therefore, closely interlinked and together determine a society's economic system. The vision may be realized only if the strategy is in harmony with the vision. This indicates that if the function of economics is to help realize a society's vision,[2] then there is no escape from also discussing the worldview of which this vision is the outcome, and then indicating the kind of strategy that is needed to make the vision a reality. One of Mawdūdī's major contributions was to discuss, in his clear and forceful style, the worldview, vision and strategy of Islam and also to show how these differed from those of prevailing economic systems.

Two economic systems with similar worldviews but different visions and strategies were dominant during the time when Muslims were struggling for independence from foreign domination. These were capitalism and communism. The crucial question for the newly-independent Muslim countries, including Pakistan, was whether they should adopt the worldview, vision and strategy of either one of these two systems, or choose a different system that would be more conducive to the realization of the Islamic vision.[3]

The critical point was the absence of a moral foundation in the strategies of either system. This does not mean that people in these societies are devoid of moral values or that justice is not one of their goals. All it means is that the system's paradigm does not assign a crucial role to moral values in the allocation and distribution of resources and the actualization of socioeconomic goals. The primary emphasis in capitalism is on the market, while that in communism is on central planning. The goals are to be realized in the former through the interaction of market forces in a competitive environment and, in the latter, through central planning in a totalitarian system where means of production were collectivized. Moral values have little direct role to play.[4] While preponderant attention is given to the efficient operation of the market or central planning, very little attention is given to the reform of the individual who operates in the market as consumer, producer, manager or worker, or performs different roles in the collectivized system. His or her tastes, preferences and behavior are taken as given in capitalism. Suggesting any changes would involve value judgments, which are not allowed. Similarly, in communism, the human being is a pawn on the chessboard of history and reform is hardly of any significance in the power struggle between different economic classes. The family, the source of the most important input of the market as well as the state, receives little attention in both systems.

The vision that Islam projects is, in sharp contrast, that of a society where the imperative is to ensure the spiritual as well as material well being of all, where the individual is free to earn his livelihood, provided he does this within the constraints of values and goals laid down by Islam,[5] where all members of society are tied to each other through strong bonds of human brother-hood, and where justice prevails, the basic needs of all individuals are fulfilled, and an equitable distribution of wealth has been attained, where the family continues to be strong and children receive the love, affection and care of both parents, and where crime, tensions and anomie are minimized and social harmony prevails.[6] The vision has moral as well as material dimensions which are interdependent, and requires an emphasis on both. Justice and brotherhood occupy a predominant place in this vision.[7] To realize this vision, the strategy cannot and does not rely predominantly on any one mechanism, like the market or the state, but rather on a number of spiritual as well as material mechanisms.[8]

In an environment where Muslim countries were weak and poor and capitalist and communist countries were far stronger and richer, it would be extremely daring for anyone to talk of a system which had not been tested in modern times. Not only this, there was an inadequate understanding of the worldview, vision and strategy of the Islamic economic system even among Muslims, in spite of their emotional attachment to Islam and their intense desire for its revival.[9] Moreover, it was necessary to counter, in a rational and convincing manner, the opposition to the Islamic system from those, both inside and outside, who had a vested interest in the continuation of the prevailing unjust system. The task was rather difficult[10] and the crucial question was who was going to bell the cat?

Mawdūdī was one of those daring souls who took up the challenge. A favorable intellectual climate had already been created to some extent by the writings of a number of scholars and the inspiring poetry of Iqbal in the Indo-Pakistan sub-continent and the movements for the revival of Islam in other Muslim countries. Even the struggle for the creation of Pakistan, along with the speeches of Muḥammad Ali Jinnah during the independence struggle, had prepared a helpful basis for the revival of Islam and raised hope that Pakistan would try to realize the Islamic vision. It was this vision, as distinct from the secularist and socialist worldview of the Indian National Congress leadership, which provided the rationale for Pakistan. Without projecting this vision, the call for the creation of Pakistan would have had no meaning and, consequently, would have received little popular support.

Mawdūdī earnestly undertook the mission of anchoring Islam in all aspects of the Muslim society of an undivided India. He wrote and lectured exten-sively on the Islamic vision,[11] different aspects of the Islamic way of life, and the strategy required for making the Islamic vision a reality.[12] The economic system of Islam was naturally an inseparable adjunct of the Islamic way of life. He indicated the essential principles of the Islamic paradigm and also defined the contours of the Islamic economic system as early as 1941 in a lecture he delivered at the Aligarah Muslim University, long before the creation of Pakistan.[13]

In this and other lectures and writings, Mawdūdī argued that the worldview and vision of Islam, since they had a moral foundation with an overwhelming emphasis on brotherhood and justice and reform of the individual, were entirely different from those of both capitalism and communism. Thus, neither of these two systems could help Muslims actualize the Islamic vision. Accordingly, he stood for a revival of Islam in a way that would ensure material prosperity along with spiritual uplift. The egalitarian tilt of Islamic values made him place considerable emphasis on need fulfillment, redistribution, and the availability of equal opportunities to all individuals to help them develop their personalities in accordance with the full potential of their aptitudes and innate abilities.[14] He considered the optimum use of all human and material resources necessary for realizing the Islamic vision. Such optimum use would not occur unless justice was ensured through satisfaction of the basic needs of the poor and needy,[15] and education was imparted to them to enable them to stand on their own feet.[16] This would require a simple lifestyle that would not be possible without kindling a moral flame in the human being.[17] Protecting the rights of duly acquired property is also indispensable.[18]

For realizing the goal of need fulfillment and rapid improvement in the economic condition of the poor, Mawdūdī's primary emphasis was on the transfer of resources from the rich to the poor. He originally (1941) emphasized that the immediate solution lay in motivating the rich to adopt the simple lifestyle of early Muslim society and to distribute the surplus income (not wealth) to the poor after fulfilling their own genuine needs (al-'afw in the Qur'ānic terminology).[19] Later on, when he seemed to have realized the difficulties that lay in the adoption of this approach in modern societies, where the altruistic spirit of the early Muslim society did not exist, he adopted a more moderate position. He now permitted Muslims to save and invest the amount left after taking care of his or her own genuine needs and fulfilling the social obligations (zakāt and 'ushr) enunciated by Islam.[20] Nonetheless, he continued to emphasize a simplicity of lifestyle and giving the poor as much of the surplus as possible. He also laid emphasis on the establishment of cooperative societies[21] and on the role of zakāt, 'ushr and the equitable distribution of a deceased person's estate in keeping with the Sharī'ah.

Mawdūdī strongly believed that the prohibition of interest could make a contribution towards the establishment of a just social order. He therefore tried to show how an interest-free financial system could be successfully established.[22] His primary emphasis in this, as in the writing of most other scholars on the subject in the initial phase, was on profit-and-loss sharing (mudārabah and mushārakah) modes of finance. The way the Islamic financial system is evolving, however, is somewhat different from this.[23] It also includes a substantial proportion of sales-based modes of financing (murābahah, *ijārah, salam* and *istisnā'*),[24] which create debt, but in a different way from interest-based loans extended by conventional banks. The difference in cash and credit prices that some ways of such financing involve (particularly *murābahah*) was considered by Mawdūdī to be equivalent to *rībah* (doubtful income) even though it was not *ribā* (interest).[25]

Mawdūdī was well aware from the outset that opting for the Islamic economic system would require a profound change in the individual himself.[26] Accordingly, he emphasized that "maximum attention should be given to the reform of the individual's attitude and character so that the root cause of evils in the human personality is uprooted."[27] This was not something new or unexpected. All the Prophets of God had given maximum priority to the reform of the individual, who was the end as well as the means of all reform and development. This was the most crucial task that lay ahead.

Mawdūdī classified moral values into two categories. One of these he called basic human values and the other Islamic values. He considered both of these to be indispensable for human development and well being.[28] In the former category, he included a number of character traits, including strong will and decision-making power, courage, diligence, readiness to sacrifice, self-control, discipline, truthfulness and integrity.[29] The general presence of these qualities in individuals in Western societies was one of the causes of their rise. Some of the traits which he included in the second category are kindness, mercy, scrupulous fairness, and purification of the self from greed, egotism, tyranny, wantonness and indiscipline so that the individual becomes, in the words of the Prophet, peace and blessings of God be on him, "the key to good and the barrier against evil."[30] Mawdūdī acknowledged frankly that both these sets of qualities were missing from a substantial proportion of the Muslim population and that this was the "crucial reason" for their decline.[31]

At the same time, Mawdūdī acknowledged in several of his other writings that there were so many different social, economic, political and historical forces influencing individual behavior that relying merely on sermons to create these qualities would not be helpful. Muslims had been listening to sermons for centuries with little transformation of their personalities. There was, therefore, a need for comprehensive socio-economic and political reform.[32] Thus, in keeping with the spirit of Islam and the writings of other great Muslim thinkers of the past, like Abū Yūsuf (d. 182H/798G),[33] al-Māwardī (d. 450/1058), Ibn Taymiyyah (d. 728/1328), Ibn Khaldūn (d. 808/1406) and Shāh Waliullāh (d. 1176/1762), Mawdūdī did not concentrate only on economic variables in his economic writings. Unlike conventional economists, he considered all aspects of an individual's life as well as his society to be interrelated; concentrating only on economic variables to solve economic problems would not take Muslim society very far in its goal of realizing the Islamic vision. In the 1941 Aligarah University address referred to above, Mawdūdī clearly emphasized this by saying, "the primary reason for the difficulty to understand and solve the economic problem of man is that some people look at it purely from an economic point of view."[34] Khurshid Ahmad has rightly reflected this idea in his introduction to Mawdūdī's *Islamic Law and Constitution* by saying, "Life is a unity. It cannot be divided into watertight compartments."[35]

The crucial problem, however, was how to bring about such comprehensive reform. The task was bound to be extremely difficult in an environment where governments were insensitive to the need for such reform, were doing little to restructure the educational system for this purpose, and where most of the *'ulamā'* were engrossed in bickering over trivial issues which had little bearing on the revival of Islam and the uplifting of Muslims.[36] In such an environment, the odds were too great against an individual scholar, no matter how hard he tried. Still, this did not shake Mawdūdī's determination or faith in the future. He established a well-disciplined organization, the Jamā'at-e-Islāmī, with sincere, hardworking, and motivated members to help him in the task.

In addition to laying great emphasis on the reform of the individual, which Mawdūdī considered to be vital for improving the well being of the people and the reform of the economic system, one of the variables that Mawdūdī considered to be extremely crucial but which has not received attention in both conventional and socialist economics is the family. Since the human being is the most important input for any economy, and the family is the primary source of this input, he attached a great deal of importance to the reform and integrity of the family. The state, society and the economy as well as the individual would all suffer if the family disintegrates. It is the family that creates the right environment for proper moral upbringing and character uplift of the new generation. It is also the family that provides love and affection to the individual, and thereby creates a proper climate for the promotion of not only peace of mind and emotional stability in the individual, but also cooperation and harmony in society. Disintegration of the family promotes bitterness and ill will and creates an environment in which the new generation does not get the kind of attention that it needs. The quality of the individual deteriorates and, with him or her, the quality of all aspects of society, including the economic.[37] It becomes difficult to sustain the economic as well as spiritual well being of society in the long-term.

Mawdūdī enumerated a number of measures that were necessary for ensuring the stability and integrity of the family.[38] While most of what he wrote in this connection was valuable, it would be difficult to agree with his emphasis on the necessity of the veil and confining women's role to the fulfillment of primarily household responsibilities. This would not only limit her contribution to the development of society, but also make her dependent on her husband for the fulfillment of practically all her needs, thereby preventing her from asserting herself and obtaining the rights Islam gives her. It is highly unrealistic to aspire for the well being of humans but

149

simultaneously confine half the population to a limited role in life. A number of eminent Muslim scholars do not consider the veil or female segregation to be a part of the Islamic values prescribed for preserving the solidarity of the family.[39]

In step with what Ibn Khaldūn wrote 600 years ago,[40] Mawdūdī also realized that directly or indirectly, political authority exercises a tremendous influence on the individual and that one of the major causes of Muslim decline was political illegitimacy.[41] It vitiated all those factors that promote development. It led to wars of succession, authoritarianism, and end of the institution of *Shūrā*. It impaired the independence of the judiciary and curbed freedom of expression. It promoted the luxury of the royal court, corruption, misuse of power and resources, inequalities of income and wealth, and social unrest.[42] Consequently, according to Mawdūdī, political reform was as indispensable as individual and social reform for economic development.[43]

This led Mawdūdī to the question of how to reform the political system. Unlike the leftists in Pakistan and elsewhere, he did not stand for the overthrow of the government. The use of force and violence had only led to destruction and misery and he, therefore, believed in gradual change through the democratic process.[44] It was necessary to win over the hearts of people in the same way as did the Prophet, peace and blessings of God be on him.[45] Mawdūdī "threw his weight in favor of the establishment and maintenance of a truly democratic order in Pakistan."[46] For this purpose, he laid maximum emphasis on "education," "resort to public pressure to prevent people from being subject to injustice," "change of leadership in the broader sense of the term," and "ultimately also political leadership."[47] He thus made individual, social and political reform an important adjunct of economic reform.[48]

Economic reform was also to be attained, like political reform, in a gradual democratic framework. He argued for a careful examination of the existing system "with a view to finding out what is malignant and hence deserves to be changed, and what is healthy and as such deserves to be preserved."[49] Mawdūdī did not blame private ownership of property for all the ills of human society. Islam allows private ownership of property and the means of production,[50] and makes it an obligation of Muslim society to protect the life, honor and property of all individuals.[51] Nationalization of all means of production was in conflict with the basic principles of Islam.[52] "The control of businesses, factories and farms by the same people who control the army, the police, the courts and the parliaments would give rise to a viciously repressive system the like of which the devil has not been able to conceive so far."[53] Means of production must in principle remain in private hands.[54] There is no justification for concentrating all decision-making in a few hands and then allowing the imposition of these decisions on the populace by all means, fair or foul.[55] Economic freedom to enable a person to earn his livelihood freely in keeping with the dictates of his conscience was as indispensable as political and social freedom.[56] At the same time, Mawdūdī was not against state ownership of some enterprises that could not be managed effectively by the private sector or of which it was not in the larger public interest to allow the private sector to manage.[57]

This raised the question of whether it was possible for the private sector to manage property in a way that would help realize general well being. The answer of communism was no, but that of both capitalism and Islam is yes. However, while capitalism generally believes that competition is by itself sufficient to rein self-interest and serve social interest, Mawdūdī asserted that competition, though necessary, was not sufficient for this purpose. He took pains to emphasize that even the competition that fitted well into the ethos of Islam was one that was fair and humane, based on the spirit of brotherhood and cooperation rather than on the concept of survival of the fittest.[58] A number of measures were needed to make competition fair and humane for the purpose of safeguarding social interest. These included the injection of a moral dimension into the economy and the playing of a positive role by the government in the economy. Problems created by private ownership of property need to be resolved, not by wholesale nationalization and regimentation, but rather by moral reform and a positive government role.

The injection of a moral dimension into the economic system would help create a sense of responsibility in the individual and make him realize that he is accountable before the Almighty. This implies that, while individuals are allowed to own and manage private property, they are not its real owners. They are, rather, only trustees.[59] They must acquire and use property in accordance with the terms of the trust, which are defined by moral values.[60] They must submit themselves to these values, which are meant to safeguard the rights of all members of society.[61] The instilling of the concept of accountability before God in the consciousness of all agents operating in the market can help moderate their pursuit of self-interest, induce them to fulfill their social obligations, and thereby help establish a just equilibrium between the interests of the individual and society.[62] In other words, Mawdūdī's emphasis was on bringing about "a happy integration of the economic and the moral."[63] Thus, he believed that economic problems could not be solved by merely relying on the interaction of market forces in a competitive environment. The 'economic' must be integrated with the "overall scheme of life based on the ethical concepts of Islam."[64]

The problem, however, is that moral checks, even when enacted by law, are not always implemented. While it is the moral obligation of the individual to be just and honest, to fulfill his obligations and abstain from doing something that would hurt others, he or she may not necessarily do so.[65] Humans need proper upbringing (in which the family plays a crucial role) and education (in which religious education needs to receive emphasis along with the mundane). Such upbringing and education will help make all participants in the economy clearly understand their responsibilities.[66]

Still, such upbringing and education, even when accompanied by the role model of the pious elite as well as social pressures, may not be sufficient to eliminate the excessive greed and self-centeredness of some people.[67] There is a further need for incentives and deterrents. There is no escape from the need for the state to play an important role.[68] It must ensure that moral values are reflected in the laws of the country and that these laws are truly observed by both high and low through effective operation of the legislative, judicial, and executive wings of the government.[69] Mawdūdī was fully aware of this need.[70] Like the great Muslim thinkers of the past, including Abū Yūsuf, al-Māwardī, Ibn Taymiyyah, Ibn Khaldūn, and Shah Waliyullah, Mawdūdī considered it the duty of the state to provide such incentives and deterrents.[71]

Mawdūdī, however, took special care to emphasize that the state should not exceed limits set by the *Sharī'ah*. It should use its coercive power only when absolutely necessary,[72] relying instead on moral reform. This is because it is also the obligation of the Islamic state to safeguard the rights of the individual and not just those of society.[73] The function of the state is not to become industrialist, trader or landlord, but rather to establish justice and use its powers and resources for the well being of the people by promoting all that is good and eradicating all that is evil.[74] Thus, within the framework of Mawdūdī's thought, the state is neither *laissez faire*, as it is in classical economics, nor totalitarian, as in communism.[75]

Unlike a number of Muslim scholars, Mawdūdī was realistic enough to accept that in order for the state to play its welfare role, income tax was a necessity, provided it is imposed with moderation and justice, and the proceeds are used efficiently and honestly for the well being of the people.[76] He also accepted the institution of insurance, provided that the elements in it which were objectionable from the Islamic point of view were reformed.[77] Mawdūdī also permitted external borrowing on interest to the extent that it was absolutely unavoidable.[78] He was also in favor of flexibility in the application of Islamic laws.[79] However, he took an extreme position on the question of birth control. He considered it to be unacceptable except when considered medically indispensable.[80] Here, he was out of step with many other scholars, who would allow birth control within certain constraints.[81]

While Mawdūdī emphasized the role of *zakāt*, *sadaqāt* (charitable contributions other than *zakāt*) and the equitable distribution of a deceased person's estate for the purpose of need fulfillment and equitable distribution of income and wealth, he did not give sufficient attention to the various techniques adopted by Western welfare states to eradicate poverty, improve wages and working conditions, promote redistribution, and provide relief to the unemployed, the aged, and the infirm. This may have been because he believed in the need for adopting the good things the West had to offer and rejecting its vices.[82] Accordingly, he may not have felt the need to specify in detail all the different ways in which Muslims could benefit from the West.

What is also missing in his writings is a discussion of the ways of accelerating growth in Muslim countries.[83] Primary reliance on redistributive methods for alleviating poverty, fulfilling needs and reducing inequalities may not lead the Muslim world very far. What is also needed is an expansion in the national income pie through economic development. Mawdūdī did not get into discussions of how development could be accelerated in Muslim countries, the kind of monetary, fiscal and commercial policies that were needed, or the techniques that could be borrowed from other countries for this purpose. As Crosland rightly pointed out, "any substantial transfer involves not merely a relative but also an absolute decline in the real incomes of the better off half of the population . . . And this they will frustrate."[84] This may also be the case in Muslim societies, even after moral transformation has taken place. Therefore, while capitalism lays greater emphasis on growth than on redistribution, Muslims cannot afford to ignore the role of economic development in reducing poverty and inequality. When they do this, they will have to draw upon the experience of other countries to the extent to which the methods used by them are compatible with *Sharī'ah*.

Mawdūdī's horizon was far wider than that of conventional economics. He was a reformer who wanted to help mankind solve the problems it was facing, in particular in his own society, which had fallen into an abyss during centuries of degeneration and foreign occupation. He saw that this would not be possible by holding on to the extremely narrow role assigned to an economist in conventional economics. He visualized the need for "carrying out a total reconstruction of human life and establishing a new social order and state and thereby ushering a new era in human society."[85] Such a transformation could not be brought about by concentrating only on economic variables. Even economic development, which was not Mawdūdī's main concern, could not be accelerated by means of such a limited approach.

In conformity with the comprehensive reform program pursued by the Prophet himself and emphasized by Muslim scholars, Mawdūdī stressed the interdependence of all aspects of society, including the moral, social, political and economic. In the economic field, his major contribution was to clearly articulate the vision, worldview and strategy of the Islamic economic system. At a time when it was fashionable to pay allegiance to 'Islamic socialism,' he not only abstained from using this term in his writings, but was also bold enough to indicate that socialism was not in harmony with Islam because of its false worldview and strategy. He discussed how moral values, closely-knit families and societies along with the market and state could together help in the realization of the Islamic vision in spite of private property. He also argued how the abolition of interest would promote social justice and how an interest-free financial system could be successfully established. Thus, in spite of not being a professional economist, his contribution to Islamic economics was significant. Mawdūdī will go down in history as one of the few great scholars who laid down the foundation for the development of this discipline in modern times. Nearly all those writing in this field in the Indo-Pakistan subcontinent as well as other Muslim countries have been influenced by and owe a debt of gratitude to him.[86]

The question that arises is why, in spite of being a powerful writer and speaker and having an unusual ability to convince people, and in spite of being successful in rallying around himself a team of dedicated and selfless workers along with innumerable sympathizers, he could not make significant headway during his lifetime in bringing about economic reform that would have helped solve the economic problems of Pakistan and improve the conditions of the underprivileged. In fact, Pakistan seems to have moved farther and farther away from the Islamic vision. It has suffered from high budgetary and balance of payments deficits and is consequently consumed by heavy debt and debt-serving burden. The rate of economic growth is low and poverty, unemployment and illiteracy are all high. Even some of the basic necessities of life (education, housing, transport and health facilities, clean water, electricity, sewage, etc.) remain inadequately supplied, particularly in areas inhabited by the poor. The Jamā'at cannot in any way be held responsible for these problems. It could have, nevertheless, helped reduce their magnitude. Its failure to do so could be due to a number of reasons, some of which are indicated below.

First, as rightly indicated by Mawdūdī himself in his writings, Pakistan has been dominated by illegitimate governments, with hardly any accountability on the part of corrupt generals, feudal lords, aristocrats and bureaucrats who have tried to serve their own vested interests at the expense of the people and country. The Jamā'at hoped to reform this state of affairs by taking part in elections. It misjudged its vote-getting ability in an environment where feudal lords and aristocrats have the mechanism to swing elections in their favor. The Jamā'at failed to win elections in a significant way. At the same time, in the process, it came into confrontation with practically all political, and even some religious, parties. This has proved to be one of the most serious obstacles in the political acceptance of its program. This does not necessarily mean that taking part in elections directly is not proper for a religio-political party. All it means is that the decision would necessarily depend on circumstances. Given the conditions prevailing in Pakistan, the better route for a small party like the Jamā'at might have been to avoid conflict and confrontation as much as possible and concentrate on creating consensus through confidence-building dialogue (Qur'ān, 16:125) on issues which are of greater importance for moral, educational, social, economic and political reform. The adoption of this route might in the long run have proved to be less costly in terms of human and material resources and more productive in terms of reviving Islam and realizing the Islamic vision.

Second, economic reform and uplift have not been a priority in the Jamā'at's program. While it carried out several campaigns for an "Islamic constitution,"

it has hardly ever carried out a campaign for reducing corruption and promoting land reform, slum clearance, and reconstruction of fiscal policy to
redress the conditions of the poor. These are of greater importance to the
poor than the constitution, which has been set aside and amended several
times by illegitimate governments to suit their vested interests. Such social-
service-oriented campaigns might have helped reduce resistance to its reform
program, increased support for its agenda, and ultimately helped enlarge its
vote bank.

Third, Mawdūdī's views on a number of controversial issues brought him
into conflict with a number of 'ulamā' and religious groups in Pakistan.[87]
The major political parties exploited this to their advantage. While opinions
on these issues by a non-political scholar might not have raised eyebrows,
they created antagonism when they came from him as a political leader.
Consequently, he could not get the kind of support he needed to win elections.
If he had abided by the Qur'ānic advice of first calling towards commonly
agreed principles (Qur'ān, 3:64), and the Jamā'at had translated his writings
into concrete policy proposals for economic reform and uplifting of the poor,
it might have met with greater success in winning the support of political
parties as well as religious groups.

Fourth, Mawdūdī himself pointed out the reasons for Sayyid Ahmad
Sirhindī and Shāh Ismā'il Shahīd's failures: they wanted to establish an
Islamic state in a society which was not mentally and morally prepared for
this and hence, not capable of shouldering the associated responsibilities.[88]
There is a great need for educating people about the high moral standards
that Islam expects from its followers. This is time-consuming. Even though
the Jamā'at has made some progress, it has not been able to make the kind
of headway needed to bring about the moral, cultural and social revolution
that Mawdūdī considered to be a prerequisite for establishing an Islamic state.
Consequently, even if the Jamā'at had won elections, the feudalistic power
structures and corrupt administrative machinery around it might have frus-
trated its efforts to fulfill the promises it had made to the electorate. Such failure
would have become an obstacle in the way of realizing its ultimate goal.

The struggle to bring about such a moral, cultural and social revolution
is bound to be an uphill task in a society where a number of ills have become
locked-in through the operation of path dependence and self-reinforcing
mechanisms over centuries of degeneration and decline in an environment
of feudalism and political illegitimacy. A strategy of gradual socio-economic
and political reform with the help of all reform-oriented parties might have
contributed to faster and greater success. Nevertheless, there is no room for
despondency, as the Qur'ān says: "Do not despair of God's mercy" (Qur'ān,
53:29). The strategy, nevertheless, has to be tailored to conditions in Pakistan.
It should be possible for a well-knit and disciplined organization like the
Jamā'at to develop and effectively implement such a strategy.

Endnotes

* Dr Chapra is grateful to Munawar Iqbal, Ausaf Ahmad, Fahim Khan, Nejatullah Siddiqi for their valuable comments on an earlier draft in the light of which the paper was finalized. He is also grateful to Khurshid Ahmad and Jalil Asghar for providing him some of Mawdūdī's works that he did not have, and to Shaikh Muḥammad Rashid for his efficient secretarial assistance.

1 Mawdūdī, IJMN, 1968a, 89.
2 For a discussion of this role of Economics, which is not generally recognized by Conventional Economists, see Chapra, 2000. There is a difference of opinion among economists on the goal of Economics. Positivists and operationalists, like Samuelson, emphasize that the role of Economics is only to describe. Logical empiricists, however, insist that explanation is the goal of Economics. By contrast, instrumentalists like Friedman emphasize that prediction is the primary function of Economics (see Caldwell, 1982). There is another goal, persuasion, which has also been emphasized (McCloskey, 1986). This, however, does not differ from explaining and predicting because it is generally not possible to persuade without convincing explanation and reliable prediction.
3 Mawdūdī, INZ, 1968b; 403–4.
4 Moral values did play an indirect role to the extent to which they influenced the behaviour and preferences of individuals. It was, however, not considered desirable to educate individuals in a way that would make these values reflected in their tastes and preferences. Nevertheless, it was not considered wrong for corporations to influence individual tastes and preferences through advertising for raising their sales and profits.
5 Moral values essentially indicate the way in which individuals are expected to behave if the humanitarian goals of brotherhood, justice, equitable distribution, strong families and freedom from crime and anomie are to be realized.
6 Discussion of the Islamic vision is spread all over the different writings of Mawdūdī. It is not, therefore, possible to give a complete citation, see Khan, 1990, 28–39.
7 Mawdūdī, MI, 1969, 379–400.
8 Mawdūdī, INZ, 1968b, 402–6.
9 *Ibid.*, 403.
10 *Ibid.*, 404.
11 See Ahmad and Ansari, 1979, 365–73.
12 Some of these lectures have been collected in *Islāmī Nizām-e-Zindagī awr us kē Bunyādī Tasawwurāt* (INZ, 1968b); see also *Let Us be Muslims* (LUM, 1985), and *The Islamic Movement: The Dynamics of Values, Power and Change* (IM, 1984). All the writings of Mawdūdī have been referred to in this paper by the abbreviation indicated on the right hand margin in the list of references.
13 This lecture was delivered in October 1941 at a function organized by the Islamic History and Culture Society, Aligarh University. The lecture was published under the title *"Insān kā Ma'āshī Mas'alah awr uskā Islāmī all"* (*The Economic Problem of Man and its Islamic Solution*, IMM, 1983) and has so far gone through several editions. The one referred to in this paper is the 1983 edition.
14 Mawdūdī, IMM, 1983, 453. See also INZ, 1968b, 453.
15 Mawdūdī, KM, 1966, 48.
16 See Ahmad and Ansari, 1979, 379.
17 Mawdūdī, IMM, 1983, 17.
18 Mawdūdī, INZ, 1968b, 452.
19 Mawdūdī, IMM, 1983, 34–6.

20 Mawdūdī, INZ, 1968b, 455 and 458.
21 Mawdūdī, IJMN, 1968a, 130.
22 *Mawdūdī, Sūd* (Interest), 1968.
23 See Chapra and Khan, 2000, for some details on how the system has actually evolved.
24 For a brief explanation of these terms, see *Ibid*, xiii–xv.
25 Mawdūdī, RM, Vol. 5, 1983, 321. While a preponderant majority of the *fuqahā'* allow the difference in cash and credit prices, some *fuqahā'* like Abū Zahrah argued against it (Abū Zahrah, 1970, 58–60).
26 Mawdūdī, INZ, 1968b, 407–8.
27 Mawdūdī, IMM, 1983, 31–32, see also Ahmad and Ansari, 1979, 380.
28 See his *Islamic Movement: Dynamics of Values, Power and Change* (IM, 1984). This booklet essentially consists of Mawdūdī's address in August 1941 at the time of formation of the Jamā'at-e-Islāmī. See in particular 94–99.
29 Myrdal includes some of these qualities in what he called the "modernization ideals" which he considered necessary for development but which were "alien" to developing countries because they "stem from foreign influences" (Myrdal, 1968, Vol. 2, 73); see, also Chapra, 1992, footnote 9 on 189.
30 Mawdūdī, IM, 1984, see in particular, 94–9.
31 *Ibid.*, 105.
32 Mawdūdī, INZ, 1968b, 400–2.
33 Wherever two years are given together hereafter, the first one refers to the Hijri year and the following to the Gregorian year.
34 Mawdūdī, EPTQ, 1963, Vol. 1, 9.
35 Mawdūdī, ILC, 1967, 3.
36 Mawdūdī, INZ, 1968b, 387–402.
37 Mawdūdī, *Pardah*, 1967, 92–3.
38 *Ibid.*
39 See, for example, Abū Shuqqah, 1990, 6 volumes.
40 For Ibn Khaldūn's analysis of the rise and fall of societies and its application to Muslim history, see Chapra, 2000, 145–172 and 173–252.
41 Mawdūdī, TID, 1992, 36–40.
42 See, KM, 1966, particularly 157–205.
43 This idea has now become a part of even Conventional Economics. The World Bank has, accordingly, emphasized that: "Development requires an effective state, one that plays a catalytic, facilitating role, encouraging and complementing the activities of private businesses and individuals. Certainly, state dominated development has failed. But so has stateless development. History has repeatedly shown that good government is not a luxury but a vital necessity. Without an effective state, sustainable development, both economic and social, is impossible" (World Bank, 1997, 111).
44 Mawdūdī, INZ, 1968b, 412.
45 Mawdūdī, KM, 1966, 55; and Ahmad and Ansari, 1979, 381.
46 Ahmad and Ansari, 1979, 380.
47 *Ibid.*, 379–80.
48 Mawdūdī, INZ, 1968b, 402.
49 Ahmad and Ansari, 1979, 381.
50 Mawdūdī, IJMN, 1968a, 127.
51 Mawdūdī, KM, 1966, 45.
52 Mawdūdī, MMZ, 1969, 105.
53 *Ibid.*, 106.
54 *Ibid.*, 106. Also Mawdūdī, RM, Vol. 4, 1983, 149–50.

55 Mawdūdī, MMZ, 1969, 108.
56 Mawdūdī, INZ, 1968b, *op. cit.*, 456.
57 Mawdūdī, RM, Vol. 4, 1983, 149–50.
58 Mawdūdī, INZ, 1968b, 454–5.
59 Mawdūdī, KM, 1966, 33.
60 Mawdūdī, INZ, 1968b, 454–8.
61 *Ibid.*, 89.
62 *Ibid.*, 456.
63 Mawdūdī, EPTQ, 1963, 189.
64 *Ibid.*, 189.
65 Mawdūdī, INZ, 1968b, 459, and RM, 1983, Vol. 4, 151.
66 Mawdūdī, EPTQ, 1963, 189–90.
67 Mawdūdī, IMM, 1983, 35.
68 Mawdūdī, EPTQ, 1963, 182; and IMM, 1983, 35.
69 Mawdūdī, EPTQ, 1963, 185; also KM, 1966, 43–4 and 66–9.
70 Mawdūdī, INZ, 1968b, 411.
71 Mawdūdī, EPTQ, 1963, 190.
72 Mawdūdī, IMM, 1983, 32.
73 Mawdūdī, INZ, 1968b, 456; and IMM, 1983, 6–7.
74 Mawdūdī, EPTQ, 1963, 178–79 and 195; and IJMN, 1968a, 173, Other scholars
of the past held the same view. For example, while Ibn Khaldūn considered the
state to be the greatest market, as a result of its large spending for the well-being
of the people, he considered it undesirable for the state to get directly involved in
economic activities (Ibn Khaldun, *Muqaddimah*, 286, 403, and 281). This would
not only reduce opportunities for the people, but also ultimately hurt the state
(*ibid.*, 281–3). Al-Dimashqī (*d. 570/1175*) also argued against the direct involvement of the state in business, saying that if the ruler participates with the subjects
in their businesses, they are ruined (al-Dimshqī, 1977, 61).
75 Mawdūdī, INZ, 1968b, 456.
76 Mawdūdī, RM, Vol. 3, 1965, 30–78, Vol. 4, 1983, 155–6; QMT, 1988, 64.
77 Mawdūdī, RM, Vol. 3, 1965, 288–93; IDN, 1968d, 135.
78 Mawdūdī, RM, Vol. 3, 1965, 312–4; Vol. 5, 1983, 195–8; and MI, 1969, 408–9.
79 Mawdūdī, MI, 1969, 422–36.
80 Mawdūdī, RM, Vol. 3, 1965, 288–93; IDW, 1968d, 135.
81 The *Fiqh* Committee of the Organization of the Islamic Conference (OIC) allows
family planning if parents consider it necessary through their mutual consent,
provided that it does not cause any harm, and the methods used for this purpose
do not violate the rulings of the *Sharī'ah* (*Majama' al-Fiqh al-Islāmī*, 1968, *Qarār*
(Resolution) No. 29, 89). Shaykh Mustafā al-Zarqā, one of the prominent jurists
of this century and a Faysal Laureate, also expressed a similar opinion (Al-Zarqā,
Fatāwā, 1999), 287–8.
82 Mawdūdī, INZ, 1968b, 397–402 and 406.
83 My attention was drawn towards this point by M. Nejatullah Siddiqi in his comments on the draft of my paper.
84 Crosland, 1974.
85 Ahmad and Ansari, 1979, 369.
86 His writings have been translated into nearly 39 languages (see Khurshid Ahmad's
introduction in Khan, 1990, p.s).
87 Certain views expressed by him in his book, (KM, 1966), raised a great deal of
controversy and severely hurt his standing in the country among the *'ulamā'*.
88 Mawdūdī, TID, 1992, 122–3.

References

Mawdūdī, Abul A'la

Abbreviation used

"Economic and Political Teachings of the Qur'ān" (1963), in M. M. Sharif, ed., *A History of Muslim Philosophy* (Wiesbaden: Otto Harrasowitz, 1963, 2 Volumes), Vol. 1, 178–98. — EPTQ

Insān kā Ma'āshī Mas'alah awr uskā Islamī Hall (1983), (Lahore: Islamic Publications Ltd., 18th ed. 1983; 1st ed., 1941), English translation. *Economic Problem of Man and its Islamic Solution* (Lahore: Islamic Publications Ltd., 2nd ed., 1970; 1st ed., 1947). — IMM

Islām awr dabt-e-Wilādat (1968d), (Lahore: Islamic Publications Ltd.). — IDW

Islām awr Jadīd Ma'āshī Nazariyyāt (1968a), (Lahore: Islamic Publications Ltd., 5th ed., 1968a; 1st ed., 1959). — IJMN

Islamic Law and Constitution (1967), (Lahore: Islamic Publications Ltd., 3rd ed., 1967; 1st ed., 1955), tr., Khurshid Ahmad. — ILC

Islamic Movement: The Dynamics of Values, Power and Change, tr. and ed. Khurram Murad (Leicester, UK: The Islamic Foundation, 1984). — IM

Islamī Nazim-e-Ma'īshat ke usūl-o-MaqāsId (1981), (Lahore: Islamic Publications Ltd., 1st ed. 1969, 6th ed. 1981). — INM

Islamī Nizām-e-Zindagī awr us kē Bunyādī Tasawwurāt (1968b), (Lahore: Islamic Publications Ltd., 3rd ed., 1968b; 1st ed., 1962). — INZ

Khilāfat-o-Mulukiyyat (1966), (Lahore: Islamic Publications Ltd., 1966). — KM

Let Us be Muslims, tr. and ed. Khurram Murad (Leicester, UK: The Islamic Foundation, 1985). — LUM

Ma'āshiyāt-ē-Islam (1969), ed. Khurshid Ahmad (Lahore: Islamic Publications Ltd.). — MI

Mas'alah Milkiyyat-ē-Zamīn (1969), (Lahore: Islamic Publications Ltd., 3rd ed. 1969, 1st ed, 1950). — MMZ

Pardah (1987) (Lahore: Islamic Publications Ltd., 19th ed., 1987; 1st ed, 1359AH/1940). — —

Qur'ān kī Ma'āshī Ta'limāt (1988), (Lahore: Islamic Publications Ltd., 1st ed. 1969, 9th ed. 1988). — QMT

Rasā'il-o-Masā'il, 5 volumes, different editions published at different times. Vol. 1 (1st ed. 1951, 17th ed. 1985), Vol. 2 (1st ed. 1954, 17th ed. 1985), Vol. 3 (1st ed. 1965, 2nd ed. 1967), Vol. 4 (1st ed. 1965, 12th ed. 1983), Vol. 5 (Delhi: Markazi Maktaba, Jamā'at-e-Islāmī, 1st ed. 1983). — RM

Sūd (1968c) (Lahore: Islamic Publications Ltd., 1st ed. 1951, 4th ed. 1968). — —

Tajdīd-o-Ihyā-e-Dīn (1992), (Lahore: Islamic Publications Ltd., 25th ed., 1992, 1st ed., 1940). — TID

Others

Abū Shuqqah (1990), 'Abd al-Halīm M., *Tahrīr al-Mar'ah fī 'Asr al-Risālah* (Kuwait: Dār al-Qalam, 1990), 6 Volumes.

Abū Zahrah (1970), *Buhūth fī al-Ribā* (Kuwait: Dār al-Buhūth al-'Ilmiyyah, 1970).

Ahmad, Khurshid, and Zafar Ishaq Ansari (1979), *"Mawlānā Sayyid Abul A'lā Mawdūdī: An Introduction to His Vision of Islam and Islamic Revival"* in Khurshid Ahmad and Zafar Ishaq Ansari. *Islamic Perspectives: Studies in Honour of Mawlānā Sayyid Abul A'la Mawdūdī* (Leicester, UK: The Islamic Foundation, 1979).

Blaug, Mark (1980), *The Methodology of Economics or How Economists Explain* (Cambridge: Cambridge University Press).

Caldwell, Bruce (1982), *Beyond Positivism: Economic Methodology in the Twentieth Century* (London: George Allen & Unwin).

Chapra, M. Umer (2000), *The Future of Economics: An Islamic Perspective* (Leicester, UK: The Islamic Foundation).

Chapra, M. Umer, and Tariqullah Khan (2000), *Regulation and Supervision of Islamic Banks* (Jeddah: IRTI/IDB).

Croslan, C. A. R. (1963), *Socialism Now* (London, Jonathan Cape).

Dimashqi, Abu al-Fadl Ja'far ibn 'Alī al- (d. 570/1175) (1977), *Al-Ishārah ilā Mahāə sin al-Tijārah*, Al-Bushra Al-Shurbaji (ed.). (Cairo: Maktabah al-Kulliyyat Al-Azhar).

Ibn Khaldun, *Muqaddimah* (Cairo: Al-Maktabah al-Tijāriyyah al-Kubrā, n.d.). See also its translation under Rosenthal (1967), and selections from it under Issawi.

Issawi, Charles (1950), *An Arab Philosophy of History: Selections from the Prolegomena of Ibn Khaldun of Tunis* (1332–1406), (London: John Murray).

Khan, Muḥammad Akram (1990), *Mawlānā Mawdūdī ke Ma'āshī Tasawwurāt* (Lahore: Maktabah Ta'mīr-e-Insāniyat).

Majma' al-Fiqh al-Islāmī (1998), *Qarārāt wa Tawsiyāt li al-Dawrāt*: 1–10, *Al-Qārārāt*: 1–97 (Jeddah: Majma' al-Fiqh al-Islāmī, 1st ed. 1988, 2nd ed. 1998).

McCloskey, D. N. (1986), *The Rhetoric of Economics* (Brighton, UK: Harvester Wheatsheaf).

Myrdal, Gunnar (1968), *Asian Drama* (New York: Twentieth Century Fund).

Rosenthal, Franz (1967), *Ibn Khaldun: The Muquddimah, An Introduction to History* (London: Routledge & Kegan Paul, 1st ed., 1958; 2nd ed., 1967), 3 Volumes.

World Bank (1997), *World Development Report* (Washington, D.C.: World Bank).

Zarqa, Mustafa al- (1999), *Fatāwā*, ed. Majd Ahmad Makkī (Damascus, Dār al-Qalam).

10

ISLAM'S CONCEPT OF LIFE REGARDING ECONOMIC MATTERS

Anwar Iqbal Qureshi

Source: *Islamic Studies*, 11:4 (1972), 297–308.

God Almighty has said in the Holy Qurā'n, "I have completed your Dīn for you". Islam claims that it provides guidance to human beings on all aspects of life. This guidance is from God, the Almighty. Therefore, it is superior in all respects to any other concept. There is no question of any misgivings in regard to this that this guidance helps human beings in leading a complete life; and that is a part of the faith of every Muslim.

From the very beginning I would like here to remove one common mis-understanding that Muslim leaders and often 'Ulemā become victims of exaggeration and high ideals. Believing that the Qur'ān is a perfect book they try to insist that they can find remedies for all our worldly ills from the Qur'ān and go on insisting for details.

It cannot be denied that teachings of the Qur'ān and its guidance are eternal and are free from the limitation of time and place. Therefore, it is quite obvious that such a book cannot go into any details which relate either to a certain place or to a certain time. Such a book can only provide guidance in regard to principles and fundamentals.

While we take stock of the Qur'ānic teachings we should keep the above mentioned principles in view. The Qur'ān is not a text book on economics nor does it discuss economic principles as such. However, it provides basic teachings regarding fundamental principles whereby the foundation of a just, progressive and balanced society may be laid and in which the basic principles of human rights in regard to economic matters are safeguarded. Teachings in respect of these high ideals are available in quite clear and unambiguous words and by acting on these teachings we can lay the basis of a very high grade society which should have an ideal system of economic and social justice. Any details which are not available about important matters in the Qur'ān are available to us from the life of the Holy Prophet (May God Almighty bless his soul) and from reliable traditions.

In the world of today, the economic system which is prevalent in most of the countries is called the Capitalistic System. Along with this in some countries we find various types of Socialistic and Communistic systems.

The late syed Sulemān Nadvī in the introduction on the writer's book 'Islam and Theory of Interest' observed:

"The superficial charm and glamour of the present European civilization has so captivated the common mind that, instead of reasoning, the expedients of Europe are adjudged to be the standard of right and wrong, and the appreciation and the condemnation of actions. The soundness of an opinion or the righteousness of an action is exclusively determined in the light of European practices and precedents; every problem or action contrary to them is evil. Hence, according to the majority of the so-called pretenders of learning and wisdom, this is the only correct approach to knowledge. Consequently we had to forsake many of our principles and we began to feel a weakness in our religious injunctions. This led many of our young men to contemplate a radical change in numerous religious matters and several modern thinkers adopted an apologetic attitude in the defence of Islam."

It has been necessary to introduce these observations here because the youth of the present generation and many leaders and intellectuals seem to be very much impressed by Socialism and Communism and try to find support for these systems in Islam.

It is our greatest misfortune that we are leaving what is pure and original and are more inclined towards substitutes which naturally are not a true copy of the original. If it is our faith that Islam provides perfect guidance for life, then why are we looking for guidance to any other system? In the world of today there are three types of economic systems which are prevalent:

(a) Capitalism.
(b) Socialism.
(c) Communism.

We shall briefly give the salient features of each of these three systems and shall also try to show what are the basic defects in these systems and that none of these could be connected with Islam. In conclusion we shall outline the teachings of Islam in the economic and social fields and show as to how Islam removes the defects of other systems and how it is better than and superior to these systems.

Capitalism

This system is also called "Free Enterprise System". Its basic principles have been taken from the famous book of Adam Smith entitled "The Wealth of Nations" which was published in 1776. The principles laid down by Adam Smith in this book were further elaborated by Robert Thomas Malthus, David Ricardo and Professor Alfred Marshal. This system is at present prevalent in most of the countries of the world, although deviations have been made from its basic principles in many countries. The biggest advocate and practitioner of this system is the United States of America. This system provides for all types of freedom to the individuals. Competition in economic life is its cardinal principle and it believes that a proper equilibrium is reached between supply and demand if economic forces are left free to find their own level. Its advocates believe that such a system is beneficial and provides for the betterment of the society as a whole.

This system provides for the non-interference by the State in the economic life, and it allows, where inevitable, such interference to the minimum and leaves economic forces quite free to work themselves. There are three cardinal principles of this system:

(a) The capitalist should have perfect freedom to invest his capital in which ever business he thinks fit.

(b) There should be full freedom in regard to the investment of capital and it should be free to move to any place where it expects the best advantage.

(c) It is accepted that no country should impose restrictions regarding the movement of capital, labour and goods.

It may be mentioned that in the world of today these ideals are more often honoured in their breach than their observance.

The golden period of the capitalistic system was from 1875 to 1914. It held sway for nearly half a century. Incidentally this was also the period when the British Empire was at its highest glory and it was said that the sun never set in this empire. It may be recalled that Great Britain was the first country which completed all the stages of Industrial Revolution (1760 to 1820). Great Britain had comparatively small population but its vast empire provided it with excessive wealth. British people have the mentality of *Banias* and all over the world they are known as a nation of shop-keepers. Therefore, they invested their capital all over the world and thereby also gained political dominance.

The second basic principle of this system is the system of free trade. Free trade was preached with great elaboration by the School of British Economists which is generally known as the Classical School of Economics and their principal members, as mentioned earlier, were Adam Smith, Ricardo and Marshal. Their teachings achieved paramount success. Their teachings were in accord with the times as Great Britian had successfully completed all the stages of Industrial Revolution while most other countries were just on its threshold. The result of this policy was that Britain got free access for its goods to most countries of the world. As according to this principle, free system of trade was paramount; it was assured that no restrictions should be placed on it. In the beginning even protection to infant industries was opposed though gradually its importance began to be recognised. We find that in the last quarter of the 19th century some textile mills were established in the undivided subcontinent. The Government of India levied a Custom Duty of 5% for revenue purposes. The Lancashire Textile Mills Owners who commanded a powerful influence in the British Parliament objected to this as they said that this duty provided protection to the Indian Textile Industry, which was against the principle of Free Trade and was against the interests of British Textiles. As a result of this pressure for some time, to counteract the effects of this small duty of 5% an excise duty was levied even on this infant textile industry of India. As the foreign dominance decreased and spirit of independence rose in many of the governed countries, the principle of protection was gradually accepted. It may be mentioned here that in the case of Indo Pakistan Sub-continent it was not accepted until 1923.

This was the first nail which was dug in the coffin of the Capitalistic System.

The second basic principle of this system is the freedom for investment of capital. There should be no restrictions on its movement and the capitalists should be free to invest their capital wherever they like. In most countries of the world in the 19th century there was a shortage of capital. The United States of America which is now so famous for its wealth, was, until the beginning of First World War in 1914, starved and heavily dependent on foreign loans and investments. Therefore, up to the First World War there was no opposition to the free movement of capital for loans or investment. But after the First World War the situation began to change. By 1929 when America was caught in the grip of Great Depression, it no longer needed foreign capital, and restrictions began to be placed on its free movement which were intensified all over the world after 1929.

The third cardinal principle of this system is the freedom of the movement of labour. This meant that a worker should be free to go anywhere he found it best to improve his lot. If wages were low, or work was not available he had the freedom to move and make his home in the U.S.A. or Canada where work was available and wages were also comparatively higher. This freedom was available up to the beginning of the First World War. It may be pointed out that now there are severe restrictions regarding the mass movement of labour in the United States, most of whose population originally came from other countries to settle down.

Now all these basic principles of this system are hedged with various restrictions in most countries of the world. The bright aspect of this system is that many developed countries of the world have reached their present stage of affluence under this system. But the greatest defect in this system is that it has opened quite widely the doors of exploitation. The question of morals in this system does not arise at all. This had led to considerable moral laxity and impropriety. This Capitalistic system provides full liberty to the capitalist to invest his capital where he can get the maximum possible rate of return on his capital investment. What effects such an investment would have on the character or the morals of the people, is no concern of the capitalist or the capitalistic system. The famous British dramatist, Bernard Shaw, remarked in his characteristic cynical style that if there is a shortage of houses for the working class but it yields less returns than the building of brothel houses, then in the capitalistic system building of brothel houses will be undertaken in preference to building of the much needed houses for the workers to provide them with necessary shelter. In the Capitalistic System, under normal circumstances, no person or government has the right to restrict the right of the capitalist regarding his choice for his investments. This leads to several undesirable consequences.

Another very great defect of this system is the evil of usury or interest which thrives under such a system. Under this system there exists no arrangements for the provision of work for the un-employed workers though some amends have been made in the recent past. Another very serious consequence of this system is that it leads to concentration of wealth in comparatively fewer hands which besides its economic ill effects has been the cause of many political evils as well. We find that in this system, there is not only large scale unemployment, but other evils like drinking, gambling, prostitution and moral delinquency also thrive. As a result of exploitation of the working class and the inability of this system to prevent unemployment, this system has come under searching criticism even by its own supporters.

Socialism and communism

The Capitalistic System was first developed in Great Britain, and it was here that protests against this system first began to be noticed. It was in Great Britain that labour as a strong political party emerged and its aims and objects were to achieve political power for the working class through constitutional parliamentary means and to introduce a socialistic economy in the country. As the British people are known for their spirit of give and take and compromise, they adopted a comparatively mild system of socialism which is known as Fabian Socialism after the name of the Fabian Society which started a campaign for this type of mild socialism.

There are various types of socialisms. Space does not permit to discuss all these varieties. Therefore, we shall confine ourselves in giving an outline of the Fabian type of Socialism.

Characterstics of Fabian socialism

1. To nationalise all industries;
2. To limit ownership of private property by heavy property taxes and still more by heavier inheritance taxes.
3. To improve the conditions of workers by:

   (a) providing better facilities of employment;
   (b) to provide relief during periods of unemployment;
   (c) to provide adequate medical facilities including facilities for surgery;
   (d) to provide cheap housing;
   (e) to provide better facilities for higher education for the children of labourers.

This movement has greatly benefited workers in the urban areas. As Britain is largely a country of towns, the benefit of this type of socialism was enjoyed by a larger majority of workers.

For the first time in the history of the world, a Parliamentary Labour Government was formed in the United Kingdom in 1929. It has come to power many times since, through parliamentary elections.

As far as moral values are concerned, there is no difference in this as compared to the capitalistic system. The moral fibre is even weaker. Drunkenness still prevails in the working class and usury and interest thrive.

Communism

This in a way is an extreme form of socialism. This system was advocated in the middle of the 19th century by Karl Marx. Practical shape to the system was given in 1917 in the Russian Revolution by Lenin and his comrades like Stalin and others.

In this system the State not only controls the means of production, it also exercises full control over distribution and consumption. Russia along with a number of its East European Satellites and Communist China are at the head of this list. Under such a system the question of any personal freedom does not arise at all. It provides for only one party which controls all the sources of the country. In such a system there exists neither any freedom for the press nor any freedom to individuals to express their views or to choose any profession for themselves or for their children. Religious freedom has been completely annihilated. Its founder, Karl Marx observed, "Religion is the opium of the People".

In the communistic system though arrangements exist for filling the stomachs of the people, their souls are completely starved. Although on paper it provides for a classless society and the difference between the rich and poor has been removed, in practical life the ruling junta, the intellectuals and writers and artists enjoy special privileges. People's tongues are sealed. During the Stalin regime lakhs of innocent people were jailed or even 'finished' for any complaint against the state. The more pronounced ones were publicly hanged.

The above, in brief, was the outline of three principal economic systems prevalent in the modern world. Islam has no truck with any of these systems. It is simply an insult to compare or link it with any of these systems.

The economic system of Islam

Now we shall proceed to examine how far Islam removes the defects of the three prevalent economic systems in the world and how far its own teachings and principles are far superior to these systems.

The outline of the three economic systems, which we have sketched above, does not provide for any moral bonds or ideals. There is complete absence of the concept of '*Ḥalāl*' or '*Ḥarām*'. In their political system the Machiavellian concept of "The end justifies the means" is their cardinal philosophy. On the other hand, Islam is strictly opposed to such a concept. For Islam means are just as important as the end. No end, however, important, is worthwhile if the means employed to achieve it are not clean. As a matter of fact, Islam insists on employing very clean means. For it the end is meaningless if achieved with improper means. In other aspects of life also Islam insists on using clean means to achieve any purpose. By introducing the concept of '*Ḥalāl*' and '*Ḥarām*', Islam has done a great service to humanity and is responsible for removing many evils which ultimately result in the destruction of a society.

The spirit of Islam and one of its cardinal principles is that every Muslim should wholeheartedly believe in the day of judgement, life after death, and be accountable for all his sins of omission and commission. He will be duly rewarded for his good deeds and obedience to the commandments of God and his Holy Prophet and will be punished for their violation. It should be a true Muslim's faith that when he does any evil in this world, when nobody sees him or detects him, God Almighty is all watching and knowing. While he can go unpunished in this world for his evil deeds, he cannot escape such punishment on the day of Judgement. While emphasising this aspect, the Holy Qur'ān lays repeated stress on the magnificence and omnipotent compassion and mercy of God. He is living, kind and forgiving to those who seek for such forgiveness and show real repentance. The doors of repentance are open all the time. The Holy Qur'ān even goes so far as to mention that no person should give up hope for mercy and compassion from God, and it is for this reason that suicide is prohibited in Islam.

But we should remember here that God Almighty has laid very great stress on *Ḥuqūq-al-'Abād* (respect for the rights of others). As far as those sins are concerned which relate to the disobedience of the commandments of God, for instance saying the daily prayers, keeping of fasts and performance of the Hajj when it is incumbent, these are all listed to be forgivable after proper repentance has been shown. But for those sins which relate to the violation of rights of other human beings, these can only be forgiven if those who have been sinned against are willing to forgive him. He can partly compensate for those by the good deeds which he has done for others. It is in this connection that one realizes the importance of Zakāt and the repeated stress laid on its giving in the Qur'ān. In the same light one should appreciate the stress laid on charity and spending money for the betterment of others. Similarly, considerable stress has been laid rgarding uprightness in worldly and commercial affairs. The Qurā'n provides for proper weights and measures and strictly warns not to indulge in malpractices. It emphasises that all agreements be properly documented and witnessed. Authentic traditions exist to provide for the rights of neighbours, to feed the hungry, to cater for the requirements of the needy and to free the debtors from the bonds of their debts.

Zakāt is a compulsory charity on the payment of which there is repeated insistence in various sections of the Qur'ān. But there is no limit to spending in the name of God i.e. for helping the poor and the more one spends, the more he is recipient of the blessings of God. Islam has not only laid stress on strengthening the moral bonds but also for the first time in the history of the world has presented the concept of Taqwa and Muttaqī.

Drinking of liquors, which is the root cause of all evils and the mainspring of immorality has been strictly forbidden. Gambling is also strictly forbidden as it gives rise to various evils. The Qur'ān insists on its believers to always tell the truth, to fulfil their promises and always to keep full weights and measures. In short there are a number of commandments in the Qur'ān for creating a very healthy and progressive society. In the Qur'ān there is a repeated stress to help the orphans and to look after their interests. Again, as mentioned earlier, it has been pointed out that while the sins committed for not following the commandments of God will be forgiven by the Almighty, the sins committed against the body politic can only be compensated by doing good for the body politic and for the public welfare. Therefore, an Islamic society creates a type of man who not only fears God but also believes in social justice and has regard for the rights of others.

The present capitalistic system, which is prevalent in most parts of the world, leads to the great evil of concentration of wealth. Concentration of wealth in a few hands is responsible for many economic and social evils. As a matter of fact it also opens the doors of corruption in the political field. It is no longer a secret that in most countries of the world the Jews exert very powerful influence on their Governments due to the large capital at their command and the Governments have to bow down even before some of their improper demands and fear their economic power. The biggest factor which helps the Jews to achieve this power is the system of interest prevalent in the modern society. Islam strictly prohibits interest. Again, one of the reasons for the concentration of wealth is that the goods are hoarded with the help of borrowed money and thereby efforts are made to buy goods and by creating a short supply they are able to charge heavy prices which they desire. Another cause for the concentration of wealth is the dealing in future and speculation instead of dealing with actual goods available in the market.

Islam has strictly prohibited hoarding and speculation and has insisted that there should be only physical buying of goods and actual deliveries must take place. If these principles are put into practice, they will result in preventing the basic causes of concentration of wealth. Another reason for the concentration of wealth is that in various religions and societies the right to inherit land has been only given to the eldest son while the other sons are deprived of the ownership of land. Feudalism gained considerable ascendency in the middle ages due to the fact that the law of eldest son only inheriting landed property was prevalent in most of the countries of the world. As far as women are concerned, there are still many western countries where they are deprived of inheritance. Therefore, it is quite obvious that under such a system wealth concentrates into a few hands. It is a golden chapter in the history of the world that Islam provides for inheritance of land not only by all sons but also by daughters and wives as well. This quite obviously prevents the concentration of wealth into a few hands. It is made incumbent for the rich to pay Zakāt to the deserving poor and emphasis has been laid on Ṣadaqāt which means spending far more than the compulsory minimum of Zakāt for the poor. The Qur'ān has gone further and it has observed that those who spend in the name of God it is as if they are lending money to God.

In the non-Islamic society there is another great evil prevalent in the form of gambling in which some gamblers even lose their wives as they put them as stakes. The evils of horse racing and betting are too well known to be emphasised here. Islam strictly prohibits all these evils.

Conflict between production and distribution of wealth in the Capitalistic System.

This conflict has been very seriously felt in the capitalist system. Although this conflict has been minimised to some extent due to the awakening in the ranks of labour and the progress of the trade unions yet the conflict is still there because the aim of this system is to earn wealth and not to distribute it justly. Neither is there any restriction regarding the legitimacy of means employed to earn this wealth.

Islam removes this conflict by its concept of Ḥalāl and Ḥarām and as if this was not enough it has created the concept of Taqwa and Muttaqi to complete the job. A God fearing Muttaqī trader or employer can neither be a party to any dishonest dealing or to any illegitimate deal. Adulteration and short measures which are the evils of the present day world Islam provides for their removal by its teachings.

During the period of Khulafā' Rāshidūn we find various examples of the just and equitable society. There are repeated commandments in the Qur'ān that those who spend their money in the way of God are the beloved subjects of God. Therefore, in the light of these very clear cut commandments and pursuasions, the question of exploitation does not arise in Islam. Islam also prohibits indulgences in extremes and insists on following a middle path. The spirit of brotherhood and equality which has been provided by Islam is further implemented by the insistence that in the Islamic society it would be the duty of the Government to provide for the basic necessities for all individuals from the public treasury. As regards payment of wages to the labour, it has been mentioned that before the sweat dries from his forehead the labourer should be paid his wages and the relationship between the labourer and the employers should be that of equality rather than of superiority and inferiority.

In short the essence of Islamic system is that it aims to create a just society in which the basic rights of everybody are equal, though the difference between the rich and the poor has been kept and there will be a disparity of incomes. However, a number of practical steps have been suggested in the Islamic system whereby this disparity can be kept to the minimum. Facing the realities of life is also the basic spirit of Islam and this system is thus distinguishable from all other systems as it provides a perfect code for the conduct of life.

11

PRINCIPLES OF ISLAMIC ECONOMICS

Masudul Alam Choudhury

Source: *Islamic Studies*, 21:2 (1982), 89–107.

Introduction

Over the years since the nineteenth century the objective of economic analysis has changed significantly. One can associate three major foci of development to it.[1] In the first half of the nineteenth century economic analysis was concerned with the problem of distribution. After 1870 it became concerned with the problem of optimal allocation of resources among competing ends. Finally, since the rebirth of macroecomomic theory in the hands of Keynes economic science became concerned with the problems of economic policy relating to employment, the generation of aggregate demand for goods and services and price stabilization. In short, modern economics has been preoccupied by the idea of one goal—the satisfaction of the economic man, Marshall's homoeconomicus, based on total, free and perfect competition.

Against this advanced and rather impressive facade of modern economics we have the niche of a new economic order. The central issue of this new economic order is efficient allocation of resources in the economy in the light of a more transcendental consideration—that of a righteous community promoting the laws of God on earth. This brings us to the central issue of the new system of economic thought commonly being termed as Islamic Economics.

Objective

The main objective of this paper is to delineate in non-technical economic language the principles of Islamic economics in as far as they constitute the philosophical basis of this economic system. We shall then look at some of the key economic instruments that translate the Islamic economic principles

171

into action. The paper will be of an introductory nature in these areas and no elaborate economic analysis of the issues is undertaken for the benefit of the common reader.

Principles of Islamic economics

1. The principle of Tawheed and Brotherhood

Islamic economics is not contented with the conventional viewpoint of economic analysis. It is instead motivated by its first cardinal principle—the principle of Tawheed and Brotherhood. Tawheed literally means unity. In the economic context it summarizes the crux of the entire essence of Islamic economics in that it teaches man how to relate and deal with other men in the light of his relationship with God. It says that behind the workings of an economy based on market exchange, the allocation of resources, the maximization of utility and profits, is a more fundamental truth—that of social justice. In Islam the capacity to understand and dispense this social justice emanates from the knowledge and practice of the principles of Quran. In this way the principle of Tawheed and Brotherhood links up our duties to men with our duties to God. In more practical terms the essence of Tawheed and Brotherhood lies in equality and cooperation. The Quran verily says, "O mankind! be mindful of your duties to your Lord who created you from a single soul and from it created its mate and from them twain has spread abroad a multitude of men and women."[2]

An immediate corollary of the principle of Tawheed and Brotherhood is the predominant note of Islamic economics, that to God alone belongs whatever is in the heavens and in the earth, and that He has made the good things for the service of man.[3] Man has been appointed as the vicegerent of God on earth and entrusted with the responsibility for the just use and distribution of the resources created by Ifim.[4]

2. The principle of work and productivity

The second basic principle of Islamic economics is that of work and labour compensation for work performed. It states that an individual's wages must be proportionate to the amount and category of the labour performed by him. The amount of labour would be measured in say, man-hours of work and the category of labour would be specific to different professions. The wages in the latter case would be constrained by the minimum of the rent determined for the category of labour in demand.

Whenever an individual acquires income greater than what is due on him by dint of his input of labour and other resources, which produce this income, he commits what is known as 'rububiyyah', i.e. sole proprietorship of the means of production. Because Islamic economic ideas hold that fundamentally all

172

means of production belong to God, so an individual by transgressing this limit commits a form of excess.

Under this category of excess are included rent on land and sharecropping, but rent on money capital is permitted.[5] As regards the prohibition of the rent on plain land, we have the 'hadith' (saying) of Prophet Muhammad, (peace may be upon him) that "He who has a land should cultivate it and should not rent it—not even for a third or fourth of its crop and not for a specific amount of food".[6] Inherent in this 'hadith' is the problem of value. Uncultivated land has not received the labour of the owner and is therefore, not liable to a price until it is exploited to produce. Thus, in the first case we have the idea of value in use and, in the second case, the idea of value in exchange.

It must be noted that rent was prohibited only on plain land and not on land in which there has been input of labour and capital by the owner. In the latter case it would be an act of injustice towards the landowner to have him forego for nothing in return, the exchange value created in the land by his labour and capital inputs. However, it is suggested strongly that this rent cannot be in crops, but in money terms. In this regard we have the following tradition mentioned by Abu Dawud, who quoted Sa'd Ibn Waqqas, a companion of Prophet Muhammad (peace may be upon him) as saying, "We used to rent land and pay the owner as rent the produce on the banks of the irrigation canals. The Prophet (peace be upon him) prohibited this and ordered us to pay rent in gold and silver."[7] Thus, while rent was prohibited on plain land, it was allowed on cultivated and used land. Sharecropping was prohibited.

3. The principle of distributional equity

The third major principle of Islamic economics is the right of society to redistribute private property. This is amply supported in several Qur'ānic verses.[8] The chief items of national incomes and transfer payments used for redistributive purposes in an Islamic economy are, 'Zakah' (tax on wealth exceeding a certain exemption level called 'Nisab'), 'Sadaqah' (voluntary charity), 'Ghanimah' (war booty), 'Fay' (property acquired in war without fighting), 'Fifth' (a part of *fay'* whose distribution pattern is similar to Zakah), 'Kharaj' (tax on lands conquered during war), 'Ushr' (Zakah on crops).

There is no order in Quran that the various sources of funds must be spent in strict accordance with the practice during the early period of Islam. It is just the broad principles of expenditure of these funds as laid down in Quran and further elaborated through the Islamic legal sources, such as 'ahadith' (traditions of Prophet Muhammad), 'fiqh' (legal study based on original sources) and 'shariah' (Islamic law as it pertains to different affairs of life), that must remain invariant. For example, the way the four-fifths of 'Ghanimah' was distributed among the Muslim soldiers in the early period of Islam was only an exigency at a time when wars were thrust on the Muslims before an Islamic state could be established. In these conditions there existed no standing army nor a state treasury to finance a standing army. Therefore, the Muslim soldiers during that early formative period were allowed their share in the war acquisitions. However, in a modern Islamic state the army could be regularly paid as are the civil servants and war acquisitions would add on to the state treasury.

Similarly, the remaining one-fifth of 'Ghanimah' can go to the state treasury to supplement organized forms of social assistance programs. The part due on the Prophet (peace be upon him) and his near of kin during the early period of Islam can now be returned to the government for public works.

Similar is the case with 'Zakah' expenditure in the form of an organized social assistance program undertaken by the state. The stated categories of expenditure of the Zakah fund can be extended to cover programs of employment creation, family welfare, rehabilitation of the aged, unemployment insurance, income support during times of economic losses and others. Even the rate of Zakah, originally fixed at 2.5 percent on all forms of assessed wealth exceeding 'Nisab' level at any given point of time can be varied but only marginally.[9]

At the more micro-level the Islamic law of inheritance helps to redistribute private property. The Quran is clear on this point.[10] The primary motive of the law of inheritance is to put a final check on the concentration of material assets in the hands of a few.

In short therefore, equitable redistribution of income and wealth is incumbent upon the Islamic state and the individual, and has to take place fundamentally on the basis of Tawheed and Brotherhood. The objective of this redistribution is to increase the productive transformation of national income and wealth for the employment and welfare of the citizens. Thus, when the early Muslim refugees evicted from Mecca found refuge in the city of Medina, they became members of that society and were treated on equal terms and not confined to camps and charities. If a refugee could cultivate land, he was given land to do so; if he had traits of trader, he was allowed to open a business; whoever could not manage, had the help of a brother in faith.

Analytic implications of the Islamic economic principles

The viability of the three major principles of Islamic economics must be tested on two grounds in order to establish the workability of an Islamic economic system. First, they must be capable of rational economic analysis. This rational economic analysis may not be of modern economics but must be consistent with economic assumptions and behaviour, normative or positive, at the micro and macro levels. Then they must also be capable of translating themselves into practical applications with the help of suitable Islamic policy instruments.

Let us first investigate the viability of the principles of Islamic economics to rational economic analysis.

1. Analytic implications of the principle of Tawheed and Brotherhood

In order to establish the principle of Tawheed and Brotherhood, Islam makes the elimination of 'Riba', i.e. interest, and the redistribution of individual and national wealth imperative. The Islamic state has established institutions to bring these policies into effect. These are discussed in the next section.

According to the neo-classical economic theory, the distributive components of the total annual gross product of the nation are used in three ways: one goes to acquire more real capital inputs for further production; the other goes as wages; the third is taken by the enterpreneur in the form of profits, interest and rents, forming in this way the capitalist's surplus value. The presence of interest rate and an initial outlay of capital then give rise to a continuous accumulation of capital. In fact, the capitalist earmarks his income for this accumulation. As capital accumulates, the rate of profit either falls or becomes constant. The rate of interest rises and consequently investment falls. In order to maintain the levels of his profits, the capitalist lowers real wages or causes unemployment.

Therefore, to facilitate the accumulation of capital in the hands of a few at the expense of lowering wages and unemployment, exploitation of the labour force sets in. The principle of equality and cooperation is, therefore, disturbed by the presence of interest in the accumulation of capital.

'Riba' in Islam does not mean interest on loan capital only. Any raising of individual or state claim of ownership beyond what Islam considers lawful is therefore, to be considered as a limit to the ownership of the means of production. This is however, not tantamount to a socialist economic doctrine on the exploitative nature of interest. The abolition of interest in Islam is considered important so as to provide a check on the exercise of the right of private proprietorship, and thereby, to end the oppression and exploitation of the labour force, while a free enterprise cooperative system is maintained.

2. Analytic implications of the principle of work and productivity

In the framework of a pure exchange economy, it can be shown that the marginal conditions for the existence of Pareto optimality (the first order conditions of efficiency in a perfectly competitive market in modern economic analysis) in the Islamic exchange system depends not only on the ratio of the marginal utilities of product and wages for the two individuals, but also on the ratio of the marginal utilities of the two individuals, owner and labour, with respect to the level of produce and wages. The significance of this result lies in the fact that under the principle of equality and cooperation and the institutions which translate this principle into practice, marginal utility of the owner depends not only on his returns from rents, but also on the wages which he has to give to the labourer equitably. Likewise, the marginal utility of the labourer depends not only on the amount of wages he receives but also on the amount of rents, which he must justly give to the employer.[11] Clearly, with respect to the ordinary exchange situation, the presence of product and wage variables in the utility functions of the two individuals introduces a distortion in the ordinarily known economic system. Therefore, with respect to the ordinary solution for the first order conditions of Pareto optimality the Islamic solution to the exchange problem given above leads to what is known as a Second Best Solution, but only with regards to the ordinarily known concept[12]. An economic Second Best solution is indeed a more realistic state of the market economy.

Once the allocational principle with regards to land rent and profit sharing has been established, Islam then allows profits on the produce of the land. Therefore, the value of the product sold in the market is determined by wages, rents and profits. Mark here the Smithian concept of the 'natural price' of a commodity.

3. Analytic implications of the principle of distributional equity

The analytical relations developed by the author elsewhere[13] on the relationship of Zakah to per capita income and Zakah to labour force activity can be succinctly summarized here to show the role of Zakah in economic activity. Zakah is found to be associated with an income multiplier effect. This can be explained via the relationships between Zakah rate and earnings through changes in the investment level. Since Zakah is imposed on idle assets only, which can be put to productive use, so economic rationality will call for a depletion of all idle stocks to make room for investment flows. Increased investment will, thereby, cause increasing income through the multiplier effect, calculated at the end of the Zakah fiscal year. Therefore, if the Zakah rate increases it will cause holders of idle capital to put them into productive use. Investment flow will cause income to rise through the multiplier effect. Hence, the multiplier is a positive function of the Zakah rate. Since the Zakah rate and the income multiplier are positively related, therefore, an increase in the Zakah rate brings about increased income through increased investment flow, which, in turn, creates higher labour force participation rate.

The principle of distributional equity implies that there is serious responsibility on the state to efficiently distribute national output among the people and institutions. This further implies that there is allowance for a good degree of government intervention in the Islamic economy. Unregulated freedom of free enterprise and the earning of exorbitant profits may at times prove injurious to society. Some may earn inordinate wealth out of profits and the availability of labour and capital in production, while others would not be able to have such easy access to these factors. But on the other hand, God has allowed equal right of usage of these factors to all. In such circumstances the strictly public common pool like the Bait al-Mal (public treasury in an Islamic state) serves to control and distribute wealth and national output according to the principle given above. Therefore, besides the obligatory tax i.e. Zakah, the individual has also to spend in the path of God for the propagation of truth. Finally, if he still has private property, this cannot be concentrated in a single hand after his death. Children and near relatives, or failing these, distant relatives, whether male or female, are lawful heirs and their shares are given by fixed percentages as stated in the Quran. Islam also recommends him to make a will for welfare projects which normally shall not exceed one-third of his property.

Policy basis of the Islamic economic principles

Let us now address ourselves to the second test of the viability of the three fundamental principles of Islamic economics, namely, how can they be translated into practical application. The practical application of the three major principles of Islamic economics to the mundane affairs of society is put into effect by four key instruments of policy on which other policy instruments can be built. They are, (1) the abolition of 'Riba', meaning interest on capital; (2) the institution of 'Mudarabah', meaning profit-loss-sharing system in Islamic economic ventures; (3) the abolition of 'Israf', meaning wasteful consumption; and (4) the institution of 'Zakah', which is an organized form of social assistance in an Islamic society financed by tax on all forms of income and wealth exceeding a certain minimum exemption level called 'Nisab.'

Let us look at these Islamic instruments of economic policy one by one.

1. Abolition of 'Riba'

Islam categorically disapproves of the existence of interest in all economic transactions. The Quranic concept of 'Riba' is not limited to loan interest. Literally, 'Riba' means excess over and above a thing, be it in money terms or in physical units of goods. When money is involved in exchange, 'Riba' refers to the form of excess that was taken by the pre-Islamic Arabs over and above the principal loaned out to another for a period of time. When commodities are exchanged by weight or measure, then there must be strict equality in such weight and measure, and immediate delivery of both goods. However, if the commodities are of different species, then equality is not insisted upon but delivery must be immediate.[14]

Modern exchange economy justifies the need for interest in order to achieve allocative efficiency as interest is assumed to cover the cost of capital in

production. By thus maintaining the recovery of capital depreciation in production, an initial outlay of capital becomes a source of a continuously
increasing stock of capital in future periods of time, and this promotes the
production process. This idea would indeed be acceptable in Islamic economics of 'Riba' if interest was in fact truly related to the actual proceeds from
production, for in this case the rate of interest would be the same as the rate
of growth of output. But in reality, the rate of interest being a pre-fixed
percentage on capital, measuring speculative and not actual cost of capital,
is an exogenous variable. It is determined outside the production system.

In the Islamic economy only the actual cost as determined by production
cost can be accounted for in compensating capital depreciation, and not the
speculative cost component. Therefore, the rate of interest is replaced by
the rate of profit, which, in turn, is determined by contractual percentage
shares in an Islamic profit-loss sharing mechanism known as Mudarabah.

2. Institution of Mudarabah

In the absence of interest in economic transactions Islamic banks would not
function as modern banks do. That is, unlike the modern banking system,
the Islamic banks would not be in a position to create as much liquidity as
they like based on a sheer notion of expected demand by creditors. This has
its logical explanation—if expectational demand for liquidity is not satisfied
when it becomes due, there will be recessionary pressures in the economy.
The economy remains below potential rate of growth, underutilization of
production capacity puts upward pressure on the cost of production. Consequently, market prices for goods and services rise. On the other hand, if
the supply of money exceeds the demand for money, there will be inflationary pressures on the economy, for now there is too much money around, but
producers decide to cut back on production capacity and investments are
subsequently not forthcoming. Incomes rise, but not due to the force of labour
productivity or technological change, but due to the supply effect of money
on prices and incomes.

In the search for monetary policies to control such recessionary or inflationary situations banks either move to an easy money supply policy or to
a tight money supply policy, respectively. The interest rate goes down and
then gets pegged in the case of easy money supply, and moves up and then
gets pegged in the case of tight money supply[15]. The interest rates, thereby,
continuously swing between the two ends over long periods of time in the
hope of creating the balance between ex-ante demand and ex-post supply of
money.

If there was no interest, the purchasing power of money would be used
up either in consumption or in investment, directly through banks operating
on the principle of profit and risk sharing in a joint enterprise in an Islamic

economy. This is the institution of Mudarabah in Islamic economics. In the presence of Mudarabah the rate of interest is replaced by a positive rate of profit[16]. A positive rate of profit arrests the problem of speculative demand for cash balances, because the ex-ante demand for money capital is reduced to an actual demand and this is based on a pure contractual sharing of profits from a joint venture in accordance with relative costs or relative capital outlays in a given production of investment.

The institution of Mudarabah, when applied to public-private sector joint ventures, is a powerful media of risk diversification. Public enterprises are found to be only marginally risk-averse in their investment behaviour, particularly, because they can easily diversify the total risk capital in the public enterprise by distributing it over a large number of investment projects.[17] Risk neutrality on the part of the public authority encourages real investment in the economy. Increased allocation of money capital into real investment reduces the amount available for consumptional expenditure but only to a certain desired level, so as to maintain an optimal allocation of capital between consumption-investment intact.

Excessive consumption is emphatically discouraged by Islam and the means to do it is the institution of Mudarabah, that automatically brings about a desired allocation of money capital between consumption-investment activity while encouraging investment into real capital.

3. Abolition of 'Isrāf'

Excessive or wasteful consumption, be it of necessaries, comforts or luxuries, and of goods or services is called 'isrāf.' The point mentioned above that the prospect for high rates of return in real investment in a Mudarabah system, increases real investment and reduces relatively consumptional expenditure, is found to control the practice of 'isrāf.'

A lower propensity to consume and a higher propensity to invest negates the basis of the neo-classical consumption theory of interest. A brief look at the Islamic investment-consumption behaviour is warranted at this point:

(i)   An Islamic society gives consumption priorities to the necessaries and comforts of life in this order. It is widely agreed upon by many Islamic scholars that the production and consumption of luxuries is prohibited in as far as this is tantamount to 'isrāf'.

(ii) Excessive production and consumption of any type of good is not recommended, for this creates wastage of factors of production and of produced goods.

(iii) Savings in the form of real investment to produce the necessaries and comforts of life and more capital goods that increase the productive capacities in the following periods of time is highly encouraged.

In an Islamic economy, therefore, the approach to the study of intertemporal allocative efficiency of modern consumer theory is replaced by the welfare analysis of income allocation predominantly into real investment. A priority area of Islamic economic theory[18] would, therefore, be Islamic welfare economics. One would first have to carefully develop the axioms of a choice theoretic approach to individual and social ordering, based on the principles of the Islamic integrated value system, particularly, as they apply to the issue of investment-consumption allocation of resources.

4. Institution of Zakah

One of the most important Quranic injunctions on Muslims is the payment of Zakah, i.e. a capital tax on accumulated wealth. Zakah is one of the five immutable pillars of Islamic faith. Literally, the word, 'Zakah' means sweetening and it is meant to purify wealth from its evil tendency to accumulate more and more in fewer and fewer hands on account of the unequal opportunities which men enjoy. Through Zakah the wealthy Muslims are made responsible individually and collectively to provide for the basic necessities of all members of the society. Islam does not object to the earning of large sums, but makes it a bounden duty of the wealthy to see that not a single soul is deprived of the basic needs of living.

A special economic significance of Zakah is that it is the avowed enemy of hoarding. A man's wealth, according to Islam, has to be spent partly on the necessaries of living and comfort, in productive investment, in charity, for the benefit of Muslims in general and in the way of God. After these whatever remains standing for a year is liable to be taxed under Zakah. Zakah revenue consists of a levy of 2.5 per cent on all idle wealth, one-tenth to one-twentieth of all agricultural produce, one-fifth of all mineral wealth, and a tax on the entire earning from capital of the nation. Zakah fund is payable to, (1) the poor, (2) the needy, (3) for the propagation of Islam, (4) for those in bondage, (5) for those in debt, (6) for the wayfarer, (7) on the functionaries who collect and distribute Zakah, as their remuneration, (8) on other noble causes for which money is required. It must, however, be clearly understood that it is only the principle behind Zakah that remains immutable in Islam, but not so the ways of collecting and distributing it on the broadest possible aspects of the eight categories of expenditure mentioned above.

Conclusion

The foreging has been a brief outline of the principles of Islamic Economics. By the terminology, 'principle', we have meant the fundamental philosophy of this system of economics. This, therefore, does not include the specific assumptions, structure and an exhaustive coverage of the instruments of policy, that would characterize the functioning of the different sectors of the Islamic economy based on the above mentioned principles.

The principles of Islamic economics would play a major role in the shaping of a new vista of development program of Muslim nations, if they are accepted as the new value system of economics. We conclude this paper by recommending that while Muslim nations are now at the threshold of a new era in joint national science and technology policies[19], that they should clearly identify their national priorities in social values and link them soundly with their economic development strategies. The harmonious blending of the two alone can put the Muslim societies on the path to a sustained, productive and meaningful growth.[20] Reddy[21] has recommended the establishment of a New International Economic Order for the fusion of the different objectives of development with the social and ethical values that found societies. In Muslim societies such values must inevitably be the Islamic values, and any form of economic development must seriously consider the potentials of Islamic economics as the basis of the New International Economic Order.

Note

This paper was presented as a popular guest lecture to students of social studies at King Abdulaziz University. The author is grateful to Dr. Z. Bashier, associate professor in the department of socio-technical studies for organizing the lecture.

References

(1) Schumpeter, J. *History of Economic Analysis*, New York, Oxford University Press, 1968.
(2) Quran. Surah 4, verse 1.
(3) Quran. Surah LV, verse 9.
(4) Quran. Surah II, verse 30–31.
(5) Sulayman, A. H. A. A. "The theory of economics of Islam", *Proceedings of the Third East Coast Regional Conference*, Muslim Students Association of the United States and Canada, April, 1968.
(6) Qayyim, Ibn-al, *Tahdhib Sunan Abu Dawud*, Vol. 5, Cairo.
(7) Qayyim, Ibn-al, op cit.
(8) Quran. Surah 59, verses 7–9.
    Quran. Surah 8, verse 41.
(9) Husaini, S. W. A. *Principles of Environmental Engineering Systems Planning in Islamic Culture: Law, Politics, Economics, Education, and Sociology of Science and Culture*, Stanford University, Report EEP—41, December, 1971.
(10) Quran. Surah 4, verse 17.
(11) The utility function of the landowner is of the form $U = U (q, w, Q)$, where, q denotes the output level, w denotes wages, Q denotes all other variables of the utility function. Note that it is now not necessary for the indifference curve between q and w to be negatively sloped. Such an instance is a peculiarity of the Islamic system and results essentially because of cooperation, which replaces

the idea of competition in a modern economy. A similar case exists with the labourer's utility function.

(12) Take the utility functions given in note (11). Let the owner's budget constraint be, $y = pq - w$, where, p denotes the price per unit of produce, so that pq denotes then the rent received by the landowner. Now, with the constants, p1' p2' we maximize the Lagrangian, $L = U1 (q, w, Q) + p1 (U2 (q, w, W) - U2^*) + p2(y - pq - w)$. The first order condition is now given by $\partial U1/\partial q + \partial U1/\partial w/(\partial U2/\partial q + \partial U2/\partial w) = (-p1)1$ on the other hand, in the ordinary exchange situation we would have,

$(\partial U1/\partial q)/(\partial U2/\partial q) = (\partial U1/\partial w)/(\partial U2/\partial w) = (-p1)0$

From the two expressions above we obtain,

$(p1)1 = (p1)0. (1 + mrs1 (q, w) / (1 + mrs2 (q, w).$

That is, $mrs1 (q, w) = b\ mrs2 (q, w) + a$.

This is a relation of the Second Best.

(13) Choudhry, M. A. "A social service model in the I-economy", *Proceedings of the seventh Annual Conference*' Association of Muslim Social Scientists, Marion College, Indiana, U.S.A., July, 1978.

(14) Muslehuddin, M. *Insurance and Islamic Law*, Lahore: Islamic Publications Limited, 1969.

(15) Bailey, M. *National Income and the Price Level*, New York, Mc Graw Hill, 1971.

(16) Choudhury, M. A. "A mathematical formulation of the principle of Mudarabah, the profit-sharing in Islam", *Proceedings of the Third Nationl Seminar*, Association of Muslim Social Scientists, Gary, Indiana, May, 1974.

(17) Choudhury, M. A. "The rate of capitalization in valuation models in an Islamic economy," paper prepared for *the Follow Up Seminar on Monetary and Fiscal Economics of Islam*, Islamabad, January 6–11. 1981.

(18) Chourdhury, M. A. *Specification of the Social Welfare Function in an Islamic Economy with Application to Cost-Benefit Analysis*, (memeo). International Centre for Research in Islamic Economics, King Abdulaziz University, Jeddah, Saudi Arabia, September, 1980.

(19) The Islamic Foundation for Science and Technology for Development (IFSTAD) is now a member body of the United Nations Program on Science, Technology and Development (see reports of IFSTAD presented at the 10th. and 11th. Islamic Conferences of Foreign Ministers, Organization of Islamic Conferences, Jeddah, Saudi Arambia).

(20) Naqvi, S. N. H. "Ethical foundations of Islamic economics," *Peshawar Journal of Development Studies*, Vol. 1, No. 1. 1978.

(21) Reddy, A. K. N. "Methodology for selection of environmentally sound and appropriate technologies," (unpublished), United Nations Environment program.

12

THESIS OF RELIGION

Normative basis of Islamic economics

Salman Ahmed Shaikh

Source: *Journal of Islamic Banking and Finance*, 28:4 (2011), 27–38.

Abstract

This paper discusses the ethical void in Capitalism which does not look prominent in welfare societies and states. But, its effects become more eminent in tough economic conditions. Unbridled pursuit of self interest, moral relativism, incentive-led economic choices and apathy to communal responsibilities would lead to a society where economic interests become the sole basis of maintaining and sustaining relationships. This inner void of identity and purpose at individual level and social void in the form of a stratified society bound together only for economic interests can be better filled with incorporating religion. Humans are much more than utility driven species, they are capable of using both instrumental and critical reasons to differentiate right from wrong and need reinforcement to adopt virtues influenced by an inner urge other than material interests as in Capitalism. This inner urge can be rekindled by looking beyond utility maximization to re-acknowledge the fundamental identity that humans are moral being than just an instrument for material advancement. Other sections of the paper provide an outline and salient features of Islamic Economics on different economic themes and perspectives for a comparative study. These provide a unique introduction to Islamic Economics in a mainstream framework.

1. Introduction: the thesis of religion

Morality is very eloquently discussed by Kant (1889/1785). He said that intentions define actions and not the consequences and not even compassion. He said that because compassion is temporary, a particular state and is not absolute. However, intentions best define the existence of morality in actions.

But, Kant did not give the method by which we could prioritize Maxims. For instance, truth and justice both are important moral values. But, what should we do if there is a conflict between the two? For illustration, if a person is known to us as murderer, but if we do not have witnesses to prove him as murderer in the court of law, should we give false testimony to convict that person?

Islam helps us to prioritize Maxims. Islam shows us that this world is not fair in all respects. A morally upright man is not necessarily the most honorable man in the world. A morally upright trader is not necessarily the richest in the world. Not all murderers have been or will be convicted in this world. Even if all murderers could have been convicted, it will not be 'naturally' possible to give equitable punishment to the murderers who have killed more than one human being.

Even if it was possible, it will not be possible to reverse the immoral actions. What happened has happened and cannot be reversed. Death is the plainest truth and if justice cannot be provided in the life of a person; then, is it not rational to believe in life after death where everyone would be given equitable rewards and punishment for one's acts and Allah by His infinite wisdom would be able to judge without any doubt the intentions behind the actions and justice will be provided to each and every one?

One can decide to do an act morally as an end in itself and not merely as means to a material end only with the knowledge of life after death and the belief in Allah. Moral act in Islam is also a means to an end i.e. to achieve eternal success and blessings of Allah. But, it is not a material end confined to this life only. In this way, the utilitarian mind is also satisfied as happiness is a relative term not achieved only by material things. The fact that moral actions even if they are not rewarded in this world will be rewarded in life hereafter satisfies the utilitarian mind.

We know what is right and what is wrong through our conscience. In matters where our conscience does not guide us, Allah intervenes and guides us through His prophets. Therefore, Prophets (peace be upon them) guide us in matters where we might not have reached the right decision about right and wrong through our conscience. For instance, interest, gambling, liquor etc. might seem useful and right; but, Allah tells us in Holy Quran that there is more harm in these things than good. (Al Baqarah: 219)

Today, we are seeing interest based system and gambling (speculative financial instruments) causing severe disorder in the economy. Similarly, the greatest asset of a human is his power to reason, his intellect, his use of wisdom and his ability to think. When we take liquor, we lose our greatest asset i.e. conscience and often do bad things which harm others also, besides us. For instance, we see people having accidents, people misbehaving with other women after taking liquor etc.

If one believes in this life only; then, that person will be more selfish to get everything in this life. If we restrict our existence confined to this world alone with no accountability in afterlife; then, I am "just" as long as I am "just" in front of the society even though there could be sins that society could have never seen me doing. Contrarily, I could be regarded as "unjust" by the society if it convicts me based on evidence which could have been untrue. Life hereafter gives all our actions the meaning by promising each and every soul the equal reward and punishment.

People can take justice in their own hands if they are allowed absolute freedom. We need institutions which can impose certain restrictions on all of us so that we can enjoy our freedom without denying freedom to others.

Islam is also such an institution which though put restrictions on one's absolute freedom (as do all other systems), but Islam not only safeguards the rights of the people, but, more importantly and fundamentally, gives meaning to the life and to our own existence.

We can use both reason and experience to believe in Allah. By way of reasoning, if we are creatures, then we are created by someone and that creator is Allah. The question that who created Allah is not valid as Allah is the creator and not the creature. Ultimate Creator needs not be created.

By way of experience, we can use empirical knowledge obtained from science to learn how the galaxies, planets, stars, rotation of the moon, rotation of the sun, rotation of the earth around sun works. How do millions of living beings sustain themselves in a universe in which even a tiny unusual interference can make life impossible on this earth? Why such a tiny interference does not happen and life continues to exist. All of this could not have been possible without accepting that this universe that is so perfect in its design was created and is being managed by Allah alone. Had there been more than one Allah, then there would not have been such 'uniformity' in the way we see universe and the way our planet earth works.

Furthermore, no meaning to life, world, man, his role and purpose can be explained without believing in Allah. Islam explains this by outlining our role that we have been created by Allah and sent in this world to be judged for our actions and will be rewarded in life hereafter if we follow the teachings of Allah i.e. to be just, kind, truthful, faithful, obedient and morally upright.

The fundamental value is freedom. Happiness results from it. Justice comes in to protect it. Humans, we see can become unjust using that freedom as speculated by Angels as well (Al Baqarah: 30). Can we provide justice and happiness in a paradigm of absolute freedom? Even when humans had little freedom in this world, we have seen them becoming unjust and then depriving the mission of providing maximum collective happiness for all.

The fundamental question is that can we provide perfect justice in this world. Can we have maximum happiness as we envision in this world. Are we or can we be absolutely free in this world?

What is of fundamental importance is the fact that this test has to be 'just'. According to Islam, everyone would be judged based on his intentions, general attitude, general behavior, and general tendencies and most importantly in matters in which one has choice clarifies that this test is just.

How can a creation like this universe, having millions of stars, reachable not within centuries even at the speed of light, all so perfectly interwoven to make life exist and that too for some time as we do not grow to be immortal by way of evolution, be explained? Not only us, none of the species can escape from natural constraints and become immortal.

Everything in this world has been created in pairs. If there is thirst, there is water. If there is moon, it needs a sun to have its light reach us. If there is man, then there is a woman. Each one alone cannot live in isolation. They are all interdependent. Similarly, this world is incomplete without a belief in life hereafter.

This world alone shows us that few people get rewards which they do not deserve, while few people do not get rewarded even when they deserve, some go through severe illness, while some live a very healthy life, while some are unjust and yet they are not given punishment, some are honest and they do not get rewarded. All these incomplete events suddenly end when we die. Then, if no one will get equitable reward and punishment, then there will be no reason why they should wait for an afterlife. They can do all the wrong things if they can avoid the law. But, even if they can, they do not always do that, they have the ability to differentiate between right and wrong inbuilt into their souls. They would like to do good acts and avoid wrong acts.

Are we our own creators? Millions of species cannot just exist in such beautiful contrast without someone responsible for it. For someone to be an ultimate creator, the Supreme Being, He has to be someone beyond the constraint of this world and nature. If the premise is that Allah created everything and nothing exists independent of His will. Then, logical conclusion would be that This Supreme Being, Allah, has to be an independent personality having no constraints of nature.

If Allah is powerful in one thing and not in another, then He is not a supreme being. If Allah is omnipotent, then, we as humans cannot predict the behavior of Allah using examples of ourselves because our frame of reference is limited and we are creatures and not ultimate creators and we have constraints.

The question arises, if Allah is omnipotent, can He be unjust. Allah knows everything, but it has nothing to do with us having a freedom to choose our way of action. A teacher sometimes knows the fate of the students, but it is the student who makes his destiny provided the teacher is just. Allah's knowledge about a person has nothing to do with the trial in question. I can, by way of my expertise, predict the result of a cricket match, but it was not me who decided the result of the cricket match in the end.

If someone is my teacher, he has the power to fail me for no reason. But, if he is just, he will do justice and will not fail me; however, it does not mean that he could not do so because of his inability, but it is because he can not contradict his own attributes and values if he was consistent (as Allah is).

Allah is just as He will only hold us accountable for our actions in which we have choice. We will not be held accountable for color, race, creed etc. Therefore, everyone has an equal chance to succeed in life hereafter.

Religion provides the answer that this universe was created by a supreme being Who created it for a purpose. Science also confirms that because it has not at all provided answers to "Why it is". In fact, science has shown that life cannot mathematically and statistically exist by chance.

We, humans have not just come in this world today and are now looking for answers. We have history behind us that tells that the Prophets came with the message of Allah and the nations which were "direct recipients" who disbelieved were punished in this world. Christians, Muslims and Jews, all believe in that history and it is our common heritage.

Shops, factories, computer programs, machines etc, are systems and they run and are operated by someone. Universe is also a system and is the most complex and a grand system. How can it just be 'the only system' that does not require a creator. All the systems mentioned above have some purpose. How can only this most grand system have no purpose?

Why there exists so much contrast in species? Why not some species just by way of chance found nothing that they could eat? Found to have body structure that is suitable in land, but they existed in sea or vice versa. The limited knowledge we have about each and every living thing and how they live and exist is just fascinating.

How could all species exist in circumstances which suit them with respect to geography, climate, body structure etc? Why then they still die and not evolve into immortality. We could not do it. None of the millions of species could do it. The extinction of species and our death signifies that someone who created us (humans) and took our lives will indeed be able to bring us to life again and that life would justify the purpose of existence and give meaning to this worldly existence.

Why none of the species became selfish enough to evolve differently so as to become a little bit superior to others etc. They would want to if they were all different kinds of animals because we as animals (if we take the evolutionists' stance) know that we are selfish to some extent, and want freedom from natural constraints.

If humans were little smarter animals, then they would have at least made some progress to get out of the natural constraints and succeed in a millions of years of history of evolution that evolutionists support.

If I am standing close to another person and if I am hit with a stick, why would only I feel the stick and not the other person? If we cannot sense each other, cannot get through our independent existence (considering we are the same types of animals), how can distinct species, one existing and one not existing, make way for each other in such a magnificent and perfect way in every detail that life becomes possible without an ultimate creator?

Can we avoid the question 'why' in any other matter of life? If we think that evolution defines a why or even if does not define it, it defines the material dispensation in this world and the human struggle and evolution in this world intellectually and physically, then we ought to believe that all the bodies of knowledge are also one way or the other biological processes.

How do we differentiate between right and wrong? It has not gone through any evolution. Speaking truth is considered (I am not saying acted upon) a right thing throughout history.

If we are not creatures, just a manifestation of nature, then, there needs to be no reason to believe anything right or anything wrong, if we will just die without any accountability in life or hereafter for our actions, then, if we can avoid the court of law, we can kill, steal, hurt etc as long as no one can hold us accountable. But, we do not think and act like that. It is because we have conscience, ability to differentiate between right and wrong. Then, we have feelings and values, and in most cases, absolute feelings and values.

It makes this belief and argument very weak that this world and universe came out just other than by way of a creator creating it. Just like everything is created by a creator as we see it and observe it, this world and universe also has to be created.

It would be normal to believe like that as it will make us consistent. But, believing that every small thing, though insignificant, needs to be created by someone, but not applying this belief to the creation of the universe is erroneous. This universe could not have come about naturally. If species could co-exist naturally and fulfill their needs naturally, why they die?

A biological process cannot describe this complex set of choices we make through our conscience to uniformly identify right from wrong.

If we restrict the scope of evolution to some aspects; then, it cannot claim to take the place of religion which is a set of comprehensive doctrine i.e. a holistic system of beliefs and practices. If evolution is restricted in just describing how, then any description of 'how' (either correct or incorrect) does not in principle contradict with the thesis of religion. One cannot avoid the question 'why' though.

Social learning theory also cannot provide the wholesome answer because social learning requires for its acceptance and relevance, a history behind some of the values which gradually need to become sacred so that the society could force them on others to believe. In the start of life, nothing could be described as such.

Birds fly in winter to avoid cold. They have built-in map and take the best route to avoid flying over sea for most time. Birds few days old and doing it for the first time in life without access to books, journals and experience can never do that as perfectly as they do neither by way of evolution nor by way of social learning. Furthermore, the process, any process, may it be evolution or a sudden big bang, or whatever, does not give any answer to 'why'.

A question arises as to why we cannot just be able to see Allah and avoid having to solve this puzzle. We cannot see Allah, because Allah has sent us here for a purpose. That purpose would be meaningless if we could see Allah through our own eyes. But, we can observe, learn within ourselves and use our intellect to search for Allah and we will find the answer, but we have to be unbiased in our search.

2. Consumer behavior theory: Islamic viewpoint

In the mainstream neo-classical economics, utility is assumed to be attained when the person himself/herself consumes the material goods which bring satisfaction, and not when he gives these goods to others. Mainstream economics allows people to have outright freedom in consuming whichever goods they like as long as they can afford them. Consumers seek maximum utility and do not have obligation to share their wealth with the poor masses apart from compulsory taxes.

This supposition has at least three problems when viewed from Islamic viewpoint.

First, with belief in Allah, a Muslim's scope of life and objective is different. His principal goal is to seek Allah's pleasure and succeed in the life hereafter. So; he is supposed to make every decision in a way to seek Allah's pleasure rather than pursuing self-pleasure and satisfaction.

Second, as per Islam, this world is a place for test and this test requires some people to be privileged and some to be deprived. The deprived and privileged are both tested for patience and thankfulness to Allah and how they take care of society and its needs. Hence, this worldview puts the focus of all human beings towards the fact that material resources they enjoy are all blessings of Allah and these are instruments for this test.

Third, as a corollary of point one, the focus of a Muslim shifts from materialism to fulfilling Allah's commands of excelling in character wholesomely. Prophet Muhammad (PBUH) said: "*Wealth is not in having vast riches, it is in contentment*".

An ideal Muslim will not indulge in lavish and conspicuous consumption due to prohibition of *Israaf* (extravagance even in lawful things), *Tabzeer* (consumption in unlawful things like liquor, free sex etc), *Hasad (jealousy)*, and having to fulfill Allah's commands and directive of *Infaq* (pay to charity), his independent and mutually exclusive choices in the wake of such controls will automatically bring about an optimal result for the society as well. Islam also creates a balance between *seclusion/self-denial* and *lavishness*. Prophet Muhammad (PBUH) taught that 'your body has rights over you'.

Diminishing Marginal Utility upon successive consumption of a commodity is a natural phenomenon and approves of the limitedness of this world and what's in it. The fundamental value is freedom. Happiness results from it. Justice comes in to protect it. Humans, as we have seen, can become

unjust using that freedom. Can we provide justice and happiness in a paradigm of absolute freedom? Even when humans had little freedom in this
world, we have seen them becoming unjust and then depriving the mission
of providing maximum collective happiness for all.

The fundamental question is that can we provide perfect justice in this
world. Can we have maximum happiness as we envision in this world. Are
we or can we be absolutely free in this world?

People can take justice in their own hands if they are allowed absolute
freedom. We need institutions which can impose certain restrictions on all
of us so that we can enjoy our freedom without denying freedom of others.

Islam is also such an institution which though put restrictions on one's
absolute freedom (as do all other systems), but Islam not only safeguards
the rights of the people, but, more importantly and fundamentally, gives
meaning to the life and to our own existence.

Moral act in Islam is also a means to an end i.e. to achieve eternal success
and blessings of Allah. But, it is not a material end confined to this life only.
In this way, the utilitarian mind is also satisfied as happiness is a relative
term not achieved only by material things. The fact that moral actions even
if they are not rewarded in this world will be rewarded in life hereafter
satisfies the utilitarian mind permanently and meaningfully.

3. Islamic perspective on factors of production & distribution

In an Islamic economy, we can classify factors of production as follows:

1 Land with natural resources.
2 Labor.
3 Physical Capital Stock.
4 Entrepreneur (Working as well as investing).

Below, we try to present details of our proposed classification.

Land with natural resources   It includes all things of value which are naturally
occurring goods such as soil, minerals, land etc and that are used in the
creation of products. The payment for the use of those resources in fixed
supply is rent. When these are sold, their compensation is profit.

Labor   Providing physical or mental exertion by way of contract for consideration in the form of wage or salary. It does not include entrepreneurial
labor as the compensation for entrepreneurial labor is the residual outcome
of the productive activity and contains an element of risk and uncertainty.

Physical Capital Stock   It includes human-made goods or produced means
of production. These are goods which are used in the production of other

goods. These include machinery, tools and buildings. The payment for the use of those resources in fixed supply is rent. When these are sold, their compensation is profit.

Physical capital stock and the factor 'land and natural resources' are differentiated on the basis of their source of existence. Physical capital stock includes human-made goods or produced means of production, whereas the factor 'land with natural resources' is not produced by humans. Both have the same compensation for their use. It is because while they are used, they do not lose their existence and hence they can be leased and traded.

One could argue that even when a production process hires a natural person providing labor, it does not consume that person and hence wage is basically the rent on human skills used. But, it is worthwhile to classify labor as a separate factor of production due to following reasons:

1) 'Physical capital stock' itself is dependent upon labor since it is man-made.

2) Termination of physical capital stock and labor from a production process could be different. When a person owning physical capital stock dies, rent will still accrue on assets in his/her ownership as long as the assets are in useful condition and as long as the contract of lease does not end. When a person providing labor dies, the factor payment ends instantly because the utility of labor or the capabilities of labor are intrinsic and are not detachable and transferable.

3) Physical capital stock is saleable and transfer of ownership is possible in them. But, in labor, transfer of ownership cannot happen. Since transfer of ownership is possible in physical stock, they can be recorded as assets.

4) Distinction has far reaching qualitative effects on behavior and management process. Expenditure on labor can only provide services or skills owned and possessed by labor which the labor willfully provides. He cannot be subjugated like physical capital stock or be traded. Only the skills are tradable and the supply of labor is much more in the hands of labor and consideration for the supply rests on factors much different from factors impacting supply of physical capital stock.

The classical economists also employed the word "capital" in reference to money. Classical economics includes money with physical human made assets/goods in Capital. Money itself has no intrinsic value and is neither a rentable asset nor a tradable commodity as per Islamic principles. If capital is combined with labor, it "*could*" produce profit, but if money alone is lent, the interest it earns is not permissible as per Islamic principles. Interest is neither a justifiable reward of money nor capital. Money holder/owner has to convert it in one of the four factors of production namely 1) land with natural resource, 2) labor, 3) physical capital stock and 4) or become an investing entrepreneur to have any justifiable compensation out of the production process.

It is necessary that we properly name this factor of production. Else, it could allow one to mix up physical assets and money in the general word 'Capital'. In classical economics literature, Capital takes different forms. A firm's assets are known as its capital, which may include fixed capital (machinery, buildings, and so on) and working capital (stocks of raw materials and part-finished products, as well as money, that are used up quickly in the production process). Financial capital includes money, bonds and shares. In classical economics, investment which increases the capital stock is also priced the same way as capital stock. Hence, classical economics considers rent on machine and interest on money as one and the same thing and the classical economics only mentions 'interest' as compensation to capital generally.

Entrepreneur It refers to an economic entity, natural person or corporation (juristic person), which undertakes the ultimate responsibility for the production process. It undertakes the responsibility to bear losses (if any) and is entitled to the entire residual positive economic outcome after rent on 'physical capital stock' and 'land with natural resource' and wages have been paid. Entrepreneur could be classified as *Working Entrepreneur* as well as *Investing Entrepreneur*. If entrepreneur is defined as an economic entity which is not entitled to a fixed compensation and that his/her compensation is based on the actual positive but residual economic outcome of the production process, then, we can introduce this classification. In Mudarabah, the Mudarib is the working entrepreneur and Rabb-ul-Maal is the investing entrepreneur. (Usmani, 2004)

By this definition and classification, we can avoid the very unnatural definition of land which also includes machines in traditional Income/Factor distribution literature in Islamic Economics. (Usmani, 2004)

By way of this classification, we are able to distinguish between assets which are natural resource and those that are human made. We are also able to distinguish between money and capital. Owner of money has to 1) buy land with natural resource and earn rent on it, or 2) need to buy physical capital stock and earn rent on it, or 3) need to become an investing entrepreneur in an Islamic economy to earn profits through enterprise. Money itself does not have any intrinsic value as per Islamic principles.

Furthermore, we are also able to include 'human capital' into the whole picture through our classification of 'working entrepreneur' and by separately including 'labor' as a distinct factor of production and qualifying 'labor' to also include 'human mental exertion'.

4. Islamic perspective on opportunity cost & time value of money

Opportunity cost is a useful concept in Economics. Some Islamic Economists argue that Islamic Economics does not recognize or give consideration to opportunity cost. Below, we try to present why this is not an appropriate approach.

4.1 Explanation of opportunity cost

If I have a job paying me $1,000 and I decide to leave it and complete my PhD. Then, the opportunity cost of going to do PhD is $1,000 of job income forgone for me. When I am considering the option of doing PhD, I must also bear in mind this opportunity cost (implicit cost) along with fees and cost of books (out of pocket costs).

Opportunity cost of an activity is the cost of best alternative forgone in its place. (Parkin, 2003). If, for example, I had another job option paying $500, then, the opportunity cost will remain to be $1,000. It is because by not doing PhD, I would have taken one of the two jobs and I will have taken the one that pays me $1,000 over the one that pays $500 if I am rational. Then, the opportunity cost of going to PhD is $1,000 of job (best alternative of the two jobs) income forgone.

Just like I cannot ask or force the university to pay me $1,000 each month for me to do PhD with the satisfaction that I have not made any 'economic loss', similarly, the owner of capital cannot ask or force the borrower to pay him/her any stipulated increase over the principal amount in a loan transaction.

4.2 Time value of money & Islamic finance

In investment for trade (which Islam allows), the investment goes through the entire process of a commercial activity that involves risk taking at each stage and any compensation on investment is strictly dependent upon the outcome of the commercial activity. The profit for the businessperson strictly depends upon the actual profit realized after taking market risk including price risk. It does not depend upon time. (Islahi, 1998)

Time value of money is the basis of interest. Time value of money is the problem for the investor to avoid keeping his/her money idle and to avoid forgoing the use of money that may bring positive value to his/her investment. However, it does not mean that the investor can demand an arbitrary increase (or is given as the case may be) as the cost of using money without taking the market and price risk.

Yes, the investor could seek ways to avoid earning an 'economic loss', but, for that, the investor cannot demand an arbitrary increase over the principal amount lent.

In a model Islamic economy, with closure of interest based Savings, Fixed/ Term deposit accounts, more money will come in stock market either directly or through mutual funds. Primary market activities will increase since companies will no longer be able to generate finance through debt. Therefore, increase in listed companies will expand the market and diversify trading opportunities for investors.

This leads us to face the problem of how to price capital in corporate finance, which we discuss briefly hereunder:

In corporate finance, Nominal GDP growth rate could be used in following valuation models:

1   It will replace R_F in Capital Asset Pricing Model.
2   It will help in calculating "Ks" and "Capitalization rate" in dividend discount model.
3   Income Bonds could be valued using Discounted Cash Flow approach. The proposed benchmark rate i.e. Nominal GDP growth rate could be used as the discount rate.
4   Free Cash Flow could be calculated using this benchmark rate.
5   In project valuation, this benchmark rate could be used to find Present Value (Indicative) of Cash Flows. This would be appropriate due to the following:

   i.   It will not lead us into falling in time value of money as we are using an enterprise or output related benchmark rather than interest based benchmark.
   ii. The Cash Flows will be themselves obtained using equity contractual modes like Mudarabah and Musharakah.
   iii. We are calculating valuation models for the investor and not for the borrower. Borrower or financee will be in no obligation to provide the returns based on these valuations. But, the investor can use this "indicative valuation results" to rank investment alternatives.
   iv. In actual distribution of income between financier and financee, profit sharing ratio would be used and applied to the gross profit earned by the financee.

Conclusion

This paper discussed the ethical void in Capitalism manifested in unbridled pursuit of self interest, moral relativism, inventive-led economic choices and apathy to communal responsibilities. This has led to a society where economic interests have become the sole basis of maintaining and sustaining relationships. Marcuse (1964) has described this phenomenon as 'One Dimensional Man' in his book. This inner void of identity and purpose at individual level and social void in the form of a stratified society bound together only for economic interests can be better filled with incorporating religion. The Islamic perspective on different important mainstream economics concepts provides the much needed addition to the literature on Islamic Economics.

References

Islami, Amin Ahsan (1998). "Taddabbur-e-Quran". Lahore: Faran Foundation

Kant's Critique of Practical Reason and Other Works on the Theory of Ethics, trans. Thomas Kingsmill Abbott, B. D., Fellow and Tutor of Trinity College, Dublin, 4th revised ed. (London: Kongmans, Green and Co., 1889).

Marcuse, Herbert (1964). One Dimensional Man. Boston: Beacon.

Parkin, Michael (2003). "Economics". USA: Pearson Education

Usmani, Muhammad Taqi (2004). "An Introduction to Islamic Finance." Karachi: Maktaba ma'ariful Quran.

Yahya, Harun (2003). "Creation of the Universe." Ankara: Harun Yahya International.

13

PHASES IN THE DEVELOPMENT OF AN ISLAMIC WORLD VIEW

Max Horten

Source: *Islamic Studies*, 11:4 (1972), 231–49. Translated by V. June Hager from *Die Philosophie des Islams*, Munich: Ernst Reinhardt, 1924.

A description of Islamic philosophy should present a "history" of world-views evolving along Arabic, Persian, Turkish, etc. lines, in this way representing the individual cultural units of the Orient. In the history of European thought, for example, one does not distinguish an intellectual unity, a common spiritual base, but rather a variety of countries and peoples; we speak of the philosophy of the Greeks, the Romans, the Italians, the Spaniards, etc. Yet the Orient is even more culturally and racially diverse than the Occident and can lay even less claim to a uniform cultural outlook. Oriental philosophy, therefore, should also be classified according to nations and races.

Until now, because of our macroscopic and superficial view, we have had to content ourselves with a collective description of the Orient, leaving deeper understanding to later times. Persia's role as the bearer of Oriental civilization somewhat compensates for the disadvantages of this treatment. Part of Persia's history is rewritten, the other countries retreat into the background, and a certain continuity is maintained in the description.

In depicting the evolution of Islamic philosophy our entire attention will be concentrated on the higher level. The development of this philosophy can be determined and observed in the midst of rapidly and colorfully changing civilizations of Oriental principalities. The rulers of former times were the exterior symbols of civilization and determined the spirit of the age; in describing the phases of Islamic philosophy, we must therefore refer to the governments of the time, and even to especially prominent princes. Here only a few lines will summarize the ancient Orient, so distant in time, yet evident and influential even today.

The oldest world-view known to us is the Sumero-Akkadian, which the "old Babylonians", Semites who emigrated from Arabia to Mesopotamia about 3000 B.C., inherited from the settled peoples of Sumer and Akkad. These were not nomads; for they conceived of their Supreme Being as sitting on a *kursī*, a chair, at the highest point in the heavens. Nomads, however, have no concept of a chair.

The most striking characteristic of the Sumero-Akkadian religion was that astronomy and theology, or religious doctrine, converged. Schools of theology and observatories were equally important. The Babylonians retained many Sumerian words in their descriptions of the gods, although they replaced others with Semitic words (i.e. *Mummu*—the all creative force), and added even more. There has been an inclination to speak of an accurate astronomy of old Babylon. However it was only much later, perhaps around 800 B.C., that a precise science of star observation developed. Moreover, there had already been a vague, popular "astronomy" before Babylon existed, in remote prehistoric times, among the peoples whose legends depict such conceptions of the heavenly processes. This prehistoric star observation suffices as a formulation of religion.

Names of gods have been preserved for us in abundance, although the system they comprise is not always clear. Teachings of various temples merge with older spirit beliefs, and to these are added notions of dynamism (i.e. the concept that stones and many inanimate objects can operate upon their environment). But it is quite evident that this religion contains an astral ingredient. We are dealing with a religion of light and revelation. In the blue sky, which may be identified as the world ocean, *Ea* reigns, the highest light, hidden in the blue depths of infinite waters which surround the earth and the lower world. From him issues *Marduk* the sun, and *Mummu* distributes the forces of both, giving life and form to everything in the universe. In light and warmth primitive man of this race experienced the mystery of religion.

The *Nabu*-concept is characteristic of this poetic and light-infatuated religion. *Nabu*, the messenger, is the sun-god in his autumn phase on September 23. He comes from the highest point in his orbit, where he was closest to *Ea*, the father-god, on June 21; from *Ea* he received revelations, which he must communicate to man during his descent from the tropic and approach to earth. (This is the explanation of the autumn phase). He is the mysterious human shape in the heavens, the model man; when later speculation speaks of the self-subsisting "human essence", the ideal man, we are instinctively reminded of *Nabu*, the prophet figure. In Islam *nabī* means prophet, derived from the root *nabā*—announce. And when Christ calls himself the Son of Man he wishes to express his mission of bringing a new revelation from God to a mankind thirsting for spiritual illumination.

The earth is surrounded by the waters of the underworld, the mighty *Tiamat*, the world dragon, who guards the realm of darkness. In this the southern part of the earth is included. The equator divides both realms. In the evening the sun descends to the world of darkness, conquers the dangers there, and reappears the next day, dispatching before it a flood of blue. The god of light behind the blue flood, the blue sky, has regained his dominion. In autumn, which has its parallel in evening, the sun sinks into the world of the dead. The planets plunge with the sun into the depths. Lucifer aspired to be God's equal. The sun in its ascent from March 21 to June 21 was striving to approach the Supreme God. Lucifer sinned through "pride" and was hurled into hell with his followers, the planets. The Yazīdī continue this myth of the seasons each succeeding year. The Logos repents his sin and penitent turns back to God, describing the orbit of the next year from December 24, the point at which the sun-god is resurrected (the birth of the new sun) to March 21 and June 21. In this way they deny the devil's existence. They "worship" the devil, i.e. they regard him as the Logos.[1]

It has often been demonstrated that the well-known Near Eastern religions such as Parsism, Mithraism, Gnosticism, Judaism, etc. originate from these Light-philosophies of the ancient Orient; and the history of religions has produced a comprehensive literature on this subject. Yet it is noteworthy that the possibilities of two entirely different lines become apparent. The true dualism conceives of light and darkness as two irreconcilable worlds. This is the foundation for the two adverse spheres in Parsism. But a different interpretation is also possible; namely that night once again becomes day, the fallen Lucifer-Logos repents (the beliefs of the Druzes are reminiscent of these ideas) and that light is always victorious. From this evolves the Light-monism peculiar to Islamic mystics, i.e. Al-Ḥallāj, who almost certainly continues the traditions of Mazdakism. This can be called Light-monism because of the doctrine that absolute evil does not exist in and of itself. Mazdak's communism is also an allusion to this, and Mazdak himself probably continued even older lines of thought. The Mandaean religion presented dualism in an extremely unusual form, while the astronomical character was emphasized by the Sabaeans in Harran in Mesopotamia, the center of the moon-religion, which extended its influence deep into Islam.

Thus when we leave the ancient Orient to study the world-view of Islam, the leap is not entirely unjustified; for the connection is clear and in this article our space is extremely limited.

In considering the world of Islam, we should be led by ideas which can reveal its essence. We have been accustomed to ask of Islam such questions as the contingencies of European cultural life seemed to demand; in the history conscious age: has Islam had an understanding of history? in the field of natural science: has Islam known an experimental physical science? in critical philosophy: has Islam used critique of the learning process? Accordingly one must also ask today: has it recognized phenomenology? Whatever happened to seem the most brightly shining star on the European intellectual horizon was regarded as the most essential.

A scientific study must seek to free itself from such relativities. Only those questions should be asked which concern the objective and essential aspects of a world system, and this system should be valued according to what it wishes to be and what it can be. The world concepts provided by Islam are intended as logical, consistent, and conceptually clear explanations of the world of sense perception, as this world appears to the Oriental. The most elevated, refined, and logical abstraction achieves this goal best, and the system is to be judged accordingly as more or less consummate. For this reason the monumental abstraction of the Buddhist world-view drew Islam into its irresistible sphere, over a thousand years ago. Here the desire for the highest abstraction is satisfied most fully. Greek and Persian ideas enter into this elevated philosophy. Only with this in mind can we correctly understand Islamic mysticism. If the ideas in Islamic mysticism are analyzed, the Greek contribution is seen to be decidedly subordinate to the Buddhist influence. Often the Persian Light-philosophy seems to compete equally with the Buddhist world-view.

A detailed study of different phases in the evolving Islamic philosophy should follow developments in the religious as well as the temporal spheres. This becomes increasingly complex. Reform movements periodically give rise to great reformers. For the Shī'a the teachings of these reformers belong to the permanent doctrine. These teachings do not lead to fresh ritual divisions; they strive to deepen and invigorate religious conscience. Theology becomes increasingly Hellenized as the possibility of assimilating Greek philosophical concepts is recognized.

For this study the developments in the temporal sphere are most important. Metaphysics embraces the most widely divergent lines of thought. Here the frame of reference changes constantly according to whether existence is differentiated from reality or identified with concrete reality. *Maya* concepts and Light-philosophy are easily adapted to these ideas. The scientific movement is familiar with experimentation and uses it zealously to determine general natural laws. The ethical movement resembles the religious movement in that it strives to increase awareness of conscience as the essence of ethics. These ideas are harmoniously assimilated into Islam, since Islamic religion and ethics place a great emphasis on conscience. (The doctrine of intention —*nīya*—is one example of this). Occasionally this basically spiritual drive is stifled by externalities; then revivalist movements appear and find fertile ground for activity in recalling Islam to its true nature. The aesthetic movement-literature and art, the emergence of rules and regulations in trade, economic development-these belong to a general study of Oriental civilization; an intellectual history, however, should not lose sight of these elements. Since 1500 much of the material wealth of the Orient, and therefore much of its political importance, have disappeared. These are all generalizations to be kept in mind when describing the evolution of Islamic philosophy.

The long series of world-views which have made their appearance in Islam reflect the outcome of clashes with constantly changing civilizations, cultures of neighboring countries and cultures of passing conquerors. These philosophies represent the levels to which Islam has risen as it received and assimilated the higher foreign cultures invading its domain. In the process Islam surrendered its graphic and culturally primitive vision and adopted the philosphical concepts typical of high civilizations.

Here the suggestion of "ascent" is not meant as a value judgement in the religious sense. In many ways the religious experience of ancient Islam is considered to have been the deepest and most powerful, although even in later times religious experiences of prophetic conviction and mysterious force have been evident, for instance in Bāb and his followers. "Ascent" is meant here only in the cultural sense; a pictorial and intuitive world view "improves" as it expresses itself in ideas and elevates these with logic and clarity to the most comprehensive abstractions. Islam has accomplished this ascent to a higher level. Since it has succeeded in this difficult task, Islam should be judged according to its own aims—that is according to the clarity of its principles expressed in the highest abstractions. These principles cannot be judged according to the subjective pre-conceptions of the critic.

Since Islam occupies a central geographic position, it has been besieged by an exceedingly large number of foreign cultures. In the process of struggling with these adversaries, Islam itself has undergone many transformations. From this perspective it is obvious that whoever describes Islam uniquely according to the Qu'rān presents this religion as it was experienced in Arabia 1300 years ago, not as it has been in the course of history, or as it is today. Contemporary Islam cannot be understood through the Qur'ān, but through contemporary interpretations of the Holy Book.

Around 700 (Umayyads 661–750), Islam, which had expressed itself in primitive Bedouin forms until that time, underwent a period of refinement, cultural enrichment, Hellenization, and Christianization. These developments took place in the centres of Egypt and Syria, where Islam, which had been considered a Judaeo-Christian sect of Arabia, strove to prove itself equal to the higher forms of Christianity. A large number of external characteristics were therefore adopted and added to the Christian ideas which had appeared in early Islam. Christian asceticism served as the example of individual, subjective piety (Ḥasan of Baṣra).

Around 800 the Arabic empire of the Umayyads had to relinquish its place in the sun to the "Persian" empire of the 'Abbāsids. The foreign ideas besieging Islam at this time were greatly encouraged. Greece, India, and Persia delivered up their treasures. A quite uninhibited assimilation of foreign elements took place, so that the liberal theologians and mystics often appear non-Muslim, as far as the substance of their ideas is concerned. Apostasies arose and the orthodoxy clung desperately to its disappearing authority.

Islam, until this time a primitive religion, entered the battle unarmed. Its adversary in the form of foreign ideas was superior. Under these conditions the extremes had to abruptly develop their positions; cultural unity seemed about to disintegrate. This period was characterized by inner contradictions and irreconcilable divisions; the task of reconstructing the unity of a culture held together by Islam was left to the future. Thus future lines of development can be predicted—fluctuations between unity and inner strife. The chasms of difference were wider and deeper in the early period, that is from about 800–1100, than at any other period of Islamic history. This was the period of the most narrow-minded biases, differences which the rivals themselves misconstrued and exaggerated. From these irreconcilable extremes the mature understanding of a later time would construct the great synthesis.

With Hārūn the development of philosophy actually begins. The previous intellectual agitations in Islam can be considered an insignificant prologue. The beginning can be easily outlined and compared to the last stage (which we will provisionally consider to be around 1900), so that general trends and tendencies are apparent.

The most distinctive characteristic of the early phase was an abrupt splintering in all directions, whereas in the end phase a wide-reaching fusion, or at least an effective rapprochment, can be observed. Thus the law of convergence is clear as the general tendency. In the first century of the 'Abbāsid reign we can identify: (1) an extremely conservative trend in theology, which clings anxiously to all the graphic depictions of religious subjects in the Qur'ān; (2) an extremely liberal trend, which can not logically be considered as remaining within the doctrinal boundaries of Islam: Naẓẓām, Thumāma; (3) a powerful Greek influence in the circle of doctors and scientists, who were soon followed by the philosophers, and who remained so far outside the narrowly defined circle of believers, that they probably smiled with a certain pity at the beliefs of the common people; (4) a mystical tendency which was so radical (Bisṭāmī), that later liberal mystics such as Junayd, Hallāj, etc. seem conservative in comparison;[2] (5) the Shī'a movement which followed the Light-cult—Hārūn even wanted to establish a holy fire temple in Mecca itself—and wished to replace the prophecy of Muḥammad with a new revelation of the Imāms (cf. Doctrine of Manifestation). The general confusion was unimaginable.

The period, therefore, was characterized by cultural disintegration. Inner tensions threatened to destroy the unity of Islam. To the following periods was left the difficult but most important task of achieving cultural unity. Even in Ghazālī's time the inner disintegration of Islam seemed inevitable. Islam's victory over this decay and division was admirable and deserves a scholarly explanation.

An equalization process began as early as about 850. Bisṭāmī "converted" from his Buddhist nihilism to a conception of an absolute and real Ground of all Being, the later ḥaqīqa-doctrine. Kindī was certainly considered heterodox, but endeavored to remain in harmony with the orthodox dogma. The government experienced the familiar conservative reaction, after it had already persecuted the conservatives with inquisition and torture. These attempts at unity are the actual core of the historical development of Islamic philosophy, and the individual trends must be observed from this perspective, to determine what is culturally essential in each.

'Soon a theological development appears, which is considered conservative by the liberals and liberal by the old conservatives—the typical manifestation of convergence. This is Ash'arī. About 900 (Sāmānids 874–999) intellectual life was in a turmoil such as it probably has never again experienced. The names Ḥallāj, Ash'arī, Māturīdī; Abū Hāshim, Juwaynī, Rāwandī; Kindī, Fārābī suggest the confusion of the period. During the reign of the 'Abbāsids Islam had undergone a "Persianization"; around 900 Mongol influences began to predominate—first of all in the composition of the army—and these increased with succeeding periods and paralleled the Persian influences. At this time the Ḥamdānids of Aleppo founded an intellectually prominent princely court.

This period is typically a time of groping attempts, of vacillating concepts, of harsh prejudices; often the new is overestimated, and what is good and essential in the old is not recognized. Therefore the *bāṭinīya* movement is significant as an attempt at reconciliation; here what is real and essential in the old is taken as the basis in order to fuse it harmoniously with the new. The period is characterized by a leaning toward mysticism. It is left to the following era to correct this imbalance and bring about more recognition of empirical reasoning. The demands of the time strongly encouraged Greek tendencies.

The theological movement had so disintegrated into conservative and liberal extremes, that a reconciliation seemed impossible. In Ash'arī a valid attempt was made; but the two schools remained sharply opposed. The trend of development however was already marked: the two extremes were doomed to defeat and the moderate faction was to be victorious; for from Ash'arī through Makkī, Bāqillānī, Ibn Fūrak, Isfarā'inī (d.1027) the line proceeded to Juwaynī and Ghazālī, to reach its climax in Rāzī (d.1210).

It soon became apparent that the present state could not continue, and future developments began to suggest themselves. First, however, Greek influences appeared on the horizon and increased the confusion, revealing the untenability of the two older theological extremes.

About 1000 (Buwayhids 932–1055) the theological storms were still raging. The orthodoxy refused to admit defeat, even though the liberals succeeded in converting several princes.

Maḥmūd of Ghaznī (998–1030) characterized the epoch. He was a fanatically orthodox follower of Avicenna. Ideas were developed and expressed in classical formulations of Aristotelian thought. Although some older scholars manifested hostility to these ideas, in general they were considered harmless. The Greek tendency reached its culmination, and proving itself properly "Islamic", assured its existence within Islam. From this time Greek ideas in ever greater numbers were accepted into Islamic theology and considered genuinely Islamic. About 900 the older liberal theology, which had been marked by Indian inclinations, had to retreat before these attacks.

The ethical-aesthetic-mystic movement also climaxes in Qushayrī (d.1074).

Because of our European and Greek biases, we are inclined to overestimate Avicenna. Yet his one-sidedness should be kept in mind. His system basically excludes the whole body of Oriental cultural values and recognizes only what is Greek. The undervaluation of the Orient sounds a strident note of discord through his work, and it is no wonder that the typical Oriental disagreed and protested. The ensuing crisis was experienced in Avicenna's school itself; from this probably derives the remark that the Master had, during the profound moments of his life, recognized the inadequacies of Greece and written his deepest conviction in his "Philosophy of Enlightenment". Nothing could give us a deeper insight into the mood of the times than this remark. It also shows us the task inherited by later periods. The spiritual depth and refinement of the Orient can not and will not be simply pushed aside. Aristotle's attitude towards metaphysics, let us say Oriental mysticism, is practically that of a materialist. Mysticism and theology now were to demand a hearing.

Around 1100 (Seljuks 1037–1194) the Nizāmīya University of Baghdad became prominent through Ghazālī. He was capable of finding a compromise between subjective mysticism, which threatened to become a perversion of Islam, and the Greek movement, which offended the orthodoxy by its many foreign elements; between the lively striving for religious intensification and the tendency towards externalization in the schools of law.

If the synthesis of Ghazālī is compared to that around 1200, one point becomes clear: it is ethical in a distinctive sense. In this respect Ghazālī resembled Socrates. Speculative questions appeared to him unresolvable, so he turned to the field of ethics. A certain scepticism is characteristic of the Muslim as well as the Greek thinker. Both concern themselves with human life and behaviour, since the doctrinal difficulties, increased by the tendencies of the time, seemed insurmountable.

With Ghazālī the former conservative and liberal movements are set aside. Their different solutions are considered unacceptable. Avicenna was responsible for this development, and Ghazālī was unable to construct an equivalent system. Thus he was confined to ethics. He strove to rescue the essence of Islamic tradition in the turmoil of the time and turned aside from the actual field of battle.

Ghazālī's solution, therefore, could not remain the final word, as it did not satisfy the need for rational treatment of the religious question. A new system had to be created for the Oriental mind, so gifted in speculative questions. Thus Ghazālī bequeathed the problems of his day to the following generation; it was for them to find the theoretical solution of which he himself had despaired.

Around 1200 (Mongol period) Islam experienced a cultural flowering, which was also evident in Spain (Almohads 1130–1269). While in the far West an attempt was made (Averroes, 1198) to commit the Greek movement to its original formulations—Aristotle's thought should not be superseded, in the East the development was quite advanced and the intellectual problem of Islam had been solved. Theology had succeeded in providing a logically satisfying answer without sacrificing anything of the essence of Islam. It had become completely Hellenized and yet highly ethical and personal, without being forced to contradict any of the words of the Prophet. The great vacillations of the former period—in Greek, mystical, liberal-theological, Christian and Indian directions—had found a middle way which reconciled "faith and knowledge, philosophy and theology".

This age also called forth the great genius of mysticism, which formulated the entire store of contemporary knowledge according to the mystical perspective and likewise reconciled "faith and knowledge" (Ibn al-'Arabī). Persian mysticism blossomed, but did not achieve maturity at this time.

After the Greek movement had produced in Avicenna an Oriental genius equal to Aristotle, it rapidly declined due to lack of diversity and also because of the philosophy of Averroes. Although Averroes represents an example of philosophical decadence, in the Latin Middle Ages he was misjudged and esteemed as an important philosopher. The peculiar attitude of the Middle Ages was responsible for this misconception. Commentaries on Aristotle were in great demand, and no thinker was expected to treat philosophical problems by dint of independent intellectual power. Averroes therefore occupied the center of the intellectual stage. The Medieval period was not acquainted with other Oriental philosophers, and Averroes was especially accessible through the Christian-Islamic border zone in Spain. An optical illusion resulted in the evaluation of philosophical contributions.

It is hoped that the significance of the period around 1200 for the intellectual development of Islam will be objectively understood in the not too distant future. The definitive conflicts between Islam and foreign influences took place at this time and in the process Islam aquired its final forms. The following case is significant: if one tries to decide whether Rāzī should be reckoned among the liberal or the conservative theologians, the impossibility of answering this question is soon recognized. He can not be included in either group. This is a clear sign that a new, third element has appeared. Neither of the two older categories can be applied to Rāzī. The era has produced a moderate movement, a school of compromise, which is the product of the former debates and which will become the crystallized rule of Islam, its *consensus*.

Rāzī and others like him do not owe their influence primarily to their creative genius; they are important because they lived in an age in which the great questions were ripe for decision and pressed for a definite solution, after vacillation had occured for several centuries.

This final crystallization of Islam is incomprehensible if the former turmoil is not kept in mind. At Rāzī's time the philosophic material had accumulated to such an extent that the old solutions of the liberal and conservative thinkers were no longer relevant. A new synthesis had to be accomplished. The analysis of this is a stimulating task; for the synthesis includes the entire wealth of former times: Greek elements (Rāzī is a disciple of Avicenna), Indian concepts of the old liberals, naive beliefs of the old conservatives, Christian and Jewish ideas which the former period had sanctioned, Persian and mystic influences which did not outrage pious Muslims. This is a prodigious synthesis which is accomplished according to the changed perspective of the times. It should be elucidated with an appreciation of its structures, and coherence, so that the fundamental problems and solutions of the time may be understood.

The years around 1300 (II-Khāns, 1295–1335) represent a period of reorganization after the first Mongol storms. Creativity blossomed in every sphere. The originality of an Ījī shows the extent to which ideas had been refined as well as the inclination to express the fruits of this refinement in concise formulas. These newly established relationships were to be wiped out by yet another invasion, then later restored to accomplish another cultural flowering.

The abundance of great works produced at this time testifies to the resiliency of the culture, which yielded very little to the confused material and political conditions of the time. The Greek movement declined rapidly because of its superficiality and materialism; it had always remained an exterior element in the practical life of Islam and a subordinate movement in its intellectual life. In addition, this movement had misunderstood the main problems of Islamic culture. Nevertheless it contributed its intellectual achievements, divested of their un-Islamic forms, to the permanent estate of Islam. Completely orthodox theologians of all the succeeding centuries including the present exhibit peculiarly Greek characteristics thanks to this Greek intellectual treasure assimilated by Islam.

Rāzī was called "the Sceptic". He had left many points undecided, and these had to be supplemented and polished in a completed system. Ṭūsī effected many improvements. The task was set for a mind which could intelligently weigh pros and cons, and such a mind was Ījī. His masterly talent for concise formulation enabled him to fulfill the mission of his age. His system is a masterpiece of the most precisely expressed ideas and became the textbook for higher schools.

Around 1400 (Timur and the Timurids 1369–1494), shortly after the storms of destruction had passed, we witness the resurgence of civilization and prompt attainment of its former cultural height. (This same tendency was apparent in the period following Genghis Khan and his descendants 1175–1307). Magnificent schools were built and the rulers put every possible means at the disposal of culture.

205

The results are masterly in form and substance. Ideas are expressed so concisely, that commentaries are necessary for a clear understanding. Whereas in Avicenna's work one feels a certain seeking and striving for what is new, the style of this period suggests confident possession and the attempt to express the richest content in the most concise form.

From the preceding period was inherited the task of arranging the great Islamic synthesis, which had been accomplished around 1200, and which the following period had refined in particular points. A tendency to include mysticism in theology is apparent. Jurjānī allocates clear definitions to mysticism. The age is threatened by satisfaction with the most recent solutions and neglect of the original sources. To offset this tendency, Fārānī feels it necessary to refer to Fārābī. Beyond the synthesis of the *mutaḥaqqiqūn*, the "true scholars", which had become Islam's permanent possession, the older period was to be preserved from oblivion. "Histories of thought" are written and all tendencies were synthesized in great surveys.

Since 1500 the history of the Near East presents a clear picture, as three lines of development emerge: Turkey, Persia, and India. These can be followed to the present time and portray the events in a certain continuity. Persia under the Ṣafawids labors within its own boundaries to restore its influence and assumes intellectual leadership. The Turks produce their own culture under the Ottomans. And in India under the Moghuls flourishes a combination of Islam, Hinduism, and Parsism, which is characterized by religious freedom. Fārānī's commentary of Fārābī (about 1496) shows how unjustified the reproach of cultural stagnation is at this time.

The Ottomans transformed Constantinople into a model of the highest culture, even in European eyes. The debates under Sulaymān the Magnificent are still renowned. Although Sulaymān demanded the strictest orthodoxy, science was pursued and open competitions were held. There was an attempt to summarize the former periods. The phenomenon of converging lines of culture again manifests itself.

Liberal and conservative tendencies are absorbed in a movement of compromise; philosophy has been included in theology; and since Ghazālī, mysticism, as ethics, has become the common property of the orthodoxy. This line of development, discernible since 1200, gains in strength as mysticism forfeits its foreign and heterodox elements; the theologians accept definitions which would have been considered heterodox by the old school. Mysticism remains synthetic, as it has always been; but in cultivated circles Islam becomes more mystical, even if this is only an ostensible mysticism; and today it is Islam which is victorious.

In Muslim India around 1600 under the Moghul emperor Akbar (1556–1605) a cultural flowering began; relationships between religions were quite modern, according to some verdicts, far surpassing modern times in tolerance. The emperor allowed complete religious freedom and attended discussions of scholars. The result was great productivity. Random samples show that independence of thought was respected and that creative and original ideas existed, even when clothed in the garb of commentaries.

In Persia the Shāh 'Abbās culture (1587–1629) occupies a position similar to that of Akbar in India; new creative works and splendid cultural activity are apparent everywhere. We outsiders simply can not comprehend the abundance of cultural achievements which have been produced between this period and our time, prejudiced as we are by the perspective of the old European schools, which did not justly understand Islamic civilization. Anything entitled "Commentary", because of this label was regarded by them as belonging to a lower order. The verdict is much different when the contents of the commentaries are fully appreciated. They exhibit a vast scope of thought and contain the whole store of past achievement, yet recognize that even the past, great as it was, was not the answer to the final questions, and that the present may and should contribute its efforts. How little blind authoritarian belief reigned in Islam is attested by the creations of this later period.

Culture attains a height which is often remembered with envy by later times, and which often shows the earlier period in a barbarian light. The ultimate achievement is the accumulation and collection of all intellectual material and the harmonizing tendencies of the time.

The period around 1700 (Nādir Shāh 1736–47) resembles the previous period of high culture around 1600; culture does not intend to live from the glory of the past, although the collective knowledge of this past in itself displays a remarkable accomplishment in its breadth and depth of thought. An astounding number of completely unknown contemporaries and older authors are cited as authorities. Any random sample suggests an amazing world, and unexpected treasures appear.

At this time we find the beginnings of a great transformation, the onset of a new period. If three main epochs of Islamic history can be defined according to the principles of exterior influences and movements of peoples, (an Arabic period to 750, a Persian period until 1200 (1258 fall of Baghdad), and a Mongol-Turkish period) so in modern times a fourth epoch must be recognized: the European. At this time European power starts to exert increasing influence on the Near East, often in the form of "invasions" by modern methods.

The greatest achievements of the period are in collecting material, although creativity is not lacking. The cultural wealth is such that in comparison the culture of Avicenna's time seems poor and meagre. The results of that early period of extremes, instability, and obscurity have become thoroughly assimilated. After a period of evolution and ferment (800–1100) followed fusion and correction (1200–1500) and the elaboration of details (1600–1900), although this last period can not be accused of lack of originality.

Since 1800 we can notice on all three fronts, Ottoman, Persian, and Indian—the emergence of reform movements which strive to imitate European civilizations, whose models are everywhere in the Orient. Egypt, which becomes independent under the Khedives, and India take the lead; conservative-leaning Turkey only feigns attempts at reform. These reforms at first concern only secular advances: engineering, business, and government. The Bābī-Bahāī religion clearly shows this. Attempts are made to modernize, yet exclude all Christian elements. The Orient feels that Christianity should be shown what true religion is, that true religion can only originate from the Orient. About 1850 the reform movement spreads to the spiritual domain. The theologians feel the need to re-examine their intellectual heritage. There is a danger that Islam may deny and abandon its own ideas. Several apostasies appear. Europeanized Muslims have laid aside their traditions, just as around 900, when typical apostates proclaimed the gravity of the age in an atmosphere of crisis. Against this, the orthodoxy raises a united voice. The struggle intensifies as the Orientals find themselves facing the western nations as political enemies. Movements of self-defence and liberation from European oppression begin in all outposts of Islam.

The demands of the time elicit a backward-looking synthesis from Bājūrī and a forward-looking synthesis from Muḥammad 'Abduh. Bāj-ūrī is inclined to retain almost all the traditional material, arranging it in a great all-inclusive framework, Muḥammad 'Abduh omits much that appears untenable, in order to make room for the imperious demands of the incoming modern age. Whatever might fetter Islam is done away with.

Since 1900 Oriental thought is marked by a deep hatred for the European intruders. The naive belief in European superiority, which characterized the first reform period, now disappears, and a conviction of self-reliance takes its place. Many flaws in the tradition are recognized, but these are not to be corrected by a passive acceptance of European cultural values, but rather by developing what is new and good from the treasures of Islam's own inheritance. Islam will not capitulate to Christianity. Only when the Oriental is respected as a human being of equal worth will understanding be possible. Contempt for foreign races does not lead to cultural progress.

Along with the refusal of what is un-Islamic, the struggle for intellectual advance characterizes modern Islam from India to Morocco. When we keep in mind the great gifts of the Oriental mind, we will not be amazed to find the East even today in a splendid renaissance of cultural activity. The University of Aligarh in India and the student circles of Jamālall-dīn Afghānī and Muḥammad 'Abduh in Egypt have been leading the movement.

Cultural satiation (since 1500) gives way to a rupture with the old and a dawning of new ideas. At the same time, much that is old proves itself relevant within the new; and the Orient can proudly observe ideas, which it has long ago preserved and refined, invading the West as "new and superior cultural values" in the form of theosophic movements. The West is apparently learning from the Orient and the Orient from the West. The way is paved for accepting a view that the empirical observation of the world does not stand in irreconcilable opposition to the speculative outlook. If the West is convinced of its superiority, the Orient displays the same conviction of its own. Clarification of these views is a task the following period will inherit from the present.

The question addressed to the future is this: will the influx of modern civilization result in the collapse of Islam?

The question is frequently answered by a thoughtless "Yes". This reply derives from a misunderstanding of the Orient and its fundamental cultural values, and perhaps from an overestimation of what is modern. For this answer the lower and intermediate levels must be ruled out. At the higher level, according to the law of converging lines of culture, the post-compromise current in theology and mysticism remain; Greek tendencies in philosophy and the liberal and conservative extremes in theology have been eliminated. In addition, following the same rule, these two directions in philosophy are now much closer together. European influences with scientific and critically-sceptical orientations are apparent as new trends. These forces operate upon Islamic tradition and thus its survival is called into question.

Yet the question as to whether Islam will endure or not must be answered in the affirmative. The basis of Islamic mysticism is the *ḥaqīqa* doctrine, the Ground of all Being as ultimate reality and ultimate truth. This idea is so broad in scope that all the achievements of experimental science can be included within it. The results of modern research do not disprove the existence of an absolute and eternal Reality beyond the reach of our understanding. The realization that mankind's religious concepts originate from primitive myths and from primitive man's naive perception of the physical universe, does not contradict the belief in an Absolute.

This observation reveals a strange fact, the answers to the ultimate questions regarding life and the world which Bisṭāmī (d.874) with his *taḍyī'*, and even before him, Indian philosophy, were able to provide, are valid today; at least they have not yet been abandoned. The oft mentioned "inferiority" of medieval and older cultures has been disproved, as far as the philosophical, or let us say metaphysical, contents are concerned. The invalidity of metaphysics is also to be refuted. We should admire former ages for their ability to construct world systems using refined abstractions.

We have come to the end of this description of Islamic philosophy. Especially in the middle and lower stratat it has presented more problems than solutions, more questions than answers; it has concentrated more on asking explanations of the future, than on summarizing the achievements of the past. The dedicated and creditable work of schools of Oriental Studies, now over one hundred years old, has not been able to reveal the secret of Oriental life and thought. Today we have progressed only enough to recognize the innumerable problems besieging us; the answers are still withheld from us. We anticipate these answers from scholars who will focus on linguistics and culture; they may be able to provide a deeper insight into the great intellectual questions which our former limited study could not penetrate.

Notes

1 World-views actively operating in the later Orient, particularly Light-philosophy, can in some cases, I believe, be traced to their tentative beginnings in ancient times (as is apparent in the preceding discussion). For literature and specific information see; Jeremias, Alfred, *Handbuch der altorientalischer Geistes Kultur*, Leipzig 1913; Winkler, Hugo, *Die babylonische Geisteskulture*, Leipzig, 1907). The question as to the age of the "scientific" astronomy of Babylon does not concern us here (for information about this see Kugler's writings), since the concepts referred to claim to be drawn from a "pre-scientific" astronomy of Babylon or even of Sumer and Akkad. The contrast between the later metaphysical and the older purely visual Naive Light-philosophy is psychologically noteworthy; this is a fascinating and convincing example of a refinement (difference) at the abstract level.

2 Different theories have been proposed concerning the genesis of mysticism, and advanced studies have increasingly revealed the complexity of the problem. Alfred v. Kremer referred to the Indian influence in 1873; in 1893 Merx pointed to Pseudo Dionysios Areopagita; Goldziher considered both Indian (compare T. Dukas' discussion. JRAS, 19–4; 125–141) and Neo-Platonic (lectures, 1910, 155F) influences; Nicholson (1903, JRAS, 303FF) discussed Greek tendencies in Dhu l-Nūn and Indian tendencies in Bistāmi. All these associations are unquestionably present; however, Gnosticism should be more emphatically stressed. Strangely enough the autochtton-Persian impact has been overlooked—proving the tendency to seek far away that which is before our very eyes. Persian mystics have the closest ties with the Shī'a; as we can percieve in their doctrine of the "pole", which, is patterned on the Imām-teaching). The essential connection with the Ḥurūfi Bektashi, and Babi-Beha'i points in the same direction. Thus the framework of the Shī'a is a circle which also encompasses these sects. The "theology of Aristotle" as well as the writings of philosophical dilettantes, may have contributed some representative themes. However these are not important in comparison to Persian ideas, attested to by Light-philosophy in the form of manifestation—doctrines. Christian ideas probably had local impact. But the foundation of the Persian mystic world-view was the manifestation-theory, to which other elements were contributed, notably: Brahmanist monism and the idea of Nirvana. The "pole" is divine in nature, in that God manifests Himself in this form as covered by a veil or a cloak. Emanation, the idea of God in all His Divinity as containing humanity in its accidental character is not intended here. Ḥallāj clearly articulates these ideas, and Wirani's verse: (Jacob; Bektuschijje, 16 A. 5) "You peer from behind a thousand disguises" shows the same manifestation—concept in the context of Light—monism, perceiving Original light as the innermost stratum of the Real, specifically manfesting itself within the world of Maya in prophetic forms—a concept of evolution entirely different from the concept of emanation.

Part 3

ISLAMIC ECONOMIC METHODOLOGY

14

ISLAMIC ECONOMIC METHODOLOGY

Mohammad Anwar

Source: *Journal of Objective Studies*, 2:1 (1990), 28–46.

The literature on Islamic economics contains comparisons of the economic views of Islam with capitalism and socialism, as well as criticism of Western economic theories and models, analyzed within the Western framework but from an Islamic perspective. Some of this literature also integrates a few Islamic economic components, mostly the prohibition of interest, into Western economic models. These studies have adequately demonstrated that Islamic economics provides better alternative than does Western economics when judged on the basis of traditional criteria, such as of equitable distribution of income, economic efficiency and stability of employment and prices. Consequently, the faith of Muslim economists in the viability of Islamic economics is gaining more strength. It has led to the introduction of some Islamic economic measures in both the private and government sectors in the Muslim world and elsewhere. The implementation of interest-free finance and the institution of zakah, however, have received the most attention.

Now there is a growing realization in the Muslim world that the process of investigation to advance the frontiers of Islamic knowledge in the social sciences is about to "take off". It is time for Islamic economists to eliminate reliance on Western methodology, revitalize Islamic methodology and devise a unanimously accepted criteria to judge the Islamicity of economic theories and to conduct economic enquiries within an Islamic framework. One way to begin this process is to Islamize modern economic theories and models. Another way is to develop economic theories independent of Western thought. These Islamic theories can be further extended to promote the growth of knowledge within an Islamic framework.

Islam is a complete code of life. Man's behaviour has to be compatible with Islamic teachings in all behavioural spheres, including religious, political, social, cultural and economic matters. Economics represents only a part of the total behaviour of man in this life. Islamization is required in all aspects of human behaviour generally studied in the social sciences. Therefore, Islamization of economics is a special case within the Islamization of the social sciences.

This paper outlines Islamic criteria for validating economic theories and models, proposes an approach for Islamizing knowledge in economics, and suggests as process whereby the discipline of Islamic economics can grow through empirical investigations and improvements in the Islamic theories and economic practices of an Islamic society.

The paper begins with an Islamic criterion for the validation of theories, economic as well as non-economic. An Islamization approach is suggested in Section II. The process of empirical investigation to facilitate the growth of knowledge within an Islamic framework is given in Section III. An overview of Western methodology for the construction and validation of economic theories in order to contrast Western methodology with Islamic methodology is given in the appendix.

I. Islamic methodology

Economics, as Lionel Robbins puts it, "is the science which studies human behaviour as a relationship between ends and scarce means which have alternative uses" (1935, 16). Economic science is essentially a tool kit for making material choices. Like other tool kits, it can be put to use in any situation. Since it refers to human behaviour, care must be exercised in adapting economic science for use in an Islamic society to make sure that the tool kit does not conflict with the fundamental behavioural postulates of Islam.

Islamic economic methodology should aim at the development of economic science, that is, it should develop economic theories that conform with Islamic economic doctrines in the discovery, exploration and utilization of the material resources of the universe. Growth in the science of Economics and other disciplines should enhance understanding of Allah's wisdom in creating the universe, and help exploit the material universe for the true betterment of humanity. Scientific discoveries, therefore, should facilitate seeking Allah's pleasure.

The Quran and the Ahadith of the Prophet Mohammad, peace be upon him, are the fundamental sources of Islamic methodology. Knowledge of the Quran and Hadith is the nucleus of Islamic methodology. The nucleus is the centre for growth around which additional knowledge can be constructed. The nucleus contains some knowledge relevant to every discipline. Knowledge in the nucleus pertaining to the economic behaviour of individuals, families, communities and society can be collected to form an "economic corpus". A "corpus" is a collection of extractions from the Quran and

214

Hadith relevant for a particular field of enquiry, including political science, sociology, law, business and economics. Derivation of corpuses from the nucleus is shown in Figure 1.

Fortunately, Waqar Hussaini, in his *Economics in the Quran*, has reported over 1400 verses on Economics out of 6226 verses in the Quran. Mohammad Akram Khan has compiled Ahadith related to economic matters in the *Economic Teachings of Prophet Mohammad (PBUH)*. Both works are essential to make the economic corpus. The corpus, in conjunction with its nucleus, contains principles, postulates, hypotheses, precepts and assumptions that are necessary for investigation, validation, advancement of Islamic economic science and Islamic Economics.

The economic corpus, along with the nucleus, should serve as a yardstick for validating economic theories and models advanced by thinkers and analysts for application in an Islamic society.

It is possible to extract political, sociological, legal and business corpuses, similar to an economic corpus, to formulate criteria for validating theories in these disciplines.

The Quran explicitly states that "in it are verses basic or fundamental; they are the foundations of the book: others are allegorical (and figurative)" (*Al-Imran, 7*). The basic and fundamental verses have established meanings that are further explained in detail in the Quran (*Hud, 1*). Therefore, the substance of the Quranic economic verses could be classified into the fundamentals and the allegorical. It is obvious, however, that all the economic statements in the Quran and Hadith need not be interpreted in their literal sense. Elements of the corpus and nucleus could very well be understood differently by different scholars. Understanding of the verses cannot be dissociated from one's personal training, innate faculties and experiences in life. Moreover, non-literal understanding of the statements in the corpus may be more beneficial than the literal one. Abdul Hamid Abu Sulayman, Director-General of the International Institute of Islamic Thought[1] agrees in the following words:

> A literal take over (adoption) of the forms and policies devised by the Prophet for his society would not only fail to work but would also fail to reflect the philosophy of Islam insofar as our society is concerned.
>
> (1968, 9)

> Accurate understanding of the philosophy involved in the Hadith is very important, because only then can the state and intellectuals properly use their imagination and creative thinking in solving the problems of contemporary society and in designing plans that would be in the context and limits of Islam.
>
> (1968, 13)

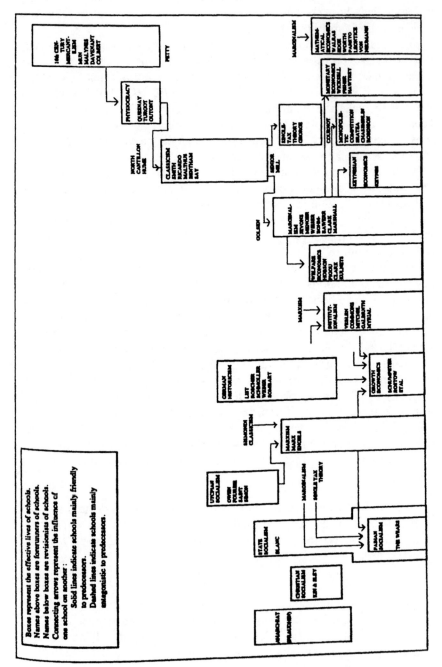

Figure 1

Mohammad Baqir al-Sadr in explaining Islamicity of different understandings of the corpus also points out in the following passage that the Quran, Hadith and Ijtihad form criteria for validating economic knowledge in Islam:

> All we shall have to do is to obtain texts of the Quranic verses and the sunan (sayings or tradition) about the sayings and practices of the Prophet, so as to gather up a number of such Islamic *ahkam* (rules of law) and conceptions by which we can reach at the end of the general economic doctrinal theories. But the understanding of the text and the discovery of the definitive content of the text requires a complicated process of Ijtihad (independent legal opinion) and not an act on plain common sense . . . since error in Ijtihad is possible because it is possible that different *mujtahids* might present different forms of Islamic economic doctrine (system) in accordance with their diverse *ijtihad.* All these forms will be considered as forms of Islamic economic doctrine because they represent exercise of the process of *ijtihad* allowed and acknowledged by Islam and patterns and norms of which it has formed. In this way as long as being a product of a legally valid *ijtihad*, they will be deemed Islamic forms irrespective of the extent of their conformity to the reality of the economic doctrine of Islam.
>
> (1983, 37–38)

In sum, the message contained in the elements of the corpus may very well be understood differently by different scholars. Even though an individual scholar is likely to stick to his own understanding during the course of his study, his understanding is likely to improve and grow through scientific research envisaged within an Islamic framework. Similar developments are needed in all walks of life, including economics, to facilitate the adoption of human behaviour espoused by Islam.

II. Islamization of economics

Mohammad Nejatullah Siddiqi (1982) has traced some of the economic writings of Islamic scholars from the early eighth century to the beginning of the nineteenth century. The study contains economic contributions of Zaid bin Ali, Abu Hanifa, Malik, Abu Yusuf and Mohammad bin Hasan al-Shaibani, in the eighth century; and of Yahya, Shafi'i, Abu Ubaid and Ahmad bin Hanbal in the ninth century. Up till 1850, Al-Mawardi, Ibn Hazm, al-Sarakhsi, al-Ghazali, Ibn Taimiyah, Ibn Khaldun, Shah Waliullah, and Jamaluddin Afghani are some of the Islamic scholars whose economic thoughts have been recorded by Siddiqi. These writings approve Schumpeter's contention that virtually all the eminent economists, at least up till 1860, were "influenced by Muslim scholars" (*Mirakhor, 1983, 5*).

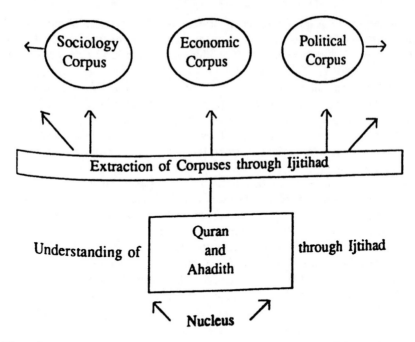

Figure 2

It is not clear, however, why the books on the history of economic thought never mention the economic contributions of Islamic scholars, although most of the basic economic problems including taxation, usury, trade, public enterprise, utility, production and prices are discussed and analyzed thoroughly in the writings of the early Islamic thinkers. Contemporary Western writers begin the history of economic thought with contributions of the Western Mercantilists, Munn and Malyanes, of the sixteenth century and go on to the physiocrats, classicists, Marxists, Keynesians and so on without any reference to Islamic thinkers before the sixteenth century or during the period covered. A chart given in Fig. 2 describes the period covered for each school of economic thought. Abbas Mirakhor (1983) has adequately demonstrated that the omission of Islamic economic contributions has left a "blind spot" in the history of economic thought.

The study of the history of knowledge clearly reveals that Western adoption of Islamic thought, in general, and of Islamic economic thought, in particular, took place until nineteenth century. Western reliance on the scientific approach of Islamic thought and its further development contributed toward great achievements in the West. But the situation in the Muslim world was the opposite. Muslims shunned Islamic traditions for developing knowledge by closing the door to ijtihad in the eleventh century. This is, at least partly, responsible for the subjugation of Muslims by non-Muslims.

Fortunately, this situation is changing now. Contemporary Muslims have recognized the loss of the traditional Islamic vitality to the West and are eager to revive their heritage and its further development in modern thought in order to re-establish the Islamic tradition of ijtihad. The process of recovery, whereby facts discovered in the West are incorporated into the framework revealed in the Quran, is called the "Islamization of knowledge".

The Islamization of knowledge involves the following steps:

(1) The corpus containing Islamically valid assumptions, institutions, percepts and postulates related to the economic behaviour of individuals and communities is extracted from the nucleus. Islamic economists are required to use their intellectual, analytical and empirical skills to develop knowledge around the economic corpus without violating the conditions in the nucleus.

(2) An Islamic economist may revive the highly sophisticated methodology of traditional Islamic scholars, such as al Shatibi or he may select promising Western economic models and theories and use them within an Islamic paradigm, i.e., he may cast them into an Islamic perspective. An autopsy or postmortem of the selected theory is necessary to know the characteristics and attributes of the assumptions, postulates and hypotheses embedded in the theory. The characteristics of the components must be compared with the elements of the economic corpus and the nucleus. The components of the selected theory may be classified into three categories: Islamic, neutral and un-Islamic. The components conforming with the principles, hypotheses and assumptions contained in the corpus are classified as Islamic. Those having universal application, irrespective of the philosophy of life and other values, are considered to be neutral vis a vis Islamic thought. The neutral components can be validated for inclusion in Islamic economic theory. Components which conflict with Islamic thought must be discarded because they are un-Islamic in character.

In essence, the selected theory can be broken into three parts: Islamic, neutral and un-Islamic. After rejecting the un-Islamic part, an economist will be left with the Islamic and neutral parts. These parts will not be good by themselves if they cannot be used to predict qualitative and quantitative changes in economic behaviour. These parts must be put together into a complete model by filling the gaps–resulting from casting aside un-Islamic elements from the model – with elements from the corpus and/or new elements derived on the basis of ijtihad. For example, if interest is discarded from a modern economic theory, a valid substitute such as a profit-share, can be plugged in as a substitute for interest to complete the model. This renovated model may be implemented in an Islamic economic system. This approach to the Islamization of economics is illustrated in Fig. 3.

In a nutshell, Islamization represents a combination of (1) a nucleus including an appropriate corpus from the Quran and Ahadith for each discipline; (2) the accommodation of functionally Islamic as well as neutral assumptions, postulates and principles from the existing non-Islamic literature;

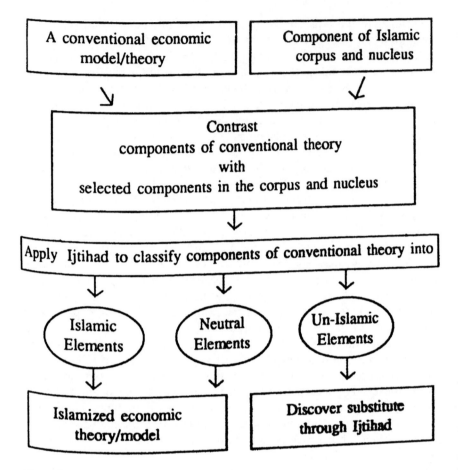

Figure 3

and (3) the addition of new thoughts consistent with the corpus developed on the basis of ijtihad.

Various aspects of the foregoing approach resemble the methodology advanced by Abdul Hamid Abu Sulayman, Mohammad Baqir al-Sadr and Isma'il al-Faruqi. For the Islamization of political science, Abdul Hamid Abu Sulayman argues:

> The two categories of current knowledge (Islamic knowledge and secular knowledge) form a tree which is unable to grow because the first category lacks the essential causes that foster growth and the second is alien to the Muslims, their lands, goals and objectives. For this reason, when one talks about reforming and reconstructing

the perspectives of Islamic knowledge and culture, one has in mind the initiation of a revival that should make them once again for production and growth.

(1985, 274)

In view of the achievements and progress made in the modern fields of knowledge, we urgently need economists, educationists, politicians, administrators, etc., who are well versed in the various affairs of social life as well. Such specialists should at the same time have first hand knowledge of the Quran and the Sunnah, which give them proper insight into the morals, values and purpose of existence as understood in Islam and validate their activities and contributions. The positive outcome of the efforts exerted by such well-equipped specialists will be development of source on which legislators can draw to meet the day-to-day requirements of the Ummah and vitalize its existence.

(1985, 273)

Mohammad Baqir al-Sadr in his celebrated work *Iqtisaduna* classifies economic studies into the "science of economics" and "economic doctrines." Knowledge pertaining to the explanation of economic laws and expressing the causes or linkages among economic events is studied in the science of economics. The study of economic doctrine focuses on the values and goals a society follows in its economic life and in the solution of its practical problems.

In his opinion, Islamic economics is an economic doctrine as it studies an economic way of life propounded by Islam. He hints at Islamization while arguing for the relevance of economic method and its application in the following words:

The need of an economic method for economic development is nothing but a need for a framework of social organisation for states to adopt, so that it is possible for economic development to be planned within this framework or the other merely by the state adopting it and adhering to it.

Thus, it is necessary that the assumed field of application, its particularities and its conditions be carefully studied so that whatever is valuable in each method by way of effectiveness in application can be observed . . . .

(1982a, xxiii–xxiv)

Isma'il al-Faruqi, the Martyr and staunch supporter of Islamization, sums up his approach in the following passage:

221

EVOLUTION OF ISLAMIC ECONOMICS

Having understood and mastered the modern disciplines as well as the Islamic legacy; having assessed their strengths and weaknesses; having established the relevance of Islam to the specific areas of inquiry of the disciplines; having identified and grasped the problems facing the ummah in its march in history as the *Khulafa* of Allah on earth; and having understood the larger problems of humankind from the standpoint of Islam which enjoins upon the Muslims to the *shuhada' ala al nas* in human history, the stage is now set for the Islamic mind to make its creative leap.

A creative synthesis must be struck between the Islamic legacy and the modern disciplines which would bridge over the gap of centuries of non-development. The legacy of Islamic learning must become continuous with the modern achievements and start to move the frontiers of knowledge to more distant horizons than the modern disciplines have envisaged. The creative synthesis must maintain the relevance to the ummah's reality by addressing itself to the problems it has already identified and analyzed.

(1982, 44–45)

Partial approach to Islamization

Articles and books published on Islamic economics take a Western model, modify one or two components of it, and label the modified model as 'Islamic'. It is not realistic to call these models Islamic. Islamicity of such models is questionable. These modified models are deceptive because most of the un-Islamic assumptions, norms, and hypotheses on which the original models were based are retained although partial adjustment is made by allowing some Islamic component(s) in those models.

Islamization, according to this paper, requires models that (1) connect Islamic norms with modern sciences, and (2) are free from all un-Islamic elements whether they be assumptions, hypotheses, postulates and/or theorems.

Building an Islamic model is akin to making a wide road through a thick forest. The modification efforts are commendable since:

(1) These are pioneer efforts toward building Islamic economic theories by breaking conventional theories into their component parts, eliminating some undesirable elements, like cutting unwanted trees and bushes from the forest, and opening more opportunities for further development. These initial efforts are also helpful in identifying remaining un-Islamic components because drilling first hole is necessary to peek into the gamut of un-Islamic structure, identify and classify components into Islamic and un-Islamic elements, and replace undesirable components with their appropriate counterparts. These efforts can certainly lead to gradual transformation of conventional theories into Islamic theories.

Alternatively, it is possible to scrutinize all components of a modern theory and reconstruct a new complete Islamic model. But this would be very complex and tedious task. This approach would be easier to adopt if ulema, policy makers, and economists jointly develop economic theories of immediate interest. Islamic universities should also train a new creed of economists that are well versed in *shariah*, and modern tools of economic analysis. The new breed can be relied to develop Islamic economic theories independently.

III. Growth of knowledge through empirical research

The standards for determining the Islamicity of an economic theory and its components were outlined above. This section will explain the role of empirical research in the growth of economic knowledge in an Islamic society. This is done by juxtaposing the Islamized economic theory with the economic realities of an Islamic society to see if the reality matches the theory. If the reality conforms to the theory under consideration, through empirical and econometric research, then probably we have a sound theory worthy of retention in Islamic economic thought.

If the theory and evidence do not match, then the source of discrepancies needs to be investigated. The conflict may be attributable to the quality of the data used in testing the theory. The data could be faulty on several grounds.

The data may be faulty in the sense that the information cannot be trusted to represent reality, even though the reality apparently is Islamic. In such cases, the quality of the data must be improved before rejecting the theory. It is possible that the data represent reality but the reality itself is un-Islamic. In this situation, the reality must be improved through appropriate measures on the part of the individuals, communities, and society. The causes of un-Islamic behaviour must be identified for rectification. Therefore, neither the theory nor evidence is at fault. In case the data is reliable, then the actual behaviour of economic agents may be un-Islamic in reality. This will require appropriate steps on the part of the communities and the Islamic state to look into the causes of the un-Islamic behaviour and adopt appropriate measures to help the economic agents improve their behaviour.

It could very well be true that the theory is Islamic, the data is of good quality but the theory is not appropriate for the situation under consideration. It would be like using an ordinary screwdriver when a phillips screwdriver is needed to do the job. In such cases, the theory needs modification for proper utilization. The theory may be revised by additions, deletions and substitutions of postulates, hypotheses and assumptions, explicit and implicit. This revised version of the theory may turn out better than the previous theory. But if the revised version is still unsatisfactory then the above process must continue until a satisfactory economic theory is obtained. The accepted theory will probably remain relevant for sometime. The theory will undergo further modifications as the realities change over time.

Knowledge in Islamic economics must increase continuously through improvement in the existing theories, economic life of people, realities and evidence. In this way, efforts to construct better theories will aid in moving closer and closer toward an economic system cherished by Islam.

Summing up, the aim of the empirical research is to identify deviations from Islamic norms in theory, practice and data. In the Western empirical economic approach, empirical analysis is aimed at acceptance or rejection of the theories with some assumed level of confidence. It is expected that a theory should represent the reality. If a theory fails to represent reality, then the theory is subject to rejection. Suggestions for improvement of reality are not part of empirical research because these investigations are not concerned with societal norms. In Islamic economics, however, both the theory and empirical evidence are subject to rejection and modification if they fail to conform with Islamic norms derived from the corpus and the nucleus.

The job of Islamic economists is to study the material dimensions for the benefit of economic agents in line with the Islamic norms spelled out in the Quran and Hadith. They must concentrate their efforts to determine how the skills of economics, both analytical and empirical, can be brought to bear on the strategic problems facing individuals, families, businesses, industries, agriculture and other sectors in an Islamic economy. Contributions to economic progress can be made by identifying weaknesses and improving upon them. The skills of Islamic economists are needed to harmonize economic theories, evidence and the actual behaviour of economic agents by casting them according to the economic principles of Islam.

Warning

As Caldwell noted, Feyerabend found in his enquiry to the question "what is so good about science?" that "scientists are as prejudiced, their opinions are as untrustworthy as anyone else's; but they are far more dangerous, because they are viewed as rational and objective" (1982, 85). Good methodology demands good people. It is people, not intellectual devices, that are good or bad. The essential methodological question is what does it take to convince oneself or others of the validity of an idea. It is no secret that people have used regressions, computers, experiments, and other methods to deceive. Although Muslim scholars are craving for revival of ijtihad, it must be remembered that it was misuse of ijtihad by people that necessitated the curtailing of ijtihad.

Appendix

A note on Western methodology

This section reflects upon two questions: What is meant by methodology in the West, and how are economic theories validated in the West? A sample of several connotations of the term methodology will reveal that methodology has different meanings for different scholars, and that there is no single definition of methodology in the West.

The criteria for validating economic theories are associated with the meanings people attach to the term methodology. Several trends and tendencies, however, have gained popularity among philosophers and economists for validating and accepting theories. These tendencies are outlined under the subsection "methodological positions" below. The aim of this appendix is to portray the contrasts between Western and Islamic methodology as it relates to growth in economic and non-economic knowledge. It will also make it clear that West has gradually acknowledged incorporation of ideological positions in scientific knowledge.

Meanings of methodology

The Library of Congress catalogues "methodology" under the category of "Philosophy, Psychology, and Religion" in its classification system because methodology has been a part and parcel of these subjects. Methodology was closely associated with epistemology and logic. But, during the course of its history, the term methodology has been put to various uses by different professions.

Accountants and statisticians employ the term methodology to express the procedures for collecting, organizing and analyzing numerical data. Social scientists use methodology to express definitions, scope, problems, methods of research, weighting and estimating procedures, standard errors and sampling techniques in methodology. Economists frequently describe their research methods under methodology. These shades of meaning given to methodology are very different from the meanings understood by philosophers. Methodology was coined to represent the philosophy of knowledge. Economic methodology, therefore, would mean the philosophy of developing economic knowledge.

Some Western scholars have raised objections to some of the uses of methodology. For example, Fritz Machlup says that the use of the term "methodology" is "a case of language pollution . . . of an irreparable sort" (1978, 6). He surveyed the meanings of methodology implied in the writings of Kant, Windelband, Royce, Croce, Max Weber, Montague, Bridgman, Whitehead, Morris Cohen, Reichenbach, Felix Kaufmann, Schutz, Carnap, Margenau, Popper, Feigl, Braithwaite, Ernest Nagel and Hempel. After a thorough analysis of the term of the use of the methodology, he settles on the following definition: methodology is the "study of the principles that guide students of any field of knowledge, and especially of any branch of higher learning (science) in deciding whether to accept or reject certain propositions as a part of the body of ordered knowledge in general or of their own discipline (science)" (1978, 54). Acceptance of this definition clearly indicates that economic methodology is a special case of general methodology.

Some scholars define methodology by indicating what methodology can do. According to Mark Blaug, "What methodology can do is to provide criteria for the acceptance and rejection of research programmes . . . what events, if they materialize, would lead us to reject that programme?" (1980, 264). Methodology represents a process of validating economic and non-economic theories. Therefore, the goal is to explain how to gain economic knowledge before the knowledge is in place, in order to make sense out of economic experiences. Some of the tasks expected of economists would include examination of the nature of axioms, theorems, postulates, and hypotheses, and the roles of historical records, fertile intuition, speculative interpretation, logical deduction, inductive generalizations, heuristic fiction, observation and experimentation, introspection, intervening variables and other non-observables.

Western methodological positions

It is very important to classify propositions and statements contained in a theory into scientific and non-scientific categories for only scientific propositions are validated by Western scholars. But what is scientific to some may not qualify as scientific to others. Each school of thought has its own vision of "scientificity". For example, Neoclassical economists believe that society is a result of interactions among selfish individuals, and so the use of statistics for validating theories is scientific. For Marxists the use of statistics is scientific but society is viewed as a reflection of class struggle. For Austrians, although society is considered to be the outcome of interactions among selfish individuals, theories are to be judged on the basis of moral rules rather than statistics because the use of statistics for validating theories, for Austrians, is unscientific. It is demonstrated in the previous sections that the best yardstick for validating theories, economic and non-economic, lies in the Qur'an, hadith and ijtihad.

Ernest Mach, Bertrand Russel, Alfred North Whitehead, and Ludwig Wittgenstein were among the influential methodologists in the Vienna Circle. They adhered to the philosophy of logical positivism. According to this philosophy, statements contained in a theory must be meaningful to acquire the status of science. Meaningfulness is accorded if the statements are either analytical or synthetic, i.e., verifiable by evidence. But verifiability requires testability which, in turn, means that the statements must be observable. Therefore, metaphysical statements are unscientific because they are unobservable. The same is true for several theoretical terms frequently used by scientists such as vacuum, magnetic fields, atoms and so on. This criteria also excluded general laws such as "all ravens are black" because the sight of one non-black raven would falsify the law.

Operationalists, like Percy Bridgman, assertively propose an operational approach according to which concepts are synonymous with the corresponding set of operations. The concepts may be defined only within the range of actual experiments. Concepts outside the range of actual experimentation are undefined and meaningless (Caldwell, 1982, 15). Instrumentalists claim that theories are only instruments. Theories are neither true nor false. The only criteria for accepting a theory should be its adequacy for given situations.

Acceptance of logical positivist criteria led to the annihilation of natural sciences as well as of all metaphysical statements. This led Karl Popper to reject the varifiability criteria and propose falsifiability as the "criterion of demarcation for distinguishing scientific from non-scientific statements" (1959, 40–42).

A. J. Ayer rejected both the verifiability and the falsifiability criteria in favour of his "weak verifiability" criterion according to which a statement is accorded empirical import if some experimental propositions could be deduced from it in conjunction with other premises that could not be deduced from those premises without these statements.

But the weak verifiability criterion could not be accepted because, as Hemple demonstrated, under this criterion any statement could assume significance and be counted scientific (see Caldwell, 1982, 21).

226

Carnap proposed two approaches to the testability problem: translatability and confirmability. The translatability criterion required that statements be translated into an empiricist language to rule out the formation of meaningless statements. Realizing that translatability was an impossible task. Carnap suggested "confirmability." According to the confirmability criterion, theories should be tested by a continuous series of experiments. If the number of positive instances increase, without a single negative instance, then confidence in the theory will grow step by step and the theories and laws will be gradually confirmed.

Another solution to accommodate non-observable terms excluded by the logical positivists was offered by logical empiricists like Hempel and Oppenheim. They favoured a "hypothetico-deductive" structure of theories. According to this approach, theories are composed of two types of statements: axioms and theorems. Axioms are primitive statements while theorems are derivative statements. Theorems can be put into observable language because they describe observable phenomena and propositions that are to be tested against reality for evaluating the theory. Axioms may be either observable or theoretical. Theories must be judged as entire systems and not by individual statements in the theories. Therefore, statements referring to non-observable entities were admitted because the direct test of each assertion in the theory became unnecessary for accepting a theory as meaningful and scientific.

In 1948, Hemple and Oppenheim also offered the "deductive-nomological" explanation for theories. They argued that every explanation consists of two parts: a sentence describing the phenomena to be explained, explanandum, and the class of those sentences which are adduced to account for the phenomena, explanan. The explanans may be classified into a list of antecedent conditions and general laws. It is asserted that "any legitimate scientific explanation must be expressible in the form of a deductive argument in which explanandum is a logical consequence of explanations. This explanation permitted universal laws, but laws of a statistical nature were admitted only if a certain likelihood of the occurrence of the event described by the explanadum can be maintained. Hence, Hempel proposed a new "inductive-probabilistic covering law model" in which explanations, comprised of sentences describing the requisite initial conditions along with statistical laws, confer upon the explanandum an inductive probability.

Logical empiricism has enjoyed a lot of respect until very recently. Its downfall began as late as 1960. Karl Popper, explaining his falsifiability criteria, argues that science advances by bold conjectures and solutions to troubling problems. Good theories make risky predictions and legitimate tests are serious attempts at falsification. A theory cannot be verified, it can only be falsified by critical refutations. Theories that survive repeated attempts at refutation are considered corroborated.

A new breed of methodologists, including Thomas Kuhn, Imre Lakatos, and Paul Feyerabend, is focusing on the dynamics of change within individual disciplines, instead of on the elaboration of models and procedural rules for understanding "how knowledge grows over time"?

Paul Feyerabend advanced "dadaist" theory of knowledge, according to which new theories emerge out of the old theories. The emerging theories use existing terms in a different sense than was accepted in the old theories. He asserts that new theories do not have to be consistent with old theories. If a new theory is to be selected on the basis of consistency then it is eliminated not because it is in disagreement with facts but because it is in disagreement with another theory (1970, 202–210).

Imre Lakatos argues that theories are the part of a larger and dynamic system within which they undergo modifications by adding, revising and deleting hypotheses. New theories emerge as a result of this constant revision. There exist a series of theories, not a single theory. For example, auxiliary clauses may be added to a previous theory to accommodate some anomaly resulting in a new theory.

Kuhn defines two concepts: normal science and paradigm. A paradigm consists of accepted laws, theories, instruments and applications. Normal science refers to research based upon past scientific achievements acknowledged as the foundation for further practice by a particular scientific community. Normal science research takes place within the framework provided by a paradigm. Both paradigm and normal science are considered prerequisites for any field to be scientific. Normal science is a puzzle-solving activity that leads to articulation and extension of the assumed paradigmatic structure. In this process, practitioners of normal science recognize anomalies or crises which inspire new discoveries and extraordinary research that are likely to lead to scientific revolution and eventual change in the paradigm. Therefore, scientists never reject an existing paradigm without a replacement. For Kuhn, persuasions and values like "accuracy, scope, simplicity, fruitfulness and the like" (1970, 261–262) are vitally important hallmarks for the scientific community to make theory choices.

Austrians, like Von Mises, claim that economic science is praxeological. The science of human action, including economics, can be verbally deduced from the axioms of the human conditions. These axioms are the basic postulates of the discipline. These are necessary and unquestionable truths about the human condition. For instance, it is maintained, a primary postulate of praxeology is that all human action is purposeful, hence, rational. The rationality axiom cannot be tested. Empirical tests of hypotheses are irrelevant and unscientific. False conclusions can result only from mistakes in verbal logic from a priori true premises. Theories are either true or false depending on their compatibility with the basic postulates. The Austrian position is opposite to that of non-Austrians. To validate theories the latter rely on empirical criteria like predictive accuracy and explanatory power, structural criteria like elegance, agreement with existing theories, and consistency; and others like generality, fruitfulness, and realism. Theories, however, are never judged on the basis of truth. As Donald McCloskey explains: "If we decide that the quantity theory of money or the marginal productivity theory of distribution is persuasive, interesting, useful, reasonable, appealing, and acceptable, we do not also need to know that it is true" (1985, 47) The marginal productivity theory is accepted because it is based on Western rationality. The quantity theory of money is accepted because of its simplicity for macroeconomic framework.

In a nutshell, Western criteria for verifying theories is that the theories be scientific. But scholars do not agree on what is scientific and what is not scientific. There are several schools of thought. A school will accept propositions and a theory as scientific only if the propositions reflect the scientificity conditions specified by the school. It is evident from the foregoing discussion that scholars validate theories on the basis of some of the conditions given below: (1) varifiability, (2) confirmability, (3) falisifiability, (4) operationatity, (5) empirical testability, (6) predictability, (7) adequacy, (8) correlations among phenomena, (9) deductiveness, (10) explanation, (11) replacement, (12) praxeology, (13) rationality, (14) expectationality, (15) logical consistency, (16) realism, (17) generality, and (18) fruitfulness.

Note

1 Presently Rector International Islamic University, Salangor, Malaysia.

References

Abu-Sulayman, Abdul-Hamid, 1968. "The Theory of the Economics of Islam" in *Contemporary Aspects of Economic Thinking in Islam*. Indianapolis: American Trust Publications.
——, 1985, "Islamization of Knowledge with Special Reference to Political Science" in *The American Journal of Islamic Social Sciences*, Vol. 2 Number 2.
Ali A. Yusuf, 1983. *The Holy Qur'an: Test, Translation and Commentary*. Brentwood: Amana Corp.
Blang, Mark, 1980. *The Methodology of Economics; or, How Economists Explain*. Cambridge: Cambridge University Press.
Caldwell, Bruce, 1982. *Beyond Positivism: Economic Methodology in the Twentieth Century*. London: George Allen & Unwin.
al-Faruqi, Isma'il, 1982. *Islamization of Knowledge*. Washington: International Institute of Islamic Thought.
Feyerabend, Paul, 1970. "Consolations for the Specialist", in *Criticism and Growth of Knowledge, edited* by I. Lakatos and A. Musgrave. Cambridge: Cambridge University Press.
Hussaini, S. Waqar Ahmed, *Economics in the Qur'an*. Mimeo.
Khan, Mohammad Akram. *Economics' Teachings of Prophet Mohammad (PBUH)*. Lahore: Islamic Research Academy. Forthcoming.
Kuhn, Thomas, 1970. "Reflections on my Critics," in *Criticism and Growth of Knowledge*, edited by I. Lakatos and A. Musgrave, Cambridge: Cambridge University Press.
McClowsky, Donald N. 1985. *The Rhetoric of Economics*. Wisconsin: University of Wisconsin Press.
Mirakhor, Abbas, 1983. "Muslim Scholars and the History of Economics: A Need for Consideration" Preliminary Draft.
Oser, Jacob, 1975. *The Evolution of Economic Thought*. New York: Harcourt, Brace & World. Inc. second edition.
Popper, Karl, 1959. *The Logic of Scientific Discovery*. New York: Harper & Row.
Robbins, Lionel, 1935. *An Essay on the Nature and Significance of Economic Science*, London: Macmillan.
as-Sadr, Mohammad Baqir, 1982a. *Iqtisaduna: Our Economics. Vol. 1*. Part 1. Teheran: World Organisation for Islamic Services.
——, 1982b. *Iqtisaduna: Our Economics*. Vol. 1, Part 2. Teheran: World Organisation for Islamic Services.
——, 1983. *Iqtisaduna: Our Economics*. Vol. 2, part 1. Teheran: World Organization for Islamic Services.
Siddiqi, M. N., 1982. *Recent Works on History of Economic Thought in Islam: A Survey*. Jeddah: International Centre for Research in Islamic Economics.

15

METHODOLOGY OF ISLAMIC ECONOMICS

Muhammad Akram Khan

Source: *Journal of Islamic Economics*, 1:1 (1987), 17–33.

1 Introduction

The main objective of the present paper is to discuss in broad and general terms methodology of Islamic Economics and to show its major differences with the methodology of economics. It would also discuss some of the methodological issues relating to Islamic economics. This paper does not intend, however, to discuss or appraise methodology of economics. A vast literature exists on this subject[1] and its restatement at this place would not add much to the pool of knowledge. In this section we intend to take up two questions: first, why do we discuss methodology of a subject especially that of economics? Second, why do we need a methodology for Islamic economics?

1.1 Why methodology at all?

Methodology of a subject investigates into the concepts, theories and basic principles of reasoning of a subject[2]. There is a wide difference of opinion on the methodology of economics. From the classical emphasis on verification of assumptions to the neoclassical falsification of predictions, the debate on methodology touches such issues as positive vs. normative, inductive vs. deductive, incorporation vs. exclusion of values, prescription vs. description, apriorism vs. empriricism, to name only some main cross-currents. Economists have taken positions on these issues and often heated debates have ensued as a result. The question arises: why a discussion of the methodology at all? The answer is that the economists are keen to reach the truth and each methodological approach claims to reach it in a surer manner as compared to the others[3]. Looking from this angle the debate on methodology is an inborn human demand. Man has been keen to reach the truth in all ages. The Quran also invites people on the plea that it is a book of sure knowledge.[4] Thus it appeals the human instinct to reach the truth. The Qur'an argues that one should discard the 'doubtful' against the 'the sure'.[5] The debate on methodology in economics (and other sciences as well) shows that there is hardly a disagreement on this basic fact. The entire debate is intended to establish clear and consistent rules to sift the true from the false.**

1.2 Need for methodology of Islamic economics

Despite the differences in various strands of methodological debate in economics there is a broad agreement on at least three points:[6]

(i) The basic assumption is that man is selfish by nature and he behaves rationally.
(ii) Material progress is a supreme goal.
(iii) Every person has an inherent tendency to maximise his material welfare and he also has the knowledge and ability for deciding what is good for him.

The Islamic view-point is quite different on these points. Firstly, it is not true that man is selfish by nature. There is an overwhelming evidence that in all civilised societies men have been motivated by altruistic motives. Altruism is a fact of life. Islam encourages people to adopt altruism and to make sacrifies for others.[7] The Quran has praised Muslims because they prefer others over themselves although they are in difficulty.[8] Caring for others is a paramount value of Islamic society. Muslim societies have a history of *waqf* institutions devoted to philanthropic activities.[9] Even in this age when the religious hold has gone weak, people in Muslim societies display a spirit of altruism. In non-Muslim societies also philanthropy is a fact of life. Only in America *22000* organisations are engaged in philanthropic activities.[10] In sum, the assumption of selfish nature of man is not supported by evidence in real life.

Secondly, the material progress is not a supreme objective in an Islamic society.[11] It is a desirable goal but is subservient to the *falah* in the *'Akhira*, should there be a conflict. The prophet (S.A.W.) led a simple life and his companions also adopted an arduous life-style. The Qur'an talks of worldly pleasures as a plaything and a fleeting joy. It seems that the primary emphasis is on the well-being of man in the *'Akhira*. It does not mean that Islam teaches monasticism or fatalism.[12] Far from it. It enjoins upon its followers a balanced attitude. Material prosperity is desirable so far it helps one to perform his duties towards God, society, family and one's own self.[13] It should be a means to achieve *falah* in the *'Akhira*. Adopting material progress as a supreme objective of life is thus alien to the Islamic framework. Thirdly,

Islam considers man incapable of knowing what is best for him.[14] Only God has perfect knowledge. The human knowledge is imperfect and man needs guidance for making various decisions in life. God in His ultimate mercy has revealed guidance for man through prophets and books. Man needs this guidance.

Thus on these basic assumptions Islamic economics has a different position. This provides, in part, need and justification for a separate methodology of Islamic economics. There is another difficulty with economics. It does not accept any source of knowledge other than the human knowledge, derived through mental hypothetico-deductive process. Thus it has closed upon itself the doors of sure knowledge available from divine sources. This has not only increased the confusion in economic thinking but has always left the question of criteria for truth unsettled. As a result there is hardly anything in economics which is universally accepted as valid and true. It seems that the entire knowledge of economics has been developed for its own sake and not for the sake of humanity.[15] The complete denial of any divine knowledge has left economics without any universally accepted framework. Almost everything is questionable, including the boundary conditions.

This is not to contend that the process of criticism and rational examination of economic theories itself is questionable. It only means that economics does not have any hard core of sure knowledge which may be treated as a point of reference and criteria for judging the truth and falsity of various theories. Therefore there is a need for a methodology which not only provides basis for sure knowledge but also eliminates confusion of contradictory theories by laying down a criterion for judging the contending theories. Since mainspring of Islamic economics is divine knowledge, it cannot accept a methodology which relies only on human knowledge.

2 Methodology of Islamic economics

2.1 The hard core

The basic function of methodology is to help in reaching the truth. The hard core of Islamic economics consists of postulates of the Qur'an and the *Sunnah* of the Prophet (S.A.W.). These postulates are divine in nature. Therefore question of their truth or falsity does not arise. They are true because of their origin. The method of Islamic economics is that for each situation reference is made, first of all, to these two sources. It is only after we do not get any guidance in these sources that human reason comes in and question of methodology arises.

For example, a number of the verses in the Qur'an lay down general principles and predictions relating to economic phenomena. We cite below some of these verses. These verses need no verification or confirmation because they have been revealed by the All-knowing God. In Islamic economics they are accepted as given. These and other verses of the Qur'an and authentic *ahadith* of the Prophet (S.A.W.) form the hard core of Islamic economics:[16]

(i) 'God takes away (gain) from usury but adds (profit) to charity' (2:276)

(ii) 'And if they had followed the teachings of Torah and the Gospel, and what has been sent down to them by their Lord, they would surely have enjoyed (blessings) from the heavens above and the earth below their feet' (5:66)

(iii) 'When they had become oblivious of what they were warned, we opened wide the gates of everything to them; yet as they rejoiced at what they were given, we caught them unaware, and they were filled with despair' (6:44)

(iv) 'And you should seek His forgiveness and turn towards Him. He will bestow the best things of life on you for a time ordained, and favour those with blessings who are worthy of grace. But if you turn away, I fear the punishment of terrible Day for you' (11:3)

(v) 'O my people, beg your Lord to forgive you, and turn to Him in repentence. He will send down rain in torrent for you from the skies and give you added strength' (11:52)

(vi) 'I shall give you more if you are grateful, but if you disbelieve then surely My Punishment is very great' (14:7)

(vii) 'But he who fails to hear my warning will have his means restricted' (20:124)

All these verses state general economic principles and make certain predictions. These predictions need no verification. They are true and Islamic economics accepts them as given. The hard core of Islamic economics consists of such axioms. They define the boundary conditions of Islamic economics. At the same time they are criteria for testing theories propounded by human beings. Any theory put forward by a human being is tested on these criteria and if there is a clear and undeniable contradiction, the theory is rejected straightaway without any further examination.

The above methodology applies only to the divine texts but not to the human interpretation of these texts. The human interpretation of these texts is open to examination and criticism. There exists a well formulated methodology (*'ilm al-usul*) to derive inferences from these texts. The Islamic economist applies the same methodology for testing the inferences from, and interpretation of, the divine texts. It is pertinent to add at this point that the methodology to interpret the Qur'an and the *Sunnah* also needs re-thinking. The scholars of the Qur'an and the *Sunnah* in the early era of Islam showed remarkable insight, imagination and vision and interpreted the basic sources in the context of their times. With the passage of time the methodology developed by them has lost relevance due to change in time and place. The entire context has undergone a major change. Therefore, there is a dire need to review the whole methodology in this age. For example, the *hadith* sources may be studied as a whole to study the rationale and objectives of the Prophet (S.A.W.) on any particular issue. The insight thus gained may be used to decide the *Shari'ah* position on an analogus contemporary question. A host of new questions in the contemporary life require the *Shari'ah* position but the scholars are unable to present an answer mainly because the existing methodology does not take them very long. The need to review the *Shari'ah* methodology is another subject, however, and it should not detain us here.[17]

2.2 *The role of reason*

The scope of Islamic economics includes study of Islamic values, analysis of real-life economic phenomena and exploration of ways and means to transform the existing economies into Islamic economies. Therefore, the hard core of Islamic economics provides direct guidance on a small number of questions. A dominant part of the economic reality requires application of human reason and intellect within the over-all divine framework. The question of methodology becomes imminent mainly in the area where human reason is applied. In this area the general principle is that if a theory does not contradict any divine text it would be open for criticism. The criticism would be on two planes: rational as well as empirical. A theory must satisfy both the criteria. It should be true on rational grounds and should also be confirmed by empirical evidence. The confirmation is sought by Popperian thesis of falsification. It means that a theory would be tested on the criterion of falsifiability. The theories which are not falsified by these two criteria would be accepted. To this extent the methodology of Islamic economics is similar to that of economics.

It further implies that the hypotheses of Islamic economics must be stated in a form that they can be falsified. In other words the hypothesis must make clear its conditions and predictions. A hypothesis would merit consideration only if it tells the situations in which it would not hold or if it specifies the conditions which would falsify it.

It may be mentioned that the falsifiability criterion applies only to theorems which ask 'how' of an economic system. It does not apply to questions of 'why' in an economic system because reason can be applied only to questions of 'how'. It cannot be applied to questions of 'why' which takes one to the domain of faith and morality. In economics the questions asked are: how markets behave? How firms take decisions? How economy responds to a certain phenomena? It does not ask 'why' because it takes economics into field of morality. Since Descartes, the West has learnt to segregate reason from faith and morality. In Islamic economics, questions of faith and moralty are quite valid. Therefore, for questions of 'why' applies the criteria of faith and morality.[18]

2.3 *Inductive or deductive reasoning*

What is the response of Islamic economics to the question of choice between inductive and deductive reasoning? The brief answer is that Islamic economics applies a combination of both the methods. But this brief answer needs qualification. Muslims are the inventors of the inductive reasoning.[19] Before the advent of Islam the ancient world did produce some great systems of philosophy but they were based on abstract speculative reasoning.[20] The Qur'an invited people to look and see. It argued on the evidence of such natural phenomena as sun, moon, day, night, rainfall, seasons, differences of colours and tongues.[21] This ignited a spirit of inquiry which led to the discovery of inductive method in research. The Qur'an cites the example of Prophet Abraham who asked for an empirical evidence for life after death.[22] The discovery of One God by Prophet Abraham also came by an empirical method.[23] At this place the Qur'an says "Thus we *showed* to Abraham the visible and the invisible world of the heavens and the earth so that he could be among those who believe" (6:75). Hence the emphasis on the word *showed* *(nuri)* refers to seeing and looking. God has used the experimental method to establish validity of metaphysical truths. It shows that for physical reality, it would be still more preferable to hold on to this method.

Therefore, in Islamic economics inductive method is only a continuation of the tradition set by Muslims in the past. But it has been argued that it is not possible to derive any scientific conclusions merely by inductive methods. The argument goes like this. Whenever a person looks around and sees a thing, there is always a *priori* thought in his mind which made him select the particular thing he saw out of the numerous others which he ignored. Therefore, the real source of knowledge is man's intellect and not observation. We do not dispute this argument. We accept that human intellect is the source of knowledge. But we want to add that there are other sources of knowledge as well. For example, revelation and institution are sources of knowledge.[24] Human mind is capable of receiving flashes of brilliant ideas which do not have any visible linkages in the empirical world or which are not result of systematic observation. The point we want to make is that the source of a theorem may be inductive or a *priori* but the Islamic economist tests it on the multiple criteria of *Shari'ah*, reason and empirical-evidence. Should we say then that Islamic economics does not use deductive reasoning at all? It cannot be said in simple words until we qualify our reply. The deductive reasoning in economics assumes a perfect knowledge of the future by economic agents. Abstract deductions are made on the basis of this assumption.[25] As a matter of fact the corpus of economic theory consists of, mainly, on these deductions. The validity of the assumption of perfect knowledge has been called into question by empiricists. Islamic economics also cannot accept this assumption as it clashes with one of the fundamental beliefs of Islam. Perfect knowledge of the future is only with Allah and man has only an imperfect knowledge.[26] Therefore, the method of abstract deductions on the assumption of perfect knowledge cannot be acceptable to Islamic economics. The whole argument can now be summed up to in one sentence. Islamic economics accepts human intellect as a valid source of knowledge but does not accept model building on the basis of deductive reasoning. Model building involves a series of deductions from initial premises, which presumes perfect knowledge of the future.

The question remains: how does Islamic economics proceed to model building? Islamic economics accepts the real life situation that individuals do not have perfect fore-knowledge and different individuals have different knowledge. Therefore, in a given situation the possible reactions could be numerous. Therefore, the only rational approach for Islamic economics is to *observe* the human behaviour in the historical and institutional setting and then hypothesise on the basis of actual knowledge. This would require adoption of unusual research methods borrowed from such disciplines as sociology, marketing, social psychology, social anthropology, history, business management and industrial relations. The sources of data would be as unusual as national accounts, company accounts, national budgets, trade practices, behaviour of employees, behaviour of farmers, etc.

2.4 Assumptions and method

The basic assumptions of economics have influenced its method as well. The economist assumes that human beings are selfish, rational, maximisers of their own material well-being and possessers of perfect knowledge in the future. These assumptions led to the hypothetico-deductive method with a limited number of variables. Islamic economics does not agree with any of these assumptions.

In Islamic economics there are high-level assumptions derived from the divine texts and low-level assumptions based on human reasoning. The high level assumptions need no verification. Therefore it dispenses with the need to discuss the validity or otherwise of these assumption. So far as low-level assumptions are concerned, they needed to be tested against the twin criteria of rationality and empirical evidence. This is a distinct position than that of economics. The western economists have argued (most prominent being Friedman) that the assumptions need not be empirically valid.[27] In fact some have gone to the extent of saying that valid predictions are possible only from invalid assumptions. Islamic economics does not accept this position on the basis of rationality and empiricism.

This leads us the question: What are high-level assumptions in Islamic economics? Firstly, man is neither selfish nor altruistic, he is both.[28] He has an inborn tendency to be selfish, to love wealth but he has also been endowed with the ability of being altruistic. Caring for others is a trait of human character which can be verified by over-whelming evidence. Secondly, by education altruistic behaviour can be cultivated and made persistent. Thirdly, human beings have imperfect fore-knowledge.[29] Therefore, all economic analyses would be carried out in a world of uncertainty. Fourthly, in the ultimate analysis, *falah* of the *'Akhira* is preferable over material progress in this world.[30] This is not an exhaustive list. More high-level assumptions may be framed from the Qur'an and the *Sunnah*.

2.5 Problem-solving

Islamic economic thought has a long history, though it has not been properly documented. Early thinkers like Abu Yusuf, Abu Ubaid, Yahya b. 'Adam, Qudama b. Ja'far, al-Mawardi, Ghazali, Ibn Taimiyya, Ibn Khaldun, Shah Wali Ullah, Afghani and thinkers of recent past like Iqbal, Mufti 'Abduhu, Rashid Rida, Mawdudi, Baqar as Sadr. Taleqeni to name a few, have almost unanimously adopted a problem solving approach.[31] They have been concerned about the economic problems of their respective times. They have written on poverty, social justice, taxation, economic balance, market imperfections and allocative role of the state. They based their arguments on the world view of Islam and brought rare insights in their respective times. Islamic economics in the contemporary era is a continuation of this tradition. Islamic economics studies the economic behaviour of individuals, households, firms and state with the following focus:

(i) Understanding the behaviour and decision-making processes.
(ii) Relating the behaviour with the *falah* of owners, employees, participants, clients, citizens and the society at large.
(iii) Hypothesising about a change path to maximise *falah* at different levels.

For example, in the first stage, a Muslim economist would *understand* how firms take various decisions regarding production, pricing and marketing of their products. In this phase, he may use with benefit the findings of neoclassical economics with a *caveat* that the assumptions of neoclassical economics are unreal and over-simplified. Therefore, the Muslim economist might have to use other disciplines such as market research, production management and social psychology. At the second stage, he would relate his *understanding* with the *falah* of the firms owners, managers, citizens and point out various trade-offs. At the third level, he would try to build models which maximises *falah* of various economic agents.

From the above discussion emerge two conclusions which are relevant to the discussion on methodology:

(i) Islamic economics is a multi-disciplinary subject. It will not be meaningful nor would it achieve its objectives if it relies only on the traditional sources of economics.

(ii) Islamic economics is a normative discipline. It does not study the economic problem for the sake of problem. It has a normative role to explore ways and means for transforming the existing economics into Islamic economies.[32] It does not deny, however, the positive content of Islamic economics. The positive content is used for normative purposes. Thus Islamic economics goes a step further to economics.

3 Comparison of two methodologies

In this section we shall summarise our discussion of the previous section to highlight distinctive features of Islamic economic methodology. First, Islamic economics uses a framework derived from the divine texts. This framework is sacred and immutable. No individual or assembly of individuals can make it redundant or irrelevant. Human criticism does not apply on the divine texts. This is distinct from the western economics where the fundamental paradigm is also subject to criticism and can also undergo change.[33] However, the interpretation of the divine texts is not sacred. But the interpretation follows the methodology developed by *Shari'ah* scholars (the *usual* methodology).

Second, Islamic economics primarily follows inductive method. It testifies the truth or falsity of the *assumptions* as well as *predictions* on the twin criterion of *rationality* and *empirical evidence*. In economics, the deductive method is more common. The assumptions need not be realistic. The real test is in the non-falsifiability of predictions. The basic assumptions of self-interest, rationality, perfect fore-knowledge, man's ability to know what is best for him have facilitated the use of deductive method by economists. Islamic economics has a different stance on these issues. Therefore, it adopts a combination of inductive and deductive methods with primarily emphasis on the former.

Third, Islamic economics builds ethical values such as justice, benevolence, moderation, sacrifice, caring for others, into analysis as behavioural parameters. The debate whether economics should contain value judgement is a lengthy one. In economics, the balance of the argument says that there is no escape from value judgements. But the economists should produce falsifiable hypothesis. In the process of hypothesis testing, personal, social or political prejudices and value judgements should be eliminated. Herein lies the road to progress in economics. In Islamic economics, so far as the matter relates to personal choices, prejudices or preferences, this approach seems to be acceptable with an important qualification. The ethical values of Islam, which have been given by the *Shari'ah* would continue to be part of economic theories and they would not be falsified by any hypothesis testing. Instead they would serve as criteria for hypothesis testing alongwith factual data. A theory which does not incorporate the *Shari'ah* ethical norms or contradicts them or leads to predictions which would defeat or dilute the ethical norms would be rejected *per se* even in the absence of any empirical evidence.

Fourth, Islamic economics is a normative discipline. It explores the ways and means to change the existing economics into Islamic economics. Economics, on the other hand, claims to be a positive science which studies the existing economic phenomena. Islamic economics is interested in changing the economic reality. Its predictions also relate to a world which has not yet ushered in. Therefore, the actual testing of Islamic economic theories would wait until an Islamic economy comes into being. However, Islamic economics also concerns itself with the transition path. Its transition theorems can be tested in the real world provided the process of transition also sets in.

Fifth, Islamic economics asks different questions than economics. It is concerned with the *falah* of man and in creating such social and institutional conditions which maximise *falah* in a society.[34] Implicitly, it visualises to pursue those research programmes which help in the maximisation of *falah*. In this way, *falah* becomes a criterion for the acceptance or rejection of a research programme. In economics no such criterion exists in unambiguous terms. As a result, research for the sake of research or knowledge for the sake of knowledge, is pursued in economics. In Islamic economics, all knowledge has a purpose. The purpose is derived from the over-all world-view of Islam.

4 Some related issues

In this section we shall discuss some related issues which often come up for discussion in the forums of Islamic economics.

4.1 Interaction with economics

Should Islamic economics discard economics and make a beginning from scratch? On this question, there are two opinions. One is that "the methodologies of western economics were developed and designed to solve problems that are peculiar to that system.[35] Therefore, the Islamic economics should discard economics altogether and develop its own theory in the Islamic framework. The other opinion is that Islamic economics should not set aside the western economic thought which accumulated over centuries. Instead, with a modesty of a learner we should cast a critical look on this pool of knowledge and should try to identify and isolate those components of thought which do not conflict either with the hard core of Islamic economics or with the rational and empirical criteria. It would be arrogance of the first order if we dismiss the entire economic thought as un-Islamic.[36] However, we should adopt the following criteria to judge the western economic thought:

(i) Compatibility with the *Shari'ah*: we should accept a theory if it does not come in conflict with the divine text or the spirit (*illal*) and objectives (*maqasid*) of the *shari'ah*.

239

(ii) We should accept a theory if it is not falsified on the twin criteria of *reason* and *empirical evidence*.

(iii) We should accept a theory if it helps solve an economic problem. Speculative knowledge which is an exercise in mental gymnastics is not of interest to Islamic economics.

At this stage we need to mention a trap into which many Muslim economists have landed themselves. The economic thought developed in the west overpowers their reason and they are pursuaded by its 'truth'. Then they try to interpret the texts of the Qur'an and the *Sunnah* in such a manner as would accommodate the economic thought of the west. They start reading the findings of the western secular economists into these primary sources. While there is no bar on the interpretation of the Qur'an and the *Sunnah* in each age, the danger is that this approach may reduce the entire discipline of Islamic economics into mockery or at least into a sub-discipline of the western economics. Thus the original objective of developing Islamic economics would be defeated. There is no hard and fast rule to remain out of this trap except that the Muslim economists should discuss their ideas widely. It is through a process of self-criticism that they can guard against this trap.

4.2 Role of revelation

The general principle of Islamic methodology is that a reference should be made to the Qur'an and *Sunnah* of the Prophet for seeking guidance on any issue. But there is a limit to which we can seek guidance from these sources. The Qur'an and the books of *ahadith* are not books on any scientific discipline or on economics. They contain broad and general principles and provide a basic framework. The details have to be worked out by people themselves in each age. But in their enthusiasm Muslim economists often try to read such meanings into the verses of the Qur'an which are not there or which need not be searched in these sources because they are common knowledge and confirmed by casual observation. The point is that if a fact can be seen and confirmed by observation or reason there is hardly any reason to search for an evidence in the Qur'an or *Sunnah*, which often has to be established by laboured interpretations. For example, there can hardly be a dispute that a well-looked-after worker would be more productive than a neglected worker. Some people have unnecessarily tried to interpret and stretch *ahadith* relating to slaves of the early Islamic era to prove this point.

A related point concerns the confusion which often takes place by not recognising the distinction between 'Islamic' and 'Islamic framework'. By 'Islamic' we mean something sacred revealed by God or enjoined by the Prophet (S.A.W.). Whatever is 'Islamic' in this sense is immutable and beyond criticism. But some people append the adjective 'Islamic' with the concepts propounded by human beings such as Islamic profit, Islamic bank, Islamic business. Sometimes the adjective 'Islamic' is not appended but the discussion implies that the writer or the speaker intends to attach a sanctity to it. This needs to be clarified. All, that is said within 'Islamic framework' need not be 'Islamic'. That is human thought and is subject to criticism.

4.3 The assumption of an ideal Islamic society

Most of the literature in Islamic economics assumes an ideal Islamic society which does not exist anywhere and the probability of its coming into being in near future is also remote. Should we continue making this assumption? The assumption of an ideal Islamic society is an analytical tool which presents a relationship of dependence between the ideal and the actual phenomena. Theories stated in this framework explain how the two phenomena are related and what are the factors which cause disturbance in this relationship. In this context it is a powerful tool.

But the Muslim economists should realise that the ideal Islamic society is a special case within a large range of possibilities. The ideal Islamic society may continue to be an ideal to be achieved. But it is also necessary that concrete social reality is also studied. This will help in shedding some of the romanticism in which many Muslim economists rejoice most of the time.

The idealism of Muslim economists has also done some harm to the scope of Islamic economics. Since the analysis is perceived in ideal Islamic conditions most of the ugly problems such as unemployment, inflation, trade cycles are simply assumed away. In ideal Islamic economy they do not exist so why study them. I think this is an overly simplistic approach. These problems are real life issues and there is no guarantee that they would not appear in an ideal Islamic economy. The Muslims in an ideal Islamic society may not behave as expected which may lead to the emergence of such problems. Therefore, the Muslim economists should face the reality and discuss the real-life problems.

5 Concluding remarks

In this era, the world at large and Muslim *Ummah* in particular are suffering from a few obstinate and insoluble economic problems such as unemployment, inflation, unequal distribution of income, poverty, balance of payments difficulties, debt overburden and international exploitation. These problems present a serious challenge to Islamic economics. If Islamic economics can present plausible solutions to these problems, it would be accepted by the world, whatever its method of inquiry. Therefore, in the final analysis it is not the method of inquiry that is important, it is the contribution that Islamic economics can make towards economic progress and prosperity. Islamic economics need not be confined to any one method. It should remain open to all the methods provided the inquiry remains within the basic framework of Islam and it satisfies the twin criteria of *reason* and *empirical validity*.

Islamic economics needs to have a name of Islamic economics and would be open to examination by Muslims and non-Muslims alike. It is ultimately the weight of its arguments and the rigour of its analysis that would fetch merit. Therefore, Islamic economics should come out of the romanticism of the ideal Islamic society. It should devote greater attention to the analysis and solution of the present day problems rather than recount the glory of Islam which it once was. It does not mean that Islamic economics should discard historical perspective. It only means that historical data need be used to learn lessons for the present rather than to rejoice in a trance of glorification.

The assumption of ideal Islamic society should also be kept as a goal to be achieved. The main occupation of Muslim economists should be to present an analysis of the application of the *Shari'ah* in the present day society. It would not only generate a theory of transition (which is missing at the present) but also provide a powerful persuasion for the unconcerned spectator to think seriously about Islamic economic system.

Notes

1 Some of the recent works which give a comprehensive view of the methodological debate are:

Mark Blaug, *The Methodology of Economics* (Cambridge: C. University Press, 1980). Bruce Caldwell, *Appraisal and criticism in economics* (Boston: Allen and Unwin, 1984). Sheilla C. Dow, *Macro economic Thought: A methodological approach* (Oxford: Basil Blackwell, 1985), A. S. Eichner, *Why Economics is not yet a science* (London: Macmillan, 1983). Daniel M. Hausman, *The Philosophy of Economics: An Anthology* (Cambridge: C. University Press, 1984), J. J. Klant, *The Rale of the Game* (Cambridge: C. University Press, 1984), Peter Willes & Guy Routh, *Economics in Disarray* (Oxford: Basil Blackwell, 1984).

2 Blaug, M. (1980), p. xi.
** We are aware of the instrumentalist 'distortion' in the debate which does not concern itself with the truth or falsity of a theory but with its usefulness or efficiency. But this approach remains only one of the many approaches, the majority adheres to the Popperian realism which through falsification of theories, tries to reach the truth of a theory.
3 Klant, J. J. (1983), p. 2.
4 Al-Qur'an, 2:1.
5 ibid. 10:36, 53:28.
6 Siddiqi, M. N. (1982), p. 18.
7 All the injunctions in the Qur'an and Hadith on *infaq*, *sila rahm*, generosity towards others are a testimony to this statement.
8 Al-Qur'an, 59:9.
9 Gilani, S. M. Ahsan, *Islami Ma'ashiyat* (urdu), Karachi: Sh. Shaukat Ali and Sons, 1962 (1947), pp. 449–450.

10 *Economist*, 23, August 1986, p. 75.

11 This is based on such Qur'anic verses as: 6:32, 14:3, 16:107, 75:20–21, 100:8.

12 Al-Qur'an categorically denies monasticism, 57:27.

13 The Prophet S.A.W. said: (Lawful) wealth for a virtuous man is an excellent thing" al-Hakim, *alMustadrik*, Vol. II, H. I. Hyderabad (India): Diara Ma'arif Nizam-yya, 1340 A.H.

14 Al-Qur'an, 4:11.

15 Sir John Hicks has observed: 'There is much of economic theory which is pursued for no better reason than its intellectual attraction: it is a good game'. (Hicks, J. R., *Causality in Economics*, Oxford: Basil Blackwell, 1979, p. viii). Also Hutchison T., "Our Methodological crises" in Peter Wiles and G. Routh, *Economics in Disarray*, Oxford: Basil Blackwell, 1984, pp. 1–21.

16 Translation of the Quranic verses has been taken from Ahmad Ali, *al-Quran: A Contemporary Translation*, Karachi: Arkash Publishing, 1984.

17 For a persuasive discussion on the subject, *see* Abu Sulayman, A. H., "Islamization of Knowledge with special reference to Political Science", *The American Journal of Islamic Social Sciences*, (2:2), December 1985, pp. 263–290.

18 Garudy, R., "The Balance Sheet of Western Philosophy", *AJISS*, (2:2), pp. 169–178.

19 One of the prayers of the Prophet (S.A.W.) bears testimony to the fact that the Prophet (S.A.W.) himself was very keen for rational explanation of natural phenomenon. He used to pray: 'God! grant me knowledge of the ultimate nature of things: *Allahumma Arina Haqa'iq al-ashya' kaniahiya*, a well known tradition found in *sufi* works such as 'Ali b. 'Uthman al Hujwiri (d.465/1072) *Kashf al-Mahjud*, p. 166, as referred to by Saeed Sheikh in his notes on Allama Iqbal's *Reconstruction of Religious Thought in Islam* (Lahore: Institute of Islamic Culture, 1986, p. 158).

20 Iqbal, (1930, 1986), p. 100.

21 al-Qur'an, 2:164, 15:16, 16:68–69, 21:33, 24:43–44, 30:48, 35:9, 36:40, 37:6, 41:12, 45:5, 50:6, 67:5, 85:1.

22 Ibid 2:260.

23 Ibid 6:75–78.

24 Ibid 16:68, 20:38, 28:7.

25 Hutchison, T., op. cit. p. 5.

26 Al-Qur'an, (e.g.) 31:34.

27 Hutchison, T., op. cit. p. 5.

28 We find verses in the Qur'an which bear witness to both the traits of human nature. For example the Qur'an says: Selfishness is ever present in human souls (4:128). At another place it says: we created man of finest possibilities (95:4).

29 Al-Qur'an, 7:188.

30 Al-Qur'an, 20:71, 20:131, 28:60, 87:17.

31 Siddiqi, M. N., *Recent works on the history of Islamic Economic Thought*, (Research paper), Jeddah: ICRIE, 1980.

32 For a detailed treatment of the issue, refer to writer's *Challenge of Islamic Economics*, Lahore: All Pakistan Islamic Education Congress, 1985, pp. 63–66.

33 For a brief account of various paradigms in economics, see Arif, M., "Towards the *Shari'ah* Paradigm of Islamic Economics: The beginning of a scientific Revolution", AJISS, Washington (2:1), 1985, pp. 79–99.

34 Khan, M. Akram *Challenge of Islamic Economics*, op. cit., pp. 2–12.

35 Sardar, Z., "Breaking Free from the Dominant Paradigm", *Inquiry*, April 1985, 41–47.

36 Khan, M. Akram, *Challenge of Islamic Economics*, op. cit., pp. 80–FF.

References

1. Al-QUR'AN.
2. ABU SULAYMAN, A. H., "Islamization of Knowledge with special Reference to Political Science", *AJISS*, Washington, (2:2), December 1985, pp. 263–290.
3. 'ARIF, Muhammad, "Towards Establishing the Microfoundation of Islamic Economics: The basis of the basics", *The Islamic Quarterly*, London, (28:2), 1984, pp. 61–72.
4. ———. "Towards a Shari'ah Paradigm of Islamic Economics: The beginning of a Scientific Revolution", *The American Journal of Islamic Social Sciences*, (2:1), July 1985, pp. 79–99.
5. ———. "Towards a Definition of Islamic Economics: some scientific considerations", *JRIE*, Jeddah, (2:2), 1985, pp. 87–103.
6. BACHARACH, Michael O. L., "The Problem of Agents' Beliefs in Economic Theory", in Baranzini, M. & R. Scazzieri, *Foundations of Economics*, Oxford: Basil Blackwell, 1986, pp. 175–204.
7. BARANZINI, M. & Roberts Scazzieri (eds.), *Foundations of Economics*, Oxford: Basil Blackwell, 1986, pp. 454.
8. BELL, D., "Models and Reality in Economic Discourse", in Daniel Bell & Irving Kristol (eds.), *The Crisis in Economic Theory*, New York: Basic Books, 1981, pp. 46–80.
9. BLAUG, Mark, *The Methodology of Economics*, Cambridge: Cambridge University Press, 1980, pp. 295.
10. BOULDING, K. E., *Beyond Economics*, Ann Arbor: The University of Michigan Press, 1986, pp. 302.
11. ———. *Economics as a Science*, Dehli: TATA McGrawhill, 1970, pp. 157.
12. BROCKWAY, G. P., *Economics: What went wrong and Why and Somethings to do about it*, New York: Basic Books, 1981, pp. 151–173.
13. CALDWELL, Bruce, *Appraisal and criticism in Economics*, Boston: Allen & Unwin, 1984.
14. DAVIDSON, P., "Post Keynesian Economics: Solving the Crisis in Economic Theory", Bell & Kristol (eds), *The Crisis in Economic Theory*, New York: Basic Books, 1981, pp. 151–173.
15. DOPFER, Kurt, (ed) "*Economics in the future*, London: Macmillan Press, 1976.
16. DOW, Sheila C., *Macroeconomic Thought: A methodological approach*, Oxford: Basil Blackwell, 1985.
17. DRUNKER, P. F., "Towards the Next Economics" in Daniel Bell & Irving Kristol (ed.), *The Crisis in Economic Theory*, New York: Basic Book, 1981, pp. 4–18.
18. ENICHNER, A. S., *Why Economics is not yet a science?* Macmillan, 1983.
19. FRIEDMAN, M., "The Methodology of Positive Economics", in Hausman, (ed.), 1984.
20. GARUDY, R., "The Balance Sheet of Western Philosophy in this Century", *AJJIS*, Washington, (2:2), December 1985, pp. 169–178.
21. al-GHAMIDY, Javed a., *Meezan* (Urdu), Vol. I, Lahore: Dar al-Ishraq, 1985.
22. GODELIER, Maurice, *Rationality and Irrationality in Economics*, New York: Monthly Review Francois Maspero, 1966).

23. HAUSMAN, Daniel M., *The Philosophy of Economics: An Anthology*, Cambridge: C. University Press, 1984.
24. HICKS, J. R., *Causality in Economics*, Oxford: Basil Blackwell, 1979.
25. HIRSHLEIFER, Jack, "The Expanding Domain of Economics", *The American Economic Review*, (75:6), December 1985, pp. 53–68.
26. HUTCHISON, T., *The Significance and Basic Postulates of Economic Theory*, New York: Kelley, 1960 (First published 1938).
27. ———, "Our Methodological Crisis" in Peter Wiles and Guy Routh (eds.), *Economics in Disarray*, Oxford: Basil Blackwell, 1984, pp. 1–21.
28. IQBAL, Allama Mohamad, *The Reconstruction of Religious Thought in Islam* (Ed: Saeed Sheikh), Lahore: Institute of Islamic Culture, 1986.
29. KAPLAN, A., *The conduct of Inquiry: Methodology for Behavioural Sciences*, New York: Thomas Y. Cromwell, 1964.
30. KATOUZIAN, Homa, *Idealogy and Method in Economics*, London: Macmillan Press, 1980.
31. KETTANI, M. 'Ali, "Science and Technology in Islam: the underlying value system", in Sardar, Z. (ed), . . . , (1984).
32. KHAN, Azmatullah & Abdul Qadir Saleem, *'Umrani 'Uloom ki Tadris ka nazriyati Pehlu'* (U) (Ideological Aspect of Teaching of Social Sciences) Islamabad: I.P.S., 1983.
33. KHAN, M. Akram, "Islamic Economics: An Outline Plan for Research", *Criterion*, Karachi: (10:4), April 1975, pp. 27–35.
34. ———, "The Economics of *falah The Criterion*, Karachi: (11:3), March 1976.
35. ———, "Economic Values in Islam" The *Criterion*, Karachi: (12:2), February 1977, pp. 14–24.
36. ———, "Economic Implications of *Tawhid, Risala* and *'Akhira*", *The Criterion*, Karachi (12: No.6&7), June–July 77, pp. 22–23.
37. ———, "Ulm e Ma'ashiyat" (Economics), in *Urdu Encyclopaedia of Islam, (08)* Lahore, 1980 (14:7–8), pp. 386–486.
38. ———, *Challenge of Islamic Economics*, Lahore: All Pakistan Islamic Educational Congress, 1985.
39. KLANT, J. J., *The Rules of the Game:* Cambridge: Cambridge University Press, 1984.
40. ———, "The Slippery Transition", in Lawson, T. & H. Pesaran, *Keynes' Economics: Methodological Issues*, London: Croom-Helm, 1985, pp. 80–98.
41. KRISTOL, I., "Rationalism in Economics", Bell & Kristol (eds), in *The Crisis in Economic Theory*, New York: Basic Books, 1981, pp. 201–218.
42. LEVINE, David P., *Economic Studies: Contributions to the Critique of Economic Theory*. London: Routledge & Kegan Paul, 1977.
43. MACHLUP, F., "The Problem of Verification in Economics", *Southern Economic Journal*, (22:1), July 1955, pp. 1–21.
44. MUSGRAVE, A., "Unreal Assumptions in Economics Theory: The F-Twist Untwisted", *Kyklos*, vol. 34, 1981, Fasc. 3, pp. 377–387.
45. NAGEL, E., "Assumptions in Economic Theory", *American Economic Review: Papers and Proceedings*, vol. 53, May 1963, pp. 211–219.
46. NASR, Hossein S. *Islamic Life and Thought*, Albany: State University of New York Press, 1981.

47. NEILD, R., "The Wider World and Economic Methodology" in Peter Wiles and Guy Routh (ed.), *Economics in Disarray*, Oxford: Black Basil, 1984, pp. 37–46.

48. NIENHAUS, V., "Epistemology, Methodology and Economic Policy: Some Thoughts on Mainstream Australia and Islamic Economics", *Humanomics*, Toronto, (1:2), 1985, pp. 10–38.

49. PHEBY, J., "Are Popperian criticisms of Keynes 'Justified'" in Lawson, J. & H. Pesaran, *Keynes' Economics: Methodological Issues*: London: Croom-Helm, 1985, pp. 99–115.

50. RAHMAN, Fazlur, *Islamic Methodology in History*, Islamabad: Islamic Research Institute, 1984 (1965).

51. ——, "Roots of Islamic Neo-Fundamentalism" in Scoddard, P. H. M. et al. (eds.), *Change and the Muslim World*, Syracuse University Press, 1981, pp. 23–35.

52. RAVETZ, J. R. "Science and Values", in Sardar, Z., . . . , 1984.

53. ROSENTHAL, F., *Knowledge Triumphant*, Leiden: E.J. Brill, 1970.

54. ROUTH, G., "What to teach to Undergraduates", in Peter Wiles and G. Routh (ed.), *Economics in Disarray*, Oxford: Basil Blackwell, 1984, pp. 240–248.

55. SARDAR, Z., (ed.) *The Touch of Midas*, Manchester University Press, 1984.

56. ——, "Islamisation of knowledge or the westernisation of Islam?" *Inquiry*, London: December 1984, pp. 40–45.

57. ——, "Breaking free from the dominant Paradigm", *Inquiry*, (2:4), April 1985, pp. 40–47.

58. SCHNEIDER, Harold K., *Economic Man*, New York: Free Press, 1974.

59. SIDDIQI, M. N., "An Islamic Approach to Economics", Paper presented at the *Seminar on Islamisation of Knowledge*, Islamabad, January 1982.

60. ——, *Islamising Economics*, Paper presented at the Third International Seminar on Islamic Thought, Kuala Lumpur, 26–31 July, 1984.

61. THUROW, Lester C., "*Dangerous Currents: The State of Economics*, London: Oxford University Press, 1983.

62. WARD, Benjamin, *What is wrong with Economics?* London: Macmillan Press, 1972.

63. WILES, Peter & Guy Routh, *Economics in Disarray*, Oxford: Basil Blackwell, 1984.

64. WISEMAN, J., (ed.) *Beyond Positive Economics*, New York: St. Martin's Press, 1983.

16

A SUGGESTED METHODOLOGY FOR THE POLITICAL ECONOMY OF ISLAM

Shamim Ahmad Siddiqi[1]

Source: *Journal KAAU: Islamic Economics*, 13:1 (2001), 3–27.

Abstract

In this paper an attempt is made to clarify some of the issues pertaining to the methodology of Islamic economics. It is argued that for any analysis in the context of Islamic economics, the behavioral norms suggested by the teachings of Islam should not be taken as the actual behavior of individuals in a Muslim society. Rather, it should be one of the goals of economic policies to provide a social environment which would *help* the inhabitants of a Muslim society to behave in an Islamically desirable way. In this regard, the importance of distribution of income and wealth is highlighted. Another focal point of this paper is that Islamic economists should be more heedful in their criticism to neoclassical economics. It is noted that a familiarity with the critical literature on neoclassic economics emanating from within the western world may provide important insights that could be helpful in finding our own solutions. Finally, to study those aspects of economics which are primarily positive in nature, the case for methodological pluralism is advocated.

1. Introduction

In the last few years several basic issues have been raised regarding the methodology of Islamic economics. In Ghazali and Omar (1989) some of the prominent Islamic economists have presented their views on different aspects of this subject. Although, a few of them have also raised questions against some aspects of contemporary literature in Islamic economics,[2] the primary theme of this volume of literature is a critique of different postulates of neoclassical economics and the need for an alternative methodology for Islamic economics. Jomo (1992) edited a collection of articles which are generally critical of the methodology currently adopted by the Islamic economists. In his critical review of Munawar Iqbal (1988), Professor Ali Khan has exposed the following deficiencies in the writings of some of the Islamic economists: (a) use of inappropriate or incorrect language (b) a lack of familiarization with the relevant literature in conventional (western) economics and (3) an unclear picture[3] of their position viz a viz the paradigms of neoclassical economics. During our numerous conversations with scholars of different fields of knowledge, economists and non-economists, Muslims and non-Muslims, even the term "Islamic Economics" has come under intense criticism.

In my opinion, in reviewing any issue pertaining to the methodology of Islamic economics, it would be quite conducive if, among other things, one can also firmly keep in the background the current debates on methodological issues among the mainstream economists which has centered around postulates of neoclassical economics, the dominant approach of our time. Islamic economists have challenged many of the assumptions of neoclassical economics. But there are many schools of Western economic thought which are also critical of certain aspects of neoclassical thinking. Post-Keynesians, institutionalists, neo-Austrians, neo-Ricardians, to name a few, have challenged different paradigms of this school. There are issues on which these critics of the neoclassical doctrine share a common line of argument but on many other matters they present competing theories. These dissenting arguments and theories may not have any direct significance to the questions posed by Islamic economists, but they can provide many insights which can be helpful in our task of presenting a detailed sketch of an Islamic economic system.

This paper, on one hand, evaluates some of the criticism put forward by Islamic economists on the prevalent methodologies of traditional (Western) economics; on the other hand, it attempts to address some questions raised by the critics of the methodology of Islamic economics. It is hoped that this process would help to move us a modest step forward towards resolving some of the issues in defining the discourse and methodology of Islamic economics.

The organization of this paper is as follows: We start with a discussion of the major themes of methodological discussion in contemporary mainstream economics. We also identify the methodological issues which are currently debated by the critics and proponents of Islamic economics. The remaining sections of the paper take up those methodological issues in detail which are currently debated in the context of Islamic economics. Section III deals with the issue of behavioral norms in the context of an Islamic economy which has been a subject of intense dissension among both the adherents and critics of the Islamic economic literature. In Section IV we present a discussion on the concept of knowledge and the way it should be used in economics. We also elaborate the idea that the methodology of physical sciences is inappropriate for economics. The deliberations and reflections of sections III and

IV provide us with an elucidating basis for the next section where we present some basic ideas on the nature of political economy of Islam. Section VI deals with the problem of jurisprudential reforms for implementation of economic reforms in Muslim countries. In section VII we argue for methodological pluralism for investigating those problems in the field of Islamic economics which are positive in nature. Finally, section VIII summarizes the main themes of this paper.

2. Major themes of methodological debate in contemporary economics

Methodological debate in mainstream economics could be divided into four broad areas. First, there is a debate about the appropriate method to be used to understand and/or evaluate economic theories. Controversy over Popperian or Lakatosian versions of falsificationism, Kuhn's historical account of periods of normal science separated by scientific revolutions and, post modernism or constructivism which emphasize the importance of rhetoric and discourse in economics, come under this category. The people involved in this debate are generally labeled as economic methodologists. The second area of methodological discussion is concerned with the relative merits of different methods of investigation in economics such as deductive, inductive, experimental, etc. The third category is related to basic assumptions made by different schools of thought about behavioural norms of individual economic agents such as rationality, utility and profit maximization, self-interest vs. altruism, subjectivity or objectivity of knowledge, etc. The fourth area deals with the scope of economics; whether it is or it should be positive or normative, is it a pure science or social science or an art. Can it be separated from other disciplines such as psychology, sociology, politics and anthropology. It is also related to the issue of how the economy works. Differences in opinion related to the last two categories provide the primary basis for different schools of thought in economics.

As far as methodological issues are concerned, Islamic economists have generally focused on the last two areas. The neglect of the first two categories is understandable. Most of the Islamic economic literature is based on Islamic principles derived from fiqh sources. Any controversies on these principles are related to the corresponding controversies in the fiqh literature and could not be resolved with any other methodological rule. Indeed, Popperian philosophy of science will regard most of Islamic economic propositions as *unscientific*. Similarly, proponents of Islamic economics who categorically regard economics as a normative subject cannot accept falsificationism as a method to advance knowledge. Islamic economists, however, do not stand alone on this point. Many economists in the western economic traditions belonging to different schools of thought have convincingly argued that economics has always been normative. For example, Warren Samuels has asserted that economics is normative because the economy is normative: the economy is made by man and what is the product of man is normative.[4] It is a result of the aggregation of individual choices through process of social or collective choice such as the market and politics. According to McCloskey "Modernism promises knowledge free from doubt, free from metaphysics, morals and personal conviction. What it is able to deliver renames as scientific methodology, the scientist's and especially the economic scientist's metaphysics, morals and personal convictions. It cannot deliver what it promises".[5]

Popperian falsificationism, in any case, is not supported by many economic methodologists.[6] There is almost a consensus among economists that merely one piece of empirical evidence against an economic theory does not refute the theory. The only version of Popperian falsificationism which finds some support among some economists is rational criticism. Similarly, economic methodologists have questioned Kuhn's idea of a single and dominant paradigm in a scientific discipline in a particular time period. According to his analysis, all research work in a particular discipline are efforts to solve some of the unsolved puzzles of the dominant paradigm until a revolution brings a new paradigm. Economists have pointed out the lively existence of different paradigms in the same time period such as Marxian, neoclassical, Keynesian and institutional economics.

One who received relatively sympathetic consideration in economics is Lakatos whose methodology of scientific research programme comes closer to what characterizes the world of economics. According to Lakatos, instead of one dominant paradigm at one time, there are competing research programmes in a scientific discipline. Each programme has a hard core which consists of assumptions which are not questionable and a protective belt consisting of a set of less important assumption which could be changed to explain any anomalies and deficiency in the theory. Lakatos then defines a progressive research program as one which not only explains away any anomalies but also predicts novel facts. A degenerating programme, on the other hand, is one which does no more than explain away anomalies. Lakatos advocates the abandoning of degenerating programmes for the progress of a particular science.[7] Economic methodologists have pointed out that research programs may go through progressive and degenerating phases and a degenerated programme can make a comeback. It would be an interesting analysis to see if research in the area of Islamic economics is a single research programme or could be classified into different overlapping and competing programmes. But any attempt to categorize them into degenerating or progressive programmes at this juncture would be a futile exercise.

As far as the second general area of methodological debate is concerned, the practice of Muslim economists suggests that they have generally accepted the principle of plurality of methods in economics.[8] Many analytical contributions in contemporary Islamic economics have been deductive in method.

The general paucity of empirical studies in Islamic economics is due to the fact that this is a new area of economics and existing data available in contemporary Muslim countries come from a different conceptual framework. Moreover, very few aspects of Islamic economic programs have so far been implemented by any Muslim country which could generate meaningful data for empirical research. A case for methodological pluralism in some areas of economics is further discussed in section VII below.

Methodological discussion in the Islamic economic literature is generally confined to categories three and four above. A critical analysis of the issues raised by both the proponents and critics of Islamic economic literature may help to determine future directions of research in Islamic economics. To this we now turn.

3. Homo economicus vs homo Islamicus

It appears that both among the adherents and the critics of Islamic economics, there is some confusion on the issue of behavior of economic agents in an Islamic economy. Some Islamic economists believe that the behavior of Muslim economic agents would be significantly different from what is assumed by the neoclassical economists. The methodology of Islamic economics, its paradigms and the resulting policy implications would, therefore, also be different.[9]

On the other hand, one of the leading critics of the Islamic economics claims that: "The suggested behavioral norms are riddled with ambiguity and also unlikely to enjoy widespread adherence in a large society. In practice, many of them would have to be treated as state-enforced laws. There is no way of ensuring, moreover, that state officials would behave in an Islamically correct behavior".[10]

Let us begin with the five basic assumptions of neoclassical economics pertaining to the behavior of economic agents which are criticized by Muslim economists:[11]

(i)   Man is selfish by nature and he behaves rationally.
(ii)   Material progress is a supreme goal.
(iii) Every person has an inherent tendency to maximize his material welfare.
(iv)   He also has the knowledge and ability for deciding what is good for him.
(v)   An individual's utility is independent of that of others.

In the rest of this section we contemplate on all these issues except (iv) which we will take up in the next section.

251

3.1 Selfishness and self-interest

Some Muslim economists have argued that the assumption of man being selfish by nature is incorrect and assert that in all civilized societies men have been motivated by altruistic motives.[12] First of all, it is important to distinguish between selfishness and self-interest. For example, when a person produces a product which he thinks has a demand in the economy (e.g., a pair of shoes), he does it in his self-interest, to make a profit and earn a living. This act can not be regarded as *selfish* as it satisfies the needs of someone else and it does not necessarily put the buyer of this product in a disadvantageous position. Although, there can be a situation in which a seller, taking advantage of the immediate need of a potential buyer, may extract a huge profit which could be considered as selfish, unethical and immoral (that some economists in the neoclassical tradition, in their blind pursuit of scienticism, may object to the use of these words is another matter). Perhaps the father of the Western classical economics had no confusion about the meaning of self-interest, when he wrote:

> "The Man has almost constant occasion for the help of his brethren, and it is in vain for him to expect it from their benevolence only. He will be more likely to prevail if he can interest their self-love in his favor, and show that it is for their own advantage to do for him what he requires of them. . . . It is not from the benevolence of the butcher, the brewer, or the baker, that we expect our dinner, but from their regard to their own interest."
>
> (Adam Smith in *Wealth of Nations* as quoted by Stigler, 1987, p. 3)

Once a person receives a profit or wage as a remuneration of his efforts, no restrictions are put on him to spend in an altruistic manner. Thus the assumption of self-interest does not imply that an individual is necessarily selfish and lacks instinct of sympathy and altruism. Irving Kristol points out that Adam Smith never conceived of the economic man of capitalism as a whole man, but only a man-in-the-marketplace. He never celebrated self-interest, per se, as a human motive. He merely pointed to its utility in a population that wished to improve its condition which was to him a normal and universal human desire. For Adam Smith, sympathy was as natural a human instinct as self-interest, and on the whole more powerful.[13] Smith never disavowed his larger view of human nature presented in *The Theory of Moral Sentiments*, which was published well before *The Wealth of Nations*.

It is important to recognize that Adam Smith's treatment of human nature was developed from a conscious rejection of Hobbes (1588–1679) who had portrayed the essence of human nature as an egoism which manifested itself as unrestrained and destructive pursuit of self-interest.[14] For Hobbes it was necessary to impose upon individuals an intensive structure of socio-political control, and the sanctions that go with them, in order to bring social cohesion to the society. Against this philosophy, eighteenth century England had two alternative perceptions: in the first case, self-interest was claimed to be adequately contained by the countervailing effect of other directed sentiments such as benevolence. In the other alternative the balance of sentiments was to be struck by means of some automatic process of social interaction. It claimed that perfectly free agents pursuing their individual self-interest in a society comprising only institutions which had developed largely without conscious human interventions including aspects of the law and the market exchange mechanism, could be relied upon to deliver an optimal social and moral outcome. Smith was influenced by all these ideas.[15]

Oakley claims that Smith had come to realize that outside the immediate family group, self-interest was dominant influence for human action. However, as societies did not explode into Hobbesian ego driven chaos, it was equally evident that some sympathetic sentiment must be keeping people from destroying each other in the struggle to maximize returns to their ego.[16] Together with Kristol's observation above, it is appropriate to claim that Smith not only realized the existence of self-interest as the driving force in *economic* affairs of human life, but considered it to be a thing which could be used both for the benefits of individuals and as a catalyst to increase the wealth of a nation. Smith related wealth of a nation to its capital stock and claimed that increase in the capital stock could push wages above the subsistence; self-interest thus promoting harmony of interest and benefiting all sections of the society.[17] As far as the economy was concerned, Smith had less faith either in benevolence or in government intervention to restrain the excesses of self-interest and its transformation into selfishness. He relied more on competition among economic agents to produce harmony of interest in the society. His unqualified opposition to the mercantilist doctrine was based on the notion that it hindered free markets and used governments for monopoly power.

Smith, however, failed to see that free style capitalism may lead to exploitation of some sections of the society through economic power which eventually leads to political power – not a terrible mistake committed in the eighteenth century. But his tacit acceptance of existing structure of land ownership and land rent (even after regarding it as an unearned income), and the institution of interest, are absolute mistakes if we look at his ideas in the framework of political economy of Islam.

In the context of Islamic economics, one has to admit the fact that human beings, in general, would behave as economic men in the market place without precluding the possibility that some economic agents may choose to behave in a somewhat *humane* way even in the market place. For example, the only neuro surgeon in a town may decide, on his own, not to charge the monopoly price of his services. But to assume that every economic agent would behave or could be made to behave in an altruistic way in the market place would be hardly tenable. Our criticism of the neoclassical school on this particular issue should be confined to the use of the word selfish and by posting a reminder as to what their spiritual father actually meant by the phenomenon of self-love.

Irving Kristol has lamented out how economics after Smith, in its pursuit of becoming something like physical science, did not remain humanistic. For example, the common sense understanding that a marginal increase in the income of the rich represents less satisfaction than a comparable marginal increase to the income of the poor, has no scientific basis in modern economic theory and one has to import a philosophical-egalitarian bias into economics to legitimize them.[18] It is perplexing to note that, the neo-Austrians, who claim to be the true heirs of 18th century Anglo-Scottish liberal enlightenment to which Smith belonged, and vehemently criticize the "scienticism" which began to envelope economic theory after Adam Smith, have themselves a tendency to reduce the human being to *economic man.*[19]

3.2 Rationality

The assumption of rationality, in the context of neoclassical economics, generally implies that an individual or group of people do not miss an opportunity to fulfil their self-interest and that they always try to maximize utility (by maximizing pleasure and minimizing pain or maximizing benefit and minimizing cost). Again, this assumption would be close to reality with two qualifications. First, in general, we confine our man to a man in the marketplace. Second, following the neo-Austrians, we treat pleasure and benefit as subjective phenomenon defined as whatever an individual (or a group of individuals) is interested in, and not something objectively given by *the economic science.* For example, an entrepreneur may like to pay his employees more than the existing wages in the industry or more bonuses than those he had originally promised. The neoclassical assumption would rule out the possibility of such act as irrational. But this act is perfectly rational if the entrepreneur is relying on the continued or extra ordinary hard work by the employees in future or to discourage them to look for another employer (efficiency wage theory). To keep a harmonious atmosphere at the work place could be another plausible reason. Not only that, it would be perfectly rational if the employer does it because he gets enormous pleasure by sharing some of his benefits (profits) with his employees and/or expects a reward in the hereafter. The last case shows that a man *could* be non materialistic even in the market place and yet he would be behaving in his self-interest!

It is thus obvious that the meaning of rationality as espoused by the neoclassical school has to be broadened in the context of Islamic economics. But there is no evident case for rejecting their concept of rationality in absolute terms. Our criticism should be restricted to the constriction of their perception.

3.3 Material welfare

As long as the assumption of material welfare is concerned, it is difficult to understand how it could not be regarded as one of the important and desirable goals of our life. How could a Muslim perform all his duties towards his Creator and his fellow human beings as asked by his Creator, without striving for material well-being for himself, his family and relatives and the community at large. This is not to reject the idea that for a true Muslim this desirable goal should be "subservient to the *falah* in *'Akhira* should there be a conflict".[20] But, one should realize the fact that we all have our shortcomings and what we are supposed to do should not be taken as what we actually do as the starting point for any economic or social analysis. The role of Islamic economics (as we will emphasize in section IV) which is certainly normative in character, is to develop an economic system with corresponding rules and regulations which would facilitate its agents to act in a desirable way.[21] This is in contrast to formulate a system which, as a starting point, assumes the behavior of individuals given as dictated by the teaching of Islam.

> Khan himself agrees that
> "Material prosperity is desirable so far as it helps one to perform
> his duties towards God, society, family and one's own self. It should
> be a means to achieve *falah* in the *'Akhira.*"[22]

But, once we admit that wealth could be an important means to achieve *falah* in the *Akhira*, his assertion that "(A)dopting material progress as a supreme objective of life is thus alien to the Islamic framework"[23] while perfectly true, becomes somewhat extraneous for economic analysis even in the context of Islamic economics. For Islamic economics the important point is that the struggle for material progress is permitted. What should further come under its premises is to empower the government to formulate proper rules and policies which would ensure fair means for this struggle and the minimization of unjustified disparities in income and wealth. However, as it is neither desirable nor possible for an economic system to quash all inequalities in income or wealth if it wishes to remain natural and efficient, a significant level of disparity in income and wealth would remain in a reformed Muslim society and people would continue to strive to push themselves into higher income strata. In a market economy, the composition of demand for consumption would be such that it may warrant production of goods and services which can come under the category of luxury, at least with reference to relatively low income groups of people. How much an individual strives for a higher level of income under the given rules of the game and then how does he spend on goods and services legally available in the market, should have to be left on his judgement. It should be the domain of Muslim educationists, sociologists, politicians and preachers to further mould the behavior of individuals to make them increasingly caring and mindful of the needs of relatively low income groups of people.

3.4 Inter-personal utility

Akram's assertion the traditional economics fails to cogitate and appropriately assimilate the question of interdependent utility, is not only correct but poses a challenge to Islamic economists. One reason why the traditional economists have failed to address this issue into their models is its intractability. The onus is, therefore, on us to accept the challenge.

4. Knowledge, subjectivism and economics as a science

Akram Khan refutes the notion that Man has knowledge and the ability to decide what is good for him. He writes

"Islam considers man incapable of knowing what is best for him. Only God has perfect knowledge. The human knowledge is imperfect and man needs guidance for making various decisions in life. God in his ultimate mercy has revealed guidance for man through prophets and books. Man needs this guidance."[24]

As Muslims, we all believe that God has true knowledge of everything, not only what we can see and experience, but also about things which we cannot observe. Out of His mercy He has given us a part of His knowledge for our guidance. But, He has chosen to keep us in dark on many aspects of our life and this world. At the same time He gave us aptitude and intellect. On many social and economic issues He has provided us direct guidance. On others, we are supposed to use our reasoning and judgements. In the first case we must accept the Knowledge provided by Him. But in the later case where we have to use our own intelligence, the nature of Knowledge we possess or discover would be different. We may claim to know something as we *Know* it although what we do know may be untrue.

According to Fritz Machlup, "(F)or my purpose, knowledge is what people think they know. Whether or not I agree with them is irrelevant for my study".[25] He emphasizes that knowledge must be studied as a system of belief and stressed that the known and the knowing are to be understood as matters of human action. That ultimately is why knowledge has a social character. What he (Machlup) did not stress is that human action is necessarily rational – purposive in any fundamental or deterministic sense; nor did he embrace the notions of apriorism or apodictic certainty".[26] Machlup, who was an economist of Austrian orientation, did not separate human knowledge from that which is revealed by God – a mistake if we see it in the context of Islamic economics. But as we can deduce from the above, he was against rejecting any source of knowledge for any social analysis as long as some people believe in it.

It is true that in contemporary Western economic thought there is no room for divine revelation to influence the structure or operation of economic institutions. Individuals (or group of individuals) may believe in divine revelation and act accordingly, but the separation of religion and state does not allow any member of the society to *demand* such institutions on religious ground even if he belongs to the majority community. Furthermore, in case of a conflict between the act of an individual (or group of individuals) and the existing law of the land, the later would prevail. For example, the Muslim communities in Western countries are not allowed to establish interest free commercial banks because the law of the land requires all banks to guarantee the depositors of their principal (and interest, in case of savings and time deposits). However, it does allow the majority, assuming that the society is run through democratic institutions, to make any laws and institutions on their own merit and without necessarily a reference to divine revelation.[27] In this sense, the neoclassical assumption cannot prohibit an individual or the majority of the society to use the knowledge available through divine sources, an important point to bear in mind in the context of Islamic economics.

The flaw of the neoclassical economics, which emanates from its attempt to equate the methodology of economics to that of physics and other natural sciences, is its assertion that there is a unique or rational way a man would behave which is objectively and naturally given to him by the economy. But as Warren Samuels has pointed out:

> "For economists and for other social scientists a key question concerns whether or to what extent, and with what qualifications, if any, epistemological criteria deemed appropriate for the study of physical reality are relevant and/or desirable for the study of man and society. This is because (1) human beings are presumably, or at least possibly, possessed of free will, at least to some extent, (2) the economy is an artifact, not (like the solar system or the galaxy) given to man, and, *inter alia*, (3) human beings can act upon or with social science knowledge and thereby change the object of study, that is, knowledge of the object of the study can affect that very object through influencing human action and choice."[28]

Similarly, Frank Knight emphasizes that human society is, not *unlike* human games, for example, soccer or poker; each is a matter of human construction and not of some prior independent reality.[29] Thus, it is possible for each society to formulate its own social and economic system commensurate with its objectives and ideology based on its own sources of knowledge.

From our perspective, the position of neo-Austrians (compared to the neoclassical doctrine[30]) is more interesting in this respect who, distracting from the neoclassical view on rationalism, define it as something which is located within the individual himself, not within something called "the economy." According to them, man acts purposefully, learns from such action, and that any existential disparity between intent and result flows from an error of knowledge.[31] Furthermore, these purposeful actions flow from "self-interest," defined as whatever it is the individual is interested in.[32] However, due to their libertarian orientation, belief in individualism and, their tendency to reduce human being to homo economicus, the neo-Austrians fail to appreciate that the individual's *self-interest* and resulting *purposeful action* can be influenced by instituting different social values based on different sources of knowledge, and alternative rules of the game for the economy. It is worth emphasizing that it is at this point where the role of Islamic economics (or any other social doctrine) becomes clear.

5. The nature of political economy of Islam

5.1 Primary objective

Monzer Kahf has correctly stated that "Any economic system should be founded on an ideology which provides the economic system with its basis and objectives on one hand and its axioms and principles on other".[33] He further adds that, "The validity of an economic system can be tested by its internal consistency, its compatibility with the systems organizing the other aspects of life, and its provision for improvement and growth".[34]

Kahf's proposition raises the following questions. What is the basic goal and objective of an Islamic economic system? On what ideology is this goal and objective based? What are its axioms and principles? Why the dominant economic doctrine of the contemporary world or *economics* is unsuitable for a Muslim society? Why Islamic economics?

According to our opinion, there are two *interrelated* basic objectives of different systems organizing economic, social and other aspects of life in a Muslim society. First, to implement the commandments of the Creator. Second, to *help* its people in leading their individual and collective life according to the teachings of Islam. The underlying ideology is that man has been put to test during his earthly life. He has been endowed with instincts for both good and the bad deeds, which is true for both Muslims and non-Muslims. The only difference when a man happens to be a Muslim is that he knows and believes what is a correct and desired behavior for him. However, just because he is a Muslim and he knows what is a preferred Islamic behavior, is no guarantee that he will *actually* behave accordingly. Timur Kuran, one of the leading critics of contemporary Islamic economics literature, has correctly pointed out the flaw in the argument of some Islamic economists who claim that the Islamic norms provide a practical solution of the modern economic problems'[35] This is not to refute that if all people in an Islamic country change their norms and behavior according to the teaching of Islam, most economic problems of the society would be solved. The point is rather that we cannot and should not base and develop a system which takes this prescribed behavior as given. It would simply be a wrong assumption. But, on the other hand, the critics of Islamic economics should also recognize the fact that a person can behave differently under different organizational set up and rules of the game.

Similarly, it would be incorrect to assume that in a Muslim society people will behave in a desired way only through moral persuasion and education. That it would help is also undeniable, and to a certain extent so will coercion. But the major part of the efforts should be centered around devising appropriate rules of the economic game and a structure of material and other social incentives which may *help* and influence people to act in a desirable way.

Another important point which is overlooked by Timur Kuran and others, and not given proper emphasis by the advocates of Islamic economics, is to recognize the differences in attitude, behavior and level of morality among individuals. That there are people in every society (Muslims or non-Muslims) with varying proportions, who possess high level of morality and/or God consciousness, is unrefutable. Nor it is impossible to devise a mechanism to locate these people and encourage them to come forward and make their contributions towards establishing an economic system based on precepts of Islam. For example, the establishment of interest-free banks would require, especially at the initial stage, competent industrialists and businessmen who are honest and prudent. According to the conventional economics, if it is conceivable that in a given circumstances an individual can lie and cheat to his benefit, then it is only proper to assume that all individuals will behave in the same manner. The implicit assumption being that a man is a man just as a stone is a stone, which would always and everywhere follow the *natural* law. We are not rejecting the fact that many individuals in contemporary Muslim society are untrustworthy, a point often raised by the critics of Islamic economics. At the same time, however, one should also realize the existence of a sizable number of people present in a Muslim (or any other) society who will not do any wrong doing because of their consciousness and/or fear of God. An economic system based on such realization will eventually favor and encourage those individuals who are honest and trustworthy.

Once we agree to the notion of differences in behavioral norms among the members of a society, and the possibility of people acting differently under a different organizational set up, it makes all the sense to claim that the goal of an Islamic economic system (as we have described above) is viable.

5.2 *What is an Islamic economic system?*

Once we have defined the primary objective of an Islamic economic system, the next step is to characterize the principal elements of that system. Islamic economists should realize that the Creator has chosen not to give a blue print of the economic system even for the period during which the Quran was revealed. Muslim intellectuals and economists of each country and for each era of history, therefore, face the challenge to construct (and reconstruct) a suitable economic system which derives its ideology and general principles from teachings of Islam and solves the economic (and other related) problems of the epoch. Muslim economists who try to find the blue print of an Islamic economic system for our time in the writings of great Fuqaha of the past, set too easy, indeed inappropriate, a task for themselves. Similarly, economists who find the contemporary Western system quite acceptable for Muslim societies, fail to envision the quintessence of an Islamic economic system. This, however, does not mean that we should reject all discourses and epistemologies in the Western economic traditions. Instead, all of these, if carefully studied and appropriately used, could be helpful in clarifying our problems and finding solutions.

5.3 *Economics or political economy?*

In a recent article, A. W. Coats points out that around the turn of the century there was a concomitant narrowing of the scope of our subject symbolized by the terminological shift from "political economy" to "economics". This move enabled economists to delegate to other social science specialists such troublesome issues as the distribution of income and wealth, the power structure and social justice".[36] Furthermore, the change was facilitated by the practice of distinguishing sharply between the *science* i.e. theory or analysis (sometimes referred to as economics proper) and the *art* of political economy i.e. the discussion of current economic problems and policies.[37] The dichotomy is based on the notion that a professional economist, like a professional engineer, is an objective scientific expert who cannot afford to consider the demand of political economy and ethics. Economics has thus become a science distinguished from art and positive distinguished from normative.

As Samuels has cautioned, one should not belittle positivism's attempt at objective, confirmable and replicable definitions of reality through its emphasis on the observable or the abstract related thereto and on properties and operations rather than ultimates, absolutes and essences. At the same time, however, it must be emphasized that positivism has been shown to have such epistemological and discursive limits as to be severely diminished in the confidence which it can accord to inquiry.[38] As soon as we admit that man is not merely an *economic man*, the economic system in which he lives ceased to remain entirely insulated from other aspects of his life. The remedy is to (re)enlarge the scope of economics. It is not only improper and unnecessary but difficult to set aside the issues of distribution of income or wealth or power structures which facilitate or expedite a particular pattern of income distribution, social justice and other social and ethical problems from economics.

For the last hundred years, the institutionalist school has struggled to keep the scope of economics broadened. It has accentuated the fact that in capitalism, allocation of resources is not achieved primarily through the market but the power structure which operates through the market by affecting the demand and supply. For instance, they stress the existence of powerful groups of labor unions, farmers and corporations. They share the view of Post Keynesians that struggle among them over the distribution of income generates both inflation and stagflation.[39] Both schools have emphasized the need for government intervention but not always for the same reason. Keynes recognized the ability of the market to allocate resources in the right directions but stressed the need for an active government to maintain full employment by controlling or expanding the volume (or aggregate demand) of economic activities. Institutionalists, on the other hand, emphasize the need to control the market for a desirable direction of resource allocation. Most of the reforms in favour of the working class in the United States have been credited to the efforts made by the founding members of this school. However, neither the post Keynesians nor the proponents of institutionalist school have been so far able to present an alternate and viable scheme of economic organization to tackle the triangular macroeconomic problems of inflation, unemployment and income distribution simultaneously without sacrificing efficiency.

In communism, the problem of distribution of income becomes the cardinal issue of economics. In order to eliminate the exploitation of workers, the process of production is carried out under a different power structure; the state takes over the roles of entrepreneur and capitalists. However, the lack of personal and/or material interest among the bureaucrats who run the enterprises results in serious inefficiencies. The events of last ten years in the communist world have decisively demonstrated the inadequacy of socialist or communist systems to solve the problems of a modern economy. They did succeed in reducing income inequalities, getting price stability and eradicating the problem of unemployment. But the cost of this achievement, in terms of the loss in efficiency, was so enormous that the system eventually collapsed.

In the context of a Muslim society, the issue of distribution of income and wealth has particular importance. Both the Qur'an and the Sunnah of Prophet, peace be upon him, give numerous instructions and principles that Muslims are supposed to follow in their individual and collective affairs. The following verse of the Qur'an is a clear instruction to both the governments and the people of Muslim societies:

> "Whatever [spoils taken] from the people of those villages God has turned over to his Apostle __ [all of it] belongs to God and the Apostle, and the near of kin [of deceased believers], and the orphans, and the needy, and the wayfarer, so that it may not be [a benefit] going round and round among such of you as may [already] be rich. Hence, accept [willingly] whatever the Apostle gives you [thereof], and refrain from [demanding] anything that he *withholds* from you; and remain conscious of God: for, verily, God is severe in retribution."
>
> (59:7; my Italic)[40]

Siddiqui (1992 b) has emphasized that this *Ayah* provides one of the basic principles of Islamic economics i.e., the government of a Muslim country has an obligation to prevent the concentration of wealth in few hands *even if* the income or wealth could have been acquired through proper means. This provides a clear justification for the government to use tax and transfer policies to impede concentration of wealth after the production process is completed.

It is quite understandable that in any society, whether their inhabitants are Muslims or not, many people would be tempted to become richer even if it is only achievable at the expense of others or by exploiting others. On the other hand, people belonging to relatively lower income groups would be jealous and envious of the rich. Such feelings are a matter of human instinct. Muslims are asked by their Creator to control these instincts:

> "O You who have attained to faith! Do not devour one another's possessions wrongfully _ *not even* by way of trade based on mutual agreement _ and do not destroy one another: for, behold, God is indeed a dispenser of grace unto you! And as for him who does this with malicious intent and a will to do wrong _ him shall We, in time, cause to endure [suffering through] fire: for this is indeed easy for God."
>
> (my Italic) (4:29–30)[41]

and

> "Hence, do not covet the bounties which God has bestowed more abundantly on some of you than others. Men shall have a benefit from what they earn, and women shall have a benefit from what they earn. Ask, therefore, God [to give you] out of His bounty: behold God has indeed full knowledge of everything."
>
> (4:32)[42]

We should admit that while many Muslims would adhere to these commandments of their Creator, others would tend to neglect the teaching. It is, therefore, inappropriate to assume that because Muslims are asked by their Creator to behave in the above manner, they will actually do so. Nor should one claim that an Islamic system, through its educational and economic policies, would be able to obliterate the causes of these natural instincts completely. But a properly designed economic system with appropriate rules and regulation, which addresses the issue of income distribution, could provide a social environment that will *help* its people to restrain and inhibit these passions.

As we have mentioned above, one way to thwart the concentration of wealth is to formulate appropriate tax and transfer policies. However, if this is the only formula, there is a danger that it may either impede economic activities and lead to inefficiency (if over-utilized) or fail to achieve the objective satisfactorily (if under-utilized). It then becomes clear that the greatest task of the political economy of Islam is to devise a production mechanism which is not only efficient and addresses the issues of unemployment and inflation, but intrinsically and endogenously tackles the problem of distribution, not leaving it as a residual issue.

One can argue that the neoclassical school does not throw away the question of distribution, it only attempts to separate this problem from that of efficiency i.e., the market is allowed to determine a major part of the production process and the resulting distribution of income pattern, but any *serious* injustice is corrected through taxation and transfer policies. However, an advantage of tackling both problems in a single and exclusive set up is that it may foster a production process which leads to a more desirable income distribution pattern intrinsically and abbreviate the extent of reliance on tax and transfer policies. Furthermore, as we have emphasized above, there is a limit to which these transfer policies can be used. This is why, under the neoclassical framework, the resolution of distributional question has manifested in accommodating the sentiments of the relatively low income groups of people against the rich instead of containing the concerns of the rich by allocating them just enough so that they remain active in the production process. There is a vast difference between these two approaches: in the former case a minimum possible part of income is allocated to low income groups of people to keep them from agitating whereas in the later approach the strategy is to allocate, through the production process, a minimum possible portion of income to the rich so that they remain in production. An important point worth noting in this context is that the neoclassical solution is a source of increasing, or at least maintaining, the gap between the rich and the poor which has been a continuous cause of resentment and indignation in many societies of the world.

In the methodology of the political economy of Islam, therefore, a central issue would be to devise a production process which, primarily through the market forces but under a different organizational set up with different rules of the game and the resulting power structure, allocates the minimum possible part of income (to the relatively rich class) to secure efficiency. This is in contrast to the neoclassical solution of redistributing a minimal part of the income (after efficient production) to avoid serious injustice and discontent. Siddiqui and Zaman (1989 a & b) and Siddiqui (1992 & 1994a) have attempted to show that replacement of interest-based transactions by those based on equity or profit and loss-sharing arrangement, can (at least to some extent) move the economy towards a desirable income distribution path without any loss of efficiency.[43] Siddiqui (1996) raises issues related to different factors of production and their returns under political economy of Islam. He points out that, in general, Muslim economists have not questioned the treatment of land, labour and their returns in neoclassical framework. However, if the distribution of income is accepted as the central focus of an Islamic economic system, the neoclassical theory of wage and its approach towards land rent must be thoroughly scrutinized. Similarly, the role of the entrepreneur in the economy and its share in income should be an important area of investigation. This is a long and difficult research agenda for students of political economy of Islam.

In his recent writings, Muhammad Umer Chapra has stressed the importance of an additional filter mechanism to assist the price system for a more desirable and equitable use of resources in the economy so that every member of the society could be assured of the basic needs of life. According to him

"Allocation of resources is to be brought about by a double layer of filters. The first filter attacks the problem of unlimited wants at the very source – *the inner consciousness of individuals* – by changing the individual's preference scale in keeping with the demands of both efficiency and equity. Islam makes it incumbent upon all Muslims to pass their potential claims on resources through the filter of Islamic values so that many of them are eliminated at the source before they are exposed to the second filter of market prices."[44]

(my italics)

Chapra also argues for categorizing all goods and services into three groups: needs, luxuries and intermediates.[45] For the last category which consists of those goods which cannot be clearly classified as basic needs or luxury, Chapra suggests the imposition of high rate of taxes or tariffs to discourage their demand. Chapra admits that in the contemporary Muslim societies conspicuous consumption has become a part of social frame of mind, and until individuals in Muslim societies stop consumption of luxury goods on a voluntary basis, it is imperative for the government to impose a ban on production or import of such goods.

Although, one can be only sympathetic with Chapra's concern for need fulfillment for all, his suggestions to achieve this goal may create some problems. For example, categorization of all goods and services into three groups would not be a trivial issue. Even if it can be made possible, when people have the means to spend as they desire, they would either try to get around the ban or find other avenues of expenditure.

As we elaborated earlier, the solution lies in improving the distribution of income in the economy so that everyone gets an income which is enough to satisfy his basic needs. The sad demise of the socialist economies is a clear proof that the task of improving distribution of income pattern and at the same time remain efficient, is not an easy one. However, for Islamic economics to provide an alternative to capitalism and socialism, we have to accept that challenge.

6. Jurisprudential reforms

In a recent article, reviewing the literature on the issue of property rights in Islam and its relevance to current political debate in the Islamic Republic of Iran, Sohrab Behdad has raised a very important issue.[46] According to him, even if Muslim economists along with the concerned political authorities in a country, on the basis of their understanding of the teaching of Islam, agree to the need and desirability of land reforms, it would be impossible to implement them unless the dominant school of Islamic jurisprudence in the country sanctions the validity of such reforms. Two points are important to note here. First of all, it should be stressed that this issue is neither confined to land reform nor to Iran where Shi'ism is the dominant school. To a certain extent, it could be conceded that religious hierarchy in Sunny sect is feeble, if not absent. For example, in the Sunny sect, whether a person holds formal religious credentials or not, or whether he belongs to a particular school of thought or not, he can still justify his position provided that his arguments are based on appropriate Islamic sources.

However, in the context of Pakistan and other Muslim countries where Sunni'ism is the dominant sect, there are two problems with most religious schools. First, the system of their religious education does not address the contemporary economic and social problems adequately. It also lacks a clear understanding of contemporary economic institutions. The second problem, which partly stems from the first one, is their unqualified allegiance and adhesion to the opinion and rulings of the leading Fuqaha of their respective schools. At times, in their obsession to follow a particular school of thought, they even overlook the very principles of fiqh and fail to give the direct teachings of The Qur'an its rightful place. A recent example is the debate on *Bai Muajjal* (deferred payments) and riba by some renowned religious scholars in two monthly journals published by two important religious groups in Pakistan.[47] It is so perplexing to see how some of them base their crucial and decisive argument on one or two passages of *AlMabsoot* and *AlHidaya* (two famous books of Hanafi fiqh) which have only an indirect implication for the subject of *Bai Muajjal*. Moreover, all of them, including those who do come up with more interesting arguments and directly refer to the Qur'an and Sunnah, fail to mention the problem of inflation even once in the whole debate.[48]

The long term solution to this problem lies in reconstructing the present system of education in Muslim countries which separates the religious and non religious education. In the short run, however, it is the responsibility of Muslim economists in general and those who have greater capability to investigate into Islamic sources of knowledge in particular (with their proficiency in Arabic language and/or Fiqh), to persuade and convince the religious authorities to reconsider their position wherever and whenever it may be necessary.

7. Methodological pluralism for positive aspects of political economy of Islam

There are aspects of economics which are universal in nature and do not hinge on a particular economic organization in any significant manner. Examples are analysis of how an increase in money supply affects general level of prices in the absence of price control or how the introduction of a social security system changes the savings and consumption behavior of individuals. In conventional economics, a number of methods are used to inquire into such phenomenon: inductive, deductive, empirical and econometric, common sense or imagination, instrumentalism, experimentalism, etc. There are adamant supporters and critics of each of these approaches. Apparently, each of them has a desire to acquire confident knowledge, if not *the* truth. But many of them have gone a bit too far in their quest to acquire such knowledge. For example, Friedman (1951) had originally argued that unrealism of assumptions in an economic model was not a matter of concern because what they neglected was not of much importance. But his followers have gone much beyond this to assert that a theory is better the more unrealistic its assumptions are. Alan Musgrave points out that Friedman's thesis of the unimportance of assumption was relevant and applicable to only those circumstances where disregarded factors were unimportant.[49] Indeed the correct way to go is neither to insist on perfectly realistic assumptions as we will never be able to model any economic phenomenon with all the complications of the real world, nor to completely disregard the real world.

The above example can be extended to all other discourses in economics. A deductive analysis can provide significant insight into a particular economic phenomenon but it would hardly ever epitomize the reality. On the other hand, observation of data can be utilized to form hypothesis which could have a potential to acquire the status of a theory, but it cannot be a direct and ready source of theory and prediction in future (which may be done in physics where the problem of parameter shift is not so serious). Similarly, instrumentalism can be applied in some cases which means accepting a theory just because it works. This is done in medicine where, for instance, aspirin is used because it does work, although its complete effects are yet to be determined. In the mean time, research is continued to obtain all possible details of its effects.[50] The same course could be followed by economists. To sum up, we quote Samuels:

> "There are varying subject-matters to which these sets of credentials may be applied; different sets of credentials may be applied to the same subject matter; no one is obligated to accept the ultimate foundations of any or all of these sets of credentials. One can work with any or all sets of credentials with varying degrees of suspension of ultimate belief."[51]

It is extremely important to realize that the task of formulating the principles of political economy of Islam, indeed a formidable one, is still in its infancy. It is pertinent for us to be more receptive to the notion that knowledge progresses through criticism.[52] Furthermore, unlike the stance of contemporary schools of thought which does not accept a criticism unless it comes from within the school of thought, or from within an epistemological perspective, we should be open to any serious criticism wherever it may come from.

8. Conclusion

The proponents of a political economy of Islam face an arduous and formidable task to restructure the systems of economy in their respective countries. Without making any attempt to deride the voluminous literature of Islamic economics, I have tried to highlight the points where some of us may have chosen an incorrect discourse and suggest an alternative path to proceed. I hope I have shown the inappropriateness of the assertion that the behavioral norms prescribed by Islam in itself provide the solution of economic problems of our time. In contrast, it is emphasized that the role of economic system is to provide an environment which would help the people in behaving in a desirable way. An important assignment for the students of political economy of Islam is to devise an efficient production mechanism which not only solves the problems of unemployment and inflation but intrinsically and endogenously addresses the issue of distribution of income.

It is pertinent for us to keep a close look at different currents of thoughts in the contemporary literature of traditional (Western) economics without being too ready to accept or reject them. Similarly, the rulings of great Fuqaha of Islam who did a tremendous job for their era, cannot be binding on us unless it is directly based on the Quranic injunctions or it still solves the problems of our time. Finally, we should be generous in accepting criticism, whether it comes from within or without. It sharpens our ideas by compelling us to do more thinking and more work. Finally, for those areas of political economy of Islam which are primarily positive in nature, we suggest that methodological pluralism is the best course of investigation and road to confident knowledge.

Notes

1 I am grateful to Dr. Abdul Naseer of the State Bank of Pakistan and Dr. S. A. Shahab of University of Brunei Darussalam who gave valuable comments on an earlier draft of the paper. I would also like to thank an anonymous referee of this Journal who pointed out a number of errors of expression in the paper and suggested corrections. Any remaining errors are solely my own.

2 For example, **Kahf, M.**, (1989, a).

3 See the review of **Iqbal** (1988) by **M. Ali Khan**, *Journal of King Abduluziz University: Islamic Economics*, Vol. 3, 1991, pp. 97–118.

4 **Samuels** (1992), pp. 85–91.

5 **McCloskey** (1985), p. 16.

6 **Backhouse** (1994), Chapter 1.

7 **Backhouse** (1994), p. 174.

8 Plurality of methods in economics or methodological pluralism is advocated by many main stream economists, for example see **Dow** (1985) and Harcourt and Hamouda (1988). This notion of methodological pluralism should be distinguished from one advocated by Caldwell who argues for *critical pluralism*, an agenda for methodologists not for economists. See Backhouse (1994, pp.4–5).

9 For example see **Khan, M. Akram**, (1989), pp. 50–52 and **Arif, Muhammad** (1989) pp. 83–84, and 91.

10 **Kuran, Timur** (1992 a) p. 39.

11 For example see **Khan, M. Akram** (1989) p.50–52; and **Zarqa, Anas** (1989) pp. 30–32 who particulary examines the treatment of interpersonal utility by the neoclassical school.

12 For example see **Khan, M. Akram** (1989), p. 51.

13 **Bell** and **Kristol** (1981), p. 206.

14 **Oakley** (1994), p. 8.

15 Hale'vey, E. as mentioned by **Oakley** (1994), p. 10.

16 **Oakley** (1994), p. 114.

17 **Oser & Brue** (1988), p. 76.

18 ibid, p. 215.

19 ibid, p. 213.

20 **Khan, M. Akram** (1989), p. 51.

21 Many Western economists have emphasized the fact economics has never been non normative and even those who believe otherwise rather unconsciously, in actuality always work under some sort of normative premises. A good discussion of this issue can be found in "Currrent Views in Economic Positivism", in **Greenway** et al. (1991).

22 **Khan, M. Akram** (1989), p. 51. He also quotes a Hadith in which Prophet (S. A. W.) said, "(Lawful) wealth for a virtuous man is an excellent thing".

23 ibid., p. 51.

24 ibid, p. 51.

25 As quoted by **Sumuels** (1992), p. 58.

26 ibid, p. 60.

27 This issue is at the core of the current controversy in Pakistan (officially an Islamic state) about the supremacy of Shariat court over the parliament. Those who support the supremacy of the parliament argue that because the majority of the members of the parliament are always Muslims, they can always make what ever laws they think are Islamic. They further claim that by giving the final authority to the Shariat Courts, the views of a particular school of thought may be imposed on the majority. On the other hand, those favoring the superiority of the Shariat Courts, argue that the present political system does not guarantee the elections of such members of parliament who would possess the necessary credentials to carry out and sustain Islamic reforms. They further claim that once a country is declared an Islamic state and Quran and Sunnah have been made the supreme sources of law through its constitution, the final authority of interpretation and the implementation of Islamic laws should be given to the Shariat courts which consist of individuals having necessary qualifications. After all, they argue, even in Western societies, the interpretation of constitution is the domain of the supreme courts.

28 **Samuels, Warren J.** (1992), p. 1.

29 ibid, p. 20. (my Italic)

30 Although the neo-Austrians are generally thought to belong to neoclassical tradition, they regard themselves as a distinct school of thought. The distinguishing elements of their thought could be found in Barry, N. P., "Austrian Economics: A Dissent from Orthodoxy", in **Greenaway**, et al (1991).

31 That error of knowledge may be the result of the inability to know (a) the knowable, due to high information cost and (b) the unknowable (e.g., uncertainty).

32 **Bell** and **Kristol**, pp. 212–13.

33 **Khar, Monzer** (1989 a), p 43

34 ibid.

35 **Timur Kuran** (1992 a), pp. 11–12.

36 Coats, A. W., Economics as a Profession, in **Greenaway** et al. (1991), pp. 120–21.

37 ibid.

38 **Samuels**, (1992), p. 13.

39 See Samuels, W. J., "Institutional Economics", in **Greenaway**, et al., (1991).

40 (59:7), as translated by Muhammad Asad in the **Message Of The Qur'an**.

41 **Asad Muhammad**, *The Message of the Qur'an*. It is important to note that in the translation of this Ayah, Asad has adopted the meaning of "ilia" as *not even* instead of its usual meaning *except*. Please see his explanatory note # 38 of Chapter IV. However, for our current purpose, any of these meanings is appropriate although the one adopted by Asad is more forceful.

42 ibid, p. 109.

43 **Siddiqui** and **Fardmanesh** (1994b) also show that the equity-based system is financially more stable.

44 **Chapra, M. Umer** (1991), p. 34.

45 **Chapra** (1992), pp. 284–5.

46 **Behdad, Sohrab** (1992).

47 Monthly *Meesaq* (Urdu), January & May (1992) published by Tanzeem-e-Islami; and Monthly *Hikmat-e-Qur'an* (Urdu), January, November–December (1992), January (1993) published by Markazi Anjuman Khuddam-ul-Qur'an, Lahore.

48 Critics of interest free banking always raise, among other things, the issue of inflation. Any discussion related to the subject of Islamic modes of finance cannot avoid this problem. For a detailed discussion on the subject, please see **Siddiqui** (1994 a).

49 As mentioned by Denis P. O'Brien in **Greenaway**, D., et al., (1991), p. 53.
50 O'Brien, D. P., in **Greenaway** et al., (1991), p. 64.
51 **Samuels** (1992), p. 14.
52 Needless to mention that this does not apply to knowledge which is bestowed on us by our Creator.

References

Arif, Muhammad, "Towards Establishing the Microfoundations of Islamic Economics: The Basis of the Basics", (1989) in **Ghazali, Aidit & Omar, Syed** (editors), *Readings in the Concept and Methodology of Islamic Economics*, Pelanduk Publications, Petaling Jaya, Malaysia.

Backhouse, Roger E. (editor), (1994), *New Directions in Economic Methodology*, Routledge, London & New York.

Behdad, Sohrab, (1992) "Property Rights and Islamic Economic Approaches", **Jomo, K. S.**, (Editor), *Islamic Economic Alternatives: Critical Perspectives and New Directions*, Macmillan Academic and Professional Ltd., London.

Bell, Daniel and **Kristol, Irving**, (1981) *The Crisis in Economics*, Basic Books, Inc., Publishers, New York.

Chapra, M. Umer, (1991) "The Need For A New Economic System", *Review of Islamic Economics*, Volume 1, No. 1.

Chapra, M. Umer, *Islam and the Economic Challenge*, (1992), The Islamic Foundation, U.K., & The International Institute of Islamic Thought, USA.

Dow, S. C., (1985), *Macroeconomic Thought, Oxford*: Basil Blackwell.

Greenaway, David, Bleaney, Michael and **Stewart, Ian M. T.**, (editors), (1991), *Companion to Contemporary Economic Thought*, Routledge, London & New York.

Harcourt, G. C., and **Hamouda, O.**, (1988), "Post keynesianism: From criticism to coherence?" *Bulletin of Economic Research*, Volume **40**, No. **1**.

Iqbal, Munawar (editor), (1988), *Distributive Justice and Need Fulfillment in an Islamic Economy*, International Institute of Islamic Economics, Islamabad and The Islamic Foundation, Leicester, U.K.

Jomo, K. S., (editor), (1992), *Islamic Economic Alternatives: Critical Perspectives and New Directions*, Macmillan Academic and Professional Ltd., London.

Kahf, Monzer, (1989 a), "Islamic Economics and its Methodology, in **Ghazali, Aidit** and **Omar, Syed** (editors), *Readings in the Concept and Methodology of Islamic Economics*, Pelanduk Publications, Petaling Jaya, Malaysia.

Kahf, Monzer, (1989 b), "Islamic Economic System: A Review", in **Ghazali, Aidit & Omar, Syed** (Editors), *Readings in the Concept and Methodology of Islamic Economics*, Pelanduk Publications, Petaling Jaya, Malaysia.

Khan, Muhammad Akram, (1989), "Methodology of Islamic Economics", in **Ghazali, Aidit & Omar, Syed** (editors), *Readings in the Concept and Methodology of Islamic Economics*, Pelanduk Publications, Petaling Jaya, Malaysia.

Kuran, Timur, (1992 a), "The Economic System in Contemporary Economic Thought", in **Jomo, K. S.**, (Editor), *Islamic Economic Alternatives: Critical Perspectives and New Directions*, Macmillan Academic and Professional Ltd., London.

McCloskey, Donald N., (1985), *The Rhetoric of Economics*, The University of Wisconsin Press, Madison, Wisconsin, USA.

Oakley, Allen, (1994), *Classical Economic Man: Human Agency and Methodology in the Political Economy of Adam Smith and J. S. Mill*, Edward Elgar Publishing Co.

O'brien, Denis P., (1991), "Theory and Empirical Observation", in **Greenaway, David**, et al., *Companion to Contemporary Economic Thought, Routledge*, London & New York.

Oser, Jacob and **Brue, Stanley L.**, (1988), *The Evolution of Economic Thought*, fourth edition, Harcourt Brace Jovanovich Publishers.

Samuels, Warren J., (1992), *Essays on the Methodology and Discourse of Economics*, The Macmillan Press Ltd., London.

Siddiqui, Shamim A., (1994 a), "Some Controversies in Contemporary Macroeconomics: An Islamic Perspective", *Review of Islamic Economics*, Volume 3. No.1.

Siddiqui, Shamim A., & **Fardmanesh, Mohsen**, (1994 b), "Financial Stability and a Share Economy", *Eastern Economic Journal*, USA, Spring, 1994.

Stigler, George J., (1987), *Essays in the History of Economic Thought*, University of Chicago Press, Chicago.

Zarqa, Anas, (1989), "Islamic Economics: An Approach to Human Welfare", in **Ghazali, Aidit** and **Omar, Syed** (editors), *Readings in the Concept and Methodology of Islamic Economics*, Pelanduk Publications, Petaling Jaya, Malaysia.

271

17

ISLAMIZATION OF ECONOMICS

The concept and methodology*

Muhammad Anas Zarqa[1]

Source: *Journal KAAU: Islamic Economics*, 16:1 (2003), 3–42.

Abstract

Could there be a science of economics that could be described as "Islamic"? If so, does this imply denial of the existence of global economic laws that encompass all social systems, both Islamic and non-Islamic? This research paper aims at finding a considered and detailed answer to these two questions through:

(a) Demonstrating that, although science is generally character-ized by its factual descriptive statements (i.e. the laws which it arrives at), there are still certain basic aspects of any science, (the social sciences in particular, including econom-ics), regarding which no researcher can help depend on a set of preconceived values.

(b) Demonstrating that, although the texts of Islamic Shari'ah (Law) are basically a source of values, yet they often contain descriptive statements about economic life.

If we replace those values on which the science of eco-nomics should be based (mentioned in 'a') by Islamic values, and if we add to the secular statements that economics has so far arrived at by the statements mentioned in 'b', we would then be able to establish an Islamic science of economics.

The paper also explains the relationship between Islamic Economics and Islamic Law and discusses a proposed work plan to Islammization of economics.

1. Introduction

1.1 Basic question

The aim of this research paper is to study the meaning and methodology of establishing the Islamic quality (Islamization) of the science of economics in particular and of the social sciences in general.[2]

272

Two major questions arise in the context of 'Islamizing' economics, in the sense of establishing it in accordance with the principles of Islamic Law. These questions are:

First: What is the relation between conventional economics and the religion of Islam?

Second: What is the relation between Islamic economics and Islamic jurisprudence?

Regarding the first question, the majority of researchers in Islamic economics have so far distinguished between an economic system and economics as a science; they emphasize that the religion of Islam provides a unique economic system. They follow this claim by saying that the science of economics does not differ from one economic system to another.

This mode of thinking, if right, entails saying that it is impossible to have an Islamic science of economics for the very same reason that does not make us expect establishing an Islamic science of mathematics or an Islamic nuclear physics. In other words, it is impossible to establish an Islamic science of economics not because Islam and the science of economics are opposed to each other, but rather because the pursuits of each are different, and because the science of economics is global in nature and indifferent to values that differ from one system to another.

Furthermore, this mode of thinking entails saying that the laws of secular economics should be accepted by an Islamic economics in the same vein that the laws of physics hold true for all countries and social systems.

On the other hand, there is another mode of thinking which claims that the science of economics is the by-product of a particular civilization and that it could never have correct laws that would hold true for different social systems. Therefore, if we need to establish an Islamic science of economics, we should cast behind our backs secular economics and start building this Islamic economics from scratch.

Each of these two modes of thinking has in it one part of the truth, but misses the other part, as we shall see in parts 2 and 3 of this paper.

Regarding the second question, some consider Islamic economics as part of *Fiqh Al Mu'amalat* (Islamic Law of Transactions); they believe that it is only "after the economic rules have been derived from the books of Shari'ah and put for discussion in independent research studies, that we would have what is called Islamic Economics".[3] Some others, on the other hand, barely see any appreciable connection between Islamic Fiqh and economics. Thus this relationship must be determined in order to clarify the connection, a matter which I shall attempt in paragraphs 4.4 and 4.6 of this paper.

1.2 Importance of the subject

This type of methodological research to economics and other social sciences is more akin to the Principles of Islamic Jurisprudence (*Usul Al-Fiqh*) than to *Fiqh* (Islamic Law). In today's terminology, it may be called "the methodology of science". Therefore, it would have been correct to entitle this research paper "Some Principles/Methodologies of Islamic Economics".

It is needless to emphasize the importance of methodology awareness in any attempt to 'Islamize' any of the sciences to avoid scattering efforts or make the vein of thoughts on the issues under consideration go in asymmetrical directions or be in conflict with the appropriate Islamic methodology. We can in no way aspire to advance Islamic Economics or any of the other Islamic social sciences before the answers to the big methodological questions related to the principles or methodology of the science first becoming clear (and I do not wish to say "first being agreed upon').

1.3 Way of writing about methodology

I do not wish to hide from the reader the secret of admitting that I write on this subject timorously as I have given it much of my thinking, read much thereon and have written so many notes and collected for years many examples to cite in substantiating my exposition.

The current research is but a small fraction of the data I have accumulated thereon. I do not pronounce this fact just to convince the reader of the validity of the conclusions I have reached on the subject, but rather to emphasize the fact that I have not embarked on this serious research without preparation and consideration. Despite all this, I am not yet completely satisfied with it. God willing, comments received from its readers might enable me to improve upon and correct it in the future.

I am increasingly convinced that its subject-matter is more difficult than it first appeared to me; differences in the terminology and modes of expression used in its discussion constitute a big hurdle that opens the door to misunderstanding, even when thoughts are in agreement. Among the difficulties enshrouding this research is that of having to address both economists and Shari'ah scholars. What is known to one of these two groups is most often not known to the other. I found that the best method of expressing ideas is by way of giving one or more illustrative examples on each idea. This is a difficult condition for the satisfaction of which I have exerted much effort, an effort that I recommend to all those who write on the subject.

1.4 The research plan

In the second part of this research, the writer shall deal with the definition and foundations of science, any science; that is to say, its essential elements and old postulates, as well as the channels through which values creep into it. In the third part of the paper, the writer shall give a conception of the plausible relation between the religion of Islam and conventional or secular economics. In the fourth chapter, the writer shall explain the essentials of Islamic economics when it comes to age and its relation to Islamic jurisprudence and conventional economics, as well as to some other branches of knowledge. The fifth part of the paper will discuss work plans for Islamization of economics.

2. Definition and constituents of science

2.1 Descriptive and normative statements

The starting point in discussing this subject is to distinguish between descriptive and normative statements. A descriptive statement describes a specific reality, as when we say, for example, an increase in rainfall results in an increase in agricultural production, or like saying that there is life on Mars. Since a descriptive statement is a statement of what is, it could also be called a predicative statement.

Opposite to these descriptive statements or propositions are **statements of value**, which express an attitude towards what should be, like saying "Solitude is better than keeping bad company" or "Telling the truth is a duty". Such statements indicate our preference of a certain state of affairs, behaviour or condition that might occur (such as the state of 'solitude' or the behaviour of 'telling the truth') to another possible state or behaviour that might occur (such as 'keeping bad company' or 'telling a lie').

Descriptive statements or propositions might be true or correct, that is, they might be consistent with reality; they might as well be false or incorrect, that is, they might not be consistent with reality. Therefore, they are amenable to testing and verification to establish their truthfulness or falsehood. Normative statements, on the other hand, do not describe a specific reality, but express a preference. Therefore, normative statements cannot be described as true (i.e. consistent with reality) or false. However, these statements are likely to be **accepted** by us if they are compatible with our values or **rejected** if they are opposed to them.[4]

It is clear from the above argument that God's ways in the Universe and Society are expressed in descriptive statements, whereas the commandments of Shari'ah (Law), any Shari'ah, are expressed in normative statements. Therefore, the content of the empirical sciences, such as physics, agriculture and medicine is often concentrated on descriptive issues, whereas the content of the Shari'ah sciences and rules of ethics often deal with normative issues.[5]

2.2 Definition and elements of science

I will not dwell long on an exact definition of science, but will seek instead to give an approximate definition that I consider to be in keeping with the Islamic conception and with other modern definitions. First, we should distinguish between science and knowledge. Knowledge is a group of facts, whereas science is but a branch of knowledge in which its facts and the results of its experiments have been assembled and codified in the form of hypotheses and general laws that are amenable to verification and testing by logic, experimentation, deduction[6] . . . etc. This definition includes empirical sciences, such as physics as well as social sciences such as economics. It also includes syntax, mathematics, *Fiqh* (jurisprudence) . . . etc.

It is to be noted that the concept of 'science' in the Qur'an and Sunnah is not limited to positive knowledge that is consistent with reality only, but includes as well **preponderant** presumptions. For this reason, Muslim jurists are in agreement to call Fiqh a science, although many of its rules are based upon presumptive evidence. They are also in agreement about the necessity of compliance with presumptive evidence, which is preponderant.

However, Shari'ah has condemned compliance with a presumptive evidence that is *not preponderant*; such type of non-preponderant presumptive evidence has not been recognized by Shari'ah as "knowledge". Muhammad Bin Ismail Al-Amin Al-Sana'ani clarified this by saying that presumption is a common word that has many meanings: doubt that makes one oscillates between the two extremes of the matter under consideration; this type of doubt is the one condemned in both the Qur'an and the Sunnah. The other meaning is 'the preponderant' side of the issue (although it does not amount to certitude); this type is not only suitable for acts of worship, but most rules of Shari'ah revolve around it.[7]

Since most of the content of social sciences, including economics, is based on presumptive evidence that is preponderant, which evidence is dependent upon observation, deduction and induction, we do not hesitate to call such disciplines 'sciences' in the Shari'ah sense too.

What are the elements of a science, i.e. what are its general constituents? For the purpose of this research, it would be suitable to divide these elements into three categories:

First essential element

Previous presumptions, or simply 'presumptions', are implicit assumptions stemming from a general view of the universe and to Man in the case of social sciences (they might also be called 'the philosophical bases of science'). An example of such presumptions in physics is the belief, prior to any research, that the universe and material therein are subject to stable laws that are amenable to discovery. Similarly, in the field of social sciences, there lies the belief that human behaviour has a certain degree of regularity and stability. Thus presumptions are in fact descriptive statements about the universe, man or society, that could be described as starting points that are explicitly or implicitly taken as bases for building science.

Second essential element

Normative values are inevitable for science to rely on. In paragraph 2.4 of this research paper, we shall point out the most important among these values.

Third essential element

This includes the descriptive side of science, i.e. all the facts, presumptions and general theories and laws related to the subject matter of science. This third element is the one that normally receives emphasis as it is considered the immediate target of science, and the element that springs to mind whenever a certain science is mentioned. It is this descriptive element that is normally subjected to verification and testing rather than the first essential element.

It is difficult to conceive of any science that does not depend on all of the three essential elements, regardless of the degree or extent of such dependence. It is noticed, however, that the role played by the first two elements in experimental sciences, such as physics and agriculture, is less than that they play in social sciences, such as economics, education and sociology in particular, where such role becomes greater. This role expands even greater in the human sciences, such as psychology, and reaches its zenith in a normative science such as the Science of Islamic Jurisprudence. (See paragraph 4.1.1 below).

It is further noticed that seldom each of the three aforementioned elements is presented distinctively or separately from the other two. Often the content of a science is presented in the mould of the third element, although the process of presentation involves, whether explicitly or implicitly, the other two.

Since many people overlook the first two essential elements of science even in their own subject of specialization, and since they do not recognize the role these two elements play in the content of a scientific discipline or its historical development, we shall give some examples for clarification in paragraphs 2.3 and 2.4 below.

2.3 Examples of earlier presumptions in science

Among the most important functions of presumptions is that they constitute the fountain from which the scientist gets his premises, which he uses to explain phenomena. For instance, when explaining the events of the Life of the Prophet, an atheist orientalist would immediately rule out an interpretation that depends on revelation or the idea of prophethood and limit himself to other assumptions. Then he tends to organize all his study and links among facts accordingly.

Similarly, the same method is applied when attempting to explain similarity among religions; that who does not recognize prophethood and revelation and takes this stance as a basic assumption would limit his interpretation of this phenomenon to the possibility of coincidence or the possible transmission of ideas by successors from their predecessors. That who believes in revelation and prophethood would have a different interpretation of the same phenomenon: the unity and sameness of the source of all religions.

Note that in the above examples the researcher (the orientalist or the student of comparative religion) seldom reveals his assumptions. However, he formulates his interpretation of events or what he presents in the name of science on the basis of these assumptions. Among the most important economic assumptions having deep repercussions on the premises and theories of this discipline are those assumptions related to man's natural disposition and motives.

2.4 Aspects of science that should depend on previous values[8]

a. **Selection of the Topics to be Discussed**: When much human and financial resources are allocated to study a certain theory, the resources left for the study of other theories grow smaller. "This claim applies to (resources allocated to) the training of new scientists and the equal time allocated to classroom instruction and the number of pages allocated in books and magazines for the various theories. Even the allocation of equal classroom time (for the various theories) is indicative of adoption of certain values.[9] Among the cases in economics one could cite as examples of the effect of previously-held values on selecting topics for research are that keen interest shown by classical economic theory in studying and analyzing the selfish economic behaviour to the neglect of studying economic behaviour that is based on self-denial or ethical motives (See example 'b', paragraph 4.1 below).

b. **Choice of Variables and Assumptions**: If we wish to study a certain phenomenon such as that of economic growth, for example, we find that this phenomenon varies with both time and place; in other words, it is subject to the influence of many variables. Without a prior theoretical analysis, the quantitative and statistical analysis of data (such as in the case of (multi-slope equations) can only prove the existence of a certain relation among the various phenomena; it cannot, by itself alone, distinguish causes and results. Therefore, one cannot by using quantitative and statistical methods alone arrive at general laws that govern the course of economic phenomena, their causes and results, unless such quantitative methods depend on a "strong theoretical orientation".[10]

Where does this theoretical orientation, which is the basis of scientific advancement and success in using quantitative methods in analysis and testing, come from? It is the result of a number of intellectual steps that could be summarized in two phases. This involves review of the variables conceived to have a possible influence on the economic event or phenomenon under consideration. Such variables are usually great in number and many of which are of non-economic nature. The second phase involves the classification of variables into three categories:

- Variables that are not related to the phenomenon under consideration.
- Exogenous variables that influence the phenomenon but are not influenced by it.
- Endogenous variables that do not only influence the phenomenon, but that are also influenced by it as well as by exogenous variables. Efforts are normally concentrated on these endogenous variables, where a number of them are selected for explanation and prediction of their individual courses.

Since social (economic and otherwise) and psychological phenomena are generally interconnected and of mutual influence, the list of variables that should be reviewed and classified when studying any particular phenomenon is very long and difficult for students of any social science to review and classify completely. What happens always is to overlook the majority of these variables and to concentrate on a limited number of endogenous and exogenous variables among them.

The steps made to select some of the variables (or, if you wish, to discard many of the variables), then to select the issues and questions to be discussed and answered (from an infinite list of questions that could be posed) are all influenced to a great extent by the pre-conceived ideas or postulates about man and society. These steps are also influenced by the implicit and explicit assumptions they adopt in their research studies, without which no discipline could be established.[11]

c. **Selection of Acceptable Research, Proof and Refutation Methods**: Any theoretical or applied research methodology adopted is often an expression of a particular conception of the world and gives importance to certain issues to the exclusion of others. Let us try to give as an example the use of quantitative and statistical methods that are in vogue in economics as well as in other social sciences. Despite their undeniable value, these methods give great importance to clear concepts that are characterized by their easy statistical measurement and low cost even if they are of limited significance or purport, or unable to arrive at the basic facts. An example of the **influence of the research methodology** adopted is those many quantitative studies (based on econometrics) dealing with the phenomenon of brain drain from the developing to the developed industrial countries. Economic variables, such as the cost of travel between the two countries involved, the average per capita income in the home country of an immigrant compared to that of the country of destination etc., were used. All these variables are easy to measure. Other more important variables, however, are ignored because they are difficult to quantify and measure, such as the social factors encouraging the immigration of brains from their home country (such as corruption and oppression) or other important personal reasons (such as the degree of a person's loyalty to his country of origin and his feeling of responsibility towards it . . . etc.).

3. Analysis of the relation between Islam and economics

It is easy to depict the relation between Islam (i.e. in its two primary sources of the Qur'an and the Sunnah and its other sources based thereon) and economics by the following simple diagram. The big circle in the diagram represents the Islamic premises or assumptions, whereas the smaller circle represents the assumptions of economics. A horizontal line separates normative assumptions (above the line) from descriptive assumptions (below the line).

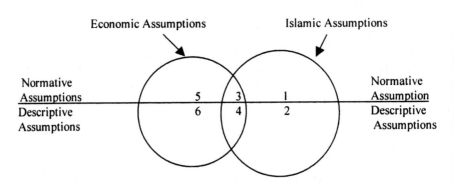

Diagram showing the relation between Islam and Economics

It is clear from the diagram that we have six distinctive categories of assumptions that have been numbered from 1 to 6. Category number 1 includes Islamic normative assumptions; number 2 includes Islamic descriptive assumptions. Categories 3 and 4 are shared between Islam and economics, where 3 includes normative assumptions that are confirmed by both Islam and economics, whereas 4 includes Islamic descriptive assumptions that are confirmed by economics. Category 5 includes normative economic assumptions about which no mention was made in the authoritative texts of Shari'ah and cannot be derived from such texts. They constitute normative assumptions that are exclusively the property of economics. Category 6 includes the descriptive assumptions of economics.

The above six categories constitute theoretical categories that none might have an equivalent in reality. It is imperative to give at least one example about each of these categories to ensure that they are not void of substance but have examples in real life. This we shall attempt in the following discussion:

First: Islamic normative assumptions (categories 1 and 3)

Here lies the bulk of authoritative Shari'ah texts from the Qur'an and the Sunnah, because all Shari'ah commands and prohibitions (in their various degrees of obligation, abomination and strict prohibition) are normative. Some of these normative assumptions are not, however, economic in nature, such as God's command "Turn not thy cheek away from men in scorn, and walk not in the earth exultantly" (31:18); others are (category 3), such as God's command "O believers, fear you God; and give up the usury that is outstanding" (2:278) or ". . . pay the alms" (2:110). All the rules governing the economic system of Islam fall within this category.

We can view category 3 from the perspective of modern economics and ask: are there any Islamic normative assumptions that are embraced by economists as well? At first glance such assumptions seem to be practically non-existent, for modern economics has always sought to avoid such normative assumptions. But as we said earlier (in 2.4), there are aspects in any science that should, by necessity, rely on certain normative assumptions, such as the selection of research topics to be discussed. One can notice that the subject of productive efficiency (which roughly refers to achieving maximum production with the least possible cost) is one of the most important issues of interest to economists, thus by virtue of such interest they implicitly express a normative preference. This is in keeping with Islam's viewpoint that prohibits waste and squandering (loss of productive efficiency is but a form of waste). It is also consistent with the objective of safeguarding wealth (*al mal*), which is one of the five major objectives of Shari'ah.

Another clear example is that of the keen interest shown by economists in analyzing economic growth (in the sense of sustained growth of the average per capita income), an issue that is compatible with Islam's interest in combating poverty and its preference of a state of affluence to that of deprivation and destitution.

Thus one can see that assumptions falling under category (3) are not empty, whether we view them from Islam's perspective or from the perspective of modern economics.

Second: Islamic descriptive assumptions (categories 2 and 4)

These assumptions **describe** a reality, refer to **a relation obtaining among variables** or **classify** facts in a certain manner. Here are a few examples of non-economic assumptions (category 2).

(a) God says about honey, "In it there is healing for people" (16:69); this is a descriptive statement showing the relation between the use of honey and the healing of certain diseases, a statement that falls within the realm of medical science.

(b) The Quran says "Our Lord, take us not to task if we forget, or make mistake" (2:286), a supplication that is indicative of the fact that there is a voluntary side to some types of forgetfulness that can be avoided, otherwise there is no justification for asking God's forgiveness for committing them. This is a descriptive statement that falls within the realm of psychology.

(c) In *Surat Al Baqarah* (2:166) God says ". . . when those that were followed disown their followers . . .". In Surat al-A'raf (7:75) He says about Salih (Peace be upon him) "The chieftains of his people, who were scornful, said unto those whom they despised. . . . . ."

The word *"mala"* originally refers to dignitaries and chieftains to whose opinions and sayings people turn back. Such group in society has been mentioned several times in the Holy Qur'an as a social predicament to acceptance of the call of God's Messengers. God says in *Surat alAhzab*, "They would say 'Our Lord, we obeyed our chiefs and great ones, and they led us astray from the way" (33:67).

The above, and some other similar verses in the Holy Qur'an, emphasize the importance of classifying people into followers and followed when analyzing society's reaction to new situations or ideas. This is a descriptive statement that falls within the domain of sociology.

Among the **economic-related Islamic assumptions** (category 4), the following could serve as examples:

(a) God says in *Surat al-Alaq*, which was the first *Surath* to be revealed, "Nay, but man doth transgress all bounds. In that he looketh upon himself as self-sufficient" (96:6–7). He also says in *Surath al-Shura*, "If God were to enlarge the provision for His servants, they would indeed transgress" (42:27). There are many traditions that also link wealth or richness to transgression, such as the Prophet's saying "Take the initiative to do (good) deeds . . . or else you would be waiting for either poverty that would make you forgetful about (initiating) such good deeds or richness that would make you transgress all bounds".[12] This is a descriptive economic statement that links affluence and richness to transgression, a statement that, as far as the author knows, has not caught the attention of economists.

(b) God says in *Surath Al-Imran*, "Fair in the eyes of men is the love of things they covet: women and sons; heaped-up hoards of gold and silver; horses branded (for blood and excellence); and (wealth of) cattle and well-tilled land. Such are the possessions of this world's life; but in nearness to God is the best of the goals (to return to). Say: Shall I give you glad tidings of things far better than those? For those that fear God are, with their lord, gardens underneath which rivers flow, therein dwelling forever, and spouses purified, and God's good pleasure. For in God's sight are (all) His servants" (3:15–16). In these verses of the Holy Qur'an there are two descriptive statements: the first is man's unlimited love of wealth. An authentic tradition has the same meaning: "Should the son of Adam possess two valleys of money, he would still love to have a third . . .".[13]

The second states that belief in God's reward in the hereafter mitigates man's unbound love of wealth in life. The first statement is shared by economists.

(c) Allah the Exalted says in *Surat Al Nisa'*, "Do not covet that whereby God in bounty preferred one of you above another . . . and ask God of His bounty" (4:32). He also says, "Stretch not thine eyes to that We have given for enjoyment to parties of them" (20:131). The Prophet (P.B.U.H.) says "Look to those who are below you (in wealth) as this is better suited to not look down scornfully to the bounties God has given to you" (Narrated by Muslim).

One could conclude from the two verses quoted above that, in seeking life's material gains, man is influenced by what others have of these gains. One could conclude from the tradition quoted above that a consumer's satisfaction of what he has is influenced by what others have, i.e. by his relative position among the total population of consumers. There are many other Shari'ah texts that emphasize the interrelatedness of individuals' behaviour and the link between the changing utility among them and the great influence external and social factors have on all that.

Such texts are incompatible with two basic assumptions in the theory of consumer behaviour and in the theory of welfare economics: the assumption that "consumers' tastes" are external variables and the assumption that changes in consumers' utility are independent of each other.

(d) God says, ". . . and if ye believe and guard against evil, He will grant you your recompense, and will not ask you (to give up) your possessions. If He were to ask you for all of them, and press you, ye would covetously withhold, and He would expose all your ill-feeling" (47:37). He also says "Hold to forgiveness . . ." (7:199) and "They ask thee how much to spend; Say "What is beyond your needs" (2:219). The descriptive

283

assumption these verses make is that there are certain limits to what could be taken from people by way of donation; should these bounds be transgressed, people would start showing hidden ill-feelings.

Third: descriptive assumptions of economics (category 6)

In spite of the famous differences in opinion among economists, economics contains many descriptive statements that capture economists' consensus of opinion, some of which shall be mentioned to point out how incorrect is the view that modern economics is nothing but a group of Western values:

(a) The Law of Engle (a German statistician), which states that the proportion of income spent on food diminishes with increase in such income.
(b) The aggregate surplus of countries posting surplus in their balance of payments equals the aggregate deficit in the balance of payments of countries posting a deficit.
(c) The value of a currency, i.e. its purchasing power, is not linked to its gold coverage.
(d) The Law of Diminishing Returns: The incremental output from successive and equal increases of one input will eventually diminish when other inputs are held constant.

POSTSCRIPT

The writer has intentionally overlooked mention of the above assumptions to avoid complicating the diagram given earlier and the discussion.

The simplest way to include the assumptions is to integrate them into our diagram under normative assumptions, where the upper part of the diagram (categories 1, 3 and 5) would include the normative assumptions and statements, leaving the lower part of the diagram (categories 2, 4 and 6) for descriptive assumptions alone.

Based on this, category 3 of the assumptions would include those normative statements or assumptions that are shared by both Islam and economics, regarding which illustrative examples have been given.

Regarding categories 1 and 5, these would include only the values or assumptions peculiar to either Islam or economics.

Fourth: two conclusions about the relation between
Islam and economics

We can draw from the above discussion two conclusions. The first is that Islam is basically a religion of guidance, the main purpose of which is to supply us with normative statements, i.e. Shari'ah rules commanding what we should do and what we should refrain from doing, or statements expressing normative preference of one situation over another. But Islam also draws our attention to some variables and supplies us with some descriptive statements that fall within some academic disciplines, such as economics, sociology and psychology. This is of great importance to the Islamization of social and human sciences and to their protection against deviation or error.

Factors, such as the myriad of variables and factors influencing social and economic phenomena, the multiplicity of descriptive statements that could be made in regard of such variables and factors, the need to disregard the greater part of such factors and to concentrate on a limited number of them (as mentioned earlier) and the inability of holding some social factors constant or of subjecting human being to laboratory experimentation – all these factors open the way for "great confusion in the social sciences and the succession of conflicting theories . . . Should understanding and reflection on the laws of the universe, existence and relations lead the Muslim astray, he would have a guardian and protector in revelation . . . thus Islamic knowledge employs, simultaneously, sources of rational and empirical inductive knowledge, along with general, deductive universal sources of knowledge (derived from revelation)".[14]

Therefore, reference by God-given Law (Shari'ah) to some of the factors and variables influencing economic life and behaviour and its supply to us of some descriptive statements are considered a valuable intellectual aid to establish an Islamic quality for the science of economics as well as for other sciences. But it is noticed that most contemporary writings about the Islamic quality of economics and other disciplines ignore the descriptive aspect of Islam, limiting their reference to the normative assumptions only.[15]

The second conclusion is that there is a common ground of interest between Islam and economics (categories 3 and 4 of the assumptions).

In the light of what has been mentioned above, we shall explain in part 4 of this paper how to achieve integration between Islam and economics, or how to establish an Islamic science of economics.

4. Essential elements and scope of Islamic economics

4.1 The relation between Islamic and conventional economics

The final result of integrating economics and Islam would be an Islamic Economics that should consist of the following assumptions:

Category 3: Islamic normative statements and assumptions. We mentioned earlier that this category would include, inter alia, the rules of the Islamic Economic System.

Category 4: Islamic descriptive statements that are related to economics.

Category 6: Descriptive economic assumptions and statements.

In other words, we shall exclude from such science category 5, which includes those normative assumptions and statements that are the exclusive property of modern economics, i.e. those that do not have an Islamic basis. Category 3 items would replace these. It is expected of this replacement to result in two types of change in the content of category 6.

The first relates to modification or correction of those assumptions that were originally based on category 5, and the addition of new assumptions (or emphasis of those ones that did not receive enough attention before) that are derived from category 3, i.e. from Islamic values and assumptions. Moreover, such replacement may result in a new and comprehensive research programme and in a wide-ranging modification of a large number of the discipline's assumptions.

(A) Let us give as an example of the possible modification to some of these assumptions the issue of possible depletion of some natural resources, which is the subject of much controversy now. One of the assumptions of Westerners is that the universe was created accidentally or as a result of the interaction among the blind forces of nature. Given this, the assumption goes on, it is not unlikely for the quantity of some natural resources to be incompatible with the needs of a decent and honourable human life. Thus when dealing with the problem of scarcity of resources and the possibility of their depletion, one of the assumptions that will be worthy of discussion based on this assumption would be that of the possible incompatibility between available resources and human needs. Much literature, statistical studies etc. on this assumption would accumulate. But owing to the nature of the subject, the very narrow scope of making it subject to experimentation and the fact that the observations made are merely hypothetical (as it is difficult to give an estimate of either the quantities that are already existing, or those that may be discovered in the future) – all these factors indicate that it would be difficult to establish or verify the error of this view in a convincing manner; its acceptance or rejection would still depend on previously-held assumptions to which the researcher sticks, either explicitly or implicitly.

However, if we take our starting point the Qur'anic verses "Verily, we have created every thing by measure"(54:49); "We have honoured the sons of Adam"(17:70); "It is We Who have placed you with authority on earth and provided you therein with means for the fulfillment of your life"(7:10); "And there is not a thing but its (sources and) treasures (inexhaustible) are with Us, but We only send down thereof in due and ascertainable measures"(15:21); "It is He Who hath created for you all things that are on earth"(2:29) – I say that if we take the above, and other similar verses, as our departure point, we will reach the assumption that earth and all that is on it have been made, by God's will, serviceable to man,[16] and that the quantities of any natural resource endowment on earth are deliberate and not haphazard; in endowing them, God has taken into consideration fulfilment of the needs of the honourable life He accepts for his servants throughout their predetermined lifespan on earth. The **only source of incompatibility** that might arise between human desires and the quantities of natural resources available would be man's misbehaviour and his deviation from the norms of production and consumption that have been ordained by God. The only solution to this problem of incompatibility would be through the correction of these deviations. Hence, the research plan and the assumptions to be given on the basis of the aforementioned basic assumption would concentrate on study of the possible relation between certain deviations in the human economic and social behaviour and the impact of such deviations on the depletion of resources.

There is room for opinions to diverge regarding the above example, which we have supplied to clarify the idea under discussion and not to prove the content of the example.

It is worthwhile here to explain the position of the economic descriptive assumptions (category 6) vis-à-vis Islamic economics. Many of these assumptions have been arrived at by non-Muslims, a matter that does not preclude their inclusion as part of Islamic economics (as it is the case with so many descriptive aspects of the empirical sciences, such as agriculture, medicine and physics). We should, however, correct, modify or re-formulate those descriptive assumptions that are founded on non-Islamic values or assumptions. We cannot ascertain in advance the extent of change that would occur to the content of category 6 as a result of this 'Islamization' process. However, this process requires great intellectual efforts, of which little has been exerted by Muslims. It is worth emphasizing that the mere act of discovering whether a particular assumption rests on non-Islamic assumptions would never be an easy task, let alone correcting or re-formulating it to make it compatible with Islamic viewpoint. The following example (B) illustrates the case in point.

(B) Many aspects of the conventional economic theory depend on the basic assumption that man is selfish by nature and that self-interest is the basic motive for his behaviour. Western economists of the neoclassical school have derived from this assumption the concepts that are suitable for 'explaining' economic behaviour, such as the consumer's utility function and the producer's objective of realizing personal gain. On this foundation is based the bulk of theories dealing with issues such as consumer's behaviour, production, the characteristics of general equilibrium under a competitive economy and the realization of such equilibrium of the conditions of Pareto's concept of the optimal distribution of resources . . . etc.

Let us now try to assume for the sake of argument that our study of the texts of the Holy Qur'an and Sunnah that relate to human behaviour has led us to a different assumption holding that there are two forces affecting human behaviour: selfishness and self-denial, which motivates us to do our duty regardless of any-personal gain. In the light of this new assumption, we start to see that conventional (secular) economics is very advanced in its analysis of the economics of selfishness, but quite lagging in its analysis of the economics of self-denial (i.e. economic behaviour motivated by ethical considerations).

Perhaps the rejection of conventional economics any interest in unselfish human behaviour could be an expression of an implicit normative attitude that is consistent with its lavish praise of the concept of the hidden hand in economics (a concept which claims that in his pursuit of self-interest, man would realize indirectly the interest of the entire society) more than an expression of a former assumption maintaining that unselfish behaviour is in fact of little importance in life.

Whatever explanation we might give to the attitude of conventional economics, our attempt to correct such attitude in a manner that would be consistent with the new assumption we adopted about the nature of human behaviour would require an extensive theoretical research programme that would modify our theories about the behaviour of the consumer and the producer, the forces influencing market equilibrium etc.

(C) Let us now try to give some examples on adding new assumptions to category 6: Muslim narrated in his Collection of Authentic *Hadiths* on the authority of Abu Hurairah that the Prophet said "Look unto those who are below you (in wealth and affluence) and do not look unto those who are above you, for this is more becoming not to look down scornfully upon the bounties that God has bestowed upon you . . .).[17] The meaning gathered from this prophetic tradition shows that the level of satisfaction (or what economists call 'utility') an individual feels vis-à-vis a certain bounty (let us assume it to be a certain quantity of consumer products) is influenced, inter alia, by his conception of his own position relative to that of other people and the bounties bestowed upon them.

This calls for our inclusion of an additional explanatory variable into the individual utility function, namely **the relative position** of the consumer, where it would be added to the traditional variable in this function, namely the quantity of commodities and services. There are many analytical results for introducing this additional variable, which results have no place for review here.

4.2 The relationship between Islamic economics and the economic history of Muslims

No doubt that study of the economic history of Muslims from the time of prophethood to the present deepens our understanding of the Islamic

ISLAMIZATION OF ECONOMICS

economic system, when Muslims tried to apply it to new events and cases. Moreover, even our understanding of the economic rules of Fiqh (such as those governing the currency in circulation and its relation to *riba*) will not be complete unless we familiarize ourselves with one side of the economic history of money used by Muslims.

However, we should not mix the events of the economic history of Muslims with the Islamic Economics, whether in its normative or descriptive aspects. This confusion often occurs in books about public finance in Islam, where the registers and financial procedures adopted and applied by Muslims are described as the Islamic financial system. It is clear that one should distinguish between the various principles underlying certain procedures; should any of such procedures have supportive legal (i.e. Shari'ah-based) evidence, then it should be considered as a part of the Islamic economic system (such as the principle of separating Zakah funds from funds of the Public Treasury (*Bait al-mal*). On the other hand, if a procedure lacks such supportive evidence, or if it is a mere executive administrative procedure that falls within the domain of what is permissible, then it should be considered a purely financial arrangement used by Muslims and does not in any way constitute a part of the Islamic financial system.

It is to be noticed that there was a period in the economic history of Muslims, which has its own normative and legislative significance. That, of course, was the period of the Prophet (P.B.U.H.) because it was the period of legislation, and the period of the Four Rightly Guided Caliphs succeeding him, for the Prophet (P.B.U.H.) says: "You should follow my path and the path of the rightly guided caliphs succeeding me; hold to them tenaciously".[18] This is known in the literature on the principles of Islamic jurisprudence and we need not dwell long on it.

4.3 Between Islamic economics and history of Muslims economic thought

A number of our predecessors have made very valuable intellectual contributions that fall, totally or partially, within the domain of modern economics. No doubt that these contributions should be subject to both study and teaching within the history of economic thought for they constitute part of it. This is all the more mandatory in the light of the fact that many Western economists are either unfamiliar with them or treat them with negligence. We have every right to be proud of such contributions, as they constitute part of our civilization.

The question that arises is do these contributions have any value outside "The History of Economic Thought"? Do they have any special Islamic value within the intellectual efforts aimed at 'Islamization' of the economy? Is the analysis offered by Al Maqrizi of the impact of money supply on price levels necessarily more 'Islamic' or correct than the analysis of the same phenomenon offered by non-Muslims? The same question could be posed in regard to the insightful economic and social views of Ibn Khaldun?

Our previous discussion allows a clear answer for such questions. Part of the economic contributions of Muslim thinkers are normative hypotheses or assumptions that have supportive evidence from Shari'ah, and thus have special significance to our efforts aiming at 'Islamization' of the economy. Some others, however, are descriptive statements (many of the analyses offered by Ibn Khaldun are of this type) that are treated analytically the same way other descriptive statements of economics are treated; we do not have to consider them more correct than others for the mere fact that they have been arrived at by Muslims. But we should add that as long as such statements are based on Islamic assumptions and are compatible with Islam's worldview, they should be accorded an advantage over other statements.

4.4 The relationship between Islamic economics and Fiqh (jurisprudence)

4.4.1 The main idea

The main difference between the science of jurisprudence and Islamic economics is that the basic objective of jurisprudence is to arrive at normative statements, which are legal judgements or rulings. These normative rulings constitute a very great proportion of juristic material. On the other hand, the objective of Islamic economics (as well as conventional economics) is to arrive at descriptive hypotheses or assumptions that diagnose reality and link the various economic phenomena.

This is the basic difference, although it has many exceptions and details, some of which have already been pointed out, some others would be given now.

Jurisprudence is basically 'knowledge of the practical rules of Shari'ah along with their supportive evidences'.[19] These rules fall into five categories: *wajib* (obligatory), *mandub* (recommended), *mubah* (permissible), *makruh* (abominable) and *haram* (forbidden, unlawful).

These five rulings are explicitly normative in nature: they give a preference to one situation or behaviour over another or consider them as equal. Thus the discharge of an obligation (or abstention from committing a prohibition) is, in the view of Shari'ah, far better than neglecting its discharge (or than committing a prohibition) etc. Thus Islamic jurisprudence is a science the majority of whose assumptions are normative in nature; they belong to the upper side of our diagram and fall under the first and third categories.[20] Despite this, *Fiqh* is not lacking in descriptive statements that are given in the course of explaining the reasons behind Shari'ah rules or pointing out their wisdom (or when applying them to new real cases, which is called in the principles of Islamic jurisprudence *'tahqiq al manat'* – ascertainment of the cause).[21] For example, wine and games of hazard are both prohibited, a rule that is normative. God has mentioned some of the reasons of the prohibition: giving rise to enmity and hatred among people and keeping people back from worshipping God and offering their obligatory prayers are some. These are descriptive rules (See Holy Qur'an, 5:91).

Just as *Fiqh* is not totally void of descriptive statements, economics (even the ordinary or conventional type) cannot but depend on some normative statements, as we mentioned in the second part of this paper. This should not make us forget that the most important elements of Fiqh are the first elements of science (i.e. normative assumptions and rules). The most important element of Islamic economics is the third element of science, namely descriptive assumptions (See paragraph 2.2).

Let us clarify the difference between economics and jurisprudence in one of the famous topics dealt with by both jurists and economists, namely the subject of monopoly. Books on Islamic jurisprudence[22] discuss the Shari'ah evidences (*adillah*) in support of the prohibition of monopoly, the commodities that should not be subject to monopoly, the conditions of prohibited monopoly and the penalty to be imposed by the ruler against the monopolist. Books on economics deal with issues such as the factors giving rise to monopoly, the types of monopoly, the effects of monopoly on income distribution, how do prices in a monopoly market differ frorn those in another similar, but competitive, market and how do the quantities sold in the two markets differ from one to the other etc. It is clear that the economist directs himself to the descriptive aspect of the phenomenon under examination, where he studies the factors influencing it and the causal relationships related to it. The jurist, on the other hand, directs himself to the normative side of the phenomenon, which is the Shari'ah rule governing it, and to the permissibility and prohibition criteria of the various forms of the phenomenon.

In the light of what has been said earlier, I do not hesitate to hold in error those who define Islamic economics in such a manner as to strip it from its descriptive content and make it synonymous to jurisprudence of transactions.[23]

We have the right to ask: is not there a relationship between the task of *Fiqh* in arriving at Shari'ah rules and the task of Islamic economics in describing and interpreting the economic phenomena related to these very same rules? The answer to this question is affirmative; there is a relationship between the two tasks, which could be summed up by saying that among the tasks of Islamic economics is to seek the economic wisdom of the rules of Shari'ah,[24] that is to analyze the results of these rules and their short and long-term impact on the economic life.[25] This will require use of the third essential element of economics, which is the descriptive side.

One of the outstanding examples about the difference between the function of economics and the function of *Fiqh* is the question of the prohibition of *riba al nasi'a*.[26] Jurisprudents have examined this issue in detail, showing the rule of Shari'ah on this question and clarifying that the rule applies to any increase in the original debt amount that is stipulated in advance, regardless of the name given to such increase (*'fa'idah'* – interest, *'umulah'* – commission, *'ta'wid'* – compensation etc).

Modern Muslim economists researched the reason for the prohibition of interest charged on loans. Among the important conclusions they reached was that the prohibition of interest on productive loans was expected to achieve two things:

- Increase economic stability; in other words, it was expected to reduce economic fluctuations at the micro and macro levels of the economy, as such interest-based financing would increase such fluctuations.[27]
- Realize higher efficiency levels in utilizing resources under certain conditions.[28]

4.4.2 More details

Shari'ah jurisprudents are in agreement that the rules of Shari'ah have not been ordained by God "for the mere purpose of bringing people under the authority of religion . . . , they were rather ordained to realize the objectives of Shari'ah in maintaining people's religious and mundane interests".[29]

Thus the Rules of Shari'ah are based on what is in the interest of people, regardless of whether the reasons for such rules are seen or hidden. In other words, these rules are based on the expected results of human behaviour and universal laws, as well as on Shari'ah weighing of benefits (manafi') against evils (mafasid); they are based on descriptive relationships (laws) that fall within the domain of different disciplines, regardless of whether these relationships are known to man or not. For those issues whose rules are supported by definitive Shari'ah textual evidence God has saved the believers the trouble of speculating about their possible results and of weighing the benefits and evils underlying such results.[30] But for those issues on which no definitive Shari'ah textual evidence has been given, proper deduction of the law or rule from its sources should be based on:

- The nature of the case under consideration and its expected results, which cannot be known except from the descriptive side of the various sciences, such as economics.
- Evaluation of these possible results in accordance with the meaning of relevant Shari'ah texts and objectives.

Jurisprudents express the idea of building Shari'ah rules on the basis of their expected results and on the legal weighing (of the benefits and evils) of such results by saying: "In every matter there are two sides, a beneficial side and a harmful one, and legal (i.e. Shari'ah-based) consideration should be given to the preponderant side".[31] That matter in which the beneficial side is preponderant gets the 'hukm' (rule or value) of 'permissible'; the more preponderant such benefit becomes, the closer it moves to the value of 'obligatory'. That in which the element of evil is preponderant is given the value of 'abominable'; once the evil element becomes more acute and outweighs the beneficial side, Shari'ah would assign it the value of 'forbidden'. What confirms the accuracy of this viewpoint, the verse in the Holy Qur'an regarding wine and games of hazard or luck:

[They ask thee concerning wine and gambling. Say: "In them is great sin, and some benefits for men, but the sin is greater than the benefit"] (2:219). [In a subsequent Verse, God ordained their total prohibition, "Ye who believe! Intoxicants and gambling, (dedication of) stones,[32] and (divination by) arrows[33] are an abomination, of Satan's handiwork: Eschew such abomination"] (5:90).

In the light of the above, one could say that in those cases regarding which a definitive hukm has been given in clear definitive Shari'ah texts, knowledge of their results and the process of weighing their benefits and evils have been done by the Lawgiver, where He has given us the entire outcome in the form of the *hukm* given. The more the text(s) of Shari'ah – that are indicative of the *hukm* – are speculative, the greater becomes the need to determine its/their expected results and evaluate them from a Shari'ah perspective. Determining the possible results of a certain course of action is a matter that falls within the domain of the various sciences, economics included.

Let us now try to give some examples about those cases in which assistance of the various sciences, including economics, is sought to interpret texts and arrive at the *hukm*. By seeking help from the various sciences we mean attempting to benefit from their information content regarding reality or the expected results of a certain behaviour. (This has been called in 2.2 the 'descriptive side' or the 'third essential element of science'). The assistance sought would be for the purpose of interpretation in accordance with the rules stipulated by the *ulama* of *usul* (jurisprudents specializing in the principles or methodology of Islamic jurisprudence) for interpreting and deducing the rules of Shari'ah.

(a)   Imam Al Shatibi says that it would be incorrect to interpret God's verse "And never will God grant to the unbelievers a way (to triumph) over the believers" (4:141) as a statement of reality, for we have seen instances of the unbeliever "having a way over the believer by capturing and humiliating him. The meaning intended should not be save that which is in keeping with what happens in reality".[34] In other words, the verse decides a Shari'ah rule, which is that a believer should not accept having the unbeliever triumph over him. Thus, according to Al Shatibi, the verse does not describe what is, but rather what should be.

Here we find that historical knowledge of what happened to Muslims at the hands of the unbelievers who occasionally managed to overpower them has been a key issue in interpreting the text of the verse.[35]

(b) Authorities on the exegesis of the Qur'an (*al mufassirun*) have differed since ancient times on the interpretation of certain verses of the Qur'an that relate to the shape of earth. Some were of the opinion that verses on the matter tilted to the side of considering earth as flat in shape, whereas others believed that these verses tilted to the side considering it round.

Now we do not doubt the correctness of the latter view, as it is consistent with what has been proven scientifically.

Examples 'a' and 'b', and many more similar ones, stem from a principle that has been adopted by trustworthy scholars of Shari'ah, of whom Ibn Taimiyah is one. In his treatise *Dar' a Ta'arud al 'Aql wa al Naql* (Repulsion of Conflict between Reason and Transmitted Texts (of Shari'ah)), Ibn Taimiyah sees that[36] it is impossible for conflict to arise between a definitive evidence that is based on reason and definitive evidence based on transmitted texts. Should there be a conflict or inconsistency between speculative evidence and definitive evidence, the scale should tilt in favour of the definitive evidence, regardless of whether it is based on reason or a transmitted text. Should there be a conflict between two speculative evidences, the scale should tilt in favour of that which is preponderant, regardless of whether it is based on reason or transmitted texts.

Therefore, tilting the scale in favour of one interpretation over other interpretations of a text by giving supportive evidence that is based on reason or other material proof is an acceptable matter. Imam Al Shatibi has explicitly supported this meaning.[37]

However, in spite of clarity and simplicity of this idea, its application requires complete mastery of the science from whose assumptions we seek help in interpreting a certain text, for many of such assumptions or statements (especially in the social sciences) have not yet attained the status of preponderant speculation (*zann rajih*) that is recognized by Shari'ah. None save those learned authorities can distinguish those assumptions that have such status.

(c) Among examples on the possibility of benefiting from the descriptive assumptions of economics in giving weight to an opinion over another, where both opinions reached through independent reasoning (*ijtihad*), is that of the *fiqhi* issue of giving, free of charge, excess water for others for them and their animals to drink, by a person who has a renewable source of water that is in excess of his own need and the need of his animals and plantations (a case known in *Shari'ah* as *'haqq al shuf'a* – preemptive right).

Jurisprudents differed on whether it is obligatory to offer, free of charge, such excess water for use by others in the irrigation of their plantations. The Hanafi, Maliki and Shafi'i schools of thought are of the opinion that foregoing consideration for such excess water is a commendable act but not obligatory. However, Imam Ahmad sees the act as obligatory, even if water is to be used for the irrigation of plantations.

Economic analysis of this case shows that giving excess water without receiving any consideration ensures efficiency in the use of natural resources and prevents its waste, which is a valid Shari'ah objective that supports Imam Ahmad's opinion on this case. This issue has been discussed in detail by the writer in a former research.[38]

(d)   Among the contemporary economic issues in which economics could help in reaching deeper understanding and tilting the balance in favour of some juristic opinions over others is that of obligatory pricing, an issue that was discussed by Muslim jurisprudents in the past and that is being discussed in detail by economists.

In case of high prices (without the existence of monopoly or connivance among merchants or without an emergency situation, such as famine), the majority of jurisprudents, based on a well-known tradition and other Shari'ah evidences, prohibit obligatory pricing and consider it illegitimate. But some other jurisprudents permit 'fair' pricing. Some contemporary jurisprudents have tended to give preponderance to the opinion of those ancient jurists who were supportive of pricing. The context does not permit elaboration on this issue. However, it has been revealed to me through a preliminary study that, given the results of modern economic analysis showing that pricing has big hidden administrative and social costs that were not known in their entirety to ancient jurists (as it is shown to the reader of their writings on the subject), nor did they capture the attention of modern jurists – these large costs accompanying pricing give preponderant weight to the view of the majority of jurists who prohibit pricing and interpret the tradition pro-hibiting it (excepting cases of monopoly, compulsion or connivance among merchants that allow the intervention of the ruler by resorting to obligatory pricing or to other measures, such as sale by compulsion etc.) in its manifest literal meaning.

(e)   It is hoped that the above examples give sufficient evidence to the fact that, in the process of interpreting legal texts and in arriving at other rules of Shari'ah reached by independent reasoning and derived from the gener-alities or texts or analogy, economic descriptive assumptions are expected to be part of the elements giving preponderant weight to one opinion over another.

If we move to Shari'ah rules that are based on Istihsan (juristic preference), we would expect economic assumptions to have a greater role to play in helping jurists arrive at the correct Shari'ah ruling. This is so because *Istihsan* to the Hanafi and Maliki schools of thought (which is called by the Hanafis "*Istihsan al-Darurah*" – preference dictated by necessity) means the abandonment of apparent analogy when its results are opposed to a preponderant interest to the Muslim or when their adoption causes a hardship to him.[39] Undoubtedly, identification of the possible results of a rule made on the basis of analogical deduction reveals whether such rule is opposed to preponderant interests or results in a hardship. Identification of the possible results of any Shari'ah rule related to the economic life is certainly a function of Islamic economics in its descriptive side.

(f)   If we move to Shari'ah rules that are based on *Istislah* (consideration of public interest), we would expect yet a greater role for Islamic economics to play than that played in *Istihsan.*

Istislah is defined as "the building of Shari'ah rules in accordance with the dictates of public interests, namely those interests to which Shari'ah has given no consideration, neither in their individual or collective capacity", but which realize the general objectives of Shari'ah in the social life of Muslims.[40] An example of these are "the rules pertaining to the affairs of public administration that regulate the interests of society . . . such as the levying of taxes on the rich when there is a need to undertake a public action, such as preparation and equipment of the army, the building of bridges, land planning, census . . . or other forms of social security required to eliminate misery and guarantee jobs for those who need it".[41]

No doubt that laying down the rules and regulations needed for the realization of such, and other similar, public interests that are in keeping with the objectives of Shari'ah requires, to a large extent, seeking the help of economics and other social and administrative sciences.

Among the important contemporary economic issues, the relevant legal rules of which are expected to be built on the basis of the principle of *Istislah* are the following:

– The extent to which it is permissible for the banking system to generate derivative money.[42]
– Determining the appropriate money supply in society. It is known that this issue has diverse and important effects on the levels of consumption, investment, prices etc.
– The rules pertaining to the distribution of the burden of public expenditures (taxes and other fees) among the various categories obligated to share them.[43]

- Determining the appropriate prices of commodities and services that should, either for natural or economic reasons, involve monopoly, such as public utilities or monopolies arising from the grant of patents.
- Rules of evaluating public investment projects.[44]

Economists see economic affairs that Muslim jurisprudents see as falling within the realm of *Istislah* as falling within the realm of economic policy (or welfare economics). Since the beginning of the 20th century. Western economists have been exerting sustainable intellectual efforts in an attempt to arrive at value-free, or objective criteria for economic policy. In other words, they have been trying to arrive at criteria that would allow giving a purely objective preponderance to one economic situation (such as free foreign trade) over another (foreign trade that is restricted by customs or other types of restrictions). The general outcome of such intellectual efforts has been agreement among economists that purely objective criteria cannot be established and that other previously-held normative values must be adopted, on the basis of which the advantages and disadvantages of competing policies could be weighed and decided in favour of a certain policy. Such values and the pertinent weighing criteria are termed "the social interest function".[45]

In other words, economists have now recognized that economic policies can never be built on the descriptive side of economics alone; they must depend also on a number of values-based judgements that are derived from a certain source outside the realm of economics.[46] It is natural that, for us, this source is nothing but our Islamic Shari'ah and all the values, *fiqhi* (i.e. juristic) rules and rules of weighing and giving preference derived from them.

In conclusion, one can say that economic rules that are based on *Istislah*, or affairs pertaining to economic policy, must be built on both Islamic law and economics, for such rules constitute the common ground shared by both subjects.

4.4.3 A comparison between the functions of Fiqh and Islamic economics

We can conclude from the above examples and clarifications that Islamic economics, in terms of its relationship with Fiqh, has the following three functions:

First: A Function Distinguishable from That of *Fiqh*: namely to describe and diagnose real events, discover the relationships that link the various economic phenomena, and to seek discovering the economic rationale of Shari'ah rules, i.e. determining their short or long run impacts in economic life. The function of *Fiqh* is to derive Shari'ah rules from their detailed supporting evidences.

Second: A Function Shared with That of *Fiqh*: namely, the function of formulating economic policies and rules that are based on considerations of public interests (*Al Masalih Al Mursalah*).

Third: The Function of Aiding *Fiqh*: namely, the function of helping the jurisprudent arrive at the Shari'ah rule itself under those circumstances in which the economic effects have special importance in tilting the balance in favour of selecting one from two or more competing opinions.

It is to be noted that the first function is of prime importance as it relates to issues of creed (*aqidah*), as understanding of the rationale behind Shari'ah rules strengthens faith and facilitates the call of people to adhere to Shari'ah.

4.5 Discussion of the opinion of Al Sadr

Muhammad Baqir Al Sadr, the learned scholar (May Allah rest his soul in peace) has devoted a short chapter in his unique book *Iqtisaduna*, entitled "Islamic Economics is not a Science".[47] The gist of Al Sadr's opinion is that Islamic economics consists of two parts:

The first is: The economic system in Islam. The function of this part is not to explain the economic life of a Muslim, but rather to call for changing it to become consistent with Islam.

The second part is the science of Islamic Economics. Its function is to give a scientific explanation of the events of the economic life of a society that applies Islam.

Thus, Al-Sadr denies the scientific quality of the first part.[48] He does not, however, dispute the scientific nature of the second part, which he explicitly calls 'science'. Therefore it does not seem to be appropriate to say that, "Islamic Economics is Not a Science" and give such statement as title of the entire chapter. I wish that he had changed his statement to "Not All Economic Systems are Scientific" since this was his intended meaning.

If we move to the function of Islamic Economics, we find that Al-Sadr has meticulously defined it as follows:[49]

First: To record and study the economic events in an Islamic society to discover the general laws that control them. This cannot be attained unless the Islamic economic system is applied in real life.

Second: To assume an Islamic social and economic reality, then to study the effects of such assumed reality and its general characteristics, as well as the salient characteristics of economic life under such assumed reality.

Although this could be done prior to the application of an Islamic economic system, it cannot mature and acquire its depth except after the application of such a system.

Thus it seems that Al Sadr limits the functioning of Islamic Economics to a Muslim society, whereas the writer sees such function to include the explanation of economic reality in any society, Muslim or non-Muslim.[50]

Proof of the writer's claim is embodied in the many examples given about the descriptive economic assumptions cited above from the Qur'an and the Sunnah. Thus, people's infatuation with wealth, the effect of wealth increase on man's inclination towards tyranny and the interconnection in utility changes among individuals, all these are general descriptive assumptions about economic life in any society, Muslim or non-Muslim. It is true that some variables and institutions may not be found in a particular society whereas they appear in another. However, this does not require that each society should have its own science of economics; a science of economics should be of such a comprehensive and general nature as to subsume under it all those special cases.

In other words, claiming that Islamic Economics is of a comprehensive and global nature is not contradicted by some features that are particular to Islamic economics, in terms of the topics it includes in the purview of its interests and studies.

For example, there would appear within the purview of Islamic Economics topics that would not normally be dealt with by Western conventional economics, such as the economics of *zakat* and *hajj*. However, this does not mean that the general descriptive and normative principles of Islamic Economics do not apply to all societies.

4.6 Conclusion regarding the essential elements of Islamic economics[51]

We conclude from the above that Islam offers a Shari'ah-based economic system that does not only consist of normative assumptions about how society's economic life should be. It also draws our attention, through the Qur'an and Sunnah, and all the conclusions and knowledge acquired on their basis, to variables, assumptions and economic descriptive assumptions that should be taken into consideration in our analyses and interpretations of life's realities, in addition to the results of observations and logical deductions reached by Muslims or others.

Islamic Economics is divided into two parts: the first is the Islamic economic system; the second is Islamic economic analysis. The bulk of the **first part** is normative in nature and deals with how economic life should be in accordance with Islam. It also clarifies the economic rationale of Shari'ah rules, **seeking in that the aid of Islamic economic analysis.**

The second part, namely Islamic economic analysis, is concerned with the analysis of the institutions and events of the economic life of societies in general, whether Islamic or otherwise, and to interpret that and know its causes and effects. It is also concerned with the formulation of Islamic policies and solutions to economic problems, **seeking in that the aid of the rules of the Islamic economic system**.

5. Work plans for Islamization of economics

5.1 A comprehensive work plan (Faruqi's Plan)

Dr. Al Faruqi (May Allah bless his soul) presented a work plan for Islamization of the various disciplines.[52] The plan consists of 12 steps that could be applied to any discipline. Collectively, these steps constitute a comprehensive map on which one could plot the progress achieved in Islamizing a certain discipline. These steps are as follows:

1. Prepare a diagram of the contents and methodology of the discipline concerned.
2. Undertake a comprehensive review of the development of the discipline concerned and its main assumptions.
3. Prepare readings culled from Islamic heritage in the subject of the discipline concerned. These books of readings should be classified in accordance with the main divisions of the discipline.
5. Analyze previous readings and determine their relation to the discipline.
6. Determine in detail the Islamic assumptions related to the discipline.
7. Evaluate Muslims' contributions to the discipline over the ages.
8. Present the major problems facing the Muslim nation that are related to the discipline.
9. Present the major relevant human problems.
10. Re-formulate the discipline from an Islamic perspective in such a manner as to realize linkages and integration between Islamic assumptions and the contributions from Islamic heritage on the one hand, and the best achievements of the discipline at present.
11. Prepare textbooks on the discipline at the university level.
12. Disseminate the contents of the discipline among specialists on a large scale.

5.2 Auxiliary work plan

We should note, however, that there is another auxiliary work plan to achieve 'Islamization' of the sciences; this plan could be called the 'auxiliary work plan' to distinguish it from the 'comprehensive work plan' mentioned earlier. This auxiliary plan involves choosing any of the subjects dealt with by a discipline and applying all or some of the aforementioned 12 points to that subject alone.

If we look at the actual course of the development of Islamic Economics during the past forty years, we will find that it is practically closer to the auxiliary plan, where the researcher chooses a particular subject, such as *riba* or development and reviews it from the perspective of modern economics and the Islamic texts and heritage. He would engage in comparing and discussing the various pertinent issues and attempt to arrive at a harmonious conception, in which Shari'ah values and rules are integrated with what he finds to be true among the assumptions of economic analysis.

The auxiliary work plan is neither an alternative to the comprehensive work plan nor opposed to it; they could both go hand in hand, as each has its own advantages and shortcomings.

Among the prominent shortcomings of the comprehensive plan is that it requires a long time and large human resources. Among its advantages is that it is a well-organized plan; its results are more reliable and comprehensive. It also allows, after achieving its first five steps, participation of large numbers of specialists in the process of 'Islamizing' the science, which is, in my opinion, the decisive advantage in the long run.

Regarding the shortcomings of the auxiliary work plan is that of the lack of a comprehensive view, which the comprehensive plan aspires to achieve. Furthermore, the topics in the auxiliary plan are often chosen in reaction to issues in which there is contradiction between Islamic rules and some of the assumptions of a certain discipline. In other words, the auxiliary method is more of a reaction to a stimuli rather than an initiator of action; it leaves initiative in the hands of non-Islamic thought and then comes to react to it.

However, an auxiliary method has some advantages; it could respond to some of the pressing questions raised within a relatively short span of time and it could be quite appropriate for university dissertations at the master and doctoral levels. (By the way, one notices that the majority of contemporary writings on comparative studies of Islamic and man-made law are done in this form).

Among the commendable achievements of the auxiliary method are those writings that appeared in the last twenty five years on the economics of money, banking and interest from an Islamic perspective. These writings have included in their subject all the steps proposed in the Faruqi's proposed comprehensive plan (except for that of university textbooks). I do not think that I would be trespassing on truth when I claim that all claims about the importance of interest (*riba*) to a modern economy have been refuted at the analytical level. On the positive side, there appeared a relatively integrated conception of a contemporary Islamic monetary and banking system, written in a language that is understood by economists, even non-Muslim ones. Some contributions to economic analysis have also appeared, demonstrating the advantages of interest-free financing over interest-based financing (in terms of efficiency and stability, as mentioned in paragraph 4.4.1). Although these advantages are not yet recognized by the majority of economists, especially that there are few among them who know and discuss them, the mere act of presenting these advantages for sound analytical discussion is by itself a big progress from the point at which we were four decades ago, when "Islam's prohibition of interest (*riba*) was generally regarded as an almost impossible proposition even among most Muslim intellectual circles".[53]

However, we should note that the achievements made by the grace of God in the economics of money and banking in Islam have been, to a large extent, the result of the establishment of many Islamic banks that helped in their achievement.

5.3 An objective look into the work plan

If we look in an objective and detailed manner, and from the perspective of contemporary research, into the third, fourth, fifth and sixth steps of Faruqi's work plan that we have just summarized, we can conclude that 'Islamizing' economics could take three simultaneous directions:

(A) First Direction: To subject Islamic economic system to a careful study that would deepen our understanding thereof, answer the contemporary questions raised about it, discover from the various Shari'ah rules general economic rules (laws) or deduce the economic rationale of some Shari'ah rules.

(B) Second Direction: To explore previous postulates and the descriptive statements related to economics and derived from the Qur'an and Sunnah or on which rules of Shari'ah are based. In fact Muslim jurisprudents do not give attention to such postulates and assumptions, as no direct practical Shari'ah rules result from them.

Therefore, the specialist himself must arrive at such postulates and assumptions by giving thought to the texts and rules of Shari'ah, review of the books on the interpretation of the Qur'an and explanations of the Sunnah related thereto, then to think about their analytical significance to his area of specialization. In view of the importance of this second orientation and the lack of attention given to it by the majority of people, we shall clarify it by giving three examples:

First Example: Many of the texts of Shari'ah that are normally classified under *raqa'iq* (texts that are meant to soften the hearts and urge them to submit to God and fear His punishment) indicate the close link between the utility functions among individuals (a negative link as in envy, and a positive link as in self-denial). This is a descriptive economic statement that is confirmed by these texts.

While it is customary in economic analysis to assume the independence of such functions from each other, to relinquish such assumption and adopt the Islamic assumption that emphasizes the link between the utility functions would have far-reaching analytic results in economic theory.[54]

Second Example: Scrutiny of Shari'ah rules prohibiting riba and permitting, at the same time, *mudarabah* (sleeping partnership) and other forms of partnership cannot be explained and justified unless one assumes that the results of investment, whether profit or loss, are not certain but speculative. This confirms that uncertainty is a previous postulate (or an implicit assumption) on which Shari'ah rules are based and a Muslim economist should adhere to it in his analysis. The importance of this issue becomes apparent when one mentions that a large portion of the theory of capital in conventional economics, and the larger part of the assumptions claiming the impossibility of abolishing interest from the economy are both based on the assumption that the results of investment are certain. This assumption collapses when it is replaced by the realistic Islamic assumption, which holds otherwise.[55]

Third Example: Many of the Shari'ah rules related to behaviour in an Islamic market and the duties of contractors therein (such as those related to the prohibition of *najash*,[56] *talaqqi al rukban*[57] or abstinence from disclosing the defects of the object of sale – generally, the rules prohibiting *khilabah* or fraudulent action in all of their forms)[58] – we say that many of these rules have no practical benefit or necessity unless we assume non-parity of the information available to the parties of the contract. This assumption of non-parity is a descriptive hypothesis on which many market-related Shari'ah texts and rules have implicitly been built.[59] Meanwhile the bulk of market analyses in modern economics, especially under a competitive market, assume, implicitly or explicitly, parity of the information available to both parties to a contract. It is clear that such descriptive assumptions or postulates are not normally mentioned in books of Fiqh, interpretation or commentary, despite their extreme analytic importance to the Islamization of economics, because of their relation to the descriptive part of this discipline.

These assumptions or postulates cannot be reached without the specialized economist receiving training in giving sustained deep thought to texts of the Qur'an, Sunnah and Shari'ah rules, seeking in such effort the aid of all possible sources that would enable him understand these texts and deduce their underlying assumptions.

No significant effort has been yet exerted to discover the Islamic descriptive assumptions and postulates. Even those who are most interested in Islamic

Economics have not yet been aware of such assumptions and postulates in the first place. (This is contrary to wide-spread awareness of Islamic values, the existence of which no one disputes). There is no way this situation could be rectified or propagate this type of contributions in the short term, for it requires people who are well versed in both Shari'ah and economics. However, it would be beneficial, in this context, to:

- publish several research papers on this subject, in which specific examples are given with detailed and careful economic analysis in order to stimulate the interest of specialists;
- compile selected texts from the Qur'an and the Sunnah, with reference to accessible commentaries thereon; and
- to assign a small group of researchers (two economists, an expert in interpretation, an expert in Sunnah and its exigesis) to undertake a quick review of the text of the Qur'an, then texts of authentic Sunnah, commenting briefly on every excerpt thought to include a descriptive statement or a postulate of Islamic Economics.

Needless to emphasize that it would be impossible to exhaust all the significance and meaning of the Shari'ah texts in this context, even if reviewed several times, each by a group of the best specialists. A realistic objective would be to plough the ground by an initial serious effort that would furnish economists with a set of Islamic descriptive assumptions and postulates that they would not have the ability to discover on their own. This is important to develop Islamic economic analysis.

(C) Third Direction: Discovery of the economic descriptive assumptions arrived at by Muslim scholars over the ages. This is the third direction to establish Islamic economics. Among the examples about these are the economic analytic assumptions of Ibn Khaldun and Al Maqrizi (unless these rest upon, or explain Shari'ah texts; if they do, then they are of type 'B' mentioned earlier).

This third direction is true and of benefit. However, I do not hesitate to consider it less important for the next phase in the development of Islamic Economics, for I believe that the decisive influences that would determine the course of this science should come the normative and descriptive assumptions mentioned in 'A' and 'B' earlier. It is worthwhile mentioning in this context that the contributions of early Muslim scholars like Abu Yusuf, author of *Al Kharaj*, and Abu Ubaid, author of *Al Amwal*, are among the richest in Shari'ah-based normative assumptions.[60]

They have high priority in the process of formulating the Islamic Economic System. Regarding the contributions of Ibn Khaldun and Al Maqrizi, these are basically descriptive and based on the two authors' own observations and analyses. I do not see according them the same priority.

5.4 Required human resources and division of labour

Scholars who could contribute to the Islamization of economics could be classified into three categories: economists, Shari'ah scholars *mukhadramun*[61] well versed in both economics and shari'ah The first two categories are available at present, but the number of scholars in the third category, which includes economists with good Shari'ah knowledge and Shari'ah scholars with good knowledge of economics, is very small indeed, which is the main obstacle on the way of Islamizing economics.

It is this third category of *mukhadramun* that could mitigate the problem of duality and dissociation of Shari'ah knowledge from conventional knowledge. It is the category which could cooperate and address the issues and coordinate work among economists and Shari'ah scholars. Thus, it could facilitate benefiting from the relatively large numbers of members of the first two categories, who could help in the Islamization process if they found someone who could speak their own language, coordinate and direct their efforts.

If we carefully review steps 3 to 7 of the Faruqi's Action Plan (par. 5.1), we will find that implementation of this Action Plan decisively depends on the presence of the third category (*mukhadramun*). This confirms the fact that scarcity of scholars in this category is the main bottleneck for the economics Islamization programme.

A possible ground for optimism regarding the mitigation of this problem lies, a few years from now, in the first groups of graduates in the departments of Islamic Economics of some universities (such as Umm Al Qura University, Imam Muhammad University and the Islamic University in Islamabad, Al Azhar University and the International Islamic University Malaysia). We hope that some of these graduates, once they complete their graduate studies, would have among them mature students who will be able to combine knowledge of both economics and Shari'ah and continue serious work towards achieving the Islamization of economics.

Notes

* The present paper is an English version of the author's Arabic paper entitled: "*Tahqiq Islamiyyat Ilm al Iqtisad: al Mafhum wa'l Manhaj*", published in Vol. 2 of this Journal in 1990 (Arabic Section). Due to vital significance of the theme presented in the paper, we reproduce it to our English readers expecting due response from them (Editor).

1 In preparing this revised version of a past research paper, I have benefited from the remarks and comments of many writers, among whom were: Late Prof. Mahmoud Abu Al Sa'ud; Dr. Muhammad Omar Zubair; Dr. Rafic Al Masri; Dr. Nejatullah Siddiqi; Dr. Ja'far Shaikh Idris, my father, the late Sheikh Mustafa Al Zarqa; Dr. Shawqi Dunya; Dr. As'ad Al Ras and the remarks and comments of three referees. To these all I would like to express my thanks. As they might not agree on what I had to say in this research paper, all faults or mistakes in thought or expression would remain my own responsibility.

2 See *Islamization of Knowledge: General Principles and Work Plan*, and its first English version by the late **Dr. Al-Faruqi, Ismail R.**, to which I will refer to in part 5 of this paper.

3 **Al-Fangari**, (1980), p. 85.

4 Descriptive statements are also called "positive statements", but we avoided the use of the word 'positive' because it also refers to a philosophical system that denies metaphysics and bases knowledge only on tested and verifiable statements of fact. Statements of value are also called "normative statements".

5 We say 'often' because even empirical sciences depend of necessity on some normative criteria. Shari'ah's normative rules may, as well, occasionally involve descriptive issues.

6 Compare with the definitions given by the Larger Oxford Dictionary. See also footnote number (48) in this paper.

7 **Al-Qasimi** (1331 H), p. 51.

8 There are many aspects other than those we shall mention in "a", "b" and "c" that depend on values. See **Samuels** (1977), pp. 475–480, where he mentioned in the realm of economics: defining the nature of the economic problem; distinguishing objectives from the means to achieve them; definition of output and cost; the concept of wealth; the concept of consumer supremacy, and many other more.

9 **Roberts** (1974), p. 54. **Lindbeck** (1971), pp. 9–12, emphasized the same idea. However, he thinks that selection of the issues to be discussed is the only value-dependent or subjective side in economics as a discipline. See also **B. Ward** (1972), p. 193.

10 Dr. I. Adelman emphasized this point in the course of her study of the phenomenon of economic growth. See other related discussions of the issue in **Samuelson** (1965), pp. 319–20; **Schumpeter**, ch. i, and in **Henderson & Quandt** (1958), pp. 1–2.

11 The economist, J. R. Hicks has rightly emphasized that economic 'theory' is by necessity a blinder that takes out of focus many of the details of reality and focuses our attention on a few elements that would become the object of theorizing and study of the relations obtaining among them.

12 Narrated by Al Tirmidhi, who classified it as a 'good' *hadith*. It is quoted also by Nawawi in his *Riyad al-Salihin*.

13 Narrated by Ibn Majah in his *Sunan* (1984), (Vol. 2, p.435, traditions # 4289). Researcher **Al 'Azami** reports about the authenticity of this *hadith*. Bukhari and Muslim narrated the *hadith* in words similar in meaning to the above wording. It was also narrated by Al Mundhiri in his *Al-Targhib wa Al Tarhib* on the authority of Anas in the following words: "Had man two valleys of money, he would have still sought a third one. Nothing can satisfy the son of Adam except earth. God would have mercy on that who has repented". Abridged version of *Al Targhib wa'l Tarhib*, by Ibn Hajar (1960), p. 161, tradition # 587.

14 **Abu Sulayman** (1982), p. 16.

15 Among the exceptions worthy of mention is the research of **Muhammad Al-Mubarak** (May Allah rest his soul in peace) entitled: *Nahwa Siyaghah Islamiyyah li Ilm al Ijtima' (Towards an Islamic Formulation of the Science of Sociology)*, which was presented to the First Conference on Islamic Education held in Makkah Al Mukarramah. He emphasizes in this paper that Islam provides us with a number of social laws and descriptive statements, giving many illustrative examples in support of this view (pp. 15–22).

16 **Al-Faruqi** (1982).

17 An Abridged Version of Muslim's Collection of Authentic Hadiths, by **Al Mundhiri** (n.d.) (Hadith # 2087).

18 Narrated by Al Tirmidhi, Ahmad and Ibn Majah in their collections of hadith. Wording of the quoted hadith is taken from Ibn Majah. See Sunan Ibn Majah, ed. by Mustafa Al 'Azami (1984), (traditions # 34 and 35).

19 This is the first article of *Majallah al Ahkam al Adliyyah*, for details please see Zarqa (1984), para 2, p. 59.

20 Juristic normative statements, or rules of Shari'ah, that are related to economic life are the backbone of the Islamic economic system. They fall under the third category of assumptions in the diagram given earlier. However, this category includes also prior economic assumptions that are not part of *Fiqh*. It is noticed also that the proper study of the Islamic economic system cannot be limited to economics-related Shari'ah rules, or to what is called '*Fiqh Al Mu'amalat*' (Jurisprudence of Transactions), it should, as well, deal with the results and economic reasons behind such rules. This would require utilization of the descriptive aspect of Islamic economics.

21 For an explanation of the relationship between ascertainment of the cause, see Dr. Al Ras (pp. 23–30).

22 See for example, *Al Mughni*, by Ibn Qudamah (1969), the chapter on *Riba* and Exchange as representative of the Hanbali School'; *Hashiat Ibn 'Abdin*, the Book on Prohibition and Permissibility, the chapter on Sale, as representative of the Hanafi School. See also a comparative juristic study by Al Duraini (1979), pp. 64–132, and 593–608 and *Al Muntaqa* commentary on *Malik's Muwatta*, by Al Baji Al Maliki (1984), Vol. 5, p. 15 forward and *Al Hisba*, by Ibn Taimiyah (1983).

23 See **Dr. Al Fangari's** statement quoted earlier in footnote 3. See also the strong counter arguments put by **Dr. Dunya** (1984), pp. 30–36, which supports the author's view.

24 I would like to thank **Dr. Nejatullah Siddiqi**, for bringing this idea into my attention and for a detailed discussion thereon.

25 Books on jurisprudence often mention briefly the causes or rationale of a Shari'ah rule, but the arrival at the relevant Shari'ah rule remains the main function of *Fiqh*.

26 Interest charged on account of delay in payment of an original debt falling due.

27 See (in English) **Zarqa** (1983/b), **Chapra** (1985, pp. 117–122) and **Khan** (1984), pp. 89–92.

28 In Arabic, see **Siddiqi** (1982), pp. 8–10 and p. 25) and **Chapra** (pp. 17–18); in English, see **Ziauddin Ahmad** (unpublished handout) and **Khan** (1984), Chapter 3. This second reference is a valuable Ph.D. thesis presented at Boston University, USA, in 1983, in which Dr. Waqar Khan proves that interest-free financing is superior in terms of efficiency to interest-based financing as long as partners adhere to the principles of honesty or as long as the cost of controls is kept within reasonable limits.

29 From the Introduction of Shaikh Abdullah Daraz to Al Shatibi's Muwafaqat (n.d.), Vol. 1, p. 3.

30 This absolutely applies to Shari'ah texts of definitive evidence. For those rules of speculative evidence, it seems that Imam Malik (May God rest his soul in peace) used to seek help, in determining their purport and limiting their absolute sense, from the descriptive expected results of the Hukm (rule). See an example about such procedure that is given by Al Qarafi related to Malik's interpretation of the tradition dealing with the issue of the Imam (Ruler) giving a supererogatory amount to a soldier fighting for the cause of God. (Al Qarafi, (1967), 25th Question, issue # 3, pp. 105–108).

31 This statement is made by my father (See, **Mustafa Al Zarqa** (1984), Vol. 1, p. 104, paragraph 26/2) as an expression of the idea emphasized by Imam Al Shatibi in his *Al Muwafaqat fi Usul Al Shari'ah*, (n.d.), Vol. 2, pp. 37 48.

32 The stones referred to here were stone altars or stone columns on which oil was poured for consecration, or slabs on which meat was sacrificed to idols. Any idolatrous or superstitious practices are here condemned.

33 The arrows referred to here were used for the division of meat by a sort of lottery or raffle. Arrows were also used for divination, i.e., for ascertaining lucky and unlucky moments, or learning the wishes of the heathen gods, as to whether men should undertake certain actions or not.

34 **al Shatibi** (n.d.), pp. 99–100.

35 Shaikh Abdullah Daraz in his marginal commentary on *Al Muwafaqat*, Vol. 1, p. 100, mentions some of the objections of Imam Shatibi to this view, where he responded to them by lending them his support.

36 I would like to thank Dr. Ja'far Shaikh Idris for bringing this to my knowledge.

37 **al Shatibi** (n.d.), p. 100.

38 See **Anas Zarqa** (1984), pargraph 4/5, pp. 14–16.

39 I have depended in my remarks on **Mustafa al-Zarqa** (1984), paragraphs 15 and 21. It is to be noted the Hanbalis, in addition to the Hanafis and Malikis depend, in deriving rules of Shari'ah, on the principle of considerations of public interests (among which is *Istihsan*). (Ibid, paragraph 30/4).

40 **Mustafa al-Zarqa** (1984), paragraph 23 forward.

41 Ibid, paragraph 29.

42 See Arabic references dealing with this issue: **Chapra** (1984) **Ma'bid Al Jarhi** (1981).

43 Among the researchers who discussed this point briefly was **Abdullah Al Thumali** (1985).

44 See two of such attempts, one by **Anas Al Zarqa**, (1982 and 1983a) and the other by **Kawthar Al Abji** (1985).

45 In Islamic economics, the source of the social interest function is generally Islamic Law. Both Imams, Abu Hamid Al Ghazali then Abu Ishaq Al Shatibi, have presented an innovative Islamic formulation of this function (although they did not give it this modern name). For more details, see **Anas Al Zarqa** (1982 and 1983a), pp. 166–256.

46 This is the basic conclusion of the well-known article of Bergson, which was published in 1938 and which constitutes one of the key supporting elements of the modern theory of welfare economics. See Samuelson's 'Foreword' to Graaff's book (in this paper's English bibliography). It is noticed that Pareto's Optimal Allocation (while all agree that it is seldom practically feasible to give preference to a certain economic policy over another based on Pareto's principle alone) depends also on some hidden assumptions or normative values; it is not, in other words, purely objectives as some economists have thought for quite a long time. (See **Heilbroner** and **Thurow** (1975), pp. 267–269).

Compensation tests, such as those suggested by Kaldor and Hicks, cannot be considered objective unless a compensation is paid to those harmed by a certain economic policy. They will be considered manifest subjective criteria, which give preference to the interests of a group of people at the expense of those of other groups. For an example, see **Reynolds** and **Smolensky** (1977), pp. 454–455. On the other hand, if a compensation is actually paid to those harmed, they would become similar to the Pareto's optimal allocation principle, which depends on hidden values, as mentioned earlier, (see **Graaff** (1967), pp. 90–92), where he shows that criteria based on compensation tests depend generally on values that are related to income distribution.

Therefore, it is correct to emphasize that neither Pareto's criterion, nor compensation tests are totally value-free and, consequently, that economic policies should, as mentioned earlier, depend on values that are derived from outside the descriptive side of economics.

47 **Al Sadr** (1968), pp. 290–294.
48 This denial of the 'scientific' quality of the first part is correct only for those who adopt a narrow definition of the word 'science', where they limit it to branches of knowledge that contain descriptive statements (laws) that are amenable to experiment. Since we have adopted a more comprehensive definition of the word 'science' that includes any organized and classified body of knowledge, study of economic ideologies and systems, including the economic system of Islam, should be considered a science. The extended definition is the one that is consistent with the concept of science in the Qur'an and Sunnah. Therefore we should not adopt the narrower definition. (See paragraph 2.2 above).
49 **Al Sadr** (1968), pp. 292–293.
50 My views about Islamic Economics are in agreement with that of **Muhammad Al-Mubarak** (1977), (May Allah bless his soul) regarding Islamic Sociology p. 14 forward. **Ba Qader** (1981), p. 22, has the same view regarding social sciences in general.
51 Compare with **Dr. Dunya** (1984).
52 **Al-Faruqi** (1982), pp. 38–53.
53 Khurshid, Ahmad's "Introduction" in **Chapra** (1985), p. 9.
54 It is known, for instance, that Pareto optimality criteria depend fully on assuming that utility functions among individuals are independent.
55 Economists do not dispute that the assumption of uncertainty is realistic and correct, although they used the assumption of certainty for simplification. However, many economists tend to quickly forget that and hold tenaciously to the results of analysis, forgetting that these results change completely when we assume uncertainty. This happened with many renowned economists. See for example the conventional analysis of the subject of time preference and the claim that the use of an interest rate is necessary for wise investment decisions. For more details, see (in English) (**Anas Zarqa** 1982 and 1983, 'a').
56 *Najash* in Arabic means 'to raise the price of a commodity offered for sale without a real interest in purchasing it, for the purpose of ensnaring other really interested buyers into bidding a price higher than the commodity's market price value'.
57 *Talaqqi Al-Rukban* in Arabic means 'the reception or meeting of merchants on horsebacks or camels and buying the commodities they carry before these merchants reach their destination towns and cities and know about their commodities' prevailing prices'.
58 See explanation **al Zarqa, Mustafa** (1964), Vol. I, pp. 404–417, paragraphs. 186–188.
59 Among those who mentioned this idea is **Awad** (1981), pp. 89–90.
60 This is apart from important descriptive contribution for Abu Yusuf that were noted by **Dunya** (1984), pp. 11–70.
61 *Mukhadramun* in Arabic is the plural of *mukhadram*, a person who lived in two different periods such as Islam and days of ignorance (*Jahihyyah*).

References

Arabic references

Al Abji, Kawther, (1405H/1985G), "*Dirasat Jadwa al Istithmar . . .*" (A Study of the Feasibility of Investment in the Light of Rules under Islamic *Fiqh*), *Majallah Abhath al Iqtisad al Islami*, Jeddah, KAAU/ICRIE, **Vol. 2, No. 2**.

Abu Sulayman, Abdul Hamid, (1982), *Al Islam wa Mustaqbal al Insaniyyah*, (Islam and the Future of Humanity), Islamabad, Research paper submitted to the Seminar on Islamization of Knowledge.

Al Asqalani, Ibn Hajar, (1960), *Mukhtasar al Targhib wa'l Tarhib* by al Mundhiri, edited by Habibur Rahman al Azami, Malegaun (India), Dar Ihya al Ma'arif, and Berut, Mu'assasah al Risalah.

——, (1373H) *Bulugh al Maram*, edited by Radwan Muhammad Radwan, Beirut, Dar al Kitab al Arabi.

Awad, Ahmad Safi al Din, (1981), *Usul Ilm al Iqtisad al Islami: al Iqtisad al Juz'i*, (Principles of Islamic Economics: Microeconomics), *Majallah Adwa' al Shariah*, Riyadh, Dar al Irshad, No. 12.

Ba Qader, Abu Bakr Ahmad, (1981), "Aslamat al Ulum al Ijtimaiyyah" (Islamization of Social Sciences), *Majallah Kulliyat al Adab Wa'l Ulum al Insaniyyah*, Jeddah, King Abaudlaziz University.

Al Baji, Abu'l Walid, (1331H), *al Muntaqa Sharh al Muwatta*, Beirut, Dar al Kitab al Arabi.

Chapra, M. Umer, (1984), *al Nizam al Naqdi wa'l Masrafi fil Iqtisad al Islami* (Money and Banking System in Islamic Economy), *Majallah Abhath al Iqtisad al Islami*, Vol. 1, No. 2, pp. 1–36.

Dunya, Shawqi, (1984), *A'lam al Iqtisad al Islami*, (The Pioneers of Islamic Economics), The First Book, Riyadh, Maktabah al Khurayji.

——, (1984), *al Nazriyyah al Iqtisadiyyah*, min Manzur Islami (Economic Theory from Islamic Perspective), Riyadh, Maktabah al Khurayji.

Al Durayni, Fathi, (1979), *al Fiqh al Islami al Muqarin*, (The Comparative Islamic Jurisprudence), Damascus, Tarbayn Press.

Al Fangari, Shawqi, (1980), *al Madhhab al Iqtisadi fi'l Islam*. (Economic System in Islam), in Muhammad Saqr (ed.), *al Iqtisad al Islami: Buhuth Mukhtarah*, Jeddah, ICRIE/KAAU.

Ibn Khaldun, (1982), *al Muqaddimah*, Beirut, Dal al Kitab al Lubnani.

Ibn Abidin, (n.d.), *Radd al Muhtar* (Known as Hashiyah Ibn Abidin), Beirut, Dar Ihyal al Kitab al Arabi.

Ibn Qudamah, (1969), *al Mughni*, edited by **Taha Sharbini**, Cairo, Maktabah al Qahirah.

Ibn Majah, (1984), *Sunan*, edited by Mustafa Azami, Al Riyadh, al Saudiah Printing Company.

Ibn Taymiyyah, (1403H/1983G), *al-Hisbah fi'l Islam* (Public Duties in Islam), edited by **Sayyid B. Muhammad Abi Sadah**, Kuwait, Dar al Arqam.

International Institute of Islamic Thought, (1986), *Islamiyyat al Ma'rifah* (Islamization of Knowledge), Washington.

Al Jarhi, Mabid, (1981), *Nahwa Nizam Naqdi wa Mali Islami*, (Towards an Islamic Monetary and Financial System), Jeddah, ICFRIE/KAAU.

Al Mubarak, Muhammad, (1977), *Nahwa Siyaghah Islamiyyah li Ilm al Ijtimat'*, (Towards an Islamic Formulation of the Science of Sociology), *al Muslim al Mu'asir*, Vol. 12, pp. 15–44.

Al Mundhiri, Abd al Azim, (n.d.), *Mukhtasar Sahih Muslim* (An Abridged Version of Muslim's Collection of Authentic Hadiths), edited by **Nasir al Din al Albani**, Kuwait, Ministry of Awqaf.

Al Qarafi, Ahmad, (1967), *al Ihkam*, edited by **Abd al Fattah Abu Ghuddah**, Aleppo, Maktab al Matbuat al Islamiyyah.

Al Qasimi, Jamaluddin, (1331 H), *Majmu Risail fi Usul al Tafsir wa Usul al Fiqh*, (Collection of Papers on Principles of Exegesis and Jurisprudence), Damascus, al Faiha Press.

Al Ra's, As'ad Muhammad, (1987), *Muqawwamat al Iqtisad al Islam* (Elements of Islamic Economics), Riyadh, King Saud University.

Al Sadr, Muhammad Baqir, (1968), *Iqtisaduna*, (Our Economics), Beirut, Dar al Fikr.

Al Salih, Subhi, (1976), *Manhal al Waridin Sharh Riyad al Salihin*, by al Nawawi, Beirut, Dar al Ilm Li'l Mala'in.

Al Shatibi, Abu Ishaq, (n.d.), *al Muwafaqat fi Usul al Shariah*, edited by **Abdullah Daraz**, Beirut, Dar al Ma'rifah.

Siddiqi, M. N., (1982), *Limadha al Masarif al Islamiyyah* (Rationale of Islamic Banking), Translated by Rafic al Masri, Jeddah, ICRIE/KAAU.

Al Thumali, Abdullah Muslih, (1985), al Hurriyyah al Iqtisadiyyah wa Tadakhkhul al Dawlah, Makkah al Mukarramah, *UQU, Ph.D. Thesis*.

Al Zarqa, Mustafa Ahmad, (1984), *Al Madkhal al fiqhi al Amm*, (A General Introduction to Jurisprudence), Damascus, al Hayat Pass.

Al Zarqa, M. Anas, (1982), *al Qiyam wa'l Ma'ayir al Islamiyyah fi Taqwim al Mashru'at*, (Islamic Values and Criteria in Project Evaluation), *al Muslim al Mu'asir*, No. 3, pp 85–105.

——, (1984), "*Nuzum al Tawzi' al Islamiyyah*", (The Islamic Distribution Systems), *Majallah Abhath al Iqtisad al Islami*, Vol. 2, No. 1, pp. 1–51.

English references

Adelman, Irma, (1961), *Theories of Economic Growth and Development*, Stanford: Stanford University Press.

Bergson, (Burk), A., (1938), "A Reformulation of Certain Aspects of Welfare Economics", *Quarterly Journal of Economics*, LII, pp. 310–34.

Chapra, M. Umer, (1985), *Towards a Just Monetary System*, Leicester, U.K.: The Islamic Foundation.

Al-Faruqi, Ismail, R., (1982), *Islamization of Knowledge: General Principles and Work Plan*, Washington, D.C.: International Institute of Islamic Thought.

Graaff, J. deV., (1967), *Theoretical Welfare Economics*. London: Cambridge University Press, (reprinted).

Heilbroner, R. L. and **Thurow, L. C.**, (1975), *The Economic Problem*, 4th Ed. Englewood Cliffs, N.J.: Prentice Hall.

Henderson, J. M. and **Quandt, R. E.**, (1958), *Microeconomic Theory: A Mathematical Approach*, New York: McGraw Hill.

Khan, Waqar Masood, (1984), Towards an Interest Free Islamic Economic System: A Theoretical Analysis of Prohibiting Debt Financing, *Ph.D. Dissertation, Boston University*.

Lindebeck, A., (1971), *The Political Economy of the New Left*, Harper.

Reynolds, M. and **Smolensky, F.**, (1977), "Welfare Economics" in **S. Weintraub**, (ed.), *Modern Economic Thought*, Oxford: Basil Blackwell.

Roberts, Marc J., (1974), "On the Nature and Condition of Social Science", *DAEDALUS*, Summer.

Samuels, Warren J., (1977), "Ideology in Economics" in **S. Weintraub**, (ed.), op. cit.

Samuelson, P. A., (1965), *Foundation of Economic Analysis*, New York: Atheneum.

Samuelson, P. A., (1967), "*Foreword*" in **Graaff**, (ed.), op. cit.

Schumpeter, J. A., (1949), *The Theory of Economic Development*. Cambridge, Mass.: Harvard University Press.

Shils, E., (1974), "Faith Utility and Legitimacy of Science", *DAEDALUS*, Summer.

Ward, Benjamin, (1972), *What is Wrong with Economics*. London: Macmillan.

Weintraub, S., (ed.), (1977), *Modern Economic Thought*. Oxford: Basil Blackwell.

Zarqa, M. Anas, (1982), "Comments on S.N.H. Naqvi's Paper" in **M. Ariff**, (ed.) *Monetary and Fiscal Economics of Islam*, Jeddah: Centre for Research in Islamic Economics.

Zarqa, M. Anas, (1983a) "The Economics of Discounting in Islamic Perspective" in **Z. Ahmad** et. al. (ed.): *Fiscal Policy and Resources Allocation in Islam*, Jeddah: Centre for Research in Islamic Economics.

——, (1983b), Stability in an Interest-free Islamic Economy: A Note, *Pakistan Journal of Applied Economics*, Karachi: Applied Economics Research Centre, Vol. II, No. 2.

18

CHOICE OF POLICY INSTRUMENTS
Specific issues

Syed Nawab Haider Naqvi

Source: S. N. H. Naqvi, *Ethics and Economics: An Islamic Synthesis*, Markfield: Islamic Foundation, 1981, pp. 129–41.

The type of Islamic economy that has been presented so far is remarkably free from the excessive collectivizing zeal of socialism as well as from the individualistic anarchism of capitalism. The Islamic approach, though laying considerable emphasis on the conscious organization of economic and social life, never draws in its web so tightly as to stifle the individual initiative completely. The general outlook is neither vindictive nor permissive, but is definitely regulatory and reformative with ethical fragrance enlivening the environment. True, ethical societies, such as Islam seeks to create, *appear* to be overbearing in terms of their "condescending" outlook on human behaviour, for the individual's unlimited freedom of choice to do what suits him best is no longer accepted as the unalterable law of nature. Indeed, in the Islamic perspective, man does not always know what is best for him: "but it may happen that ye hate a thing which is good for you, and it may happen that ye love a thing which is bad for you" (2:216). Such an attitude, despite its apparent autocratic overtones, promotes an atmosphere of certainty in which the cult of unrestrained, unaltruistic individualism has no place. However, the *creative* instincts of man are allowed to flower so that they can contribute the most to collective welfare.[1] The ultimate thrust of Islamic reform is to press both the organization and the individual, in proportion to the "capacities" of each, into the cause of establishing a society based on the ethical principles of Islam. To achieve such a synchronization of man's many behavioural facets, the State will have to assume a predominant, even a patronizing, role in an Islamic system.

Translated onto the economic plane, the government in an Islamic economy will have to use both "direct" and "indirect" economic controls to regulate overall economic activity. Furthermore, in order to ensure a socially desirable *and* Islamically legitimate redirection of productive resources, it will be essential for the government to attain the "commanding heights" of the economy. However, the choice of policy instruments in a fully-fledged Islamic economy will be constrained in two principal ways:

(i) *Ribā*, or anything resembling it, will not be among the set of allowable policy instruments.[2] As pointed out in the previous chapter, an alternative Islamically acceptable principle of capital pricing will have to be found.

(ii) No policy sustaining, or exacerbating, unlimited private property rights will be allowed.

In general, any set of economic policies which have the effect of permanently creating or exacerbating social inequities, cannot be condoned on any pretext whatsoever – e.g. that of economic growth. For an Islamic economy will be committed not just to the achievement of material prosperity but to enhancing the *quality* of life as well. Subject to these constraints, the policymakers in an Islamic economy will be free to choose an appropriate policy package, containing direct as well as indirect controls, even though the exact proportion in which these two types are combined must remain a matter of economic expediency.

Direct controls

In an Islamic economy, the government will have to play a predominant role to: (i) direct investment resources into socially desirable channels; (ii) ensure that the scarcest of real resources – e.g. capital – is allocated most economically among legitimate competing uses; (iii) provide enough, but just enough, monetary resources to accommodate the financial needs of the commodity-producing sector in order to avoid excessive fluctuations in economic activity; and (iv) ensure an adequate provision for those who live below the "poverty line".

(i) Investment controls

To make sure that investment activity, in both the public and the private sectors, conforms to the overall socio-economic priorities of an Islamic economy, it will be essential to regulate it in considerable detail. In doing so, it will be essential for the policy-makers to make sure that: (a) capital is priced at its scarcity value to ration it and ensure its most economical use; and (b) private profitability of investment decisions is made to approximate its social profitability to prevent under-expansion of socially desirable production.[3] This is particularly true of industries in which sizeable external economies exist. For the satisfactory fulfilment of these objectives it will be necessary to adopt a system which gives discretionary, *but not arbitrary*, powers to the government, while making full allowance for allocative efficiency.

Investment auctioning

An economically valid procedure for achieving the above-mentioned objectives will be for the government to auction investment authorizations to the prospective investors, through the banking system and financial institutions. These authorizations will be sold to the highest bidders through the market mechanism. Such an arrangement will make it possible for the investors to take into account the scarcity price of capital, which will be high and positive in a capital-scarce economy, in making investment decisions. In order to prevent an unnecessary "cornering" of investment authorizations by a few "resourceful" bidders, and also to reflect social investment priorities, the auctions will take place periodically according to the following scheme.

The government, in consultation with the Planning Agency and other responsible authorities, will parcel out total investment resources into several categories of investment, *to be specified in an investment schedule.* Each broad category of investment in the investment schedule will be assigned an upper monetary limit. Auctioning will stop in a particular category once the monetary limit assigned to it has been reached. This system will achieve both of the objectives stated above and ensure that investment resources are not all forced into those uses which are considered to be the most profitable from the point of view of individual investors but have a low social profitability. It will also prevent over-capitalization and excess capacity through an economic use of scarce resources and will make sure that the average capital/labour ratio remains in line with the resource-endowment pattern of the country.

The question may be raised: does this scheme have an element of *ribā* built into it? The answer is in the negative. All that is happening under the proposed scheme is that investors will be allowed possession of investment resources only at a scarcity price. The scarcity price of capital is not fixed in advance: *it is determined by the supply of and demand for investible funds.* The scheme has the added merit that it avoids the arbitrariness that goes with a system designed to control the level and composition of investment entirely through administrative investment sanctioning. Administrative procedures in such a system become tangled for the simple reason that the magnitude of excess demand for capital at the going rate of interest, which is generally low, is too large to be cut down through detailed rationing procedures. The proposed system will perform the rationing function at a reletively low administrative cost since the price of capital so determined will reflect its true opportunity cost.

(ii) Income distribution policies

Fiscal, monetary and exchange rate policies affect, directly and indirectly, the accrual of money incomes to various classes of income recipients. This should be obvious enough because all measures regulating income flows must have income distributional implications. However, the problem of income distribution has to be tackled in an explicit way. Corresponding to any specified growth strategy, the entire economic superstructure, involving production, consumption and exchange, must be geared explicitly to the attainment of the most desirable income distribution pattern in an Islamic economy. This must involve such diverse elements as land reforms, a specific programme of maximizing the production of wage goods, and an improvement of the public distribution system, including its extension to the rural poor as well. Such an "amphibious" attack on the distribution problem, mostly through direct regulatory measures, is essential because not only does growth imply a specific distribution of income, but the reverse relationship also holds: the most desirable pattern of effective demand will produce the socially optimal production mix.

In view of the complexity of this problem, the government will have to: (i) provide basic needs at reasonable prices through the adoption of consumption subsidy schemes which may require the establishment of a network of fair price shops; (ii) initiate wide-ranging land reforms to bring about an equitable distribution of land; (iii) make a co-ordinated effort to improve the living standards of the rural poor; and (iv) provide new job opportunities to the under-employed and landless labourers. Jobs such as the construction of roads, dams, irrigation projects, etc. should help solve the problem of underemployment to a large extent and result in the provision of a basic infrastructure. Another source of employment creation could be small-scale and cottage industries. Incidentally, such a policy will also help lower the average capital/labour ratio, a distinct advantage in a capital-scarce economy.

(iii) Nationalization of banks

In order to achieve the "commanding heights", the process of monetary creation will have to be controlled directly by the government. In an Islamic economy, the "optimal" money supply can best be determined by the government, since it will also be regulating both the level and composition of production and consumption. Indeed, this follows from the argument of the previous chapter: an active government role in the production process implies an even greater degree of control of the process of money creation. Furthermore, as the objective of the economic policy in an Islamic economy is to provide a framework for growth with reasonable price stability, a nearly complete dovetailing of the financial and the real sectors of the economy will have to be arranged. As pointed out above, such a reform will also be essential for abolishing *ribā* in due course. Added to this is the problem of meeting the "allowability" constraint, which again would call for a credit policy not only to supplement purely economic policies but also to enforce the ethical requirements of an Islamic economy.

Indirect controls

(i) Monetary policy

It may be said that the argument in the previous paragraph does not *necessarily* lead to an unambiguous recommendation for an outright nationalization of banks, since there are indirect ways of controlling money supply and, through it, the level and composition of investment. Unfortunately, an Islamic Central Bank would not have too many "degrees of freedom" in exercising a decisive control on money supply through indirect means for the sheer lack of a sufficient number of policy instruments. The traditional policy instruments, like the Bank Rate and the Open Market Operations, *will no longer* be permitted in a *ribā*-free Islamic economy.[4] The only orthodox policy instruments still available to the Central Bank in an Islamic economy will be moral suasion and the power to change the statutory deposit ratios for regulating the lending activities of the commercial banks.[5]

Profit-sharing arrangements

It has been noted in the literature on Islamic Economics that, while an Islamic Central Bank will lose the interest rate as a regulatory device, it will gain another policy instrument in the form of profit-sharing arrangements. According to this system, the commercial banks will be participating in productive activities by investing deposit money on an equity-participation basis, sharing in both the losses and the profits. The profits and the losses will then be distributed over the total deposit accounts in a specified proportion.[6] Firstly, while it is true that the system by itself is Islamically legitimate, this fact does not necessarily mean that it is also the best principle on the basis of which an exploitation-free Islamic economy should be run. The crucial fact that will ultimately determine the feasibility of such an arrangement depends on our vision of the structure of the Islamic economy. For the financial flows merely reflect the physical production and consumption relationships characterising a particular economic system. If these structural physical relationships are Islamically unjust, the superimposition of even an Islamically just financial arrangement may end up making the system even more unjust if only through the chaos that such an artificial symbiosis will promote. This is just a restatement of a point noted several times in this book that capitalism cannot be "Islamized" just by the transposition of a single policy instrument from an Islamic economic system.

317

The economic viability of the proposed profit-sharing system cannot be established through *a priori* reasoning; it must be tested on an economy-wide basis before any meaningful evaluation of it is possible.[7] As pointed out in the previous chapter, this is because the return on investment becomes a function of business conditions in general and of the efficiency with which the enterprise is being run. Hence, an element of uncertainty is introduced into the investor's expectations. Hence, to hedge against the probability of a loss, ways and means must be found, through some kind of deposit insurance scheme, to guarantee the safety of the *nominal* values of deposits. If no such explicit risk-insurance system is evolved, not only the banking system, but the entire economy will become highly "unstable", since the proposed system will make it hypersensitive to even small changes in business fortunes. Disturbances originating in one part of the economy will be transmitted fully, indeed in a magnified form, to the rest of the economy, which will, in effect, become a house of cards. Thus the "shock-absorbing" characteristics of the present limited-liability principle, on which the modern banking system rests, will be lost under the proposed profit-sharing system. This will be a big loss, since the policy-makers will, in effect, be losing their capacity for on-the-spot "trouble shooting": economic crises, instead of remaining "localized", will always be "generalized" under the proposed reform.

Secondly, to run the profit-sharing system in an efficient way, it will be necessary to recruit a large technical staff to assess the profitability of investment projects. True, some kind of a scrutiny of the viability of investment projects is done even now, but an economy-wide shifting to an equity-based system will increase this type of job several-fold, quantitatively and qualitatively. Indeed, business firms and banks will have to revise the existing accounting procedures, which at present allow a kind of camouflage operation to be carried out with impunity. The outcome will be a substantial increase in overhead expenses, cutting deeply into the distributable net profit margins. This will result in a lowering of the rate of return accruing to the depositors. Thirdly, even assuming that this system may be used as a replacement for interest-bearing deposits, or even as a mode of lending, it can certainly not be employed as a policy instrument to influence economic activity in the same way as *changes* in the rate of interest are used by monetary authorities. The proposed arrangement does not possess any flexibility in that profit (loss) margins, calculated *ex post*, cannot be varied at the discretion of the Central Bank.

It follows from this discussion that indirect monetary controls will be substantially reduced in importance in an Islamic economy, for the simple reason that not many of the traditional policy instruments will be available, while the ones suggested in their place, like profit-sharing, are not really workable. At least so it appears *a priori*. This leads to the inevitable conclusion that nationalization of the entire banking system is an integral part of the Islamic reform.

(ii) Fiscal policy

It also follows that, to the extent that indirect monetary controls become less important, fiscal policy will gain in importance for laying out the preconditions of a just Islamic economy. In particular, tax and expenditure policies will become significant policy instruments in the general category of indirect controls. And this may turn out to be one of the strengths of an Islamic economic system, because fiscal policy can in general be more effective than monetary policy in restoring full-employment equilibrium.[8] Furthermore, as pointed out in the previous chapter, reliance on public saving (investment) will be enhanced at the expense of private saving (investment), implying that a high rate of taxation will be an essential feature of a *ribā*-free, welfare-oriented Islamic economy.

(iii) Tax policy

In an Islamic economy the primary emphasis will be on broadening the tax base rather than on increasing the tax rates. The Islamic ethics demand that, except in a few cases, participation in the activity of giving should be *universal*, i.e. by both the rich and the not-too-poor: "Those who spend (of that which Allah hath given them) in ease and in adversity . . ." (3:134). Indeed, there is no way to attain salvation except through giving of what one treasures most: "Ye will not attain unto piety until ye spend of that which ye love" (3:92). Tax rates will have to be raised high enough to equalize the burden on the tax-payers but the marginal tax rates will not be oppressively high: "No-one should be charged beyond his capacity" (2:233). Indeed, once the tax base has been substantially broadened, there will be no need of too high tax rates anyway. An implication of such a reform is that a proper balance will have to be achieved between the so-called direct and indirect taxes. However, the main thing is not so much the balance between direct and indirect taxes *per se*, as the economic consequences of both in terms of the basic policy objectives of an Islamic economy, in particular social justice.

Furthermore, the tax policy will be used *primarily* as a revenue-raising device to allow the government to perform its substantially enlarged role in an Islamic economy. Hence, the income-equalizing and incentive functions of the tax policy will have to be relatively de-emphasized. The incentive function will be deflated in proportion to the decreased importance of private saving and investment. Income equalization will be done primarily by reducing drastically the size of private property and by establishing an elaborate social security system. However, in so far as the private sector does play a role in the production process – mostly in the production of consumer goods – an appropriate *tax-cum-subsidy* policy will have to be evolved to induce a socially desirable and Islamically legitimate composition of production and consumption. (Remember the "allowability" constraint noted in Chapter 3.)

It is interesting to note that such a general approach accords with the modern thinking on public finance which aims at broadening the tax base and lowering the tax rates. Furthermore, the modern taxonomic approach warns against "over-straining" any one policy instrument in the pursuit of multiple policy objectives. Experience has shown that using the tax policy for multifarious, often contradictory, purposes tends to weaken its functions as a revenue-raising device by substantially narrowing the tax base. Furthermore, several studies have shown that a tax policy is particularly ineffective in bringing about an equitable distribution of income and wealth.

The best that can be done in this direction is to equalize the tax burden on the tax payers.[9] Also, the traditional direct-indirect taxonomy is generally de-emphasized in modern literature on public finance in favour of a more analytical approach relating the total tax package to its effects on equity, capital formation, allocative efficiency, etc.[10]

An important element of the Islamic tax policy is the *Zakāt* levy (i.e. poor due), which will be *one of the many taxes* imposed in an Islamic economy. It is levied at a flat rate on all wealth, including income that remains unused for one full year, i.e. savings. Since, except for those who are very poor, all have to pay *Zakāt*, the tax base is greatly broadened, giving the entire population a sense of participation and responsibility. Furthermore, this levy is yet another example of Islam's unitary philosophy in which economic expediencies merge with ethical considerations: the payment of *Zakāt* is also a means of spiritual salvation.

A distinguishing feature of *Zakāt* is that it links tax policy with expenditure policy. Not only its rate and base but also the mode of its expending has been specified in the Holy Qur'ān. Furthermore, since, by and large, *Zakāt* is supposed to be levied and spent at the local level, the link between tax and expenditure becomes *visible*. The tax payers know exactly where and how the tax proceeds can be spent. This should be a great help in improving fiscal accountability and facilitating tax collection, which should be bigger because tax evasion will be minimal.

(iv) Public expenditure policy

In the context of a welfare-oriented society, such as Islam's, a conscious expenditure policy assumes great importance, since a tax policy is by and large ineffective in promoting social equity. This is because private consumption, curtailed through compulsory measures and a voluntary renunciation of wasteful expenditure, will have to be replaced by a substantial enlargement of public expenditure. This shift of emphasis, in terms of the resultant change in the composition of total national expenditure, is in accord with the *requirement* that a legitimate and an economically efficient consumption basket be produced to satisfy the needs of the poor.[11]

The broad priorities of public expenditure should accord with the overall requirement of ensuring social justice, statically and dynamically. A direct implication of this statement is that a judicious division will have to be made between the needs of immediate consumption and the necessity to provide for capital formation. However, constrained by the requirements of financing economic growth, public expenditure, at any given point of time, should aim at equalizing expenditure levels across various income groups. Starting from a situation where gross inequalities of income prevail, the focus of expenditure policy will be on alleviating the lot of the poor, the sick, the old, the unemployed and the orphans. It has already been noted that *Zakāt* proceeds must be spent, as laid down in the Qur'ān, primarily on relieving immediate hardships, without creating a permanent class of hangers-on and social parasites. In fact, there is emphasis in the Qur'ān that the needs of those who are genuinely hard-pressed but otherwise won't ask for help – out of self-respect, that is – must be given priority: "(Alms are) for the poor who are straitened for the cause of Allah, who cannot travel in the land (for trade). The unthinking man accounteth them wealthy because of their restraint. Thou shalt know them by their mark: They do not beg of man with importunity" (2:273).

In general, public expenditure must reflect the "fact" that in an Islamic economy the State must play a substantial role, not only as a catalyst but as an active agent of change, in the dynamic process of moving the economy towards the Islamic ideal. In the area of stabilization policy, the State will also have to engage in large public works programmes to generate employment opportunities in distress areas and also to shore up effective demand in times of depression. Indeed, the appropriate budgetary policies will have to be adopted to lessen excessive fluctuations in the business cycles – *a la* Equilibrium axiom.

Summary

The policy-makers will have to evolve, through the inevitable process of trial and error and learning-by-doing, an optimal policy package to meet the requirements of social justice in a growing Islamic economy. Direct controls will, in general, receive a heavier weight than indirect controls in the overall policy package. The State will have to attain the "commanding heights" for ensuring that scarce resources are redirected for priority uses, subject to the overall allowability constraint. This will entail nationalization of banks and all or most of the capital-goods-producing industries. Furthermore, direct investment controls will have to be exercised for the same reason. Monetary policy will have to be supplemented by fiscal policy, which will gain in importance as a regulatory device.

It may be objected that a substantial expansion of a socially just and efficient public sector will require a quantum jump in the supply of appropriate expertise. This may be a tall order for most of the skill-poor Muslim countries to meet. True, but the skill gap will have to be explicitly recognized (indeed, created) and gradually closed through the promulgation of universal education, without which the Islamic society will *never* take root. There should be no complacency that all this can be done in a short time. Creating an infrastructure of skills is even more difficult a task to accomplish than putting together socially desirable physical and economic infrastructures. Yet, this has to be done, and let nobody think that it is going to be easy. Restructuring of societies is a hard enough job, *but doing it along ethical lines* is truly a Herculean task. To think that the introduction of *Zakāt* and the abolition of *ribā* will solve all the problems is to put these two significant elements of the Islamic reform out of their essential "general-equilibrium" context of a comprehensive, wide-ranging Islamic reform, which seeks to establish a society or system free of social, economic and moral exploitation.

Notes

1 Russell [4] has argued that man's actions are largely controlled by instincts, which are of two kinds: creative and possessive. The success of any organization depends on its ability to control and regularize the latter while providing maximum opportunities for the former through individual or group autonomy.
2 For instance, according to some Muslim jurists, the renting of bare land on a sharecropping basis is also forbidden, because it *resembles ribā*. The selling of a tree with unripened fruits for a fixed sum of money is also prohibited in Islam.
3 All the more so, because in an Islamic economy there are restrictions on what can and should be included in the consumption basket. Not all productive activities will therefore be "allowable". It may be noted that, in an Islamic economy, not only the feasibility constraints, but also the "allowability" constraints will be binding. Sec Chapter 3, *Supra*.
4 Open Market Operations, in the strict sense of the term, will not remain meaningful because of the absence of interest-bearing securities in an Islamic economy. All the more so because one of the primary aims of Open Market Operations, namely to influence the interest rate *structure*, will no longer be relevant in such an economy. (It has, however, often been argued that Open Market Operations in the *equity* market should remain meaningful in an Islamic economy.) The argument that these policy instruments are not very effective anyway, even in an interest-based system, is irrelevant since it implies the recommendation that steps be taken to make them more effective. For instance, the Bank Rate in Pakistan remained unchanged (and ineffective) during the 1950's and 1960's; but this observation points to the conclusion that the correct policy should have been to raise it. (It has in fact been raised since then.) What we are arguing in the text is that such a policy instrument, irrespective of its effectiveness in the real world, will not be available to the Muslim policy-makers.
5 However, these policy instruments will not provide a really effective handle to the Central Bank for control of the money supply, particularly when excess liquidity exists in the banking system. Furthermore, when, as was the case in Pakistan during the Sixties, banks and insurance companies are owned by industrialists, it becomes well-nigh impossible for the Central Bank to influence, through indirect monetary policy, either the level or the composition of credit creation, which, in turn, greatly impairs its capacity to control the process of money creation. That

being the case, the government can hardly exercise any effective control on either the level or the composition of investment in the economy.

6 This is the well-known *Mudāraba* principle, which has been held Islamically valid by Muslim jurists. The advocates of this system consider this to be a complete replacement, as a policy instrument, of a positive rate of interest, an opinion which the present author does not share. A brief discussion of an amended *Mudāraba* scheme is given in the Appendix to Chapter 7. It is interesting to note that, according to Ibn Hazm, the institution of *Mudāraba* is not based on the Holy Qur'ān or on any of the Holy Prophet's traditions. It was only a custom of the pre-Islamic Arabs: "*Mudāraba* was practised in pre-Islamic Arabia. The tribe of Quraish had no other livelihood but trade. The old people, women, children and orphans used to give their capital on the basis of *Mudāraba* to the merchants for a certain part of the profit" [2, p. 247]. It is important to note his observation that "all the loss in *Mudāraba* was borne by the capital owner and not by the merchant, who took the capital for the purpose of trade" [2, p. 248].

7 It may be noted that the proposed system is being tried on a *limited basis* in some Muslim countries. No authoritative studies are yet available on the operational viability and efficiency of this system. But even if such a system succeeds on a *partial basis*, this is no guarantee that it will do so on an economy-wide basis as well. This is because in the latter case, it will require *all* the savers to become risk-takers, something that does not happen when this system is one of the many possibilities open to investors, the option to invest in interest-bearing deposits being not ruled out. The risk-takers may take this form of investment, while the risk-averters will not opt for it. In this case, the preference structure of the investors remains intact while it does not when the system is adopted on an economy-wide basis. A psychological reform, or rather indoctrination, will be required to make risk-takers of us all. But is it really necessary to go to such lengths? The present author would give a negative answer.

8 It is common knowledge that a tight fiscal policy and an easy monetary policy constitute a superior policy mix to the one in which an easy fiscal policy is combined with a tight monetary policy. The rate of capital formation will tend to be higher in the former case than in the latter case.

9 See, for instance, A. C. Harberger [1].

10 For instance, see R. A. Musgrave and P. Richman [3].

11 However, the solution to the problem is not as easy as it sounds. To produce an Islamically-legitimate consumption basket, for which there is an effective demand, cannot be arbitrarily foisted upon the people but must be decided upon through the process of trial and error. Economic considerations, political expediency and ethical requirements will all play a part in determining the "contents" of such a consumption basket – something not fixed for all times to come.

References

1. Harberger, A. C. *Fiscal Policy and Income Distribution*. Princeton, U.S.A. 1974 (Mimeographed)
2. Hazm, Ibn. *Al-Mulhallā* (Arabic). Vol. 8. Cairo: Idara al Muniriyya. 1350 A.H.
3. Musgrave, R. A., and Peggy Richman. "Allocation aspects: Domestic and International." In *The Role of Direct and Indirect Taxes in the Federal Revenue System*. (A Conference Report of the National Bureau of Economic Research and the Brookings Institution.) Princeton, N.J. (USA): Princeton University Press. 1964.
4. Russell, Bertrand. *Authority and the Individual*. London: Unwin Books. 1949.

Part 4

PIONEERS OF ISLAMIC ECONOMICS

19

SHIHĀB AL-DĪN IBN ABĪ'L-RABĪ'

On management of personal and public wealth[1]

S. M. Hasanuz Zaman

Source: *Islamic Studies*, 31:3 (1992), 365–74.

Introduction

The facts about the career of Shihāb al-Dīn Aḥmad ibn Muḥammad ibn Abī'l-Rabī' (H 218–272) are still shrouded in obscurity;[2] but his brief treatise entitled *Sulūk al-Mālik fī Tadbīr al-Mamālik* (Conduct of the Master in the Management of the Kingdoms), places him among the rank of major Muslim writers who have dealt with the subject of politics and statecraft as a science. The book was caligraphed by Muḥammad 'Alī al-Krurāsānī in H 1286, and published the same year (in Arabic), under the auspices of Muḥammad 'Ārif Pāshā. It comprises 152 pages.

The theme of the treatise is to emphasise that moral and material welfare can be achieved only by following the way of the Prophet (peace be upon him). Al-Rabi' devotes a whole chapter to the discussion on the standards and the methods of achieving moral and spiritual perfection, and another chapter to the pre-requisites of material welfare. In this part, he dilates upon the need for acquisition of knowledge and its various branches as well as upon social, and family life. This chapter also includes his views on wealth (*māl*), dealing mainly with sources of earning, household budget, and home economics.

The last chapter deals with politics and political economy. An interesting part of the discussion covers budget-making and public expenditure, describes significance of material resources for the public exchequer and the ways of increasing these resources. The book concludes with selected aphorisms of early thinkers and sages.

Discussion on the evolution of society by al-Rabī' is not much different from earlier discussions by sociologists. It is, however, distinct in listing the bare necessities which have compelled man to organize himself in a society.

While food, clothing, shelter and medicare are treated as bare necessities by Muslims and non-Muslims alike, the institution of marriage is held equally important by the Muslims who consider it an important factor in stabilizing family life and in the prevention of moral laxity. Needless to point out that this attitude is inspired by the sayings of the holy Prophet (peace be upon him) that articulately emphasised the institution of marriage. (p. 101)

The pattern of Islamic life is based on faith which encompasses the economic behaviour also. No economic system, and especially the Islamic economic system, can successfully and effectively function unless personal as well as social ethics are disciplined. The basic premise of al-Rabīʿ rests on his claim that the best and the most efficient administration depends on the best moral orientation not only of the rulers (and of administrations) but also of the entire population. The people should be moulded, early in life, into acquiring excellent character. In order to ensure that moral values are properly inculcated in the individuals, a child, al-Rabīʿ advises, should be taught that show of greediness is bad behaviour and that the consumption of food is a matter of secondary importance. He should be trained to content himself with simple food and to do service to others. Generosity and philanthropy should become his habits. Moreover, he should be taught to have contempt for gold and silver and refrain from hearing vain and boastful talk. (p. 83)

It is no wonder, therefore, that emphasis on ethics occupies a central place in the conduct of the individual as well as of the ruler and his functionaries. Personal character and a sound and stable society occupy a place higher than the material goods and belongings. A man should acquire wealth through just and honest means. Every profession is not dignified;[3] one should, therefore, choose that profession which is most beneficial to the people and is respected by all and sundry. (p. 88)

Al-Rabīʿ considers village people to be the basic unit on which the entire population depends. But these villagers have no direct link with the general population which gets articles of use from the business people who, in turn, obtain there articles from the village people. He advises the ruler to show magnanimity to the good people among them and try to ameliorate their condition. The welfare of any people depends, inter-alia, on the following factors:

1. Defence and internal security to protect people from enemies.
2. Internal peace and maintenance of law and order.
3. Levy of taxes on the well-to-do, according to their ability, for the maintenance of the poor and the destitute.
4. Providing of justice.

In the entire treatise, tabulations outnumber the descriptive statements. Without having a look at the manuscript it is not possible to conceive how the author could have actually arranged his charts and tables. It is also not possible for us to claim that the editor of the treatise might have re-arranged his descriptions in the form of charts and tables. Anyhow, the editor himself mentions that this work has been written in a unique fashion (*namaṭ gharīb wa ṭarz 'ajīb* (p. 15) which leads us to deduce that the tabular form, that the editor chose, had been, in some way or the other, arranged by the author himself. This is what the words *namaṭ gharīb* and *ṭarz 'ajīb* imply. The aim behind adopting this style was to facilitate the study of the available material on the subject. He was inspired to do so by a similarly arranged book written by someone on the subject of physical health (*Kitāb Mushajjar fī Ḥifẓ Ṣiḥḥat al-Badan*). The book is described as the collection of relevant discussion that suits the subject matter. (pp. 3–4)

1. On wealth and money

Al-Rabī' discusses wealth (*māl*) on two different places. In chapter 3 he has discussed personal wealth but in the last chapter he deals with public exchequer or the ruler's treasury. His approach is identical towards both kinds of wealth.

Al-Rabī's discussion on the need and significance of *māl* (wealth) in context of personal wealth reveals that by this term he means money. His description of the origin of money is not different from what his predecessors had given. According to him, system of money had to be devised in order to set a standard of value and to find out a medium of exchange. A man who possesses money has control over all the things that he needs. (p. 75)

2. On household budgeting

Under the title of *māl* in chapter 3, he proceeds very systematically to prove the significance of wealth and of the use of money. *Māl*, according to him, is necessary for physical existence. In order to rear cattle and to grow fruit, preserve it, and make it worth consumption, it is necessary to set up workshops and manufacturing units. This gives rise to civilisation wherein the producer and craftsmen are inter-dependent. Money is necessary (p. 75) in order to benefit all these producers and workers. According to his tabular presentations, personal management of money requires that three points should be kept in mind.

a. Earning;
b. Maintenance or security (*ḥifẓ*), and
c. Expenditure.

Earning requires that one should refrain from getting money through injustice, fraud, duress, undignified and disgraceful profession, dishonesty, false accounting and lies. Security or maintenance (*ḥifẓ*) of money calls for consuming less than, not even equal to, earning, and investing in avenues of quick turn over. Proper spending requires avoiding inessential expenditure without refraining from spending on worthy causes or on family. In addition to these compulsory considerations one should stick to the following ethical rules of spending:

i.   Spend on proper requirements but refrain from satisfying personal pleasures and sensous desires.
ii. Spend on meeting the accepted obligations without being prodigal.
iii. Follow a standard of living which befits one's own class. (p. 76)

3. On public policy and government spending

Al-Rabī' devotes relatively more space to discussion on public policy and government spending. Delineating the duties of a ruler to look after the well-being of the country, he divides the population of a region into two categories (p. 118) and assigns separate duties to both categories i.e. People engaged in agriculture, and townmen.

i. Policy towards agriculturists

It is the duty of the ruler to:

a. arrange for water supply for personal requirements and for irrigation.
b. remove the difficulties faced by the farmers in order to stop them from abandoning their farms and thus taking to other professions.
c. levy taxes in accordance with the norms of justice and the *Sharī'ah*, to avoid the possibility of any injustice and tyranny.

The author considers all the three requirements as categorical. (p. 118)

The infra-structure required for a village includes abundant supply of fresh water, fair climate, availability of provisions, proximity to grazing grounds and supply of firewood in addition to open suburbs and protection from enemies. (p. 118)

ii. Policy towards townsmen

There are five reasons for living in a town:

a. Peace and convenience.
b. Protection of wealth.
c. Protection of women's privacy.
d. Availability of necessary goods.

e. Freedom of pursuing a profession and of obtaining necessary articles of use.

In case either of the five objectives is missing, the town is not worth living in. (p. 118)

The infra-structure that is necessary for setting up a town includes:

a. abundant supply of fresh water.
b. wide and open roads for unhampered flow of traffic.
c. setting up of a sufficient number of markets so that there is easy access to all amenities; and
d. lodging such number of craftsmen and scholars as can cater to the needs of the population without forcing them to frequent other towns for satisfying these needs.

These factors are, in addition to fair climate, security of the town from the enemies, construction of a central mosque and planning of population taking into consideration homogeneous groups. (pp. 120–121)

4. Management of exchequer and budgeting

Discussion on public treasury follows almost the same pattern as his ideas on personal wealth. He highlights the necessity and significance of money to the ruler and its protection and growth. Wealth, according to him, is the strength and succour of a ruler. Its management calls for the fulfilment of four conditions.

i.   Realization of the fact that money is necessary for defence preparations, for strengthening the weak, for eradicating evils and for repaying debts. It also satisfies all human needs.
ii. The ruler should store money in the safest place under his personal supervision.
iii. The ruler should appoint a thoroughly trustworthy person as custodian of the treasury, who should be wealthy, pious and of a contented nature. Moreover, he should not be dishonest or self-indulgent.
iv. The ruler should persuade his people to exert for the prosperity of the country. He should fully realize that to fight a war he needs money. It is money with which military hardware is bought without which a war cannot be fought. Under the same heading, al-Rabī' persistently emphasises upon the ruler to urge his people to increase their incomes and to reprimand them for not doing so. This means that he is fully alive to the fact that state of a country's treasury is dependent upon the prosperity and affluence of the people. The second point that transpires from this emphasis is that in the author's time the government did not possess sizable financial resources. (p. 133)

While al-Rabī' advocates that coffers should be full, he also recommends measures to improve the financial position of the country. It is here that he discusses the strategy of budgeting, which describes the relationship between revenues and expenditure. In respect of revenues he stresses two points:

i.   The conduct of the ruler should not violate *Sharī'ah*.[4]
ii. He should not discard the sources of income made available by just and lucky officials. (p. 119)

Expenditure also requires two considerations:

a.   Spending on lawful heads whenever really necessary.
b.   Spending generously but remaining within the means. (p. 119)

While comparing revenue and expenditure, al-Rabī' discusses three different situations of a budget and the impact of each. He favours a surplus budget on its own merits. His arguments in respect of the three situations are:

i.   A country whose income is more than expenditure is stable and its policies are sound. Its surplus income can be used during hard times. (p. 119)
ii. When expenditure is more than income, the country is unstable and its policies are unsound. This situation would lead the country to ruin. (p. 119)
iii. Expenditure equals income. Such a country is well-off during conditions of peace and normalcy but becomes weak during hard times. In case the country is hit by a calamity, its population becomes restless and its enemies make mischiefs. (p. 119)

5. On the policy towards general public

Among the policies that are exclusively related to the rulers is also the policy towards public which, inter-alia, includes:

i.   Keeping a watch on the availability of residential units and provisions and on their prices.
ii. Refraining from subjecting the people to false promises and fears.
iii. Adopting a method of benefiting the public which is generally accepted. Such a method is always the most effective.
iv. Eliminating the causes of dispute so that it becomes difficult for the people to lay hands on the property of others. (p. 107)[5]

Al-Rabī' classifies people into seven main categories, each of which is further divided into the sub-categories of good, bad and average. Good

people are law-abiding patriots. They need to be encouraged and respected
and should be entrusted with important assignments. Bad people are immune
to good counsel and are uncontrolable. If they are impervious to punishments
and there is no hope of their reformation, they should be exiled to distant
areas to protect people from their transgressions. Average people comprise
professionals and have both good and bad traits. A physician-like treatment
is required for reforming them. (pp. 112–113)

According to al-Rabī', all these categories of people can be controlled in
the following manner:

a. They should be involved in their professional jobs in such a way that no
    free time is left for them to indulge in evil practices.
b. They should be stopped from prying into the affairs of the ruler.
c. The ruler should levy taxes on the well-to-do according to their ability
    to pay and should treat everyone in the same manner.
d. He should be available at all times to listen to the people's grievances
    and provide full justice to the oppressed.
e. He should protect the citizens from enemies through improving the
    fortification of the city.

    He should protect the citizens from plunderers so that they are not
    deprived of provisions. (p. 114)

6. On 'adl (justice)

In addition to his ideas on wealth and money, home economics, public
policy and budgeting, and policy towards public, al-Rabī' like any other
Muslim thinker on economics, emphasises the role of 'adl (justice) in economics and politics. His discussion on justice is to be found on three different
places under separate headings. While enumerating the components of a state
(p. 105), he lays down 'adl (justice) as one of the components, besides the
ruler, population, and statecraft (tadbīr). 'Adl also forms a basis for the successful functioning of a government.[6] A relatively more detailed discussion
on 'adl appears later on (pp. 116–117), in which he delineates the universal
recognition, significance, aspects, and requirements of 'adl. 'Adl, according
to al-Rabī', has three aspects (p. 87):

i.   'Adl that is required in man's discharge of his obligations to Allah.
ii. 'Adl that is required to protect the rights of the predecessors.[7]
iii. Reciprocal 'adl that protects each others' rights in the society.

These rights include lending and borrowing, discharging the trust, paying
the debt, giving true evidence, and doing good deeds.

A man possessing the quality of 'adl should, according to al-Rabī', be
faithful and honest, merciful, should keep his promise, be truthful, balanced

in putting a thing in its proper place and bound to the norms of justice. This quality is as essential in a common man and in government functionaries as is it is in a ruler. (p. 117)

Passing references to the significance of *'adl* are frequently made in context of the behaviour of a ruler and of the functionaries of the government. For example, tabulating the pre-requisites of a ruler he enlists the abundance of wealth as the fifth pre-requisite and treats it as one of the essentials of a government. He claims that affluence can be achieved through practising *'adl* in respect of the wealth of the citizens and through keeping the country prosperous. It is *'adl* that makes the country inhabited and prosperous, and brings in stability. (p. 74) It will be found that the thrust of his emphasis on *'adl* is more social and moral than economic in nature.

7. On the qualifications of functionaries

Al-Rabī' not only describes the character that a ruler should possess along with the administrative qualities that he should develop, but also lays down the qualifications that are necessary in government functionaries. Among these functionaries are included the incharge of revenues (*Kātib al-Kharāj*), and the collector (*'Āmil*) who works under him in the field. Al-Rabī' lays down (p. 128) the following qualifications for the *Kātib al-Kharāj:*

i.   He should be adept in the art of making canals and water courses (for irrigation).
ii.   He must have thorough knowledge of technicalities of surveying and making estimates of crops.
iii.   He must know arithmetic and fractions.
iv.   He must be conversant with the art of construction of bridges.
v.   He must know what crop should be grown.
vi.   He must know the appropriate time of sowing a crop and the trend of prices.
vii.   He must have knowledge of difference crops of the year and the seasons.
viii.   He must be fully alive to the rights and duties of the *Bayt al-Māl*.

The collector (*'Āmil*) is supposed to meet the following requirements:

a.   He must have perfect knowledge about the affairs of the forest and farms.
b.   He must collect money from the public without harassing them in order to add to the resources of the exchequer.
c.   He should act justly and should not spend public money on unnecessary heads.
d.   He must be just, pious, and should be considerate to the people. (p. 133)[8]

Notes and references

1 The ideas expressed in this paper are the personal views of the author and do not necessarily represent the views of the organization he belongs to.

2 According to al-Zirkalī (al-A'lām, 1:195), his date of birth is H 218, but the fact that he is believed to have belonged to the period of Caliph Mu'taṣim and that he has himself paid tribute to the Caliph who died in the year H 228 (CE 1842), when Shihāb al-Dīn should have been only ten years old, leads us to doubt the year 218 of Hijrah (CE 833) as the date of his birth. It is unbelievable that a ten years old boy can write such a book on politics. The tribute that he paid to the Caliph reads as follows: "The people of this era are fortunate to have among them a monarch possessing the qualities of . . . in the person of Amīr al-Mu'minīn Mu'taṣim Billāh" (pp. 12–13). According to a recent study of the work, reference to Mu'taṣim has been treated as a mistake in decipherment of the probable word Musta'ṣim which dates him to seventh Hijrah century (Nājī al-Tikritī, ed. Beirut, 1978, p. 7 sqq.). If this theory is accepted, the significance of the book, excepting its unique style and arrangement, is much reduced. The arguments adduced in the book are, however, debatable and do not provide us with a conclusive evidence about his period nor do they provide us any details about Ibn Abī'l-Rabī'.

3 Al-Rabī' is not the first to distinguish good professions from bad. His predecessor, Muḥammad al-Shaybānī (d. H 1890) was perhaps the first to dilate upon the issue in greater detail (Kitāb al-Iktisāb, p. 35 sqq.). In any case, for Muslim thinkers, the factor that determines the nobility or otherwise of a profession is the worker's relationship with Allah and benefit of the profession to the public.

4 It should not be difficult to comprehend the relevance of practices in revenue collection which are against Sharī'ah. Obviously such practices imply levying of unjust taxes, unfairness in assessment, and oppression in collection.

5 The text is vague. Perhaps it points out legislation that stops from transactions involving jahl and gharar (ignorance and uncertainty) and from acts of the property-owners that harm others.

6 This is in addition to punishment that protects the government; pardon that reflects the glamour of authority; and piety that creates prestige and reverence.

7 By the rights of predecessors, al-Rabī' means proper burial of the dead, repayment of their debt, and looking after their orphans and the like.

8 Bibliography:

Ibn Abī'l-Rabī', Shihāb al-Dīn Aḥmad ibn Muḥammad, Sulūk al-Mālik fī Tadbīr al-Mamālik (n.p., Muhammad 'Alī al-Khurāsānī, H 1286).

Al-Shaybānī, Muḥammad ibn Ḥasan, al-Iktisāb fī' Rizq al-Mustaṭāb (Cairo, H 1357).

Al-Zirkalī, Khayr al-Dīn, al-A'lām, second edition (n.p., n.d.).

Nājī al-Tikrītī (ed), Sulūk al-Mālik fī Tadbīr al-Mamālik (Beirut, 1978).

20

ECONOMICS OF IBN KHALDUN REVISITED

Abdol Soofi

Source: *History of Political Economy*, 72:2 (1995), 387–404.

Introduction

A close look at the writings of the Middle Eastern and North African scholars who lived in the Middle Ages (roughly between A.D. 476–1500) reveals an immense body of theoretical knowledge pertaining to the humanities and behavioral and social sciences. A partial list of the scholars who wrote on these issues includes Abu Yusuf (eighth century), Abul-Fadl Al-Dimishgi (ninth century), Al-Farabi (tenth century), Al-Ghazali (eleventh century), Nasiruddin Tusi (thirteenth century), Ibn Taimiya (fourteenth century), and Ibn Khaldun (fourteenth century).

Of this tradition, the most prominent figure is Abdel Rahman Ibn Khaldun of Tunis (1332–1406), who was a diplomat, jurist, historian, politician, sociologist, and economist. Unlike the writings of his predecessors and contemporaries, his writings on economic topics transcend the tradition of making disjointed remarks on and isolated references to important questions of political economy. Ibn Khaldun's rationalistic approach to economic reasoning, his power of abstraction, and his pioneering work in developing economic models are unparalleled among the writers of medieval times. In fact, his theories bear striking resemblance to those later developed independently by Thomas Malthus and John Maynard Keynes, among others. Had Ibn Khaldun's fourteenth-century work been available to Western economists earlier, his influence on economic theory and policy surely would have been significant. However, it is in a retrospective light that Western economists now "rediscover" Ibn Khaldun.

Ibn Khaldun's work was introduced to the West when some of his writings were translated into French by Silvestre de Sacy in 1806 (Schmidt 1967). In the field of economics, primarily due to the efforts of Mohammad Aly Nashat

(1945), Charles Issawi (1950), Joseph Spengler (1964), Jean David Boulakia (1971), M. Yassine Essid (1987), and Timur Kuran (1987), Ibn Khaldun is relatively well known. Nashat's work is an abridged version of his dissertation in Arabic, which was presented to the faculty of Economie Politique at the University of Fouad el Awal in Egypt. Nashat makes an effort to appraise Ibn Khaldun's economics in light of the economic theory known to him in the 1940s. His analysis, however, contains certain errors, omissions, and mis-interpretations. Issawi's treatment of Ibn Khaldun's economic ideas is mainly for the purpose of introducing his thought to English readers in the form of selected passages translated from *al-Muqaddimah*.[1]

The articles by Spengler and Boulakia do not discuss the technical details that are integral to the development of economic theory in *al-Muqaddimah*. Essid and Kuran correctly see Ibn Khaldun's economics in the context of a broader sociopolitical-historical system; nevertheless, in dealing with the subject, they both confine their comments to some general statements pertaining to his contribution to the theory of politico-economic cycles, and by doing so, they neglect his many other contributions to economic theory.

This article aims to develop a searching, critical evaluation of the economic aspects of the Khaldunian system. I will attempt to place Ibn Khaldun's economics in the context of the intellectual history of economics by taking an inventory of his knowledge of economic theory. Simultaneously, I recognize that Ibn Khaldun's economic ideas were developed in the context of his discovery that there is a historical pattern to the development of societies, an insight he realized after, or just prior to, completing his writing of *The Book of Examples and Register of Subject and Predicate Dealing with the History of the Arabs, Persians, and Berbers.*[2]

A general methodological note is in order at this point. I agree with Essid (1987) and Kuran (1987) that Ibn Khaldun's was a unified theory in matters of state and sovereignty. At the same time, I deny the validity of Essid's argument that, taking the absolutist approach[3] in studying separate aspects of Ibn Khaldun's writing, in isolation from his system as a whole, will frag-ment its unity. Essid writes, "Later commentators, dazzled by the importance of Ibn Khaldun's works, plunged into analyzing isolated aspects of his writings from the points of view of specific fields of knowledge and, in the process, fragmented its unity" (1987, 90). Essid does not show why focusing on one aspect of the system, while recognizing the totality of it, will distort or undermine it. By taking an absolutist approach in studying Khaldunian economics, I intend to verify whether his contribution to economics stands on its own feet.

Of course the absolutist approach has its critics. Some historians of economic thought may dismiss the absolutist approach of judging past theories by modern theoretical standards as too harsh. The absolutists may respond by asserting that following the relativist approach in doctrinal history and not recognizing the theoretical contributions of early writers will

337

result in what Paul Samuelson called "the sophisticated-anthropomorphic sin" (Blaug 1962, 1).

In this context and to avoid such a sin, I shall first discuss Ibn Khaldun's thought on various economic topics and then relate his work to that of Greek philosophers and of more recent Western writers who have rediscovered his ideas. Furthermore, I shall use modern theory to identify the principal weaknesses in his theories. It shall become clear that this approach establishes him as a first-rate economic theorist, even according to the high scientific standards of the twentieth century.

Ibn Khaldun's epistemology

Before discussing some of Ibn Khaldun's economic ideas, a note on his methodology is in order. He was a rationalist with little patience for the rambling, observational style of some of his contemporaries and predecessors: "Ibn Al Mokafa came across some of the questions treated by us but his work is lacking in proofs . . . [and] Judge Al Tartouchi classified his book in a manner similar to us; however, he collects well-known sayings in support of his assertions and does not investigate the truth by means of rational arguments" (Nashat 1945, 381).

Unlike many other Moslem scholars, Ibn Khaldun was not interested in explanations that certain socioeconomic realities were the fulfillment of the will of Allah. In contrast, he writes, "We find the universe governed by an accurate system through which prevails the law of cause and effect" (Nashat 1945, 382). He devoted himself to discovering the natural laws that he believed governed the development of societies. He writes, "We must study human society and distinguish its essential features from its accidental ones and trace the social laws that are at work within it and use them as criteria as to the value of historical assertions" (380–81). The scientific approach permeates his writing, particularly his economic theories. It is through the power of abstraction that Ibn Khaldun was able to develop insight into many socioeconomic and political phenomena.

Value theories

Value theory forms the foundation of classical and Marxian political economy. A discussion of theories of value is present in *al-Muqaddimah*, but it does not occupy such a prominent role in Ibn Khaldun's writings as it does in the classical and Marxian systems. His treatment of the determinants of value of commodities in many respects resembles, but is not as well developed as, the theories of value independently worked out by Smith, Ricardo, and Marx centuries later. Additionally, his remarks associating utility and prices— derived from his observations about real estate—are a prelude to a utility theory of value.

338

Labor theory of value

Although Moslem writers had alluded to labor as an important source of value as early as the seventh century,[4] Ibn Khaldun in his *al-Muqaddimah* developed the rudiments of a significant labor theory of value. The parallels between Adam Smith's labor theory of value and Ibn Khaldun's labor theory of value are striking, especially since the two evolved completely independently. Smith started his labor theory of value by positing that "labour was the first price, the original purchase-money that was paid for all things. It was not by gold or by silver, but by labor, that all the wealth of the world was originally purchased" (1937, 30). Ibn Khaldun developed his value theory from the assumption that "there is nothing here [originally] except the labor, and [the labor] is not desired by itself as acquired [... but the value realized from it].... Carpentry and weaving, for instance, are associated with wood and yarn [the respective craft needed for their production]. However, in the two crafts [first mentioned] the labor [that goes into them] is more important, and its value is greater.... It has thus become clear that gains and profits, in their entirety or for the most part, are value realized from human labor" (Ibn Khaldun 1958, 2:313–14).[5] Earlier, he had defined "profit" as the part of income "that is obtained by a person through his own effort and strength" (1958, 2:312). Here, however, he divides the total product—the gains—into used and unused parts. He writes "sustenance ... is [the part of the profit] that is utilized" (2:314)—a concept that Karl Marx would later call "necessary labor."

For modern readers Ibn Khaldun's use of the term profit is problematic. However, it should be clear from this passage that what Ibn Khaldun calls profit or gain is in fact total production. In discussing the constituent parts of the gain, he explains that a man's "profits will constitute his livelihood, if they correspond to his necessities and needs. They will be capital accumulation, if they are greater than [his needs]" (2:311–12). Therefore, his fourteenth-century division of the total product of labor into "sustenance" and "capital accumulation" is similar to the Marxian notion of "necessary" and "surplus" labor. In considering labor a commodity, "in as much as incomes and profits represent the value of the labor of their recipients" (Issawi 1950, 85), Ibn Khaldun was one step ahead of Karl Marx again.

Ibn Khaldun's thought on another aspect of value theory, an "invariable" unit of measurement, resembles David Ricardo's approach. Ricardo, developing his own labor theory of value, selected gold as his static unit because it is a commodity produced by a method that averages two extremes of production: "the one where little fixed capital is used, the other where little labor is employed, as to form a just mean between them" (in Meek 1956, 110).

Ibn Khaldun also reasoned that gold and silver could be considered commodities of "invariable" measures of value, explaining that "God created the two mineral 'stones,' gold and silver, as the [measure of] value" (2:313).

Furthermore, gold and silver are what "the inhabitants of the world, by preference, consider treasure and property [to consist of]. Even if, under certain circumstances, other things are acquired, it is only for the purpose of ultimately obtaining [gold and silver]. All other things are subject to market fluctuations, from which [gold and silver] are exempt" (2:313).[6] By this analogy, I neither intend to imply that Ibn Khaldun's selection of precious metals as "invariable" measures of value was based on in-depth analyses comparable to those that characterized Ricardo's selection procedure, nor do I mean to suggest that Ibn Khaldun was consciously in search of an invariable unit of measurement in the modern sense. My comments are aimed at showing that both men happened to select precious metals for their purposes. From the foregoing discussion it is clear that Ibn Khaldun had a rudimentary labor theory of value, a prelude to the consistent, well-formulated, and sophisticated versions of the theory by Ricardo and Marx.

Subjective value theory

Ibn Khaldun also had touched upon utility as a source of the value and determinant of the price of a product. Of course, such discussions were nothing new, since many centuries before, Xenophon as well as Aristotle had associated the utility of an object to its price (Lowry 1987a).[7]

Therefore, since the intellectual contributions of classical Greek philosophers were known to the Moslem scholars, it is not surprising that Ibn Khaldun incorporated their ideas in his discussions about real estate:

> For towards the end of a dynasty, and the setting up of a new state, real estate loses its attractiveness, owing to the poor protection afforded by the state and the general conditions of chaos and ruin: its utility is diminished and its price falls, hence it is acquired for a small sum. . . . Now when the new state has firmly established itself and order and prosperity have returned and the country has rejuvenated itself, real estate becomes once more attractive, owing to its great utility, and its price once more rises.
>
> (Issawi 1950, 76)

Clearly, Ibn Khaldun's remarks regarding utility theory of value, like his insights with respect to labor theory of value, were rudimentary. Moreover, this passage is an isolated remark. Ibn Khaldun did not pursue this line of reasoning elsewhere in his work, and there are no indications that he was cognizant of the doctrinal significance of his statements. Based on Ibn Khaldun's more substantive treatment of objective value theory and his isolated, casual remarks on the relationship between the utility of real estate and its prices, I conclude nonetheless that Ibn Khaldun held a labor theory of value.

The theory of income distribution and growth

In a section dealing with the economic consequences of oppression, Ibn Khaldun presents elements of an income distribution theory that are somewhat similar to, but of course not as concise or well developed as, those in the marginal productivity theory of income distribution. In a passage quoted above, he considers labor as a commodity and states that "incomes and profits represent the value of the labor of their recipients" (Issawi 1950, 85). Elsewhere, he argues that "the income which a man derives from the crafts is, therefore, the value of his labor" (71).

This last statement is yet a long way from the notion that the real wage rate is equal to the marginal physical product of labor in equilibrium. Nevertheless, one can discern the rudiments of such a theory by reviewing Ibn Khaldun's association of the value of labor and the income of the laborer. He distinguishes between wage incomes and profit incomes, as evidenced by his statement on labor as the source of income and profit, quoted above. Although he recognized the contribution of circulating capital to the productive process, he failed to distinguish between the sources of wage and profit incomes. "In certain crafts, the cost of raw materials must be taken into account, for example, the wood and the yarn in carpentry and in weaving. . . . In other occupations than crafts, too, the value of labour must be added to [the cost of] the produce" (Issawi 1950, 71). He also states that "the cost of labour affects the price of grain" (72). Discussing Moslem agricultural production in the regions with relatively unproductive soil, he again insists that the price of a product ought to include all costs incurred in the production of the product. The Moslems "were forced to apply themselves to improving the conditions of those fields and plantations. This they did by applying valuable work and manure and other costly materials. All this raised the cost of agricultural production, which costs they took into account when fixing their price for selling" (Issawi 1950, 73).

In general, Ibn Khaldun did not discuss capital accumulation and its effects on economic growth at great length. A few scattered remarks dealt with expansion of commercial capital through fluctuation in prices of hoarded commodities and appreciation of real estate. Capital accumulation, Ibn Khaldun wrote, "is achieved only by a few and is achieved only rarely through market fluctuations, through the acquisition of a great deal of [real estate], and through the upgrading of [real estate] as such and its value in a certain city" (Ibn Khaldun 1958, 2:285). In an environment where fixed capital was rather scarce, neglecting the contribution of the fixed capital to the total product is indeed understandable. Clearly, in a predominately mercantilist economy, the development of a full-fledged capital theory would be nearly impossible. Nevertheless, if we define capital theory to be concerned with the implications of the means of production for theories of price, production, and distribution, then Ibn Khaldun did have a capital theory of sorts.

He did not explicitly introduce the effect of rent on the price of a product, although the above passage concerning the effect of marginal land on the price of agricultural output clearly implies that he was aware of the relationship. Therefore, I conclude that Ibn Khaldun had formulated a cost of production theory of prices in the late fourteenth century. Furthermore, he understood quite clearly that total production is divided into wage share and profit share, although his theory falls short of explicitly specifying that the factor shares are determined by the marginal productivity of the factors of production. Incidentally, it is instructive to see Ibn Khaldun's description of the relationship between the quality of land and the prices of the agricultural products. His theory may be compared with Ricardian rent theory, which explains rent as pure economic profits accruing to the most fertile farms. According to this theory, the market price of a given farm product is determined by the high marginal cost of production of the least fertile land; thus the most fertile lands with lower marginal costs of production acquire the difference between their cost and the higher market price as rent on the land.

Theories of economic development and forty-year cycles

Ibn Khaldun has a remarkable theory of sociopolitical-economic cycles, beginning with an explanation of how increased productivity results from specialization, division of labor, and exchange. He was familiar with and critical of the writings of Aristotle and Plato on specialization and division of labor.[8] "We find in the book of Aristotle on Politics, a fit part; however, it does not exhaust the subject and is lacking in proofs and there is some confusion in it" (1958, 1:81). He stated that higher productivity and exchange increase community welfare by enabling the members of the economy to satisfy their needs as well as allowing them to consume luxury commodities.

> The individual human being cannot by himself obtain all the necessities of life. All human beings must cooperate to that end in their civilization. But what is obtained through the cooperation of a group of human beings satisfies the need of a number many time greater [than themselves]. Furthermore, if the labor of the inhabitants of a town or city is distributed in accordance with the necessities and needs of those inhabitants, a minimum of that labor is needed. Consequently, it is spent to provide the conditions and customs of luxury and to satisfy the needs of the inhabitants of other cities. They import [the things they need] from [people who have a surplus] through exchange or purchase.
>
> (1958, 2:271–72)

By the way, it is interesting to note a fourteenth-century concept of "necessities" and "luxuries":

> It should be known that all markets cater to the needs of people. Some of these needs are necessities, foodstuffs, for instance, such as wheat and barley; corresponding foods, such as beans, chickpeas, peas, and other edible grains; and wholesome foods such as onions, garlic, and the like. Other things are conveniences or luxuries, such as seasonings, fruits, clothes, utensils, mounts, all the crafts, and buildings.
>
> (276)

By specialization and division of labor, some producers are able to generate surplus products, and through exporting to other communities and satisfying the luxury wants of the consumers, these producers are able to amass a great deal of wealth.

Ibn Khaldun's description of productive processes implies a production function with a single variable input: labor. He argues that the labor input of a city determines the total output of that community. "When there is more labor, the value realized from it increases among the [people]" (1958, 2:272). Higher output, given that output required for the sustenance of the people is fixed in size, implies higher output of luxury goods. Furthermore, higher income derived from higher labor input generates an effective aggregate demand that absorbs the entire surplus. The increased spending on luxury goods further increases production of existing luxury products, stimulates creation of new industries, and provides additional incentives for people to enter into the manufacture of luxury commodities.

His explicit statements on the relationship between private spending on the one hand and the output and income effects of these expenditures on the other hand preceded by centuries the Malthusian theory of gluts and the Keynesian theory of incomes and expenditures.

> If, therefore, much labor is used, its total value rises. Consequently, the income of such a community will necessarily rise, and prosperity will soon lead to luxury and refinement. . . . Now the demand for such things attracts men skilled in their production; this leads to prosperity in such crafts and services, higher incomes for those engaged in them, and a rise in the income and expenditure of the whole community.
>
> This increase in prosperity leads to a further increase in economic activity which leads to a rise in incomes and increasing luxury, the new wants so created will lead to the creation of new industries and services, with consequent increases in income and prosperity. And this process can go on two or three times, because all the new activities minister to luxury, unlike the original activities which ministered to necessities.
>
> (Issawi 1950, 92–93)

The above interactive, dynamic processes closely resemble the concept of an expenditure multiplier as it was first developed by Bertil Ohlin in 1927 and later by Richard F. Kahn (Uhr 1989). Unlike the refined expenditure multiplier concept of the twentieth century, however, Ibn Khaldun's expenditure multiplier process runs out of steam after a few rounds of effect (Issawi 1950).

He was correct in stating that incomes and expenditures are equal in an ex post sense. "Income and expenditure balance each other in every city. If income is large, the expenditure is large, and vice versa. And if both income and expenditure are large, the inhabitants become more favorably situated, and the city grows" (1958 2:275).

This quotation clearly shows that Ibn Khaldun saw aggregate demand as an important determinant of national income and economic growth, a concept that is central to the modern Keynesian theory of national income determination and growth theory.

Moreover, he understood that private expenditure was only one method of increasing national income, recognizing that state spending and taxation had a similarly stimulating effect on business conditions. The celebrated Laffer-curve analysis of the effect of taxation on government revenues closely resembles the insightful discussion of the same topic in *al-Muqaddimah*. Ibn Khaldun warned against curtailing government spending, as well as against the imposition of high taxation on the people, both of which would reduce aggregate demand in the economy and ultimately reduce government tax revenues. Second, he strongly cautioned against increasing taxation or other forms of government revenue collection:

> It should be known that attacks on people's property remove the incentive to acquire and gain property. People, then, become of the opinion that the purpose and ultimate destiny of [acquiring property] is to have it taken away from them. . . . Civilization and its well-being as well as business prosperity depend on productivity and people's efforts in all directions in their own interest and profit. When people no longer do business in order to make a living, and when they cease all gainful activity, the business of civilization slumps, and everything decays.
>
> (1958, 103–4)

He returns to the subject later. "As the tax rate goes beyond moderate rate, the tax payers compare their tax liabilities with their profits and become pessimistic, and as a result do not promote economic growth and development. A large number of people refrain from productive economic activities, thus causing a decline in the accrued tax revenue to the state" (1958, 537–38). He listed a number of actions that he considered unjust, including levying of "a duty not required by the religious law" (537–38). All injustices, including excessive taxation, have the devastating economic consequences enumerated above.

He believed that some government spending was essential to maintain high aggregate demand and create economic prosperity.

> For it is the goods demanded by the state which enjoy the highest sales. Other goods, not demanded by the state but only by private individuals, can not compare with them, for the state is the greatest market, spending on things without too nice a calculation.
>
> (Issawi 1950, 73)

> Cities have a highly developed civilization and their inhabitants are very prosperous, and the dynasty is at the root of it, because the dynasty collects the property of the subjects and spends it on its inner circle and on the men connected with it who are more influential by reason of their position than by reason of their property. The money comes from the subjects and is spent among the people of the dynasty and then among those inhabitants of the city who are connected with them. They are the largest part [of the population]. Their wealth, therefore, increases and their riches grow. The customs and ways of luxury multiply, and all the various kinds of crafts are firmly established among them.
>
> (Ibn Khaldun 1958, 2:287)

> Government serves as the world's greatest market place. . . . Now, if the ruler holds on to property and revenue, or they are lost or not properly used by him, then the property in the possession of the ruler's entourage will be small. The gifts which they, in their turn, had been used to give their entourage and people, stop, and all their expenditures are cut down. They constitute the greatest number of people [who make expenditures], and their expenditures provide more of the substance of trade than [the expenditures of] any other [group of people]. Thus [when they stop spending], business slumps and commercial profits decline because of the shortage of capital. Revenues from the land tax decrease, because the land tax and taxation [in general] depend on cultural activity, commercial transactions, business prosperity, and the people's demand for gain and profit.
>
> (2:102–3)

This line of reasoning is similar to the theory of underconsumption as the basis for the Malthusian theory of gluts and the Keynesian theory of insufficient aggregate demand. The Malthusian solution to the problem of recurring gluts resulting from an excessive rate of profits and the ensuing unsustainable rate of capital accumulation is familiar. "There must therefore be a considerable class of persons who have both the will and power to consume more material wealth than they produce, or the mercantile classes could not continue profitably to produce so much more than they consume. In this class the landlords no doubt stand pre-eminent" (Malthus 1960, 400). The Keynesian theory of inadequate aggregate demand in advanced industrial economies and Keynes's methods of remedying the problem are too well known to require documentation.

The significance of public works and the important role of the government in the economic development of a community were a well-established fact centuries before Ibn Khaldun wrote his *al-Muqaddimah*. Abu Bakr Muhammad al-Turtushi, a twelfth-century Hispano-Moslem writer quoting from a Coptic history of Egypt, describes how the pharaoh "invested 800,000 dinars in agriculture, opening a canal and building dykes and water-channels, making free allowances of fodder to the poorer farmers so that they might be able to keep some working animals, bringing more land into cultivation, providing tools, and paying extra labor to help with the sowing and general farm-work" (Grice-Hutchinson 1978, 68).

Ibn Khaldun asserts that the expansion phase of the cycle lasts about forty years, comparable to an individual's physical power and biological growth. "When a man has reached the age of forty, nature stops growing for a while, then starts to decline. It should be known that the same is the case with sedentary culture in civilization, because there is a limit that cannot be over-stepped" (Ibn Khaldun 1958, 2:291–92).

What is the most immediate cause of the cyclical downturn? Ibn Khaldun attributes the decline in the "civilization of a dynasty" to demand-pull and cost-push inflation. He theorized that the sedentary lifestyle of the city dwellers leads to their preferences for luxury items. This, combined with the higher incomes of the consumers in the city, increases demand for luxury products. On the supply side, craftsmen and laborers realize that their skills and labor are in high demand, and without the urgent need to work because of the abundance of necessities in town, they request high wages. At the same time, employers with high income and "money to waste" are willing to employ craftsmen at a wage rate that is greater than "the ordinary worth of labor." He writes:

> Then, when a city has a highly developed, abundant civilization and is full of luxuries, there is a very large demand for those conveniences and for having as many of them as a person can expect in view of his situation. This results in a very great shortage of such things. . . . Prosperous people used to luxuries will pay exorbitant prices for them, because they need them more than others. Thus, one can see, prices come to be high.
>
> Crafts and labor also are expensive in cities with an abundant civilization. There are three reasons for this. First, there is much

need [of them]. . . . Second, industrial workers place a high value on their services and employment. . . . Third, the number of people with money to waste is great, and these people have many needs for which they have to employ the services of others and have to use many workers and their skills. Therefore, they pay more for [the services of] workers than their labor is [ordinarily considered] worth, because there is competition for [their services] and the wish to have exclusive use of them. Thus, workers, craftsmen, and professional people become arrogant, their labor becomes expensive, and the expenditures of the inhabitants of the city for these things increase.

(1958, 2:277)

The result is an upward pressure on the price level: "a city with a large civilization (population) is characterized by high prices in business and high prices for its needs" (2:292). Feeling the inflationary pressure, the government levies customs duties to meet the rising expenditures. The customs duties raise the sales prices because the merchants pass on the tax burden to the consumers: "small businessmen and merchants include all their expenses, even their personal requirements, in the price of their stock and merchandise. Thus, customs duties enter into the sales prices" (2:293).

Finally, high prices and high taxes lead to the financial bankruptcy of an increasing number of people and to general business and moral decline. "One person after another becomes reduced in circumstances and indigent. Poverty takes hold of them. Few persons bid for the available goods. Business decreases, and the situation of the town deteriorates" (2:293). Sedentary life styles and preference for luxury goods also have deleterious effects on the morality of the people:

Corruption of the individual inhabitants is the result of painful and trying efforts to satisfy the needs caused by their (luxury) customs. . . . Immorality, wrongdoing, insincerity, and trickery, for the purposes of making a living in a proper or an improper manner, increase among them. The soul comes to think about (making a living), to study it, and to use all possible trickery for the purpose. People are now devoted to lying, gambling, cheating, fraud, theft, perjury, and usury.

(2:293)

Thus, internal decay and economic slump set the stage for withering away of the state (dynasty) and urban society. At such an opportune time, nomads with the moral characteristics of frugality, courage, and independence will conquer the city and establish a new, vigorous order and dynasty, according to Ibn Khaldun's predictions.

Such is the Khaldunian theory of politico-economic cycles. Even with the high standards of modern economics, this is a cohesive and logically consistent

347

theory of cycles that contains many elements of economic analysis that were later developed by Malthus and Keynes.

Monetary theory

Ibn Khaldun, like many of his predecessors, had a clear understanding of the functions of money. He explicitly discussed money in terms of its functions as the measure and store of value, as described above. Otherwise, his contribution in this area is rather limited.[9]

However, he did have a keen insight into the role money plays in the circulation of commodities:

> The quantity [of money] existing in the hands of men circulates and is transmitted from generation to generation. And it probably circulates from country to country and from state to state. . . . Thus if such wealth has decreased in North Africa, it has not diminished in the land of the Franks or Slavs. . . . For it is social effort, the search for profit and the use of tools that cause the increase or decrease of the quantity of precious metals in circulation.
>
> (Issawi 1950, 77)

Contrary to modern monetary theory, Ibn Khaldun argued that the presence of money does not stimulate economic activity. The profit motive, social organization and efforts, and the use of capital are the factors that determine the volume of trade and, therefore, the quantity of money in circulation. In support of his theory he cites examples of prosperous economies that had no gold mines—gold mines being the source of the money supply—and then refers to the Sudan as a country with an ample supply of gold but without prosperity. However, in discussing the inflation problem he gives a transaction-demand argument that tends to resemble the quantity theory of money.

> Conveniences, foodstuffs, and labor become very expensive. As a result, the expenditures of the inhabitants increase tremendously in proportion to the civilization of [the city]. A great deal of money is spent. Under these circumstances, [people] need a great deal of money for expenditures, to procure the necessities of life for themselves and their families, as well as all their other requirements.
>
> (Ibn Khaldun 1958, 2:280)

Ibn Khaldun clearly understood the transactions demand for money. Furthermore, his statement implies that the demand for real balances changes only with expansion of the level of economic activity and that increased demand for nominal balances is due to inflationary pressure. Of course, Ibn Khaldun did not consider inflation to be a purely monetary phenomenon;

for him, initially demand-pull and then cost-push were causes of inflation. Thus, we must conclude that his monetary theory, in general, contradicts the quantity theory of money. However, Ibn Khaldun made one statement that alluded to the equation of exchange: "the money spent in each market corresponds to [the volume of business done in it]" (Ibn Khaldun 1958, 2:273). However, as mentioned above, he did not claim that there is a one-to-one correspondence or even a casual relationship between the quantity of money and the general price level.

So far as Ibn Khaldun's monetary theory is concerned, I conclude that he understood the functions of money, the role money plays in circulation of commodities, and the transactions demand for money. Nevertheless, he fell short of indicating how money can affect general economic activities.

Summary and conclusion

The above analysis has dealt with a wide spectrum of Ibn Khaldun's economic thought, including theories of value, distribution, growth and development, money, prices, public finance, business cycles, inflation, rent, and benefits of trade. There are numerous other subjects, particularly in microeconomics, that for brevity's sake are excluded here but which will be dealt with on a separate occasion.

Several observations are in order. First, accepting Schumpeter's statement that "most statements of fundamental facts acquire importance only by the superstructures they are made to bear and are commonplace in the absence of such superstructures" (1954, 54), I observe that Ibn Khaldun's discovery of fundamental economic, sociological, and historical facts constitutes a superstructure that is logically sound and cohesive. Thus, instead of sporadic facts, the superstructure gives rise to what has been called the Khaldunian System (Essid 1987). Second, Ibn Khaldun's contributions to economic theory have been referred to as the "economic thought of Islam" (Spengler 1964; Essid 1987). As observed in this article, this substantial body of economic knowledge was discovered again later and expanded by theorists such as Smith, Malthus, Ricardo, Marx, and Keynes. Ibn Khaldun's economic thought is related to Islamic doctrines as much as the Western writers' ideas are related to the Judeo-Christian tradition. Since Marxian or Keynesian economics are not considered to be economics of Judaism or Christian economics, respectively, then one should probably not label Ibn Khaldun's economics as "Islamic economics." Khaldunian economics is a system of logical, cohesive thought that was based on his economic observations in fourteenth-century North Africa. In spite of his strong religious convictions and his repeated references to God, the prophet Mohammad, and Koranic verses, his economic analyses were not based on any religious doctrines. In fact, as discussed in section 2 above, Ibn Khaldun was in search of the natural laws that govern the development of societies. He was a keen observer of the social, economic, political, and historical phenomena of his contemporary culture and that of preceding times. With the power of abstraction he was able to identify and articulate relationships between the essential economic variables. He was a superb model-builder for his time.

Finally, it is regrettable Ibn Khaldun's work was not known to Western economists in the late fourteenth century. Translation of *al-Muqaddimah* into European languages would have expedited the progress of economics, potentially obviating a great deal of work on the part of Western writers.

Notes

I am grateful to Professors Brian Peckham and Carl G. Uhr and to anonymous referees for helpful comments on an earlier draft of this paper. This research was partially supported by a grant from the University of Wisconsin-Platteville.

1 *Al-Muqaddimah*, meaning "the prolegomena," was intended to be an introduction to a book with the title *General History of Ibn Khaldun*. It nevertheless became a major treatise on social sciences in its own right and was published separately in 1379. In this study, I use two translations of *al-Muqaddimah*: one in English by Franz Rosenthal (Ibn Khaldun 1958) and the other in Persian (Farsi) by Mohammad Parvin Gonabadi (Ibn Khaldun 1957).
2 This work is also known as the *General History of Ibn Khaldun* (see note 1).
3 There are two approaches in studies of doctrinal history: the absolutist and the relativist. The absolutist approach concentrates on the strictly intellectual development of a discipline irrespective of socioeconomic conditions that may have given rise to the development of the theories. The relativist approach, in contrast, perceives theories as reflections of the socioeconomic conditions of the theorists' time; hence, it puts more emphasis on historical development that may have given rise to the theory than its logical consistency and analytical integrity.
4 A. B. Shirazi attributes the following statement to Imam Baghar, a seventh-century Shiite saint: "Money is nothing but a medium of exchange, and it is the labor power of the Moslems that has put Roman's gold and silver at our disposition" (1985, 58).
5 In all the quotations from Ibn Khaldun 1958, the contents of the brackets were added by the translator, Franz Rosenthal.
6 This view of acquisition of precious metals (money) as the ultimate aim of all economic activities is identical to the thesis that liberal economists, including Adam Smith, wrongly attributed to the mercantilists. For an interesting discussion of this controversy, see Suviranta 1923, chap. 5.
7 I am indebted to an anonymous referee for bringing this point to my attention.
8 For the Greek philosophers' writing on specialization and division of labor, see Lowry 1987b, p. 8.
9 As Lowry (1987b, 20–21) indicates, Aristotle had a clear understanding of the functions of money.

References

Blaug, Mark. 1962. *Economic Theory In Retrospect*. 3d ed. Cambridge: Cambridge University Press.

Boulakia, Jean David C. 1971. Ibn Khaldun: A Fourteenth-Century Economist. *Journal of Political Economy* 79:1105–18.

Essid, M. Y. 1987. Islamic Economic Thought. In *Pre-Classical Economic Thought*, edited by S. Todd Lowry. Boston: Kluwer Academic Publishers.

Grice-Hutchinson, Marjorie. 1978. *Early Economic Thought in Spain: 1177–1740*. London: Allen & Unwin.

Ibn Khaldun, Abdel Rahman. 1957. *Muqaddimah-eh Ibn Khaldun I*. Vol. 1. In Farsi, translated by Mohammad-eh Parvin-Gonabadi. Tehran: Sherkat-eh Entesharat-eh Elmi Va Farhangi.

———. 1958. *The Muqaddimah: An Introduction to History*. 3 vols. Translated by Franz Rosenthal. London: Routledge & Kegan Paul.

Issawi, Charles. 1950. *An Arab Philosophy of History*. London: John Murray.

Kuran, T. 1987. Continuity and Change in Islamic Economic Thought. In *Pre-Classical Economic Thought*, edited by S. Todd Lowry. Boston: Kluwer Academic Publishers.

Lowry, S. Todd. 1987a. *The Archaeology of Economic Ideas: The Classical Greek Tradition*. Durham: Duke University Press.

———. 1987b. The Greek Heritage in Economic Thought. In *Pre-Classical Economic Thought*. Boston: Kluwer Academic Publishers.

Malthus, Thomas R. 1968. *Principles of Political Economy*. New York: A. M. Kelley.

Meek, R. L. 1956. *Studies in Labor Theory of Value*. 2d ed. New York: Monthly Review Press.

Nashat, M. A. 1945. *Ibn Khaldun Pioneer Economist*. Cairo: Imprimerie Nationale Boulac.

Schmidt, N. 1967. *Ibn Khaldun: Historian, Sociologist, and Philosopher*. New York: AMS Press.

Schumpeter, A. J. 1954. *History of Economic Analysis*. Edited by Elizabeth B. Schumpeter. New York: Oxford University Press.

Shirazi, A. B. 1985. *Masael-eh Eghtesadi* (Economic Problems). Tehran: Moaseseyeh Anjuman-eh Ketab.

Smith, Adam. 1937. *The Wealth of Nations*. New York: Random House.

Spengler, J. J. 1964. Economic Thought of Islam: Ibn Khaldun. *Studies in Society and History* 6:268–306.

Suviranta, B. 1923. *The Theory of the Balance of Trade in England. A Study in Mercantilism*. Helsingfors, Finland.

Uhr, G. Carl. 1989. A Retrospective View of the Stockholm School of Political Economy and That of J. M. Keynes. Paper presented at the 31st Annual Conference of the Western Social Science Association, 28 April.

21

A MEDIEVAL APPROACH TO SOCIAL SCIENCES: THE PHILOSOPHY OF IBN KHALDUN

Some historical notes and actual reflections

Giovanni Patriarca

Source: *Journal of Markets & Morality*, 13:1 (2010), 175–88.

In the history of Islamic philosophy Ibn Khaldun deserves a place of honor. His analytical method is a perennial contribution to the analysis of social dynamics. His critique of the omnipotence of the state, his denunciation of high fiscal spending, and his exaltation of political freedom show him to be a precursor of modern political science and of classical liberalism. His imperishable fame survives today, particularly for the *Muqaddima*, prologue to an ambitious work on the universal history never brought to an end: the *'Ibar*. In this work, Ibn Khaldun affirms repeatedly that it is not the amount of money reserve or precious metals that is the measure of a country's prosperity but the division of labor between the inhabitants. This, in fact, generates a "virtuous circle" that augments productivity in a right distribution of roles and risks.

Due to global changes and new geopolitical assets, a renewed interest in the Islamic culture and the richness of its philosophy has appeared in Western universities and institutions. A particular outlook is rightly oriented toward the first centuries of Islam in which—apart from the conquests and territorial expansions—a new culture tried to find a proper way between the Judeo-Christian and Greco-Roman traditions. Especially during the Middle Ages many thinkers contributed significantly to the development of the human civilization by translating many Greek philosophers' works and commenting on them in precious books. On this basis, we can properly affirm that a variety of matters were studied with originality and skillfulness: from mathematics to geography and physics to law. Not so far from the collapse of the Muslim domination of Spain, Ibn Kaldun was emblematic in understanding the importance and the contradictions of a declining empire.

Ibn Khaldun's life is so rich with events and vicissitudes that it assumed epical tones. A legendary aura of impassibility and courage against all difficulty accompanies the figure of this distinguished scholar of society and magisterial interpreter of history. Capable of a synthetic and farsighted comprehension of the events in a period that very often saw the ascent and decline of sovereigns and kingdoms, he was not afraid of changing allegiances and duties in an incessant saga of intrigues and betrayals. Some have seen in him an indomitable hero, others a free thinker with the typical characteristics that would have been depicted later in the Renaissance's Machiavellism. The survival law in a region of hard social disputes and bloody rebellions shows historically that his chamelionlike decisions matured thanks to an unusual sagacity and an acumen worthy of admiration.

Recent research has shown some interesting aspects that were not completely expressed in previous years. His critiques of the omnipotence of the state, his denunciation of the high fiscal charging, and his exaltation of freedom show him to be, contrary to some rhetoric, a precursor of modern political science and classical liberalism. Discovered by Western historiography in the late nineteenth century, this approach is strictly connected by a veil of misunderstood geniality that has characterized, at least until present times, all the researches and monographs of his works and their intrinsic value. Ibn Khaldun's method, deeply analytical and rigorous, has been mistakenly shown by some Western lectors to be a forerunner of the positivist theories of history to be considered, exaggerating in the contents and arguments, an idol *ante litteram* of historical materialism.[1]

The forced westernization, moreover, in the structural and philological studies is fruit of an unclear scientific hermeneutics with an evident attempt at manipulation that has depicted him as a scholar out of the canonical schemes of the Islamic culture. Accepting this would be as inauthentic for Khaldun himself as it would be for the history of Arab-Islamic culture and philosophy. We cannot agree with a posterior interpretation that wants, with the force of secularization and ideology, to reduce all philosophy to a pure human science devoid of any spiritual heritage and religious tradition.[2] This academic celebration, sometimes laborious and politically factious, has been transferred—especially during the period of decolonization in Northern Africa—to the Arab cultural circles that have viewed him, rightly, as a scrupulous and methodical interpreter of the ancient origins of contemporary adversities and vicissitudes. H. Corbin, one of the most important Orientalists, did not hesitate to criticize the westernizing excesses in the interpretation of Ibn Khaldun.[3] We agree with him in clarifying, *in primis*, that Ibn Khaldun is not an isolated case who suddenly appeared in history: He is a son of his time, of his land, and of the Islamic culture.

He was born, in fact, in Tunis in 1332 into an influential Arab-Andalusian family coming from Seville—at that time in the hands of the *Christian Reconquista*—with ancient origins in the Hadramawt. The years of adolescence were characterized by a solid general education according to the traditional Islamic teachings. The Maranid Invasion (1347/1349) had opened the doors of the town to eminent scholars and literates. Unfortunately, a grave pestilence, commonly known in the annals of universal history as the Black Death,[4] decimated the population, and Tunis was reduced to a ghost town.[5] He lost his parents and the majority of his teachers and friends.[6] He left us a meticulous description of this apocalyptic disaster:

> Civilization in both the East and the West was visited by a destructive plague which devastated nations and caused populations to vanish. It swallowed up many of the good things of civilization and wiped them out. It lessened the power of the dynasties and curtailed their influence. It weakened their authority. Their situation approached the point of annihilation and dissolution. Civilization decreased with the decrease of mankind. Cities and buildings were laid waste, roads and way signs were obliterated, settlements and mansions became empty, nations and tribes grew weak. The entire inhabited world changed.[7]

The splendor of the past was finished, leaving an "intellectual emptiness"[8] that pushed Ibn Khaldun to find refuge from his malaise and his loneliness in the town of Fez, the nerve center of North African cultural life and important commercial crossing where everyone was engaged to "build mansions and palaces of stone and marble decorated with ceramic plaques and arabesques. They passionately sought out silken robes, fine horses, good food and jewels of gold and silver. Well-being, comfort and luxury were everywhere."[9] There, he accepted a position in the administration of the Sultan Abu Ishak (1350), profiting by the presence of eminent scholars in the town and taking advantage of their teachings. The experience in this office did not last long because the invasion of *Afrikiya* by the Amir Abu Yazid (1352) caused disorders throughout the region. From that moment, his life was characterized by a series of adventurous and sudden changes in perspective. He lived in several places in Northern Africa, giving his services to a cohort of several sovereigns and despots with different tasks among which was the position of courtier's poet to the Sultan Abu Salim. The Sultan's environment was not very suitable because of hostility and antagonism. Fortunately, he obtained permission to reach Granada where he was received with honor and appreciation. During that period, he had the occasion to visit Seville—the town in which the memory of his family and his ancestors was still alive—where he was received by Peter the Cruel who prayed him insistently to remain, having perfectly understood his innate qualities as a statesman and promising him in exchange the restitution of all the properties and goods of his family.

He, instead, made the journey back toward the African coasts and reached the town of Bougie where he offered his services at the cohort of 'Abu Abd Allah Muhammad, old companion of conspiracy during his stay in Fez (1365). This experience was also very brief because of the invasion of the Emir of Constantine in the spring of 1366. After some peregrinations, he found refuge in Biskra at the cohort of the Banu Muzni. In this period, notwithstanding the serious intentions to dedicate himself to letters and reflections, he did not hold back, on account of a visceral desire to take part actively in the events of history, from the conjures and complots among the sovereigns of the region (Marinids, Hafsids, and other local despots). In that geographical context it was as easy to have the honor of the thrones as to fall in the dust and blood. His insistent participation in the political activities caused legitimate suspicions of secret machinations and betrayals.

He retired in the residence of Banu Salama in a locality—not so far from the city of Frenda—suitable to the concentration and studies where he found the right inspiration to write his most important work: the *Muqaddima*. At the end of his stay at the castle of Banu Salama, he felt the desire to come back to Tunis where he obtained permission by the Hafsid cohort to dedicate himself to the redaction of his *'Ibar*, whose first copy would be given to the Sultan Abu 'l-'Abbas. Such a success and glory were cause for jealousy and envy. With the pretext of a pilgrimage to Mecca, he took the occasion to abandon his hometown, avid with wickedness and perfidy against him, to which he would return no more.

He arrived in Cairo, the capital of Mameluke, and at first sight he had a marvelous impression of magnificence. Very famous is his description of the town as "the mother of the world, great center of Islam, mainspring of the sciences and the crafts."[10] In another passage, rich with emotive emphasis and sincere admiration, he writes:

> I saw there moons and stars shining among its scholars (*ulama*): on seeing the Nile, I thought I was seeing the river of paradise; one would say that its waters came from heaven, and spread everywhere good health, as well as fruits, flowers and riches. I saw the city filled with passers-by, and its bazaars of merchandise. We did not stop talking about this city for a long time and admiring its great and beautiful buildings."[11]

The contact with the metropolis and its fervent cultural activity was a stimulus for his character keen with curiosity and knowledge. His notorious fame brought him to teach in the University of Al-Azhar, the most prestigious school of the town, where his courses in *malikit fikh* were attended by so great a number of students that he achieved the title of *kadi* (1384). Al-Hafiz Ibn Hajar, present at the lectures, described his teacher with these words: "He was very eloquent, an excellent essayist and exhibited a deep knowledge of the subjects, particularly those relating to the state."[12]

A great tragedy awaited him. His family, which finally had obtained the permission to reach him by the intercession of the Sultan Al-Zahir Barkuk, would never reach the port of Alexandria because of a disastrous shipwreck near the Bengasi's coast. In addition to this personal suffering, there was a strong chauvinism of the local cultural elites who saw an excess of power in the hands of a "stranger." For this reason, he was obliged to resign his position (1385), dedicating himself primarily to the teaching in different schools of the town. This engagement absorbed him entirely for fourteen years. In 1399, he was recalled again to the task of *kadi* that he would leave a few months later when he was obliged to follow Al-Nasir in the expedition toward Damascus where Tamerlan had already imposed his power. He was received by the cohort of the dreadful leader by whom he was cordially entertained. It is said, in fact, that Tamerlan was so deeply impressed by the wisdom and culture of Ibn Khaldun that he invited him to remain at his service. Knowing the surly disposition and vindictive character of the Mongol chief, he did not hesitate to accept, provided that he would return to Cairo to retrieve his books without which he would not have been able to live and continue in his studies. By this stratagem, testimony of elevated skills of shrewdness and astuteness, he could come back to Cairo where he died in 1406.

As we have seen, his life was a series of tragic fatalities and sudden changes, due also to his longing for power and his personal ambition. Thanks to his pen, we have much information on Northern Africa in those troubled times. His imperishable fame survives today, particularly for the *Muqaddima*, prologue to an ambitious work on the universal history never brought to an end: the *'Ibar*. This work shows some historical gaps, especially regarding the dynasty of the Almohads[13] and does not realize the assumptions and premises of the prologue. Among the other works, the *Ta'rif*—a biography rich with detailed particulars—and the *Shifa' al-sa'il*, a treaty of mystics—written presumably at the end of his life—whose authenticity is still a motif of discussion, deserve to be mentioned.

The first draft of the *Muqaddima* belongs to the period of voluntary exile at the residence of Ibn Salama (1375/1379). In it appears all the richness of his thought in which the traditional disciplines of the Islamic pedagogy are joined to an impassive capacity of analysis,[14] the fruit of his whirling political adventures and of a clear psychological investigation not only of the powerful individuals but, primarily, of social groups. The author's intention is, without any doubt, laudable and innovative: It deals with "an encyclopaedic synthesis of any necessary cultural and methodological knowledge that permits the historian to produce a truthful scientific work."[15] Considering the method of his predecessors too slavish to transcribe the exploits of the leaders and devoid of a sane thirst for critical analysis, he applies a new definition of history: To understand the past it is necessary to explain the social, cultural, economic, moral, and religious aspects. In fact, history finds its value in properly investigating the conditions of the nations and in understanding the effects of tyranny and of arbitrary policies on the collective mentality as well as in analyzing the qualities of the prince, the defense of the state, the devotion of the army, and the inclination of the sovereign toward commerce and exchange for the well-being of the nation. To these important points is connected the inquiry on the greediness and avarice of the prince regarding his people, which in the long run could become sedition; thus bringing the nation toward a form of degeneration and anarchy.

In an ode dedicated to the Sultan Abul Abbas, upon the occasion of the consignment of the first copy of the *Muqaddima*, he explains poetically his *modus investigandi*:

> *Here in the histories of time and peoples*
> *Are lessons the morals of which are followed by the just.*
> *I summarized all the books of the ancients*
> *And recorded what they omitted.*
> *I smoothed the methods of expression*
> *As if they submitted to my will.*
> *I dedicate it, a glory, to your realm,*
> *Which shines, and is the object of pride.*
> *I swear that I did not exaggerate*
> *A bit of exaggeration is hateful to me.*[16]

The criterion that moves his investigation starts from the assumption of the conformity to reality (*kanun al-mutabaka*) as a term of comparison of any historical event. In this perspective, his effort to understand the reason of evolution in history in a ceaseless aetiological research of the "social laws," that determine each case in question, appears evident. In order to realize scientifically a correct interpretation, it is necessary that this science be independent (*'ilm mustakill bi-nafsih*). Additionally, the investigation's first object has to be civilization (*al-'umran al-bashari*) intended as the merging of the characteristics of the social facts in their integrity. Without lingering in the description of the six chapters of the *Muqaddima*, it is important to present their intrinsic value.

At the beginning, there is a socioanthropological study on the influence of the environment of human nature arriving at the description of the first nomad civilizations (*'umran badawi*). The concept of *'umran* contains in itself a plurality of meanings: from inhabitated geographical place to society *stricto et lato sensu.*[17] From here, the interest comes to the first institutional forms and their evolutionary characteristics until arriving at the more developed and sophisticated forms of social aggregation in an urban and sedentary context (*'umran hadari*). In this way, he analyzes the modalities of commerce and the development of manufacturing activities and their indissoluble contribution to the flourishing of a thriving society where philosophy, culture, and art bloom freely and without impediment.

The complex methodological *organon* shows a concrete study of the historical dynamics in which appear *in nuce* the *Idealtypen* of the *Verstehende Methode* with the analysis of the structural dichotomies such as town/countryside, nomad/sedentary society, and tribal solidarity/individual egoism.[18] This global vision of history permits Ibn Khaldun to formulate an economic theory characterized by the cyclicity in which the state, originally, has a limited power, and the taxation is at a relatively low level so that it allows a constant growth of production and consumption. After this phase (*first and second generation*) the state concentrates in itself all the power augmenting the fiscal charging and reducing the freedom of initiative and spirit of enterprise to which follows an evident diminution (*third generation*) of consumption and production. The final phase (*fourth generation*) is a strong economic stagnation whose principal effect is the paralysis of the state.[19] This cyclical analysis can be adapted to different historical situations because, according to C. Isawi, in societies with the same structure, similar laws and social mechanisms reign even if such societies are separate in time and space.

In this theory of evolution and decline—in which are analyzed all the symptoms and evils of a society that appear, grow, and die—the *'asabiyya* plays a fundamental role. It is—according to the different and punctual definition of the historians of Ibn Khaldun—public spirit, social solidarity, group's cohesion, common will, *Lebenskraft*.[20] This sense of common belonging and "reciprocal solidarity inspired at the fight for life"[21] binds each member of the community in a widespread effort toward a common aim. To this *Volksstreben* is connected the destiny of the society because the *'asabiyya* is "*die motorische Kraft in staatlichen Geschehen.*"[22] It joins the individuals through those agreements (*asaba*) that bind the survival of the group with respect to a common code of values. In the historical parabola of each civilization, it is possible to read "the development, the acmes and the deterioration"[23] of these solidarity bonds that are the intrinsic force. This capacity to offer his service for the general interests, sacrificing egotism appears to Ibn Khaldun to be the necessary condition for cooperation and public action.

To fortify spirits and political power is necessarily a common religious conviction that is considered a spiritually bonding agent. "A dynasty—Ibn Khaldun affirms—that begins its history supported by the religion doubles the force of *'asabiyya* that helps it in its formation."[24] In its cyclical paths, a civilization is in the beginning characterized by a common religion and a strong spiritual and ascetic union among the members. After years, the state or the political authority becomes the unique administrator of the religious sphere, which assumes a merely social value, abandoning the original mystical sense. Society begins to lose that centripetal force of defense, and the enjoyment of riches substitutes for the spirit of sacrifice and ascetic practice. This generational path marks the end of social solidarity and of common good. The 'asabiyya of the origins loses its strong spiritual characterization until being completely substituted by another emerging and different social movement.

Concerning his concept of social development, Ibn Khaldun affirms repeatedly that it is not the amount of money reserves or precious metals that is the measure of the prosperity of a country but the better specialization or division of the work between the inhabitants. This, in fact, generates a "virtuous circle" that augments the productivity in a right distribution of roles and risks: The artisan receives a reward for his work, the merchant deserves his profit by virtue of the risks, the authorities have the right to compensation for the services and the protection of public and private goods.[25] This social task, anyway, should not be misunderstood: it does not justify a constant interference in the private sphere and in the free development of human activities because

> attacks on people's property remove the incentive to acquire and gain property. People, then, become of the opinion that the purpose and ultimate destiny of acquiring property is to have it taken away from them. When the incentive to acquire and gain property is gone, people no longer make any efforts to acquire any. The extent and degree on which property rights are infringed upon determines the extent and degree to which the effort of the subjects to acquire property slackens. The disintegration of civilization causes the disintegration of the status of dynasty and ruler.[26]

In the *Muqaddima*, Ibn Khaldun is convinced that an oppressive government brings about the ruin of public prosperity[27] and that

> one of the greatest injustices and one which contributes most to the destruction of civilization is the unjustified imposition of tasks and the use of subjects for forced labor. . . . An injustice even greater and more destructive of civilization and the dynasty is the appropriation of people's property by buying their possessions as cheaply as possible and then reselling them at the highest possible prices by means of forced sales and/or purchases. . . . If no trading is being done in the markets, the subjects have no livelihoods and the tax revenue of the ruler decreases or deteriorates, since . . . most of the tax revenue comes from customs duties on commerce. It should be

known that all these practices are caused by the need for money on the part of dynasty and ruler. . . . The ordinary income does not meet the expenditure. Therefore, the ruler invents new sorts and kinds of taxes, in order to increase the revenues and to be able to balance the budget. . . . The need for appropriating people's property becomes stronger and stronger. In this way, the authority of the dynasty shrinks until its influence is wiped out and its identity is lost and it is defeated by an attacker.[28]

The first symptoms of this delegitimation of the original power are, in fact, strictly connected to tax regulation. Very often without the personal stimulus to productivity and engagement, the society itself is condemned to implode in the apathy caused by a political system that is coercive and disrespectful toward individual freedom. Concerning this, he affirms in a famous statement that "it should be known that at the beginning of a dynasty, taxation yields a large revenue from small assessments. At the end of a dynasty, taxation yields a small revenue from large assessments."[29] In this precise anticipation of the Laffer Curve, he explains very clearly that having lost their austere habits and having increased their luxurious necessities, the sovereigns impose a heavy taxation on their subjects, pushing up the level of the old taxation to enlarge their benefits. The effect of this augmentation is the diminishment of the economic activity. In this delicate situation, the government seems to have no other solution than a depreciation of the money that generates an infinite series of evils as Al-Makrizi, a distinguished Egyptian disciple of Ibn Khaldun, demonstrated in depth in his works,[30] reaffirming the precise statement that "it should be known that treasures of gold and silver are no different from other minerals. It is civilization that produces them in abundance or causes them to be in short supply."[31]

Ibn Khaldun's work, from every point of view, is worthy of admiration. His empirical method goes beyond the cold transcription of the events to be correctly defined as "historical science" in which the law of cause and effect and the distinction between essential and accidental are the starting point for any historical definition.[32] He, presenting his scientific criterion, affirms to have chosen "a remarkable and original method"[33] to comment "on civilization ('umran), on urbanization and on the essential characteristics of human social organization in a way that explains to the reader how and why things are as they are."[34]

Y. Lacoste even comes to affirm that if "Thucydides invented history, Ibn Khaldun turned it into a science."[35] Even though, not without a bit of reticence and sarcasm, some have described the philosophy of Ibn Khaldun as *ancilla sociologiae*,[36] it would be incorrect not to concede that it is rightly meritorious from a straightforward philosophical perspective. His thought is the fruit of a perfect synthesis in which sociology and social psychology and political science and economy appear as auxiliary sciences to history in a complex unity. Ibn Khaldun admonishes that "it is necessary that the historian knows the fundamental principles of the art of government, the true character of events, the difference between the nations, the countries and the times in which observe the costumes, the uses, the behavior, the opinions and religious sentiments and all the circumstances that influence the society."[37]

The work of Ibn Khaldun was more often made the object of a comparative analysis with the philosophy of N. Machiavelli, but if "the great Florentine instructs us in the art of governing people, he does make it as a foresighted politician. Ibn Khaldun was able to analyze the social phenomenon as a deep economist and philosopher, a fact that invites us to see in his work such a critical methodology totally unknown in his epoch."[38] At the end of this brief article dedicated to the social thought of Ibn Khaldun and in accord with A. J. Toynbee, eminent historian of the civilizations, we can say that "[Khaldun] has conceived and formulated a philosophy of history that is undoubtedly the greatest work of its kind that has ever yet been produced by any mind in any time and place."[39]

Notes

1 "His importance lies in the unique feat, for the time, of having been able to rationalize the subject of history and to reflect upon its methods and purposes. In marked contrast with the static or eschatological conceptions of contemporary Christian historiography was his dynamic thesis that the process of historic growth is subject to constant change, comparable to the life of the individual organism. He made clear the cooperation of psychic and environmental factors in the evolution of civilization. There was a pre-Marxian flash in his observation that the usages and institutions of peoples depend upon the way in which they provide their subsistence." H. E. Barnes, *A History of Historical Writing* (New York: Dover Publishing, 1963), 96.

2 I. A. Ahmad, "Islam and Markets," *Religion & Liberty* 6, no. 3 (May–June 1996): 6.

3 H. Corbin, *Storia della Filosofia Islamica* (Milano: Adelphi, 1991), 290.

4 "In the short span of five to ten years, the Black Death had an immediate and dramatic effect on all aspects of political, social, economic, cultural, and intellectual life." See *Dictionary of the Middle Ages*, vol. 2, s.v. "Black Death."

5 "It is now clear that the Black Death was fully as devastating in the Near East as it was in Europe. And in the long term its implications were far worse, since in the Near East this epidemic initiated a series of recurrences of the disease which struck more frequently and with greater severity than Europe. In particular, pneumonic plague, the disease's most lethal form, continued to reappear in the Near East after the Black Death; and whereas the plague had disappeared from most parts of Europe by the seventeenth century, it was still a recurrent and common scourge in the Near East until the late nineteenth century, when the advent of modern plague epidemiology made it possible to suppress the disease." See *Dictionary of the Middle Ages*, vol. 9, s.v. "Plagues in the Islamic World."

6 The calamity "folded the carpet with all there was on it [and] the notables, the leaders and all the learned died, as well as my parents on whom be God's mercy." (Ibn Khaldun, *Muquaddima: An Introduction to History*, trans. Franz Rosenthal (Princeton: Princeton University Press, 1993), 1:64.

7 Ibn Khaldun, *Muqaddima*, 1:64.
8 M. Talbi, "Ibn Khaldun," *The Encyclopaedia of Islam* (Leiden: Brill, 1991), 825.
9 Ibn Khaldun, *Histoires des Berbères et des dynasties musulmanes de l'Afrique septentrionale*, trans. Baron De Slane, vol. 4. (Algiers: n.p., 1852–1856), 180.
10 Ibn Khaldun, *Muqaddima*, 3.274.
11 Quotation of the *Ta'rif*, 246–47, in *Ibn Khaldun in Egypt*, ed. W. J. Fischel (Berkeley: University of California Press, 1967), 19.
12 Quotation in M. A. Enan, *Ibn Khaldun* (New Delhi: Kitab Bhavan, 1984), 66.
13 M. Talbi, "Ibn Khaldun," 829.
14 "In the *Muqaddima* he gives examples of how misunderstanding of history leads workers, artisans, teachers, and other people of low status to aspire to political power and authority that they cannot really possess. These examples helped him come to terms with the true position of the scribe. In the early days of Islam, he points out, the scribe was a minister of state and a member of ruling elite. In his own time the true political rulers were the sultans, the royal families, and the chiefs of the tribes that supported them. Now the scribe was only a servant. From history he could gauge his realistic prospects, temper his ambition, and re-establish his respect for the legitimacy of the established dynasties and the given social order." See *Dictionary of the Middle Ages*, vol. 7, s.v. "Ibn Khaldun."
15 M. Talbi, "Ibn Khaldun," *The Encyclopaedia of Islam* (Leiden: E. J. Bril, 1991), 829.
16 Enan, *Ibn Khaldun*, 56.
17 Concerning this controversial point, Y. Lacoste affirms that "Ibn Khaldun does not, as is so often claimed, make any basic distinction between nomadic and sedentary groups. His views are much more complex and far-reaching. He did not study the rural population alone, but the entire population of the area, and its various social, intellectual, and material activities (material in sense of production and consumption). He uses the term *umran* to refer to this totality. Both De Slane and Rosenthal translate this as 'civilization,' which limits Ibn Khaldun's concept considerably by suggesting an explicit comparison with 'barbarism' and 'savagery.' The word *umran* derives from the Arabic root *amr*, meaning to live somewhere, to live with someone, to cultivate land, to make prosperous, to have a house, to have a fixed abode." Y. Lacoste, *Ibn Khaldun: The Birth of History and the Past of the Third World* (London: Verso Editions, 1984), 93.
18 L. Baeck, *The Mediterranean Tradition in Economic Thought* (London: Routledge, 1994), 115.
19 Ibid., 117.
20 W. J. Fischel, *Ibn Khaldun in Egypt* (Berkeley: University of California Press, 1967), 153–54; and Y. Lacoste, *Ibn Khaldun*, 110–27.
21 S. Noja, *Breve storia dei popoli dell'Islam* (Milano: A. Mondadori, 1997), 154.
22 F. Rosenthal, *Ibn Khalduns Gedanken ueber den Staat* (Munich: n.p., 1932).
23 S. Noja, *Breve storia dei popoli dell'Islam* (Milano: A. Mondadori, 1997), 155.
24 Ibn Khaldun, *Muqaddima*, 2.325.
25 L. Baeck, *The Mediterranean Tradition in Economic Thought* (London: Routledge, 1994), 116.
26 Ibn Khaldun, *Muqaddima*, 2.103–4.
27 Ibid., 1.106.
28 Ibid., 2.123.
29 Ibid., 1.89.
30 Enan, *Ibn Khaldun*, 99–100.
31 Ibn Khaldun, *Muqaddima*, 2.235.
32 M. Mahdi, *Ibn Khaldun's Philosophy of History* (Chicago: University of Chicago Press, 1991), chaps. 3 and 4.

33 Ibn Khaldun, *Muqaddima*, 1.10.
34 Ibid.
35 Y. Lacoste, *Ibn Khaldun*, 142.
36 H. Corbin, *Storia della Filosofia Islamica* (Milano: Adelphi, 1991), 288.
37 Ibn Khaldun, *Muqaddima*, 1.6.
38 S. Colosio, "Contribution à l'etude d'Ibn Khaldun," *Revue du Monde Musulman*, 24 (1914): 334.
39 A. J. Toynbee, *A Study of History*, vol. 3 (Oxford: Oxford University Press, 1934), 322.

References

Ahmad, I. A. 1996. "Islam and Markets." *Religion & Liberty* 6, no. 3 (May–June): 6–8.

——. 1971. *The Political Economy of Classical Islamic Society*. Chicago: University of Chicago Press.

Ahmad, K., ed. 1980. *Studies in Islamic Economics*. Leicester, U.K.: The Islamic Foundation.

Al-Azmeh, A. 2003. *Ibn Khaldun: An Essay in Reinterpretation*. Budapest: Central European University Press.

Badawi, A. 1972. *Histoire de la Philosophie en Islam*. Paris: Librairie Philosophique J. Vrin.

Baeck, L. 1994. *The Mediterranean Tradition in Economic Thought*. London: Routledge.

Barnes, H. E. 1963. *A History of Historical Writing*. New York: Dover Publishing.

Bosworth, E. et al., ed. 1991. *The Encyclopaedia of Islam*. Leiden: E. J. Brill.

Colosio, S. 1914. "Contribution à l'etude d'Ibn Khaldun." *Revue du Monde Musulman*, 26: 308–38.

Corbin, H. 1991. *Storia della Filosofia Islamica*. Milano: Adelphi.

Hernandez, M. Cruz. 1981. *Historia del Pensamiento en el Mundo Islamico*, vol. 2. Madrid: Alianza Universal.

D'Ancona, ed. 2005. *Storia della Filosofia nell'Islam medievale*. Torino: Einaudi.

Enan, M. A. 1984. *Ibn Khaldun*. New Delhi: Kitab Bhavan.

Fischel, W. J. 1967. *Ibn Khaldun in Egypt*. Berkeley: University of California Press.

Gottfried, R. 1984–1986. *Dictionary of the Middle Ages*. Edited by J. Strayer et al. New York: C. Scribner's Sons.

Hourani, A. 1991. *History of the Arab Peoples*. Cambridge: Harvard University Press.

Khaldun, Ibn. 1852–1856. *Histoires des Berbères et des dynasties musulmanes de l'Afrique septentrionale*. Translated by Baron De Slane. Algiers: n.p.

——. 1993. *The Muquaddima: An Introduction to History*. Translated by Franz Rosenthal. Princeton: Princeton University Press.

Lacoste, Y. 1984. *Ibn Khaldun: The Birth of History and the Past of the Third World*. London: Verso Editions.

Mahdi, M. 1991. *Ibn Khaldun's Philosophy of History*. Chicago: University of Chicago Press.

Noja, S. 1997. *Breve storia dei popoli dell'Islam*. Milano: A. Mondadori.

Rosenthal, F. 1932. *Ibn Khalduns Gedanken uber den Staat*. Munich: n.p.

Schmidt, N. 1967. *Ibn Khaldun: Historian, Sociologist and Philosopher*. New York: AMS Press.

Toynbee, A. J. 1934. *A Study of History*. Oxford: Oxford University Press.

22

ISLAMIC ECONOMICS

A reflection on al-Ghazali's contributions

Amer Al Roubaie and Shafiq A. Alvi

Source: Paper presented at the International Conference on al-Ghazali's Legacy: Its Contemporary
Relevance, 24–27 October 2001, Kuala Lumpur, International Institute of Islamic Thought and
Civilization.

Introduction

The aim of this paper is to highlight the contributions of Abu Hamid al-
Ghazali's (1058–1111) thought on economics with regard the ongoing debate
concerning the construction of the Islamic economic system. The underlying
objective of our study is to interpret some of al-Ghazali's ideas about the
nature of man and its relevance to the present efforts by Muslim scholars to
formulate a working framework for the functioning of the Islamic economy.
Such analysis increases the prospects of shedding some light on the behavioral conduct of the economic agents with respect to allocation of resources
and blanching the need of both material and spiritual. According to al-
Ghazali, the ultimate aim of man's action in this life is to seek the pleasure
of the hereafter without of course neglecting life in this world. To do so,
man must equip himself with the correct knowledge of God and the world
in order to fulfill the Ibadat, for which he is being created, and earn the
mercy of Allah. Guided by both the rational soul and the highest ethical
and moral standards ultimately bring him happiness and satisfaction.

Abu Hamid al-Ghazali, also known as Hujjat al-Islam or the proof of
Islam, is among the most distinguished scholars in the history of Islam. His
fields of scholarship comprise a wide range of subjects including theology,
logic, philosophy, science and tasawwuf. Al-Ghazali's fame brought him to
become president of the Nizamiyya academy in Baghdad, one of the most
prestigious schools of learning in the Muslim world at the time. His emphasis
on the importance of knowledge and action in the realization of man's ultimate
objectives, i.e. serving God, underlines the significance of knowledge in the

overall development of human societies. The current state of underdevelopment in the Muslim World today is largely due to the failure of Muslims to pursue policies and programs for advancing scientific research and promoting a knowledge-based development. The future prospect and development in Muslim societies will depend on their ability to contribute to various fields of knowledge as well as on the capacity to disseminate information and modern technologies. In Islam, acquisition of knowledge is necessary not only to increase man's material desires but also to meet his spiritual needs. Al-Ghazali emphasis on the importance of knowledge refers to necessary knowledge, which directly points to the revelation about God.

Early Muslim scholars were interested in the developments of the physical sciences with little attention paid to investigation in social sciences. Historically, no model can be found to represent a well-defined system outlining the economic determinants of an Islamic economy. However, Muslim scholars at different times have discussed several economic issues, but mainly within the framework of Islamic jurisprudence and religious teachings. During various phases in its duration, the Islamic civilization achieved considerable progress in the field of economics through increasing productivity and improvement in individual welfare.

Emergence of Islamic economics

In recent years, a substantial amount of literature has been written about Islamic Economics reflecting the interest of Muslim scholars in reviving some of the lost Islamic heritage in the field of economics. The debate about the subject is relatively young and therefore studies in Islamic history add valuable contribution to the field. It was the Conference on Islamic Economics held in Jeddah, Saudi Arabia in 1976 that gave birth to the present body of literature on the subject. Since then a surge of research and studies have been done to identify the main determinants of the Islamic economic system. The aim of these efforts is to provide adequate analysis that incorporates the guidelines of Islam as well as to construct a methodology applicable to improve the existing socio-economic conditions in Muslim societies. The failure of the Western economic methodology in promoting sustained growth underlines the urgency for an alternative approach to development in Muslim countries. Despite their factor endowments and financial wealth, income per capita of an individual Muslim has remained very low compared with that of the industrialized countries as well as the rest of the world on average. After long and bitter colonial experiences, a great deal of the Islamic heritage has been lost leaving Muslims far behind in the quest for knowledge, education and socio-economic progress. Poverty, income inequalities, illiteracy, corruption, mismanagement and lack of public participation are so common that it is impossible for a contemporary secular economic system to solve. In addition, the high degree of dependence by Muslim countries on world markets, poor institutional bodies and weak infrastructures has continued to obstruct their path toward recovery. The ultimate objective of development in Islam is to increase self-sufficiency by helping Muslims to improve their productive capacity and reduce dependence on others.

The aim of Islamic economics is to provide an alternative to the existing economic system(s) by developing a body of knowledge constituting an ethical and moral approach to man's economic problems. In Islam, economics cannot be separated from the rest of man's action in attribution to achieve fallah, i.e. success, by combining the satisfaction of both this life and the hereafter. The dynamism of the Islamic economic system comprises a set of moral and ethical principles meant to enforce justice, freedom and cooperation. Not only the material aspects and love for worldly life are satisfied under the Islamic system, but also man's spiritual need should be met. In other words, the objectives of economics in Islam are to create a balance between man's basic material desires and his spiritual needs. These two aspects of man's life are both important for his achieving fallah.

Man's behavior in the economic sphere should be a reflection of his knowledge of the religious guidelines concerning conduct in the market place. It is not the purpose of this study to dwell in detail on the main fundamentals governing individual behavior, but rather to highlight some of al-Ghazali's views and their relevance to contemporary economics. Without any doubt, the contribution of al-Ghazali to the body of knowledge about the subject will be of great significance. By doing so, we will be able to increase our understanding about the behavioral functions of the Islamic man in fulfilling his duties and responsibilities as God's representative on earth. The Islamic economic system is a reflection of man's behavior in order to gain, compete and operate freely in the market place. Imam al-Gazali sums up Islam 'as equally striving for earning on the one hand and striving in the cause of God on the other.'

The apparent stagnation of the sciences within the Islamic civilization followed by long colonial domination led to the decay of these institutions in different parts of the world. The recent literature on Islamic economics has emphasized the need for re-instituting Islamic values aimed at freeing the Muslim world from its current economic problems including poverty and inequalities. Among the main institutional bodies to be re-instated are those of the Zakat, prohibition of Riba, individual freedoms and rights, ethical and moral principles, knowledge, work and the active role of the state. Market practices according to these guidelines endorse economic justice and promote development by allowing fair distribution of income and wealth and provide equal opportunity to all individuals. These economic guidelines of the Shari'ah, may not be clearly stated and have to be interpreted, consist of a wide range of measures in all market activities including production, consumption and distribution. So far the body of literature on Islamic economics has covered a wide range of issues but is still far from being complete to meet the rising demand for research.

Economics has been man's immediate concern since the first day of his existence and despite the fact that civilizations are born and then decline, man's concern for economics remains more pressing than ever before. Hunting and gathering of food were the first profession man learned to master not only to sustain himself but also to guarantee his security. As Ibn Khaldun explains "God created and fashioned man in a form that he can live and subsist only with the help of food. He guided man by a natural desire for food and instilled in him the power that enables him to obtain it."[1] In the Arabian Desert, the Arabs lived for thousands of years moving from one place to another in search of food to feed themselves and their animals. The Qura'n (Quraish: 107:1-4) makes reference to the Quraish for being blessed by Allah for providing them with the means that guaranteed their need for food and security. It says: "For the Familiarity of The Quraish, their Familiarity with the journeys By winter and summer, Let them worship the Lord of this House, who provides them with food against hunger and with security against fear." Today, the economic problem as manifested in global poverty and the desperate needs of millions of people for their daily survival represents one of the greatest challenges facing humanity. Instead of using beneficial knowledge to overcome the forces of nature and help fellow human beings, man becomes his own enemy by preventing others from the fruits of the knowledge to sustain their own survival. Food security has been amongst the most important issues being considered both locally and internationally. The future prospects for solving man's problems will depend on the ability to increase this beneficial knowledge, and hard work.

Although al-Ghazali's teachings fall within the domain of religion, and related sciences owing to his reflection on man's character and pattern of conducts, al-Ghazali's approach is unique in the sense that both knowledge and action are important for fulfilling man's duties. In this respect he recognizes the applications of knowledge through action to enhance the capability of man towards achieving the main objective in life. Al-Ghazali believed that the link between this world and the hereafter involves both knowledge and action. In modern contemporary economics, allocation of resources and the various organizational, managerial and administrative activities represent a body of knowledge that when put into practice increase the productivity of factors input. Al-Ghazali recognized that man could only achieve fallah in the hereafter through his worldly actions. He states that man must survive through his own work to meet his basic essentials in life. In the present debate about Islamic Economics, works are regarded as not a form of worship but also to achieve fallah in both worlds. Wealth accumulation and rapid change can be realized through knowledge and hard work.

Consumer behavior

Among other things, Muslim economists have begun to analyze the behavioral patterns of the 'Islamic Man' vis-à-vis the Secular Man of Western modernity. To establish a linkage between religion and individual behavior is vital for defining the principles of conduct in the market place. Similar to other branches of knowledge in Islam, economics derives its main premises from the religion of Islam itself. In other words, economic transactions and financial practices must be guided by ethical and moral teachings of Islam, a necessary qualification for man to be God's representative. Being vicegerent implies in the economic sense that man is put in a position of trust to allocate resources in the most efficient way to promote justice and equity among all. In Islam, Allah is the absolute owner and therefore, man is not supposed to act in a manner that will lead to mismanagement, excessive consumption, deterioration of quality, waste and a monopoly over these resources. It is not because of man's basic need but his greed that causes shortages, inequalities and excessive exploitation. Resources are Allah's bounty to man to be shared by all men as well as other creatures in a manner to promote sustainability and ensure justice. The Qur'an (Hud: 11:6) endorses this by stating: "There is no moving creature on earth but its sustenance Dependent on Allah."

Modern conventional economics is a product of western modernity, which has been in the making for several centuries. Modernity is a secular process of social change endorsing worldly principles based on man's experience towards achieving self-motivated objectives. It is individual freedom and action toward maximizing self-interests that the philosophy of modern economics rests upon. Adam Smith the father of modern economics argues that the collective benefit of a society is served indirectly through the hidden arms of its individuals. Such analysis however, implies that man is a rational being capable of making his own decisions with regard to his interests are best served. Unfortunately, this is not the case as far as man's behavior is concerned. Several centuries of colonial domination has proven that man is exploitative by nature driven by greed and self-interest. Today, globalization, which is guided by the principles of 'liberal democracy' is nothing more than an extension of the old colonial system aimed at serving interests of a few at the expense of the rest of the world. Never before has the world experienced inequalities and injustices now prevalent.

In Western economic tradition, the behavioral functions of the rational man is linked to his animal soul and not necessarily to his rational soul. He maximizes his personal self-interests in the form of profit or utility without guidance neither from religion nor from the interests of others or the community. In contrast, the action of the Islamic man involves both implementing the principles of religion and the interest of others. In other words, works with sincere action and intention is considered a form of worship in Islam. That is to say the verse in the Qur'an (Az-Zariyat: 51:56) "I have only created Jinns and men, that they may serve Me." implies that man by striving to earn his rizq, i.e. earning, he at the same time performing Ibadah. "Work takes precedence over worship, as shown for example in the saying of Abu Sulayman al-Darani (a companion of the Prophet): "Earn your bread first, then devote yourself to worship."[2] Furthermore, one of the qualities of God al-Musabbib implies that works are an expression of thankfulness to God and that by abandoning work is an expression of disobedience. According to al-Gazali man is obliged to fulfill three things in life, food, shelter and clothing.[3]

The current debate concerning the behavior of the Islamic man is directed at the implementation of the Shar'iah norms of conduct in the market place. In contemporary economics, the behavior of the economic agent is a reflection of the social, cultural, political and economic determinants. Al-Ghazali describes the 'goods of the soul' to comprise two aspects: faith and good character.[4] The former is linked to the knowledge of God as outlined in the Qur'an and Sunnah whereas the later includes all the praiseworthy of the soul. However, these two features represent the main path to achieve happiness. Implementing such guidelines, in addition to its knowledge requirement, man must also prove through the means of action his conduct. Thus in al-Ghazali rules of conduct both knowledge and action is necessary for achieving the state of happiness.

One action that leads man to achieve his desired objectives is what al-Ghazali calls kasb al aish or earning a living. In contemporary economic language, the means for earning kaseb is described by economic activities constituting various professions, market operations, and rule of conducts. Thus al-Ghazali's reflection on such matters as ethics, knowledge, action, trade, occupation, money and wealth could provide valuable insight to the role that economics plays in the development of Muslim societies. The current discourse on Islamic economics involves many aspects of al-Ghazali's teachings and therefore by incorporating these ideas into the present literature will consequently enhance our understanding about individual behavior and the functioning of the market. Given the injustices and inequalities of contemporary economics both at the national and international levels, al-Ghazali's thoughts on the inner psychology of man and his ethical and moral conduct will lead to economic justice and promote cooperation. Already, the literature on Islamic economics has brought to light ideas and concepts of several Muslim scholars whose writings can be traced back to different historical periods. There is no doubt that al-Ghazali's views on human behavior especially economic matters from this perspective will be a valuable contribution to the main determinants of the contemporary body of knowledge on economics.

The importance of knowledge

The quest for knowledge constitutes the crux of al-Ghazali teachings. He clearly states that 'morality and good conduct are not possible without it.'[5] Knowledge is the product of the human intellect, a faculty that distinguishes man from animals. And the highest of all knowledge is spiritual knowledge, which comes either from 'self-cultivation' or 'is revealed directly.' According to al-Ghazali all knowledge including the sciences is the result of the functioning of the intellect and that the true nature of knowledge becomes evident when man begins to understand the 'true nature of things'[6] including God, the soul, and so forth. However, knowledge that man usually acquires has no limitation depending on experience and spirituality. Al-Ghazali divides sciences into two groups, the religious sciences needed for the purification of the soul; and the intellectual sciences, which comprise the knowledge of human worldly conducts. For al-Ghazali, the most important knowledge is the knowledge of God and that the purity of man's action will depend on the achievement of this form of knowledge. The highest degree of man's purity lies in his conduct towards fulfilling his religious duties as well as in his understanding the true knowledge of God. However, man can never be perfect since perfect knowledge is the property of God only. These also represent eternal knowledge bearing absolute truths that can only be assigned to the qualities and actions of God. The nearest to God man can reach will be linked to the acquisition of eternal knowledge. Al-Ghazali argues that the knowledge of this world is not only useful for man to obtain for supporting his substances but also as a means for learning the knowledge of God. In other words, learning about the knowledge of the world enhances man's knowledge about the soul, attributes of God, and so forth.

The acquisition of knowledge is essential for two important reasons: it is, firstly an apprehension of objects and their significance, and secondly a guide to conduct.[7] The concept of knowledge has a broad meaning reflecting man's ability to think and act in the way of doing things to gain control over nature and enjoy the bounty of Allah. In the words of the Prophet, acquisition of knowledge in Islam is a duty upon Muslims both male and female. Similarly, the Qur'an goes further by stating that those who fear Allah most are the people of knowledge. However, knowledge in Islam is meant to guide man for achieving fallah in this life and the Hereafter. In this respect, knowledge is not only important to guide man to follow the commandments of Allah as outlined in the Qur'an, but also to help him conduct his daily affairs in seeking sustenance. The act in the way of sustenance can be defined in terms of the economic activities that man usually follows to go about earning his rizq. From an Islamic point of view both this life and the next are connected and therefore any action in this life is complementary to earning the pleasure of Allah in the next. As a matter of fact the next life depends on man's action in this one. In this respect, the acquisition of knowledge is important for man's happiness in both worlds.

Al-Ghazali also links the concept of knowledge to the principles of Kasb. He mentions the hadith of the Prophet, which states: Seeking knowledge is a duty of every Muslim male and female. Al-Ghazli says the man who is seeking Kasb needs the knowledge of Kasb.[8] The knowledge of action in acquiring Kasb is imperative in knowing what to avoid. To put in contemporary perspectives simply implies information that will be useful for the market. So according to al-Ghazali knowledge about trade is essential for a trader because it helps to avoid misconduct.

In addition to knowledge, Al-Ghazali also emphasizes the importance of capital in both its financial and physical forms. He states that industries and crafts can only be made possible through finance (mal) and tools or equipment (Adawat)[9] Fittingly, these are the two most important ingredients for modern production. In contemporary economies both knowledge and technology are vital for socio-economic development.

Ethical and moral conduct

In Islam, ethics describes the rules of man's conduct according to the principles of the Qur'an and the Sunnah of the Prophet. In other words, ethics is strictly the "body of injunctions laid down in the Qur'an for the practical conduct of life and fully exemplified in the practice of the Holy Prophet throughout his life."[10] Al-Ghazali considers the Prophet as the ideal perfect man, par excellence, in all aspects of life.

Al-Ghazali's ethical teachings are defined in relation to the fulfillment of religious beliefs or Ibadats. In this respect, the concept of action in al-Ghazali involves "the study of actions directed towards God, of actions directed towards one's fellow-man and family and in society, of purification of the soul from vices and of its beautification with virtues."[11] Thus the principle of ethics in al-Ghazali includes a wide range of individual actions covering all his activities. Although, al-Ghazali did not specifically mention economics, his concept of ethics also involves the rules of conduct in the market place. Being guided by the guidelines of the Shar'iah, the Islamic man is acting according to his rational soul. Such behavior is a reflection of his knowledge of God as well as of his understanding of the ethical guidelines in relations to his conduct with other people. We must also point out that al-Ghazali considers action by man as a means to help him not only in achieving his sustenance in this life but also in the next one. "Moral principles are to be learnt with a view to applying them to practical life."[12] The Western man on the other hand, acts according to his own self-interest without guidance from religion.

Islam endorses ethical relations and rules of conduct among individuals at every level. The Shar'iah guidelines are Divine orders containing a set of ethical and moral rules to guide man in his quest for fallah. As a religion, Islam is not confined to limited or narrow aspects of human life but covers every single human activity both physically and mentally. In this respect, human conduct is a derivative of the divine laws of Islam, which involve ethical and moral principles. Man can only obtain God's satisfaction by following these ethical laws via action supported by faith and knowledge. According to al-Ghazali "faith, knowledge and action are the fundamentals of religion."[13] Furthermore, he considers knowledge as the key to man's progress towards achieving happiness in both its material and physical dimensions, i.e. 'knowledge is the basis for virtuous life.' Thus, for a Muslim to acquire knowledge becomes a form of fulfilling his Ibadah. Knowledge enables man to enhance his ethical conduct as well as bring him closer to Allah.

Man's moral behavior involves two dimensions: one his relation to God; and two towards his fellow human beings. To fulfill such duties, man requires knowledge in order to be able to implement the shar'iah requirements concerning his Ibadah or duties towards God as well as towards other men. Being a member of the community it becomes incumbent upon man to act in a spirit of cooperation or what al-Ghazali calls haqq al-abad. Every other member must act in a similar spirit if the society is to make progress and forge forward. The fulfillment of such duties towards others is a moral duty that obligates all members of the community to cooperate in order to have the interest of all served. Observing such moral guidelines in business transactions is also necessary if justice is to be served. Al-Ghazali speaks of 'causing harm' in case injustices are practiced in the market place and therefore people must refrain themselves from committing such acts. For example, a general harm could result from an economic transaction if a seller withholds part or all his produce in order to charge higher prices in future. Al-Ghazali uses the term ihtikar or monopoly to describe the negative effects of such practices and the harm made to the general public by the actions of some individuals. Hoarding for the sake of taking advantage of future profits is not allowed in Islam, particularly with the case of commodities needed for sustenance. This may result in injustice being done to those with a limited income, the elderly, or the unemployed. Similarly, in modern conventional economics the consequences of monopolies and their impact on markets are discussed. Moral behavior however, goes beyond the prevention of monopolies include weight, measurement, defects and any other transaction that may violate Islamic ethical guidelines. From an Islamic point of view, trade including earning profit is encouraged but not to the extent of exploitation. Prices must be fair and not too high so as not to do harm to poor people. Traders and businessmen working in the market are entitled to earn enough money to support their families as well as to have extra for spending in the way of Allah. Al-Ghazali recognizes the importance of natural resources and the need for taking care of earth's resources in meeting man's basic needs, which include food, and shelter. He also classifies professions into four categories: agriculture, weaving, construction and hunting.[14] In addition, al-Ghazali makes reference to services where people can be paid for renting out their property or animals. This is rather interesting owing to the fact that al-Ghazali recognized services as an economic activity. In present day economics, services account an important aspect of economic activities.

The role of capital

Incorporating al-Ghazali's thoughts on knowledge, action, ethics and human psychology into the current debate on Islamic economics can be useful to remedy the state of economic underdevelopment in Muslim countries. In addition, al-Ghazali views can also be seen to provide incentive to the process of capital accumulation. On one hand, he emphasizes moderation in consumption and on the other hand he strongly argues against hoarding. In the developing economy both measures are essential for increasing savings and investment, which are badly needed for broadening the economic base and increasing productivity. Al-Ghazali stands on consumption limited only to the necessities of life and any extra wealth must be spent in the way of Allah. In contemporary economics, substantial portion of income earned is allocated for luxury products. Moderation, or what al-Ghazali calls wasat, implies that extravagance spending be eliminated or curtailed to the minimum reducing in the process waste and luxury expenditures. Furthermore, by not hoarding the unused funds increases circulation of money. In poor countries such tendency has the power to accelerate economic activities by generating demand via spending or through channeling the extra funds into the economy either through direct spending or indirectly via the banking system. To build upon such system and cultivate the benefit of dishoarding, there is a need for building financial institutions to mobilize the extra funds for investment in productive enterprises.

The other aspect of al-Ghazali stimulus spending is the expenditures on religious or in the way of Allah. These are voluntary expenditures and the effects of which could also be productive in terms of the economic gain to the country. Perhaps the most important item among these is the Zakat. On one hand the Zakat provides means to spend for the poor and needy and also provides incentive for capital to be invested instead of being held idle. Thus in al-Ghazali interpretation, economic development can be designed to involve knowledge and action as well as the principle of economic moderation in consumption and controlling waste. This concept can also be suitable to promote sustainable development by balancing the needs against the environment. Similarly, the economy will be in a position to achieve self-sufficiency by allowing resources to be shared in a manner to satisfy the necessities.

Al-Ghazali classifies the spending of wealth or mal into three categories.[15]

1. To be spent on oneself in the form of worship (Ibada) or in a way of enhancing his ibada, in other words, if man has to fulfill his religious

obligation of performing the Hajj. In the second case, al-Ghazali considers spending on such necessities as food, shelter and clothing equally important in promoting his spiritual life. Al-Ghazali emphasizes the need for meeting man's basic essentials in order to reduce the risk of poverty. He considers poverty is evil, which prevents man from performing his religious duties.

2. To be spent on other people in the form of charity or Sadaqh to be given to those who are in need, protection and payment for people who are hired to work for you. Al-Ghazali states that such spending increases social harmony and improves cooperation amongst men.
3. Spending for supporting public projects such as building mosques, bridges, roads and so on. This kind of spending falls under the category of Waqf where man expects to be rewarded in the hereafter by allocating part of his wealth to worldly projects befitting the needy and poor in the community. The prophet in one of his sayings encouraged such charitable contribution.

Al-Ghazali also states that there are three disadvantages connected to wealth and money that may lead to disobedience and to committing sins. He classifies the negative effects of wealth into three categories.

1. Wealth causes temptation leading to deviation from fulfilling the ibadah.
2. It leads to luxurious life style by encouraging man to become excessive in spending.
3. Wealth keeps man from remembering Allah. Al-Ghazali considers anything that keeps man busy from performing his religious duties from of loss.

Classification of professions and crafts

Al-Ghazali classifies resources into three categories; minerals for production of equipment and money; plants to be used for producing medicine and animals for the purpose of producing meat and for transportation. Man's engagement with these resources, according to al-Ghazali is a cause of corruption of his heart by keeping him busy with worldly affairs creating in him bad features like arrogance, greed, jealousy, deceit and pride. Furthermore, being engaged physically with the development of these resources reflects the rise of professions, industries and crafts. In order for man to utilize the existing resources he has to make use of them by modifying their natural form using various methods and techniques as prescribed in the forms of crafts and industries. By doing so, man's relation to worldly affairs is therefore defined by two dimensions: One in the form of his love for life which is linked to the heart; and Two the action or works linked to himself. However, al-Ghazali's interpretation of the allocation of resources is to help man to reach the ultimate goal in life, which is his salvation and serving Allah. He considers, these resources as a vehicle, which can be expressed in the form of fulfilling these ibadats, to carry him into the next life. In this context, the vehicle is the human body, which needs nourishment reflecting the desire for food, shelter and clothing. According to al-Ghazali these means for human survival cause man to be obsessed with life and cause him forget about the real purpose of his creation.

An important outcome of al-Ghazali's classification of economic activities is the need for specialization and exchange, upon which modern economics rests. In the former case al-Ghazali stresses on the fact that man cannot work on his own, without the skills of others, for production towards providing the main means for sustenance could be difficult without them. In the present day economy, specialization in various fields is a necessary condition for market operations. In this process also enter the various forms of management, organization and the process for making decisions, which require special kinds of training, which arise due to the same process that al-Ghazali mentions. On the other hand, al-Ghazali shows that specialization in production as well as in skills lead to the necessity of the market where products produced or skills acquired can be exchanged or obtained. He seems to have recognized that without the exchange, a society would remain undeveloped. To facilitate such an exchange, he considered money to be the main instrument.

The other important aspect of al-Ghazali economic contribution is the role that capital plays in the advancement of industries and crafts. He argues: "these industries can not be developed except with the use of capital, (mal) and tools. Capital represents the resources of the earth and everything on it, which is useful. Among the most beneficial are those related to food, shelter, stores, markets, farms, tools, animals, and so forth."[16] He also says that these professions cannot be practiced unless man is able to learn them through knowledge and hard work.

It seems that al-Ghazali understood well the operation of the market by arguing that supply creates demand. He indicates that the need for tools springs from other economic activities such as building a house or a farm needs the services of others. He includes animals in the tools by stating that a merchant may need to transport his commodities so he rents of the animals of others in exchange of wages (he calls Ijara).

Market activities

Al-Ghazali regards man's short stay in this life as a means to obtain eternal happiness of the life to come. In preparing himself to achieve such ultimate objectives, man's actions must have the combination of both worldly and spiritual contents. On the one hand, man must earn his kasb to maintain his sustenance. On the other hand, he should make sure that his religious duties are not sacrificed for the love of this world. To equip himself with the tools needed for earning the pleasure of Allah, man must use both knowledge and action to implement the shar'iah principles, and to fulfill the duties assigned to him by religion.

Al-Ghazali places great importance on earning kasb through work in order to attain a higher ideal in the hereafter. In a similar manner, man has to satisfy his material needs for maintaining an adequate living standard. Such an engagement in economic activities, however, should not make him obsessed with the materialistic nature of this life, rather he must be sure to balance his work for sustenance in this world with the goals of attaining higher satisfaction in the next. In this respect, the present debate about the material and spiritual dimensions of the Islamic man is in conformity with al-Ghazali's reflections on man's action and conduct in order to achieve his ultimate objectives. In recent literature on Islamic economics, the concept of balancing the material and spiritual aspects of human conduct has received substantial acceptance. Al-Gazali sums up man's action toward kasb in three principles (1) fair dealing, (2) justice and (3) beneficence. Acting upon implementing such objectives, man's conduct must be in conformity with the ethical and moral obligations outlined by the religion of Islam.

The key to fulfilling these criteria is the acquisition of knowledge. Earning knowledge for the sake of improving one's conduct is incumbent upon every Muslim both male and female, says the Prophet. Learning about kasb is equally important in order to promote correct and just criteria in decision making as well as in dealing with others. Market freedoms must ensure that the interest of every man is protected according to the guidelines of the shar'iah. In other words no man has the right to sanction, monopolize, or obstruct the operations of business activities at the expense of others. Al-Ghazali emphasizes that the Islamic spirit of cooperation is necessary in dealing with economic activities to the extent that man must 'wish for others what he wishes for himself.' In this regard, al-Ghazali puts the interests of the general population above the interests of the individual to prevent market manipulation and to establish justice for all. In Islam economic conduct is directly linked to the interest of the community and therefore, wide divergences in income inequalities, monopolies and unjust practices among members of the society are not acceptable. In other words, the interest of earning kasb by individuals must be balanced against the interests of the community by endorsing equitable and fair distribution of gain from market activities.

Under the current contemporary economic system, unjust practices, inequalities and exploitation are the main causes of the widespread poverty in Muslim societies. It is the love of money and materialistic life that causes man's failure to act in accordance with the ethical and moral principles, towards his fellow man. Such unethical behavior can only be justified by the actions of the animal soul, which implants in man the undesirable conducts of greed, self-interest, love for money, and an overall negligence of his duties toward God.

It is worth mentioning however, that work for the sake of earning kasb is important to pay for the necessities of life, which include food, shelter and clothing. Beyond this, the additional wealth earned must be spent in the way of Allah to increase a spiritual dimension and strengthen the principles of religion. Monopoly and market manipulation aimed at taking advantage of market shortages are disallowed in Islam. A deliberate interference in market activities by hoarding food and accumulating wealth for the sake of future profit is condemned by the Prophet. Stocking food for future gain will hurt the poor member of the society at a time of need and bad harvest. "In the same way the use and circulation of counterfeit coins is prohibited by Islam. The most important part of the teachings of the Prophet, in so far as they bear upon the principles of trade, barter and production of wealth, the Prophet emphasizes the pervading spirit and guiding principles of equality and justice. It is sinful to corner any food-stuff merely for personal gain, for this means oppression of and tyranny over, the common people. In business matters and economic relations, honesty and just dealings are emphatically enjoined."[17]

In addition to the principle of being just, al-Ghazali adds the notion of Ihsan or benevolence to market conduct. Practicing justice is necessary in promoting fairness and preventing exploitation, but benevolence is equally essential to achieve the ultimate satisfaction and to purify the soul in earning the pleasure of Allah in the next life. The dimensions of Ihsan involve every act performed by man including his relation to economics. "Al-Ghazali defines benevolence as an act which benefits persons other than those from whom the act proceeds without any obligation."[18] For economic conduct to facilitate transactions at the level of Ihsan al-Ghazali points out six criteria. (1) Acting to help those in need should be made in accordance to the spirit of coop-eration and not by exploiting them by charging them higher prices. The highest level of Ihsan will be achieved by eliminating profit all together. (2) A poor man working hard to earn his rizq must be supported by giving him more than the price he is charging. Such an act will have a positive effect not only in terms of lifting him out of poverty but also in increasing the velocity of circulation. (3) A lender should act according to the principles of Ihsan in case more time is needed for debt re-payment. At times of difficulty, the lender must help the debtor by reducing the burden of the debt. (4) It is honorable for a debtor to pay back his debt without being asked or reminded to do so. (5) It is part of Ihsan to allow people to return or replace goods purchased. Such an act reduces waste by allowing goods to be utilized with regard to their usefulness. (6) In case sales are made on the basis of deferred payment, sellers should not press for payments if buyers are in difficulty. However, the concept of Ihsan in al-Ghazali's teachings is a reflection of his sufi commitment to purification of the soul through good deeds aimed at achieving the goal of religion, and gaining the pleasure of Allah.[19]

Engaging oneself in trade, al-Ghazali says should not divert a man from his ultimate aim: performing Ibadah. In other words, he should not trade the hereafter in the business of this life through earning profit and making money. He considers man's most valuable capital to be the religion itself and that man should strive towards strengthening his religion and trade with this in mind.[20] He accepts the fact the man must have a share in this life but the share of the hereafter is more important. Al-Ghazali lists seven criteria that a trader must follow if he has to observe Shar'ah guidelines. (1) He must have good intention by conducting himself with the religious code of conduct. (2) People who are capable of starting a trade must do so in order to prevent other Muslims from starving. He also states that diversity in business and industry is essential for the survival of the community. He goes into detail to describe the conditions for establishing an industry and profession. (3) The business of this life should not interfere with the aim of achieving fallah in the hereafter. A man in business must fulfill his religious duties by starting his day in the mosque and performing his daily prayers. (4) Even during market activities, man should not forget about the remembrance of Allah. (5) Traders should not spend all their time in trade. They have to limit the time devoted to earning what is sufficient for living and not to live in luxury. (6) It is important to avoid trading in forbidden products. (7) Traders must ensure that the principles of justice are taken care of in every transaction otherwise they will be responsible for any misconduct.[21]

Al-Ghazali's economic thought can better be defined as a subsistence economy aimed at providing the basic necessities for human survival. To a large extent, such an economy implies self-sufficiency by reducing the dependency on others and allowing the community to practice sustainable methods to meeting its basic needs. The following of such criteria could have a positive impact on market conduct by implementing principles of economic justice and by eliminating poverty. Also, to promote cooperation among individuals that will strengthen the social organization and increase the welfare of the community at large. Similarly it is to prevent man from begging, which from an Islamic point of view is a condition synonymous with kufr. To facilitate economic transactions and to establish moral and ethical conduct al-Ghazali views the operation of the market in the following ways. (1) Being engaged in a profession or trade is considered a fulfillment of duty on the part of man towards his family and also to help him avoid asking for zakat. A capable man guided by correct knowledge and action will be producing more wealth than what he needs for himself and his family. Such a condition increases wealth and hence the strength of the community and by using the additional wealth it helps those who serve religion such as teachers. (2) Engagement in trade and business must create opportunities for other people to work. Today, economic policies in most countries are designed to provide incentive for individuals and companies to create employment opportunities, particularly for those with limited capabilities. (3) Economic activities should not divert man from his main aim to seek pleasure in the next life. In other words, economic activities in the way of seeking kasb are an integral part of performing ibadah, the rewards of which will be reserved for the hereafter. (4) All prohibited transactions must be avoided. It is necessary that no forbidden products be produced or distributed to ensure the purity of the market and enhance the ethical conduct among participants. Riba, pork and alcohol are among some of the forbidden products. Everything else accepted according to the shar'iah is encouraged. (5) There must be moderation in the way man conducts trade by this means to avoid being greedy.

Al-Ghazali provides details about what he calls Knowledge of Kasb or Ilm al-Kasb. He says that the knowledge of kasb is a duty upon those who are engaged in it. A trader needs this knowledge in order to avoid bad business practices. Under present market conditions, having knowledge simply means information about the various aspects of the market in order to help in making business decisions. He also emphasizes the importance of contracts in business transactions. To enforce the validity of transactions a trader should avoid doing business with children, mentally disturbed people, the blind, and slaves. Similarly, certain products should not be put for sale in the market such as liquor, dogs and pork. Ivory taken from an elephant or even the dishes and other tools made from it are also included among the items that should be avoided in trade. This is rather interesting if we look at the preset situation as far as trade in ivory is concerned. Elephants have been slaughtered and trade in ivory is causing many people to worry that if such practices continue elephants may become extinct.[22] Similarly, trade in insects, snakes and rats are also disallowed.

Al-Gazali emphasized the need for a medium of exchange to facilitate transactions in the market place. He criticizes the barter system for its deficiency in providing accurate measures for exchange of commodities and demands for the use of money in exchange. He says: "If a person wants to buy food in exchange for dress he does not know how much food to be exchanged for the cloths. Such transactions involve several other commodities, which cannot be facilitated. Therefore, there is a need for a medium of exchange to equalize between items and this can be done through a long lasting metal like gold, silver and cooper. This in turn, required minting and the establishment of specialized monetary exchanges for printing."[23]

Al-Ghazali also asserts that some professions require efforts and training which people do not pay attention to in their youth forcing them later to steal or coming with excuses as to why they cannot work. The existing of such groups in the community lead to rise of the number of unemployed causing people becoming lazy and try to convince those with wealth their inability to earn living. In contemporary economy, specialization in production and obtaining skills are necessary to obtain employment.

According to al-Ghazali, in pursuing his needs man must be able to acquire the necessities for living, which include adequate food to feed his family, shelter and clothing. In modern terminology, simply means meeting the basic needs for maintaining minimum living standards. Although the concept of basic needs is not clearly specified in terms of the amount needed for satisfying man's requirements, al-Ghazali speaks about moderation or waste and that the closer a man can be to the limit of sustenance or essentials, the higher his reward in the hereafter will be. Beyond the means required to meet man's necessities, wealth is likely to be hoarded implying that a portion of it will not be used in circulation.

Conclusion

In this paper a brief discussion about some of al-Ghazali's thoughts on economics is presented. Despite the fact that al-Ghazali expressed these views about 1000 years ago, the opinions he furnished are in conformity with the methodology concerning various subjects in contemporary economics. His emphasis on ethics, morality, wealth, division of labour, money and trade are among the most pressing economic challenges facing Muslims today. Interest in Islamic economics in recent years, has given substantial importance to the history of economic thought and the contribution of early Muslim scholars to the field of economics. The concept of the Islamic man can be greatly enhanced by drawing on al-Ghazali teachings, particularly those of ethics, morality, knowledge, and personal conduct. Similarly, he looked at Islam as a universal religion the principles of which comprise all humanity. The notion of present day globalization is a reflection of the same world that al-Ghazali projected long ago. His call for cooperation amongest men, moderation in consumption, beneficent use of wealth and capital, and the need for balancing between the interest of the individual and that of the public represent important steps in constructing a just economic system. Al-Ghazali regards man's action during his lifetime as a reflection of fulfilling God's commands, which will grant him ultimate happiness in the hereafter. After all man is at a loss and the most valuable things he leaves behind are a good son, beneficial knowledge and charity. So says the Prophet.

Notes

1 See Louise E. Sweet (ed.), People and Cultures of the Middle East, Volume 1, (New York: The Natural History press, 1970), p. 3
2 Fuad I. Kuri "Work in Islamic Thought", Al-Abhath, Quarterly journal of the American University of Beirut, Vol. XXI, December 1968, Nos. 2,3,4, p. 10.
3 Al-Ghazali, Abu Hamid, Ihya Ulum ad-Din, Volume 3, (Beirut: Dar ul Khair, 1990), p. 394.
4 Muhammad Abul Quasem, The Ethics of Al-Ghazali (Delmar: Caravan Books, 1978), p. 59.
5 Muhammad Umar ud Din, The Ethical Philosophy of Al-Ghazali, (Lahore: SH. Muhammad Ashraf, 1962), p. 78.

6 Ibid, p. 79.
7 See Ibid, p. 80.
8 See Al-Ghazali, Ibid, Vol. 2, p. 127.
9 Ibid, Vol. 3, p. 396.
10 Muhammad umar ud Din, Ibid. P. 51.
11 Muhammad Abul Quasem, Ibid. p. 22.
12 Ibid. P. 25.
13 Muhammad Umar Ud Din, Ibid. p. 261.
14 See Al-Ghazali, Ibid. Vol. 3, P. 395.
15 See Al-Ghazali, Ibid., Vol. 4, p. 10.
16 Al-Ghazali, Ibid. Vol. 3, p. 396.
17 Muhammad Umar Ud Din, Ibid., p. 241.
18 Ibid. p. 241.
19 Al-Ghazali, Ibid. Vol. 2, pp. 147–151.
20 Ibid. Vol. 2, p. 151.
21 See Al-Ghazali, Vol. 2, pp. 151–157.
22 See Al-Ghazali, Ibid. Vol. 2, p. 128.
23 Ibid. 397.

23

IBN TAIMIYAH'S CONCEPT OF MARKET MECHANISM

Abdul Azim Islahi*

Source: *Journal of Research in Islamic Economics*, 2:2 (1985), 51–60.

Introduction

The main objective of this paper is to study and analyse the concept of the market mechanism as seen by Ibn Taimiyah. The paper will also attempt to compare his views with those of some other Muslim thinkers and Western writers until mid-eighteenth century. The first section is devoted to the analysis of Ibn Taimiyah's views and the last two sections are meant for comparison.

The concepts of demand and supply are most fundamental in the science of economics. They are the essence of market mechanism. But the idea of classifying all market forces into these two broad categories and of price determination through demand and supply was a very late development in the history of economic thought. According to Schumpeter, "As regards the theory of the mechanism of pricing, there is very little to report before the middle of the eighteenth century . . . (Schumpeter, p. 305). Yet it is interesting to discover that as early as the thirteenth century Ibn Taimiyah (1263–1328 CE/661–728AH) had a concept of market mechanism.

Market mechanism as conceived by Ibn Taimiyah

Ibn Taimiyah had a clear notion of the prices in a free market being determined by the forces we now call demand and supply. He says:

"Rise and fall in prices is not always due to injustice (*zuln*) of some people. Sometimes its reason is deficiency in production or decline in Import of the goods in demand. Thus if the desires for the good increase while its availability decreases, its price rises. On the other hand if availability of the good increases and the desires for it decrease, the price comes down. This scarcity or abundance may not be caused by the action of any people; it may be due to a cause not involving any injustice or, sometimes, it may have a cause that invovies injustice. It is Allah the Almighty who creates desires in the hearts of people . . .".

(Ibn Taimiyah, 1381, vol.8, p. 523)[1]

From the preceding statement of Ibn Taimiyah it appears that one prevailing opinion at his time held rising prices to be the result of injustice or malpractices on the part of sellers. The original word used by him is '*zulm*' which means transgression or injustice. Here it is used in the sense of manipulations by sellers leading to imperfections in the market, like hoarding. According to Ibn Taimiyah this is not always true. He states the economic reasons for the rise and fall of prices and the role of market forces in this regard.

Ibn Taimiyah mentions two sources of supply – local production and import of the goods demanded (*ma yukhlaq aw yujlab min dhali'k al mal al matlub*). '*al matlub*' has its root 't.i.b.' which is the synonym of the word 'demand' in English. To express demand for a good he uses the phrase '*raghabat fi'l shai*', i.e. desires for the good. Desire which reflects needs or 'taste' is one of the important determinants of demand, the other being the income. This second factor is not mentioned by Ibn Taimiyah.

A change in supply, the other market force beside demand, is described by him as an increase or decrease in availability of the good. He had already noted the two sources of supply: local production and import.

The aforementioned statement suggests that Ibn Taimiyah is referring to what we now call shifts in demand and supply functions, though he did not state them as such. That is, more being demanded at the same price and less being supplied at the same price or conversely, less being demanded and more being supplied at the same price leading to an ultimate decline of the price. He combines two different changes in one. No doubt, if a decreased supply accompanies an increase in demand, rise in the price will be more pronounced. Similarly, if an increase in supply is associated with a decrease in demand, the fall in the price will be larger, because both changes help the movement of price in the same direction. However, it is not necessary to combine the two changes or to find their occurrence simultaneously. *Cetris paribus*, we can experience the same result if only one of them changes. For example, if demand decreases while supply remains the same, price will come down and vice versa. A number of such possibilities can be imagined, which seem to be implied in Ibn Taimiyah's above statement. In his book al *Hisbah fi'l Islam*, Ibn Taimiyah describes the two changes separately as he says:

383

"If people are selling their goods according to commonly accepted manner without any injustice on their part and the price rises due to decrease of the commodity (*qillat al shai'*) or due to increase in population (*kathrat al Khalq*), then this is due to Allah".

(Ibn Taimiyah, 1976, p.24)

Here he gives the reasons for increase in price to be either a decrease of commodity, or an increase in population. "Decrease of commodity", can be appropriately translated as a decrease in supply. Similarly, an increase in population is more likely to cause an increase in market demand, so it can be translated as increase in demand. An increase in price due to a decrease in supply or due to an increase in demand is characterised as an act of God, implying the impersonal nature of the market mechanism.

In the preceding passages Ibn Taimiyah has distinguished between an increase in price due to market forces and one which is caused by people's injustice, e.g. hoarding – a distinction that provides a ground for price regulation by authorities. Ibn Taimiyah was a strong supporter of price control in the case of imperfection in the market; but he was against such controls if price rises were caused by the market forces of demand and supply. (Islahi, pp.79–90; Kahf, and al Mubarak, pp.107–125).

It should be noted here that in the texts quoted above Ibn Taimiyah analyses the effect of the changes in demand and supply on prices but he does not note the effect of high or low prices on quantity demanded and supplied (i.e., a movement along the same curve from one point to another). At one place in '*al Hisbah*' he reports with approval the view of an earlier jurist Abul Walid (1013–1081 CE-403-474AH) that "administrative setting of too low a price that leaves no profit results in a corruption of prices, hiding of goods (by sellers) and destruction of people's wealth" (Ibn Taimiyah, 1976, p.41). This awareness of the supply drying up should the price fall too low brings Ibn Taimiyah very close to indicating a direct relationship between the quantity supplied and price.

On another occasion, in his *Fatawa* he gives some of the factors that affect demand and consequently price. He says (Ibn Taimiyah, 1383, vol.29, pp.523–525):

(a) "People's desire (*al raghabah*) is of different kinds and varies frequently. It varies according to the abundance or scarcity of the good demanded (*al matlub*). A good is much more strongly desired when it is scarce than that when it is available in abundance.

(b) "It varies also depending on the number of demanders (*tullab*). If number of the persons demanding a commodity is large, its price goes up as against when their number is small.

(c) "It is also affected by the strength or weakness of the need for the good and by the extent of the need, how great or small is the need for it. If

384

the need is great and strong, the price Will increase to an extent greater than if the need is small and weak.

(d) "(The price also varies) according to (the customer) with whom exchange is taking place (al mu'awid). If he is rich and trustworthy in paying debts, a smaller price from him is acceptable (to the seller) which (price) would not be acceptable from one known for his insolvency, delay in payment or denial of payment due.

(e) "Also (the price is influenced) by the kind (of money) paid in exchange; if it is in common circulation (naqd ra'ij), price is lowered which is not the case if payment is made in money less common in circulation. Like dirham and dinar these days in Damascus where payment in dirhams is the common practice.[2]

(f) "This is because the purpose of contracts is (reciprocal) possession by the two parties (to the contract). If the payer is capable of payment and is expected to fulfill his promise, the objective of the contract is realised with him contrary to the case if he is not fully capable or faithful regarding his promise. The degrees of capability and faithfulness differ. This applies to the seller and the buyer, the lessor and the lessee, the bride and the groom in marriage. The object of the sale is sometimes (physically) available and sometimes it is not. The price of what is available is lower than the price of what is not (physically available). The same applies to the buyer who is sometimes able to pay at once as he has money, but sometimes he does not have (cash) and wants to borrow (in order to pay) or sell the commodity (to make payment). The price is lower in the former case.

(g) "The same applies to one who rents out (an object). He may be in a position to deliver the benefits to which the contract entitles so that the lessee can avail of these benefits without any (further) costs. But sometimes the lessee cannot avail of the benefits without (additional) costs as happens in villages visited by oppressors in authority or by robbers, or in places infected by predatory animals. Obviously the (rental) price of such land is not at par with the rental price of land which does not require this (additional cost)."

As we have noticed earlier, Ibn Taimiyah takes 'desire in the sense of demand. Subsequently he uses the exact word 'al matlub' and 'al talibun' for the goods demanded and for demanders respectively. In his analysis of increasing and decreasing prices. Economic and non economic factors and individual and collective actions are mentioned together.

To say that a scarce good is much more strongly desired than one available in abundance is to conceive of demand and supply as interdependent which is not true, generally speaking. Ibn Taimiyah records it as a psychological fact he observed: that some individuals finding a good in short supply may expect it to be in shorter supply in future and hence increase their demand for that good now.

An increase in the number of demanders causing an increase in price is an economic phenomenon and it is one of the cases of a change in the market demand functions. Smallness or largeness of need as distinct from its intensity may refer to the commodity's place in the total basket of goods needed by the consumer. Should this interpretation be correct, Ibn Taimiyah is associating intensity of need, coupled with its relatively large size as a proportion of the totality of his consumption expenditure, with high prices. In contrast, a less intensely felt need for a commodity needed in a small quantity in proportion to the totality of his needs will be a cause for lower prices.

The next point (i.e., (d) above) relates to sale on credit. It deals with a specific case not very relevant to an analysis of market prices, except when this becomes the general case so that sellers have to take into account the uncertainties regarding payment.

The matter of price in terms of silver coins being lower (para (e) above) is a reference to the peculiar monetary situation in Damascus at that time. The reason might have been an increasing quantity of alloy in gold coins or the frequent unfavourable changes in dinar and dirham ratio, as testified by the history of that period (Qalaqshandi, vol. 3, p. 438; Maqrizi, vol. 1, p. 899). It should be noted that towards the end of his reign, Nasir Muhammad b. Qalawun – the Sultan contemporary to Ibn Taimiyah forbade people to sell or buy gold. All were obliged to surrender their gold to the mint and take dirhams in return. (Maqrizi, vol.2, p.393). This also might have been responsible for relatively higher prices in terms of dinars.

The specific individual case of charging a lower price for a commodity presently available and a higher price for that which is not presently available in the market (para (f) above) can be interpreted as a case of extra payment being made for procuring the commodity which is difficult to come by. Ibn Taimiyah has noted this case along with the case of the cash price for a commodity being lower than its price when payment is deferred. This he had already noted (in (d) above).

The example given in (g) aims at making the point that any Costs which must be incurred by the buyer in order to utilise a rented object have to be taken into account by the one who rents out the object. Ibn Taimiyah finds a common element between the cases d, e, f and g: uncertainties or costs involved cause prices to be different from what they would have been without them. This, in it self, is a significant contribution to economic analysis. Add to this his awareness of the effects of changes in supply and demand on prices. It will be interesting, therefore, to compare his ideas in this regard with those of some other Islamic thinkers and Western writers until the advent of Economics during mid-eighteenth century.

Price formation as seen by some other Muslim thinkers

The earliest record of increase and decrease of production with respect to price changes I was able to find is in Abu Yusuf (731–798 CE/113–182AH). But instead of giving any theoretical account of demand and supply and their effect on prices, he states, "There is no definite limit of cheapness and dearness that could be ascertained. It is a matter decided from the heaven" not known how? Cheapness is not due to plentifulness of food, nor dearness is due to scarcity. They are subject to the command and decision of Allah. Sometimes food is plentiful but still very dear and sometimes it is too little but cheap" (Abu Yusuf, p. 48).

In the above passage, Abu Yusuf denies a common impression of the negative relationship between supply and price. It is true that price does not depend on supply alone. Equally important is the force of demand. Therefore, increasing or decreasing price is not necessarily related to decrease or increase in production. Insisting upon this point Abu Yusuf says that there are some other reasons also, which he fails to mention "for the sake of brevity" (Abu Yusuf, p.48). What are those factors? What did he keep in his mind? Whether changes in demand, or changes in money supply of the country, or hoarding and hiding of goods, or all of these? It remains to be explored whether he or any of his contemporaries touched these points.

In the opinion of Siddiqi, the context in which Abu Yusuf discussed the issue of prices i.e. proportional agricultural tax (*nizam al muqasamah*) is better and more justifiable than fixed land tax (*nizam al misahah*), did not require an explicit and detailed description of all the factors involved. (Siddiqi, 1964, pp.79–80, 85–87).

Ibn Khaldun (1332–1404 CE/732–806AH) is another important figure in whose writings we find description of both demand and supply in respect of rise and fall of prices. In his famous work '*al Muqaddimah*', under the heading 'Prices in Towns', he divides the goods into necessaries and luxuries. According to him, when a city expands and its population increases, prices of necessaries decrease comparatively and those of luxuries increase. The reason given by him is that the foodstuffs and similar commodities being the necessaries of life get the first and the foremost attention of every man and thus their supply increases; causing prices to fall. On the other hand, the production of luxuries and conveniences does not attract the attention of every one, while their demand increases due to changes in life patterns causing their prices to increase. In this way Ibn Khaldun gives a reasonable account of demand and supply and their effect on prices. He also notes the role of competition among the demanders and increasing cost of supply due to taxation and other kinds of duties in the towns. (Ibn Khaldun, pp. 288–289).

At another place Ibn Khaldun describes the effect of increased or decreased supply on prices. He says:

EVOLUTION OF ISLAMIC ECONOMICS

"... When goods (brought from outside) are few and rare, their prices go up. On the other hand, when the country is near and the road safe for travelling, there will be many to transport the goods. Thus they will be found in large quantities, and the price will go down".

(Ibn Khaldun, p.314)

The foregoing quotations show that like Ibn Taimiyah, Ibn Khaldun also considers both demand and supply to be important in determination of prices. Ibn Khaldun then goes on to say that a moderate profit boosts trade whereas very low profits discourage traders and artisans and very high profits decrease demand (Ibn Khaldun, pp.315–316). Indeed, Ibn Khaldun goes beyond Ibn Taimiyah in his clear mention of the elements of competition and different costs of supply on which Ibn Taimiyah is not very explicit. After his statement of demand and supply, Ibn Khaldun cites examples of different goods and their supply in different countries and their high or low prices according to their availability. He merely makes these observations but does not prescribe any price control policy. He seems to be more concerned with the facts while Ibn Taimiyah is interested in policy issues. Ibn Taimiyah does not confine his analysis to discussing the effect of increase and decrease in demand and supply on prices, but he opposes fixation of any price as long as market forces work normally. In the case of imperfection in the market or injustice on the part of suppliers he recommends price control. (Ibn Taimiyah, 1976, pp.25–51; Islahi, pp. 79–90; Kahf; and Mubarak, pp. 107–125). At one place in the *Muqaddimah*, Ibn Khaldun examined the depressing effect of state trading on the prices of goods sold by private competitors and suppliers, (Ibn Khaldun, pp.223–224) but it has nothing to do with the price control policy.

Western thinking on price mechanism until mid-eighteenth century

According to the historians of economic thought, the Greek philosophers Aristotle and Plato could not present a theory of price formation by the operation of supply-demand mechanism in the market. (Gordon, p.46; Schumpeter, p.60). Almost the same is the case with the famous scholastic thinker Thomas Aquinas (1225–1274 CE) whose ideas influenced an epoch.

At the beginning of this paper we have noted Schumpeter's remark on the theory of the mechanism of pricing on the part of Western writers. He did not find much worth mentioning before the middle of eighteenth century. He has also said there that, "The contributions of even the brightest lights, such as Barbon, Petty, Locke, do not amount to much, and vast majority of the Consultant Administrators and Pamphleteers of the seventeenth century were content with the kind of theory they found or could have found in

Pufendorf." (Schumpeter, p.305). Samuel Von Pufendorf (1632–94) a Swedish jurist was born more than three hundred years after Ibn Taimiyah. We have no access to the works of Pufendorf whom Schumpeter held to be the leader of so many thinkers. The only reference to his contribution given by Schumpeter is as follows: "Distinguishing value in use and in exchange (*or pretium eminens*), he (Pufendorf) lets the latter be determined by the relative scarcity or abundance of goods and money. Market price then gravitates towards the costs that must normally be incurred in production" (Schumpeter, p. 122).

This brief quotation on the substance of Pufendorf's contribution is not sufficient for a critical examination or a comparison with Ibn Taimiyah's contribution. To say that value in exchange or price is determined by the relative scarcity or abundance of goods and money is more related to a quantity theory of money than the theory of the mechanism of pricing. And perhaps, that is what Schumpeter also meant, because Barbon,[3] Petty (1623–1687), and Locke (1632–1704) whom he mentioned in this connection were more concerned about the effect of money supply on prices than any thing else. Credit for discovery of the quantity theory of money is usually given to a French jurist Jean Bodin (1530–1596) who developed it in 1568 in a "Reply to the Paradoxes of M. Maletroit" (Speigel, p.89). Although implied in this theory is the application of demand and supply analysis to money, it is a different subject. Ibn Taimiyah did not apply demand and supply to money. At one occasion only, he said, "The authority should mint the coins (other than gold and silver) according to the just value of people's transaction, without any injustice to them . . . and a ruler should not start business in money by purchasing copper and minting coins and thus doing business with them . . ." (Ibn Taimiyah, 1381, p.469).

Apart from Jean Bodin, Pufendort, Barbon, Petty and Locke, there are other Western writers before Adam Smith who used the analysis of demand and supply to explain changes in price. Schumpeter does not mention them. But Barry Gordon, in his book *Economic Analysis Before Adam Smith* mentions John Nider (1380–1438), Navarrus (1493–1586), Luis Molina (1536–1600) and Lessius (1554–1632) and gives a brief account of each. Stating Nider's views he says, "Moreover, by as much as a greater number of men have need of a commodity and desire to possess it, whereas the available supply of it is less, by so much is it more likeky to be estimated and sold at a higher price" (Gordon, p. 232). Gordon writes about Navarus that "He was an opponent of a system of stationary price fixation, arguing that when the goods were abundant, it was quite unnecessary and that when they were scarce, the system might do the welfare of the community more harm than good . . . A new emphasis was lent to the operation of supply determinants and the idea of "a market' was brought into sharper focus" (Gordon, p. 239). According to Gordon, Molina explained, "If, for example goods are supplied at retail in small quantities, they will command a higher unit price than in bulk. He is the first among scholastics to use the word competition" (Gordon;

p.240). And about the Belgian Jesuit, Lessius, Gordon writes, "Not only variation in supply conditions, but a wide range of other forces, quite properly, influence the making of prices. Among the factors he lists as relevant are following . . . the goods themselves, and their abundance or scarcity; the need for them and their usefulness; the sellers and their labour, expenses, risks suffered in obtaining the goods in transporting and storing them; the manner of the sale, whether offered freely, or on demand; the consumers, and whether there are few or many, and whether money is plentiful or scarce" (Gordon, p.269).

Conclusion

It is clear from the above that until the mid-eighteenth century, no Western author could present an analysis of demand and supply better than Ibn Taimiyah did in the 13th–14th century. Only Leonard Lessius added a few important variables affecting prices which are not found explicitly in writings of Ibn Taimiyah, such as cost of production and the risks suffered in obtaining the goods, and transporting and storing them, etc. Ibn Taimiyah also discussed different forms of imperfection in the market and advocated a detailed policy of price control where market forces were not allowed to work. We have already examined it elsewhere (Islahi, pp.79–90).

Notes

* The author is highly indebted to Prof. M. N. Siddiqi, Dr. M. Anas Zarqa and two anonymous referees for their substantial comments on earlier drafts of this paper.

1 The Arabic text of this as well as the subsequent quotations from Ibn Taimiyah are reproduced in the Appendix, numbered in the sequence they appear in the text.
2 For an explanation, see what follows the quotation.
3 Known for his book 'Discourse of Trade' (1690).

Appendix: Arabic texts

(١) "إن الغلاء والرخص لا تنحصر أسبابه في ظلم بعض بل قد يكون سببه قلة ما يخلق. أو يجلب من ذلك المال المطلوب، فإذا كثرت الرغبات في الشيء وقل المرغوب فيه: ارتفع سعره، فإذا كثر وقلت الرغبات فيه انخفض سعره. والقلة والكثرة قد لا تكون بسبب من العباد وقد تكون بسبب لا ظلم فيه، وقد تكون بسبب فيه ظلم. والله تعالى يجعل الرغبات في القلوب".

(ابن تيمية: مجموع فتاوى شيخ الإسلام أحمد بن تيمية، الرياض، مطابع الرياض ١٣٨١ المجلد٨، ص ٥٢٣).

(٢) " فإذا كان الناس يبيعون سلعهم على الوجه المعروف من غير ظلم منهم وقد ارتفع السعر إما لقلة الشيء وإما لكثرة الخلق فهذا إلى الله ".

(ابن تيمية: الحسبة في الإسلام، تحقيق عزام، س. قاهرة، دار الشعوب ١٩٧٦م).

(٣) " قال أبو الوليد ووجه ذلك أنه بهذا يتوصل إلى معرفة مصالح الباعة والمشترين. ويجعل للباعة في ذلك من الربح ما يقوم بهم ولا يكون فيه إجحاف بالناس وإذا سعر عليهم من غير رضى بما لا ربح لهم فيه ذلك إلى فساد الأسعار وإخفاء الأقوات وإتلاف أموال الناس". (ابن تيمية: الحسبة، ص ٤١).

(٤) "فرغبة الناس كثيرة الاختلاف والتنوع، فإنها تختلف بكثرة المطلوب وقلته. فعند قلته يرغب فيه مالا يرغب فيه عند الكثرة. وبكثرة الطلاب وقلتهم، فإنما كثر طالبوه يرتفع ثمنه، بخلاف ما قل طالبوه. وبحسب قلة الحاجة وكثرتها وقوتها وضعفها، فعند كثرة الحاجة وقوتها ترتفع القيمة مالا ترتفع عند قلتها وضعفها وبحسب المعاوض. فإن كان مليًا، دينًا: يرغب في معاوضته بالثمن القليل، الذي لا يبذل بمثله لمن يظن عجزه أو مطله أو جحده.

وبحسب العوض فقد يرخص فيه إذا كان بنقد رائج مالا يرخص فيه إذا كان بنقد آخر دونه في الرواج: كالدراهم، والدنانير بدمشق في هذه الأوقات، فإن المعاوضة بالدراهم هو المعتاد.

وذلك أن المطلوب من العقود هو التقابض من الطرفين، فإذا كان الباذل قادرًا على التسليم، موفيًا بالعهد، كان حصول المقصود بالعقد معه؛ بخلاف ما إذا لم يكن تام القدرة أو تام الوفاء. ومراتب القدرة والوفاء تختلف.

وهذا يكون في البائع وفي المشتري، وفي المؤجر، والمستأجر، والناكح والمنكوحة، فإن المبيع قد

يكون حاضرًا، وقد يكون غائبًا، فسعر الحاضر أقل من سعر الغائب، وكذلك المشتري قد يكون

قادرًا في الحال على الأداء، لأن معه مالاً، وقد لا يكون معه لكنه يريد أن يقترض أو يبيع السلعة.

فالثمن مع الأول أخف.

وكذلك المؤجر قد يكون قادرًا على تسليم المنفعة المستحقة بالعقد بحيث يستوفيها المستأجر

بلا كلفة، وقد لا يتمكن المستأجر من استيفاء المنفعة إلا بكلفة؛ وقد لا يتمكن المستأجر من استيفاء

المنفعة إلا بكلفة؛ كالقرى التي يتنابها الظلمة من ذي سلطان أو لصوص؛ أو تنتابها السباع، فليست

قيمتها كقيمة الأرض التي لا تحتاج إلى ذلك".

(ابن تيمية: مجموع فتاوى في الإسلام ابن تيمية، الرياض، ١٣٨٣ ، مجلد٢٩، ص٥٢٣- ٥٢٤).

(٥) "وإذا قلت وعزت غلت أثمانها، وأما إذا كان البلد قريب المسافة والطريق سابل بالأمن

حينئذ يكثر ناقلوها فتكثر وترخص". (ابن خلدون، المقدمة، دار الفكر، ص٣١٤).

(٦) "ولهذا ينبغي للسلطان أن يضرب لهم فلوسًا تكون بقيمة العدل في معاملاتهم؛ من غير

ظلم لهم. ولا يتجر ذو السلطان في الفلوس أصلاً؛ بأن يشتري نحاسًا فيضر به فيتجر فيه".

(ابن تيمية: مجموع فتاوى شيخ الإسلام أحمد بن تيمية، مجلد رقم ٢٩، ص ٤٦٩).

References

Abu Yusuf, *Kitab al Kharai*, Beirut, Dar al Ma'rifah, 1979.

Gordon, B., *Economic Analysis Before Adam Smith*, London, Lewes Reprint Ltd., 1979.

Ibn Khaldun, *al Muqaddimah*, Beirut, Dar al Fikr, n.d.

Ibn, Taimiyah, *Majmu' Fatawa Shaikh al Islam Ahmad b. Taimiyah*, Riyadh, al Riyadh Press, vol. **8**, 1381; vol. **29**, 1383.

——, *Al Hisbah fi'l Islam*, ed. Azzam, S., Cairo, Dar al Sha'b, 1976.

Islahi, A. A., *Economic Views of Ibn Taimiyah*, Aligarh Muslim University (Ph.D. Thesis), 1980, unpublished.

Kahf, Monzer, 'Economic Views of Ibn Taimeyah' in *Universal Message*, Karachi, vol. **4**, No. **2**. July 1982; vol. **4**, No. **3**, August 1982, first published in al *Ittihad*, Plainfield, Indiana, 1977.

al Maqrizi, Taqiuddin, Ahmad b. Ali, *Kitab al Sulak Ii Ma'rifat al Duwal Wal Muluk*, ed. Ziadeh, M. M., Cairo, Lajnah, al Talif Wa'I Tarjamah, 1956.

al Mubarak, Muhammad, *Ara' Ibn Taimiyah fi'l Dawlah wa mada Tadakhkhuliha fi'l Majal al Iqtisadi*, Beirut, Dal al Fikr, 1970.

al Qalaqshandi, Abul Abbas Ahmad b. Ali, *Subh al A'sha*, Cairo, Dar al Kutub al Khudaiwiyah, 1913.

Schumpeter, J. A. *History of Economic Analysis*, London, George Allen and Unwin Ltd., 1972.

Siddiqi, M. N., 'Abu Yusuf ka Ma'ashi Fikr' (Urdu) in *Fikr-o-Nazar*, Aligarh, vol. **5**, No. **1**, January, 1964, pp.79–80, 85–87.

Speigel, H. W., *The Growth of Economic Thought*, New Jersey, Prentice Hall Inc., 1971.

24

THE FINANCIAL REFORMS OF THE CALIPH AL-MUʿTAḌID (279–89/892–901)

Ahmad Al-Hasan

Source: *Journal of Islamic Studies*, 18:1 (2007), 1–13.

Introduction

This study examines a historical phenomenon during the caliphate of al-Muʿtaḍid bi-llāh Aḥmad b. Ṭalḥa (r. 279–89/892–901), namely the remarkable finance-generating policies of his administration. When al-Muʿtaḍid succeeded to the caliphate, the State Treasury (*bayt al-māl*)[1] was virtually empty apart from some few dirhams,[2] on account of the circumstances faced by and the actions of his predecessor, caliph al-Muʿtamid ʿalā-llāh Aḥmad b. al-Mutawakkil (r. 259–79/869–92). First, there had been the internal revolts, especially the Zanj rebellion, which lasted some fifteen years, from 255/868 to 270/883.[3] Second, some of the major Islamic territories had seceded, notably Egypt and al-Shām, controlled by the Tulunids (254–92/868–96),[4] and Persia, governed by the Saffarids (254–87/867–900).[5] The secession of these regions naturally terminated the flow of revenues from them to the ʿAbbasids' capital in Baghdad, especially the land taxes, which were the state's main source of financial support at that time.[6] The third factor was the irresponsible behaviour of the caliph's vizier, Ismāʿīl b. Bulbul (d. 279/892), who squandered state funds by distributing them among his own companions and supporters.[7]

During the reign of al-Muʿtaḍid, various new measures and procedures were adopted to avoid financial shortfalls and increase state funds; these were so successful that by the end of his caliphate there were more than nine million dinars[8] of ready money in the State Treasury.[9]

The present study examines the measures and procedures adopted in order to bring about this sound financial footing and does so under the successive headings of political, financial and economic, and administrative measures.

1 Political measures

Undoubtedly, the caliph, on account of his position of authority over all state affairs, was able to play a leading role in influencing the state's financial health, positively or negatively.[10] Caliph Al-Muʿtaḍid brought a number of good qualities to the role of head of state—political astuteness, a strong personality, and wide military experience.[11] These qualities had a positive effect in improving the state's finances and the condition of the State Treasury generally.

Al-Muʿtaḍid's authority manifested itself in different aspects of state management. His control of the army was unchallenged so that the period of his reign did not witness any revolt or disorder. This was a huge achievement, since during many periods of political instability and financial adversity the army had caused serious problems for the caliphs and, on occasions, even assassinated caliphs: for example, before al-Muʿtaḍid's caliphate—during the reigns of al-Mustaʿīn bi-llāh Aḥmad b. al-Muʿtaṣim (248–52/862–66),[12] al-Muʿtazz bi-llāh Muḥammad b. al-Mutawakkil (252–55/866–68),[13] and al-Muhtadī bi-llāh Muḥammad b. al-Wāthiq (255–56/868–69),[14]—and after it—during the reigns of al-Muqtadir bi-llāh Jaʿfar b. al-Muʿtaḍid (295–320/907–32)[15] and al-Qāhir bi-llāh Muḥammad b. al-Muʿtaḍid (320–22/932–34).[16] As al-Muʿtaḍid was able to control the army and keep it obedient to himself, he could use it as his tool to further his caliphal aims—among them the restoration to his rule of a number of regions, such as Rayy,[17] ʿAmid,[18] Mārdīn,[19] and Mawṣil (Mosul).[20] The recovery of these regions added new income, in the form of taxes, to the State Treasury. The wars between the caliph's army and the seceders led to the accumulation of large quantities of spoils.[21] However, al-Muʿtaḍid had sufficient wisdom to refrain from wars against those with strong military support, such as the Tulunids in Egypt and al-Shām, and the Saffarids in Persia. The reasoning behind this was that there could be no guarantee of a final victory and, in any case, the seceders posed no direct threat to the central government—rather, they acknowledged the ʿAbbasid caliphate.[22] In addition, any war against them would have necessitated vast sums of money beyond the capacity of the caliph to raise, at a time when funds were required for far more pressing needs.[23] Caliph al-Muʿtaḍid had no doubt learnt this wisdom in earlier days when he was one of the prominent leaders during the war against the Zanj revolt (255–70/868–83).[24] He had learnt the diplomacy of blending flexibility with firmness.[25]

Indeed, the exercise of this policy instilled a sense of fear into the caliph's possible enemies, so that the Tulunids sent him large sums in tribute, amounting to 450,000 dinars annually, and the provinces of Qinnasrīn and al-ʿAwāṣim were returned to the caliph's rule[26] in exchange for acknowledgment by al-Muʿtaḍid of their right to govern the other provinces that they occupied.[27] In similar manner, and for a like purpose, the Saffarids sent four million dirhams.[28] Later, when they were defeated by the Samanids, a family still loyal to the 'Abbasids and governing the territories of Māwarā' al-Nahr,[29] the whole land of Persia came under the control of the 'Abbasids and al-Mu'taḍid sent his tax-collectors into these lands.[30]

The acquisition of these lands and the revenue raised from them were in fact the chief means of improving the situation of the central Treasury. Moreover, the evident strength of the caliph and his acknowledged control over the army led, in general, to improved political stability, which had various positive financial results. The central Islamic state did not lose any more territories, which meant that there was both no loss of income and an overall improvement in economic conditions in the Islamic state so that (as al-Mas'ūdī notes) price levels were low at this time.[31] Low prices benefited both the people and the government. The government benefited because low prices held down demands for higher wages among the army and made government projects less costly to finance. The people benefited because, in this period of stability and security, traders felt safe in doing business, and so markets were generally brisk. This again benefited the government as additional taxes could be levied on the shops.[32]

2 Financial and economic measures

During al-Mu'taḍid's reign, the government took many financial and economic measures to increase the state's income. The first concern was with financial resources and, primarily, the income from taxation on agricultural lands, which, in particular the land tax (kharāj),[33] formed the most important source of revenue for the State Treasury. Early in his reign, in 282/895, al-Mu'taḍid introduced a significant modification, known as al-Nayrūz al-mu'taḍadī, in the system of land taxation by delaying the date on which payment was due, normally 11th April, until the time when the crops ripened, for which the date was fixed to 17th June every year.[34] In this way, he solved the problem people had of paying the tax just when they were without money, when the harvesting season was still months away. This had, in fact, been a difficulty up to the time of al-Mu'taḍid's accession[35] and hindered the government in collecting the land tax from the people, who, to save themselves from the hardship, sometimes deceived government officials as to the actual sum due, or simply delayed payment. Al-Mu'taḍid's reform benefited both parties—the people, who were enabled to pay the land tax at a time when they had the money, and the government, which was able to collect the tax on a regular basis at the full value.

A second measure introduced by al-Mu'taḍid was to lend money for the purchase of seeds and cattle, as a form of assistance enabling the people to improve their agriculture and husbandry, and to exploit their lands in the best way.[36] This measure again benefited the government, albeit indirectly, as it was later able to collect more land tax in view of the improved yields.

Further evidence of al-Muʿtaḍid's concern to maintain a steady income from agricultural lands is reflected in his policy after quelling internal revolts. So, for example, when the caliphal army defeated the Carmathians[37] in battle, killing many of them, the army did not pursue the beaten foe, in order (as al-Ṭabarī reports) to save the Sawād lands[38] from adverse effects since the Carmathians were peasant workers on those lands.[39]

The ʿAbbasid government was also concerned not to transfer the tenancy of those lands, since they brought in a steady income to the Treasury.[40]

The ʿAbbasid state also owned lands known as 'the Sultanic Lands' (ḍiyāʿ al-sulṭāniyya), which produced a large revenue for its Treasury. So, for example, it is reported that the total income of the Sultanic Lands in the time of al-Muʿtaḍid and his son, al-Muqtafī bi-llāh ʿAlī b. al-Muʿtaḍid, in addition to the revenue from the Sawād, the land of al-Ahwāz, and the lands situated to the east and west of Baghdad, amounted to 46,830,000 dinars.[41] There were, in addition, the tax revenues on agricultural lands known as iqṭāʿ[42] and ījār.[43]

Recognizing the importance of income from agricultural lands, the government paid particular attention to the means of their irrigation in order to ensure that they had sufficient water to sustain yields. Their improvements in irrigation systems again benefited both the people and the government. So, for example, Caliph al-Muʿtaḍid gave orders for the removal of stones blocking flow at the mouth of the River Dujayl, so that the water might flow freely to the agricultural lands.[44] He also paid out 1,300 dinars to close up one outflow (bathq).[45] Moreover, the government was particularly concerned to resolve disputes over water rights, such as that between the people of the Bādūrayā[46] and those of the Sāriyah regions. The importance attached by Caliph al-Muʿtaḍid to a proper resolution of this problem was reflected in his sending as negotiators some of his highest officers of state, including the vizier, al-Qāsim b. ʿUbayd Allāh (d. 291/903); the army commander, Badr (d. 289/901); and the secretary of state, Abū l-ʿAbbās Aḥmad b. Muḥammad b. al-Furāt (d. 291/903). They listened to both sides of the dispute before reporting to the caliph, who finally gave his decision as to the correct resolution of the problem.[47]

In fact, these various concerns for the prosperity of agriculture led ultimately to a good income from the lands. The clearest example of this is the fact that the income from the land tax on the Sawād lands of Iraq rose to 28,000,000 dirhams, a level which had not been experienced since the caliphate of ʿUmar b. al-Khaṭṭāb (13–23/634–643).[48]

As a general procedure to counter shortfalls in the State Treasury, al-Muʿtaḍid exercised careful economy to minimize expenses.[49] Thus, he limited the quantities of food consumed by his servants and court retinue and by so doing saved a large amount of money.[50] Also, he reduced the work days of his governors from six to five per week and thereby managed to save 4,770 dinars annually.[51] In addition, he extended the periods for salary payments to some of his governors and required them to pay for the fodder for their riding animals out of their own salaries, again saving thousands of dinars.[52] Al-Muʿtaḍid also found other ways of saving costs, as, for instance, when he required the landlords who were to benefit from irrigation works on the River Dujayl to cover the costs, amounting to around 4,000 dinars.[53]

He took pains, in addition, to ensure that government supplies were obtained at their actual prices and in this way too saved money for the Treasury. For example, when he was with his army engaged in warfare at the city of Dīnawar[54] and the prices rose to very high levels, he quickly left that place because, as reported, he was in need of supplies but the prices were too high in the immediate neighbourhood.[55] Similarly, when a thief stole a large army payroll from the house of the army paymaster (ṣāḥib ʿaṭāʾ al-jaysh), the caliph personally investigated the case, with great skill and determination, until he had recovered the official funds from the thief.[56]

Among the sources of additional income for the Treasury were the confiscations (al-muṣādarāt). The confiscation policy implemented by al-Muʿtaḍid was not like that, for example, employed in the time of Caliph al-Muqtadir bi-llāh,[57] but was rather used as a system of punishment for offences against state authority. It was used, for example, against the vizier of Caliph al-Muʿtamid ʿalā-llāh, Ismāʿīl b. Bulbul, together with some of his supporters, who exhausted the State Treasury.[58] Aḥmad b. al-Ṭayyib was also punished by the confiscation of 50,000 dinars for his part in trying to instigate a dispute between al-Muʿtaḍid and some nobles.[59]

3 Administrative measures

A number of al-Muʿtaḍid's measures were particularly concerned to regulate financial administration and thereby reinvigorate the State Treasury. Soon after al-Muʿtaḍid succeeded to the caliphate, his government made an inventory of needs and expenses. Then al-Muʿtaḍid ordered the vizier, Abū l-Qāsim ʿUbayd Allāh b. Sulaymān (d. 288/900), to fit expenditure to actual income.[60] The government also listed its requirements in detail and the exact cost of each requirement.[61] This accurate accounting enabled officials to know the exact amount of necessary expenses and to keep them within that limit. Practically, it helped achieve a balanced budget and avoid the shortfall in funding that commonly occurred when expenditure exceeded income.

Another administrative procedure was to take from tax-collectors a guarantee (ḍamān), allowing them to collect land taxes from a region provided they guaranteed to pay the government annually a pre-agreed sum, regardless of the actual amount collected.[62] During the caliphate of al-Muʿtaḍid, the ḍamān performed an important function and came to be used in a variety of ways. At the beginning of his caliphate, the Treasury was empty and the government desperately needed to achieve financial solvency so that all the necessities—particularly the salaries of army personnel—could be paid and instability in the state avoided. Therefore, the government made an agreement, in the form of a *ḍamān*, with a businessman called Aḥmad b. Muḥammad al-Ṭā'ī, who was to obtain money from certain regions and pay the government a specific sum of money in advance.[63] This and other similar arrangements enabled the government to secure a continuous inflow of cash, at the same reducing the administrative responsibility of the government towards the lands in its possession.

In fact, the main financial administration was done by the secretary of state, Abū l-'Abbās Aḥmad b. Muḥammad b. al-Furāt, who had overall responsibility for the financial affairs of the state. He was highly qualified in financial matters and accounting (*ḥisāb*), and had an extensive knowledge of the state's agricultural lands and their taxes.[64] These qualifications led to his being appointed to financial responsibility for the state in the early days of al-Mu'taḍid's caliphate (from 279/892).[65] He was well trusted, not only by the caliph himself,[66] but also by the army commander, Badr,[67] and the vizier, 'Ubayd Allāh b. Sulaymān.[68] So, as his opinions in financial matters were held in high regard, he was given wide authority in financial affairs to serve the State Treasury.[69] Moreover, Abū l-'Abbās was firmly convinced of the need for the government to hold ready money in hand so as to secure political stability, and of the severe results if it were not available. He himself asserted that political dominance depended on money, as soldiers would cease to listen and obey if they were not paid their dues. Without financial backing, there would be a failure in political governance, bloodshed, insecurity along the roads, and a general increase in prohibited activities.[70] He also felt that he had primary responsibility for the state's finances,[71] a view which inspired him to work for the increase of state income. The expertise of Abū l-'Abbās b. al-Furāt was apparent from the early days of al-Mu'taḍid's caliphate, when Abū l-'Abbās, with his brother Abū al-Ḥasan 'Alī b. Muḥammad, persuaded Aḥmad al-Ṭā'ī to place some areas of Iraq under the *ḍamān* system. This was to prove the means of resolving the current financial straits, and to have himself made responsible for the state's financial affairs.[72]

The policy of Abū l-'Abbās stood on four main principles. First, he used only qualified persons to manage financial affairs. The most prominent of these were Abū l-Ḥasan 'Alī b. Aḥmad b. al-Furāt (d. 312/924),[73] Muḥammad b. Dāwūd b. al-Jarrāḥ (d. 296/909),[74] and 'Alī b. 'Īsā b. Dāwūd b. al-Jarrāḥ (d. 334/946).[75]

Second, the financial administration was greatly improved by Abū l-'Abbās establishing a new central department, the *Dīwān al-Dār*, under the responsibility of Abū l-Ḥasan b. al-Furāt.[76] This *Dīwān* was later divided into two sections, the *Dīwān al-mashriq* (the office for the east), under the responsibility of Muḥammad b. Dāwūd b. al-Jarrāḥ,[77] and the *Dīwān al-maghrib* (the office for the west), under the responsibility of 'Alī b. 'Īsā b. Dāwūd b. al-Jarrāḥ.[78]

Third, Abū l-'Abbās was at pains to exercise direct supervision and keep an accurate account of all matters, whether relating to work or employees.[79] This gave him reliable information about his office, enabling him to issue clear directives and advice based on real facts and his own experience. It also led to a reform of financial administration and prevented errors, abuses, and underhand dealings. Abū l-'Abbās was able to discover cases of fraudulent reduction of the amount of land tax due from some people—for instance, in the case of the Narsī family, who were responsible for some territories beyond the Euphrates and owned agricultural lands there. They reduced the tax they were liable to pay, as recorded in the register. Abū al-'Abbās spotted this act of exploitation and forced the Narsī family to repay the full amount held back from the government, a sum amounting to 300,000 dinars.[80] On another occasion, when one of the landlords bribed a government employee to reduce his land tax, the direct supervision of Abū al-'Abbās enabled him to discover the fraud and to impose a severe punishment on the guilty person.[81] Thus, the close supervision of fiscal affairs saved the government from major financial losses and, at the same time, deterred anybody from emulating the kinds of fraud that had been discovered and punished.

Fourth, Abū l-'Abbās sought to limit the intervention of those who had more power than himself in the government and might have a bad influence in setting the government budget. So, when Caliph al-Mu'taḍid wanted to requisition a plot of land to be used as an open square (maydān) opposite his palace, Abū l-'Abbās did not immediately execute this order passed to him by the vizier, but approached the caliph directly about the matter. He explained to him that this plot of land was worth 200,000 dinars as agricultural land and could produce 200,000 dirhams of revenue for the State Treasury annually. Following this discussion, the caliph changed his mind and chose an alternative site.[82] Similarly, instead of implementing the instruction of Badr, the army commander, to distribute agricultural lands to his companions, Abū l-'Abbās went to meet Badr and persuaded him of the dangerous consequences of this action, which would produce a shortage of funds in the Stare Treasury. As a result, Badr countermanded the order he had given.[83] All of these examples illustrate Abū l-'Abbās' readiness to reason with state officials in order to save money for the State Treasury by limiting unnecessary expenditure.

In conclusion, therefore, it may be stated that budgetary solvency was regained under al-Mu'taḍid not by imposing new charges on the people—not by increasing the rates of existing taxes, nor by introducing new ones—rather, as we have seen, al-Mu'taḍid treated the people with consideration.[84] All the political, financial, and administrative procedures that we have described combined to increase income and achieve budgetary solvency. The secret of this success was the harmony that existed between the leading officials in the government of Caliph al-Mu'taḍid. This is reported by the most experienced recorders of the state's dīwāns, who state that at any time a meeting might be held between the caliph (al-Muʿtaḍid), the vizier (Abū l-Qāsim ʿUbayd Allāh b. Sulaymān), a *dīwān*-writer (Abū l-ʿAbbās b. al-Furāt), and the army commander (Badr), so that the management of these four was continuous, affairs were well organized, building projects were always progressing, and there were no cash-flow problems. As a result, after all expenditures had been met, there remained in the State Treasury a surplus of no less than nine million dinars of ready money.[85]

Notes

1 For details about *bayt al-māl*, see ʿAlī b. Muḥammad al-Māwardī, *al-Aḥkām al-sulṭāniyyab wa-l-walāyat al-dīniyyah* (Cairo: Dār al-Fikr, 1973), 213–15; Cl. Cahen, 'Bayt al-māl', *EI²* art. (i. 1131–7); Khawlah al-Dujayfī, *Bayt al-māl* (Baghdad: Wizārat al-Awqāf, 1976).

2 Hilāl b. al-Muḥassin, *al-Ṣābī, Tuḥfat al-umarāʾ fī taʾrīkh al-wuzarāʾ* (Cairo: Dār Iḥyāʾ al-Kutub al-ʿArabiyyah, 1958), 13; M. A. Shaban, *Islamic History: A New Interpretation, 750–1055/132–448* (Cambridge: Cambridge University Press, 1986), 119.

3 Muḥammad b. Jarīr al-Ṭabarī, *Taʾrīkh al-rusul wa-l-muluk* (Beirut: Dār Suwaydan, n.d.), ix. 410 f., 477 f., 504 f., 520 f., 577, 633; Abū l-Ḥasan ʿAlī b. al-Ḥasan al-Masʿūdī, *Murūj al-dhahab* (Beirut: Dār al-Maʿrifa, 1982), iv. 194 f., 207 f.

4 Al-Masʿūdī, *Murūj*, iv. 382 f. For details about the Tulunids, see H. A. R. Gibb, 'Ṭulūnids', *EIʾ* art. (viii. 834–6); Ḥasan Ibrāhīm Ḥasan, *Taʾrīkh al-Islām*, (Beirut: Dār Iḥyāʾ al-Turāth, 1964), iii. 126 f.

5 Al-Ṭabarī, *Taʾrīkh*, ix. 382–6, 476, 507, 516–20, 544 f., x. 76 f.; Ḥasan, *Taʾrīkh*, iii. 65–9; C. E. Bosworth, 'Ṣaffārids', *EI²* art. (viii. 795–8).

6 See Muḥammad al-Rayyis, *al-Kharaj wa-l-nuẓum al-māliyya*, (Cairo: Dār al-Anṣār, 1977), 3 f., 85 f., 369 f.

7 Al-Masʿūdī, *Murūj*, iv. 228; al-Ṣābī, *Tuḥfat al-umarāʾ*, 13.

8 Ibid, 209; al-Masʿūdī, *Murūj*, iv. 232.

9 Muḥammad b. Yaḥyā al-Ṣūlī, *Akhbār al-raḍī li-llāh wa-l-muttaqī li-llāh min kitāb al-Awrāq* (Beirut: Dār al-Masīra, 1979), 115; Abū l-Faraj ʿAbd al-Raḥmān b. al Jawzī, *al-Muntaẓam fī tawārikh al-muluk wa-l-umam* (Beirut: Dār al-Fikr, 1995), vii. 340. Other sources mention different sums: forty million dirhams (al-Masʿūdī, *Murūj*, iv. 232); gold to the value of ten million dinars (Ibn al-Jawzī, *al-Muntaẓam*, vii. 340); more than ten million [units of measure unspecified] (Ismāʿīl b. Kathīr, *al-Bidāya wa-l-nihāya* (Beirut: Dār al-Fikr, 1996), ix. 94).

10 By way of illustrating the negative effect of caliphal influence on the state's economic health, we may cite al-Muqtadir bi-llāh Jaʿfar b. al-Muʿtaḍid, who managed to lose the seventy million dinars during his reign that had been accumulated in the State Treasury by the beginning of his caliphate. See Aḥmad b. Muḥammad b. Miskawayh, *Tajārib al-umam* (Baghdad: Maktabat al-Muthannā, 1914), i. 238.

11 Al-Ṣūlī, *Akhbār* (the sequel to *Shadharāt min kutub mafqūda*), 429 f.; al-Masʿūdī, *Murūj*, iv. 232; Ibn al-Jawzī, *al-Muntaẓam*, vii. 274, 254; Hugh Kennedy, 'al-Muʿtaḍid billāh', *EI²* art. (vii. 760).

12 Al-Masʿūdī, *Murūj*, iv. 144, 162–5.

13 Ibid, 166, 177 f.

14 Ibid, 182, 184 f.

15 Ibn al-Jawzī, *al-Muntaẓam*, viii. 119.

16 Ibid, 125 f., 141 f.

17 Al-Ṭabarī, *Taʾrīkh*, x. 36f.

18 Ibid, 70. 'Amid was considered as the greatest city in Diyār Bakr (Yāqūt al-Hamawī, *Muʿjam al-buldān*, (Beirut: Dār Ṣādir, 1986), i. 56.

19 Al-Ṭabarī, *Taʾrīkh*, x. 31, 39.

20 Ibid, 37 f.; ʿAlī b. ʿAbd al-Karīm b. al-Athīr, *al-Kāmil fī l-taʾrīkh* (Beirut: Dār Ṣādir, 1965), vii. 466 f.; al-Masʿūdī states more generally that the west and east were opened for him and that he defeated most of his opponents (*Murūj*, iv. 232).

21 Al-Ṭabarī, *Taʾrīkh*, x. 38, 41; Ibn al-Jawzī, *al-Muntaẓam*, vii. 278. For details on the government policies and military acitivites of Caliph al-Muʿtaḍid, see Shaban, *Islamic History*, 124 f.; H. Bowen, *The Life and Times of ʿAlī b. ʿĪsā* (Cambridge: Cambridge University Press, 1928), 44 f.

22 H. Kennedy, *The Prophet and the Age of the Caliphs* (London: Longman, 1980), 183.

23 Some of the pressing needs are recorded in al-Ṣābī, *Tuḥfat al-umarāʾ*, 15–26.

24 Al-Ṭabarī, *Taʾrīkh*, ix. 557–70, 603, 606, 625, 631 f., 637–41, 646, 649 f.

25 Kennedy, *The Prophet*, 183; id. ʿal-Muʿtaḍid billāh', *EI²*, art. vii. 760).

26 Al-Ṭabarī, *Taʾrīkh*, x. 70.

27 Ibid.

28 Ibid, 30, 71; al-Masʿūdī, iv. 237; Shaban, *Islamic History*, 119.

29 On the Samanids, see C. E. Bosworth and Y. Crowe, 'Sāmānids', *EI²* art. (viii. 1025–31).

30 Al-Ṭabarī, *Taʾrīkh*, x. 77, 84; Ibn al-Jawzī, *al-Muntaẓam*, vii. 321, 329.

31 Al-Masʿūdī, *Murūj*, iv. 232, Fārūq ʿUmar, *al-Khilāfah al-ʿAbbāsiyya fī ʿaṣr al-fawḍa al-ʿaskariyya* (247–334/861–946) (ʿAmmān: Dār al-Shurūq, 1998), 49.

32 There were taxes on the markets of Baghdad from the early years of the ʿAbbasid dynasty. See e.g. Aḥmad b. Wāḍiḥ al-Yaʿqūbī, *Taʾrīkh al-Yaʿqūbī* (Beirut: Dār Bayrūt, 1960) ii. 399. It seems almost certain that these taxes continued as they were an acknowledged right of the state during ʿAbbasid times.

33 The word *kharāj* is used by al-Māwardī to denote land tax (*Aḥkām*, 146 f.; see also Cl. Cahen, art. 'Kharādj', *EI²* art. (iv. 1030); al-Khwārizmī uses it to mean land taken under treaty, distinguished from *fayʾ*, the term for land got through conquest (Muḥammad b. Aḥmad b. Yūsuf al-Khwārizmī, *Mafātiḥ al-ʿulūm* (Cairo: Maktabat al-Kulliyyat al-Azhariyyah, 1981), 39; see also Qudāmah b. Jaʿfar, *al-Kharāj wa-ṣināʿ at al-kitāba*, (Cairo: Dār al-Rashīd, 1981), 204. The word *kharāj* is also used in a number of other senses, such as 'wages' (i.e. as equivalent to *ajr* or *ʿaṭāʾ*) and poll-tax (*jizya*). See e.g. Abū Yūsuf Yaʿqūb b. Ibrāhīm, *Kitāb al-Kharāj* (Beirut: Dār al-Maʿrifa, 1979), 23; and within the same publication: Yaḥyā b. Ādam, *al-Kharāj*, 22 f., and Ibn Rajab al-Ḥanbalī, *al-Istikhrāj li-aḥkām al-kharāj*, 4 f.

34 Al-Ṭabarī, *Taʾrīkh*, x. 39 (al-Ṭabarī adds in explanation that the caliph wished to make payment of this tax easier for his people), ʿAbd al-ʿAzīz al-Dūrī *Taʾrīkh al-ʿIrāq al-iqtiṣādī fī l-qarn al-rābiʿ al-hijrī* (Beirut: Markaz Dirāsat al-Waḥda al-ʿArabiyya, 1995), 59; Adam Mez, *al-Ḥaḍāra al-Islāmiyya fī l-qarn al-rābiʿ al-hijrī* (Beirut: Dār al-Kitāb al-ʿArabī, 1969), 208; Shaban, *Islamic History*, 119.

35 Al-Ḥasan b. ʿAbd Allāh al-ʿAskarī *al-Awāʾil* (Beirut: Dār al-Kutub al-Islāmiyya, 1987), 218–20; Aḥmad b. ʿAlī al-Maqrīzī, *al-Mawāʾiz wa-l-Iʿtibār bi-dhikr al-khiṭaṭwa-l-āthār*, (Cairo: Maktabat al-Thaqāfa al-dīniyya, n.d., 273–5; al-Dūrī, *Ṭāʾrīkh*, 60 f.; Mez, *al-Ḥaḍāra*, i. 208.

36 Al-Muḥassin b. ʿAlī al-Tanukhī, *Nishwār al-muḥāḍara wa-akhbār al-mudhākara*, (Damascus: al-Majmaʿ al-ʿIlmī al-ʿArabī, 1930) viii. 66; Fārūq, *al-Khilāfa*, 49; al-Dūrī, *Taʾrīkh*, 61; al-Dujaylī, *Bayt al-māl*, 156.

37 On the Carmathians, see W. Madelung, 'Karmaṭī', *EI²* art. (iv. 660–5).

38 A region in Iraq known as the Sawād, meaning 'the black', perhaps on account of the shade of its date palms and other vegetation. It stretches from Ḥadītha

(near Mawṣil) as far as ʿAbbādān, along a strip of land between al-ʿUdhayb (near Qadisiyyah) and Ḥulwān. See Yāqūt, *Muʿjam*, iii. 272.

39 Al-Ṭabarī, *Taʾrīkh*, x. 82.

40 Al-Ṣābī, *Tuḥfat al-umarāʾ*, 280 f.

41 Ibn Miskawayh, *Tajārib*, i. 240 f.; al-Dujaylī, *Bayt al-māl*, 197.

42 Al-Ṣābī, *Tuḥfat al-umarāʾ*, 209. Al-Khwārizmī explains the term *iqṭāʾ* as referring to land given as a gift of property by the ruler (*Mafātīḥ*, 40). See further Cl. Cahen, 'Iḳṭāʿ'', *EI²* art., iii. 1088–91; al-Dūrī, *Taʾrīkh*, 44–64.

43 Al-Ṣābī, *Tuḥfat al-umarāʾ*, 209. The *ījār* was a tax fief, i.e. a piece of land exempted from entry by tax-collectors, but whose owner had to pay to the government a specified sum of tax (al-Khwārizmī, *Mafātīḥ*, 40).

44 Al-Ṭabarī, *Taʾrīkh*, x. 46; Ibn al-Jawzī, *al-Muntaẓam*, vii. 490.

45 Al-Ṣābī, *Tuḥfat al-umarāʾ*, 184; al-Dujaylī, *Bayt al-māl*, 123.

46 A city situated on the west side of Baghdad. See Yāqūt, *Muʿjam*, i. 317.

47 Al-Ṣābī, *Tuḥfat al-umarāʾ*, 278–280; al-Dūrī, *Taʾrīkh*, 61; Bowen, *Life and Times of ʿAlī b. ʿĪsā*, 47 f.

48 Al-Ṣābī, *Tuḥfat al-umarāʾ*, 209; Muḥammad b. Aḥmad al-Maqdisī, *Aḥsan al-taqāsīm fī maʿrifat al-aqālīm*, (Beirut: Dār Ihyāʾ al-Turath al-ʿArabī, 1987), 118; al-Dujaylī, *Bayt al-māl*, 43.

49 Ibn al-Jawzī, *al-Muntaẓam*, vii. 260.

50 Al-Masʿūdī, *Murūj*, iv. 232.

51 Al-Ṣābī, *Tuḥfat al-umarāʾ*, 27; Shaban, *Islamic History*, 120; M. M. Ahsan, *Social Life under the Abbasids 170–289 AH, 786–902 AD* (London: Longman, 1979), 285.

52 Al-Ṣābī, *Tuḥfat al-umarāʾ*, 16, 19.

53 Al-Ṭabarī, *Taʾrīkh*, x. 46.

54 A city near to Qarmīsīn (Yāqūt, *Muʿjam*, ii. 545).

55 Ibid, 36 f.

56 Al-Masʿūdī, *Murūj*, iv. 248 f.

57 Ibn Miskawayh, *Tajārib*, i 239 f.; al-Dujaylī, *Bayt al-māl*, 194–9.

58 Al-Masʿūdī, *Murūj*, iv. 229; al-Ṣābī, *Tuḥfat al-umarāʾ*, 12.

59 Al-Masʿūdī, *Murūj*, iv. 259; al-Ṣūlī, *al-Awrāq*, 424 f.

60 Al-Ṣābī, *Tuḥfat al-umarāʾ*, 241. For details of the state's needs, see 15 f.

61 Ibid.

62 Al-Dujaylī, *Bayt al-māl*, 88.

63 Al-Ṣābī, *Tuḥfat al-umarāʾ*, 14 f.; Mez, *al-Ḥaḍāra*, i. 246; Shaban, *Islamic History*, 120 f.

64 Al-Ṣābī, *Tuḥfat al-umarāʾ*, 12, 191, 208.

65 Ibid, 12 f.; Bowen, *Life and Times of ʿAlī b. ʿĪsā*, 30 f.; D. Sourdel, 'Ibn al-Furāt', *EI²*.

66 Al-Ṣābī, *Tuḥfat al-umarāʾ*, 207 f.; Bowen, *Life and Times of ʿAlī b. ʿĪsā*, 31.

67 Al-Ṣābī, *Tuḥfat al-umarāʾ*, 20.

68 Ibid, 13 f.

69 Ibid, 200, 202 f., 241, 278, 290 f.

70 Ibid., 200.

71 Ibid.

72 Ibid, 13 f.

73 Ibid, 12 f., 286.; Mez, *al-Ḥaḍāra*, i. 181 f.; D. Sourdel, 'Ibn al-Furāt', *EI²* art. (iii. 767).

74 Al-Ṣābī, *Tuḥfat al-umarāʾ*, 286 f.; D. Sourdel, 'Ibn al-Djarrāḥ', *EI²* art. (iii. 750).

75 Al-Ṣābī, *Tuḥfat al-umarāʾ*, 286 f.: Mez, *al-Ḥaḍāra*, i. 185 f.; H. Bowen, "Alī ibn ʿĪsā', *EI²* art. (i. 386–8); Kennedy, *The Prophet*, 188 f.

76 Al-Ṣābī, *Tuḥfat al-umarāʾ*, 148; Bowen, *Life and Times of ʿAlī b. ʿĪsā*, 46. Sourdel, 'Ibn al-Djarrāḥ', *EI²* art. (iii. 750).

77 Al-Ṣābī, *Tuḥfat al-umarā'*, 148; Bowen, *Life and Times of 'Alī b. 'Īsā*, 46; id. 'Ibn al-Djarraḥ', 750.
78 Al-Ṣābī, *Tuḥfat al-umarā'*, 149; Bowen, *Life and Times of 'Alī b. 'Īsā*, 46; id. "Ali ibn 'Īsā', 386.
79 Al-Ṣābī, *Tuḥfat al-umarā'*, 205, 220.
80 Ibid, 191 f.
81 Ibid, 217–20.
82 Ibid, 280 f.
83 Ibid, 200.
84 Aḥmad b. 'Abd al-Wahhāb al-Nuwayrī, *Nihāyat al-Arab fī funūn al-adab*, (Cairo: al-Hay'a al-Miṣriyyah al-'Ārnma li-l-Kitāb, 1984), xxii. 359 (citing Thābit b. Qurra (d. 288/900)); Jalāl al-Dīn 'Abd al-Raḥmān al-Suyūṭī, *Ta'rīkh al-khulafā'*, (Beirut: Dār al-Jīl, 1988), 431, where al-Suyūṭī describes the situation of the people during the caliphate of al-Mu'taḍid as good, and states that they enjoyed security and welfare.
85 See note 8 above; also Bowen, *Life and Times of 'Alī b. 'Īsā*, 44.

25

THE CONTRIBUTION OF MUḤAMMAD BĀQIR AL-ṢADR TO CONTEMPORARY ISLAMIC ECONOMIC THOUGHT

Rodney Wilson

Source: *Journal of Islamic Studies*, 9:1 (1998), 46–59.

Bāqir al-Ṣadr had little contact with other leading contemporary writers and critics of Islamic economics. This was partly because he was a Shīʿī scholar living in comparative isolation in Najaf, whose activities were restricted by an oppressive regime. Unlike these other reformist writers, al-Ṣadr had no formal training in mainstream neo-classical economics, although he had a good knowledge of Marxist economics, the basic assumptions of which he rejected vehemently.

Apart from studies by Nejatullah Siddiqi[1] and Mohamed Aslam Haneef,[2] there has been little comparative work on contemporary Islamic economic thought. There would appear to be much scope for further work. Haneef looked at five authors—Muhammad Mannan, Nejatullah Siddiqi, Syed Naqvi, Monzer Kahf, Sayyid Taleghani—and Bāqir al-Ṣadr. This paper concentrates on al-Ṣadr, but draws some comparisons with the work of Umer Chapra, Nejatullah Siddiqi, and Syed Naqvi, in the case of the latter two drawing on more recent writings which were published after Haneef had completed his original study.[3]

How al-Ṣadr's thinking would have developed had he not been executed in 1980 under the orders of Saddam Hussein must be a matter of conjecture, but his economic writing has received an increasing amount of international attention since his death, initially from Hanna Batatu,[4] and more recently from Chibli Mallat.[5] His major work in this field, *Iqtiṣādunā: Our Economics*,[6] influenced to varying degrees later writings, notably Chapra's *Islam and the Economic Challenge*,[7] Naqvi's *Islam, Economics and Society*,[8] and Siddiqi's *The Role of the State in the Economy*.[9]

This paper is organized thematically, starting with a review of al-Ṣadr's definition of Islamic economics. There is an evaluation of al-Ṣadr's critique of Marxism and capitalism, his views on wealth and income distribution, and his ideas on finance. One crucial question is why al-Ṣadr's ideas have not been even more influential, given the undoubted quality of his work.

Al-Ṣadr's economics

al-Ṣadr had a clear and inspiring vision of what an ideal Islamic economy would be like. He defines Islamic economics as: 'the way Islam prefers to follow in the pursuit of its economic life and in the solution of its practical economic problems in line with its concept of justice'.[10] His approach was holistic, and it can be categorized as 'juristic-economic' with the moral valuation of economic actions playing the central role. In economic terms al-Ṣadr could be described as a micro-economist, his interest being in how markets worked, including financial markets, and how transactions could be justly conducted, the latter being the distinctive Islamic economic perspective.

The claims which al-Ṣadr made for Islamic economics were extremely cautious, as he recognized its methodological limitations. Islamic economics was not seen as a substitute for secular mainstream economics, as the former was concerned with justification, but the latter with explanation. While al-Ṣadr's central concern was moral values, he nevertheless believed that there were natural universal laws of economics which could not be disregarded as they explained economic phenomena and events. These included the laws of supply and demand and the notion of diminishing returns, which were not capitalist laws, but general laws which manifested themselves irrespective of the prevailing economic system. For al-Ṣadr these laws should be respected, not resisted, as they constituted a guarantee for human contentment provided that the economic system ensured that all members of society were free to participate in economic activity.

There are inevitably limitations to al-Ṣadr's work. Although he developed arguments and identified important economic issues, he did not predict the major social changes that occurred before and after his death. He devoted excessive attention to socialism, a doomed system, and underestimated the adaptability of capitalism. Nor did he have much to say about the advantages and disadvantages of international trade; indeed his work implicitly assumes a closed economy.

Syed Naqvi, who has perhaps done more to develop a methodology for Islamic economics than any other writer, acknowledges the contribution of al-Ṣadr.[11] Both al-Ṣadr and Naqvi see Islamic economics as inseparable from Islamic ethics, but the latter sees his approach as axiomatic and inductive since he believes the workings of an Islamic economy can be seen in the behaviour of Muslim society.[12] al-Ṣadr, by contrast, started from the *Sharī'a*, and deduced the principles by which Muslims should manage their economic affairs.[13] For al-Ṣadr the workings of particular Muslim economies fell far short of the ideal, but that was the essence of the moral challenge.

Islamic man in society

al-Ṣadr did not see himself as being naively idealistic; rather he saw Islamic economics as being both realistic and moral.[14] Too much should not be expected of economic agents, as all humans are fallible and have limited abilities. Egoism is a natural human condition which cannot be denied. However, moral behaviour can be developed and encouraged, and the young in particular made aware of their social responsibilities. Governments can of course intervene, but mere intervention is not a substitute for individual virtue. al-Ṣadr asserted that, although governments could impose taxes on the better off to help the poor, this would be ineffective unless the richer members of society were really committed to improving the welfare of their poorer brethren.

Furthermore, it is not only the end which is important, but also the means. This is why Islam provides for *Zakāt*, a voluntary wealth tax which Muslims pay in recognition of their social responsibilities. This fosters good behaviour by the more prosperous, by giving them choice through its voluntary nature, in a way that compulsory taxation cannot. *Zakāt* thus helps both rich and poor, and has a moral as well as a material dimension, whereas compulsory redistributive taxation helps only the poor in solely material terms.

Siddiqi, by contrast, is more doubtful about the potential for social solidarity in modern urban industrialized societies. He sees the state playing the key role, with compulsory *Zakāt* collection,[15] and redistribution to help the poor and needy, although this assumes a benevolent and socially responsible government. The state's role in directly productive activity should be limited, however, as bureaucracies tend to be rigid and inflexible, and the state cannot have as much information as those actually involved in market transactions. Rather the state's prime role should be the administration of social justice, but this cannot be successfully imposed by coercion. State intervention is most likely to be successful, according to Siddiqi, if its aims and ideas of what constitutes justice are in line with those of the individuals in the society being governed.[16]

Chapra always believed in a more limited role for the state than Siddiqi. His views were more in line with al-Ṣadr's thinking, as he does not see widespread government intervention as being necessary, and excessive regulation as being desirable, but rather believes the state should try to strike a balance between private and social interest, referring to the *Sharī'a* for basic guidance, and using democratic channels of consultation.[17] Like al-Ṣadr, Chapra stresses the need to encourage individual responsibility, and writes about the importance of invigorating the human factor by ensuring that individuals are morally motivated.[18]

Naqvi's position is also closer to those of Chapra and al-Ṣadr than that of Siddiqi; indeed he refers with approval to al-Ṣadr's stress on the state providing a social balance when discussing ethics and the role of government.[19] Nevertheless, Naqvi envisages the state's role in the economic sphere as being fairly extensive, especially if the 'justice as fairness' principle is to apply. Naqvi believes that the Rawls concept of social order is close to the Islamic ideal in spirit, if not in letter.[20]

Critique of Marxism and capitalism

In al-Ṣadr's major work, *Iqtiṣādunā: Our Economics*, the subtitle gives a clue to the subject-matter: 'An objective study consisting of the examination and criticisms of the economic doctrines of Marxism, capitalism and Islam as concerns the fundamentals and details of their ideas'. al-Ṣadr condemned the limitations of both the Marxist and capitalist systems. For him the differences can be characterized in the following scheme, which is both simple and admirable for its clarity.

The nature of the economic problem.

System	Problem
Capitalism	Scarcity of resources
Marxism	Form of production and distribution
Islam	Wants of man

al-Ṣadr saw capitalism as more a matter of doctrine than of scientific laws. He identified its three basic principles as the universal application of private property rights, the unconstrained exploitation of these rights, and the absolute sovereignty of the consumer. Although al-Ṣadr was vehemently opposed to Marxism, his critique of capitalism bears resemblances to those who take a Marxist perspective. In his rejection of the universality of the economic assumptions which he believed underpin capitalism, he seemed to equate these with the model of the classical economist, David Ricardo,[21] but there was no reference to any neo-classical economists or any of the many schools of mid-twentieth-century economic thought.

Chapra, by contrast, has read widely, and is able to draw on the critiques of capitalism by a wide range of Western writers from John Kenneth Galbraith to the American Marxists, Baran and Sweezy, and even refers to the Christian critique of capitalism by R. H. Tawney.[22]

al-Ṣadr may have been less widely read than Chapra, but his economic ideas provided clear and coherent alternatives to those that political economists associate with capitalism and Marxism. He believed that it is through work that private property rights are acquired.[23] He had a labour theory of ownership, which was quite different from the Marxist labour theory of value, since value for al-Ṣadr was determined through exchange. He stressed the principle of multi-faceted ownership, a mixed economy with private, public, and state ownership, public ownership applying to natural resources and state ownership to utilities.[24]

Private ownership and inheritance

For al-Ṣadr private ownership was recognized as legitimate, but there were moral constraints on the exercise of these rights. Ultimately property is held in trust for God, and the exercise of rights must at the same time be seen as morally accountable action. Chapra shares this view, but stresses that private property and the profit motive are necessary to motivate producers towards greater efficiency and improved quality.[25] For Chapra, however, responsible property ownership means that it should be used for the common good, with God-given resources not destroyed or wasted, the emphasis being on sustainability, so that future generations may also benefit. Futhermore, like al-Ṣadr, Chapra believes that private property should be acquired through work or inheritance, as stipulated under the *Sharī'a* law, and that property should not be disposed of if it would undermine the well-being of the owner's family and adversely affect their inheritance rights.[26]

Respect for private property rights and inheritance does not, however, justify maintainance of a *status quo* where there is a very uneven distribution of land, and al-Ṣadr acknowledges that the history of private property is full of injustice and exploitation.[27] Other contemporary Islamic economic writers have more to say on land reform, notably Chapra and Naqvi. Chapra believes the concentration of the ownership of the means of production in Muslim countries is a major impediment to development, and asserts that without land reform the mass poverty of the rural populations cannot be relieved.[28] Chapra admits that the *Sharī'a* does not set any limit on the size of landholding, but if its goals are to be realized (*maqāṣid al-Sharī'a*), land reform measures stipulating ceilings on acreage owned may be necessary.

Naqvi sees a potential conflict between the Islamic inheritance laws and the Islamic ethical principle that the interests of cultivators take precedence over those of non-cultivating landlords. He believes most Muslim scholars have failed to address the issue of inheritance rights when the property itself was not acquired legitimately, although he does not name those he criticizes.[29] In essence the issue is whether the Islamic position on inheritance is purely non-consequentialist, or if the need for social and economic justice is paramount. Naqvi is in agreement with al-Ṣadr in seeing labour as the source of property rights, but goes on to point out how private ownership of land which is not self-cultivated may therefore be viewed as unjustified.[30] Most radical of all is Siddiqi, who goes furthest in urging widespread land reform, and even the transfer of some of the shares in joint stock companies to the poor.[31] al-Ṣadr had less knowledge of modern companies, and *Iqtiṣādunā* is more about economic management in general and less about particular sectors of an economy or institutions for corporate governance.

Income and wealth distribution

al-Ṣadr's theory of distribution was well thought out and, arguably from a moral perspective, preferable to Marxist theory. Like other Islamic economists, he was less concerned with the relative shares of income and wealth, but he stressed the provision of basic needs so that all men can live with dignity. He distinguished between three groups in society:

(1) those who through their talents and abilities could provide for themselves a high standard of living;
(2) those who could only provide for their basic needs through their work;
(3) the physically or mentally weak who could not sustain themselves through their own efforts.

Society has an obligation to help the latter, but not by excessively penalizing those in the first group. For if work is penalized, this 'means a death blow to the most important power that pushes the economic system ahead'.[32]

In his discussion of income distribution and need, it is notable that al-Ṣadr makes more reference to Marxist economics than Qur'ānic writing. Although he condemns the Marxist assumptions, he keeps returning almost obsessively to Marxist theories and concepts, as if this is the benchmark against which Islam's superior system of distribution should be measured. The first and richest group referred to above are equated with capitalists, and the second with the workers. While these two groups are embroiled in their class struggle, the third group, those who can do little or no work because of their physical or mental frailty, are neglected.[33]

Although there are differences in emphasis between contemporary Islamic economic writers, there is a common view that *Zakāt* and the Islamic inheritance system are insufficient in themselves to ensure a just distribution of resources. Supporters of *Zakāt* have been disappointed at the experience of countries where it has been widely used, notably the Sudan.

al-Ṣadr was more concerned with the principles of *Zakāt* than Chapra, who focuses on the practicalities. Chapra points out that *Zakāt* is not a substitute for a modern social insurance system that provides for unemployment benefit, health care, and pensions.[34] *Zakāt* can help those who fall through a social insurance safety net, but Chapra sees it as a temporary form of assistance to enable poor Muslims to stand on their own feet. According to Chapra, *Zakāt* can be used to finance education or training, or to provide capital grants to expand self-employment. Siddiqi is more cautious about using *Zakāt* to help self-employment, but he does not rule it out, instead saying that further investigation is needed.[35]

Theory of Islamic finance

Islamic economics is often most noted for its approach to finance, and the prohibition of *ribā*, the addition to the principal of a loan. al-Ṣadr, like most Islamic economists, believed that interest was an unjustifiable reward. In *Iqtiṣādunā* a parallel was drawn between the notion that there could be no reward without work or effort and interest which was assigned to the unjustifiable remuneration category.[36] There is little discussion of banking in *Iqtiṣādunā*, however, which is a book about principles, not practice. It was al-Ṣadr's later work on Islamic finance, *Al-Bank al-lāribawī fī l-Islām*,[37] that was more concerned with Islamic banking, although he was not acquainted with the theories of modern finance. There was no attempt to justify his position on *ribā* against modern theories of interest-rate determination, largely because he was unaware of liquidity preference and loanable fund theories, and did not discuss neo-classical economic notions such as opportunity cost or time preferences.

al-Ṣadr distinguished between commercial capital and the tools of production, the former referring to the finance and the latter to physical capital such as machinery. The worker uses his tools of production to earn wages, but he may also be innovative in how the tools are used and developed. It is notable that al-Ṣadr saw the worker, not the financier, as the potential entrepreneur.[38] As an entrepreneur the worker may earn a share in the possible profits resulting from any innovation, but it is the financier, not the entrepreneur, who is responsible for covering any losses. It is this that justifies the financier's return in the form of a share in any profits the commercial venture generates. A financier cannot earn a return under conditions of certainty, as this would constitute *ribā*.

In Islamic economics a financier can only be rewarded for direct participation in a business venture. al-Ṣadr did not explore the various types of risk taking or consider how financiers can also be rewarded for the collection and interpretation of information. Nor did he consider the issue of interest as a reward for simply deferring consumption. However, in *Al-Bank al-lāribawī fī l-Islām* al-Ṣadr examined how bank depositors could be rewarded through being entitled to a share in the bank's profits on the basis of *muḍaraba* participatory finance.[39] al-Ṣadr also considered how banks themselves can finance businesses through *muḍāraba*, but he did not examine some of the most popular forms of Islamic financing which were subsequently to develop, notably *murābaḥa* (cost plus trade finance) and *ijāra* (leasing).

al-Ṣadr's isolation from other Arab writers in Egypt and the Gulf who were concerned with Islamic finance resulted in his ideas having less practical influence. The Palestinian writer Sami Homoud was to have the greatest influence on the Islamic banking practices adopted by the new Islamic commercial banks and the Islamic Development Bank in the 1970s and 1980s. Homoud worked out how the principle of *murābaḥa* could be applied to finance exports and imports during a period when trade was booming for the Muslim states of the Gulf because of the oil price rises of 1974 and 1979. Homoud was able to attend numerous Islamic banking and finance conferences, vigorously promoting his ideas, while al-Ṣadr made few trips away from Najaf, where his movements became increasingly restricted by the Saddam Hussein regime.

There was even a neglect of al-Ṣadr's work on the notion of two-tier *muḍāraba*, which correctly distinguished between the relationship of bank depositors with their bank on the one hand, and the bank with the business being financed on the other. Nejatullah Siddiqi's work on *muḍāraba* was much more widely quoted, even from the time of his early publications in Lahore, although it was his later works on *Banking without Interest*[40] and *Partnership and Profit Sharing in Islamic Law*[41] that were to serve as textbooks for upwardly mobile Islamic bankers concerned to get to grips with the principles of their subject.

It would be incorrect to regard Islamic finance as a negative constraint simply because it concerns a number of prohibitions. Essentially it is about economic justice: how reward can be morally justified. Islam is not against making money, and there is no inherent conflict between the material and the spiritual. However, what is important is how money is made. Wages and salaries are seen as legitimate rewards for work. Islamic writers recognize rent as a proper reward for ownership responsibilities. Profits are also seen as legitimate and are discussed by al-Ṣadr, even though this was not specifically in terms of being a return for risk taking and the anxieties that often entails.

Interest is not seen as a justifiable reward, as it involves no work or effort. Merely making money from money is regarded as sterile, since no wealth creation is involved on the part of the provider of the capital.[42] The borrower may be creating wealth, and may be taking considerable risks, but these are not being shared by the financier, who will be expecting an interest payment which is unrelated to the returns from the transaction or project being financed. In practice, interest rates in Western economies are determined by macro-economic conditions, as interest rates are the main tool of monetary policy. Interest is seldom related to the returns on what is being funded. Islamic economists believe that returns on finance should be determined in accordance with how it is used, that is at the micro-economic level, not through macro-economic policy changes which bring unjustified gains or losses to the lender or borrower.

Acknowledgements to al-Ṣadr in later writing

Both Chapra and Siddiqi refer to al-Ṣadr in their own work, acknowledging his role in the development of contemporary Islamic economic thought. Chapra, for example, cites with approval al-Ṣadr's view that poverty and deprivation are caused by the absence of a morally defined framework of human relationships between the rich and the poor.[43] Siddiqi supports al-Ṣadr's case for a minimum guaranteed standard of living for all in an Islamic state.[44]

al-Ṣadr's views on the role of the state, and the principle of multi-faceted ownership, have also been noted by later writers. In Chapra's earlier book, *Towards a Just Monetary System*,[45] there are two references to al-Ṣadr, one concerned with his economic thinking and the second with finance, which will be dealt with later. When reviewing al-Ṣadr's economic thinking Chapra stresses the substantial role envisaged in *Iqtiṣādunā* for the private sector and the 'considerable scope for individual freedom in Islam within a framework of Islamic goals and values'.[46]

This point is taken up by Timur Kuran, the Turkish American commentator on contemporary Islamic economics. He sees al-Ṣadr as a sophisticated writer who rejects the view that 'an Islamic economy is a static structure consisting of fixed norms, an invariable *Zakāt* system, and a financial system equipped with an unchanging set of instruments'.[47] Rather, writers such as al-Ṣadr 'incorporate processes of change into their accounts of the Islamic economy by asserting that the holy laws of Islam accommodate all the necessary flexibility'.[48]

Kuran sees al-Ṣadr's major contribution as being to provide the ideological support to attempts to restructure the Iranian economy along Islamic lines. He categorizes al-Ṣadr with Sayyid Taleghani and Abdulhasan Bani Ṣadr and other Shīʿī writers, although it can be argued that denominational differences between Sunnī and Shīʿī writers have little relevance in Islamic economics. al-Ṣadr of course had Shīʿī followers, in particular Abdulhasan Bani Ṣadr,[49] who was briefly President of Iran in the early days of the Islamic Republic, and Ali Rahnema,[50] the Iranian-born, but Paris-based, economist.

Ayatollah Khomeini, the spiritual leader of Iran and power behind the Islamic revolution, knew al-Ṣadr in Najaf, and was undoubtedly influenced by him, although Khomeini himself had little interest in economics. Hanna Batatu makes clear, however, that there were personal differences between the exiled Iranians in Najaf and their Arab Shīʿī brethren,[51] perhaps reflecting cultural and linguistic differences. This was arguably of greater significance than the Sunnī-Shīʿī divide. It would be misleading to speak of a distinctive *Shīʿī* Islamic economics, and this is certainly not a division that al-Ṣadr would have wished to see emerge.

Chapra also acknowledges al-Ṣadr's contribution to the theory of Islamic commercial banking,[52] and although he does not spell out exactly what it is, the reader is referred to al-Ṣadr's book *Al-Bank al-lāribawī fī l-Islām*. Chibli Mallat provides a much more explicit discussion of al-Ṣadr's contribution to Islamic commercial banking theory by stressing how he distinguished between a bank's relationship with its depositors and with the businesses it was financing. In conventional banking the two are separated, whereas an Islamic bank acts as a true intermediary by bringing the parties together.[53]

Al-Ṣadr's influence in retrospect

Despite these acknowledgements of al-Ṣadr's contribution to the development of Islamic economic thought, and efforts of Mallat to bring both *Iqtiṣādunā* and *Al-Bank al-lāribawī fī l-Islām* to the attention of a wider readership among those concerned with Middle Eastern and Islamic studies generally, al-Ṣadr's writings have not received the attention they deserve. Following al-Ṣadr's interest in promoting his ideas amongst young Muslims and students, Dr Mohammed Almoussawi of the Muslim Youth Association of the United Kingdom has organized conferences on al-Ṣadr's work at the University of London's School of Oriental and African Studies in April 1996 and at the University of Westminster in April 1997, both of which were well attended, although the papers were unpublished. There seems to be no co-ordination between this organization and the much more active Leicester-based Islamic Foundation which Chapra and Siddiqi support. The latter puts together ring-bound volumes of its conference papers, and has a long list of publications, but none on al-Ṣadr.

Why has al-Ṣadr's work remained on the margin despite its intellectual depth? One problem has been the poor dissemination of his work, which was originally published in Arabic in Beirut. Although a summary of and abstracts from *Al-Bank al-lāribawī fī l-Islām* are provided in Mallat's study,[54] the whole text has never been translated, and the Arabic text is not widely available. *Iqtiṣādunā* was translated into English by the Peermahomed Ebrahim Trust of Pakistan working on behalf of the Board of Writing, Translation and Publication of World Organization for Islamic Services of Tehran, but the translation was far from satisfactory, and the distribution very limited. Indeed it is difficult to get hold of the work and few libraries have it. It was the deficiencies in this translation that prompted Ian Howard of Edinburgh University to translate parts of *Iqtiṣādunā* in various issues of the Islamic studies magazine, *Al Sarat*. But this magazine is no longer published, the editions concerned are out of print, and it was never widely distributed in any case.

In contrast, Syed Naqvi's work was published by a major British publisher, Kegan Paul, and the work of Umer Chapra and Nejatullah Siddiqi is widely distributed by the Islamic Foundation. These Islamic economists write in English, which has become the language of debate for Islamic economics. Accessibility inevitably affects subsequent work. Originally the historian of

Islamic economic thought, Mohamed Aslam Haneef, had intended to work on al-Ṣadr for his doctoral thesis for the University of East Anglia, an author suggested by the well-known Malaysian economist, J. S. Jomo. Being Malaysian himself, however, with a limited grasp of Arabic, Haneef decided to undertake a comparative study covering the five Islamic economists mentioned earlier, Muhammad Abdul Mannan, Nejatullah Siddiqi, Syed Naqvi, Monzer Kahf, and Sayyid Mahmud Taleghani, devoting only one chapter to al-Ṣadr.

al-Ṣadr was also a writer of his times, much influenced by Marxist currents of economic thought. Although he rejected the materialism of Marx, and its treatment of history as being determined solely by economic forces, al-Ṣadr was influenced by Marxist thinking in terms of methodology and subject categorization. As Marxist economic philosophy has fallen out of favour in recent years with the demise of communism, al-Ṣadr's work has in one sense become dated, not least as Islamic economics itself has moved on, and now accommodates some of the most recent developments in neo-classical economic theory, such as transactions theories of information and search and the modelling of expectations, concepts of which al-Ṣadr was unaware. Former leftist writers who were influenced by al-Ṣadr, such as Ali Rahnema,[55] have changed their positions, and now see much merit in mainstream economic approaches. Other Islamic thinkers see Islam in terms of postmodernist relativism, although this has yet to be worked out in a postmodernist economic perspective.[56] Syed Naqvi comes closest with his concept of Islamic economic man, but he is not explicitly postmodernist, and indeed may not wish to be categorized as such, even implicitly.

It would be incorrect to assert that al-Ṣadr has been marginalized because he was Shīʿī, as the denominational differences within Islam do not correspond to different currents in Islamic economic thought, which are more influenced by political outlook and academic background. The other writers do not even refer to al-Ṣadr as Shīʿī. Furthermore, in the 1970s al-Ṣadr was called in to advise the then newly established Kuwait Finance House, the first Islamic bank in the Emirate, which is largely staffed by Sunnī Muslims. Being Shīʿī and Iraqi did not seem to be a disadvantage. Although contact between Iranian and Arab Islamic bankers is limited, they do meet freely at commercial conferences on Islamic finance, and institutions such as the Geneva-based Dār al-Māl al-Islāmī have both Sunnī and Shīʿī employees.

How al-Ṣadr's own thinking would have developed had his life not come to such an untimely end is difficult to say. He would certainly have been despondent about the failure of any Islamic banks or financial institutions to be allowed to develop in his native Iraq, but encouraged by developments elsewhere. Not all aspects of Iran's Islamic economy would probably have met his approval, despite the Islamic banking legislation of 1983. Perhaps he would have been most heartened by developments in countries such as Malaysia where Islamic financing is increasingly used for major contracts, a country he never had the good fortune to visit.

415

Notes

1 M. Nejatullah Siddiqi, *Muslim Economic Thinking: A Survey of Contemporary Literature* (Leicester: Islamic Foundation, 1981).
2 Mohamed Aslam Haneef, *Contemporary Islamic Economic Thought: A Selected Comparative Analysis* (Kuala Lumpur: S. Abdul Majeed for Ikraq, 1995).
3 The scope of Haneef's work was determined by 1990, and his Ph.D. awarded from the University of East Anglia in 1994. The author was external examiner.
4 Hanna Batatu, 'Iraq's Underground Shi'a Movements: Characteristics, Causes and Prospects', *Middle East Journal*, 35: 4 (1981), 578–94.
5 Chibli Mallat, *The Renewal of Islamic Law: Muḥammad Bāqir as-Ṣadr, Najaf and the Shi'i International* (Cambridge: Cambridge University Press, 1993).
6 Muḥammad Bāqir al-Ṣadr, *Iqtiṣādunā: Our Economics* (Tehran: World Organization for Islamic Services, 1982), and various issues of *Al Sarat*, edited by Ian Howard of Edinburgh University. The author would like to thank Ian Howard for providing personal copies.
7 M. Umer Chapra, *Islam and the Economic Challenge* (Leicester: Islamic Foundation, 1992).
8 Syed Nawab Haider Naqvi, *Islam, Economics and Society* (London: Kegan Paul International, 1994).
9 Siddiqi, *The Role of the State in the Economy: an Islamic Perspective* (Leicester: Islamic Foundation, 1996).
10 al-Ṣadr, *Iqtiṣādunā: Our Economics*, vol. 2, part 2, p. 6.
11 Naqvi, op. cit. xxiv–xxv.
12 Ibid. 20.
13 al-Ṣadr, *Iqtiṣādunā: Our Economics*, vol. 1, part 2, pp. 57–8.
14 Ibid. 62–3.
15 Siddiqi, op. cit. 19–20.
16 Ibid. 1.
17 Chapra, op. cit. 223–4.
18 Ibid. 251–2.
19 Naqvi, op. cit. 65.
20 John Rawls, *A Theory of Justice* (Cambridge, MA: Harvard University Press, 1971). Naqvi also refers to John Rawls, 'Justice as Fairness: Politics not Metaphysical', *Philosophy and Public Affairs*, 14: 3 (1985), 223–51.
21 al-Ṣadr, op. cit., vol. 1, part 2, pp. 20–1.
22 Chapra, op. cit. 62–9.
23 al-Ṣadr, op. cit., vol. 1, part 2, p. 117.
24 Ibid. 124–8.
25 Chapra, op. cit. 41.
26 Ibid. 207. This parallels the discussion in al-Ṣadr, op. cit., vol. 1, part 2, p. 125.
27 Mallat, op. cit. 132.
28 Chapra, op. cit. 263–4.
29 Naqvi, op. cit. 101.
30 Ibid. 100.
31 Siddiqi, op. cit. 32.
32 al-Ṣadr, op. cit., vol. 1, part 2, p. 120.
33 Ibid. 119.
34 Chapra, op. cit. 274–5.
35 Siddiqi, op. cit. 33.
36 Mallat, op. cit. 162–3.
37 al-Ṣadr, *Al-Bank al-lāribawī fī l-Islām*, 7th edn. (Beirut: Dār al-Ta'āruf lil-Maṭbū'āt, 1981).

38 Mallat, op. cit. 163–4.
39 Ibid. 169–73.
40 Siddiqi, *Banking without Interest* (Leicester: Islamic Foundation, 1983).
41 Siddiqi, *Partnership and Profit Sharing in Islamic Law* (Leicester: Islamic Foundation, 1985).
42 Michael Ainley, 'A Central Bank's View of Islamic Banking' in Muazzam Ali (ed.), *European Perceptions of Islamic Banking* (London: Institute of Islamic Banking and Finance, 1996), 12.
43 Chapra, op. cit. 12.
44 Siddiqi, op. cit. 14.
45 Chapra, *Towards a Just Monetary System* (Leicester: Islamic Foundation, 1985).
46 Ibid. 67 and 78, n. 1.
47 Timur Kuran, 'Islamic Economics and the Islamic Subeconomy', *Journal of Economic Perspectives*, 9: 4 (1995), 155–73. Quotation from p. 160.
48 Ibid.
49 Abdulhasan Bani Ṣadr, *Work and the Worker in Islam* (Tehran: Hamdani Foundation, 1980).
50 Farhad Nomani and Ali Rahnema, *Islamic Economic Systems* (London: Zed Books, 1994).
51 Batatu, op. cit. 594.
52 Chapra, *Towards a Just Monetary System*, 154 and 182, n. 8.
53 Mallat, op. cit. 168–9.
54 Mallat, op. cit. 164–82.
55 Nomani and Rahnema, op. cit.
56 Akbar S. Ahmed, *Postmodernism and Islam: Predicament and Promise* (London: Routledge, 1992).